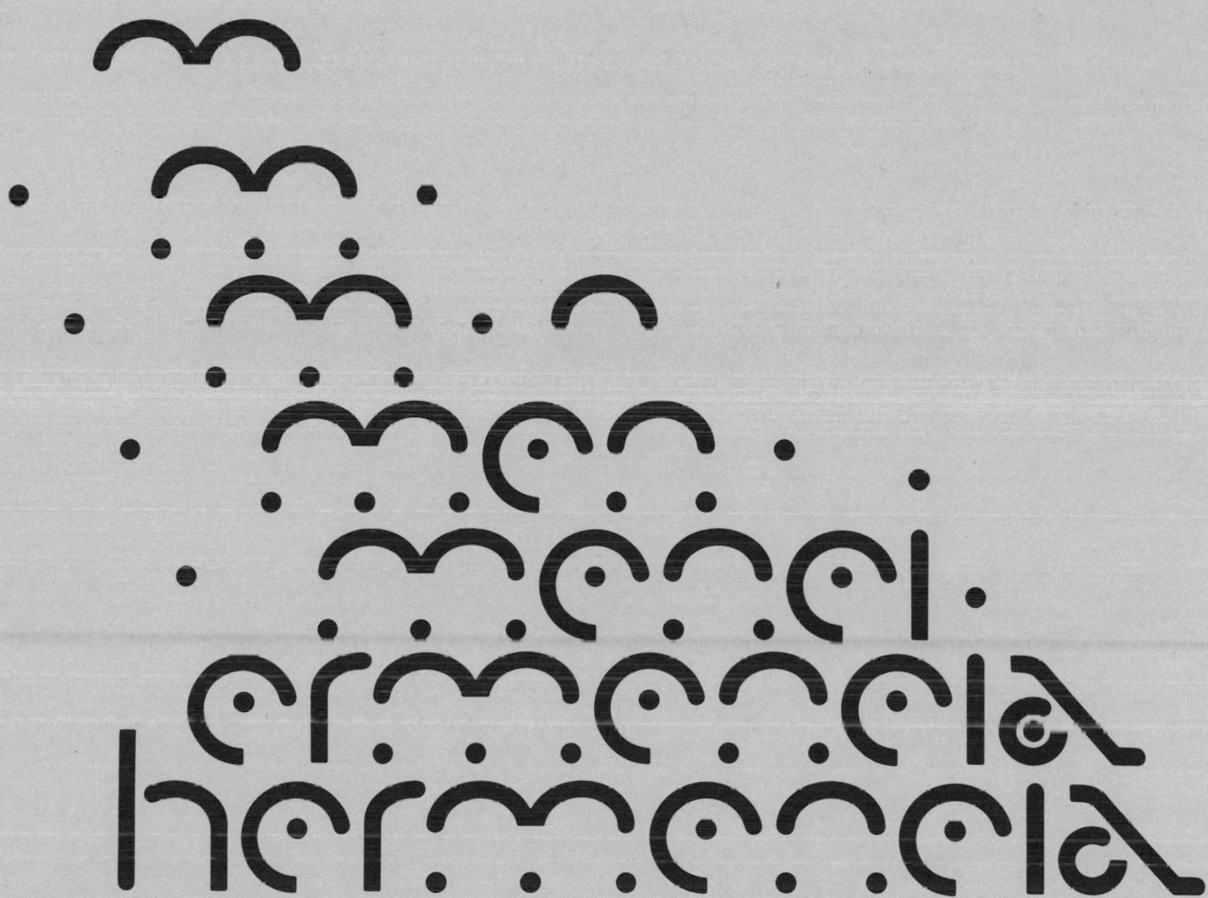
hermeneia

Hermeneia
—A Critical
and Historical
Commentary
on the Bible

Colossians and Philemon

A Commentary on the Epistles to the Colossians and to Philemon

by Eduard Lohse

Translated by
William R. Poehlmann and
Robert J. Karris

Edited by
Helmut Koester

Fortress
Press

Philadelphia

Translated from the German *Die Briefe an die Kolosser und an Philemon* (1st edition) by Eduard Lohse. Kritisch-Exegetischer Kommentar über das Neue Testament begründet von Heinrich August Wilhelm Meyer, 14. Auflage. © Vandenhoeck & Ruprecht, Göttingen, 1968.

Library of Congress Catalog Card Number 76-157550
ISBN 0-8006-6001-3

Printed in the United States of America

Type set by Maurice Jacobs, Inc., Philadelphia

MEMORIAE
FRATRIS DILECTISSIMI
WALTER LOHSE
QUI
EREPTUS EST NOBIS
PRAEMATURA MORTE
ANNO SUAE AETATIS XVIII
VOCATUS ULTIMAM IN HORAM
ANNO DOMINI MCMXLIIII

ΧΡΙΣΤΟΣ Η ΖΩΗ ΗΜΩΝ

The Author

Eduard Lohse became Bishop of the Evangelical Church of Hannover, Germany, in 1971. Earlier he had been Professor of New Testament Theology at the University of Göttingen. A contributor to Kittel's *Theological Dictionary of the New Testament*, he has also published *Märtyrer und Gottesknecht* (1955), *Israel und die Christenheit* (1960), *Das Ärgernis des Kreuzes* (1969), and, in English, *History of the Suffering and Death of Jesus Christ* (1967).

Contents

Foreword

The name *Hermeneia*, Greek ἑρμηνεία, has been chosen as the title for the commentary series to which this volume belongs. The word *Hermeneia* has a rich background in the history of biblical interpretation as a term used in the ancient Greek-speaking world for the detailed, systematic exposition of a scriptural work. It is hoped that the series, like the name, will carry this old and venerable tradition forward. A second, entirely practical reason for selecting the name lay in the desire to avoid a long descriptive title and its inevitable acronym or worse, an unpronounceable abbreviation.

The series is designed to be a critical and historical commentary to the Bible without arbitrary limits in size or scope. It will utilize the full range of philological and historical tools including textual criticism (often ignored in modern commentaries), the methods of the history of tradition (including genre and prosodic analysis), and the history of religion.

Hermeneia is designed for the serious student of the Bible. It will make full use of ancient Semitic and classical languages; at the same time English translations of all comparative materials, Greek, Latin, Canaanite, or Akkadian, will be supplied alongside the citation of the source in its original language. The aim is to provide the student or scholar in so far as possible with the full critical discussion of each problem of interpretation and with the primary data upon which the discussion is based.

Hermeneia is designed to be international and interconfessional in the selection of its authors, and is so represented on its board of editors. On occasion, distinguished commentaries in languages other than English will be published in translation. Published volumes of the series will be revised continually, and eventually new commentaries will be assigned to replace older works in order that the series can be open-ended. Commentaries are also being assigned for important literary works falling in the categories of apocryphal and pseudepigraphical works of the Old and New Testament, including some of Essene or Gnostic authorship.

The editors of *Hermeneia* impose no systematic-theological perspective (directly or indirectly by the selection of authors) upon the series. It is expected that authors will struggle fully to lay bare the ancient meaning of a biblical work or pericope. In this way its human relevance should become transparent as is the case always in competent historical discourse. However, the series eschews for itself homiletical translation of the Bible.

The editors are under a heavy debt to Fortress Press for the energy and courage shown in taking up an expensive and long project the rewards of which will accrue chiefly to the field of biblical scholarship. The translators of this volume are Mr. William R. Poehlmann of Harvard University (first half of Colossians) and Dr. Robert J. Karris, O.F.M., of the Catholic Theological Union at Chicago (second half of Colossians and Philemon). Mr. Poehlmann also assisted in the editing of the Manuscript, Miss Judith Dollenmayer undertook the meticulous task of copy-editing with skill and tact and Mr. Harold W. Attridge of Harvard University aided in the proof-reading. To all who were involved in the production of this volume, the editors wish to express their gratefulness for their untiring efforts which resulted in an unusually harmonious experience of cooperation.

The editor responsible for this volume is Helmut Koester of Harvard University.

June 1971

Frank Moore Cross, Jr.
For the Old Testament
Board of Editors

Helmut Koester
For the New Testament
Board of Editors

Reference Codes

1. Abbreviations

Abbreviations used in this volume for sources and literature from antiquity are the same as those used in the *Theological Dictionary of the New Testament*, ed. Gerhard Kittel, tr. Geoffrey W. Bromiley, vol. 1 (Grand Rapids, Michigan and London: Eerdmans, 1964), xvi–xl. Some abbreviations are adapted from that list and can be easily identified.

In addition, the following abbreviations have been used:

ad loc.	*ad locum*, at the place or passage discussed
ANF	*The Ante-Nicene Fathers: Translations of the Writings of the Fathers Down to A.D. 325*, eds. Alexander Roberts and James Donaldson (Buffalo: The Christian Literature Publishing Company, 1885–97; reprinted by Wm. B. Eerdmans Publishing Company, Grand Rapids, Michigan, 1951–56)
ASNU	Acta Seminarii Neotestamentici Upsaliensis
AThANT	Abhandlungen zur Theologie des Alten und Neuen Testaments
ATR	*Anglican Theological Review*
b.	Babylonian Talmud, usually followed by abbreviated title of tractate
BBB	Bonner Biblische Beiträge
BHTh	Beiträge zur Historischen Theologie
BWANT	Beiträge zur Wissenschaft vom Alten und Neuen Testament
BZ	*Biblische Zeitschrift*
BZNW	Beihefte zur Zeitschrift für die neutestamentliche Wissenschaft und die Kunde der älteren Kirche
CBQ	*The Catholic Biblical Quarterly*
CD	The Cairo Genizah Damascus Document
cf.	confer, compare with
col.	column(s)
ed.	editor, edited by
[Ed.]	Editor of this volume of Hermeneia
ET	English translation
EvTheol	*Evangelische Theologie*
ExpT	*The Expository Times*
FRLANT	Forschungen zur Religion und Literatur des Alten und Neuen Testaments
HNT	Handbuch zum Neuen Testament, ed. Hans Lietzmann and Günther Bornkamm
HTR	*The Harvard Theological Review*
IB	The Interpreter's Bible
ibid.	in the same place
ICC	International Critical Commentary, ed. S. R. Driver *et al.*
idem	the same (person)
item	also, in addition
j.	Jerusalem Talmud or Palestinian Talmud, usually followed by abbreviated title of tractate
JBL	*Journal of Biblical Literature*
JPTh	Jahrbücher für protestantische Theologie
JQR	*The Jewish Quarterly Review*
JTS	*The Journal of Theological Studies*
KD	*Kerygma und Dogma: Zeitschrift für theologische Forschung und kirchliche Lehre*
KEK	Kritisch-exegetischer Kommentar über das Neue Testament, begründet von Heinrich August Wilhelm Meyer
KIT	Kleine Texte für Vorlesungen und Übungen, ed. Hans Lietzmann
Loeb	The Loeb Classical Library, founded by James Loeb, ed. E. H. Warmington (Cambridge, Mass., and London: Harvard University Press and Heinemann, 1912ff.)
NF	Neutestamentliche Forschungen
NGG	Nachrichten von der Gesellschaft der Wissenschaften zu Göttingen
NIC	The New International Commentary on the New Testament
NovTest	*Novum Testamentum: An International Quarterly for New Testament and Related Studies*
NPNF	*A Select Library of the Nicene and Post-Nicene Fathers of the Christian Church*, 1st Series, ed. Philip Schaff (New York: The Christian Literature Company, 1886–90)
NTAbh	Neutestamentliche Abhandlungen
NTD	Das Neue Testament Deutsch (Neues Göttinger Bibelwerk), ed. Paul Althaus and Gerhard Friedrich
NTS	*New Testament Studies*
p. (pp.)	page(s)
P. Grenf.	I, *An Alexandrian Erotic Fragment and Other Greek Papyri, chiefly Ptolemaic*, ed. B. P. Grenfell (Oxford: Clarendon Press, 1896). II, *New Classical Fragments*, ed. B. P. Grenfell and A. S. Hunt

(Oxford: Clarendon Press, 1897)

P. Osl. — *Papyri Osloenses*, ed. S. Eitrem and L. Amundsen, vols. 1–3 (1925–36)

P. Rainer — *Corpus Papyrorum Raineri*, ed. C. Wessely (1895)

P. Strassb. — *Griechische Papyrus der Kaiserlichen Universitäts– und Landesbibliothek zu Strassburg*, ed. F. Preisigke, vol. 1 (Leipzig: 1906–12), vol. 2 (Leipzig: 1920)

PSI — *Publicazioni della Societa Italiana: Papiri Greci e Latini*, vols. 1–11 (1912–35), vol. 14 (1957)

Q — Qumran documents:

- 1 QH — Hodayot, the Psalms of Thanksgiving
- 1 QHf — Hodayot Fragment
- 1 QM — Milḥamah, the War of the Children of Light against the Children of Darkness
- 1 Q *34* — Fragment of 1 QM
- 1 QpHab — Pesher Habakkuk, the Commentary on Habakkuk
- 1 QpPs — Pesher on Psalms, the Commentary on Psalms
- 1 QS — Serek hay-yaḥad, the Rule of the Community
- 1 QSa, b — Adjuncts to the Rule of the Community
- 4 QCry — Astrological Cryptic Document

RAC — *Reallexikon für Antike und Christentum*, ed. Theodor Klauser

RB — *Revue Biblique*

RechSR — *Recherches de Science Religieuse*

rev. — revised by

RGG — Die Religion in Geschichte und Gegenwart: Handwörterbuch für Theologie und Religionswissenschaft

RHPR — *Revue d'Histoire et de Philosophie Religieuses*

RHR — *Revue de l'Histoire des Religions*

SAH — Sitzungsberichte der Heidelberger Akademie der Wissenschaften

SBT — Studies in Biblical Theology

ST — *Studia Theologica*

s.v. — *sub verbo* or *sub voce*, under the word (entry)

TDNT — *Theological Dictionary of the New Testament*, ed. Gerhard Kittel

ThLZ — *Theologische Literaturzeitung*

ThQ — *Theologische Quartalschrift*

ThZ — *Theologische Zeitschrift*

tr. — translator, translated by

[Trans.] — translator of this volume of Hermeneia

[trans. by Ed.] — translated by editor of this volume of Hermeneia

TTK — *Tidsskrift for Teologi og Kirke*

TU — Texte und Untersuchungen zur Geschichte der altchristlichen Literatur

TWNT — *Theologisches Wörterbuch zum Neuen Testament*, ed. Gerhard Kittel

UCL — Universitas Catholica Lovaniensis: Dissertationes ad gradum magistri in facultate theologica

UNT — Untersuchungen zum Neuen Testament

UPZ — *Urkunden der Ptolemäerzeit* ed. W. Wilcken, vol. 1 (1922–27), vol. 2 (1933-57)

v (vss) — verse(s)

VD — *Verbum Domini*

v.l. — *varia lectio*, variant reading

vol. — volume(s)

WMANT — Wissenschaftliche Monographien zum Alten und Neuen Testament

WUNT — Wissenschaftliche Untersuchungen zum Neuen Testament

ZAW — *Zeitschrift für die alttestamentliche Wissenschaft*

ZNW — *Zeitschrift für die neutestamentliche Wissenschaft und die Kunde der älteren Kirche*

ZSTh — *Zeitschrift für systematische Theologie*

ZThK — *Zeitschrift für Theologie und Kirche*

2. Short Titles of Commentaries, Studies, and Articles Often Cited

Commentaries on Colossians and Philemon as well as a few basic reference works are cited by author's name only.

Aalen, "Begrepet"
Sverre Aalen, "Begrepet plaeroma i Kolosser- og Efeserbrevet," *TTK* 23 (1952): 49–67.

Abbott
T. K. Abbott, *The Epistles to the Ephesians and to the Colossians*, ICC (Edinburgh: T. & T. Clark, 1897).

Bammel, "Versuch zu Col 1:15–20"
Ernst Bammel, "Versuch zu Col 1:15–20," *ZNW* 52 (1961): 88–95.

Bauer
Walter Bauer, *A Greek–English Lexicon*, tr. William F. Arndt and F. Wilbur Gingrich (Chicago: University of Chicago Press, 1957, ²1965).

Benoit, "Rapports littéraires"
Pierre Benoit, "Rapports littéraires entre les épîtres aux Colossiens et Éphésiens," in *Neutestamentliche Aufsätze, Festschrift für Joseph Schmid* (Regensburg: 1963).

Betz, *Lukian*
Dieter Betz, *Lukian und das Neue Testament: Religionsgeschichtliche und paränetische Parallelen*. TU 76 (Berlin: 1961).

Bieder
Werner Bieder, *Der Kolosserbrief* in: Prophezei (Zürich: 1943).

Bieder
Werner Bieder, *Der Philemonbrief* in: Prophezei (Zürich: 1944).

Bieder, *Mysterium Christi*
Werner Bieder, *Das Mysterium Christi und die Mission: Ein Beitrag zur missionarischen Sakramentalgestalt der Kirche* (Zürich: 1964).

Billerbeck
Hermann Strack and Paul Billerbeck, *Kommentar zum Neuen Testament aus Talmud und Midrasch* 6 Vols. 2nd ed. (München: 1954–61).

Bjerkelund, *Parakalô*
Carl J. Bjerkelund, *Parakalô: Form, Funktion und Sinn der parakalô–Sätze in den paulinischen Briefen*. Bibliotheca Theologica Norvegica (Oslo: 1967).

Blass–Debrunner
F. Blass and A. Debrunner, *A Greek Grammar of the New Testament and Other Early Christian Literature*, tr. and rev. Robert W. Funk (Chicago: University of Chicago Press, 1961).

Blinzler, "Lexikalisches"
Josef Blinzler, "Lexikalisches zu dem Terminus τὰ στοιχεῖα τοῦ κόσμου bei Paulus," in *Studiorum Paulinorum Congressus Internationalis Catholicus*, 1961, 2. Analecta Biblica 18 (Rome: 1963), 429–43.

Bornkamm, *Early Christian Experience*
Günther Bornkamm, *Early Christian Experience*, tr. by Paul L. Hammer (New York and Evanston: Harper & Row, 1969).

Bornkamm, *Aufsätze* 1, 2
1 – Günther Bornkamm, *Das Ende des Gesetzes: Paulus–studien*. Beiträge zur Evangelischen Theologie 16 (München: 1952).
2 – Günther Bornkamm, *Studien zu Antike und Christentum, Gesammelte Aufsätze*, vol. 2. Beiträge zur Evangelischen Theologie 28 (München: 1959).

Bornkamm, "Die Hoffnung"
Günther Bornkamm, "Die Hoffnung im Kolosserbrief—Zugleich ein Beiträg zur Frage der Echtheit des Briefes," in *Studien zum Neuen Testament und zur Patristik, Festschrift für Erich Klostermann*. TU 77 (Berlin: 1961), 56–64.

Braun, *Qumran* 1
Herbert Braun, *Qumran und das Neue Testament*, vol. 1 (Tübingen: 1966).

Bultmann, *Theology*
Rudolf Bultmann, *Theology of the New Testament*, vol. 1, tr. Kendrick Grobel (New York: Charles Scribner's Sons, 1951); vol. 2, tr. Kendrick Grobel (New York: Charles Scribner's Sons, 1955).

Bultmann, "Neues Testament und Mythologie"
Rudolf Bultmann, "Neues Testament und Mythologie," in *Kerygma und Mythos 1*, ed. Hans Werner Bartsch (Hamburg: ²1951).

Casel, "Kultsprache"
Odo Casel, "Zur Kultsprache des heiligen Paulus," *Archiv fur Liturgiewissenschaft* 1 (1950).

Charles, *APOT*
R. H. Charles, ed. *The Apocrypha and Pseudepigrapha of the Old Testament in English, with Introductions and Critical and Explanatory Notes to the Several Books*, vols. 1 and 2 (Oxford: Clarendon Press, 1913).

Conzelmann
Hans Conzelmann in Hermann W. Beyer, Paul Althaus, Hans Conzelmann, Gerhard Friedrich, Albrecht Oepke, *Die kleineren Briefe des Apostels Paulus*. NTD 8 (Göttingen: ¹⁰1965).

Conzelmann, *Outline*
Hans Conzelmann, *An Outline of the Theology of the New Testament*, tr. John Bowden (New York and Evanston: Harper & Row, 1969).

Dahl, "Formgeschtl. Beobachtungen"
Nils Alstrup Dahl, "Formgeschichtliche Beobachtungen zur Christusverkündigung in der Gemeindepredigt" in *Neutestamentliche Studien für Rudolf Bultmann*. BZNW 21 (Berlin: 1954, ²1957).

Daube, *NT and Rabbinic Judaism*
David Daube, *The New Testament and Rabbinic Judaism*. Jordan Lectures in Comparative Religion 2, 1952 (London: University of London, Athlone, 1956).

Deichgräber, *Gotteshymnus und Christushymnus*
Richard Deichgräber, *Gotteshymnus und Christushym-*

nus in der frühen Christenheit: Untersuchungen zu Form, Sprache und Stil der frühchristlichen Hymnen. Studien zur Umwelt des Neuen Testaments 5 (Göttingen: 1967).

Deissmann, *LAE*
Adolf Deissmann, *Light from the Ancient East, The New Testament Illustrated by Recently Discovered Texts of the Graeco-Roman World*, tr. Lionel R. M. Strachan (New York: George H. Doran, 1927).

Deissmann, *Paul*
Adolf Deissmann, *Paul, A Study in Social and Religious History*, tr. by William E. Wilson (London: Hodder & Stoughton, 1926).

Delling, "Merkmal der Kirche"
Gerhard Delling, "Merkmal der Kirche nach dem Neuen Testament," *NTS* 13 (1966–67): 297–316.

Dibelius, *Aufsätze* 2
Martin Dibelius, *Botschaft und Geschichte: Gesammelte Aufsätze* 2, *Zum Urchristentum und zur hellenistischen Religionsgeschichte*, in Verbindung mit Heinz Kraft, herausgegeben von Günther Bornkamm (Tübingen: 1956).

Dibelius-Conzelmann, *The Pastoral Epistles*
Martin Dibelius and Hans Conzelmann, *The Pastoral Epistles*, tr. by William Buttolph, Hermeneia (Philadelphia: Fortress Press, 1972).

Dibelius–Greeven
Martin Dibelius and Heinrich Greeven, *An die Kolosser, Epheser, an Philemon*. HNT 12 (Tübingen: [3]1953).

Easton, "Ethical Lists"
Burton Scott Easton, "New Testament Ethical Lists," *JBL* 51 (1932): 1–12.

Eckart, "Exegetische Beobachtungen"
Karl-Gottfried Eckart, "Exegetische Beobachtungen zu Kol. 1:9–20," *Theologia Viatorum* 7 (1959–60): 87–106.

Ellingsworth, "Colossians 1:15–20"
P. Ellingsworth, "Colossians 1:15–20," *ExpT* 73 (1961–62): 252f.

Eltester, *Eikon im NT*
Friedrich Wilhelm Eltester, *Eikon im Neuen Testament*. BZNW 23 (Berlin: 1958).

Feuillet, "La Création"
André Feuillet, "La Création de l'Univers 'dans le Christ' d'après l'Épître aux Colossiens (1:16a)," *NTS* 12 (1965–66): 1–9.

Feuillet, *Le Christ sagesse*
André Feuillet, *Le Christ sagesse de Dieu d'après les épîtres Pauliniennes*. Études bibliques (Paris: 1966), 163–273.

Foerster, "Irrlehrer"
Werner Foerster, "Die Irrlehrer des Kolosserbriefes" in *Studia Biblica et Semitica, Festschrift für Th. Vriezen* (Wageningen: 1966), 71–80.

Francis, "Humility"
F. O. Francis, "Humility and Angelic Worship in Col. 2:18," *ST* 16 (1962): 109–34.

Friedrich, "Philemonbriefe"
Gerhard Friedrich in Hermann W. Beyer, Paul Althaus, Hans Conzelmann, Gerhard Friedrich, Albrecht Oepke, *Die kleineren Brifee des Apostel Paulus*. NTD 8 (Göttingen: [10]1965).

Friedrich, "Lohmeyers These"
Gerhard Friedrich, "Lohmeyers These über das paulinische Briefpräskript kritisch beleuchtet," *ThLZ* 81 (1956): 343–46.

Fridrichsen, "ΘΕΛΩΝ"
Anton Fridrichsen, "ΘΕΛΩΝ Col 2:18," *ZNW* 21 (1922): 135–37.

Gabathuler, *Jesus Christus, Haupt der Kirche*
Hans-Jakob Gabathuler, *Jesus Christus, Haupt der Kirche—Haupt der Welt: Der Christushymnus Colosser 1:15–20 in der theologischen Forschung der letzten 130 Jahre*. AThANT 45 (Zürich: 1965).

Gewiess, *Christus und das Heil*
Josef Gewiess, *Christus und das Heil nach dem Kolosserbrief*. Unpub. Diss. (Breslau: 1932).

Grässer, "Kol 3, 1–4"
Erich Grässer, "Kol 3, 1–4 als Beispiel einer Interpretation secundum homines recipientes," *ZNW* 64 (1967): 139–68.

Greeven, "Prüfung der Thesen von J. Knox zum Philemonbrief"
Heinrich Greeven, "Prüfung der Thesen von J. Knox zum Philemonbrief," *ThLZ* 79 (1954): 373–78.

Harrison, "Onesimus"
P. N. Harrison, "Onesimus and Philemon," *ATR* 32 (1950): 268–94.

Haupt
Erich Haupt, *Die Gefangenschaftsbriefe*. KEK 8–9 (Göttingen: 1902).

Hegermann, *Schöpfungsmittler*
Harald Hegermann, *Die Vorstellung vom Schöpfungsmittler im hellenistischen Judentum und Urchristentum*. TU 82 (Berlin: 1961).

Heitmüller, *Im Namen Jesu*
Wilhelm Heitmüller, *Im Namen Jesu: Eine Sprach- und religionsgeschichtliche Untersuchung zum Neuen Testament speziell zur altchristlichen Taufe*. FRLANT[2] (Göttingen: 1903).

Hennecke–Schneemelcher 1, 2
Edgar Hennecke, *New Testament Apocrypha*, ed. Wilhelm Schneemelcher, tr. ed. R. McL. Wilson, vol. 1 (Philadelphia: Westminster, 1963); vol. 2 (Philadelphia: Westminster, 1964).

Holtzmann, *Kritik*
Heinrich Julius Holtzmann, *Kritik der Epheser- und Kolosserbriefe* (Leipzig: 1872).

Jang, *Philemonbrief*
L. Kh. Jang, *Der Philemonbrief im Zusammenhang mit dem theologischen Denken des Apostels Paulus*. Unpub. Diss. (Bonn: 1964).

Jervell, *Imago Dei*
Jacob Jervell, *Imago Dei: Gen 1, 26f im Spätjuden-*

tum, in der Gnosis und in den paulinischen Briefen. FRLANT 58 (Göttingen: 1960).

Kamlah, *Form*
Erhard Kamlah, *Die Form der katalogischen Paränese im Neuen Testament*. WUNT 7 (Tübingen: 1964).

Käsemann, *Aufsätze 1, 2*
Ernst Käsemann, *Exegetische Versuche und Besinnungen*, vol. 1 (Göttingen: 1960); vol. 2 (Göttingen: 1964).

Käsemann, *Essays*
Ernst Käsemann, *Essays on New Testament Themes*, tr. W. J. Montague. SBT 41 (Naperville: Alec R. Allenson, 1964).

Käsemann, *Leib Christi*
Ernst Käsemann, *Leib und Leib Christi: Eine Untersuchung zur paulinischen Begrifflichkeit*. BHTh 9 (Tübingen: 1933).

Käsemann, "Römer 13:1–7"
Ernst Käsemann, "Römer 13:1–7 in unserer Generation," *ZThK* 56 (1959): 316–76.

Kittel, "Kol 1, 24"
Gerhard Kittel, "Kol 1,24," *ZSTh* 18 (1941): 186–91.

Klein, *Die Zwölf Apostel*
Günther Klein, *Die Zwölf Apostel: Ursprung und Gehalt einer Idee*. FRLANT 77 (Göttingen: 1961).

Knox, *Philemon*
John Knox, *Philemon Among the Letters of Paul, A New View of its Place and Importance* (New York and Nashville: Abingdon Press, [2]1959).

Kramer, *Christ, Lord, Son of God*
Werner Kramer, *Christ, Lord, Son of God*, tr. Brian Hardy. SBT 50 (Naperville: Alec R. Allenson, 1966).

Koester, "The Purpose"
Helmut Koester, "The Purpose of the Polemic of a Pauline Fragment (Philippians III)," *NTS* 8 (1961–62): 317–32.

Kremer, *Leiden Christi*
Jacob Kremer, *Was an den Leiden Christi noch mangelt: Eine interpretationsgeschichtliche und exegetische Untersuchung zu Kol. 1, 24b*. BBB 12 (Bonn: 1956).

Kümmel, *Introduction*
Introduction to the New Testament, founded by Paul Feine and Johannes Behm, re-ed. Werner Georg Kümmel, tr. A. J. Mattill, Jr. (New York and Nashville: Abingdon, 1966).

Kuhn, "Epheserbrief"
K. G. Kuhn, "Der Epheserbrief im Lichte der Qumrantexte," *NTS* 7 (1960–61): 334–46.

Larsson, *Christus*
Edvin Larsson, *Christus als Vorbild: Eine Untersuchung zu den paulinischen Tauf- und Eikontexten*. ASNU 23 (Uppsala: 1962).

Lietzmann, *Römer*
Hans Lietzmann, *An die Römer*. HNT 8 (Tübingen: [4]1933).

Lightfoot
J. B. Lightfoot, *St. Paul's Epistles to the Colossians and to Philemon* (London and New York: Macmillan, [3]1879, [4]1892).

Lohmeyer
Ernst Lohmeyer, *Die Briefe an die Philipper, an die Kolosser und an Philemon*. KEK 9 (Göttingen: [9]1953, [13]1964).

Lohmeyer, *Probleme*
Ernst Lohmeyer, "Probleme paulinischer Theologie, I. Briefliche Grussüberschriften," *ZNW* 26 (1927): 158–73; reprinted as *Probleme paulinischer Theologie* (Darmstadt and Stuttgart: 1954), 9–29.

Lohse, "Christologie und Ethik"
Eduard Lohse, "Christologie und Ethik im Kolosserbrief," in *Apophoreta, Festschrift für Ernst Haenchen*. BZNW 30 (Berlin: 1964), 156–68.

Lohse, "Christusherrschaft und Kirche"
Eduard Lohse, "Christusherrschaft und Kirche im Kolosserbrief," *NTS* 11 (1964–65): 203–16.

Lohse, *Märtyrer und Gottesknecht*
Eduard Lohse, *Märtyrer und Gottesknecht: Untersuchungen zur urchristlichen Verkündigung vom Sühnetod Jesu Christi*. FRLANT 46 (Göttingen: 1955).

Lührmann, *Offenbarungsverständnis*
Dieter Lührmann, *Das Offenbarungsverständnis bei Paulus und in paulinischen Gemeinden*. WMANT 16 (Neukirchen: 1965).

Lyonnet, "Colossiens"
Stanislas Lyonnet, "L'Épître aux Colossiens (Col 2, 18) et les mystères d'Apollon Clarien," *Biblica* 43 (1962): 417–35.

Lyonnet, "L'hymne christologique"
Stanislas Lyonnet, "L'hymne christologique de l'Épître aux Colossiens et la fête juive du Nouvel An," *RechSR* 48 (1960): 92–100.

Lyonnet, "St. Paul"
Stanislas Lyonnet, "St. Paul et le gnosticisme: la lettre aux Colossiens" in *Le Origini dello Gnosticismo*, ed. U. Bianchi (Leiden: 1967), 538–61.

Masson
Charles Masson, *L'épître de Saint Paul aux Colossiens* in Commentaire du Nouveau Testament 10 (Neuchatel and Paris: 1950).

Maurer, "Die Begründung der Herrschaft Christi"
Christian Maurer, "Die Begründung der Herrschaft Christi über die Mächte nach Kolosser 1, 15–20," *Wort und Dienst* NF 4 (1955): 79–93.

Mayerhoff, *Der Brief an die Colosser*
Ernst Theodor Mayerhoff, *Der Brief an die Colosser, mit vornehmlicher Berücksichtigung der drei Pastoralbriefe kritisch geprüft* (Berlin: 1838).

Merk, *Handeln*
Otto Merk, *Handeln aus Glauben: Die Motivierungen der paulinischen Ethik*. Marburger Theologische Studien 5 (Marburg: 1968).

Michaelis, *Einleitung*
Wilhelm Michaelis, *Einleitung in das Neue Testament* (Bern: [3]1961).

Michaelis, *Gefangenschaft*
Wilhelm Michaelis, *Die Gefangenschaft des Paulus in*

Ephesus und das Itinerar des Timotheus, Untersuchung zur Chronologie des Paulus und der Paulusbriefe. NF 1, 3 (Gütersloh: 1925).

Moule
C. F. D. Moule, *The Epistles of Paul to the Colossians and to Philemon* in The Cambridge Greek Testament Commentary (London and Edinburgh: Marshall, Morgan & Scott, 1957).

Moule, H. C. G., *Colossian Studies*
H. C. G. Moule, *Colossian Studies, Lessons in Faith and Holiness from St. Paul's Epistles to the Colossians and Philemon* (London: Pickering & Inglis, [2]1926).

Moulton, *Prolegomena*
James Hope Moulton, *A Grammar of New Testament Greek*, vol. 1, *Prolegomena* (Edinburgh: T. & T. Clark, [3]1919).

Moulton–Turner
James Hope Moulton, *A Grammar of New Testament Greek*, vol. 3, *Syntax*, by Nigel Turner (Edinburgh: T. & T. Clark, 1963).

Münderlein, "Die Erwählung"
Gerhard Münderlein, "Die Erwählung durch das Pleroma, Bemerkungen zu Kol. 1.19," *NTS* 8 (1961–62): 264–76.

Mussner, *Christus das All*
Franz Mussner, *Christus, das All und die Kirche: Studien zur Theologie des Epheserbriefes*. Trierer Theologische Studien 5 (Trier: 1955).

Neugebauer, *In Christus*
Fritz Neugebauer, *In Christus*—ΕΝ ΧΡΙΣΤΩΙ*: Eine Untersuchung zum paulinischen Glaubensverständnis* (Göttingen and Berlin: 1961).

Norden, *Agnostos Theos*
Eduard Norden, *Agnostos Theos, Untersuchungen zur Formengeschichte religiöser Rede* (Leipzig: 1913 = Darmstadt: [4]1956).

Percy, *Probleme*
Ernst Percy, *Die Probleme der Kolosser– und Epheserbriefe*. Acta reg. Societatis Humaniorum Litterarum Lundensis 39 (Lund: 1946).

Preiss, *Life in Christ*
Théo Preiss, *Life in Christ*, tr. Harold Knight. SBT 13 (London: SCM Press, 1954).

Radermacher, *Grammatik*
Ludwig Radermacher, *Neutestamentliche Grammatik, Das Griechische des Neuen Testaments im Zusammenhang mit der Volkssprache*. HNT 1, 1 (Tübingen: [2]1925).

Reicke, "Verständnis"
Bo Reicke, "Zum sprachlichen Verständnis von Kol 2, 23," *ST* 6 (1952): 39–53.

Reitzenstein, *Erlösungsmysterium*
Richard Reitzenstein, *Das iranische Erlösungsmysterium* (Bonn: 1921).

Reitzenstein, *Mysterienreligionen*
R. Reitzenstein, *Die hellenistischen Mysterienreligionen* (Leipzig and Berlin: [3]1927).

Rengstorf, "Mahnungen an die Frau"
Karl Heinrich Rengstorf, "Die neutestamentlichen Mahnungen an die Frau, sich dem Manne unterzuordnen" in *Verbum Dei manet in aeternum, Festschrift für Otto Schmitz*, ed. Werner Foerster (Witten: 1953), 131–45.

Reumann, "OIKONOMIA-Terms"
John Reumann, "OIKONOMIA-Terms in Paul in Comparison with Lucan *Heilsgeschichte*," *NTS* 13 (1966–67): 147–67.

Rigaux, "Révélation des Mystères"
B. Rigaux, "Révélation des Mystères et Perfection à Qumrân et dans le Nouveau Testament," *NTS* 4 (1957–58): 237–62.

Robinson, "A Formal Analysis"
James M. Robinson, "A Formal Analysis of Colossians 1:15–20," *JBL* 76 (1957): 270–87.

Robinson, "Hodajot-Formel"
James M. Robinson, "Die Hodajot-Formel in Gebet und Hymnus des Frühchristentums" in *Apophoreta: Festschrift für Ernst Haenchen*. BZNW 30 (Berlin: 1964), 194–235.

Roller, *Das Formular*
Otto Roller, *Das Formular der paulinischen Briefe*. BWANT 4, 6 (Stuttgart: 1933).

Sanders, "Literary Dependence"
Ed Parish Sanders, "Literary Dependence in Colossians," *JBL* 85 (1966): 28–45.

Schaff
Philip Schaff, ed. *A Select Library of the Nicene and Post–Nicene Fathers*, 1st Series (New York: The Christian Literature Company, 1889).

Schattenmann, *Prosahymnus*
Johannes Schattenmann, *Studien zum neutestamentlichen Prosahymnus* (München: 1965).

Schenke, "Widerstreit"
Hans-Martin Schenke, "Der Widerstreit gnostischer und kirchlicher Christologie im Spiegel des Kolosserbriefes," *ZThK* 61 (1964): 391–403.

Schille, *Frühchristliche Hymnen*
Gottfried Schille, *Frühchristliche Hymnen* (Berlin: 1962, [2]1965).

Schlier, *Christus*
Heinrich Schlier, *Christus und die Kirche im Epheserbrief*. BHTh 6 (Tübingen: 1930).

Schlier, *Epheser*
Heinrich Schlier, *Der Brief an die Epheser* (Düsseldorf: [5]1965).

Schlier, *Galater*
Heinrich Schlier, *Der Brief an die Galater*. KEK 7 (Göttingen: [12]1962).

Schmithals, *Apostelamt*
Walter Schmithals, *Das kirchliche Apostelamt: Eine historische Untersuchung*. FRLANT 79 (Göttingen: 1961).

Schmithals, *Die Gnosis*
Walter Schmithals, *Die Gnosis in Korinth*. FRLANT 66 (Göttingen: [2]1965).

Schrage, *Einzelgebote*
Wolfgang Schrage, *Die konkreten Einzelgebote in der paulinischen Paränese* (Gütersloh: 1961).

Schroeder, *Die Haustafeln*
D. Schroeder, *Die Haustafeln des Neuen Testaments: Ihre Herkunft und ihr theologischer Sinn*. Unpub. Diss. (Hamburg: 1959).
Schubert, *Pauline Thanksgivings*
Paul Schubert, *Form and Function of the Pauline Thanksgivings*. BZNW 20 (Berlin: 1939).
Schweizer, *Church Order*
Eduard Schweizer, *Church Order in The New Testament*, tr. Frank Clark. SBT 32 (London: SCM Press, 1961).
Schweizer, *Erniedrigung*
Eduard Schweizer, *Erniedrigung und Erhöhung bei Jesus und seinen Nachfolgern*. AThANT 28 (Zürich: [1]1955, [2]1962).
Schweizer, *Neotestamentica*
Eduard Schweizer, *Neotestamentica: deutsche und englische Aufsätze 1951–1963; German and English Essays 1951–1963* (Zürich: 1963).
von Soden
H. von Soden, *Die Briefe an die Kolosser, Epheser, Philemon; die Pastoralbriefe* in Hand-Commentar zum Neuen Testament 3, 1 (Freiburg i.B. and Leipzig: [2]1893).
Spicq, *Agape*
Ceslaus Spicq, *Agape in the New Testament*, tr. Marie Aquinas McNamara and Mary Honoria Richter, vol. 2 (St. Louis: B. Herder, 1965).
Staab, *Gefangenschaftsbriefe*
Karl Staab, *Die Gefangenschaftsbriefe* in Regensburger Neues Testament 7 (Regensburg: [3]1959).
Staerk, *Gebete*
Willy Staerk, *Altjüdische liturgische Gebete*. KIT 58 (Berlin: [2]1930).
Tachau, '*Einst*' und '*Jetzt*'
P. Tachau, '*Einst*' *und* '*Jetzt*' *im Neuen Testament*. Unpub. Diss. (Göttingen: 1968).
Tannehill, *Dying and Rising*
Robert C. Tannehill, *Dying and Rising with Christ: A Study in Pauline Theology*. BZNW 32 (Berlin: 1967).
Vincent
Marvin R. Vincent, *The Epistles to the Philippians and to Philemon*. ICC (Edinburgh: T. & T. Clark, 1897, [5]1955).
Vögtle, *Tugend– und Lasterkataloge*
Anton Vögtle, *Die Tugend– und Lasterkataloge im Neuen Testament: Exegetisch, religions– und formgeschichtlich untersucht*. NTAbh 16, 4.5 (Münster i.W.: 1936).
Wagenführer, *Die Bedeutung Christi*
Max Adolf Wagenführer, *Die Bedeutung Christi für Welt und Kirche: Studien zum Kolosser– und Epheserbrief* (Leipzig: 1941).
Wegenast, *Verständnis*
Klaus Wegenast, *Das Verständnis der Tradition bei Paulus und in den Deuteropaulinen*. WMANT 8 (Neukirchen: 1962).
Weidinger, *Die Haustafeln*
Karl Weidinger, *Die Haustafeln: Ein Stück urchristlicher Paränese*. UNT 14 (Leipzig: 1928).
Weiss, *Untersuchungen zur Kosmologie*
Hans–Friedrich Weiss, *Untersuchungen zur Kosmologie des hellenistischen und palästinischen Judentums*. TU 97 (Berlin: 1966).
Wendland, *Literaturformen*
Paul Wendland, *Die urchristlichen Literaturformen*. HNT 1, 3 (Tübingen: [2, 3]1912).
Wengst, *Formeln*
K. Wengst, *Christologische Formeln und Lieder des Urchristentums*. Unpub. Diss. (Bonn: 1967).
Wibbing, *Tugend– und Lasterkataloge*
Siegfried Wibbing, *Die Tugend– und Lasterkataloge im Neuen Testament und ihre Traditionsgeschichte unter besonderer Berücksichtigung der Qumran–Texte*. BZNW 25 (Berlin: 1959).
Wickert, "Philemonbrief"
Ulrich Wickert, "Der Philemonbrief—Privatbrief oder apostolisches Sendschreiben?" *ZNW* 52 (1961): 230–38.
Wilckens, *Weisheit*
Ulrich Wilckens, *Weisheit und Torheit: Eine exegetische–religionsgeschichtliche Untersuchung zur 1 Kor 1 und 2*. BHTh 26 (Tübingen: 1959).
Wildberger, "Das Abbild Gottes"
H. Wildberger, "Das Abbild Gottes" ThZ 21 (1965): 245–59, 481–501.
Zahn, *Introduction*
Theodor Zahn, *Introduction to the New Testament*, tr. ed. Melanchthon Williams Jacobus and Charles Snow Thayer (New York: Charles Scribner's Sons, [3]1917).

Editor's Note

The English translation of the Epistles to the Colossians and to Philemon printed in this volume was made by the translators on the basis of the Greek text, but they tried to reflect the author's exegetical decisions and consulted his German translation throughout.

The translators are also responsible for all translations of other biblical texts, but they have followed the *Revised Standard Version* wherever possible.

Translations of ancient Greek and Latin texts are taken from the *Loeb Classical Library* in all instances in which no particular source for the translation is identified. In all other cases, the source of the translation is given in brackets [ ]; or it is noted that the translators have rendered the text into English [Trans.].

Whenever available, recent scholarly works are cited in their published English versions. Quotations from literature not available in English translation have been rendered by the translators. In several instances, a published English translation proved unsatisfactory; in such cases, the translators have given their own rendering as indicated by a note in brackets.

With respect to all scholarly publications which are available in the English language, we have not preserved the author's references to the original publications in other languages, except in the Bibliography. Though it seemed desirable to maintain such references, it would have overburdened the footnotes considerably.

The Bibliography has been supplemented by a few additional entries which have appeared since 1968. These titles are marked by an asterisk (*).

The endpapers in this book are from the Chester Beatty Biblical Papyri and are reproduced by courtesy of the Chester Beatty Museum, Dublin, Ireland. The front endpaper is a reproduction of a complete fragment of Colossians 2:23—3:11; the back endpaper is an enlarged detail from the same fragment.

Colossians

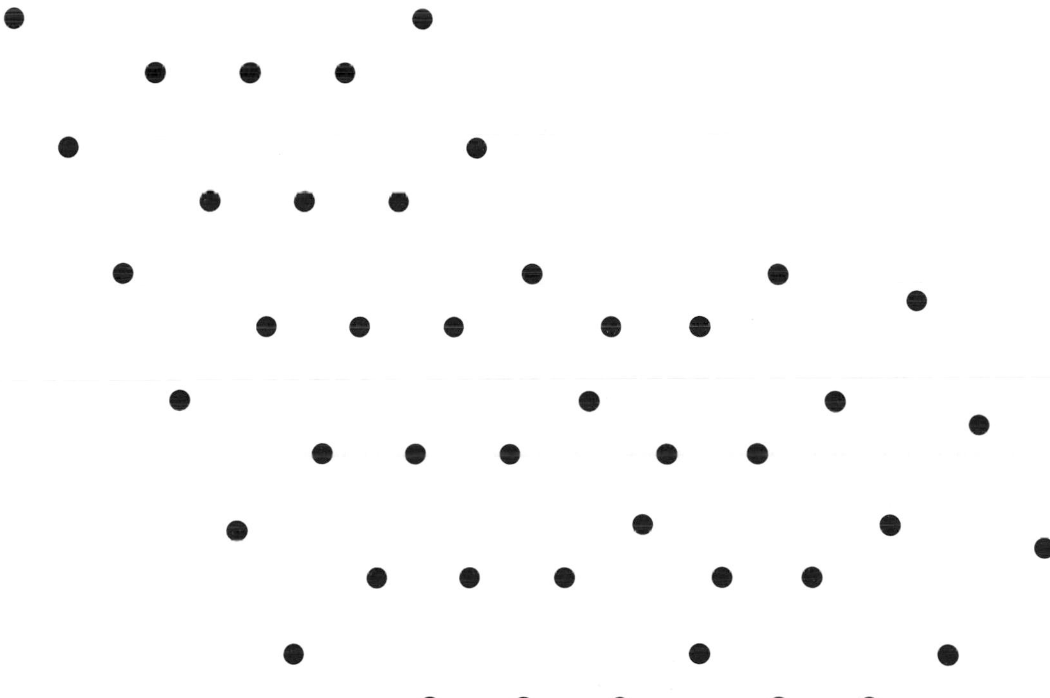

1. The community in Colossae

The saints in Colossae, who are addressed as faithful brothers in Christ (1:2), were not brought to faith in Jesus Christ as Lord by Paul himself, for during his missionary work in Asia Minor (2:1) the apostle never reached Colossae in the upper valley of the Lycus. However, the good news which he proclaimed principally in the larger cities and centers of commerce was quick to spread. Christians who belonged to communities which Paul had founded carried the gospel farther into the interior of Asia Minor, so that communities sprang up not only in Colossae but also in nearby Laodicea and Hierapolis (2:1; 4:13, 15). No firsthand information concerning the beginnings of these communities has survived; thus any information about the founding of the Christian community in Colossae and its situation must be derived from the letter itself.

There are many allusions to the heathen past of the letter's recipients. They are reminded that they were once estranged, with a hostile mind involved in evil deeds (1:21); it is said that they were dead in sins and in uncircumcision of the flesh (2:13). Thus they were heathen who heard the good news through Epaphras (1:7f and 4:12f) and accepted it. In baptism they experienced the creative power of God who raised them to new life (2:12), who forgave their sin (1:14; 2:13), and who raised them with Christ (3:1) in order that they might henceforth conduct their lives under the dominion of Christ (1:13f). The proclamation, which was discerned to be the truth (1:5f), had been presented as teaching (1:17) which had been shaped into a distinct form in the tradition (2:6f). Of this tradition, particular elements, fixed in their wording, were cited in this letter: there is the hymn which sings of the universal dominion of the exalted Christ (1:15–20); the sentences which deal with baptism and God's act in the cross of Christ (2:12–15); lists of deeds which the Christians should put away and avoid (3:5, 8) as well as a definition of the attitude to be practiced in conduct (3:12); and, finally, the series of exhortations directed to Christians in various stations of life (3:18–4:1). The community is reminded of this familiar teaching and made aware of the consequences which necessarily follow from it: to confess Christ as the Lord who holds in his hands the rule over the whole world, and to be obedient to him in all phases of life.

Until now the community has, in fact, been faithful to this teaching. It holds firmly to the faith, has demonstrated its love to all the saints, and knows of the hope which is prepared in the heavens (1:4f). The word of truth, which the community had once heard, is now active among them, growing and bearing fruit (1:5f).

What is decisive now, however, is that the community, rooted and built up in Christ, established in the faith, continue its resolute loyalty to the received teaching (2:7). Thus the appeal to persevere, to be regular in prayer, to be watching with thanksgiving, and to be constant in intercession (4:2 f). There is a call to let wisdom guide one's conduct of life and to make the most of the time (4:5). In addition, the community is again assured that it had received the genuine truth in the instruction of Epaphras, its founder (1:6f). Epaphras, a witness of the gospel who is expressly legitimized by the apostle, again, as previously, puts himself fully into the work. His activity and intercession, which he makes before God in prayer for the community, have but one aim, "that you may stand forth perfect and be filled with everything that is God's will" (*ἵνα σταθῆτε τέλειοι καὶ πεπληροφορημένοι ἐν παντὶ θελήματι τοῦ θεοῦ*, 4:12).

The situation in the community, as is evident from this letter, corresponds completely to the image of a community which is obedient to the apostolic gospel. Admittedly, illustrative features which might come from actual experience and personal acquaintance are missing from the description. Rather, it is kept quite general, and conventional phrases state how genuine Christians in all places ought to live in the "love in the Spirit" (*ἀγάπην ἐν πνεύματι*, 1:8).

2. The occasion for the letter

Although the community's life and conduct offer no cause for reprimand, the author of the letter is deeply worried that the community, unsuspecting and innocent as it is, may be led astray by false teaching and become the victim of deceivers. For this reason the community is urgently warned and admonished concerning the distinction between correct and false preaching: "Be on your guard that no one snares you by philosophy and empty deceit" (*βλέπετε μή τις ὑμᾶς ἔσται ὁ συλαγωγῶν διὰ τῆς φιλοσοφίας καὶ κενῆς ἀπάτης*, 2:8). This warning points out the danger which threatens the community. Some persons have appeared who call their teaching "philosophy" (*φιλοσοφία*) which apparently refers to the secret information of the divine ground of being, the proper perception of the "elements of the universe" (στοιχεῖα τοῦ κόσμου, 2:8, 20), and the way which must be taken in order to be in the proper relation to them. These elements of the universe, represented as strong angelic powers, determine not only the cosmic order but the destiny of the individual. Thus man must serve them in cultic adoration and follow the regulations which they impose upon him (2:16–23): careful observance of the particular holy times—festivals, new moon, Sabbath (2:16)—as well as imposed abstinence from certain food and drink.

The outline of this teaching can be inferred from the polemical statements in the letter's second chapter. This teaching could have made some impression even on Christians, for it promised protection from cosmic powers and principalities. A Christian might have supposed that he had not (or not sufficiently) received such protection in the Christian proclamation and in the pronouncement of the forgiveness of sins. In addition, adherents of this teaching, as well as members of the community who paid attention to them, presumably supposed that this "philosophy" could very easily be united with Christian faith. Indeed, faith is only brought to its true completion by this combination. This, however, raises the critical question: is the preaching of the gospel to be drawn into that varicolored mesh of the syncretism of late antiquity, or is the proclamation of the crucified, resurrected and exalted Christ to be taken as the exclusively valid answer which applies to all man's questions and searchings?

In order to oppose this "philosophy," the letter to the Colossians at its very beginning refers back to the hymnic confession with which the community is familiar (1:15–20); from this hymn the letter develops its message, in which Christ is proclaimed as Lord over all the world. In him the whole fullness of deity dwells bodily (2:9); he is the head of all powers and principalities (2:10), he is the head of his body, the Church (1:18). The whole fullness and the forgiveness of sins, as well as the gift of new life (1:12–14; 2:12–15), has come to the man who has been buried with Christ in baptism and has been raised with him by faith in the power of God who raised Christ from the dead (2:12). This man cannot and may not devote himself to a worship of angels and to enslaving regulations, for he has already died with Christ to the elements of the universe (2:20). On the one side is Christ, as he was preached and received in faith, and on the other is "philosophy" (φιλοσοφία) which in truth is "empty deceit" (κενὴ ἀπάτη, 2:8). This opposition ought to be clearly and sharply perceived by the community through the aid of the apostolic teaching which is once again presented to them.

3. The structure of the letter

The letter to the Colossians begins with the introductory greetings (1:1–2); to this are joined the thanksgiving for the good state of the community (1:3–8) and the plea that they may progress in knowledge and in conduct of life (1:9–11).

The first, instructional portion is introduced by the summons to hymnic praise and the quoting of the Christ-hymn (1:12–20). Then the hymn is applied to the community: the word of reconciliation is pronounced to them (1:21–23). Indissolubly connected with the correct proclamation, however, is the office of the apostle, who has been commissioned to proclaim Christ as the Lord among the Gentiles (1:24–2:5). As the apostolic gospel in its basic meaning is elucidated, presuppositions are created for warding off the false teaching which threatens the community (2:6–23). This refutation is given in two parts: first, from the confession of Jesus as Lord, it follows that his dominion includes everything—thus also the principalities and powers (2:6–15); second, for all those who belong to this Lord it is simply impossible to worship the cosmic elements and to obey their regulations (2:16–23).

The second, hortatory portion is equally determined by the theme of the universal dominion of Christ: those who have been raised with Christ are to seek that which is above (3:1–4). That means, however, that they are to put to death what is earthly, i.e., to put off the old being, to take off the old man and put on the new man. Under the governance of love the new man is active and the word of Christ proves effective. Through Christ, thankful praise is brought to God the Father (3:5–17). Next, the letter demonstrates how in reality obedience to the Kyrios ought to be carried out, in view of the various social positions in which individual members of the community live (3:18–4:1). The hortatory section ends with several admonitions addressed to the entire community (4:2–6).

The concluding section contains personal messages, greetings and short instructions (4:7–18).

Just as there is the unfolding of the universal scope of the dominion of Christ in the first two chapters of the letter, the third and fourth chapters give an exposition of the ways in which the lordship of Christ includes all areas of our life. Teaching and exhortation are thus closely bound to one another. As Christ is Lord over all (1:15–20), so his own people should do all in the name of the Lord Jesus (3:17).[1]

4. Time and origin of the letter

Paul is in prison (4:3, 10), but where he is imprisoned is not stated. Likewise there is no indication of the particular time when the letter was composed. The community is urged, however, to remember the apostle in prison (4:18). His suffering, which he must endure for the sake of his commission (4:3, 10), is of a piece with his apostolic office. He completes vicariously for the church—that is, the body of Christ—what is still lacking of the eschatological afflictions of Christ (1:24). Paul has been entrusted with the proclamation among the Gentiles (1:27); therefore the community at Colossae lies within the sphere of his official responsibility. Although it does not know the apostle personally, the community must realize that he is struggling and that he is laboring for it (2:1). Even though he is physically distant, he is close to the community in spirit (2:5) and speaks to it with the apostolic word.

Since this letter gives no indication of the place or time of its composition, the only way to determine its place in the *corpus Paulinum* and to clarify the problem of its origin is by a thoroughgoing comparison with the other Pauline letters. The use and connections of words, the structure and sequence of sentences must all be investigated in depth and compared with the world of thought and manner of expression in the other Pauline letters to churches. Above all, however, the theological content of Colossians must be made explicit in such a way that its statements about christology, ecclesiology, teaching concerning the apostolic office, eschatology, and its understanding of baptism are considered in their relation to the theology of other Pauline letters. The letter to the Ephesians will be continuously taken into account here, since it has extensive similarities to Colossians in language, style and theology. In certain passages Ephesians reads like the first commentary on Colossians, though admittedly it does more than explicate the thoughts of Colossians: it also expands them into concepts of its own.[2] While in these analyses and in the exegesis of Colossians we shall speak of the "author" or the "apostle," this does not imply a decision concerning the Pauline or non-Pauline origin of the letter to the Colossians. Rather, this question will be left open and be answered only later, after considering all points of view which must be taken into account.

1 The word "all" and related words appear with extraordinary frequency in Colossians: 1:4, 6, 9–11, 15–20, 28; 2:2f, 9f, 13, 19, 22; 3:8, 11, 14, 16f, 20, 22; 4:7, 9, 12. These passages are like a red thread drawn through every section of the letter.

2 Concerning the question of the relation of Ephesians to Colossians, I will note here only that Colossians has, in any event, chronological priority; cf. the comprehensive treatment in Werner Georg Kümmel, *Introduction to the New Testament*, tr. A. J. Mattill, Jr. (New York and Nashville: Abingdon, 1966), 253f. See also Ernst Percy, *Die Probleme der Kolosser- und Epheserbriefe* (Lund: 1946), 360–433, and Pierre Benoit, "Rapports littéraires entre les épîtres aux Colossiens et Éphésiens," in *Neutestamentliche Aufsätze, Festschrift für Joseph Schmid* (Regensburg: 1963), 11–22, reprinted in *Exégèse et Théologie* 3 (Paris: 1968), 318–334. However, cf. also John Coutts, "The Relationship of Ephesians and Colossians," *NTS* 4 (1957–58): 201–07. Indeed, Ephesians could be considered as not directly dependent upon Colossians, but as dependent upon hymnic–liturgical and catechetical traditions which were independently used in each letter (cf. Nils A. Dahl, "Der Epheserbrief und der verlorene erste Brief des Paulus an die Korinther" in *Abraham Unser Vater, Festschrift für Otto Michel*, Arbeiten zur Geschichte des Spätjudentums und Urchristentums 5 [Leiden: 1963], 71f, and the works listed in footnote 1, p. 71). However, as Kümmel, *Introduction*, 253ff states, it is by far the more probable assumption that the author of Ephesians knew Colossians and had a copy of it. Cf. also W. Ochel, "Die Annahme einer Bearbeitung des Kolosserbriefs im Epheserbrief," Unpub. Diss. (Marburg: 1934). In the exegesis detailed attention will be given to the manner in which the statements of Colossians are taken up and further developed in Ephesians.

1 Introductory greeting

1 **Paul, an apostle of Christ Jesus through the will of God, and Timothy, the brother, 2/ to the saints in Colossae, the faithful brothers in Christ; grace and peace from God our Father.**

The introduction of Col gives the name of Paul, adds the title of apostle, and states that Timothy also is sending this letter. There follow the naming of the recipients and the greetings that wish them grace and peace. Both verses, then, correspond to the outline of the formula used in all the Pauline letters.[1]

The Pauline prescript follows the oriental model for a letter and employs this in a Hellenized form; the content, however, reveals a decisive Christian influence.[2] Whereas the Greek form for a letter, together with the name of the sender and the addressee, uses the verbal form χαίρειν (to greet), the oriental model is characterized by its two-fold form.[3] First: the name of the sender and that of the addressee; second: the greeting in the form of direct address: peace be with you! Thus an edict of King Nebuchadnezzar opens with the words "King Nebuchadnezzar to all peoples, nations and languages that dwell in all the earth: peace be multiplied to you!" (Dan 3:98 ⌊4:1⌋). The letter which the leader of Jewish insurrectionists sent to a subject begins in this manner: "From Simon ben Kosheba to Jeshua ben Gilgola and the people of his company: peace!"[4] The introduction of a letter can be made more extensive by the addition of decorative epithets or explanatory remarks, and by making the greeting more verbose.[5] In any case, the basic structure of the formula remains the same.

In the prescript of the Pauline letters the sender and addressee are described as Christians, and the greeting is "grace and peace" (χάρις καὶ εἰρήνη). Occasionally in Jewish letters one finds "mercy" (ἔλεος)[6] alongside "peace" (εἰρήνη), but never "grace" (χάρις). Perhaps it was significant in the choice of this word that "grace" clearly reminds one of the usual Greek greeting (χάρις: χαίρειν).

In any case, "grace" clearly expresses the fact that the reference is to that "peace" which has been inaugurated by God's eschatological action (cf. Lk 2:14). The content of the greeting of "peace" is thus more clearly defined by the wish for grace. At the close of the letters this wish is regularly taken up again: "the grace of our Lord Jesus Christ be with you" (ἡ χάρις τοῦ κυρίου ἡμῶν Ἰησοῦ

1 Cf. Paul Wendland, *Die urchristlichen Literaturformen*, HNT 1, 3 (Tübingen: ^{2,3}1912): 411–17; Ernst Lohmeyer, "Probleme paulinischer Theologie, I. Briefliche Grussüberschriften," *ZNW* 26 (1927): 158–73; reprinted in *idem*, *Probleme paulinischer Theologie* (Darmstadt and Stuttgart: 1954), 9–29; Hans Lietzmann, *An die Römer*, HNT 8 (Tübingen: ^{4}1933), 22; Otto Roller, *Das Formular der paulinischen Briefe*, BWANT 4, 6 (Stuttgart: 1933); Gerhard Friedrich, "Lohmeyers These über das paulinische Briefpräskript kritisch beleuchtet," *ThLZ* 81 (1956): 343–46; Johannes Schneider, "Brief," *RAC* 2, 564–76.

2 This was correctly recognized by Lohmeyer, *Probleme*, 9–29, contrary to Schneider, "Brief," 575, who states "Paul adopted the Greek model for letters but he reconstructed and expanded it for Christian content."

3 The Greek model for letters appears in several passages in the NT: Jas 1:1 "James, a servant of God and of the Lord Jesus Christ, to the twelve tribes in the dispersion greetings." (Ἰάκωβος θεοῦ καὶ κυρίου Ἰησοῦ Χριστοῦ δοῦλος ταῖς δώδεκα φυλαῖς ταῖς ἐν τῇ διασπορᾷ χαίρειν). Cf. also Acts 15:23, 29; 23:26, 30 *v. l.*

4 Cf. J. T. Milik, "Une lettre de Siméon Bar Kokheba (Pl. XIV)," *RB* 60 (1953): 276–94; *idem*, *Discoveries in the Judaean Desert* 2, ed. P. Benoit, J. T. Milik, R. de Vaux (Oxord: 1961), 159–61.

5 Examples from Rabbinic literature are found in Hermann Strack and Paul Billerbeck, *Kommentar zum Neuen Testament aus Talmud und Midrasch* 3 (München: 1961), 1.

6 2 Bar 78:2 "Thus says Baruch, son of Neriah, to the brethren carried into captivity: Mercy and Peace be with you."

Χριστοῦ μεθ' ὑμῶν 1 Thess 5:28).[7] Though 1 Thess 1:1 has only the short, quick introduction, "Grace to you and peace" (χάρις ὑμῖν καὶ εἰρήνη), there is usually the addition "from God our Father and the Lord Jesus Christ" (ἀπὸ θεοῦ πατρὸς ἡμῶν καὶ κυρίου 'Ιησοῦ Χριστοῦ Gal 1:3).[8]

■ **1** The statement concerning the sender agrees verbatim with the opening of 2 Cor, "Paul, an apostle of Christ Jesus by the will of God, and Timothy, the brother." (Παῦλος ἀπόστολος Χριστοῦ 'Ιησοῦ διὰ θελήματος θεοῦ καὶ Τιμόθεος ὁ ἀδελφός 2 Cor 1:1). At the head of the letter is the name of Paul, the name which the apostle used in the Hellenistic-Roman world instead of the Jewish "Saul" (שָׁאוּל: Σαῦλος).[9] Directly following is the title by means of which the official character of this writing to the community is indicated. Paul has been called by the will of God[10] to be the ambassador plenipotentiary of the exalted Lord (cf. Gal 1:1, 15f),[11] and thus he speaks to the community by virtue of the authority which was granted him. As the apostle to the Gentiles who holds the commission to proclaim the Good News to the heathen, he is *the* Apostle.[12] In Col no mention occurs of any apostle except Paul. There is no need to defend his status against attacks such as those made in Galatia and Corinth against the office of Paul (cf. Gal 1:1, 10–12; 1 Cor 9:1, 3; 2 Cor 10–13). There is also no need to gain the approval of the community for Pauline proclamation, or support of the mission's work to the heathen, as was the case in the letter to the Romans (cf. Rom 1:1–7, 8–17; 15:22f). The unique position of the apostle is undisputed, so that Paul is presented as an apostle only in the opening verse; throughout the remainder of the letter the title is not mentioned again.

Beside Paul is Timothy, his helper and co-worker. He is also mentioned in the salutation of 2 Cor and Phil (2 Cor 1:1; Phil 1:1), and in the beginnings of both Thess he is named with Silvanus (1 Thess 1:1; 2 Thess 1:1). Those who send the letter with Paul and are cited at its

7 Cf. also Gal 6:18; 1 Cor 16:23; 2 Cor 13:13; Rom 16:20; Phil 4:23; Phlm 25; 2 Thess 3:18; Col 4:18; Eph 6:24; 1 Tim 6:21; 2 Tim 4:22; Tit 3:15.

8 Cf. also 1 Cor 1:3; 2 Cor 1:2; Rom 1:7; Phil 1:2; Phlm 3; 2 Thess 1:2; Eph 1:2; 1 Tim 1:2; 2 Tim 1:2; Tit 1:4. Since the salutation lacks the articles, Lohmeyer supposed that their basis was a liturgical formula which Paul employed. Friedrich has correctly objected that the lack of the article is to be explained otherwise: just as the Hebrew greeting "peace" שָׁלוֹם has no article, so also "grace and peace" do not have it. Since, however, in the attributive use of nouns, the article is used according to the main substantive, the words dependent upon "grace and peace" follow without articles (Friedrich, "Lohmeyers These," 345f). On the other hand, the wish for "grace" at the end of the letter ("peace" does not appear here) uses the article for "grace": ἡ χάρις μεθ' ὑμῶν (Col 4:18 and elsewhere).

9 Cf. Acts 13:9 "But Saul, who is also called Paul" (Σαῦλος δέ, ὁ καὶ Παῦλος). Also cf. Ernst Haenchen, *Die Apostelgeschichte*, KEK 3 (Göttingen: [14]1965), *ad loc.* The Jews in the Greek-speaking areas took names which most closely approximated the sound of their Hebrew or Aramaic names; e.g., Silas:Silvanus (Σιλᾶς: Σιλουανός); Jesus:Jason ('Ιησοῦς:'Ιάσων). Cf. Adolf Deissmann, *Bible Studies*, tr. by A. Grieve (Edinburgh: T. & T. Clark, 1901), 314f.

10 In 1:9 and 4:12 the "will" (θέλημα) of God means the will which is to be fulfilled in the conduct of the Christian's life. Here, however, the "will" (θέλημα) of God is the will which elects, which made Paul an apostle (cf. 2 Cor 2:1; Eph 1:1; 2 Tim 1:1).

11 "Christ" (Χριστός) is no longer thought of as a title, but is connected with "Jesus" as a double name. Concerning the placing of "Christ" first, cf. Ernst von Dobschütz, *Die Thessalonicher-Briefe*, KEK 10 (Göttingen: [7]1909), 61. Also Lietzmann, *Römer*, 23; Otto Michel, *Der Brief an die Römer*, KEK 4 (Göttingen: [12]1966), 34, n. 4. There is also the sequence "of Jesus Christ" ('Ιησοῦ Χριστοῦ) in Gal 1:12; 3:22; Rom 1:4, 6, 8; 16:25, 27; Phil 1:11, 19), cf. Fritz Neugebauer, *In Christus* — ΕΝ ΧΡΙΣΤΩΙ: *Eine Untersuchung zum Paulinischen Glaubensverständnis* (Göttingen and Berlin: 1961), 46.

12 Concerning the problem of the early Christian apostolate, cf. Karl-Heinrich Rengstorf, "'Απόστολος," *TDNT* 1, ed. Gerhard Kittel, tr. Geoffrey W. Bromily, vol. 1 (Grand Rapids, Michigan and London: Eerdmans, 1964), 407–47; Gerhard Sass, *Apostelamt und Kirche: Eine theologisch-exegetische Untersuchung des paulinischen Apostelbegriffs*, Forschungen zur Geschichte und Lehre des Protestantismus 9, 2 (München: 1939); Hans von Campenhausen, "Der urchristliche Apostelbegriff," *ST* 1 (1947–48): 96–130; Eduard Lohse, "Ursprung und Prägung des christlichen Apostolates," *ThZ* 9 (1953): 259–75; Harald Riesenfeld, "Apostel," RGG[3] 1, 497–99; Günther Klein, *Die zwölf Apostel: Ursprung und Gehalt einer Idee*. FRLANT 77 (Göttingen: 1961); Walter Schmithals, *Das kirchliche Apostelamt: Eine historische Untersuchung*, FRLANT 79 (Göttingen: 1961); Jürgen Roloff, *Apostelamt—Verkündigung—Kirche: Ur-*

beginning (with the exceptions of Rom and Eph) did not have a hand in its composition.[13] Their names appear alongside Paul's in order to testify to the community that they, like the apostle, preach and teach the one gospel (cf. Gal 1:2). Timothy supported Paul with untiring loyalty; he carried reports and instructions to communities and continuously reminded them of the apostle's word (cf. 1 Cor 4:17; Phil 2:19–24). In all probability, however, no personal connection existed between Timothy and the community in Colossae, for his name is not mentioned again either in the letter or in the list of those greeting others. His name appears, then, in the salutation, just as he is placed in other letters alongside Paul as a trustworthy helper (cf. 2 Cor 1:1). At the same time, however, his position is clearly distinguished from the apostle's, for Paul alone is the apostle, while Timothy is "the brother" (ὁ ἀδελφός). As a Christian brother he is likewise closely connected to the sender and to the recipients of the letter.

■ **2** Although the letter is directed to the Christian community in Colossae, the word "church" (ἐκκλησία) is not in the address. The absence of this description is surely not to be explained by the supposition that the apostle is writing to a community unknown to him and that he therefore wishes to avoid an official–sounding expression.[14] There is, indeed, no mention of "church" (ἐκκλησία) in the salutation of Rom, but the word is also missing in the address to the community in Philippi, with which Paul had an especially cordial relation (Phil 1:1). As a matter of fact, only in the letters to Thessalonica, Corinth and Galatia are the recipients called "church" or "churches." In the letters to Rome, Philippi, Ephesus and Colossae the term "saints" (ἅγιοι) appears instead of "church." But, as 1 Cor 1:2 shows, these do not indicate any difference in meaning, for Paul turns to the Corinthians with the words "to the church of God which is in Corinth" (τῇ ἐκκλησίᾳ τοῦ θεοῦ τῇ οὔσῃ ἐν Κορίνθῳ), and then adds as an explanation "to those sanctified in Christ Jesus, called to be saints" (ἡγιασμένοις ἐν Χριστῷ Ἰησοῦ, κλητοῖς ἁγίοις, cf. also 2 Cor 1:1). Since in the salutations of the letters the Greek word ἅγιοι is never used as an adjective, but always appears as a noun,[15] τοῖς ἁγίοις in the address of Col is clearly meant to be a noun: "to the saints."[16] Whether the community, therefore, is addressed as "church" or as "saints," the meaning is always that these are the holy people whom God has chosen for himself in the end–time. As those who call upon the name of the Lord, they are his own.

That which is holy (ἅγιος) has been withdrawn from profane usage and singled out as God's exclusive possession. Thus Israel is God's holy people (Exod 19:6) who shall be holy because he is holy (Lev 11:44; 19:2; etc.). His community is not holy by reason of its own power, but by reason of God's election. The community at Qumran, accordingly, understood itself as "the people of the saints of the Covenant" (1 QM X, 10. עם קדושי ברית), who

sprung, Inhalt und Funktion des kirchlichen Apostelamtes nach Paulus, Lukas und den Pastoralbriefen (Gütersloh: 1965); Traugott Holtz, "Zum Selbstverständnis des Apostels Paulus," *ThLZ* 91 (1966): 321–30.

13 According to Roller, *Das Formular*, 21, Paul made use of a secretary when composing his letters, so "that the letter was drafted by another party according to the instructions of the apostle and perhaps on the basis of short notations on a small wax tablet. Then the rough copy was approved, perhaps even corrected by Paul, who then signed the final copy." For a critique of the secretary-hypothesis, cf. Percy, *Probleme*, 10–14; Wilhelm Michaelis, *Einleitung in das Neue Testament* (Bern: [3]1961), 242–44; Kümmel, *Introduction*, 178, 252f, 263f.

14 Thus T. K. Abbott, *The Epistles to the Ephesians and to the Colossians*, ICC (Edinburgh: T. & T. Clark, 1897), *ad loc.*

15 Cf. Rom 1:7 "To all God's beloved in Rome, who are called to be saints" (πᾶσιν τοῖς οὖσιν ἐν Ῥώμῃ ἀγαπητοῖς θεοῦ, κλητοῖς ἁγίοις); Phil 1:1 "To all the saints in Jesus Christ who are at Philippi" (πᾶσιν τοῖς ἁγίοις ἐν Χριστῷ Ἰησοῦ τοῖς οὖσιν ἐν Φιλίπποις); and Eph 1:1 "To the saints who are [at Ephesus] and faithful in Christ Jesus" (τοῖς ἁγίοις τοῖς οὖσιν [ἐν Ἐφέσῳ] καὶ πιστοῖς ἐν Χριστῷ Ἰησοῦ).

16 Since the article is missing before "faithful brothers" (πιστοῖς ἀδελφοῖς), one might suppose that ἁγίοις is to be connected with πιστοῖς as an adjective of "brothers" (ἀδελφοῖς) so as to read "holy and faithful brothers." Cf. C. F. D. Moule, *The Epistles of Paul to the Colossians and to Philemon* in The Cambridge Greek Testament Commentary (London and Edinburgh: Marshall, Morgan & Scott, 1957), *ad loc.* But see above and the foregoing footnote.

lived according to the law and will of God.[17] As the company of saints of God to whom the hidden mystery has been revealed (1:26), the Christian community is the people of his own possession in the midst of a world that is given to another faith; they are the called and elect community of the end–time. "God's chosen ones, holy and beloved" (ἐκλεκτοὶ τοῦ θεοῦ ἅγιοι καὶ ἠγαπημένοι 3:12) are all those who have been baptized in the name of the Kyrios Jesus Christ and placed in his dominion (cf. 1 Cor 6:11). They are the "church," the body of the Christ whose dominion extends to the whole cosmos (1:18, 24).[18] As the individual communities (4:16), and even as the little band which meets in a house (4:15), they are assembled as God's holy people.

The indication of location is closely connected with the characterization of the community as "saints." Normally this indication is connected with "church" by the genitive[19] or by the phrase "which is in" (τῇ οὔσῃ ἐν). Sometimes the phrase "to those who are in" (τοῖς οὖσιν ἐν) is connected with "to the saints."[20] Yet in the case of Col, the location is mentioned in an almost incidental manner.[21] By means of the brief description "to the saints in Colossae," the community of Colossae, which was in close contact with the neighboring communities of Laodicea (2:1; 4:13–16) and Hierapolis (4:13), is singled out for address as the letter's recipient.

Colossae

The ancient city of Colossae,[22] well known since earliest antiquity,[23] was situated in the upper valley of the Lycus River, surrounded by high mountains. Herodotus already described it as a "great city in Phrygia" (7,30.1 πόλιν μεγάλην Φρυγίης). He reported that here the Lycus disappeared into the earth, emerging five stadia away to flow into the Meander. There is, however, no indication of a subterranean watercourse for the river at this location. Either Herodotus mistakenly made an incorrect report or the bed of the river was altered by one of the severe earthquakes which have continuously plagued this region for centuries. The route which led from the East to Ephesus in the West went through Colossae. King Xerxes and his army traveled through this city (Hdt. 7,30) as later did Cyrus the Younger with his soldiers. In his description of the march of Cyrus, Xenophon calls Colossae an "inhadited city, prosperous and large" (*An.* 1.2.6 πόλιν οἰκουμένην, εὐδαίμονα καὶ μεγάλην). Later, however, the city declined considerably in importance, so that two generations before Paul, Strabo speaks only of a "town" (12.8.16 πόλισμα).

Despite its favorable position, Colossae lost its prominence in the course of time.[24] The reason for this is found chiefly in the fact that Laodicea, only a

17 Cf. also 1 QM III, 5; VI, 6; XVI, 1; etc. Also, Heinz–Wolfgang Kuhn, *Enderwartung und gegenwärtiges Heil; Untersuchungen zu den Gemeindeliedern von Qumran*, Studien zur Umwelt des Neuen Testaments 4 (Göttingen: 1966), 90–93.

18 Cf. Eduard Lohse, "Christusherrschaft unh Kirche im Kolosserbrief," *NTS* 11 (1964–65): 203–16; Gerhard Delling, "Merkmale der Kirche nach dem Neuen Testament," *NTS* 13 (1966–67): 303f.

19 Cf. Gal 1:2 "to the churches of Ga atia" (ταῖς ἐκκλησίαις τῆς Γαλατίας). Also 1 Thess 1:1; 2 Thess 1:1.

20 Cf. 1 Cor 1:2 "To the church of God which is at Corinth" (τῇ ἐκκλησίᾳ τοῦ θεοῦ τῇ οὔσῃ ἐν Κορίνθῳ); also 2 Cor 1:1. For Rom 1:7; Phil 1:1; Eph 1:1, cf. above, p. 7, n. 15.

21 Cf. Ernst Lohmeyer, *Die Briefe an die Philipper, an die Kolosser und an Philemon*, KEK 9 (Göttingen: ^{9}1953, ^{13}1964), *ad loc.*, "No other letter of Paul so disregards the historical particulars."

22 Cf. especially J. B. Lightfoot, *St. Paul's Epistles to the Colossians and to Philemon* (London and New York: Macmillan, ^{3}1879, ^{4}1892), 1–22; W. M. Ramsay, *The Cities and Bishoprics of Phrygia* 1 (Oxford: 1895), 208–34; Theodor Zahn, *Introduction to the New Testament*, tr. ed. Melanchthon Williams Jacobus and Charles Snow Thayer (New York: Charles Scribner's Sons, ^{3}1917), 447–49; Martin Dibelius and Heinrich Greeven, *An die Kolosser, Epheser, An Philemon*, HNT 12 (Tübingen: ^{3}1953), 4.

23 The Greek authors usually spell the name of the city Κολοσσαί (Hdt. 7, 30; Xenoph., *An.* 1.2.6; Strabo 12.8.13; etc.). Later the spelling Κολασσαί occurs; Col 1:2 gives the name as Κολοσσαί (in the mss. ℵ [A] B D E F G L d e f g vg arm Clem Alex). Later textual witnesses, however, give the form Κολασσαί (I K pm). The superscript, added later, says πρὸς Κολοσσαεῖς (ℵ B^{c} D E F G L it vg) or πρὸς Κολασσαεῖς (p^{46} A B* I K P pm).

24 Pliny the Elder, *Hist. nat.* 5.(41) 145, says in his description of Phrygia that "its most famous towns besides the ones already mentioned are Ancyra, Andria, Calaenae, Colossae . . ." (*Oppida ibi celeberrima praeter iam dicta, Ancyra, Andria, Calaenae, Co-*

short distance away, had developed into a prosperous city during the first century B.C. (Strabo 12.8.16). This city, situated west of Colossae, was founded by Antiochus II (261–246 B.C.) who named it after his wife, Laodice. Under Roman rule Laodicea became the seat of the judicial district (*conventus*) of Cibyra, which was part of the province of Asia.[25] Not far away, on the north side of the valley, was the city of Hierapolis which was likewise important in New Testament times, particularly because it was famous for its healing springs (Strabo 13.4.14). There was commerce in wool in these cities, for sheep were herded in the meadows and on the slopes of the Lycus valley. The wool was dyed—in fact "Colossian" was used as a technical description for a particular color of wool (Strabo 12.8.16)—and then woven. Also living in these cities were many Jews whose ancestors had been settled in Phrygia by Antiochus III (Josephus, *Ant.* 12.147–53).

When, under Roman rule, the governor, Flaccus, prevented the Jews from sending to Jerusalem the temple tax which had been gathered, he came into possession of twenty pounds of gold from the district of Laodicea and one hundred pounds of gold from the district of Apamea (Cicero, *Or.* 59 [*pro Flacco*] 28). From this large sum it is possible to calculate approximately the number of Jews involved: about 11,000 Jewish men in the district of Laodicea (wives, children and slaves were exempted from paying this tax), and about 55,000 in the district of Apamea.[26]

Tacitus reported that in the seventh year of Nero (60–61 A.D.) Laodicea "was laid in ruins by an earthquake, but recovered by its own resources without assistance from ourselves" (*tremore terrae prolapsa nullo a nobis remedio propriis opibus revaluit, Annales* 14.27). It is, however, uncertain whether and to what extent Colossae also was struck by this earthquake which destroyed Laodicea. Later Orosius wrote "in Asia three cities, Laodicea, Hierapolis and Colossae, have fallen by earthquakes" (*in Asia tres urbes, hoc est Laudicia, Hierapolis, Colossae, terrae motu conciderunt, Historiae adversum paganos* 7.7.12). It is not certain, however, whether this report refers to the same event which Tacitus records. In any case, Laodicea was subject to frequent earthquakes (cf. *Sib.* 3.471; 4.107f). The citizens of Laodicea were able to rebuild their city with their own resources (without the aid of the Roman government). Colossae, on the other hand, was overshadowed by its neighboring city and completely lost its importance. Probably it later fell victim to an earthquake and was not rebuilt. There are various later references to Chonai (Χῶναι) as a Christian episcopal city, built in the vicinity of what was once Colossae.[27] The name of Colossae, however, disappeared from history.

The saints in Colossae are furthermore designated "faithful brothers in Christ" (πιστοὶ ἀδελφοὶ ἐν Χριστῷ). The word πιστός can be used for God's faithfulness as well as for that of man.[28] In this sense, "faithful" (πιστός) is used several times in Colossians in order to emphasize the absolute reliability of Paul's co-workers (1:7; 4:7, 9). In this passage, however, "faithful" does not have this sense of reliability but rather the sense of being "believing," i.e., Christian (cf. Eph 1:1).[29] The Colossians have obediently accepted God's election, whereby the believing ones have been singled out as saints, and now they follow this election in confident trust. The saints are faithful brothers in Christ,[30] not by natural relation, but rather because they have been joined together by

lossae). This sentence, however, does not mean that Colossae remained more important in Pliny's time. Rather, these are places now named on account of their previous greatness, and thus differ from the cities which had been mentioned before (*praeter iam dicta*): Hierapolis, Laodicea and Apamea. Cf. Dibelius–Greeven, p. 4.

25 Cf. Pliny the Elder, *Hist. nat.* 5 (29) 105; and Cicero, *Att.* 5.21.

26 Cf. Lightfoot, p. 20.

27 Cf. Lightfoot, 68f; also Zahn, *Introduction*, 448.

28 For God's "faithfulness" cf. 1 Cor 1:9; 10:13; 2 Cor 1:18; 1 Thess 5:24. For man's "faithfulness" cf. 1 Cor 4:2, 17; 7:25.

29 Cf. Gal 3:9 "with Abraham who had faith" (σὺν τῷ πιστῷ Ἀβραάμ); 2 Cor 6:15 "what has a believer in common with an unbeliever?" (τίς μερὶς πιστῷ μετὰ ἀπίστου). Cf. also Rudolf Bultmann, *TDNT* 6, p. 214.

30 The phrase "in Christ" (ἐν Χριστῷ) expresses, as does the term "faithful," what later was described as "Christian." Cf. 1 Cor 1:2 "sanctified in Christ Jesus" (ἡγιασμένοις ἐν Χριστῷ Ἰησοῦ); Phil 1:1 "to the saints in Christ Jesus" (τοῖς ἁγίοις ἐν Χριστῷ Ἰησοῦ); Eph 1:1 "faithful in Christ Jesus" (πιστοῖς ἐν Χριστῷ Ἰησοῦ); and also 1 Thess 1:1

God's act as members of the one *familia Dei.*[31]

The formula "in Christ" (ἐν Χριστῷ)[32], in Col as in the other Pauline letters, expresses that those who are "in Christ" are shaped by the Christ–event,[33] or live in the dominion of the exalted Lord. The "brothers in Christ" (ἀδελφοὶ ἐν Χριστῷ 1:2) are the Christian brothers who, as members of the body of Christ, are drawn together into a community. The proclamation which is broadcast to all the world is directed toward the goal "that we may present every man perfect in Christ" (ἵνα παραστήσωμεν πάντα ἄνθρωπον τέλειον ἐν Χριστῷ 1:28). The "faith in Christ Jesus" (πίστις ἐν Χριστῷ Ἰησοῦ 1:4) sets man free for the love and hope of the Christian. The new life "in Christ" signifies the conduct of life in obedience to the Kyrios. In the exhortation of chapters 3 and 4, "in the Lord" (ἐν κυρίῳ) takes the place of "in Christ" in order to develop this summons. It is a matter of conducting oneself "as is fitting in the Lord" (ὡς ἀνῆκεν ἐν κυρίῳ 3:18) or as it is "pleasing in the Lord" (εὐάρεστόν ἐστιν ἐν κυρίῳ 3:20). Concerning Tychicus it is said that he is "a beloved brother, a faithful minister, and a fellow servant in the Lord" (ἀγαπητὸς ἀδελφὸς καὶ πιστὸς διάκονος καὶ σύνδουλος ἐν κυρίῳ 4:7). Archippus, also, is to be reminded of the "ministry" (διακονία) which he has received "in the Lord" (4:17).

In Col there is the repeated use of the expression "in whom" (ἐν ᾧ) or "in him" (ἐν αὐτῷ), as in Ephesians.[34] In various contexts they describe Christ as the one who originates and completes the work of salvation.[35] The statement of 1:16 is within a hymnic quote, "in him all things were created" (ἐν αὐτῷ ἐκτίσθη τὰ πάντα). Christ is the agent of creation through whom the whole creation has its continuance (ἐν αὐτῷ 1:17). The hymn continues: "in him all the fullness was pleased to dwell" (ἐν αὐτῷ εὐδόκησεν πᾶν τὸ πλήρωμα κατοικῆσαι 1:19). A phrase from tradition also appears in 1:14, "in whom we have redemption, the forgiveness of sins" (ἐν ᾧ ἔχομεν τὴν ἀπολύτρωσιν, τὴν ἄφεσιν τῶν ἁμαρτιῶν). Col appropriates this previously known statement in order to show the community that in Christ there is given the fullness of salvation. In him not only are "hidden all the treasures of wisdom and knowledge" (πάντες οἱ θησαυροὶ τῆς σοφίας καὶ γνώσεως ἀπόκρυφοι 2:3) but also "in him the entire fullness of diety dwells bodily" (ἐν αὐτῷ κατοικεῖ πᾶν τὸ πλήρωμα τῆς θεότητος σωματικῶς 2:9). Those who have been baptized into him have died with him and are raised to new life: "in him you were also circumcised with a circumcision not made by hands" (ἐν ᾧ καὶ περιετμήθητε περιτομῇ ἀχειροποιήτῳ 2:11); "in him you were also raised" (ἐν ᾧ καὶ συνηγέρθητε 2:12); and "you have your fullness in him" (καὶ ἐστὲ ἐν αὐτῷ πεπληρωμένοι 2:10).

The salutation is formulated with similar brevity. Grace and peace come from God, upon whom as their Father the faithful call with complete confidence (cf. Gal 4:6; Rom 8:15). In 1 Thess 1:1 there is an even shorter form, "grace to you and peace" (χάρις ὑμῖν καὶ εἰρήνη).[36] In all other Pauline letters the introductory greeting always names the Kyrios Jesus Christ along with God the Father. For this reason, later copyists considered the greeting of Col to be too short and supplied the addition "from the Lord Jesus Christ," but in doing so they

and 2 Thess 1:1. In the Col passage here, the mss A D * G pc lat add "Jesus" (Ἰησοῦ) to the words "in Christ" (ἐν Χριστῷ).

31 The first two verses are quite familiar in the world of Pauline expressions which generally characterize the Pauline letter openings. The word "faithful," like the word "will" (θέλημα), is used in the salutation with a meaning different from the one used in the rest of the letter (cf. above, p. 6, n. 10).

32 Concerning the Pauline formula "in Christ" (ἐν Χριστῷ), cf. the investigation of Neugebauer, *In Christus* (which has extensive references to other literature). Cf. also M. Bouttier, *En Christ*, Études d'histoire et de philosophie religieuses 54 (Paris: 1962); also Albrecht Oepke, *TDNT* 2, 541–43; Rudolf Bultmann, *Theology of the New Testament*, vols. 1 and 2, tr. Kendrick Grobel (New York: Charles Scribner's Sons, 1951, 1955), secs. 34, 36; and Hans Conzelmann, *An Outline of the Theology of the New Testament*, tr. John Bowden (New York and Evanston: Harper & Row, 1969), 208–12. Cf. also below on Col 1:4.

33 Cf. Neugebauer, *In Christus*, 175–79. Also *idem*, "Das Paulinische 'In Christo'," *NTS* 4 (1957–58): 136f.

34 For ἐν ᾧ cf. Col 1:14, 16; 2:3, 11ff. For ἐν αὐτῷ cf. 1:17; 2:9f, 15. For the passages in Eph, cf. Fritz Neugebauer, *In Christus*, 179–81.

35 Cf. Dibelius–Greeven, p. 9.

36 Of course, before this has come the closer description of the recipients as a Christian community: "in God the Father and the Lord Jesus Christ" (ἐν θεῷ πατρὶ καὶ κυρίῳ Ἰησοῦ Χριστοῦ).

confirmed that the shorter version is the original text.[37] Since Christology is the point of central significance in Col, it would certainly be mistaken to endeavor to search out theological reasons which might have led to the shortening of the greeting formula. The form of Pauline letters is not a rigid schema which would forbid any variations. Rather, there is a consistently recognizable basic structure which is subject to change or reshaping in all the letters; thus no salutation agrees verbatim with another. Whereas Galatians has a salutation that is considerably expanded by a detailed reference to the Christ–event (Gal 1:3–5), Col begins with the terse statement: "grace to you and peace from God our Father" (*χάρις ὑμῖν καὶ εἰρήνη ἀπὸ θεοῦ πατρὸς ἡμῶν*).

37 The textual addition *καὶ κυρίου* Ἰησοῦ Χριστῷ appears in ℵ A C I 𝔎 G al it vg. The shorter version is found in B D pm it vg^{codd} sy Or.

1 Thanksgiving

3 We thank God, the Father of our Lord
Jesus Christ, always when we pray for
you, 4/ because we have heard of your
faith in Christ Jesus and of the love
which you have for all the saints, 5/ for
the sake of the hope which lies prepared
for you in heaven; about this [hope]
you have heard before in the word of
truth, the gospel 6/ which is present
among you–just as it is in the whole
world, bearing fruit and growing, just as
it is among you–from the day you heard
and understood the grace of God in
truth; 7/ as you learned from Epaphras
our beloved fellow servant, who is a
faithful minister of Christ on our behalf
8/ and who has made known to us your
love in the Spirit.

Very often, letters from the Hellenistic period opened with a thanksgiving to the gods or the divinity.[1] There is evidence of this beginning as early as the Third Century B.C.,[2] and, as the examples become more numerous in the following centuries,[3] a clear pattern of thanksgiving emerges. These begin with "thanks be to the gods" (*χάρις τοῖς θεοῖς*) or "I (or we) give thanks to the gods (or to the god)" (*εὐχαριστῶ* [*εὐχαριστοῦμεν*] *τοῖς θεοῖς* [*τῷ θεῷ*]), to which an occasional assurance is added that the gods are being faithfully called upon at all times. Following this are reasons for this gratitude, referring to the particular benefits or the gracious actions of the divinity. Finally, it is emphasized that the sender of the letter has many thankful thoughts concerning the addressee.[4] This form of thanksgiving also entered Hellenistic Judaism, as is indicated in 2 Macc 1:10ff, where a letter from the Jews in Jerusalem to those in Egypt is cited. Upon the introductory words of "Greeting, and good health" (*χαίρειν καὶ ὑγιαίνειν*) there follows "having been saved by God out of grave dangers, we thank him greatly" (*ἐκ μεγάλων κινδύνων ὑπὸ τοῦ θεοῦ σεσῳσμένοι μεγάλως εὐχαριστοῦμεν αὐτῷ* 2 Macc

1 Cf. Wendland, *Literaturformen*, 413f; Roller, *Das Formular*, 63f, 463f; and Paul Schubert, *Form and Function of the Pauline Thanksgivings*, BZNW 20 (Berlin: 1939), 158–79.

2 The oldest witness appears in a letter fragment from about 260 B. C.: "Ptolemaeus to Heraclides, greeting. If you are well, and if the objects of your care and other concerns are to your mind I should be glad and *much gratitude* would be due *to the gods;* I myself am also in good health . . ." (Πτολεμαῖ[ος] *Ἡρακλείδει χαίρειν. εἰ ἔρρωσαι καὶ ὧν πρόνοιαν ποιεῖ καὶ τἄλλα σοι κατὰ λόγον ἐστιν εἴ<η> ἂν ὡς ἐγὼ θέλω καὶ τοῖς θεοῖς πολλὴ χά[ρι]ς, ὑγίαινον δὲ καὶ [α]ὐτός . . .* *PHibeh* 79).

3 The letter of a woman named Isias to her husband Hephaestion is an example from the second century B.C.: "Isias to her brother (husband?) Hephaestion, greeting. If you are well and other things are going right, it would accord with *the prayer which I make continually to the gods*. I myself and the child and all the household are in good health and *think of you always* . . . for the news that you are well *I straightway thanked the gods*." (Ἰσιὰς Ἡφαιστίωνι *τῶι ἀδελφῶ[ι χαί(ρειν)]. Εἰ ἐρρωμέννωι <σοι> τἆλλα κατὰ λόγον ἀπαντᾶι, εἴη ἂν ὡς τοῖς θεοῖς εὐχομένη διατελῶ, καὶ αὐτὴ δ' ὑγίαινον καὶ τὸ παιδίον καὶ οἱ ἐν οἴκωι πάντες σου διὰ παντὸς μνείαν ποιούμενοι . . . ἐπὶ μὲν τῶι ἐρρῶσθα[ί] σε εὐθέως τοῖς θεοῖς εὐχαρίστουν . . .* *PLond*. 42, 1–10 = *Wilcken Ptol*. 1, 59.1–10) [trans. from Loeb, *Select Papyri* 1, 283].

4 This is shown in a letter of an Egyptian named Apion who, in the second century A.D., served in the Roman fleet and wrote to his father, wishing him and the rest of the family good health. He then continues, "*I thank the Lord Serapis* that he saved me so quickly when I was in danger at sea" (*Εὐχαριστῶ τῷ κυριῷ Σεράπιδι, ὅτι μου κινδυνεύσαντος εἰς θάλασσαν ἔσωσε εὐθέως*. *BGU* 2, 423, 6–8; cf. Adolf Deissmann, *Light from the Ancient East, The New Testament Illustrated by Recently Discovered Texts of the Graeco–Roman World*, tr. Lionel R. M. Strachan [New York: George H. Doran, 1927], 179–83, where the translation is found). A *ὅτι* clause states the rea-

1:10f). God is the object of thanks, which is emphasized by "greatly" (μεγάλως) and for which the reason is given by reference to the saving act of God.[5]

The apostle Paul adopted this customary Hellenistic epistolary model, and at the beginning of his letters he offers a thanksgiving to God, the Father of Jesus Christ, in order to praise him for all that he has brought about in the community.[6] The introductory thanksgiving reveals a fixed structure found in all Pauline letters. In a shorter form, thanks is expressed to God, an adverb of time is added, and the reason for the thanks is given in a ὅτι clause: "*I give thanks to God always* for you for the grace of God which was given to you in Christ Jesus *because* in every way you were enriched in him. . ." (εὐχαριστῶ τῷ θεῷ πάντοτε περὶ ὑμῶν ἐπὶ τῇ χάριτι τοῦ θεοῦ τῇ δοθείσῃ ὑμῖν ἐν Χριστῷ Ἰησοῦ, ὅτι ἐν παντὶ ἐπλουτίσθητε ἐν αὐτῷ 1 Cor 1:4).[7] The other, more elaborate form similarly begins with giving thanks to God, such as are always brought before him in the apostle's prayers. Then a first participial construction is used to elucidate the adverb of time. After this a second participial construction states the particular occasion for the giving of thanks. At the conclusion of the thanksgiving there is an admonition to the letter's recipients: "*I thank my God always when remembering you* in my prayers, *hearing of* the love . . . *that* the sharing of your faith may promote . . ." (εὐχαριστῶ τῷ θεῷ μου πάντοτε μνείαν σου ποιούμενος ἐπὶ τῶν προσευχῶν μου, ἀκούων σου τὴν ἀγάπην . . . ὅπως ἡ κοινωνία τῆς πίστεως σου ἐνεργὴς γένηται . . . Phlm 4–6)[8] [Trans.].

Col presents the more completely developed form of the thanksgiving: "we thank God . . . always when we pray for you, because we have heard of your faith" (εὐχαριστοῦμεν τῷ θεῷ . . . πάντοτε περὶ ὑμῶν προσευχόμενοι, ἀκούσαντες τὴν πίστιν ὑμῶν 1:3f). The assurance that they are mentioned in prayer is taken up again later: "Therefore, . . . we have not ceased to pray for you and to ask"; it is then connected with a ἵνα clause having exhortatory content: "that you may be filled with the knowledge of his will . . ." (διὰ τοῦτο καὶ ἡμεῖς . . . οὐ παυόμεθα ὑπὲρ ὑμῶν προσευχόμενοι καὶ αἰτούμενοι ἵνα πληρωθῆτε τὴν ἐπίγνωσιν τοῦ θελήματος αὐτοῦ 1:9). The participial construction "giving thanks" (εὐχαριστοῦντες 1:12) is joined to this construction in a rather loose way, and three long relative clauses are added (1:13, 15, 18b), leading to the conclusion "And you, who were once estranged and hostile-minded . . . he has now reconciled" (καὶ ὑμᾶς ποτε ὄντας ἀπηλλοτριωμένους καὶ ἐχθροὺς . . . νυνὶ δὲ ἀποκατήλλαξεν 1:21–23).[9] This unusually long sentence construction actually is disrupted by its content. The words "give thanks" (εὐχαριστοῦντες 1:12) do not connect with "we thank God" (εὐχαριστοῦμεν τῷ θεῷ 1:3), but rather the community is called upon to join in the hymn of praise. In the three relative clauses (1:13, 15, 18b), traditional phrases are quoted which then are, in conclusion, explicated in direct application to the community (1:21–23). The structure of the whole composition is: a thanksgiving (1:3–8), an intercession (1:9–11), praise and a hymn (1:12–20), and finally, the application and the demand of reconciliation (1:21–23).

Verses 3–8 form a single sentence, which is, however, difficult to follow.[10] The reasons for the thanksgiving are given by the words "because we have heard of your faith . . . and of the love . . . for the sake of the hope" (ἀκούσαντες τὴν πίστιν ὑμῶν . . . . καὶ τὴν ἀγάπην . . . . διὰ τὴν ἐλπίδα); following this, several subordinate clauses are added. These are v 5b (ἣν προηκούσατε) which is related to the hope of the Christians; v 6a which refers to the world-wide scope of the proclamation (καθ-

son for the thanks, cf. also "I shall give thanks before all the gods because you have clothed me" [Trans.]. εὐχαριστ[ή]σω πα[ρ]ὰ πᾶσι τοῖς θεοῖς, ὅτι σύ με ἐνδέδυκ[α]ς *PGiess.* 1,77,7f.). Further examples may be found in Schubert, *Pauline Thanksgivings*, 158–79.

5 For an analysis of the letter, cf. Schubert, *Pauline Thanksgivings*, 117–19.

6 Gal is the only example of not using the "I give thanks" (εὐχαριστῶ) or the like to lead into the theme of the letter; rather, the writer uses the abrupt "I am astonished" (θαυμάζω, Gal 1:6).

7 Cf. also 1 Thess 2:13; Rom 1:8; 2 Thess 1:3; 2:13.

8 Cf. 1 Thess 1:2–5; Phil 1:3–11; Eph 1:15–17. Cf. Schubert, *Pauline Thanksgivings*, 51f and 65f as well as the table on pp. 54f.

9 Cf. Schubert, *Pauline Thanksgivings*, 14–16. The most extensive thanksgiving is found in 1 Thess. It involves the first three chapters and gathers the report concerning the beginnings of the community, as well as news about the apostle's condition, under the phrase "we give thanks to God" (εὐχαριστοῦμεν τῷ θεῷ 1 Thess 1:3–3:13).

10 For an analysis, cf. Dibelius–Greeven, p. 5.

ὡς καὶ ἐν παντὶ τῷ κόσμῳ ἐστὶν καρποφορούμενον καὶ αὐξανόμενον); the words "just as it is among you" (καθὼς καὶ ἐν ὑμῖν 6b) point back again to the preaching presented to the community; "as you learned from Epaphras" (καθὼς ἐμάθετε ἀπὸ Ἐπαφρᾶ 7). Thus the following structure appears in the sentence:

"we give thanks" (3a)
  "when we pray" (3b)
    "because we have heard . . . faith . . . love" (4)
      "because of the hope" (5a)
      "concerning which . . .
      you have heard before" (5b)
        "just as it is in the whole world" (6a)
        "just as it is among you" (6b)
      "as you learned from Epaphras" (7)
    "who has made known to us" (8)

εὐχαριστοῦμεν (3a)
  προσευχόμενοι (3b)
    ἀκούσαντες τὴν πίστιν . . . καὶ τὴν ἀγάπην (4)
      διὰ τὴν ἐλπίδα (5a)
      ἣν προηκούσατε (5b)
        καθὼς καὶ ἐν παντὶ τῷ κόσμῳ (6a)
        καθὼς καὶ ἐν ὑμῖν (6b)
      καθὼς ἐμάθετε ἀπὸ Ἐπαφρᾶ (7)
    ὁ καὶ δηλώσας ἡμῖν (8)

Verses 7 f. lead back to the relation of the apostle and the community, so that the thanksgiving leads into the intercession (1:9–11).

■ **3** The thanksgiving does not begin with "I give thanks," but with "we give thanks," as in the letters to the Thessalonians.[11] Although the plural form is used here, there is no difference in meaning between it and the singular form.[12] From time to time in Col "we" and "us" appear,[13] but it is still the apostle as an individual who speaks.[14] The thanksgiving and the intercession of the letter continue the plural form, but it is later replaced by the singular, as shown in the phrases, "of which (the gospel) I, Paul, became a minister" (οὗ ἐγενόμην ἐγὼ Παῦλος διάκονος 1:23); "now I rejoice . . . and I complete" (νῦν χαίρω . . . καὶ ἀνταναπληρῶ 1:24); and "of which (the church) I became the minister" (ἧς ἐγενόμην ἐγὼ διάκονος 1:25).[15] The voice of the apostle is to be heard throughout the whole letter, since it is he who is toiling for the community, suffering for it, and lifting his hands to God in prayer for it.

The prayer of thanks is offered to God the Father. The term "father" was also used frequently in the milieu of the New Testament as a title for God.[16] Among the Greeks, Zeus was called the "father of men and of gods" (πατὴρ ἀνδρῶν τε θεῶν τε Hom. *Od.* 1:28; *Il.* 1.544);[17] this expresses the view of a natural relation between God and man in general. In Israel, however, this thought could never have been applied to the relation between God and man. The Old Testament references to Yahweh

11 Cf. 1 Thess 1:2; 2:13; 3:9; 2 Thess 1:3; 2:13.

12 Lohmeyer, *ad loc.*, fails to notice that "we give thanks" or the like is also found in the Thess letters, and that the change from singular to plural is merely stylistic—that is, it does not affect the content. He states that "The 'we' placed here can probably be explained from the position of the apostle vis-à-vis the community at Colossae. He is not close enough that it would be possible to use an 'I', yet he is not far enough removed so that he would have to resort to the impersonal passive form." But this is all beside the point.

13 Cf. Rom 1:5. The words "through whom we have received grace and apostleship" (δι' οὗ ἐλάβομεν χάριν καὶ ἀποστολήν) are clearly referring to Paul's apostolic office alone. Also, the sentence of 1 Thess 3:1f, "Therefore when we could bear it no longer, we were willing to be left behind at Athens alone and send Timothy," (διὸ μηκέτι στέγοντες ηὐδοκήσαμεν καταλειφθῆναι ἐν Ἀθήναις μόνοι, καὶ ἐπέμψαμεν τὸν Τιμόθεον), is explained by 1 Thess 3:5, "For this reason, when I could bear it no longer, I sent . . ." (διὰ τοῦτο κἀγὼ μηκέτι στέγων ἔπεμψα).

14 Cf. Karl Dick, *Der schriftstellerische Plural bei Paulus* (Halle: 1900); Ernst von Dobschütz, "Wir und Ich bei Paulus," *Zeitschrift für systematische Theologie* 10 (1933): 251–77; F. Blass and A. Debrunner, *A Greek Grammar of the New Testament and Other Early Christian Literature*, tr. and rev. Robert W. Funk (Chicago: University of Chicago Press, 1961), sec. 280.

15 Cf. also 2:1, 4f; 4:4, 7, 11, 13, 18.

16 Cf. Ernst Lohmeyer, *The Lord's Prayer*, tr. John Bowden (London: Collins, 1965), 32–62; Gottfried Quell and Gottlob Schrenk, *TDNT* 5, 945–1022; Joachim Jeremias, *The Prayers of Jesus*, tr. John Bowden and John Reumann, SBT, 2d Series 6 (Naperville: Alec R. Allenson, 1967), 11–66.

17 For further material cf. Gottlob Schrenk, *TDNT* 5, 952f.

as father are always to his actions toward and with his people, who understand themselves as having been chosen by him. For this reason they call him their father.[18] Since Israel is God's child, it has a binding obligation of obedience to him (Deut 14:1ff), for he called Israel as his son (Hos 11:1) and established a covenant with his people. When God was also praised as father in Judaism it was because he is the lord and king of his people.[19] The Christian community prayed to God using the word "Abba," and it also retained this Aramaic invocation in Hellenistic Christianity.[20] God has shown himself to be father by his action, in that he raised Jesus Christ from the dead (cf. Gal 1:1). He is father of his community which professes this lord as the risen, exalted, and present Christ, using the words "Lord Jesus Christ" (Phil 2:11; cf. 1 Cor 12:3 *κύριος Ἰησοῦς Χριστός*).[21]

"We give thanks to God the Father of our Lord Jesus Christ" (*Εὐχαριστοῦμεν τῷ θεῷ πατρὶ τοῦ κυρίου ἡμῶν Ἰησοῦ Χριστοῦ*).[22] These solemn sounding words are different from the normal short formulation "I give thanks to God" (*εὐχαριστῶ τῷ θεῷ* 1 Cor 1:4) or "we give thanks to God" (*εὐχαριστοῦμεν τῷ θεῷ* 1 Thess 1:2). They also differ from the more personal formulation preserved in Phil 1:2, "I give thanks to my God" (*εὐχαριστῶ τῷ θεῷ μου*), but they are most reminiscent of Rom 1:8, "I give thanks to my God through Jesus Christ" (*εὐχαριστῶ τῷ θεῷ μου διὰ Ἰησοῦ Χριστοῦ*). The name of the Kyrios, which did not appear in the introductory greeting, is now stated at the beginning of the thanksgiving and closely associated with the designation of God as father. The language used in early Christian liturgy is present in this expression, which is found in Col only in 1:2f, 12 and 3:17. The phrase "God, the Father of our Lord Jesus Christ," has been shaped by the confession of God as the Father and Jesus Christ as Lord (cf. 1 Cor 8:6), and is employed in the elevated speech of 2 Cor 11:31, "the God and Father of our Lord Jesus Christ, he who is blessed forever" (*ὁ θεὸς καὶ πατὴρ τοῦ κυρίου Ἰησοῦ Χριστοῦ . . . ὁ ὢν εὐλογητὸς εἰς τοὺς αἰῶνας*).[23]

When the apostle thinks of the community in his prayers, he is always filled with thanks toward God. The adverb "always" (*πάντοτε*) is further explained by "when we pray for you" (*προσευχόμενοι*)[24]. Whenever the apostle prays to God[25] he thanks him for all that he has given to the community; the apostle also intercedes for them.[26]

■ **4** The occasion for the thankful prayer derives from the good reports which have been given about the community's situation. Paul could say of the Thessalonians that they were a paragon for all believers in Macedonia and Achaia, and that their faith in God had become known everywhere (1 Thess 1:7f). Concerning the Roman community, he could say that their faith was spoken of in all the world (Rom 1:8). Thus the faith and love of the

18 Cf. Deut 32:6; Jer 3:4–9; 31:9; Isa 63:16; Mal 1:6; 2:10.

19 Cf. the invocation אָבִינוּ מַלְכֵּנוּ cf. Willi Staerk, *Altjüdische liturgische Gebete* KIT 58 (Berlin: ²1930), 27–29. For further examples cf. Schrenk, *TNDT* 5, 978–82; and Jeremias, *Prayers*, 15–29.

20 Cf. Gerhard Kittel, *TDNT* 1, 5–6.

21 Concerning the Christological title Kyrios (*κύριος*), reference must be made to the latest, extensive investigations: Siegfried Schulz, "Maranatha und Kyrios Jesus," *ZNW* 53 (1962): 125–44; Werner Kramer, *Christ, Lord, Son of God*, tr. Brian Hardy, SBT 50 (Naperville: Alec R. Allenson, 1966); Ferdinand Hahn, *Titles of Jesus in Christology*, tr. Harold Knight and George Ogg (New York: World, 1969); Philip Vielhauer, "Ein Weg zur neutestamentlichen Christologie? Prüfung der Thesen Ferdinand Hahns," *EvTh* 25 (1965): 24–72; reprinted in *idem*, *Aufsätze zum Neuen Testament*, Theologische Bücherei 31 (München: 1965), 141–98.

22 There were several attempts made to assimilate *θεῷ* with the usual reading, e. g., by adding the article *τῷ* (D* G Chrys) or by placing a *καί* after *θεῷ* (ℵ A 𝔎 pl vg). The word *Χριστοῦ* ("of Christ") is missing only in B 1739 and assuredly must be read here.

23 Cf. the introductory greetings of the Pauline Letters and the opening praise, "Blessed be the God and Father of our Lord Jesus Christ" (*εὐλογητὸς ὁ θεὸς καὶ πατὴρ τοῦ κυρίου ἡμῶν Ἰησοῦ Χριστοῦ* 2 Cor 1:3; Eph 1:3; 1 Petr 1:3; also Rom 15:6).

24 For *πάντοτε* cf. 1 Thess 1:2; 1 Cor 1:4; Rom 1:10; Phil 1:4; Phlm 4; 2 Thess 1:3. For *προσευχόμενοι* cf. 1 Thess 1:2 *μνείαν ποιούμενοι ἐπὶ τῶν προσευχῶν ἡμῶν* (mentioning you in our prayers). Cf. also Rom 1:9; Phil 1:3; Phlm 4; Eph 1:6.

25 I.e., usually at the prescribed times of prayer: morning, noon, and evening. Cf. Günther Harder, *Paulus und das Gebet*, Neutestamentliche Forschung 10 (Gütersloh: 1936), 8–19.

26 Instead of "for" (*περί*), B D G* al have *ὑπέρ* (cf. v. 9 "for you" *ὑπὲρ ὑμῶν*) in order to show more clearly that "for the benefit of" is meant. For the interchange of *περί* and *ὑπέρ*, cf. Blass–Debrunner, sec. 299, 1.

community in Colossae are praised, and connected with this is a reference to hope.[27]

The triad of faith, love and hope is found repeatedly in the Pauline letters.[28] In 1 Thess it is connected with the three concepts of "work," "labor," and "steadfastness" (*ἔργον, κόπος, ὑπομονή* 1 Thess 1:3) in order to describe the life of the community in a comprehensive, summarizing way. 1 Thess 5:8 joins the triad with a quote from Isa 59:17, "put on the breastplate of faith and love, and for a helmet the hope of salvation" (*ἐνδυσάμενοι θώρακα πίστεως καὶ ἀγάπης καὶ περικεφαλαίαν ἐλπίδα σωτηρίας*). The scriptural passage has only two objects, breastplate and helmet; if the three concepts of faith, hope and love are nevertheless brought into connection with them, obviously this triad was already a fixed expression. Since Paul uses this formula in his earliest known letter, the thesis that this triad was first formed in his argumentation with the Corinthian enthusiasts is untenable. This thesis would have it that a fourfold Gnostic formula was transformed by Paul for polemical purposes into the triad of faith, hope and love.[29] Rather than altering a gnostic formula, Paul placed a traditional early Christian triad at the close of the hymn of love in order to emphasize love as the greatest among the three (1 Cor 13:13).[30] In this formula "faith" always holds first place, for faith is the source of a Christian life which demonstrates its capabilities in love and hope. The sequence and connection of these concepts with one another clearly indicate the genuinely Christian character of the triad.

First mentioned is the "faith" of the community, which is described as the status of the believers, as is also done in Rom 1:8. The additional phrase "in Christ Jesus" (*ἐν Χριστῷ Ἰησοῦ*) does not refer to the content, but rather to the realm in which "faith" lives and acts.[31] Those baptized "into Christ" (*εἰς Χριστόν* Rom 6:3) have been incorporated into the body of Christ (1 Cor 12:13). Thus they have been wrested from the power of sin, of the law, and of death, so as to live from now on "in Christ" (*ἐν Χριστῷ*). They have been freed for a new life in obedience to the Kyrios.[32] Just as they were made members of Christ's body by the action of God, in faith they also appropriate salvation and persevere in it. Thus the words "faith in Christ Jesus" (*πίστις ἐν Χριστῷ Ἰησοῦ*) indicate not only the source but also the accomplishment of life under the dominion of the exalted Christ.

Faith verifies itself in love as the "faith working through

27 Cf. Eph 1:15 "because I have heard of your faith in the Lord Jesus and your love for all the saints" (*ἀκούσας τὴν καθ᾽ ὑμᾶς πίστιν ἐν τῷ κυρίῳ Ἰησοῦ καὶ τὴν ἀγάπην τὴν εἰς πάντας τοὺς ἁγίους . . .*), and v 18 "what is the hope to which he has called you" (*τίς ἐστιν ἡ ἐλπὶς τῆς κλήσεως αὐτοῦ*).

28 Cf. Richard Reitzenstein, *Historia Monachorum und Historia Lausiaca*, FRLANT 7 (Göttingen: 1916), 100–02, 238–55; *idem*, "Die Formel 'Glaube, Liebe, Hoffnung' bei Paulus," *NGG* (1916): 367–416; *ibid.* (1917): 130–51; Adolf von Harnack, "Über den Ursprung der Formel 'Glaube, Liebe, Hoffnung' " in *Aus der Friedens– und Kriegsarbeit* (Giessen: 1916), 3–18; A. Brieger, *Die urchristliche Trias Glaube, Hoffnung, Liebe* Unpub. Diss. (Heidelberg: 1925); Ethelbert Stauffer, *TDNT* 1, 710; Günther Bornkamm, "The More Excellent Way (I Corinthians 13)," in *Early Christian Experience*, tr. by Paul L. Hammer (New York and Evanston: Harper & Row, 1970), 186f; and also the commentaries on 1 Cor 13:13.

29 Reitzenstein proposed that there was a four-part Gnostic sequence of "faith, knowledge, love, hope" (*πίστις, γνῶσις, ἔρως, ἐλπίς*). Paul, accordingly, removed "knowledge" (*γνῶσις*) and replaced *ἔρως* with *ἀγάπη*. For a critical discussion of Reitzenstein, cf. especially von Harnack, "Über den Ursprung," and Walter Schmithals, *Die Gnosis in Korinth*, FRLANT 66 (Göttingen: ^{2}1965), 135f.

30 Besides the tri-partite formula, the connection of both faith and love (*πίστις, ἀγάπη*) is also customary. Both describe the Christian status of the communities (1 Thess 3:6; Gal 5:6, 22; 2 Cor 8:7; Phlm 5; 2 Thess 1:3; Eph 6:23). In addition, there are several passages where various other words are associated with these two: "Steadfastness" (*ὑπομονή* 1 Tim 6:11; 2 Tim 3:10) or "peace" (*εἰρήνη* 2 Tim 2:22) or "purity" (*ἀγνεία* 1 Tim 4:12). Quite often, however, "faith" and "hope" appear together (Col 1:23; Tit 1:1f; Heb 6:11f; 1 Pet 1:21).

31 The words "in Christ Jesus" (*ἐν Χριστῷ Ἰησοῦ*) are thus not connected to "your faith" (*τὴν πίστιν ὑμῶν*) as though they were its object. The object of faith Paul usually places in the genetive (Gal 2:16, 20; 3:22; Rom 3:22, 26; Phil 3:9) or else connects it by using "toward" (*πρός* Phlm 5) or "in" (*εἰς* Col 2:5).

32 Cf. above, p. 8 on 1:2. For literature consult accompanying note.

33 Cf. Ceslaus Spicq, *Agape in the New Testament*, trans. Marie Aquinas McNamara and Mary Honoria Richter, vol. 2 (St. Louis: B. Herder, 1965), 243–45.

34 The mss 𝔎 al sy^{p} assimilate the text to Eph 1:15, *τὴν ἀγάπην τὴν εἰς πάντας τοὺς ἁγίους*.

love" (πίστις δι' ἀγάπης ἐνεργουμένη Gal 5:6).[33] As Paul wrote to Philemon, "hearing of your love and of the faith which you have toward the Lord Jesus and of the love for all the saints" (ἀκούων σου τὴν ἀγάπην καὶ τὴν πίστιν ἣν ἔχεις πρὸς τὸν κύριον καὶ τὴν ἀγάπην εἰς πάντας τοὺς ἁγίους Phlm 5), so here the report of the community's active love stands beside that of their genuine faith (cf. Eph 1:15). Through love, Christians are to be servants of one another (Gal 5:13), and the word "all" before "saints" (πάντας ἁγίους) accentuates the breadth of love.[34] No distinctions are made, for love enfolds all the saints as the "bond of perfection" (3:14 σύνδεσμος τῆς τελειότητος) and is shared equally by all.

■ **5** Faith bases itself on the unique, eternally valid Christ-event, and confesses its binding power; love is active in the present in that it is extended to all the saints. In a corresponding manner, hope is directed to the anticipated consummation.[35] In this passage of Col, however, this third member of the triad does not follow in exact correspondence to the other two members. The words "for the sake of the hope" (διὰ τὴν ἐλπίδα) are only attached here in loose fashion,[36] so the reference to the "hope" (ἐλπίς) is somewhat contrasted with the previous words, and this gives "hope" (ἐλπίς) particular emphasis. "Faith" and "love" are the hallmarks of the Christian life of the community, but "hope" refers to the content of the message which the community heard and accepted. This hope makes them capable of remaining firm in faith and of practicing love to all the saints.[37]

Paul connects hope most closely with faith.[38] It is not oriented toward that which is visible, because we do not hope for what we are able to see (Rom 8:24f). Rather, hope is based on faith, which trusts in God's promises "in hope against hope" (παρ' ἐλπίδα ἐπ' ἐλπίδι Rom 4:18) and it does not disappoint because it is sure of God's love (Rom 5:5). Faith provides a firm foundation for hope so that it strives forward and confidently awaits the fulfillment of what is anticipated.[39] Hope already shapes the present through the disposition of hoping, for "love hopes all things" (ἡ ἀγάπη . . . πάντα ἐλπίζει 1 Cor 13:7), and Rom 12:12 exhorts to "rejoice in hope" (τῇ ἐλπίδι χαίροντες). This hoping is directed toward the goal ahead, the fulfillment and realization of the promises made by God. Thus in Rom 8:24f, hope can be understood as the content of hope as well as the disposition of the "hoping:" "For in this hope we are saved. Now hope that is seen is not hope, for who hopes for what he sees? But if we hope for what we do not see, we wait in patience." (τῇ γὰρ ἐλπίδι ἐσώθημεν· ἐλπὶς δὲ βλεπομένη οὐκ ἔστιν ἐλπίς· ὃ γὰρ βλέπει τις, τί καὶ ἐλπίζει; εἰ δὲ ὃ οὐ βλέπομεν ἐλπίζομεν, δι' ὑπομονῆς ἀπεκδεχόμεθα).

In contrast to this understanding of hope as "hope by which something is hoped" (*spes qua speratur*), the hope of Col may be described as "hope which is hoped for" (*spes quae speratur*).[40] Hope, understood as the content of hope, already lies prepared in the heavens. This manner of speaking takes up a common parlance, for "lies prepared" (ἀπόκειται) was said of that for which one waited.[41] Thus in the Persian court it was customary to enter the names of deserving men in the official records so that royal thanks or the title of benefactor was, so to

35 Cf. Lightfoot, *ad loc.*, who makes reference to Pol. *Phil* 3:3, "faith . . . which is the mother of us all, while hope follows after and love of God and Christ and neighbor goes before" (. . . πίστιν, ἥτις ἐστιν μήτηρ πάντων ἡμῶν, ἐπακολουθούσης τῆς ἐλπίδος, προαγούσης τῆς ἀγάπης εἰς θεὸν καὶ Χριστὸν καὶ εἰς τὸν πλησίον).

36 For this reason they cannot be immediately connected to the main verb (cf. Charles Masson, *L'épître de Saint Paul aux Colossiens*, Commentaire du Nouveau Testament 10 [Neuchatel and Paris: 1950], *ad loc.*, and the exegetes named in Masson, p. 90, n. 3) so as to explain the passage as J. A. Bengel *ad loc.* does "from [the greatness of the object of] hope it is evident how great a cause of thanksgiving there is for the gift of faith and love," in *Gnomon*, ET ed. Andrew R. Fausset, tr. James Bryce, vol. 4 (Edinburgh: T & T Clark, 1858), 157. Rather, the cause for thanks has already been given by the mention of the good report about life in the community ("because we have heard" (ἀκούσας 1:4).

37 Percy, *Probleme*, 477f, has correctly contended that the consideration which holds that the hope of reward is the driving motive behind brotherly love, is quite beside the point.

38 Cf. Rudolf Bultmann, *TDNT* 2, 530–32.

39 Cf. 1 Thess 4:13; 5:8; Gal 5:5; Rom 8:20; etc.

40 Cf. Günther Bornkamm, "Die Hoffnung im Kolosserbrief—Zugleich ein Beitrag zur Frage der Echtheit des Briefes," *Studien zum Neuen Testament und zur Patristik, Festschrift für Erich Klostermann*, TU 77 (Berlin: 1961), 56–64.

41 Cf. Friedrich Pfister, "Zur Wendung ἀπόκειταί μοι ὁ τῆς δικαιοσύνης στέφανος," *ZNW* 15 (1914): 94–

speak, secured for them.[42] Following this custom, Hellenistic rulers had favors prepared for their loyal servants.[43] This expression can also be used for describing the fate which the deity determines for man. That which is set for him will certainly overtake him, be it evil destined for him by fate,[44] the wrath of the gods upon those who live an immoral life,[45] or be it death, which takes all men.[46] The victor in a contest can shout with joy that the victory prize of a crown is prepared for him (2 Tim 4:8);[47] so also Christians are given the promise that all that is contained in their hope is kept for them in the proper place. This place is the heavens, which signifies that the precious inheritance is kept in readiness with God, with the exalted Christ.[48] The hope of the Christian community is indeed directed toward nothing other than its Lord, who is enthroned at God's right hand (3:1) and is himself the "hope of glory" (*ἐλπὶς τῆς δόξης* 1:27). This hope is the gospel's content (1:23). Admittedly this precious content of hope is above, and still hidden from men's view, but it shall be revealed "when Christ is revealed" (*ὅταν ὁ Χριστὸς φανερωθῇ* 4:3).

The believers' thinking and searching, therefore, is directed toward that which is above (3:1). This shifts the concept of "hope" from a temporal-eschatological orientation to one which has spatial characteristics. In Col, then, hope rather than love is praised as the greatest among the triad of faith, love and hope. For this reason, hope can simply be described as the content of the good news as such; faith and love have their ground in this content.[49]

The community has already heard of the heavenly hope and all that is involved in it (cf. 1:23), for the phrase "heard before" (*προ-ηκούσατε*) refers to the beginning which Epaphras made by his preaching and teaching (cf. 1:7f). The community received the gospel (*εὐαγγέλιον*) in a "word" (*λόγος*) that consisted of fixed traditional formulas (cf. 1 Cor 15:3–5; Rom 1:3f).[50] This "word" is described as "the word of truth" (*λόγος τῆς ἀληθείας*). "Word of truth" is what God has spoken and revealed to men. Thus the psalmist pleads "take not the word of truth . . . out of my mouth" (Ps 119:43). The introduction to the instruction in the commandments of God states "And now, my children, hearken to the words of truth in order to work righteousness" (*καὶ νῦν ἀκούσατε, τέκνα μου, λόγους ἀληθείας, τοῦ ποιεῖν δικαιοσύνην* *Test. Gad.* 3:1). The same phrase is used for

96; Friedrich Büchsel, *TDNT* 3, 655; Dibelius–Greeven, *ad loc.*; Martin Dibelius and Hans Conzelmann, *The Pastoral Epistles*, Hermeneia (Philadelphia: Fortress Press, 1972), for 2 Tim 4:8; Bauer, *s.v.*

42 Cf. Pfister, "Zur Wendung," 94.

43 Cf. the inscription of Antiochus I of Commagene: ". . . but the priests shall take care of them, and the kings, officials and all private persons shall stand by them, since the favor of the gods and heroes *will be laid up* [as a reward] for their piety." Trans. from Frederick Clifton Grant, *Hellenistic Religions: The Age of Syncretism* (New York: The Liberal Arts Press, 1953), 24; text in Ditt. *Or*. 383, 186–91: *ἀλλ' ἐπιμελείσθωσαν μὲν αὐτῶν ἱερεῖς, ἐπαμυνέτωσαν δὲ βασιλεῖς τε καὶ ἄρχοντες ἰδιῶταί τε πά[ν]τες· οἷς ἀποκείσεται παρὰ θεῶν καὶ ἡρώων χάρις εὐσεβείας.*

44 Cf. Iamblichus, *De mysteriis* 8,7 "the evils prepared by fate" (*τὰ ἀπὸ τῆς εἱμαρμένης ἀποκείμενα κακά*) [Trans.].

45 Cf. Wilcken, *Ptol*. 1, 144, 47, "Wrath is prepared by the gods for those not choosing to live according to the highest good." (*'Απόκειται γὰρ παρὰ θε[ῶ]ν μῆνις τοῖς μὴ κατὰ τὸ βέλτισθον πρ[οαι]ρουμένοις ζῆν*) [Trans.].

46 Cf. *Epigr. Graec.* 416, 6 "knowing that for all mortal men it is appointed to die" (*εἰδὼς ὅτι πᾶσι βροτοῖς τὸ θανεῖν ἀπόκειται*); also 4 Macc 8:11 "before you [is] death" (*ἀποθανεῖν ἀπόκειται*) and Heb 9:27 "it is appointed for men to die once" (*ἀπόκειται τοῖς ἀνθρώποις ἅπαξ ἀποθανεῖν*). — *ἀπόκειται* can also indicate that which is given to a person as something which must be done: cf. Lucian, *De Syr. dea* 51 "The young man to whom Fortune has given this adversity . . ." (*ὁ νεανίης, ὅτῳ τάδε ἀποκέαται*). Cf. Hans Dieter Betz, *Lukian und das Neue Testament: Religionsgeschichtliche und paränetische Parallelen*, TU 76 (Berlin: 1961), 78.

47 Cf. also 2 Macc 12:45 "But if he was looking to the splendid reward that is laid up for those who fall asleep in godliness . . ." (*εἶτ' ἐμβλέπων τοῖς μετ' εὐσεβείας κοιμωμένοις κάλλιστον ἀποκείμενον χαριστήριον*).

48 In Eph 1:18, "hope" appears alongside "inheritance" (*κληρονομία*). Cf. also 1 Petr 1:4 "an inheritance . . . kept in heaven for you" (*κληρονομίαν . . . τετηρημένην ἐν οὐρανοῖς εἰς ὑμᾶς*). According to Jewish hope, the treasure in heaven is the precious good which awaits the pious. Cf. 4 Ezra 7:14; 2 Bar 14:12; 24:1, etc.

49 Cf. Bornkamm, "Die Hoffnung," 64.

enjoining men to appropriate divine understanding, "Hear the word of truth and receive the knowledge of the Highest" (*Od. Sol.* 8:8). The good news is expressed in the "word of truth" (**λόγος ἀληθείας** Eph 1:13), in the "word of God" (**λόγος τοῦ θεοῦ** 1 Cor 14:36),[51] in the "word of the Lord" (**λόγος τοῦ κυρίου** 1 Thess 1:8; 2 Thess 3:2), in "the message of reconciliation" (**λόγος τῆς καταλλαγῆς** 2 Cor 5:19) and in "the word of life" (**λόγος ζωῆς** Phil 2:16). In Col 3:16 it is the "word of Christ" (**λόγος τοῦ Χριστοῦ**) which shapes the life of the community. The "truth" (**ἀλήθεια**) of the word is perceived in the hearing and obedient acceptance of the word.[52] This word of truth is offered only by the apostolic proclamation. Thus Polycarp reminds the Philippians of the "wisdom of the blessed and glorious Paul, who when he was among you in the presence of the men of that time, taught accurately and steadfastly the word of truth, and also when he was absent wrote letters to you . . ." (**σοφία τοῦ μακαρίου καὶ ἐνδόξου Παύλου, ὃς γενόμενος ἐν ὑμῖν κατὰ πρόσωπον τῶν τότε ἀνθρώπων ἐδίδαξεν ἀκριβῶς καὶ βεβαίως τὸν περὶ ἀληθείας λόγον, ὃς καὶ ἀπὼν ὑμῖν ἔγραψεν ἐπιστολάς** Pol. *Phil.* 3:2). The gospel which Paul set forth in word and writing contains the correct teaching, to which the communities should adhere and on which they can rely.

■ **6** This "word of truth of the gospel" (**λόγος τῆς ἀληθείας τοῦ εὐαγγελίου**) also came to the Colossian community and, remaining there,[53] it gained its sure place in their lives.[54] However, not only did this word come to Colossae, but it was proclaimed in all places. The reference to the catholic character of the message, as added by the "just as" (**καθώς**), is also found in the introductory thanksgivings of other Pauline letters.[55] Paul greets the community in Corinth with the words "with all those who in every place call upon the name of our Lord Jesus Christ, both their Lord and ours" (**σὺν πᾶσιν τοῖς ἐπικαλουμένοις τὸ ὄνομα τοῦ κυρίου ἡμῶν Ἰησοῦ Χριστοῦ ἐν παντὶ τόπῳ αὐτῶν καὶ ἡμῶν** 1 Cor 1:2), and he praises the communities in Thessalonica and Rome that their faith is known to all.[56] The gospel is bearing fruit in all the world; its growth is unfolding.[57]

The participles "bearing fruit and growing" (**καρποφορούμενον καὶ αὐξανόμενον**),[58] which are in apposition to "the gospel,"[59] characterize the power of the gospel. In the Old Testament, "to bear fruit and to grow" (פָּרָה וְרָבָה) is commonly used as a combination, but it is

50 Conerning *εὐαγγέλιον*, cf. Gerhard Friedrich, *TDNT* 2, 707–36.

51 For *λόγος ἀληθείας* also see 2 Cor 6:7; 2 Tim 2:15; Jas 1:18. For *λόγος τοῦ θεοῦ* also see 2 Cor 2:17; 4:2; Rom 9:6; Phil 1:14; Col 1:25, etc.

52 Cf. Rom 10:14; Acts 2:37; 13:7, 44; 19:10; 1 John 2:7; etc. For *ἀλήθεια* cf. Rudolf Bultmann, *TDNT* 1, 243f.

53 For "be present among" (*παρεῖναι εἰς*) cf. "be present with" (*παρεῖναι πρός*) in Gal 4:18, 20; Acts 12:20.

54 For "which is present among you" (*τοῦ παρόντος εἰς ὑμᾶς*), cf. the explanation of John Chrysostom, *ad loc.* "he means, it did not come and go away, but that it remained and was there." [Trans. from NPNF 13, 259]. (*οὐ παρεγένετο, φησί, καὶ ἀπέστη, ἀλλ' ἔμεινε καὶ ἔστιν ἐκεῖ*).

55 However, one can hardly say that a "just as" (*καθώς*) clause "belongs to the set style of one of the thanksgiving–patterns which can be ascertained in Paul's writings" (Dibelius–Greeven, p. 6, against Schubert, *Pauline Thanksgivings*, pp. 31, 46). For a comparison with similar "just as" phrases in the Pauline corpus cf. Percy, *Probleme*, 243–45.

56 1 Thess 1:8f; Rom 1:8 and cf. 2 Thess 1:3f. Cf. also 1 Thess 2:14; the community in Thessalonica experienced persecution from their own countrymen, "as they (the Jewish Christians in Palestine) did from the Jews" (*καθὼς καὶ αὐτοὶ ὑπὸ τῶν Ἰουδαίων*). In 2 Thess 3:1 the community is urged to pray "that the word of the Lord may speed on and triumph, as it did among you" (*ἵνα ὁ λόγος τοῦ κυρίου τρέχῃ καὶ δοξάζηται καθὼς καὶ πρὸς ὑμᾶς*). Cf. Percy, *Probleme*, 51. Synagogue inscriptions frequently have a greeting of peace, which is for this place and all places in Israel (יהי שלום במקום הזה ובכול מקומות ישראל). Cf. Samuel Klein, *Jüdisch-Palästinisches Corpus Inscriptionum* (Wien: 1920), Nos. 6 und 8; and Hans Lietzmann and Werner Georg Kümmel, *An die Korinther I/II*, HNT 9 (Tübingen: [5]1969), *ad* 1 Cor 1:1–3.

57 Col does not speak here of the "faith", i.e. the situation of faith in the community; but, pointing to the spread of the gospel, the author chooses a more objective formulation.

58 The words "and growing" (*καὶ αὐξανόμενον*) are not in the Imperial (𝔎) text, which attempts to shorten the expression.

59 Following Lohmeyer and Dibelius–Greeven, *ad loc.*

never used in a figurative sense. In the LXX, the divine command for the creation is "grow and be multiplied."[60] The figurative use of "bearing fruit" is expressed in the words עָשָׂה פֵּירוֹת (produce fruit),[61] which was translated into Greek by *καρποφορεῖν*. The middle form of this verb[62] used in this verse is replaced in v 10 by the more common active form, although no difference in meaning exists. The Christians should conduct their lives "bearing fruit and growing."[63] In Judaism the law was recognized as having power to produce fruit and thus lead to glory,[64] but the Christian community confesses that the gospel bears fruit and grows.[65] According to 1 Cor 3:7f, God grants the growth so that "the word of God increases" (*ὁ λόγος τοῦ θεοῦ ηὔξανεν* Acts 6:7; 12:24; 19:20) and faith flourishes (2 Cor 10:15).[66] In the spreading and unfolding of the gospel it is not the person of the messenger, not his skillful manner of presenting the word which plays the decisive role. Rather, it is God himself who is at work in that he fills the whole world with the sound of the good news.[67]

The Christians in Colossae have shared in this world–wide action of God's word since the day when they first heard the gospel. The train of thought is brought back from the world–wide aspect of the proclamation to the beginning of the community by means of a second "just as" (*καθώς*) clause. This beginning was already mentioned in v 5 and now the "heard before" (*προηκούσατε*) is continued with the "you heard" (*ἠκούσατε*). The reference to the time, "from the day" (*ἀφ' ἧς ἡμέρας*),[68] indicates when the community was incorporated into the growth of the gospel which spreads itself throughout the whole world: This happened when they responded in faith to the proclamation of God's act of grace. The concept of "gospel" (*εὐαγγέλιον* v 5) is taken up in the words "the grace of God" (*τὴν χάριν τοῦ θεοῦ*). The divine demonstration of grace occurred in the Christ–event, so it is true that "you know the grace of our Lord Jesus Christ, . . . who for your sake became poor that by his poverty you might become rich" (*γινώσκετε γὰρ τὴν χάριν τοῦ κυρίου ὑμῶν Ἰησοῦ Χριστοῦ, ὅς δι' ὑμᾶς ἐπτώχευσεν, ἵνα ὑμεῖς τῇ ἐκείνου πτωχείᾳ πλουτήσητε* 2 Cor 8:9). All this is then contingent upon not accepting the grace of God in vain (*μὴ εἰς κενὸν τὴν χάριν τοῦ θεοῦ δέξασθαι* 2 Cor 6:1). The sole content of the gospel is this munificent "grace" (*χάρις*) of God; both concepts can thus be brought together in the phrase "the gospel of the grace of God" (*εὐαγγέλιον τῆς χάριτος τοῦ θεοῦ* Acts 20:24).

By the phrase "grace of God" (*χάρις τοῦ θεοῦ*) a connection is made to the reference to the gospel in v 5; therefore "in truth" (*ἐν ἀληθείᾳ*) is not to be understood as an adverb (i.e., truly), but rather as a reference to the previous description of the gospel. Thus "in truth" (*ἐν ἀληθείᾳ*) corresponds to "in the word of truth" (*ἐν τῷ λόγῳ τῆς ἀληθείας* v 5), and signifies that the community understood the word presented to them as the truth.[69] The "truth of God" (*ἀλήθεια τοῦ θεοῦ*, Rom 1:18, 25; 3:7; 15:8) has made the apostle its servant so that he confesses "For we cannot do anything against the truth, but only for the truth" (*οὐ γὰρ δυνάμεθά τι κατὰ τῆς ἀληθείας ἀλλὰ ὑπὲρ τῆς ἀληθείας* 2 Cor 13:8). The gospel, presented "in the word of truth" (*ἐν λόγῳ*

60 In LXX Gen 1:22, 28. Cf. also Gen 8:17; 9:1, 7; Jer 3:16; 23:3.

61 Cf. Billerbeck 3, 625. It is used for the producing of sin, e.g., *b Qid* 40a.

62 Cf. Bauer, *s.v.* Several other verbs can appear on occasion in their middle voice instead of the expected active: cf. Blass–Debrunner, sec. 316.

63 For further examples of *καρποφορεῖν*, "to bear fruit (i.e. of the believers)," cf. below p. 29 on 1:10.

64 Cf. 4 Ezra 9:31 "Today I sow my law in you and it shall bring forth fruit in you and you shall gain everlasting glory." Cf. also 4 Ezra 3:20.

65 Cf. John Chrysostom, *ad loc.*, " 'Bearing fruit' in works. 'Increasing' by the accession of many, by becoming firmer; for plants then begin to thicken when they have become firm." (*καρποφορούμενον διὰ τὰ ἔργα, αὐξανόμενον τῷ πολλοὺς παραλαμβάνειν, τῷ μᾶλλον στηρίζεσθαι, καὶ γὰρ ἐν τοῖς φυτοῖς τότε πυκνὰ γίνεται, ὅταν στηριχθῇ τὸ φυτόν*) [Trans. from NPNF 13].

66 About "to grow" (*αὐξάνειν*) in Col, cf. also below, on 1:10; 2:19.

67 Cf. also Pol. *Phil.* 1:2 "Your firmly rooted faith, which was famous in past years, still flourishes and bears fruit unto our Lord Jesus Christ" (*ἡ βεβαία τῆς πίστεως ὑμῶν ῥίζα, ἐξ ἀρχαίων καταγγελλομένη χρόνων, μέχρι νῦν διαμένει καὶ καρποφορεῖ εἰς τὸν κυρίον ὑμῶν Ἰησοῦν Χριστόν*).

68 Concerning the phrase "from the day" (*ἀφ' ἧς ἡμέρας*), cf. 1:9 and Matt 22:46 "from that day" (*ἀπ' ἐκείνης τῆς ἡμέρας*); Acts 20:18 "from the first day from which" [Trans.] (*ἀπὸ πρώτης ἡμέρας ἀφ' ἧς*); Matt 24:38 "until the day" (*ἄχρι ἧς ἡμέρας*). Also cf. Lk 1:20; 17:27; Acts 1:2.

ἀληθείας 2 Cor 6:7), is proclaimed as the truth which is correctly understood only when it is conceived as God's generous mercy (Gal 2:5, 14, 21). To deny this message is to "have fallen away from grace" (Gal 5:4 *τῆς χάριτος ἐξεπέσατε*). If in these passages "truth" means the only appropriate consequence which is to be drawn from the gospel, then the term "truth" thereby acquires the meaning of correct teaching and correct faith.[70] This meaning is developing specifically in a situation where a need exists to ward off false teaching, against which the true proclamation must be expounded.[71]

In line with the introductory thanksgiving, Paul again admonishes the community to seek correct understanding.[72] This concerns the "knowledge of all that is good" (*ἐπίγνωσις παντὸς ἀγαθοῦ* Phlm 6) or the "knowledge" (*ἐπίγνωσις*) and "discernment so that you may approve what is excellent" (*αἴσθησις εἰς τὸ δοκιμάζειν ὑμᾶς τὰ διαφέροντα* Phil 1:9f).[73] In these passages, "understanding" is related to "discernment" and the probing of things which a Christian ought to do and leave undone. Accordingly in Col, the content of the gospel is said to be the object of "understanding" (*ἐπιγινώσκειν*). The "word of truth" (cf. 2 Cor 6:7; Col 1:5; Eph 1:13) is opposed to all perversion of the truth, and must be clearly distinguished from all that is counterfeit. This association of "knowledge" and "truth" assumes considerably greater importance in the later New Testament writings. Very frequently, they employ the phrase "to come to the knowledge of the truth" as the equivalent of "to become a Christian."[74] Preservation of the "knowledge of the truth" (*ἐπίγνωσις ἀληθείας*) characterized the Christian.[75] The false teachers and all who listen to them have turned away from the truth and have lost the right way (1 Tim 6:5; 2 Tim 2:18; 4:4; Tit 1:14).

Col repeatedly emphasizes the correct knowledge and thus indicates to the community how it can unmask and fend off false teaching. The community knows well what the "word of truth" is (1:5); it had gained the correct knowledge when it accepted the truth (1:6). This includes the knowledge of God's will (1:9f) and thus obligates the community to actualize this "knowledge" in obedient activity. It is necessary to hold fast to the "knowledge of the mystery of God" (*ἐπίγνωσις τοῦ μυστηρίου τοῦ θεοῦ* 2:2), and that means to be continually aware that in Christ "are hid all the treasures of wisdom and knowledge" (*πάντες οἱ θησαυροὶ τῆς σοφίας καὶ γνώσεως ἀπόκρυφοι* 2:3). The concept of "knowledge" reappears in the exhortations (3:10) in order to make the point clear that correct understanding should become visible in the conduct of the new man's life. The beginning which was made when the community understood "the grace of God in truth" (*τὴν χάριν τοῦ θεοῦ ἐν ἀληθείᾳ*) also determines the way which it should follow unerringly.

■ **7** A third "just as" (*καθώς*) phrase[76] indicates how

69 Cf. Dibelius–Greeven, *ad loc*. They point to the comparable passage Epict. *Diss*. 1.4.31f, "(to discover) the truth" (*τὴν ἀλήθειαν* [*εὑρεῖν*]) is taken up again by "(to show) the truth touching happiness" (*τὴν ἀλήθειαν τὴν περὶ εὐδαιμονίας* [*δεῖξειν*]).

70 Cf. Rudolf Bultmann, *TDNT* 1, 243f.

71 Cf. 1 Tim 6:5; 2 Tim 2:18; 3:8; 4:4; Tit 1:14. Also compare the language usages in the Qumran writings. The community had withdrawn from the world of falsehood and committed itself to undivided obedience to the law of God. The doers of the law are "Men of Truth" (אנשי האמת 1 Qp Hab VII, 10; cf. also 1 QH XI, 11; XIV, 2) who have willingly shown that they will stand for God's truth הנדבים לאמתו 1 QS I, 11; V, 10). They have gained knowledge (ידע, דעת) of the truth (1 QS IX, 17; 1 QH VI, 12; IX, 10; X, 29; XI, 7; 1 QHf I, 9) and demonstrate this by loyal observance of the Torah.

72 Cf. Günther Bornkamm, "Faith and Reason in Paul," in *Early Christian Experience*, 29–46. For the Jewish background of the concept of understanding (*ἐπιγινώσκειν—ἐπίγνωσις*), cf. below p. 25 concerning 1:9.

73 Cf. Martin Dibelius, "'Επίγνωσις ἀληθείας," in *Neutestamentliche Studien für Georg Heinrici*, Untersuchungen zum Neuen Testament 6 (Leipzig: 1914), 176–89; reprinted in *idem*, *Aufsätze* 2, 1–13, esp. p. 4.

74 Examples in 1 Tim 2:4; 2 Tim 3:7; also 1 Tim 4:3; 2 Tim 2:25; Tit 1:1; Heb 10:26; 2 John 1.

75 Cf. Dibelius, *Aufsätze* 2, p. 2 "And so *ἐπίγνωσις ἀληθείας* (knowledge of the truth) means Christian knowledge which originates from correct teaching and which has effect in life." Cf. also Rudolf Bultmann, *TDNT* 1, 706–07.

76 The insertion of a *καί* (𝔎 pl) after *καθώς* assimilates to other passages using *καθὼς καί* (1 Thess 4:1; Rom 1:13; Col 3:13).

this hearing and knowing came about: Epaphras brought the good news to Colossae, and the community learned the gospel from him. Usually Paul describes the acceptance of the gospel as "hearing," "obeying," or "believing," and it is seldom characterized as "learning." In Rom 16:17 it is "teaching" (**διδαχή**) what is "learned" (**μανθάνειν**),[77] in 1 Cor 4:6 it is the correct interpretation of the scriptures (cf. also 1 Cor 14:31, 35), in Phil 4:9 it is instruction in the tradition.[78] In the Pastorals the "learning" that is concerned with false teaching and leads to empty knowledge (1 Tim 5:13; 2 Tim 3:6f) is contrasted with correct learning, linked with "sound teaching" (**ὑγιαίνουσα διδασκαλία**).[79] If, in Col, the community is reminded of what they learned from Epaphras, it is being bound to the instruction in the correct doctrine which it has received and should maintain.

The name of Epaphras[80] vouches for the fact that the community has been instructed in the true faith. As a disciple and helper of the apostle, he has also shared his imprisonment (cf. Phlm 23: "my fellow prisoner" **ὁ συναιχμάλωτός μου**) and is now present with him. Despite physical separation, Epaphras knows that he is very closely bound to the community (4:12f).[81] Even though Paul himself did not organize the community, it can be assured that the true apostolic gospel was proclaimed to them. Epaphras is expressly legitimized by Paul as an authorized missionary since it is confirmed that he is a servant of Christ who participates in the same work as the apostle (cf. 4:12).[82] Servants are chosen by God and predestined for his service. "Servant of God" is a title of honor in the Old Testament—given to Abraham (Ps 105:42), Moses (Ps 105:26; 2 Kings 18:12; Dan 9:11), Joshua (Jos 24:29; Jud 2:8), David (2 Sam 7:5; Ps 89:4, 21) and other great religious figures.[83] The prophets are also God's servants[84] to whom he has revealed his mysteries.[85] Whom God has made his servant may not declare his own thoughts and opinions, but must faithfully repeat the message entrusted to him. Thus the apostle of Jesus Christ is a "servant of Christ Jesus" (**δοῦλος Χριστοῦ Ἰησοῦ** Gal 1:10, Rom 1:1; Phil 1:1).[86] Epaphras is called "beloved fellow servant" (**ἀγαπητὸς σύνδουλος**); this is not only the expression of the apostle's undivided confidence, but also the confirmation of the official commission which he has received.[87] As a representative of the apostle he is authorized for his office and by the authority given to him, he guarantees the genuine transmission of the apostolic gospel.[88]

In addition to the title "fellow servant" (**σύνδουλος**) there is also that of "faithful minister of Christ" (**πιστὸς διάκονος τοῦ Χριστοῦ**).[89] Just as the apostle is a "minister of Christ" (**διάκονος Χριστοῦ** 2 Cor 11:23; cf. Eph 3:7), his co–workers in the communities are also instruments of God, mere ministers "through whom you have believed" (**δι' ὧν ἐπιστεύσατε** 1 Cor 3:5; cf. 2 Cor 6:4). Thus Timothy is a minister of God (1 Thess 3:2; 1 Tim 4:6) as well as Tychicus, a "minister in the Lord" (**διάκονος ἐν κυρίῳ** Col 4:7; Eph 6:21). Epaphras, then, is also called a "minister of Christ" and as such he has met the highest requirement which can be set for a minister, for he has shown himself to be completely faithful (cf. 1 Cor 4:2, 17). This confirmation of reliability (cf. Col 4:7, 9; Eph 6:1; 1 Pet 5:12) is all the more important

77 Cf. Karl Heinrich Rengstorf, *TDNT* 4, 406–12.

78 Alongside "to learn" (μανθάνειν), the terms "to receive" (παραλαμβάνειν) and "to hear" (ἀκούειν) are used.

79 Cf. 2 Tim 3:14; Tit 3:14; also cf. 1 Tim 2:11; 5:4, 13.

80 The name Ἐπαφρᾶς is a shortened form of Ἐπαφρόδιτος (cf. Blass–Debrunner, sec. 125.1) and is used elsewhere. Cf. *CIG* 1.268.7; 2.1820.1; 1963.1; 2248.4; and Ditt. *Syll.* 3.1112.26; 1243.34; also cf. Bauer, *s.v.*

81 Epaphras probably came from Colossae, cf. 4:12 "who is one of you" (ὁ ἐξ ὑμῶν).

82 Concerning the use of "servant" in Paul's writings, cf. Karl Heinrich Rengstorf, *TDNT* 2, 270–79; Gerhard Sass, "Zur Bedeutung von δοῦλος bei Paulus," *ZNW* 40 (1941): 24–32.

83 Cf. Ps 105:26 "He sent Moses *his servant*, and Aaron *whom he had chosen*."

84 For the prophets, cf. Am 3:7; 1 QS I, 3; 1 Qp Hab II, 9; VII, 5; etc.

85 Apc 1:1; 10:7; 11:18; etc.

86 Cf. Rengstorf, *TDNT* 2, 277.

87 The term "fellow servant" (σύνδουλος) appears again only in 4:7 and nowhere else in the Pauline letters.

88 Cf. Theodoret, *ad loc.* "He gave him much praise, marking him as a beloved fellow servant and faithful minister of Christ, so that by it he might be more worthy of greater respect." [Trans.] (πολλοῖς δὲ αὐτὸν ἐκόμισεν ἐγκωμίοις, ἀγαπητὸν καὶ σύνδουλον καὶ πιστὸν τοῦ Χριστοῦ διάκονον ἀποκαλέσας, ἵνα αὐτοῖς πλείονος αἰδοῦς ἀξιώτερος γένηται).

89 Cf. Hermann Wolfgang Beyer, *TDNT* 2, 89.

since Paul himself has been unable to visit the communities. Rather, by means of his disciples—who are likewise faithful ministers of Christ and trustworthy messengers of the gospel—the apostle has, so to speak, worked among them. Consequently the train of thought as well as the weight of textual witnesses make the reading "on our behalf" preferable.[90] Epaphras is the apostle's authorized representative in Colossae, who has worked and will work in the community in the apostle's stead.

■ **8** Epaphras has brought to the apostle news about the life and conduct of the community. He reports, as it were, to the apostle to the Gentiles who is also responsible for Colossae.[91] What he has to report is hinted at in the words "your love in the Spirit" (*τὴν ὑμῶν ἀγάπην ἐν πνεύματι*). The love which is active in the entire community marks all of its conduct. Its whole life is filled with this love which is generated by the Spirit, and it enables it to aid all the saints (cf. v 4).[92] This "love in the Spirit" (*ἀγάπη ἐν πνεύματι*) also determines the community's relation with the apostle, for it has heard his word and is assured of his prayers for it.

This further reference to the happy state of the community completes the arc which describes the train of thought in the thanksgiving. The good report which was made concerning the life of the Christians also has future implications, in the form of obligations. The community will continue to be active in faith and love, it will set its sights toward that which hope has prepared in heaven, and unfalteringly will hold to the apostolic gospel as it was received at the beginning.

---

90 For "on our behalf" (ὑπὲρ ἡμῶν) the witnesses are p[46] ℵ B A D* G Ambst. The other reading, "on your behalf" (CΨ 33 ℜ lat sy, ὑπὲρ ὑμῶν), gives the sentence a different meaning: Epaphras remains with Paul (cf. 4:12) and represents the community in his support of the imprisoned apostle. The alteration from "on our behalf" (ὑπὲρ ἡμῶν) to "on your behalf" (ὑπὲρ ὑμῶν) is perhaps due to the influence of 4:12 (ὑπέρ ὑμων).

91 The phrase "made known" (δηλοῦν) as in 1 Cor 1:11 "For it has been reported to me by Chloe's people . . ." (ἐδηλώθη γάρ μοι περὶ ὑμῶν, ἀδελφοί μου, ὑπὸ τῶν Χλόης).

92 The words "in the Spirit" indicate the means by which the "love" receives its strength; cf. Rom 15:30 "by the love of the Spirit" (διὰ τῆς ἀγάπης τοῦ πνεύματος) and Gal 5:22 "But the fruit of the Spirit is love" (ὁ δὲ καρπὸς τοῦ πνεύματός ἐστιν ἀγάπη). In the Pauline letters are many prepositional attributives which are post-positional and without articles (cf. Blass–Debrunner, sec. 272. [Trans.]). Cf. Percy, *Probleme*, 54–61. The concept "spirit" (πνεῦμα) is seldom used in Col and then only in formal expressions. It occurs once more in 2:5; cf. furthermore "spiritual" (πνευματικός) in 1:9 and 3:16.

1

Intercession

9 **Therefore, from the day we heard of it we are also not ceasing to pray for you and to ask that you may be filled with the knowledge of his will in all wisdom and insight worked by the Spirit, 10/ to conduct lives worthy of the Lord, toward all good pleasure that you bear fruit in every good work and grow through the knowledge of God, 11/ [being] strengthened with all power according to the might of his glory for all endurance and patience.**

The intercession is closely connected with the preceding thanksgiving.[1] The phrase of v 3, "we thank . . . always when we pray for you" (εὐχαριστοῦμεν . . . πάντοτε περὶ ὑμῶν προσευχόμενοι) is connected to v 9 by the words "therefore . . . we have not ceased to pray for you" (διὰ τοῦτο καὶ ἡμεῖς . . . οὐ παυόμεθα ὑπὲρ ὑμῶν προσευχόμενοι). Beyond this, several words and phrases which were used in the thanksgiving reappear in vss 9–11:

9 "from the day"—v 6 "from the day"
ἀφ' ἧς ἡμέρας—ἀφ' ἧς ἡμέρας

9 "we heard"—v 4 "we heard"
ἠκούσαμεν—ἀκούσαντες

9 "the knowledge"—v 6 "understood"
τὴν ἐπίγνωσιν—ἐπέγνωτε

10 "bearing fruit . . . and growing"—v 6 "bearing fruit and growing"
καρποφοροῦντες καὶ αὐξανόμενοι—καρποφορούμενον καὶ αὐξανόμενον

10 (cf. v 9) "in the knowledge"—v 6 "understood"
τῇ ἐπιγνώσει—ἐπέγνωτε

In both sections "all" (or other translations of πᾶς) serves to emphasize the concepts it modifies:

4 "the love which you have for *all* the saints"
τὴν ἀγάπην ἣν ἔχετε εἰς πάντας τοὺς ἁγίους

6 "in the *whole* world"
ἐν παντὶ τῷ κόσμῳ

9 "in *all* wisdom and insight worked by the Spirit"
ἐν πάσῃ σοφίᾳ καὶ συνέσει πνευματικῇ

10 "*fully* pleasing to him in *all* good works"
εἰς πᾶσαν ἀρέσκειαν, ἐν παντὶ ἔργῳ ἀγαθῷ

11 "with *all* power . . . for *all* endurance and patience"
ἐν πάσῃ δυνάμει εἰς πᾶσαν ὑπομονὴν καὶ μακροθυμίαν

The resumption of these phrases and concepts clearly indicates that the thanksgiving and intercession are closely connected.[2]

Following the main verb, "we have not ceased to pray" (οὐ παυόμεθα . . . προσευχόμενοι v 9) there is a ἵνα-clause which gives the intent of the prayer, "that you may be filled," (ἵνα πληρωθῆτε). Then an infinitive construction of purpose ("to conduct lives" περιπατῆσαι) is added with the participles "bearing fruit . . . growing . . . being strengthened" (καρποφοροῦντες καὶ αὐξανόμενοι . . . δυναμούμενοι v 10). Loosely joined to this is the participial phrase "giving thanks" (v 12 εὐχαριστοῦντες), which then introduces the invitation to the hymn which the community should begin to sing.

■ **9** The word "therefore" (διὰ τοῦτο) makes an inferential connection and carries forward the train of thought. Paul often uses the particle καί (and) with the sense of "also" or "then,"[3] and in this case it belongs to the verb.[4] There is no particular emphasis in the "we" (ἡμεῖς), for it merely expresses the identity of those who

1 Concerning the connection of thanksgiving and intercession in the Pauline letters, cf. above pp. 12f.

2 Cf. Schubert, *Pauline Thanksgivings*, 89, "Col 1:9–12 is, structurally speaking, the ἵνα–clause of the Colossian thanksgiving and is very explicitly paraenetical."

3 Cf. 1 Thess 2:13 "for this reason we *also* thank" [Trans.] (καὶ διὰ τοῦτο καὶ ἡμεῖς εὐχαριστοῦμεν) and Rom 3:7 "why *then* am I still being condemned as a sinner?" [Trans.] (τί ἔτι κἀγὼ ὡς ἁμαρτωλὸς κρίνομαι). Cf. Lietzmann, *Römer*, p. 46; and also 1 Thess 3:5; 2 Cor 6:1; Rom 5:3; 8:11, 24; 9:24; 13:6; 15:14, 19; Eph 1:15 etc.

4 Cf. Dibelius–Greeven, *ad loc.*

are thanking and praying.[5] Ever since the apostle has heard reports about the community they have been closely bound to each other.[6] He has been making constant and earnest prayers for them, similar to 1 Thess 1:2; 2:13; Rom 1:9; and Eph 1:15. This is also indicated by the use of both "to pray" (προσευχόμενοι) and "to ask" (αἰτούμενοι).[7] This prayer is made to God with great intensity so that he may grant it.[8]

The intent of the prayer is what appears in the ἵνα-clause,[9] and only God can effect[10] the fulfillment of this request.[11] The life of the community should be completely shaped by the gifts which God provides (cf. Rom 15:13f).[12] The "knowledge" (ἐπίγνωσις) for which the community intercedes is not that of higher worlds, but rather concerns the "will of God" (θέλημα θεοῦ). The will of God demands an obedience that is visible in one's actions. This view of "knowledge" (ἐπίγνωσις) is determined by Jewish presuppositions,[13] such as have been clearly developed in the writings of the Qumran community.[14] God, without whose will nothing takes place, teaches all understanding (1 QS XI, 17f; III, 15). He reveals what is hidden and makes his mysteries known (1 Qp Hab XI, 1; 1 QS V, 11; 1 QH IV, 27; etc.). The will of God is made known to the members of the covenant community in the covenant, i.e., the legal statutes given by God (1 QS III, 1; VIII, 9f). This knowledge includes the obligation to do the will of God (1 QS I, 5; IX, 13; etc.) and to conduct one's life according to the will of God.[15] Some of the gifts which are granted to those who lead their lives under the direction of the Spirit of Truth are "understanding" (שכל), "intelligence" (בינה), and "mighty wisdom" (חכמת גבורה) in 1 QS IV, 3. These three appear in the prayer in Col as "knowledge" (ἐπίγνωσις), "wisdom" (σοφία), and "insight" (σύνεσις). Wisdom and understanding were regarded by the Qumran community as gifts of God which were received through the spirit (cf. רוח דעת 1 QS IV, 4; 1 Q Sb V, 25). He who prays praises God as the "God of understanding" (אל הדעות) and says "And I, gifted with understanding, I have known Thee, O my God, by the Spirit which Thou hast given to me" (1 QH XII, 11f).[16] "Thou hast favored me, Thy servant, with the Spirit of Knowledge" (1 QH XIV, 25 ברוח דעה).[17] Corresponding to this view of understanding as a gift from God is that of the Christian community, for they count "wisdom" (σοφία) and "insight" (σύνεσις)

5 Thus it is not emphatic, "we, too" as Lohmeyer, *ad loc.*, has it.

6 Eph 1:15f summarizes the statements of Col 1:4f and 9: "For this reason, because I have heard of your faith in the Lord Jesus and your love toward all the saints, I do not cease to give thanks for you, remembering you in my prayers . . ." (διὰ τοῦτο κἀγώ, ἀκούσας τὴν καθ' ὑμᾶς πίστιν ἐν τῷ κυρίῳ Ἰησοῦ καὶ τὴν ἀγάπην τὴν εἰς πάντας τοὺς ἁγίους, οὐ παύομαι εὐχαριστῶν ὑπὲρ ὑμῶν μνείαν ποιούμενος ἐπὶ τῶν προσευχῶν μου).

7 The middle voice of the verb αἰτεῖσθαι (to ask) appears in only one other place in the Pauline corpus, Eph 3:20. The active form αἰτεῖν is used in 1 Cor 1:22 for the Jews' demand for signs. Cf. also Eph 3:13. If the words καὶ αἰτούμενοι in the mss. B and K are deleted, the text is assimilated to the usual expression: προσευχόμενοι (to pray) by itself.

8 Cf. Mk 11:24 "Therefore I tell you, whatever you ask in prayer, believe that you receive it, and you will." (πάντα ὅσα προσεύχεσθε καὶ αἰτεῖσθε, πιστεύετε ὅτι ἐλάβετε, καὶ ἔσται ὑμῖν).

9 The word ἵνα (that) often appears after a verb of requesting; cf. Blass–Debrunner, sec. 392, 1c.

10 The passive form πληρωθῆτε (that you be filled) paraphrases the name of God: "may God fill you." Cf. Gerhard Delling, *TDNT* 6, 291.

11 Cf. Phil 1:9 "And it is my prayer that your love may abound more and more, with knowledge and all discernment, . . . v 11: filled with the fruits of righteousness which come through Jesus Christ . . ." (καὶ τοῦτο προσεύχομαι, ἵνα ἡ ἀγάπη ὑμῶν ἔτι μᾶλλον καὶ μᾶλλον περισσεύῃ ἐν ἐπιγνώσει καὶ πάσῃ αἰσθήσει . . . v. 11 πεπληρωμένοι καρπὸν δικαιοσύνης τὸ διὰ Ἰησοῦ Χριστοῦ).

12 For the use of the accusative with the passive, cf. Blass–Debrunner, sec. 159, 1. Cf. 1 Cor 12:13 "we . . . were made to drink of one Spirit" (ἓν πνεῦμα ἐποτίσθημεν).

13 Correctly noted by Lohmeyer, *ad loc.*

14 Cf. Eduard Lohse, "Christologie und Ethik im Kolosserbrief" in *Apophoreta, Festschrift für Ernst Haenchen*, BZNW 30 (Berlin: 1964), 167; also W. D. Davies, " 'Knowledge' in the Dead Sea Scrolls and Matthew 11:25–30," *HTR* 46 (1953): 113–139, reprinted in *Christian Origins and Judaism* (Philadelphia: Westminster, 1962), 119–144.

15 E.g., 1 QS V, 10; III, 9, 20; VIII, 18, 21; IX, 6, 8f, 19; 1 Q Sb I, 2; V, 22; 1 QH IV, 21, 24; VI, 6; XVII, 24.

16 The Hebrew text: ואני משכיל ידעתיכה אלי ברוח אשר נתתה בי.

17 This statement relates directly to the OT view (cf.

as God's gifts, brought by the Spirit.[18]

Similarly, in the instruction of primitive Christianity, understanding of the will of God is always connected with the command to follow God's will and to do it. The servant "who knew his master's will but did not make ready or act according to his will" will receive a severe beating (*γνοὺς τὸ θέλημα τοῦ κυρίου αὐτοῦ καὶ μὴ ἑτοιμάσας ἢ ποιήσας πρὸς τὸ θέλημα αὐτοῦ* Lk 12:47). Only those who do the will of the Father who is in heaven will enter into the kingdom of God (Mt 7:21).[19] The Jew is reminded "you know his will" (*γινώσκεις τὸ θέλημα* Rom 2:18), and Paul asks this in order to ask what the Jew's situation is regarding obedience to the commandments recognized as God's will. The Christian community, however, is told "understand what the will of the Lord is" (*συνίετε τί τὸ θέλημα τοῦ κυρίου* Eph 5:17). Whoever does the will of God shall receive the fulfillment of the promise (Heb 10:36; cf. 13:21). "But he who does the will of God abides for ever" (*ὁ δὲ ποιῶν τὸ θέλημα τοῦ θεοῦ μένει εἰς τὸν αἰῶνα* 1 Jn 2:17).[20]

Since the intent of this prayer of intercession is that the community be filled with the understanding of God's will, the train of thought moves toward exhortation.[21] The correct understanding of God's demonstration of his grace, as this is proclaimed in the gospel (cf. 1:6; 2:2), is also understanding of his will which binds one to his commandments and directs the conduct of the believers (cf. 3:10). God's will is understood through probing (Rom 12:2), leads to sanctification (1 Thess 4:3), and is praised with thanksgiving (1 Thess 5:18). Not only "knowledge" (*ἐπίγνωσις*), but also "wisdom" (*σοφία*) and "insight" (*σύνεσις*) are characterized by this practical orientation and are thus opposed to a speculative view of "wisdom." "Wisdom" and "insight" are linked frequently, not only in the tradition of the Old Testament and Judaism,[22] but also in Greco–Roman philosophy.[23] Aristotle regarded "wisdom or intelligence and prudence" as the highest virtues (*ἀρεταί*) of the human intellect (*σοφίαν μὲν καὶ σύνεσιν καὶ φρόνησιν Eth. Nic.* 1, 13, p. 1103a). Wisdom (*σοφία*) is the perfect form of knowledge (*Eth. Nic.* 6, 11, p. 1141a).[24] Intelligence (*σύνεσις*) however, is subordinate to prudence (*φρόνησις*), because in distinction from prudence, intelligence can only judge, but it cannot command (*Eth. Nic.* 6, 11, p. 1143a).[25] Among the Stoics, wisdom was defined as the "knowledge of the affairs of both the gods and men." (*ἐπιστήμη θείων τε καὶ ἀνθρωπείων πραγμάτων*).[26] In striving after knowledge, man attempts to comprehend in a knowledgeable way the interrelatedness of the entire universe. Col, however, clearly does not presuppose the view developed by Hellenistic philosophy. Instead, it follows the tradition of the Old Testament and Judaism, joining wisdom and insight with the understanding of the will of God. The believer has received a rich measure of insight (2:2), i.e., the "knowledge of God's mystery, Christ" (*ἐπίγνωσις τοῦ μυστηρίου τοῦ θεοῦ, Χριστοῦ*), in whom all the treasures of "wisdom" (*σοφία*) and "knowledge" (*γνῶσις*) are hidden (2:2f). This wisdom is distinguished from everything that only has the "appearance of wisdom" (2:23 *λόγον σοφίας*), and those who are filled with it have the obligation henceforth to "conduct yourselves wisely"

Lohmeyer, *ad loc.*) wherein wisdom and understanding are gifts of the Spirit; cf. Ex 31:3: Bazaleel is filled with "the Spirit of God" (רוּחַ אֱלֹהִים), i.e., "with wisdom and with intelligence and with knowledge" (בְּחָכְמָה וּבִתְבוּנָה וּבְדַעַת). In the LXX this is *πνεῦμα θεῖον σοφίας καὶ συνέσεως καὶ ἐπιστήμης*, ("with the divine Spirit of wisdom, and of insight, and of understanding" [Trans.]). Cf. also Ex 35:31, 35; Deut 34:9; Isa 29:14 (=I Cor 1:19); 1 Chr 22:12; 2 Chr 1:10f; Job 12:13; Dan 1:17; Sir 39:6, 9f; Isa 11:2 where רוּחַ חָכְמָה וּבִינָה = *πνεῦμα σοφίας καὶ συνέσεως* ("Spirit of wisdom and insight"; [Trans.]).

18 *Contra* Lohmeyer, *ad loc.*, who states, "by means of a single word . . . Paul has 'Christianized' the matter: the wisdom is also 'Spirit–given'." (Translator's note: the German "geistgegeben" refers to the Greek *πνευματικῇ*.)

19 Cf. Jn 4:14; 7:17; 9:31; Acts 13:22.

20 Further examples appear in Gottlob Schrenk, *TDNT* 3, 57–59.

21 Cf. Schubert, *Pauline Thanksgivings*, 89, "All Pauline thanksgivings have either explicitly or implicitly paraenetic function."

22 Cf. above p. 25, n. 17. Also, cf. Deut 4:6; Dan 2:20; Bar 3:23. In like manner, the adjectives "wise" (*σοφός*) and "understanding" (*συνετός*) are often used together; cf. LXX Deut 1:13, 15; 1 Kg 16:18; Isa 3:3; 19:11; 29:14; Jer 4:22; Hos 14:10; Eccl 9:11; Dan 1:4; and, in the NT, Mt 11:25, par.; etc.

23 Cf. Lightfoot, *ad loc.*

24 Cf. Ulrich Wilckens, *TWNT* 7, 471f.

25 Cf. Hans Conzelmann, *TWNT* 7, 877.

26 For examples, cf. Wilckens, *TWNT* 7, 473.

(ἐν σοφίᾳ περιπατεῖτε 4:5).

Since "wisdom" and "insight" are so intimately connected, the preceding "all" (πάσῃ) and the following "worked by the Spirit" (πνευματικῇ) are also to be joined to these two terms.[27] Wisdom and insight are not virtues which man could achieve by his own ability;[28] rather, they are granted by God as gifts of the Spirit.[29] For this reason the request is made of God that he grant this gift in full measure; this gift is basically different from all "earthly wisdom" (σοφία σαρκική 2 Cor 1:12) or the "wisdom of men" (σοφία ἀνθρώπων 1 Cor 2:5, 13) or the "wisdom of this world" (1 Cor 2:6). Thus the phrasing "in *all* wisdom and insight worked by the Spirit" (ἐν πάσῃ σοφίᾳ καὶ συνέσει πνευματικῇ). Wisdom and insight should, however, unfold in a comprehensive sort of activity: "in *all* good works" (1:10 ἐν παντὶ ἔργῳ ἀγαθῷ).

■ **10** This correct understanding actualizes itself in the fulfillment of the right conduct of life.[30] In Greek, the word "to conduct a life" (περιπατῆσαι)[31] is an infinitive of purpose, and corresponds to the Hebrew התהלך-הלך.[32] As the teaching of the Qumran community expresses it, the conduct of a person's life can proceed in the obstinacy of a guilty heart and lead to evil events (1 QS I, 6f; II, 14, 26; etc.). However, man should not be led by the spirit of perversity to travel that path; rather, he should be led by the spirit of truth (1 QS III, 18f) that he "may live perfectly before him in accordance with all that has been revealed" (1 QS I, 8f; cf. also II, 2; III, 9, 20f; etc.).[33] When he does this he will be "walking in the way of His delight" (1 QS V, 10 והתהלך ברצונו). Thus, as one who has freely pledged himself, he will "cling to all His commandments according to His will" (1 QS V, 1 צוה לרצונו), "to do the will of God" (1 QS IX, 13 לעשות את רצון אל). Consequently he will no longer act according to what seems to be good to him (CD III, 12 לעשות איש את רצונו); rather, nothing will be pleasing to him except what is also pleasing to God (1 QS IX, 24 וחולת רצון אל לוא יחפוץ).

This passage states that the Christian should lead a life that is "fully pleasing" (εἰς πᾶσαν ἀρέσκειαν). The Greek word ἀρέσκεια usually signifies the behavior by which one seeks to gain favor, and thus most often is used with a negative connotation.[34] But this word can also be used in the positive sense of the recognition from society or God which one receives regarding his behavior.[35] This word was used repeatedly in Hellenistic Judaism to mean what was "well pleasing to God." Thus Philo writes that the Levites left their parents, children, brothers and all other mortal kin "for the sake of being well pleasing to God" (ἕνεκα ἀρεσκείας θεοῦ Fug. 88). "Those who are minded to live with God for their standard and for the good pleasure of Him who truly is . . ." [Trans.] will despise carnal pleasures (*Spec. Leg.* 1.176 κατὰ θεὸν καὶ πρὸς τὴν τοῦ ὄντως ὄντος ἀρέσκειαν). True relation and friendship are recognized by only one sure sign, the effort to please God (ἡ πρὸς θεὸν ἀρέσκεια *Spec. Leg.* 1.317). The first man is described as a "citizen of the world" (κοσμοπολίτης) and "he earnestly endeavored in all his words and actions to please the Father and King" (πάντα καὶ λέγειν καὶ πράττειν ἐσπούδαζεν εἰς ἀρέσκειαν τοῦ πατρὸς καὶ βασιλέως *Op. Mund.*

27 Cf. Abbott, *ad loc.*

28 Cf. Eduard Schweizer, *TDNT* 6, 437, n. 704. Cf. Col 1:8 "your love in the Spirit" (τὴν ὑμῶν ἀγάπην ἐν πνεύματι). The word πνεῦμα appears again in Col only in 2:5, and πνευματικός only in 3:16.

29 Concerning the Jewish background of this formulation, cf. above, p. 25.

30 The concept "understanding" (ἐπίγνωσις) from v 9 is taken up again at the end of v 10, "through the knowledge of God" (τῇ ἐπιγνώσει τοῦ θεοῦ). The texts Ψ and 1611 al place the preposition ἐν before this word, and the Imperial text clearly endeavors to smooth this over by changing it to εἰς τὴν ἐπίγνωσιν τοῦ θεοῦ (for the knowledge of God). But this destroys the sense of the statement, for understanding is not the goal of growth, but rather, genuine growth is made possible by understanding.

31 The Koine text adds ὑμᾶς (you) for clarification, i.e., "to conduct your lives." Cf. 1 Thess 4:1, τὸ πῶς δεῖ ὑμᾶς περιπατεῖν (how you ought to live) and Eph 4:17, ὑμᾶς περιπατεῖν (you [must] live).

32 Cf. Blass–Debrunner, sec. 392.

33 Numerous phrases which sound similar could be added: "walk in the way of Thy truth" (1 QH IV, 21, 24; VI, 6f); "walk before Thee" (1 QH VII, 14); "walk in all that Thou lovest" (1 QH XVII, 24); "walk according to the command of the law" (CD XIX, 4). Cf. also 1 QS VIII, 18, 21; IX, 6, 8f, 19; 1 Q Sb I, 2; V, 22; CD I, 20; etc.).

34 Cf. Werner Foerster, *TDNT* 1, 456; Bauer, *s. v.*

35 Cf. *Inscr. Priene* 113.73 "for the pleasing of the populace" (trans.) (πρὸς τὴν εἰς τὸ πλῆ[θος] ἀρέσκειαν); and *P. Oxy.* IV.729.24 "they shall irrigate . . . to the satisfaction of Serapion" (ποιήσονται τοὺς ποτισμοὺς . . . πρὸς ἀρεσκί[αν] τοῦ Σαραπίωνος).

144).[36] Where the meaning of ἀρέσκεια is clearly indicated by the context, Philo uses this word for divine pleasure without further explanation. God demands of the soul that it tread every path that will please him (διὰ πασῶν ἰέναι τῶν εἰς ἀρέσκειαν ὁδῶν *Spec. Leg.* 1.300). Of course, the motivations which lead men to please God are of many different sorts: "For however different are the characters which produce in them the impulses to do my pleasure" (οἱ τρόποι διαφέρουσιν, ἀφ' ὧν ποιοῦνται τὰς πρὸς ἀρέσκειαν ὁρμάς *Abr.* 130).

Col uses the short expression "fully pleasing" (εἰς πᾶσαν ἀρέσκειαν) to modify the phrase "conduct your lives" (περιπατῆσαι), but it does not state who is to be the one to acknowledge such well pleasing conduct.[37] Thus several questions must be raised: was a secular expression taken into Christian speech?[38] Is the reference to the good pleasure of the community chosen by God?[39] Or is it not rather a reference to the good pleasure of God?[40] The latter meaning, which places God as the sole judge of human conduct, is not only supported by the context, but is suggested above all by a comparison with the sentences previously cited from the writings of the Qumran community. No human tribunal may pass judgment on the conduct of the community; this is for God alone to do. Just as the pious Jew is intent on conducting his life in accordance with God's will and on finding God's "good pleasure" or "favor" (רצון), so it is with the conduct of the community: their only goal is to please God.[41] Since this applies to *all* areas of life, the words are "toward *all* good pleasure" (εἰς πᾶσαν ἀρέσκειαν),[42] for everything depends on pleasing God (cf. θεῷ ἀρέσαι Rom 8:8) or to be pleasing to him (cf. εὐάρεστοι αὐτῷ εἶναι 2 Cor 5:8). Or Paul can say that one should think "how to please the Lord" πῶς ἀρέσῃ τῷ κυρίῳ 1 Cor 7:32) or "how one must live and please God" (πῶς δεῖ. . . περιπατεῖν καὶ ἀρέσκειν τῷ θεῷ 1 Thess 4:1).

This description of the conduct of the Christian life closely follows the Jewish conceptions already known at the time, but this traditional world of thought was given a clearly Christian orientation by the words "worthy of the Lord" (ἀξίως τοῦ κυρίου). Paul often describes the life conduct of the Christians by a closer characterization of the verb περιπατεῖν:[43] "conduct your lives by the Spirit" (πνεύματι περιπατεῖτε Gal 5:16); "in us, who conduct ourselves not according to the flesh but according to the Spirit" (ἡμῖν τοῖς μὴ κατὰ σάρκα περιπατοῦσιν ἀλλὰ κατὰ πνεῦμα Rom 8:4); "we live by faith" (διὰ πίστεως περιπατοῦμεν 2 Cor 5:7); "let everyone lead the life . . . in which God has called him" (ἕκαστον ὡς κέκληκεν ὁ θεός, οὕτως περιπατείτω 1 Cor 7:17); "to lead a life worthy of God" (εἰς τὸ περιπατῆσαι ὑμᾶς ἀξίως τοῦ θεοῦ 1 Thess 2:12); and "let your manner of life be worthy of the gospel of Christ" (ἀξίως τοῦ εὐαγγελίου τοῦ Χριστοῦ πολιτεύεσθε Phil 1:27).[44] The phrase "worthy of the Lord" (ἀξίως τοῦ κυρίου) does not only demand behavior that is worthy and suitable; it binds the conduct of the Christian to undivided obedience to the Kyrios. He is the Lord over all powers and principalities, he has received dominion over all things, and he is the Lord over his own, so that they can conduct themselves "worthy of the Lord" only if they follow the summons given in 2:6, "as therefore you re-

---

36 Cf. also *Spec. Leg.* 1, 297 "for the pleasure of God" [Trans.] (πρὸς ἀρέσκειαν θεοῦ); and *Congr.* 80 "for honor and pleasure of God" (trans.) (θεοῦ τιμῆς καὶ ἀρεσκείας ἕνεκα).

37 Cf. Foerster, *TDNT* 1, 456 " 'to every kind of pleasing attitude'; towards whom is not clearly specified."

38 Cf. Dibelius–Greeven, *ad loc.*, with reference to Phil 4:8.

39 Cf. Lohmeyer, *ad loc.*

40 Cf. Theodoret, *ad loc.* "so that you may accomplish all the things that are pleasing to God" [Trans.] (ἵνα πάντα τὰ ἀρέσκοντα τῷ θεῷ διαπράττησθε).

41 In the texts from Qumran, the suffix makes it clear that God's "good pleasure" (רצונך) is meant. In Greek the suffix can be absent and the word can still have the same meaning. Cf. 1 QH IV, 32f בני רצונו (sons of His good pleasure) = Lk 2:14 ἄνθρωποι εὐδοκίας (men of good pleasure [Trans.]). Also, cf. 1 Cor 16:22 מרנא תא (Our Lord, come!) = Rev 22:20 ἔρχου κύριε Ἰησοῦ (Come, Lord Jesus).

42 The noun ἀρέσκεια is a hapaxlegomenon in the NT, but the verb ἀρέσκειν appears several times.

43 Cf. Heinrich Seesemann, *TDNT* 5, 944f.

44 Cf. also Eph 4:1 "to lead a life worthy of the calling" (ἀξίως περιπατῆσαι τῆς κλήσεως).

45 Both participles καρποφοροῦντες καὶ αὐξανόμενοι (bearing fruit and growing) are in the nominative case instead of the accusative which is actually demanded by connecting them to the verb περιπατῆσαι. The participial expressions, therefore, follow rather independently. Knox's assumption that this pair of Greek words was a slogan of the false teachers against whom this letter was written, remains an unproven supposition. Cf. Wilfred Lawrence Knox,

ceived Christ Jesus the Lord, so conduct yourselves in him" (ὡς οὖν παρελάβετε τὸν Χριστὸν Ἰησοῦν τὸν κύριον, ἐν αὐτῷ περιπατεῖτε).

The images of bearing fruit and growing were used to illustrate the increase of the gospel in all the world (1:6); now these images[45] are applied to the conduct of the believers.[46] If the good news has been accepted in that it is recognized to be the truth (1:6), then this knowledge (cf. 1:9) leads to the growth and maturing of the fruit.[47] Thus the words τῇ ἐπιγνώσει τοῦ θεοῦ do not indicate growth "in the knowledge of God" but rather by what means the growth is produced: "through the knowledge of God." The bearing of fruit and increasing which are effected by the knowledge of God, however, become visible "in every good work" (ἐν παντὶ ἔργῳ ἀγαθῷ).[48]

The demand for good works appears regularly in Jewish exhortatory material. Thus, in the opening of the Qumran *Community Rule*, the admonition which is to guide the pious ones in all their life conduct states that the sons of light should "abstain from all evil" but "cling to all good works" (1 QS I, 4f). Paul, too, says that faith is active (Gal 5:6) and that all men, but especially those of the household of faith, should be the recipients of good works (Gal 6:10 and 2 Cor 9:8). Civil authorities are not the only ones who pay attention to what citizens do, and approve good works (Rom 13:3). God himself inquires concerning actions when he judges, and on this basis he will pass judgment (Rom 2:7–10; 2 Cor 5:10; etc.). Yet men's deeds can never open the way to salvation, for Paul is adamant that "a man is justified by faith apart from the works of the law" (Rom 3:28). Without any mention of the relation between faith and works,[49] Col states the admonition that is so much a part of common Christian exhortation: the community should manifest its growth and maturation through good works. The words "in every" (παντί) again underscore the point that this demand extends to all actions and dealings of the Christian.[50]

The exhortations in the deutero-Pauline letters continue to put stress on the demand for good works. We are God's "workmanship, created in Christ Jesus for good works which God prepared beforehand that we should walk in them" (ποίημα, κτισθέντες ἐν Χριστῷ Ἰησοῦ ἐπὶ ἔργοις ἀγαθοῖς, οἷς προητοίμασεν ὁ θεὸς ἵνα ἐν αὐτοῖς περιπατήσωμεν Eph 2:10). Right conduct of life and good works go hand in hand. False teachers are unmasked when their actions are considered, for they are "unfit for any good deed" (πρὸς πᾶν ἔργον ἀγαθὸν ἀδόκιμοι Tit 1:16). The proclaimer is therefore charged to remind the community continuously "to be ready for every good work" (πρὸς πᾶν ἔργον ἀγαθὸν ἑτοίμους εἶναι Tit 3:1). This is important, for by good works even faith is now recognized (1 Tim 2:10; 5:10; 2 Tim 2:21; 3:17; etc.). Col takes up this common demand. If, during

St. Paul and the Church of the Gentiles (Cambridge: Cambridge University Press, 1939), 149, n. 5; 156f.

46 Cf. the parable about the four kinds of soil. The seed that fell on good soil "brought forth fruit, growing up and increasing" [Trans.] (ἐδίδου καρπὸν ἀναβαίνοντα καὶ αὐξανόμενα Mk 4:8 and par.). The explanation of the parable applies this; these are the ones who "hear the word, accept it and bear fruit" (οἵτινες ἀκούουσιν τὸν λόγον καὶ παραδέχονται καὶ καρποφοροῦσιν Mk 4:20 and par.).

47 For the comparison of "bearing fruit" (καρποφορεῖν) with the conduct of the believers, cf. Rom 7:14, "in order that we may bear fruit to God" (ἵνα καρποφορήσωμεν τῷ θεῷ). For that of "growing" (αὐξάνεσθαι), cf. 2 Cor 10:15, "as your faith increases" (αὐξανομένης τῆς πίστεως ὑμῶν); Eph 4:15 "we are to grow up in every way into him" (αὐξήσωμεν εἰς αὐτὸν τὰ πάντα); 1 Pt 2:2 "that by it (i.e., pure spiritual milk) you may grow up to salvation" (ἵνα ἐν αὐτῷ αὐξηθῆτε εἰς σωτηρίαν); 2 Pt 3:18 "But grow in the grace and knowledge of our Lord and Savior Jesus Christ" (αὐξάνετε δὲ ἐν χάριτι καὶ γνώσει τοῦ κυρίου ἡμῶν καὶ σωτῆρος Ἰησοῦ Χριστοῦ).

48 Since "bearing fruit and growing" (καρποφοροῦντες καὶ αὐξανόμενοι) form a pair of concepts, these verbs also connect "through the knowledge of God" (τῇ ἐπιγνώσει τοῦ θεοῦ) with "in every good work" (ἐν παντὶ ἔργῳ ἀγαθῷ), though Dibelius–Greeven *ad loc.* take this differently. The growth comes about through the understanding, and produces good works. Cf. Abbott, Lohmeyer, *ad loc.*; and Percy, *Probleme*, 123, n. 93.

49 Cf. the letter of James, whose collection of exhortatory sayings is guided by the theme that "faith" (πίστις) without "works" (ἔργα) is "dead" (νεκρά), as seen in Jas 2:17, 26. Cf. Eduard Lohse, "Glaube und Werke—zur Theologie des Jakobusbriefes," *ZNW* 48 (1957): 1–22.

50 Cf. also 2 Cor 9:8 "that you . . . may provide in abundance for every good work" (ἵνα . . . περισσεύητε εἰς πᾶν ἔργον ἀγαθόν); and 2 Thess 2:17 "establish them in every good work and word" (στηρίξαι ἐν παντὶ ἔργῳ καὶ λόγῳ ἀγαθῷ).

their pagan days, the Colossians expressed their hostility toward God by "doing evil deeds" (ἐν τοῖς ἔργοις τοῖς πονηροῖς 1:21; cf. 3:7), they should now manifest their knowledge of the truth "in all good works" (ἐν παντὶ ἔργῳ ἀγαθῷ). Whatever the Christians may do "in word or in deed" (ἐν λόγῳ ἢ ἐν ἔργῳ), everything should be done "in the name of the Lord Jesus, giving thanks to God the Father through him" (πάντα ἐν ὀνόματι κυρίου Ἰησοῦ, εὐχαριστοῦντες τῷ θεῷ πατρὶ δι' αὐτοῦ 3:17).

■ **11** In order to be able to maintain this life conduct worthy of the Lord, the community is to be strengthened and filled with the power of God. This reference to the might of divine glory which strengthens the life of the believers again employs Jewish expressions.[51] Those praying in the Qumran community are aware that God's "power" (גבורה) supports them, and they confess "the rock of my steps is the truth of God and His might is the support of my right hand" (1 QS XI, 4f). Only by the Spirit of God is the conduct of the children of men made perfect, "that all His creatures might know the *might of His power*, and the abundance of His mercies toward all the sons of His grace" (בכוח גבורתו 1 QH IV, 31–33). The "might of God" (גבורת אל) assists the warriors in the struggle against the hosts of Belial, so that they hold the field and win the battle.[52] Supported by God's power (1 QS XI, 19f; 1 QH XVIII, 8; etc.), the pious man is certain that God reveals his glory and power, that by the judgment over the wicked he is glorified and shows his power in the pious man in the presence of the sons of men (1 QH II, 24 f). Thus God is praised with the words "it is in Thy purpose to do mightily (להגביר) and to establish all things for Thy glory" (לכבודכה 1 QH XVIII, 22). At Qumran the community's praise of God rose to this height of elaborate description which circumloquated his sublimity: "Summit of Glory and Almighty Eternal Majesty" (1 QS X, 12).[53]

The admonishing intercession of Col takes up such fulsome expressions of God's praise by praying: may God's might (δύναμις) strengthen (δυναμοῦν)[54] the community. In this way the power of his glory will demonstrate itself,[55] for God remains true to himself and acts in agreement with (κατά) the demonstration of his power and glory he has already made.[56] The words "power" and "glory" (κράτος, δόξα) often appear in doxologies together, used to praise God: "to him belong glory and power for ever and ever." (ᾧ ἐστιν ἡ δόξα καὶ τὸ κράτος εἰς τοὺς αἰῶνας τῶν αἰώνων).[57]

God's mighty power should strengthen the community "for all endurance and patience" (εἰς πᾶσαν ὑπομονὴν καὶ μακροθυμίαν). The word "endurance" (ὑπομονή) signifies the kind of perseverance which is to be proven in battle by holding the position one has taken against all enemy attacks.[58] By this "endurance" it will become evident whether the Christian is able to hold out and stand firm.[59] "Endurance" also persists in "good works" (ἔργον ἀγαθόν Rom 2:7), and it produces "character" (δοκιμή Rom 5:4). It also perseveres through suffering (2 Cor 1:6) and maintains unwaveringly the certain hope of the fulfillment of the divine promises (Rom 8:25; 15:4). Thus the "endurance" of the community should prove a steadfast power of resistance in every respect (πᾶσα).[60]

51 Cf. Lohse, "Christologie und Ethik," 167.

52 Cf. 1 QM I, 11, 14; III, 5, 8; IV, 4, 12; VI, 2, 6; etc.

53 The Hebrew text is רום כבוד וגבורת כול לתפארת עולם.

54 The verb δυναμοῦν "to strengthen" is used elsewhere in the NT only in Heb 11:34 and Eph 6:10 *v.l.* The form ἐνδυναμοῦν appears in Rom 4:20; Phil 4:13; Eph 6:10; 1 Tim 1:12; 2 Tim 2:1; 4:17.

55 Cf. the intercession of Eph 1:18f "what is the immeasurable greatness of his power in us who believe, according to the working of his great might" (τί τὸ ὑπερβάλλον μέγεθος τῆς δυνάμεως αὐτοῦ εἰς ἡμᾶς τοὺς πιστεύοντας κατὰ τὴν ἐνέργειαν τοῦ κράτους τῆς ἰσχύος αὐτοῦ).

56 Cf. Lk 1:51 "He has shown strength with his arm" (ἐποίησεν κράτος ἐν βραχίονι αὐτοῦ).

57 Cf. 1 Pt 4:11 and 1 Pt 5:11; Jude 25; Rev 1:6; 5:13. In the NT κράτος is never used for human power, and is not used by Paul elsewhere, although it occurs in the deutero-Pauline letters, e.g., Eph 1:19; 6:10; 1 Tim 6:18.

58 Cf. the concept מעמד which can designate the perseverance of the faithful, according to the Qumran texts: 1 QH II, 22; XI, 13; XVI, 13; etc.

59 Cf. Lk 8:15 "and (they) bring forth fruit with patience" (καὶ καρποφοροῦσιν ἐν ὑπομονῇ).

60 Cf. Friedrich Hauck, *TDNT* 4, 586–88.

61 The words אֶרֶךְ אַפַּיִם and μακροθυμία stand for God's patience which does not give way to his anger (Ex 34:6f; Num 14:18; etc.) as well as for the human virtue which should correspond to divine forbearance, Eccl 7:8ff. Cf. Johannes Horst, *TDNT* 4, 376–79.

"Endurance" refers to defence against all opposition from without, and thus "patience" (*μακροθυμία*) is directed toward the relationship with one's fellowmen. It means the deep breath which enables one to wait patiently.[61] Paul reckons "patience" (*μακροθυμία*) as one of the fruits of the Spirit (Gal 5:22), praises love for its "being patient" (*μακροθυμεῖν* 1 Cor 13:4), and urges the community "be patient with them all" (*μακροθυμεῖτε πρὸς πάντας* 1 Thess 5:14).[62] The Christians are summoned to "put on . . . patience" (*ἐνδύσασθε . . . μακροθυμίαν* Col 3:12) and thus are reminded that patience springs from the divine source of power which also enables them to endure. Thus the words "endurance" and "patience" together are the sure sign of the loyal Christian, for he is not swayed from his hope by any power, nor does he grow weary in love.[63]

As the exegesis has shown, verses 9–11 are full of words and expressions which come largely from Jewish tradition. If one should remove the basis given for the life conduct of the Christian, the words "worthy of the Lord" (*ἀξίως τοῦ κυρίου* 1:10), then the rest of this passage could easily appear in a Jewish text.[64] The early Christian style of prayer is to a rather great extent rooted in the *OT*–Jewish heritage. But this close reliance on Jewish tradition finds reason also in the subject matter.[65] The great emphasis on the knowledge of God's will and the consequent obligation to conduct one's life obediently have been thoughtfully placed at the opening of the letter in order to oppose a speculative understanding of "wisdom" to this sober description of wisdom wrought by the Spirit. The intercessions in Pauline letters always have an exhortatory accent,[66] and so Col emphasizes that correct understanding is "understanding of his will" (*ἐπίγνωσις τοῦ θελήματος αὐτοῦ*). God's will, however, demands obedience in leading a life that is worthy of the Lord.[67]

62 For "patience" as used by Paul, cf. Horst, *TDNT* 4, 382–85.

63 Both concepts also appear together in the *Test. Jos.* 2:7 ". . . endurance is a mighty charm, and patience giveth many good things." (*μέγα φάρμακόν ἐστιν ἡ μακροθυμία, καὶ πολλὰ ἀγαθὰ δίδωσιν ἡ ὑπομονή*). Cf. also 2 Cor 6:4, 6; 2 Tim 3:10; Jas 5:10f; 1 *Clem* 64; Ign *Eph* 3:1.

64 One could achieve the same effect by understanding the word *κύριος* in the Jewish sense of the title for God.

65 Mention need only be made of the numerous Jewish parallels to the petitions of the Lord's Prayer. Cf. Billerbeck 1, 406–24; Lohmeyer, *The Lord's Prayer*, 32–62; Karl Georg Kuhn, *Achtzehngebet und Vaterunser und der Reim*, Wissenschaftliche Untersuchungen zum Neuen Testament 1 (Tübingen: 1950); Joachim Jeremias, *The Lord's Prayer*, tr. John Reuman, Facet Books, Biblical Series 8 (Philadelphia: Fortress Press, 1964), reprinted in *idem*, *Prayers*, ch. 3.

66 Cf. also pp. 13, 26 above.

67 Karl-Gottfried Eckart, "Exegetische Beobachtungen zu Kol. 1:9–20," *Theologia Viatorum* 7 (1959–60); 87–107; and "Urchristliche Tauf- und Ordinationsliturgie (Kol 1:9–20, Acts 26:18)" *Theologia Viatorum* 8 (1961–62): 23–37. Eckart has accurately observed that verses 9–12 contain traditional expressions. He pushes this insight too far, however, when he maintains that the whole complex (1:9–20) is a baptismal liturgy. This ignores the fact that in Pauline letters the intercessions always have an exhortatory orientation. Above all, it overlooks the fact that verses 9–20 are composed from variously formed pieces and do not constitute a complete liturgical unit. Thus it is incorrect to characterize verses 9–12 as a tightly-formulated liturgical exhortation ("Exegetische Beobachtungen," 99) and to exclude the words "according to the might of his glory" (*κατὰ τὸ κράτος τῆς δόξης αὐτοῦ*) as a secondary interpretational addition (*ibid.*, 92).

I. Theological Instruction
The Universal Lordship of Christ

Colossians 1:12–20

1

Thanksgiving and Hymn

12 With joy give thanks to the Father, who
had authorized you to participate in the
lot of the holy ones in the light.
13 He has delivered us from the tyrannical
rule of darkness and transferred us into
the domain of his beloved Son's rule,
14 in whom we have redemption, the forgive-
ness of sins.
15 He is the image of the invisible God,
the firstborn before all creation;
16 for in him all things were created
in the heavens and on earth,
the visible and the invisible,
whether thrones or dominions, powers
or principalities, all things are created
through him and for him;
17 and he is before all things,
and in him all things are established,
18 and he is the head of the body, that is, of
the church.
He is the beginning,
the firstborn from the dead,
in order that he might be the first in all
things;
19 for in him all the fullness was pleased to
dwell
20 and through him to reconcile all things to
him, making peace through the blood
of his cross, through him, whether on
earth or in the heavens.

Without pause, the intercession changes into a summons to give thanks. Although the words "with joy give thanks" (*μετὰ χαρᾶς εὐχαριστοῦντες*) are loosely attached to the preceding, like the participles "bearing fruit and growing" (*καρποφοροῦντες καὶ αὐξανόμενοι*) and "being strengthened" (*δυναμούμενοι*) in 1:10f, they express a new thought in their context. The subject is no longer the conduct of life of the believers; rather the community is now urged to praise God[1] with thanksgiving, as they are reminded of the saving action of God extolled in the confession. This summons is made in vss 12–14 utilizing traditional phrases recognizable not only by the participial style, *τῷ ἱκανώσαντι* (v 12 "who has been authorizing us"), and the relative style, *ὃς ἐρρύσατο* (v 13 "he [who] has delivered us"), *ἐν ᾧ ἔχομεν* (v 14 "in whom we have"), but also by the appearance of a series of terms not used otherwise, either in Col or in the *corpus Paulinum*. The word "to authorize" (*ἱκανόω*) reoccurs only in 2 Cor 3:6, and there it is used for the apostolic ministry. The noun "part" (*μερίς*) comes up again only in 2 Cor 6:15, a section which was hardly composed by Paul (2 Cor 6:14–7:1) but probably goes back to

1 In Jewish texts the participle often appears with an imperatival meaning. Cf. David Daube, "Participle and Imperative in I Peter," in Edward Gordon Selwyn, *The First Epistle of St. Peter* (Oxford: Oxford University Press, ^{2}1947 = ^{3}1949), 467–88; *idem*, *The New Testament and Rabbinic Judaism*, Jordan Lectures in Comparative Religion 2, 1952 (London: University of London, Athlone, 1956), 90–105; Eduard Lohse, "Paränese and Kerygma im 1. Petrusbrief," *ZNW* 45 (1954): 75f. In primitive Christian exhortation the participle is repeatedly used in this sense. Cf., e.g., Rom 12:9 *ἀποστυγοῦντες τὸ πονηρόν, κολλώμενοι τῷ ἀγαθῷ* (*hate* what is evil, *hold fast* to what is good!). Since the participle *εὐχαριστοῦντες* (give thanks) is only loosely attached to the preceding verses, the translation as an imperative is com-

pre–Pauline tradition.[2] The word *κλῆρος* (lot), and the phrases *ἅγιοι ἐν τῷ φωτί* (saints in light), *βασιλεία τοῦ υἱοῦ τῆς ἀγάπης αὐτοῦ* (kingdom of his beloved son) are without parallels in the Pauline letters. The Greek word *ἐξουσία* is otherwise not used with the meaning of "(domain of) tyrannical rule" (1:13); in 1:16 and 2:10 it signifies the cosmic powers and principalities. The word *ἀπολύτρωσις* (redemption) used in the sense of "the forgiveness of sins" (*ἄφεσις τῶν ἁμαρτιῶν*) is part of the theological language of the primitive Christian community. This can be seen in the sentences of confessional type in Rom 3:24f; 1 Cor 1:30 as well as Eph 1:7, 14; 4:30.

The reasons for the summons to give thanks to the Father are given in the participial phrase *τῷ ἱκανώσαντι ὑμᾶς* (1:12 "who has authorized you") and in the relative sentence *ὃς ἐρρύσατο* (1:13 "he [who] has delivered"). The reference to the redemption wrought by Christ (1:14) makes the transition to the Christological statements which are more broadly developed in the hymn. Vss 12–14 thus are placed before the Christ-hymn as a sort of introit which introduces the solemn hymn sung by the community.[3]

■ **12** The sound of joy ought to open the singing of this hymn—that is, the words *μετὰ χαρᾶς* ("with joy") are not to be drawn into the previous sentence, but are to be connected to the *εὐχαριστοῦντες* ("give thanks"). Just as prayers are said with joy (cf. Phil 1:4), the praise of the community should be with jubilation: "rejoice with unutterable joy" (*ἀγαλλιᾶσθε χαρᾷ ἀνεκλαλήτῳ* 1 Pt 1:8, cf. 4:13). As a fruit of the Spirit (Gal 5:22), "joy" (*χαρά*) fills the life of the community and expresses itself in the "rejoicing" (*ἀγαλλίασις*) by which God is thanked for keeping his promises and inaugurating salvation (Acts 2:46). This thankful praise to God is borne along by eschatological joy: "Rejoice always, pray constantly, *give thanks* in all circumstances" (*Πάντοτε χαίρετε, ἀδιαλείπτως προσεύχεσθε, ἐν παντὶ εὐχαριστεῖτε* 1 Thess 5:16–18); "Rejoice in the Lord always; again I will say, rejoice . . . in everything by prayer and thanksgiving let your requests be made known to God" (*χαίρετε ἐν κυρίῳ πάντοτε· πάλιν ἐρῶ, χαίρετε . . . ἐν παντὶ τῇ προσευχῇ καὶ δεήσει μετὰ εὐχαριστίας τὰ αἰτήματα ὑμῶν γνωριζέσθω πρὸς τὸν θεόν* Phil 4:4–6).[4]

The words "with joy give thanks" (*μετὰ χαρᾶς εὐχαριστοῦντες*)[5] are directed to the whole community and therefore cannot be viewed as a connecting link to the prayer of thanksgiving, which opens the letter with the apostle's thanks to God for the good condition of the community.[6] Paul never closes the intercessions in his letters with thanksgiving or with a summons to it.[7] It is not impossible to construct a connection between the apostle's prayer and the summons "with joy give thanks" (*μετὰ χαρᾶς εὐχαριστοῦντες*) by supplying the intermediary thought that the good condition of the community had necessarily to be expressed in a prayer of thanksgiving;[8] after all, there is no longer any mention of the condition of the community. Rather, the community is asked to receive the word and to offer a hymn of praise to God the Father for his eschatological act of salvation, which he has rendered to them and to all

---

pletely justified. Cf. also the liturgical context of 1 QS I, 18ff; 18f has יהיו הכוהנים והלויים מברכים את אל ישועות ("The priests and the Levites *shall bless* the God of salvation"); 19f has וכול העוברים בברית אומרים ("And all those entering the Covenant *shall say*"); 21f has . . . והכוהנים מספרים ומשמיעים ("And the priests *shall recite* . . . *and shall declare*"); 22 has והלויים מספרים ("And the Levites *shall recite*"); 24 has [וכול] העוברים בברית מודים ("all those entering the covenant *shall confess*").

2 Cf. Joseph A. Fitzmyer, "Qumran and the Interpolated Paragraph in 2 Cor 6:14–7:1," *CBQ* 23 (1961): 271–80.

3 Cf. Eduard Norden, *Agnostos Theos* (Leipzig: 1913 = Darmstadt: [4]1956), 250–54; Ernst Käsemann, *Essays on New Testament Themes*, tr. W. J. Montague, SBT 41 (Naperville: Alec R. Allenson, 1964), 152f; Günther Bornkamm, *Aufsätze* 2, 196f; Eduard Lohse, "Christologie und Ethik", 165. Cf. also below, p. 40, n. 63.

4 Cf. also Phil 1:3f "I give thanks . . . making prayer with joy" (*εὐχαριστῶ . . . μετὰ χαρᾶς τὴν δέησιν ποιούμενος*).

5 The insertions of *καί* (and) after *μετὰ χαρᾶς* ("with joy") and of *ἅμα* (at the same time) after *εὐχαριστοῦντες* ("give thanks") in the mss p^{46} and B are secondary textual expansions. Cf. Blass–Debrunner, sec. 425.2.

6 The secondary reading *ἡμᾶς* (us) in A C 𝔎 D G pm also would not achieve a connection. Cf. below p. 35, n. 19.

7 Correctly observed by Lohmeyer, *ad loc.*

8 Thus Dibelius–Greeven, *ad loc.*, in that they explain

the world.[9]

The verb **εὐχαριστεῖν** (to give thanks) does not appear often in the LXX, and does so only in books which lack a Hebrew original.[10] In the Psalms the summons to thanksgiving is given by the hiphil form of ידה (to know), and this form is usually translated in the LXX as **ἐξομολογεῖσθαι** (to confess, to praise) as in the LXX Ps 135:1, 2, 3, 26; 137:1, 2, 4; etc. The noun form תודה becomes **ἐξομολόγησις** (confession, praise) as in LXX Josh 7:19; Ps 41:4; 92:4; 95:6; etc. Later, in the linguistic usage of Hellenistic Judaism, **ἐξομολογεῖσθαι** (to confess, praise) was replaced by **εὐχαριστεῖν** (to give thanks). Thus Philo almost always uses the latter verb as the expression for thanks offered to God.[11] In view of this transition from **ἐξομολογεῖσθαι** to **εὐχαριστεῖν**, Origen can state that "to say 'I confess' is the same as saying 'I give thanks' " (*Orat.* 6 **τὸ ἐξομολογοῦμαι ἴσον ἐστι τῷ εὐχαριστῶ**) [Trans.]. The Greek **εὐχαριστεῖν** thus corresponds to the Hebrew ידה in the hiphil, which served to introduce the song of thanks and praise.

The Hodayoth, hymns of praise of the Qumran community, begin with a stereotyped and frequently used opening "I thank you, O Lord, for . . ." (אודכה אדוני כי). Thus 1 QH II, 20 continues "for you have placed my soul in the bundle of the living" and v 31 has "for you have (fastened) your eye upon me." Also, I QH III, 19 has "for you have redeemed my soul from the Pit." The one praying speaks in the first person singular, addresses God as his Lord, and then bases his laudatory prayer of thanks by making reference to God's action. If these introductory phrases are translated into Greek, they become **εὐχαριστῶ (ἐξομολογοῦμαί) σοι, κύριε, ὅτι.**[12] Of course the whole community is able to join in this praise; thus there is the first person plural "we praise your name" (1 Q 34, 3, 1, 6 and also cf. 1 QS I, 24; CD XX, 28). In the place of the כִּי-**ὅτι** (*because* . . .) clauses, a relative clause (אֲשֶׁר-**ὅς**) can also give the reason for the thanksgiving: "let us give thanks to the Lord our God *who* is putting us to the test as he did our forefathers" (**εὐχαριστήσωμεν κυρίῳ τῷ θεῷ ἡμῶν, ὅτι πειράζει ἡμᾶς κατὰ καὶ τοὺς πατέρας ἡμῶν** Jdth 8:25).

The Christian community expresses its praise of God in formulations which were shaped by Judaism. Thus the hymn of the twenty-four elders in the book of Revelation opens with these words, "We give thanks to you, Lord God almighty, who is and who was, that you have taken your great power and begun to reign" (**εὐχαριστοῦμέν σοι, κύριε ὁ θεὸς ὁ παντοκράτωρ, ὁ ὢν καὶ ὁ ἦν, ὅτι εἴληφας τὴν δύναμίν σου τὴν μεγάλην καὶ ἐβασίλευσας** Rev 11:17). In the eucharistic prayers of the Didache the form is "we give thanks to you, O Holy Father" (**εὐχαριστοῦμέν σοι, πάτερ ἅγιε** 10:2), and "above all we give thanks to you because you are mighty" (**πρὸ πάντων εὐχαριστοῦμέν σοι, ὅτι δυνατὸς εἶ** 10:4). Unlike the form of the Hodayoth of the Qumran community, in these Christian texts it is not an individual "I," but rather the "we" of the community which is calling on God the Father. Beyond this, however, the praise and thanks given to God are rendered in the same words as in Jewish prayers.[13]

The same form of a summons to praise[14] which was taken over from Judaism is also the basis for the words "with joy give thanks to the father" (**μετὰ χαρᾶς εὐχαριστοῦντες τῷ πατρί**).[15] The Father[16] is praised because he has effected salvation and redemption in Christ—as the participial phrase **τῷ ἱκανώσαντι ὑμᾶς** (1:12 "who has authorized you") and the relative clause **ὃς ἐρρύσατο** (1:13 "who has delivered us") show by way of an additional explanation.[17] Even though there is one instance in the Hodayoth where the author of the prayer

---

that Paul understood the prayer of thanksgiving as "infused prayer," *oratio infusa*.

9 Cf. James M. Robinson, "Die Hodajot-Formel in Gebet und Hymnus des Frühchristentums" in *Apophoreta: Festschrift für Ernst Haenchen*, BZNW 30 (Berlin: 1964), 194–235. Also, Fritzlothar Mand, "Die Eigenständigkeit der Danklieder des Psalters als Bekenntnislieder," *ZAW* 70 (1958): 185–99; Günther Bornkamm, "Lobpreis Bekenntnis und Opfer," in *Apophoreta*, 46–63.

10 E.g., Jdth 8:25; Wisd Sol 18:2; 2 Macc 1:11; 10:7a; 12:31; 3 Macc 7:16.

11 Cf. Robinson, "Hodajot-Formel," 198f. The songs which the Therapeutae sing are called "songs of thanksgiving" (*οἱ εὐχαριστήριοι ὕμνοι*) in Philo, *Vit. Cont.* 87; cf. also *Ebr.* 94 and 105.

12 Cf. Robinson, "Hodajot-Formel," 208.

13 Cf. *ibid.*, p. 210f. Further examples are cited there; one of these may be quoted in full: *Const. Ap.* 8, 38, 1, "We give thanks to you for all things, Master and Ruler of All, that you have not taken away your mercies" (*εὐχαριστοῦμέν σοι περὶ πάντων, δέσποτα παντοκράτορ, ὅτι οὐκ ἐγκατέλιπες τὰ ἐλέη σου*) [adapted from ANF 7, 475].

14 Cf. Theodoret, *ad loc.*, who explains the verb *εὐχαριστεῖν* by means of *ὑμνεῖν* (to sing hymns): "we

says that his father does not know him and his mother abandoned him to God, and continues: "You are a father to all (the sons) of your truth" (1 QH IX, 35), nevertheless no other passage of the writings of the Qumran community calls God "Father." In the introductory words of the Hymns of Thanksgiving he is always called "Lord." The Christian community, however, prays to God as the Father.[18] As Father of Jesus Christ (1:3), he is our Father (1:2), to whom "thanksgiving" (*εὐχαριστία*) is given through the Kyrios Jesus Christ (3:17). The use of the aorist participle in the Greek *τῷ ἱκανώσαντι* ("who has authorized") points to a definite act of God. The community is reminded that he has authorized "*you* to participate in the lot of the holy ones in light" (*εἰς τὴν μερίδα τοῦ κλήρου τῶν ἁγίων ἐν τῷ φωτί*).[19]

The Greek nouns "part" and "lot" (*μερίς–κλῆρος*) are close to each other in meaning and are often used together in the Old Testament. Thus, *μερίς* ("share," "part") is usually the translation of חֵלֶק, sometimes also for נַחֲלָה. Also *κλῆρος* ("lot") can stand for נַחֲלָה, but as a rule it is the translation for גּוֹרָל, which is never translated as *μερίς*. The tribe of Levi did not receive a "portion and lot" (Deut 10:9 חֵלֶק וְנַחֲלָה—LXX *μερὶς καὶ κλῆρος*) as did its brothers when the land was distributed (cf. Deut 12:12; 14:27, 29; 18:1). The two concepts חלק (part) and נחלה (lot) are often used to describe the part or share received in the apportionment of the land (Deut 32:9; Josh 19:9).[20] Both *μερίς* and *κλῆρος* designate what is apportioned and thus can be employed with transferred meaning to indicate that which is determined as each man's portion—be it reward or punishment (cf. Isa 57:6; Jer 13:25). Particularly they indicate participation in the salvation accomplished by God. The pious man can rejoice that "The Lord is the portion of my inheritance" (LXX Ps 15:5 *κύριος ἡ μερὶς τῆς κληρονομίας μου*). Once the inheritance in the promised Land was taken as a visible demonstration of participation in the fulfillment of the promise; now men are similarly divided according to the portion which falls to them. With this meaning, the terms חלק and נַחֲלָה are often used in the writings of the Qumran community.[21] Men have a portion in the realms of two spirits (1 QS IV, 15), in that of the spirit of truth and that of the spirit of perversity. They conduct their lives and actions according to each man's portion (1 QS IV, 16 "according to the lot of each man" לפי נחלת איש; cf. also IV, 24). God has established both spirits, set hatred between them, and determined the portion or lot of each man. On one side is the lot of Belial (1 QS II, 5 גורל בליעל),[22] of perversity (1 QS IV, 24), of darkness (1 QM I, 11; XIII, 5), and of the sons of darkness (1 QM I, 1). On the other is the lot of God (1 QS II, 2 גורל אל),[23] of truth (1 QM XIII, 12), and of light (1 QM XIII, 9; CD XIII, 12). Thus the opposition is stated, "For they

sing hymns (of thanks) to the benevolent Master that he has made us, who are unworthy, to share the light of the holy ones" [Trans.] (*ὑμνοῦμεν δὲ τὸν φιλάνθρωπον δεσπότην, ὅτι ἡμᾶς ἀναξίους ὄντας κοινωνοὺς ἀπέφηνε τοῦ τῶν ἁγίων φωτός*).

15 Cf. Robinson, "Hodajot–Formel," 230–33.

16 The texts ℵ* (G) 69 it vg^{cl} sy^{p} insert *θεῷ* (to God) before *πατρί* ("to the Father"); and 104 pm offer the reading *τῷ θεῷ καὶ πατρί* (to God and to the Father).

17 Cf. Nils A. Dahl, "Anamnesis," *ST* 1 (1947): 86f, who certainly connects the concept "to give thanks" (*εὐχαριστεῖν*) too quickly with the celebration of the Eucharist.

18 The words "the Father" appear without apposition in phrases which have received their stamp in the liturgy, e.g., Gal 4:6; Rom 8:15; Phil 2:11, as well as in creedal sentences, e.g., 1 Cor 8:6; Rom 6:4.

19 The variant *ἡμᾶς* (us) in A C 𝔎 D G pm is an assimilation to the first person plural of the confessional style preserved in vss 13 and 14. The mss. D G 33 pc it alter *ἱκανώσαντι* ("qualified") to read *καλέσαντι* (called), and B has both *καλέσαντι καὶ ἱκανώσαντι*. The verb *ἱκανοῦν* appears again in the NT only in 2 Cor 3:6, concerning the qualification of the apostle for his ministry. For *ἱκανός* (qualified, worthy) cf. 1 Cor 15:9 and 2 Cor 3:5. In the LXX only the passive form *ἱκανοῦσθαι* "to be made worthy" appears, as indeed outside the NT the passive is generally used. Cf. Bauer, *s.v.*

20 For the connection between "part" and "lot" (*μερίς–κλῆρος*) cf. further LXX Gen 31:14; Num 18:20; and also Acts 8:21 "you have neither part nor lot" (*οὐκ ἔστιν σοι μερὶς οὐδὲ κλῆρος*). Further examples are in Werner Foerster, *TDNT* 3, 759–61.

21 Cf. Lohse, "Christologie und Ethik," 165.

22 Also 1 QM I, 5; IV, 2; XIII, 2.

23 Also 1 QM XIII, 5; XV, 1; XVII, 7.

are the lot of darkness, whereas the lot of God is that of (eternal) light" (1 QM XIII, 5f [Trans.]). The side on which man is placed is determined by God's election. To those whom he has chosen, God "has granted . . . a share in the lot of the Holy Ones (וינחילם בגורל קדושים) and has joined their assembly to the Sons of Heaven for a Council of the Community" (1 QS XI, 7f [Trans.]). Although the term קדושים (holy ones, saints) is used several times as a self-description by the Qumran community,[24] this cannot be its meaning in this context. In both halves of the parallel structure of the sentences there is a correspondence between "the Holy Ones" and "the Sons of Heaven." Thus the "Holy Ones" are the angels in heaven,[25] with whom the community of the elect on earth will be joined by God's merciful act.[26]

The "holy ones" (ἅγιοι) are the angels, and the Christian community has been authorized to participate in their "portion of the lot" (μερὶς τοῦ κλήρου)—this is unmistakably clear from the parallel statements from the Qumran community.[27] So the host of those chosen by God is joined to the angels and they are likewise called "Holy Ones." As God's possession, they are holy ones (cf. 1:2 "saints") who will receive the heavenly inheritance. In contrast to the darkness which rules the godless world, the light is truth, redemption, salvation and the nearness of God. Light (φῶς) thus characterizes the domain in which God has placed his own by his action.[28] The terms "part" and "lot" are joined together in the phrase "to participate in the lot" and this expresses the same thought as was already indicated by the reference to the content of "hope" which is stored up in heaven for the saints (1:5). Here again the concept does not have temporal-eschatological connotations, but rather a spatial orientation.[29] By his unfathomable mercy, God has now *already* made his own capable of participating in the heavenly inheritance with the holy ones, and also capable of conducting themselves in the light.[30]

■ **13** Sharing the inheritance of the holy ones in light, however, means that God has delivered us from the domain of the power of darkness and placed us in the domain of the rule of his beloved Son. V 13, composed of two corresponding lines, adds a substantiating explanation to v 12. It switches from the second person plural used in the summons of v 12 to the first person plural. In a credal statement the community pronounces that it has been freed by God's redeeming act.[31] The Greek ῥύεσθαι (to save, rescue, deliver) is usually the LXX translation of the Hebrew hiphil of נצל, and it describes God's helping and saving intervention.[32] He delivered his people from the hands of the Egyptians (Exod 14:30; Judg 6:9, 13), from bondage (Exod 6:6), and from the hands of all its foes (Judg 8:34). This deliverance occurs according to his great mercy (Neh 9:28), according to his mercy (LXX Ps 32:18f), for his name's sake (LXX Ps 78:9). Just as he assisted the whole of his people, so also he shows his saving help to the pious individual by delivering him from the hand of his persecutor (2 Sam 12:7) and by assisting him against his foes (LXX Ps 7:2). The Qumran community also spoke its praises of the liberating act of God: the host of those who follow the teacher of righteousness are saved by him from the house of Judgment (1 Qp Hab VIII, 2), but idols are not able

24 Cf. 1 QM III, 5; VI, 6; X, 10; XVI, 1; etc. Cf. above, p. 8, n. 17.

25 Cf. Martin Noth, "The Holy Ones of the Most High" in *The Laws of the Pentateuch*, tr. D. R. Ap-Thomas (Philadelphia: Fortress, 1967), 215–28; Christianus Henricus Wilhelmus Brekelmans, "The Saints of the most High and their Kingdom," *Oudtestamentische Studiën* 14 (1965): 305–29; Robert Hanhart, "Die Heiligen des Höchsten," *Hebräische Wortforschung, Festschrift für W. Baumgartner*, Supplement to VT 16 (Leiden: 1967), 90–101.

26 Cf. also Wisd Sol 5:5. The godless, full of remorse, ask concerning the righteous one, "Why has he been numbered among the sons of God? And why is his lot among the holy ones?" (πῶς κατελογίσθη ἐν υἱοῖς θεοῦ καὶ ἐν ἁγίοις ὁ κλῆρος αὐτοῦ ἐστιν). For the rabbinic word usage, cf. Billerbeck 3, 625.

27 Cf. also Eph 1:18; Acts 20:32; 26:18; and also Ernst Käsemann, *Leib und Leib Christi: Eine Untersuchung zur paulinischen Begrifflichkeit*, BHTh 9 (Tübingen: 1933), 142, 147; as well as Lohmeyer, *ad loc.*

28 The words "in the light" (ἐν τῷ φωτί) do not belong only to the preceding word, but rather to the whole phrase.

29 Cf. Abbott, Dibelius–Greeven, *ad loc.*

30 The word "light" (φῶς) does not here mean the "transcendent realm of salvation where God dwells" (thus Conzelmann, *ad loc.*), but simply the domain into which God has transferred the saints and which, therefore, determines their conduct of life here and now. Cf. the parallels in the texts of Qumran.

31 The subject of the relative clause (ὅς) is God. This clearly distinguishes vss 13f from the relative clauses of vss 15 and 18, in which Christ is the subject of the relative clauses.

32 Cf. Wilhelm Kasch, *TDNT* 6, 998–1003.

to save their worshippers on the day of judgment (1 Qp Hab XII, 14). The covenant of God assures all those who live according to its commandments that he will save them from all snares of the Pit (CD XIV, 2). Those praying praise God in the words "You have redeemed my soul from the hand of the mighty" (1 QH II, 35), and "You have redeemed my soul from the Pit" (1 QH III, 19).

The Christian community prays to God "deliver us from evil" (Mt 6:13 ῥῦσαι ἡμᾶς ἀπὸ τοῦ πονηροῦ) and awaits its Lord "who delivers us from the wrath to come" (τὸν ῥυόμενον ἡμᾶς ἐκ τῆς ὀργῆς τῆς ἐρχομένης 1 Thess 1:10). The anxious question "who will deliver me from this body of death?" (τίς με ῥύσεται ἐκ τοῦ σώματος τοῦ θανάτου τούτου Rom 7:24) is answered by the confession in Col 1:13, God "has delivered us from the power of darkness" (ἐρρύσατο ἡμᾶς ἐκ τῆς ἐξουσίας τοῦ σκότους). The Greek ἐξουσία corresponds to the Hebrew concept מֶמְשָׁלָה and designates the "domain of power."[33] Thus the Qumran texts speak of the "dominion of Belial" (ממשלת בליעל) which now exercises its power over the sons of darkness (1 QS I, 18, 23f; II, 19; 1 QM XIV, 9). It can also be called the "dominion of his malevolence" (ממשלת משטמתו 1 QS III, 23) or the "dominion of perversity" (ממשלת עולה, 1 QS IV, 19) or even the "dominion of wickedness" (ממשלת רשעה, 1 QM XVII, 5f).[34] The two realms to which men belong are characterized by the contrast of light and darkness—on one side the lot of Belial and the sons of darkness, on the other the lot of the Holy Ones and the sons of light.[35] By contrasting the terms "light" (φῶς) and "darkness" (σκότος),[36] the Christian confession also indicates that a change of dominion has taken place[37] which is absolutely determinative for the life of the believer.[38]

Much like a mighty king who is able to remove whole peoples from their ancestral homes and to transplant them to another realm,[39] so God is described as taking the community from the power of darkness[40] and transferring it "to the domain of the rule of his beloved Son" (εἰς τὴν βασιλείαν τοῦ υἱοῦ τῆς ἀγάπης αὐτοῦ).[41] The word βασιλεία (rule, domain of rule), the counterpart of the previous word ἐξουσία (power), corresponds to the Hebrew מַלְכוּת. According to 1 QM VI, 6, kingly rule will belong to the God of Israel, who is terrible in the glory of his rule (מלכות, 1 QM XII 7). The "covenant of kingly rule over his people" (ברית מלכות עמו) is given to the scion of David according to divine promise for everlasting generations (4 Q Patriarchal Blessings, 4). In the age of salvation, Israel will receive rule and exercise it (1 Q Sb V, 21; 1 QM XIX, 8). The eschatological concept "the kingdom of heaven" (מַלְכוּת הַשָּׁמַיִם) is taken up in the preaching of Jesus and given unprecedented urgency: God's rule is coming, it is at hand (Mk 1:15, par.). Wherever Paul mentions the "rule of God" (βα-

33 Cf. LXX 4 Kg. 20:13; Ps 113:2; 135:8f; Isa 39:2; Jer 28(51): 28; etc.

34 The connection ממשלת חושך = ἐξουσία τοῦ σκότους (dominion of darkness) appears in 1 QH XII, 6; it is not, however, used there in a figurative sense, for the one praying declares that he wishes to praise God "at the beginning of the dominion of darkness", i.e., in the evening.

35 For Belial and darkness, cf. 1 QS II, 5; 1 QM I, 1, 5, 11; IV, 2; XIII, 2; etc. For the Holy Ones and light, cf. 1 QS I, 9; II, 16; XI, 7f; 1 QH XI, 11f; etc.

36 Cf. Hans Conzelmann, *TWNT* 7, 424–46, esp. 443.

37 Lk 22:53 also uses the words "the power of darkness" (ἐξουσία τοῦ σκότους). At his arrest Jesus says to those taking him "But this is your hour, and the power of darkness" (αὕτη ἐστὶν ὑμῶν ἡ ὥρα καὶ ἡ ἐξουσία τοῦ σκότους).

38 Cf. 2 Cor 6:14 "What fellowship has light with darkness?" (τίς κοινωνία φωτὶ πρὸς σκότος); 1 Pt 2:9 ". . . who called you out of darkness into his marvelous light" (τοῦ ἐκ σκότους ὑμᾶς καλέσαντες εἰς τὸ θαυμαστὸν αὐτοῦ φῶς); Eph 5:8 ". . . for once you were darkness, but now you are light in the Lord" (ἦτε γάρ ποτε σκότος, νῦν δὲ φῶς ἐν κυρίῳ); and 1 Clem 59:2 "through whom (i.e., Christ) he called us from darkness into light" (δι' οὗ ἐκάλεσεν ἡμᾶς ἀπὸ σκότους εἰς φῶς). Concerning this subject, cf. below p. 38, n. 49.

39 Cf. Josephus, *Ant.* 9, 235, who uses the same Greek verb. The Assyrian king Tiglath–Pileser took captive the populace of areas of Palestine which he had conquered and "transported them into his own kingdom" (μετέστεσεν εἰς τὴν αὐτοῦ βασιλείαν).

40 Cf. Chrysostom, *ad loc.*, who explains "from the power" (τῆς ἐξουσίας) by the words "from the tyranny" (τῆς τυραννίδος).

41 The Greek verb μεθιστάναι signifies the transferring from one place to another, cf. 1 Cor 13:2 "to remove mountains" (ὄρη μεθιστάναι) and cf. also Acts 19:26. It may also mean transferring in the sense of removing (Lk 16:4; Acts 13:22). But it does not mean a "lifting up" or a "being carried off" (*contra* Lohmeyer, *ad loc.*, who has "entrücken").

σιλεία τοῦ θεοῦ) in his letters, the futuristic meaning of the concept is presupposed, just as throughout primitive Christian proclamation. The future kingdom of God and the inheriting of the "kingdom" are repeatedly mentioned,[42] but only in 1 Cor 15:23–28 does Paul speak of Christ's kingly rule. Christ, who is now raised and exalted, must reign until he puts all enemies under his feet. At the end, however, Christ shall give the "rule" to God so that God may be all in all. Thus the "rule" of Christ has temporal limits and the objective of preparing the way for the rule of God which will endure forever.[43] In contrast to this, Col opposes the "power of darkness" (ἐξουσία τοῦ σκότους) to the "rule" of the beloved Son, without mentioning a temporal limit. The domain of Christ's rule into which the faithful have been transferred mediates salvation to them here and now, for they have already been raised with Christ (2:12), resurrected with him for a new life (3:1f). There is no waiting for the future consummation; rather, what 3:11 states applies to the salvation now proclaimed and appointed: "Christ is all and in all" (πάντα καὶ ἐν πᾶσιν ὁ Χριστός).

The hebraizing Greek construction ὁ υἱὸς τῆς ἀγάπης αὐτοῦ ("the son of his love," i.e. "his beloved son")[44] corresponds to the usual expression ὁ υἱὸς ὁ ἀγαπητός (Mk 1:11, par; 9:7, par; 12:6, par.) or ἠγαπημένος (Eph 1:6 "the Beloved").[45] As the heavenly voice in the baptismal story proclaims, God has revealed Christ as his beloved Son (Mk 1:11, par). The resurrected Christ is appointed Son of God (Rom 1:4) and has been enthroned at God's right hand (Rom 8:34; Col 3:1; Acts 2:34f; etc.). The aorist forms ἐρρύσατο (delivered) and μετέστησεν (transferred) point to baptism as the event through which the change from one dominion to another has taken place, in that we have been wrested from the power of darkness and placed in the "kingdom" of the beloved Son of God.[46] This does not mean that those baptized have been taken up into a transcendent realm of light.[47] There is no mention of an enthusiastic anticipation of the consummation. Rather, just as darkness designates those who are lost, light characterizes the rule of Christ,[48] which here and now shapes the life and conduct of those who are baptized.[49]

42 Cf. 1 Thess 2:12; Gal 5:21; 1 Cor 6:9f; 15:50; 2 Thess 1:5; and also 1 Cor 4:20; Rom 14:17. In Col 4:11 "kingdom of God" (βασιλεία τοῦ θεοῦ) is used as a fixed formula, "fellow workers for the kingdom of God" (σύνεργοι εἰς τὴν βασιλείαν τοῦ θεοῦ). Eph 5:5 mentions the "inheritance in the kingdom of Christ and of God" (κληρονομία ἐν τῇ βασιλείᾳ τοῦ Χριστοῦ καὶ θεοῦ).

43 The "rule" of Christ is "as it were, an already present, representative 'forerunner' of the βασιλεία τοῦ θεοῦ (rule of God) and is exercised by the exalted Christ." Since according to apocalyptic ideas the messianic interregnum can only begin at the Parousia, "the βασιλεία of 1 Cor 15:24 cannot be identified with it," Hans-Alwin Wilcke, *Das Problem eines messianischen Zwischenreiches bei Paulus*, AThANT 51 (Zürich: 1967), 99 [Trans.].

44 This is clearly a Semiticism (cf. Blass–Debrunner, sec. 165) and not a poetic Attic manner of expression which "had come down into the market place" (thus Dibelius–Greeven, *ad loc.*; from J. H. Moulton, *A Grammar of New Testament Greek*, vol. 1, *Prolegomena* [Edinburgh: T. & T. Clark, ³1919], 74).

45 The beloved Son is the only son, cf. Gen 22:2. Further examples are cited by Lohmeyer, *ad loc.* Eduard Schweizer, "Dying and Rising with Christ," *NTS* 14 (1967–68): 5, n. 3, considers the possibility that the expression "the beloved son" could have been taken "from a first line of the hymn quoted in 1:15–20"; "for . . . it occurs rather frequently in Egyptian texts . . . together with the concept of the image of God (v. 15)." Cf. below, p. 41, n. 64.

46 Cf. Käsemann, *Essays*, 158–61; Bornkamm, *Aufsätze* 2, 190f; and Eduard Schweizer, *TWNT* 8, 370.

47 *Contra* Lohmeyer, Conzelmann, *ad loc.*

48 This meaning for the concepts of light and darkness is assured by the parallels from the Qumran texts. This should not be taken to mean that the author of Col had direct contact with the writings or the tradition of the Qumran community. Rather, certain concepts and ideas from the teaching of this community had been accepted in the Hellenistic synagogue—cf. the Testaments of the Twelve Patriarchs!—and in this way also became known to the Christian community. Cf. below, note 49 and Braun, *Qumran* 1, p 226.

49 In Acts 26:18 almost the same words are used to formulate the commission given to Paul outside Damascus: to open the eyes of the Gentiles, "that they may turn from darkness to light and from the power of Satan to God, that they may receive forgiveness of sins and a share among those who are sanctified by faith in me." (τοῦ ἐπιστρέψαι ἀπὸ σκότους εἰς φῶς καὶ τῆς ἐξουσίας τοῦ σατανᾶ ἐπὶ

■ **14** The relative clause, "in whom we have" (ἐν ᾧ ἔχομεν)[50] speaks of the new life which we have received in Christ. The word ἀπολύτρωσις ("redemption"),[51] which was seldom used in Greek at this time,[52] designates liberation from imprisonment and bondage.[53] In the New Testament the term is used with an eschatological sense when there is mention of the hope of the "redemption of our bodies" (ἀπολύτρωσις τοῦ σώματος ἡμῶν Rom 8:23), or of the "day of redemption" (Eph 4:30 ἡμέρα ἀπολυτρώσεως, cf. also Eph 1:14). Most often, however, the "redemption" is recognized as having already taken place: Christ has become our "redemption" (1 Cor 1:30), and "redemption" means nothing other than "forgiveness of sins" (ἄφεσις τῶν ἁμαρτιῶν Col 1:14; Eph 1:7).[54] Normally, however, Paul seldom speaks of the forgiveness of sins. He understands ἁμαρτία (sin) as a power which found entrance into the world through Adam's deed (Rom 5:12) and since then has exercised its tyranny over men. Its power, however, was broken by Christ's cross (Rom 8:3), for he was made to be sin for us so that in him we might become the righteousness of God (2 Cor 5:21). Where there is mention of the forgiveness of sins in the Pauline letters,[55] it is a matter of a common Christian expression.[56] Rom 3:24 is based on a Jewish–Christian creedal statement which Paul takes up in order to substantiate and develop his understanding of the "righteousness of God" (δικαιοσύνη θεοῦ).[57] God has accomplished "redemption" in Christ. The "passing over former sins" (πάρεσις τῶν προγε-

---

τὸν θεόν, τοῦ λαβεῖν αὐτοὺς ἄφεσιν ἁμαρτιῶν καὶ κλῆρον ἐν τοῖς ἡγιασμένοις πίστει τῇ εἰς ἐμέ). This sentence elucidates the turning from darkness to light as a turning from "the power of Satan" (ἐξουσία τοῦ σατανᾶ) to God. Whoever has turned to him receives, as a member of the community of salvation, a share among the saints through faith in Christ. This means he receives forgiveness of sins. The use of the contrast between the concepts of light and darkness in connection with the conversion to the God of Israel is already known from the Hellenistic synagogue, as *Joseph and Asenath* shows in 8:9 (49:19–21) "Lord God of my father Israel, the Most High and mighty God who brings all things to life and calls *from the darkness to the light* and from error to truth and from death to life . . ." (κύριε ὁ θεὸς τοῦ πατρός μου Ἰσραήλ, ὁ ὕψιστος καὶ δυνατὸς θεός, ὁ ζωοποιήσας τὰ πάντα καὶ καλέσας ἀπὸ τοῦ σκότους εἰς τὸ φῶς καὶ ἀπὸ τῆς πλάνης εἰς τὴν ἀλήθειαν καὶ ἀπὸ τοῦ θανάτου εἰς τὴν ζωήν). Again 15:12 (62:11–13) has "Blessed is the Lord your God who sent you *to deliver me from the darkness* and to bring me from the foundations of the abyss itself *into the light*" (εὐλογητὸς κύριος ὁ θεός σου, ὁ ἐξαποστείλας σε τοῦ ῥύσασθαί με ἐκ τοῦ σκότους καὶ ἀναγαγεῖν με ἀπὸ τῶν θεμελίων αὐτῆς τῆς ἀβύσσου εἰς τὸ φῶς). (Trans. adapted from E. W. Brooks, *Joseph and Asenath*, Translations of Early Documents, Series 2, Hellenistic–Jewish Texts [London: SPCK, 1918].) Cf. also Christoph Burchard, *Untersuchungen zu Joseph und Aseneth*, Untersuchungen zum Neuen Testament 8 (Tübingen: 1965), 102, n. 3.

50 The ms. B reads ἔσχομεν (we had) and thereby assimilates with the aorist in v 13.

51 Cf. Friedrich Büchsel, *TDNT* 4, 351–56.

52 Examples for the use of ἀπολύτρωσις (redemption) begin to appear only from the second and first century B.C. onward, and in the LXX it is used only in Dan 4:34 for the "redemption" of Nebuchadnezzar from his insanity. Cf. Büchsel, *TDNT* 4, 351; and Bauer, *s.v.* For the subject matter, cf. also *Test Zeb* 9:8 "He shall redeem all the captivity of the sons of men from Beliar" (αὐτὸς λυτρώσηται πᾶσαν αἰχμαλωσίαν υἱῶν ἀνθρώπων ἐκ τοῦ Βελίαρ); *Test Joseph* 18:2 "And you shall be redeemed by the Lord from all evil" [Trans.] [illegible]) παντὸς κακοῦ λυτρωθήσεσθε διὰ κυρίου). The Qumran community understood itself to be "the people whom God redeemed" [Trans.] (עם פדות אל 1 QM I, 12) or to be the "poor whom you have redeemed" (אביוני פדותכה 1 QM IX, 9). Cf. also 1 QM XIV, 5, 10; XV, 1; and XVII, 6.

53 Examples in Büchsel and Bauer, see preceding note.

54 There is here no connection with the practice of freeing a slave from captivity. Deissmann, *LAE*, p. 330, however, points to the freeing of slaves in antiquity. On this matter, cf. Werner Elert, "Redemptio ab hostibus," *ThLZ* 72 (1947): 265–70.

55 Cf. Rudolf Bultmann, *TDNT* 1, 511–12.

56 Primitive Christian usage on this subject took up the language of the OT and of Judaism. There are many passages in the writings of the Qumran community which mention the forgiveness of sins (סלח, נשא) or the atonement (כפר). Cf. 1 QS I, 23–26; II, 8; III, 6–12; IX, 4; XI, 14; CD II, 4f; III, 18; IV, 9f; XIV, 19; 1 QH IV, 37; VII, 35; IX, 13, 34; X, 21; XI, 9, 31; XIV, 24; XVI, 16; XVII, 12, 15, 18; etc. For rabbinic evidence see Billerbeck 1, 113f and 421.

57 Cf. Ernst Käsemann, "Zum Verständnis von Römer 3, 24–26" in *Aufsätze* 1, 96–100; also Eduard Lohse, *Märtyrer und Gottesknecht: Untersuchungen zur urchristlichen Verkündigung vom Sühnetod Jesu Christi*,

γονότων ἁμαρτημάτων Rom 3:25)[58] is guaranteed by the expiatory death of Christ. Reference to his vicarious death is also made in Eph 1:7, "in him we have redemption through his blood, the forgiveness of our trespasses" (ἐν ᾧ ἔχομεν τὴν ἀπολύτρωσιν διὰ τοῦ αἵματος αὐτοῦ, τὴν ἄφεσιν τῶν παραπτωμάτων).[59] Yet the forgiveness of sins is received in baptism. In the baptism of John was expectation of the future "forgiveness of sins" (ἄφεσις ἁμαρτιῶν) on the day of judgment which was drawing near (Mk 1:4; par). In primitive Christian baptismal practice, however, the "forgiveness of sins" was granted directly (Acts 2:38).[60] Thus, in the book of Acts the forgiveness of sins can be cited repeatedly as the content of salvation.[61] By defining "redemption" as "forgiveness of sins," in agreement with the common Christian understanding, the summons to praise clearly refers to baptism.[62] This, in turn, indicates in what sense the following hymn is to be understood.[63] All speculations about knowledge of higher worlds are confronted by the assertion that nothing can surpass nor supplement the forgiveness of sins. This is so because the sovereign rule of Christ is present where there is forgiveness of sins; and with forgiveness of sins everything, life and blessings everlasting, has in fact been granted.

FRLANT 46 (Göttingen: 1955), 149–54.

58 The word πάρεσις (passing over) does not mean something like "overlooking," but has the same sense as ἄφεσις, i.e., forgiveness. Cf. Rudolf Bultmann, *TDNT* 1, 511.

59 Several late witnesses insert the words "through his blood" (διὰ τοῦ αἵματος αὐτοῦ), from Eph 1:7, in Col 1:14 (35 1912 al vg[cl] sy[h]).

60 The phrases of a creedal type in Rev 1:5 also refer to baptism: "To him who loves us and has freed us from our sins by his blood" (τῷ ἀγαπῶντι ἡμᾶς καὶ λύσαντι ἡμᾶς ἐκ τῶν ἁμαρτιῶν ἡμῶν ἐν τῷ αἵματι αὐτοῦ). Cf. Eduard Lohse, *Die Offenbarung des Johannes*, NTD 11 (Göttingen: [2]1966), 16; and Peter von der Osten-Sacken, "Christologie, Homologie, Taufe—Ein Beitrag zu Apc Joh 1:5f," *ZNW* 58 (1967): 255–66.

61 E.g., Acts 5:31; 10:43; 13:38; 26:18; also Mt 26:28; Lk 1:77; 24:47; Heb 9:22; 10:18.

62 There is certainly no allusion to the Jewish Day of Atonement as Lohmeyer, 43–46; 52f, would like to find. Cf. below pp. 45f. This thought plays an important role in the epistle to the Hebrews, but not in this passage, where the concepts "redemption" and "forgiveness of sins" were taken from the primitive Christian tradition.

63 Cf. Käsemann, *Essays*, 158–67, prefers to see the whole context, vss 12–20, as a baptismal liturgy. Karl-Gottfried Eckart, "Exegetische Beobachtungen zu Kol. 1:9–20," *Theologia Viatorum* 7 (1959–60): 87–106, also wishes to incorporate vss 9–11 into the baptismal liturgy, which then consists of three parts: the exhortation (1:9–11), the responsory which is the adjunct confession of the one baptized (1:13f), and the Christ-hymn (1:15–20). It is, however, difficult to speak of a liturgy. Vss 9–12 express the intercession of the apostle. Vss 12–14 deal with the event of baptism—and also take up traditonal phrases—but they do not form any continuous liturgical context. Cf. also Leonhard Fendt, *ThLZ* 76 (1951): 532; Dibelius-Greeven, 11; Bornkamm, *Aufsätze* 2, 196, n. 19a; Eduard Schweizer, *Neotestamentica: deutsche und englische Aufsätze* 1951–1963; *German and English Essays* 1951–1963 (Zürich: 1963), 293, n. 1; Reinhard Deichgräber, *Gotteshymnus und Christushymnus in der frühen Christenheit: Untersuchungen zu Form, Sprache und Stil der frühchristlichen Hymnen*, Studien zur Umwelt des Neuen Testaments 5 (Göttingen: 1967), 78–82. Bornkamm notes correctly that "One must be satisfied with the statement that the content of 1:12–14 is the event of baptism and that 1:15–20 is allied with it." Although Käsemann asserts "The writer of the letter evidently found vv 13–14 already connected with the hymn" (*Essays*, altered by *trans.* p. 153), it is quite uncertain whether this connection already existed in the oral tradition. For there is a difference in the concepts and terminology used by the two passages, and also a change in style (v 13 has a relative clause in the style of a confession; vss 15–20 lack the word "we" introducing the community as speaking, and the "you" by which it is addressed). It is more probable that the author of the letter joined various pieces of tradition together and, by means of the entire context he produced, indicated how the Christ-hymn ought to be understood.

The Christ–hymn: 1:15–20

The quotation of a hymnic unit begins in v 15 and extends to v 20.[64] By inserting the hymn into the letter's train of thought a certain tension arises regarding its present context. The previous vss 13–14 preserve the style of a confession ("us," "we"); vss 15–20, however, make no mention of the confessing community, but instead only demonstrate the world–wide validity and effect of the Christ–event. What follows is an explanation which interprets the hymn and applies it to the community with the words: "he has reconciled you" (1:21–23). The reconciliation is thereby no longer understood in a cosmic context; rather it is related to the community which is addressed by the word of reconciliation.

Style and language identify vss 15–20 as a hymnic section which has been appropriated from the tradition. Christological statements about exaltation are introduced twice by a relative clause (ὅς ἐστιν 1:15, 18b),[65] and each in turn is followed by a causal clause beginning with ὅτι (1:16, 19). Vss 17 and 18 respectively are joined to the preceding by a καὶ αὐτός ("and he . . ."), and v 20 is attached by καὶ δι' αὐτοῦ ("and through him"). The hymn is concluded by the pleonastic phrase, "making peace by the blood of his cross, through him, whether on earth

64 Since the quotation begins with a relative clause, at least one brief line must have preceded this clause in the original hymn. It could have been something like "blessed be the Son of God" etc. (cf. above p. 38, n. 45). Hans Jakob Gabathuler has provided a critical report of the research on the exegesis of 1:15–20 in his *Jesus Christus, Haupt der Kirche—Haupt der Welt: Der Christushymnus Colosser 1:15–20 in der theologischen Forschung der letzten 130 Jahre*, AThANT 45 (Zürich: 1965). In addition to the commentaries, the following investigations of the hymn must be especially noted:

Eduard E. Norden, *Agnostos Theos, Untersuchungen zur Formengeschichte religiöser Rede* (Leipzig:1913= Darmstadt: ⁴1956), 250–54.

Günther Harder, *Paulus und das Gebet*, Neutestamentliche Forschung 10 (Gütersloh: 1936), 46–51.

Max Adolf Wagenführer, *Die Bedeutung Christi für Welt und Kirche: Studien zum Kolosser– und Epheserbrief* (Leipzig: 1941).

Ernst Percy, *Probleme*, 68–78.

Charles Masson, "L'hymne christologique de l'épître aux Colossiens I, 15–20," *Revue de Théologie et de Philosophie* NS 36 (1948): 138–42.

Ernst Käsemann, "A primitive Christian baptismal liturgy," *Essays*, 149–68.

E. Unger, *Christus und der Kosmos: Exegetisch–religionsgeschichtliche Studie zu Kol 1, 15ff.* Unpub. Diss. (Vienna: 1953).

Lucien Cerfaux, *Le Christ dans la théologie de saint Paul*, Lectio Divina 6 (Paris: ²1954), 298–301; =*Christus in der Paulinischen Theologie* (Düsseldorf: 1964), 245–47.

Christian Maurer, "Die Begründung der Herrschaft Christi über die Mächte nach Kolosser 1, 15–20," *Wort und Dienst* NF 4 (1955): 79–93.

James M. Robinson, "A Formal Analysis of Colossians 1:15–20," *JBL* 76 (1957): 270–87.

Eduard Lohse, "Imago Dei bei Paulus" in *Libertas Christiana: Festschrift für F. Delekat*, Beiträge zur EvTh 26 (Munich: 1957) pp. 126–30 *idem*, "Christologie und Ethik," 160–64.

Jacob Jervell, *Imago Dei: Gen 1, 26f im Spätjudentum, in der Gnosis und in den paulinischen Briefen*, FRLANT 58 (Göttingen: 1960), 197–226.

Karl–Gottfried Eckart, "Exegetische Beobachtungen," 87–106.

Ernst Bammel, "Versuch zu Col 1:15–20," *ZNW* 52 (1961): 88–95.

Harald Hegermann, *Die Vorstellung vom Schöpfungsmittler im hellenistischen Judentum und Urchristentum*, TU 82 (Berlin: 1961), 88–157.

Eduard Schweizer, "Die Kirche als Leib Christi in den paulinischen Antilegomena," *ThLZ* 86 (1961): 241–56 =*Neotestamentica*, 293–316. *Idem*, "The Church as the Missionary Body of Christ," *NTS* 8 (1961–62): 1–11 =*Neotestamentica*, 317–29.

P. Ellingsworth, "Colossians 1:15–20 and its Context" *ExpT* 73 (1961–62): 252f.

Gottfried Schille, *Frühchristliche Hymnen* (Berlin: 1962; ²1965), 81f.

Johannes Schattenmann, *Studien zum neutestamentlichen Prosahymnus* (Munich: 1965), 16–18.

André Feuillet, *Le Christ sagesse de Dieu d'après les épîtres Pauliniennes*, Études bibliques (Paris: 1966), 163–273.

Nikolaus Kehl, *Der Christushymnus Kol 1, 12–20*, Stuttgarter Biblische Monographien 1 (Stuttgart: 1967).

Richard Deichgräber, *Gotteshymnus und Christushymnus in der frühen Christenheit: Untersuchungen zu Form, Sprache und Stil der frühchristlichen Hymnen*, Studien zur Umwelt des Neuen Testaments 5 (Göttingen: 1967), 143–55.

K. Wengst, *Christologische Formeln und Lieder des Urchristentums*, Unpub. Diss. (Bonn: 1967), 163–74.

65 For the use of relative clauses at the opening of a hymnic quote, cf. Phil 2:6; 1 Tim 3:16; 1 Pt 2:22; Heb 1:3.

or in the heavens" (εἰρηνοποιήσας διὰ τοῦ αἵματος τοῦ σταυροῦ αὐτοῦ, δι' αὐτοῦ εἴτε τὰ ἐπὶ τῆς γῆς εἴτε τὰ ἐν τοῖς οὐρανοῖς). The verses of the hymn contain an impressive number of terms which either do not appear at all elsewhere in the Pauline corpus, or are used otherwise with a different meaning. Verse 15 has "image of God" (εἰκὼν τοῦ θεοῦ) which is used again only in 2 Cor 4:4 as a Christological predicate in the formula–sentence: "who is the image of God" (ὅς ἐστιν εἰκὼν τοῦ θεοῦ).[66] In the whole New Testament, ὁρατός (1:16 "visible") appears only here, and while ἀόρατος (1:15f "invisible") appears a few times (Rom 1:20; 1 Tim 1:17; Heb 11:27) it is never used elsewhere as a contrast to ὁρατός ("visible"). The Pauline letters do not mention θρόνοι ("thrones") elsewhere, and only Eph 1:21 uses κυριότης (1:16 "dominion"). The intransitive form συνεστηκέναι (1:17 "to be established") is otherwise not used by Paul. In a Christological context Paul speaks of Christ as ἀπαρχή (1 Cor 15:20 "first fruits"), but never as ἀρχή (1:18 "beginning").[67] The words πρωτεύειν ("to be the first") and εἰρηνοποιεῖν ("to make peace") are hapaxlegomena in the New Testament. The word κατοικεῖν (1:19 "to dwell") reoccurs in Col 2:9, but this verse refers back to the hymn, and again in Eph 3:17. Eph 2:16 contains the only other use of ἀποκαταλλάσσειν ("to reconcile"). The blood of Christ is mentioned by Paul only in connection with traditional primitive Christian phrases which have to do with the vicarious death of Christ,[68] and the combination αἷμα τοῦ σταυροῦ αὐτοῦ (1:20 "blood of his cross") is without parallel.

These observations exclude the possibility that the author of this letter could have composed these verses himself by using traditional phrases.[69] Rather, this is a quotation from a primitive Christian song which celebrates the unique dignity of the exalted Lord and which contains two strophes, each introduced by the Greek relative clause ὅς ἐστιν ("He [who] is . . ." 1:15, 18b).[70] The first strophe states that all things were created in him, through him, and for him, so that the second strophe deals with reconciliation which is established as cosmic peace by the bearer of the divine fullness. Thus creation and reconciliation, cosmology and soteriology are dealt with in order to praise Christ as the Lord of the cosmos, who is the head of the body and whose reign encompasses all things.

It is clear, moreover, that the author of the letter did not incorporate the hymn without alterations; rather, he inserted short interpretive additions and thus accentuated it in certain ways. Above all, it is curious that at the end of the first, cosmologically oriented strophe, Christ is suddenly referred to as the "head of the body, the church" (1:18a κεφαλὴ τοῦ σώματος τῆς ἐκκλησίας). Considering its content, this statement would have to be connected with the second strophe which is characterized by soteriological statements. The structure of the hymn, however, places it in the first strophe. The difficulty in the arrangement of 1:18a is solved when the words τῆς ἐκκλησίας ("of the church") are taken as an interpretive addition, as Ernst Käsemann has argued

66 1 Cor 11:7 says of man that he is the "image and glory of God" (εἰκὼν καὶ δόξα θεοῦ).

67 The word ἀρχή with the meaning "beginning" appears in the *Corpus Paulinum* only in Phil 4:15 and 2 Thess 2:13, but as a variant reading: ἀπαρχήν (B G 33 al f vg sy[h]) or ἀπ' ἀρχῆς (ℵ Ψ 𝔎 D pm it sy[p]). (Cf. the RSV footnote *ad loc.* [trans.]). With the meaning "principality" it appears in 1 Cor 15:24; Rom 8:38; Col 2:10, 15; Eph 1:21; 3:10; 6:12. In Tit 3:1 the civil authorities are called ἀρχαί.

68 Rom 3:25; 1 Cor 10:16; 11:25, 27; cf. also Eph 1:7; 2:13. Also, cf. Lohse, *Märtyrer und Gottesknecht*, 138–41.

69 Thus Dibelius–Greeven, p. 10: "The situation has caused Paul to speak of things which otherwise . . . he only touches upon with allusions." [Trans.] Also, Maurer, "Die Begründung der Herrschaft Christi," 84; H. C. G. Moule, *Colossian Studies, Lessons in Faith and Holiness from St. Paul's Epistles to the Colossians and Philemon* (London: Pickering & Inglis, 1926), 58–62; Kümmel, *Introduction*, 242. Feuillet, *Le Christ sagesse*, 246–73, maintains that the author of Col took up a hymn which he had composed at an earlier date: "Col 1:1–15 may well be regarded as the summit of Pauline Christology" [Trans.].

70 An analysis of the hymn must begin with the parallel structure of these two relative clauses. Attempts to demonstrate another division of the hymn ignore its strophic structure. Lohmeyer, *ad loc.*, wants to reconstruct the two strophes, each with seven lines, which begin at 1:15 and 1:18; each strophe would be preceded by a unit of three lines (1:13f; 1:16c, 17). For a critique of this analysis, see especially Käsemann, *Essays*, 149–51. Dibelius–Greeven, *ad loc.*, place the beginning of the first strophe at 1:15 and the second at 1:18a: "He is the head . . ." (καὶ αὐτός ἐστιν ἡ κεφαλὴ κτλ). Masson *ad loc.* proceeds in an altogether different manner: by leaving out 1:18a, he constructs five strophes of four cola each. These four cola are built according to the rule of *parallelismus membrorum:* 1:15–16a; 16b–c; 17–18b; 19–20a; 20b–c. For a critical discussion of this, cf. Ellingsworth, "Colossians 1:15–20," 252f, and Gabathuler, *Jesus Christus, Haupt der Kirche*, 42–49, 61–66.

convincingly.[71] Originally, then, the reference was to Christ as the head of the body, i.e., of the cosmos. However, inserting "of the church" (τῆς ἐκκλησίας), the author of the letter gave the term "body" (σῶμα) a new interpretation which corresponds to his understanding of the church as the body of Christ (cf. 1:24).[72] It is also clear that there is a secondary expansion at the end of strophe two. The text says that he has made peace "through the blood of his cross, through him" (διὰ τοῦ αἵματος τοῦ σταυροῦ αὐτοῦ, δι' αὐτοῦ). This double "through" (διά) has continuously given rise to critical reflection, so that several copyists deleted the "through him" (δι' αὐτοῦ) in order to achieve a smoother text (e.g.: B D * G I al latt Or). It is hardly possible that "through him" was subsequently added to the text. The words "through the blood of his cross" (διὰ τοῦ αἵματος τοῦ σταυροῦ αὐτοῦ) indicate, rather, an addition[73] which follows the thrust of Pauline theology and points to the cross as the place where reconciliation was accomplished. By means of these two glosses the hymn's statements receive solid historical reference. The reconciliation which relates to the whole world originated in the vicarious death of Christ; the rule of Christ, however, is a present reality in his body, the church.

It is difficult to determine whether the original form of the hymn has been rediscovered after these two additions have been removed, or whether the text contains further secondary supplements. As concerns the structure of both strophes, not only is the first one (vss 15–18a) a good bit longer than the second (vss 18b–20), but there is no exact formal correlation between the individual lines. Thus, one must examine whether it is possible to reconstruct a more properly balanced structure of the original hymn.

The enumeration "whether thrones or dominions, powers or principalities" as well as the phrase "whether on earth or in the heavens" (εἴτε θρόνοι εἴτε κυριότητες εἴτε ἀρχαὶ εἴτε ἐξουσίαι v 16; εἴτε τὰ ἐπὶ τῆς γῆς εἴτε τὰ ἐν τοῖς οὐρανοῖς v 20), were described by Eduard Norden as "superfluous ornamental trimming" which is "foreign to the nature of the Semitic, but quite acceptable to that of the Hellenistic mind"; they were therefore, he judged, added secondarily.[74] Indeed, many exegetes have agreed with this view and have asserted that the author of the letter inserted these words in order to be able to polemicize against the worship of cosmic powers—a practice with which he must come to grips in chapter two.[75] But it must be noted that "thrones or dominions" (θρόνοι καὶ κυριότητες) are not mentioned again either in Col or in the Pauline *corpus*.[76] It is difficult to ascribe the coupling of these two terms to the vocabulary of the author or of his opponents without further ado.[77] This only leaves one to suppose that such an addition could already have been made in the oral tradition. Concerning the concluding phrase, "whether on earth or in the heavens" (εἴτε τὰ ἐπὶ τῆς γῆς εἴτε τὰ ἐν τοῖς οὐρανοῖς), it must be said that it recalls the beginning of the hymn[78] and, as a reference to the cosmic dimensions of the reconciliation, it achieves an appropriate conclusion. Since the second strophe lacks an exact counterpart for the two clauses which start with καὶ αὐτός ("He" or "and he" in tr. of vss 17, 18a),[79] several exegetes have called vss 17 and 18a an insertion[80] which stands out syntactically and narrows the cosmological horizon of the two parallel strophes of vss 15f and 18b–20.[81] Actually, however, the two clauses serve to underscore in pleonastic phrases the words "all things" (τὰ πάντα) which are repeatedly used; thus it is out of

---

71 Cf. Käsemann, *Essays*, 150–53. Wagenführer, *Die Bedeutung Christi*, 62f, recognized the problem, but he considered "of the church" (τῆς ἐκκλησίας) as a later gloss inserted into the text of Col.

72 Contrary to Käsemann (*Essays*, 151–53), the words "the church" are not due to an earlier Christian re-editing of a pre-Christian hymn, but rather stem from the author of Col—as the comparison with 1:24 shows.

73 Convincingly established by Käsemann, *Essays*, 151–53.

74 Norden, *Agnostos Theos*, 261; cf. Hegermann, *Schöpfungsmittler*, 91.

75 Cf. Robinson, "A Formal Analysis," 282f, who also reckons "the visible and the invisible" (τὰ ὁρατὰ καὶ ἀόρατα) to be an insert, and takes the view that both phrases were necessitated by the controversy with the Colossian heresy. So also Hegermann, *Schöpfungsmittler*, 91f; Schweizer, *Neotestamentica*, 293f; Hans-Martin Schenke, "Der Widerstreit gnostischer und kirchlicher Christologie im Spiegel des Kolosserbriefs," *ZThK* 61 (1964): 401. Eckart, "Exegetische Beobachtungen," 104–06, omits only the phrase in v 16, but not that in v 20, like Deichgräber, *Gotteshymnus und Christushymnus*, 146f.

76 The word κυριότης (dominion) appears again only in Eph 1:21. Cf. above p. 42.

77 The words ἀρχαὶ and ἐξουσίαι (principalities and powers) are resumed in 2:10 and 15 in the explanation and application of the hymn.

78 Cf. Käsemann, *Essays*, 151–53.

79 But cf. v 20, "and through him" (καὶ δι' αὐτοῦ).

80 Maurer, "Die Begründung der Herrschaft Christi," 82f; Schweizer, *Neotestamentica*, 295; cf. also, Gabathuler, *Jesus Christus, Haupt der Kirche*, 128f.

81 Thus Bornkamm, *Aufsätze* 2, 197, n. 20.

the question that they narrow the cosmic perspective. Furthermore, the formal structure of vss 17 and 18a is explained by their position in the context of the hymn, in which they serve as a summary that brings the first strophe to a conclusion.[82]

An exactly parallel structure for the strophes can only be achieved through deletions and transpositions. For reasons of form, Eduard Bammel and Eduard Schweizer view v 18c as an addition made by the author of the letter because the result clause ("in order that" ἵνα) does not fit the structure of the whole.[83] Yet the verb πρωτεύειν (to be first) is a hapaxlegomenon in the New Testament and thus may scarcely be claimed for Pauline vocabulary. James M. Robinson transposes v 18a to the close of the hymn and connects it with the result clause ("in order that") of v 18c, which has no formal counterpart in the first strophe.[84] Thus the hymn would end in this manner: "and he is the head of the body in order that he might be the first in all things" (καὶ αὐτός ἐστιν ἡ κεφαλὴ τοῦ σώματος, ἵνα γένηται ἐν πᾶσιν πρωτεύων).[85] These alterations, however, meddle too much with the given text and do not give evidence sufficient to make probable the hypothesis of two strophes of exactly parallel structures.[86] It is hardly probable that a primitive Christian hymn would have consisted of regularly constructed verses and strophes; rather, the individual strophes probably differed in structure and were composed in the free rhythm of hymnic prose.[87] For this reason the attempt to discover the original form of the hymn must proceed with caution.[88]

Aside from the two glosses in vss 18a and 20, which clearly reveal the theology of the author of the epistle, all the other phrases which are considered to be additions to an originally shorter hymn are actually statements which draw out further the lines already plotted in the hymn. Thus there is no valid reason for reckoning with further interpretive additions. The two strophes do not correspond to each other in all details, yet there are the marked beginnings "he (who) is" (ὅς ἐστιν) of vss 15 and 18, and the two following predications of Christ. There are the two ὅτι clauses ("for in him," vss 16 and 19), and also the two conclusions considering the cosmic dimension of Christ's rule which round out the strophes (vss 16b, 20b). Thus the structure of these two strophes can be presented in this manner:

He is the image of the invisible God,
The first-born before all creation,
For in him all things were created
In the heavens and on earth,
The visible and the invisible,
Whether thrones or dominions, principalities or powers;
All things are created through him and for him;
And he is before all things
And in him all things are established
And he is the head of the body, [the church].
He is the beginning,
The first–born from the dead,
In order that he might be the first in all things,

82 Hegermann, *Schöpfungsmittler*, 92f, who would like to achieve two equally long strophes, excludes "all things were created through him" (τὰ πάντα δι' αὐτοῦ καὶ εἰς αὐτὸν ἔκτισται v 16c) and also "and he is before all things" (καὶ αὐτός ἐστιν πρὸ πάντων v 17) as being repetitious of "the first born" (πρωτότοκος v 15).

83 Ernst Bammel, "Versuch zu Col 1:15–20," *ZNW* 52 (1961): 94; and Schweizer, *Neotestamentica*, 294.

84 Robinson, "A Formal Analysis," 280–82. Robinson's reconstruction is not free of arbitrary meddling with the text. Instead of 1:19, he has assigned 2:9 to the second strophe, and has deleted "making peace" (εἰρηνοποιήσας) in v 20 in favor of "he has reconciled" (ἀποκαζήλλαξε) which he inserts as the predicate.

85 *Ibid.*, 285. Robinson asserts that the Christ–hymn in Phil ends with a result clause (ἵνα), cf. Phil 2:10f.

86 Bammel has attempted to establish a chiastic structure for the hymn, but this principle of division does violence to the hymn when it is carried out. If it is not even evident to what degree vss 15a and 16c as well as vss 18a and 20a are supposed to correspond to each other in chiastic arrangement, then it is altogether impossible to demonstrate the chiasm in its particulars. The phrases "whether thrones or dominions, principalities or powers" (εἴτε θρόνοι εἴτε κυριότητες εἴτε ἀρχαὶ εἴτε ἐξουσίαι), according to Bammel, are said to correspond to each other as b' a' a' b'. Yet if "thrones" (θρόνοι) and "powers" (ἐξουσίαι) can be set in relation to each other, they can no longer be understood in an angelological sense. Finally, in order for this schema to hold, v 18c, "in order that he may be the first in all things" (ἵνα γένηται ἐν πᾶσιν αὐτὸς πρωτεύων) must be omitted as an addition while the gloss in v 20 must be retained).

87 Cf. Ernst Haenchen, "Probleme des johanneischen 'Prologs'," *ZThK* 60 (1963): 309; reprinted in *idem*, *Gott und Mensch, Gesammelte Aufsätze* (Tübingen: 1965), 118.

88 In order to obtain two parts of 151 syllables each, Schattenmann, *Prosahymnus*, 16–18, places v 13f before v 18b–20 so that a Christ–hymn (vss 13, 18b–20) follows a Logos–hymn pertaining to God (vss 12, 15–18a). For a critique of this arbitrary proce-

For in him all the fullness was pleased to dwell
And through him to reconcile all things toward him,
Making peace [through the blood of his cross]
through him
Whether on earth or in the heavens.

ὅς ἐστιν εἰκὼν τοῦ θεοῦ τοῦ ἀοράτου,
πρωτότοκος πάσης κτίσεως,
ὅτι ἐν αὐτῷ ἐκτίσθη τὰ πάντα
ἐν τοῖς οὐρανοῖς καὶ ἐπὶ τῆς γῆς,
τὰ ὁρατὰ καὶ τὰ ἀόρατα,
εἴτε θρόνοι εἴτε κυριότητες εἴτε
ἀρχαὶ εἴτε ἐξουσίαι·
τὰ πάντα δι᾽ αὐτοῦ καὶ εἰς αὐτὸν ἔκτισται·
καὶ αὐτός ἐστιν πρὸ πάντων
καὶ τὰ πάντα ἐν αὐτῷ συνέστηκεν,
καὶ αὐτός ἐστιν ἡ κεφαλὴ τοῦ σώματος [τῆς
ἐκκλησίας]·
ὅς ἐστιν ἀρχή,
πρωτότοκος ἐκ τῶν νεκρῶν,
ἵνα γένηται ἐν πᾶσιν αὐτὸς πρωτεύων,
ὅτι ἐν αὐτῷ εὐδόκησεν πᾶν τὸ πλήρωμα κατοικῆσαι
καὶ δι᾽ αὐτοῦ ἀποκαταλλάξαι τὰ πάντα εἰς
αὐτόν
εἰρηνοποιήσας [διὰ τοῦ αἵματος τοῦ σταυροῦ
αὐτοῦ] δι᾽ αὐτοῦ
εἴτε τὰ ἐπὶ τῆς γῆς εἴτε τὰ ἐν τοῖς οὐρανοῖς.

Where did this hymn come from, and what conditions, known from the history of religions, determined its characteristics? Ernst Käsemann thought that once the two additions "of the church" (τῆς ἐκκλησίας v 18a) and "through the blood of his cross" (διὰ τοῦ αἵματος τοῦ σταυροῦ αὐτοῦ v 20) were removed, a hymn remained that no longer displayed any specifically Christian characteristics. Thus he viewed it as a pre-Christian Gnostic text which deals with the supra-historical, metaphysical drama of the Gnostic redeemer. Creation and redemption are related constituents in the myth of the primeval man and redeemer who breaks into the sphere of death as the pathfinder and leader of those who belong to him.[89] Yet this thesis is hardly convincing. First of all, the Christian character of the phrase "first-born from the dead" certainly can not be doubted.[90] Furthermore, it must be pointed out that the words of v 19 speak of God's decree of election with the Old Testament term "to be pleased" (εὐδοκεῖν)—a phrase that wants to be understood as a statement about the unique event of divine revelation in Christ, quite comparable to the sentences in the prologue of the Gospel of John.[91] In contrast to the non historical myth of Gnosticism, this refers to God's definite and defining act. Finally, the repeated references to the divine creation correspond to Old Testament and Jewish tradition, even though the formulation is expressed in Hellenistic language, and the words "in him" (ἐν αὐτῷ), "through him" (δι᾽ αὐτοῦ), and "for him" (εἰς αὐτόν) recall Stoic phrases. These observations lead to the conclusion that the history of religions background of the conceptions in this hymn is to be sought in Hellenistic Judaism.[92]

This definition of the background is to be differentiated from Ernst Lohmeyer's exposition of the history of religions presuppositions.[93] Using the concept of reconciliation (*Versöhnung*) mentioned in v 20 as a starting point, Lohmeyer maintains that the whole hymn can be unraveled by means of this catchword, and should be understood against the background of the Jewish Day of Atonement (*Versöhnung*).[94] On the Day of Atonement, Israel receives the pronouncement of the forgiveness of sins; the Creator and Lord of the whole world turns to his people, so that creation and reconciliation are brought close to one another. According to Lohmeyer, the statements of this hymn similarly revolve around the two foci of creation and reconciliation. The Jewish institutions, however, are said to have been abolished in Christ, for he is not only the essence and fulfillment of the Law, but also of Jewish rites.[95] "Just as the existence of the world rests trustingly in the rite of atonement, so it also rests in this particular figure of Christ, who 'reconciles all

---

dure cf. the review by Gottfried Schille, *ThLZ* 92 (1967): 36.

89 Käsemann, *Essays*, 154–56. Ulrich Wilckens follows him in his *Weisheit und Torheit; Eine exegetische–religionsgeschichtliche Untersuchung zu 1 Kor 1 und 2*, BHTh 26 (Tübingen: 1959), 200–02.

90 Cf. Ernst Percy, "Zu den Problemen des Kolosser- und Epheserbriefes," *ZNW* 43 (1950–51): 184; Schweizer, *Neotestamentica*, 297, n. 11; *idem*, *Erniedrigung und Erhöhung bei Jesus und seinen Nachfolgern*, AThANT 28 (Zürich: [1]1955), 103, n. 465.

91 Cf. Lohse, "Christologie und Ethik," 162f.

92 Concerning the cosmological conceptions as developed in Hellenistic Judaism, cf. Hans-Friedrich Weiss, *Untersuchungen zur Kosmologie des hellenistischen und palästinischen Judentums*, TU 97 (Berlin: 1966).

93 Lohmeyer, pp. 43–47.

94 Stanislas Lyonnet, "L'hymne christologique de l'Epître aux Colossiens et la fête juive du Nouvel An," *RechSR* 48 (1960): 92–100, began with Lohmeyer's statements and attempted to demonstrate that v 20 presents allusions to the Jewish liturgy for the New Year's festival.

95 Lohmeyer, p. 45.

things'."[96] The picture of Christ, however, is drawn here in accordance with the "myth of the primeval man, or in Jewish terms, the eschatological Son of Man, which is closely connected with a new cosmological view of Adam."[97] Yet the term "to reconcile" (ἀποκαταλλάξαι v 20) does not allude, even remotely, to a connection with Jewish conceptions of sacrifices and of the great Day of Atonement; moreover, the synagogue did not connect the Day of Atonement with the concept of creation.[98] Finally, the myth of the primeval man or the expectation of the Son of Man presents a motif that is completely separate from the concepts which were related to the Day of Atonement. Thus this motif likewise does not help to explain the hymn.[99]

The exalted Christ is called "the image of God, the first-born of all creation" (εἰκὼν τοῦ θεοῦ, πρωτότοκος πάσης κτίσεως), and he is also called "the beginning" (ἀρχή). With these designations the hymn relates to the characterizations which Hellenistic synagogues gave to Wisdom. They praised Wisdom (σοφία) as created before all creatures, as the first-born of God, the primordial beginning—in view of creation as well as of the redemption she grants as the mediatrix of salvation. In the Jewish Diaspora, moreover, there was much borrowing from the concepts of popular Hellenistic philosophy, and there was certainly no total ban against influences from the syncretistic milieu. However, the Christian communities, which in many cases arose directly from the circles of Hellenistic Judaism, expressed their confession of Christ as the Kyrios with the aid of the terminology developed in the synagogue, which itself had assimilated its Old Testament inheritance with oriental concepts and Greek thought. The words "all," "all things" (πᾶν, πάντα) appear repeatedly from the beginning to the end of the hymn as the leading keynote which is joined with another recurrent expression, "in him" (ἐν αὐτῷ), in order to praise the rule of the exalted Christ which encompasses all things.

This hymn was clearly familiar to Christians in Asia Minor,[100] and the author of Col takes it as the point of departure for his argumentation. This is done in order to demonstrate to the community that Christ holds in his hands dominion over all the world, and that he is the head of his body, the church. Whoever belongs to this Lord and has received the forgiveness of sins has thus also been wrested from the enslaving dominion of the cosmic powers and raised with Christ to new life.

■ **15** Christ is the "image of the invisible God" (εἰκὼν τοῦ θεοῦ τοῦ ἀοράτου)—thus the hymn begins. This title of sovereignty, as well as the following phrase "first-born before all creation" (πρωτότοκος πάσης κτίσεως), recall the story of creation: "In the beginning God created the heavens and the earth" (Gen 1:1); he created man "in his own image, in the image of God he created him" (Gen 1:27). Yet even though the term "image" (εἰκών) suggests Gen 1:27, it is out of the question to interpret it as a direct reference to the biblical account of creation.[101] When the word εἰκών is defined as the "image" of the invisible God, the Hellenistic understanding of this term is to be assumed. God is invisible,[102] but he allows himself to be known wherever he wills to

96 Lohmeyer, p. 46.
97 *Ibid.*
98 Cf. Gabathuler, *Jesus Christus, Haupt der Kirche*, 36.
99 Cf. Käsemann's pertinent critique of Lohmeyer: ". . . while, from the angle of the comparative study of religion [his interpretation] tries without exception to reach an understanding of the passage on the basis of Jewish premises, he does not draw the conclusion that would he to the point, i.e., an approach in strictly historical categories. Instead he remains in a phenomenological orientation which gets no further than the uncovering of suprahistorical–metaphysical 'facts' and his thought therefore does not actually commence from Judaism but from Hellenism." (Trans. from *Aufsätze* 1, p. 39, n. 21; cf. *Essays*, p. 155, n. 1).
100 Certainly the hymn was known and sung by more than one community—not by the Colossians alone. It was doubtless the common property of communities in Asia Minor, so that one can neither speak of a "Colossian" hymn nor of a "heretical" one—not to mention that, at this period, the sharp distinction between orthodoxy and heresy did not yet exist, but became established only later. Cf. Walter Bauer, *Rechtgläubigkeit und Ketzerei im ältesten Christentum*, BHTh 10 (Tübingen: 1934); 2d edition, 1964, ed. Georg Strecker.
101 This explanation was advocated above all by C. F. Burney, "Christ as the 'ΑΡΧΗ of Creation (Prov. VIII 22, Col. I 15–18, Rev. III 14)" *JTS* 27 (1926): 160–77. Paul supposedly gave a meditative exposition of the first words of the Bible (In the beginning) in Col 1:15–18, exegeting Gen 1:1 via Pr 8:22 as follows:
B[erêshîth] = 'in *rêshîth*'—
ἐν αὐτῷ ἐκτίσθη τὰ πάντα

be known, i.e. he is revealed in his "image."[103]

Plato had already called the cosmos the visible image of God (*Tim.* 92c); likewise, in the Hellenistic age the world was considered God's "image." The cosmos was created by God "in his image" (κατ' εἰκόνα αὐτοῦ *Corp. Herm.* 8.2)[104] so that "The Aeon then is an image of God; the cosmos is an image of the Aeon" (ἐστὶ τοίνυν εἰκὼν τοῦ θεοῦ ὁ αἰών, τοῦ δὲ αἰῶνος ὁ κόσμος *Corp. Herm.* 11.15) and the whole cosmos can be called ". . . a great God, and an image of Him who is greater . . ." (ὁ μέγας θεὸς καὶ τοῦ μείζονος εἰκὼν *Corp. Herm.* 12.15).[105] In the beginning was the eternal God, then came the world, and then came man "who has been made in the image of the cosmos" (κατ' εἰκόνα τοῦ κόσμου γενόμενος *Corp. Herm.* 8.5). Man, then, is to render "praise and thanks in full measure to God, and revering God's image (the Cosmos), not unaware that he himself is a second image of God. For there are two images of God; the Cosmos is one, and man is another . . ." (*laudes gratesque maximas agens deo, eius imaginem venerans, non ignarus se etiam secundam esse imaginem dei, cuius sunt imagines duae mundus et homo.* Pseud. Apul. [*Asclepius*] 10). This understanding of the term "image," which uses this term to refer to the divine revelation,[106] was taken over by Hellenistic Judaism and transferred to "Wisdom."[107] She was already praised by Pr 8:22, which states that Yahweh created her at the beginning of his work as the first of his acts of old, before the creation of the world. In Wisd Sol 7:26 she is called an "image of his [God's] goodness" (εἰκὼν τῆς ἀγαθότητος αὐτοῦ), which makes known the goodness of God. Philo describes Wisdom as " 'beginning' and 'image' and 'vision of God' " (ἀρχὴν καὶ εἰκόνα καὶ ὅρασιν θεοῦ *Leg. All.* 1.43), in that he grants to her the same dignity as to the Logos, which itself is called " 'the Beginning' and the Name of God and His Word and the Man after His image and 'he that sees,'

B[*erêshîth*] = 'by *rêshîth*'—
πάντα δι' αὐτοῦ ἔκτισται
B[*erêshîth*] = 'into *rêshîth*'—
πάντα εἰς αὐτὸν ἔκτισται
Rêshîth = 'Beginning'—
αὐτός ἐστιν πρὸ πάντων
Rêshîth = 'Sum-total'—
τὰ πάντα ἐν αὐτῷ συνέστηκεν
Rêshîth = 'Head'—
αὐτός ἐστιν ἡ κεφαλὴ τοῦ σώματος
Rêshîth = 'First–fruits'—
ὅς ἐστιν ἀρχή, πρωτότοκος ἐκ τῶν νεκρῶν

Some exegetes have agreed with this thesis: W. D. Davies, *Paul and Rabbinic Judaism: Some Rabbinic Elements in Pauline Theology* (London: S.P.C.K., 1948, ²1955), 150–52; Moule, *ad loc.*; Edvin Larsson, *Christus als Vorbild: Eine Untersuchung zu den paulinischen Tauf– und Eikontexten*, ASNU 23 (Uppsala: 1962), 190–96. This thesis would presuppose that the passage was an exegesis of the Hebrew text, but the insight that 1:15–20 is a citation of a Hellenistic Christian hymn does away with this assumption. Moreover, it cannot be carried through in particulars without the aid of artificial explanations, and it is not sufficient for comprehension of the whole context—for this would be necessary if ἀρχή (beginning) from the second strophe is to be included. For a critique, cf. Jervell, *Imago Dei*, p. 200, n. 107; Gabathuler, *Jesus Christus, Haupt der Kirche*, 26–29; Feuillet, *Le Christ sagesse*, 189–91.

102 For this theme, cf. Rom 1:20; 1 Tim 1:17; Acts 14:17; 15:23–28; Heb 11:27; Jn 1:18. Furthermore, cf. Rudolf Bultmann, "Untersuchungen zum Johannesevangelium: B. Θεὸν οὐδεὶς ἑώρακεν πώποτε", *ZNW* 29 (1930): 169–82; reprinted in *idem*, *Exegetica: Aufsätze zur Erforschung des Neuen Testaments* (Tübingen: 1967), 174–92; also Erich Fascher, *Deus invisibilis: Eine Studie zur biblischen Gottesvorstellung*, Marburger Theologische Studien 1 (Marburg: 1931), 41–77.

103 For the concept εἰκών (image), cf. Gerhard Kittel, Gerhard von Rad, Hermann Kleinknecht, *TDNT* 2, 381–97; Friedrich–Wilhelm Eltester, *Eikon im Neuen Testament*, BZNW 23 (Berlin: 1958); Jervell, *Imago Dei*, esp. 214–26; and Hans Wildberger, "Das Abbild Gottes," *ThZ* 21 (1965): 245–59, 481–501.

104 Translations for *Corp. Herm.* based on text of *Corpus Hermeticum* by A. D. Nock and A.–J. Festugière (Paris: 1945) and with help of *Hermetica* by Walter Scott (Oxford: Clarendon Press: 1924). (Trans.)

105 Cf. Hermann Kleinknecht, *TDNT* 2, 388f.

106 In the Hellenistic ruler–cult it was said that the appearance of the ruler was the event of the deity's epiphany. Cf. the inscription on the Rosetta Stone, where it is stated that Ptolemaeus Epiphanes was the "living image of Zeus, the son of the sun" (εἰκόνος ζώσης τοῦ Διός, υἱὸς τοῦ Ἡλίου Ditt. *Or.* 90.3; [Trans.]. Hans Wildberger, "Das Abbild Gottes," 496–501, rightly reminds us that the Egyptian view of the king as the image of God entered Hellenistic syncretism and must have had some significance for the development of speculations about Wisdom in Egyptian Judaism.

107 Cf. Weiss, *Untersuchungen zur Kosmologie*, 189–210; 265–75.

that is Israel" (ἀρχὴ καὶ ὄνομα θεοῦ καὶ λόγος καὶ ὁ κατ' εἰκόνα ἄνθρωπος καὶ ὁ ὁρῶν, 'Ισραήλ, προσαγορεύεται *Conf. Ling.* 146).[108] Philo describes "Wisdom" (σοφία), as well as the Logos, as "the perfect way . . . which leads to God" (τελείαν ὁδὸν τὴν πρὸς θεὸν ἄγουσαν *Deus Imm.* 142f; *Migr. Abr.* 175). Wisdom was present at the beginning of creation but found no dwelling–place on the earth and returned to heaven (1 En 42:1f).[109] According to apocalyptic expectations she will reappear in the last times when her spirit will dwell in the Son of Man; he will act in the power of Wisdom and he will execute judgment (1 En 49:1–4). Thus Wisdom is not only the mediatrix of creation but also of salvation, and cosmology and soteriology are related to one another in the myth of Wisdom.

The Christian community applied the concept "image" to Christ so as to praise him as the one in whom God reveals himself.[110] As the "image" of the invisible God, he does not belong to what was created, but stands with the creator who, in Christ, is acting upon the world and with the world.[111] He is absolutely superior to the cosmos, i.e., the whole creation on earth and in heaven.[112] Therefore the first title of majesty is followed by the second, "first–born before all creation" (πρωτότοκος πάσης κτίσεως).

The characterization of the pre–existent Christ as the first–born before all creation likewise accords with Jewish speculation about Wisdom.[113] In the beginning of his work, Yahweh created Wisdom (Pr 8:22), and, created before all things (Sir 1:4), she rejoices: "From eternity, in the beginning, he created me" (πρὸ τοῦ αἰῶνος ἀπ' ἀρχῆς ἔκτισέν με Sir 24:9).[114] She is present with God (Wisd Sol 9:9) and has possession of his throne (Wisd Sol 9:4). She is the "first–born mother of all things" (*primogenita mater universorum*, Philo, *Quaest. in Gen.* 4:97). Thus it can be said of her that "she exists before heaven and earth" (πρὸ οὐρανοῦ καὶ γῆς αὐτὴν ὑπάρχειν Aristobulus, in Eus., *Prep. Ev.* 7.14.1). Philo also calls the Logos, as well as Wisdom, the "first–born son" (πρωτόγονος υἱός *Conf. Ling.* 146; *Agric.* 51; *Som.* 1.215).

The description of the pre–existent Christ as the "first–born before all creation" (πρωτότοκος πάσης κτίσεως) is not intended to mean that he was created first and thereby began the succession of created beings. Rather, it refers instead to his uniqueness,[115] by which he is

108 Concerning the designation of Logos as "image," cf. also Philo, *Conf. Ling.* 97, 147; *Fug.* 101; *Som.* 1.115, 239; 2.45. Philo also employed the concept "image" in his anthropology, in that he relates Gen 1:27 to the ideal primeval man who was created according to God's image, and yet relates Gen 2:7 to the earthly man (*Leg. All.* 1.31; *Op. Mund.* 134).

109 According to other traditions, Wisdom found her dwelling–place in Israel, the people of the Law (Sir 24:7, 11).

110 The problem disputed in the ancient church, whether the image of the invisible God was visible or not (cf. Lightfoot, *ad loc.*), thus comes to nothing. Cf. also Eltester, *Eikon im NT*, 148f; Jervell, *Imago Dei*, 219.

111 In a later writing, the *Epistula Apostolorum*, Christ says to his disciples, "I am wholly in the Father and the Father in me after his image and after his form and after his power and after his perfection and after his light, and I am his perfect word." Trans. from H. Duensing in Edgar Hennecke, *New Testament Apocrypha*, ed. Wilhelm Schneemelcher tr. ed. R. McL. Wilson, vol. 1 (Philadelphia: Westminster, 1963), 201. Cf. Jervell, *Imago Dei*, 255, n. 201.

112 Cf. Maurer, "Die Begründung der Herrschaft Christi," 86.

113 Concerning "first–born" (πρωτότοκος), cf. Edward Augustine Cerny, *Firstborn of Every Creature* (Col. 1:15), Unpub. Diss. (Baltimore: 1938); B. R. Brinkman, *The Prototokos Title and the Beginnings of its Exegesis*, Unpub. Diss. Gregoriana (Rome: 1954); Wilhelm Michaelis, "Der Beitrag der Septuaginta zur Bedeutungsgeschichte von πρωτότοκος," in *Sprachgeschichte und Wortbedeutung, Festschrift für Albert Debrunner* (Bern: 1954), 313–20; *idem*, "Die biblische Vorstellung von Christus als dem Erstgeborenen," *ZSTh* 23 (1954): 137–57; *idem*, *TDNT* 6, 871–81; A. W. Argyle, "Πρωτότοκος πάσης κτίσεως (Colossians I:15)," *ExpT* 66 (1954–55): 61f; *idem*, "Colossians I:15," *ibid.*, 318f; T. W. Buckley, *The Phrase "Firstborn of Every Creature" (Colossians I:15) in the Light of its Hellenistic and Jewish Background*, Unpub. Diss. Angelicum (Rome: 1962); Alfred Hockel, *Christus der Erstgeborene: Zur Geschichte der Exegese von Kol.* 1,15 (Düsseldorf: 1965).

114 Cf. T. Francis Glasson, "Colossians 1:18, 15 and Sirach 24," *JBL* 86 (1967): 214–16.

115 The first–born is installed in kingly power by God, LXX Ps 88:28 "And I shall make him the first–born, higher than the kings of earth" (κἀγὼ πρωτότοκον θήσομαι αὐτόν, ὑψηλὸν παρὰ τοῖς βασιλεῦσιν τῆς γῆς). In Judaism, not only the messianic king, but also Israel, the Patriarchs and the Torah are given this title of distinction. Examples are given

distinguished from all creation (cf. Heb 1:6).[116] The point is not a temporal advantage but rather the superiority which is due to him as the agent of creation who is before all creation.[117] As the first–born he stands over against creation as Lord.[118]

■ **16** This statement about the unique position of the pre–existent Christ now receives more explicit proof: "in him all things were created." The use of the passive form, "were created" (*ἐκτίσθη*) signifies that God is the creator. The clause "in him all things were created" (*ἐν αὐτῷ ἐκτίσθη τὰ πάντα*) is taken up again by the words "all things are created through him and for him" (*τὰ πάντα δι' αὐτοῦ καὶ εἰς αὐτὸν ἔκτισται*). There the aorist form is replaced by the perfect form of the verb in order to express the creation's continuing existence. All of this in turn connects with the sentence, "And he is before all things and in him all things are established" *καὶ αὐτός ἐστιν πρὸ πάντων καὶ τὰ πάντα ἐν αὐτῷ συνέστηκεν* v 17). In these phrases reminiscences of Stoic formulations are clearly evident:[119] Marcus Aurelius states, "O Nature . . . all things come from you, subsist in you, go back to you" (*ὦ φύσις, ἐκ σοῦ πάντα, ἐν σοὶ πάντα, εἰς σὲ πάντα* M. Ant. 4.23.2 [adapted from Loeb trans.]. Nature, which is pervaded by divine powers, is origin, continuation and goal.[120] The final unity of all that exists is expressed by this succession of prepositions, which appears almost a play on words.[121] God and nature are viewed together and are one. This view which was widely spread by Hellenistic popular philosophy[122] was subject to a particular diffraction in

---

by Wilhelm Michaelis, *TDNT* 6, 873–76, and Billerbeck 3, 256–58, 626. Since the Col passage uses this designation in the context of the idea of creation's agent, it is surely related to the Jewish speculation about Wisdom.

116 Cf. Justin, *Dial*. 100.2 "the first–born of God and before all creatures" (*πρωτότοκον μὲν τοῦ θεοῦ καὶ πρὸ πάντων τῶν κτισμάτων* [Trans.]). Cf. also *Dial*. 84.2; 85.2; 138.2. Theodoret, *ad loc*. "not as having the creation for a sister, but as having been born before all creatures" (*οὐχ ὡς ἀδελφὴν ἔχων τὴν κτίσιν, ἀλλ' ὡς πρὸ πάσης κτίσεως γεννηθείς* [Trans.]. Theodore of Mopsuestia, *ad loc*. "not concerning time alone, but concerning first honor also . . . honored above every creature" (*οὐκ ἐπὶ χρόνου ἀλλ' ἐπὶ προτιμήσεως...παρὰ πᾶσαν κτίσιν τιμώμενος* [Trans.]).

117 Cf. Wilhelm Michaelis, *TDNT* 6, 877–80; Maurer, "Die Begründung der Herrschaft Christi," 85; Eltester, *Eikon im NT*, 138f; Jervell, *Imago Dei*, 225.

118 Concerning the exegesis of the early Church on this passage, cf. Lightfoot, *ad loc*. When Isidore of Pelusium (*Epist*. 3.31) accentuates *πρωτοτόκος* he gives the word an active meaning, i.e., "to (have been) born first, that is, to have made the creation" (*πρῶτον τετοκέναι, τουτέστι, πεποιηκέναι τὴν κτίσιν* [Trans.]. Cf. Lightfoot, Abbott, *ad loc*.

119 Cf. Norden, *Agnostos Theos*, 249f, 347f.

120 Cf. (Pseudo) Aristotle, *Mund*. 6(397b), "It is indeed an ancient idea, traditonal among all mankind, that all things are from God and are established . . . through God" (*ἀρχαῖος μὲν οὖν τις λόγος καὶ πάτριός ἐστι πᾶσιν ἀνθρώποις ὡς ἐκ θεοῦ πάντα καὶ διὰ θεοῦ συνέστηκεν*). Pseudo Apuleius (Asclepius) 34; "For God is all things; from him are all things and all things are dependent on his will . . . from God and in God and through God are all things . . ." (*omnia enim deus et ab eo omnia et eius omnia voluntatis . . . omnia enim ab eo et in ipso et per ipsum.* [Trans.]). *Corp. Herm*. 5.10 states "all things are in Thee . . . all things are from Thee" (*πάντα δὲ ἐν σοί, πάντα ἀπὸ σοῦ* [Trans.]). The Paris magical papyrus 4.2838 has "for all things are from Thee, and in Thee, Eternal One, all things come to their end" (*ἐκ σέο γὰρ πάντ' ἐστὶ καὶ εἰς <σ'>, αἰών[ι]ε, πάντα τελευτᾷ* Preis, *Zaub*. 1,162). Further formulas from magical texts are in M. Berthelot, *Collection des Anciens Alchimistes Grecs* (Paris: 1888), 84, 143, 169, 442.

121 Cf. Seneca, *Epist*. 65.8, "Accordingly, there are five causes, as Plato says: the one 'from which' (material), the one 'by which' (agent), the one 'in which' (formal), the one 'according to which' (exemplary), and the one 'for which' (final). Last comes the result of all these. Just as in the case of the statue . . . the one 'from which' is the bronze, the one 'by which' is the artist, the one 'in which' is the form which is adapted to it, the one 'according to which' is the pattern imitated by the maker, the one 'for which' is the purpose in the maker's mind, and, finally, the result of all this is the statue itself." (*Quinque ergo causae sunt, ut Plato dicit: id ex quo, id a quo, id in quo, id ad quod, id propter quod, novissime id quod ex his est. Tamquam in statua . . . id ex quo aes est, id a quo artifex est, id in quo forma est, quae aptatur illi, id ad quod exemplar est, quod imitatur is, qui facit, id propter quod facientis propositum est, id quod ex istis est, ipsa statua est.* [Loeb trans. adapted].)

122 Cf. Philo, *Cher*. 125, "for to bring anything into being needs all these conjointly, the 'by which,' the 'from which,' the 'through which,' and the 'for which,' and the first of these is the cause, the second the material, the third the tool or instrument, and the fourth the end or object." (*πρὸς γὰρ τὴν τινος*

Hellenistic Judaism. It was impossible to identify the God of Israel with nature, and the faith of Israel could not be dissolved into a pantheistic world view.[123] The breadth of creation, therefore, which was called into existence by God's act can well be described in Stoic terms. God, however, remains Lord of creation; he does indeed act creatively in nature, but also stands against it as its ruler.[124]

From the Hellenistic synagogue, this confession of God the creator, formulated in Stoic phrases, was appropriated by the Christian community and joined together with its confession of Christ. Thus 1 Cor 8:6 reads "Yet for us there is one God, the Father, from whom are all things and for whom we exist, and one Lord Jesus Christ through whom are all things and through whom we exist" (*ἡμῖν εἷς ὁ θεὸς ὁ πατήρ, ἐξ οὗ τὰ πάντα καὶ ἡμεῖς εἰς αὐτόν, καὶ εἷς κύριος Ἰησοῦς Χριστός, δι' οὗ τὰ πάντα καὶ ἡμεῖς δι' αὐτοῦ*). The community praises God "For from him and through him and to him are all things" (*ὅτι ἐξ αὐτοῦ καὶ δι' αὐτοῦ καὶ εἰς αὐτὸν τὰ πάντα* Rom 11:36). It praises Christ as the agent of creation in whom, through whom and for whom all things were created.[125]

Through Wisdom Yahweh founded the earth, as it is already stated in Pr 3:9. Wisdom narrates: "when he established the heavens, I was there, when he drew a circle on the face of the deep, when he made firm the skies above, when he established the fountains of the deep, when he assigned to the sea its limit, so that the waters might not transgress his command, when he marked out the foundations of the earth, then I was beside him, like a master workman; and I was daily his delight, rejoicing before him always, rejoicing in his inhabited world and delighting in the sons of men" (Pr 8:27–31). It is "Wisdom," according to Philo, "through whom the universe came into existence" (*δι' ἧς τὰ ὅλα ἦλθεν εἰς γένεσιν* *Fug*. 109), for God created heaven and earth through Wisdom.[126] The Christian confession appropriates this view of Wisdom's role as the agent of creation and transfers it to Christ in order to express the universal validity of the Christ–event (cf. 1 Cor 8:6). All creation owes its existence to the pre–existent Christ.[127] "All things were made through him and without him was not anything made that was made" (*πάντα δι' αὐτοῦ ἐγένετο, καὶ χωρὶς αὐτοῦ ἐγένετο οὐδὲ ἓν ὃ γέγονεν* Jn 1:3). "He is the radiance, the glory of God and the very stamp of his essence, upholding the universe by his word of power" (*ὃς ὢν ἀπαύγασμα τῆς δόξης καὶ χαρακτὴρ τῆς ὑποστάσεως αὐτοῦ, φέρων τε τὰ πάντα τῷ ῥήματι τῆς δυνάμεως αὐτοῦ* Heb 1:3).[128]

All things have been created in him, that is, through him.[129] The fullness of what "all things" (*τὰ πάντα*) means is depicted more exactly by the addition: every-

---

γένεσιν πολλὰ δεῖ συνελθεῖν, τὸ ὑφ' οὗ, τὸ ἐξ οὗ, τὸ δι' οὗ, τὸ δι' ὅ· καὶ ἔστι τὸ μὲν ὑφ' οὗ τὸ αἴτιον, ἐξ οὗ δὲ ἡ ὕλη, δι' οὗ δὲ τὸ ἐργαλεῖον, δι' ὃ δὲ ἡ αἰτία). Cf. Weiss, *Untersuchungen zur Kosmologie*, 269–72, for further examples.

123 Cf. Conzelmann, *ad loc.*

124 Philo, *Cher.* 125, "Because God is the cause, not the instrument, and that which comes into being is brought into being *through* an instrument, but *by* a cause." (ὅτι ὁ θεὸς αἴτιον, οὐκ ὄργανον, τὸ δὲ γινόμενον δι' ὀργάνου μὲν ὑπὸ δὲ αἰτίου πάντως γίνεται).

125 It should be noted that the prepositions ἐν (in), διά (through), and εἰς (for) are used, but not ἐκ (from). "From whom are all things" (ἐξ οὗ τὰ πάντα) is said of God in 1 Cor 8:6. He is and remains the creator, but the pre–existent Christ is the mediator of creation.

126 Cf. the Targum Neofiti 1 for Gen 1:1. Cf. also Siegfried Schulz, *Komposition und Herkunft der Johanneischen Reden*, *BWANT* 5,1 (Stuttgart: 1960), p. 31, n. 137 (cf. also his pp. 58–62). When the Qumran texts say in various ways that God has created all things in his wisdom (1 QH I.7.14f, 19, etc.), this does not presuppose any hypostasization of Wisdom, but rather it is the description of the manner and way of divine action.

127 Cf. Eduard Schweizer, *Erniedrigung*, 103.

128 Cf. also Heb 2:10 "for whom and by whom all things exist" (δι' ὃν τὰ πάντα καὶ δι' οὗ τὰ πάντα), and Barn 12:7 "the glory of Jesus, for all things are in him and for him" (τὴν δόξαν τοῦ Ἰησοῦ, ὅτι ἐν αὐτῷ πάντα καὶ εἰς αὐτόν).

129 The phrase "in him" (ἐν αὐτῷ) is therefore to be understood in an instrumental sense, as is shown by the religious background, i.e., Jewish speculations about Wisdom. To understand the phrase as referring to location is only possible on the basis of quite different history of religions backgrounds: in the Platonic understanding, the Ideas have their "place" in the Logos or in Sophia; cf. Philo, *Op. Mund.* 20 "the universe that consisted of ideas would have no other location than the divine reason" (οὐδ' ὁ ἐκ τῶν ἰδεῶν κόσμος ἄλλον ἂν ἔχοι τόπον ἢ τὸν θεὸν λόγον). But this understanding is not applicable [to Col] because "all things" (τὰ πάντα) can-

thing that is in the heavens and on earth.[130] There are no exceptions here,[131] all things visible and invisible[132] are included. Even the cosmic powers and principalities were created in him. "Thrones" (*θρόνοι*) and "dominions" (*κυριότητες*) (cf. 1 Cor 8:5) were occasionally specified in Judaism among the heavenly hosts of angels;[133] "principalities" (*ἀρχαί*) and "powers" (*ἐξουσίαι*) are often named as being supermundane beings and powers.[134] In such enumerations it does not matter whether the list is complete or whether the angelic powers are arranged in the order of their particular classes.[135] The emphasis is rather that all things that exist in the cosmos were created in Christ. Thus he is Lord of the powers and principalities (cf. 2:10, 15; Eph 1:21; 1 Pt 3:22).

All things were created "through him and for him" (*δι' αὐτοῦ καὶ εἰς αὐτόν*).[136] This clause continues the statements made about Christ's mediation of creation. "Through him" (*δι' αὐτοῦ*) takes up the preceding "in him" (*ἐν αὐτῷ*), and "for him" (*εἰς αὐτόν*) completes the line. Whereas in Stoic praise of nature the self–contained harmony of all things is described with the words *εἰς σὲ πάντα*,[137] the phrase *εἰς αὐτόν* ("toward/

not be interpreted as the world of ideas since "the visible things" (*ὁρατά*) in v 16 are part of "all things" (Eltester, *Eikon im NT*, 140, n. 74). Another approach postulates the Gnostic myth of the primal man as the history of religions background of the hymn. Then the "in him" would have to be interpreted to mean that all things have their place "in him (locally);" thus Käsemann, *Essays*, 156–58; Dibelius–Greeven, *ad loc.*; Eltester, *Eikon im NT*, 140, n. 74; Jervell, *Imago Dei*, 226; Fred B. Craddock, " 'All things in Him,' a Critical Note on Col. I:15–20" *NTS* 12 (1965–66): 78–80. It is in fact not impossible, albeit not at all certain (cf. Hegermann, *Schöpfungsmittler*, 70 and *passim*), that concepts from the myth of the primal man have influenced Jewish Wisdom speculations. In these speculations, however, Wisdom is always viewed as the master builder through whom creation is [being] done. Since the statements about the mediation of creation by Christ are certainly shaped by these concepts (cf. Hegermann, *Schöpfungsmittler*, 96; André Feuillet, "La Création de l'Univers 'dans le Christ' d'après l'Epître aux Colossiens (I.16a)" *NTS* 12 (1965–66): 1–9; *idem*, in *Le Christ sagesse*, 202–10), the phrase "in him" is to be taken in an instrumental sense, not one of location. Not only does the following phrase "through him" (*δι' αὐτοῦ*) argue for this interpretation, but also the parallel statements from 1 Cor 8:6 and Jn 1:3 assert this.

130 Cf. Sir 24:5f. Wisdom says "Alone I have made the circuit of the vault of heaven and have walked in the depths of the abyss. Over the waves of the sea, over the whole earth, and over every people and nation I have established my rule" [Trans.] Wisd Sol 18:6 says of the Logos, "The Logos . . . touched the heavens and strode along the earth" [Trans.]

131 The mss A (C) and ℜ pl insert *τά* before *ἐν τοῖς οὐρανοῖς* (to read "the things in the heavens"), and A C ℜ D and G pl supply this article before *ἐπὶ τῆς γῆς* (to read "the things on the earth").

132 Cf. Plato, *Phaed.* 79a " 'Now,' said he, 'shall we assume two kinds of existences, one visible, the other invisible?' " (*θῶμεν οὖν βούλει, ἔφη, δύο εἴδη τῶν ὄντων, τὸ μὲν ὁρατόν, τὸ δὲ ἀιδές*).

133 Cf. 2 En 20:1. Enoch reports "and I saw there (i.e. in the seventh heaven) a very great light and fiery troops of great archangels, incorporeal forces, and dominions and orders and governments, cherubim and seraphim, thrones and many–eyed ones, nine (ten) regiments . . ." Cf. Gottlieb Nathanael Bonwetsch, *Die Bücher der Geheimnisse Henochs: Das sogenannte slawische Henochbuch*, TU 44.2 (Berlin: 1922), 18f; A. Vaillant, *Le Livre des Secrets d'Henoch* (Paris: 1952), 22f. According to Test Levi 3:8, in heaven "there are thrones snd dominions in which they always offer praise to God" (*εἰσὶ θρόνοι, ἐξουσίαι, ἐν ᾧ ὕμνοι τῷ θεῷ προσφέρονται*).

134 Cf. 1 Cor 15:24; Rom 8:38; Eph 1:21; 6:12. Cf. 2 En 61:10, ". . . all the host of the heavens, and all the holy ones above, and the host of God, the Cherubin, Seraphin and Ophannin, and all the angels of *power*, and all the angels of *principalities*, and the Elect One, and the other *powers* on the earth (and) over the water . . ." Further examples in Billerbeck 3, 583; cf. also G. H. C. Macgregor, "Principalities and Powers: the Cosmic Background of Paul's Thought," *NTS* 1 (1954–55): 17–28.

135 For "whether–or" (*εἴτε–εἴτε*) as the formal means of composing such enumerations cf. 1 Cor 3:21–23: "For all things are yours, whether Paul or Apollos, or Cephas or the world or life or death or the present or the future, all are yours; and you are Christ's; and Christ is God's" (*πάντα γὰρ ὑμῶν ἐστιν, εἴτε Παῦλος εἴτε Ἀπολλῶς εἴτε Κηφᾶς, εἴτε κόσμος εἴτε ζωὴ εἴτε θάνατος, εἴτε ἐνεστῶτα εἴτε μέλλοντα, πάντα ὑμῶν, ὑμεῖς δὲ Χριστοῦ, Χριστὸς δὲ θεοῦ*). In 1 Cor 12:13 the dissolution of all earthly opposites into the membership of Christ's body is shown by "whether Jews or Greeks, whether slaves or free" (*εἴτε Ἰουδαῖοι εἴτε Ἕλληνες, εἴτε δοῦλοι εἴτε ἐλεύθεροι*).

136 The ms p^{46} begins this clause with "for" (*ὅτι*); cf. v 16a.

137 "All things . . . go back to you" M. Ant. 4.23.2. Also

to him") which refers to Christ[138] receives a different meaning; all things are created "toward" him.[139] In this way not only the statements about the origin of creation are summarized, but also the goal of creation is indicated: creation finds its goal in no one save Christ alone.[140]

■ **17** He is "before all things" (**πρὸ πάντων**), which means that as the pre–existent one[141] he is Lord over the universe.[142] This refers back to the designation "first–born before all creation" (**πρωτότοκος πάσης κτίσεως**) and it emphasizes once again the unique position of Christ as Lord over the cosmos.[143] Not only is the universe created in him and by him, but it is also established permanently in him alone. In Platonic and Stoic philosophy the verb **συνεστηκέναι** (to be established, to continue, exist, endure) was used to denote the wonderful unity of the entire world.[144] This conviction is most ancient and was shared by all men "that all things are from God and are constituted . . . by God" (**ὡς ἐκ θεοῦ πάντα καὶ διὰ θεὸν συνέστηκεν** Pseudo Aristotle, *Mund.* 6 [p. 397b]).[145] Hellenistic Judaism used the same words to express the belief that God's creation is firmly established. Philo speaks of the four "first principles" (**ἀρχαί**) and "potentialities" (**δυνάμεις**), "from which the world has been established (**ἐξ ὧν συνέστηκεν ὁ κόσμος** *Rer. Div. Her.* 281); or of the opposites in the structure of the world, "of which the whole world is composed" (**ἐξ ὧν ἅπας ὁ κόσμος συνέστηκε** *Rer. Div. Her.* 311).[146] The divine Logos, indeed God himself, is the unifying bond which includes all things and holds them together:[147] "And by his word all things hold together" (**ἐν λόγῳ αὐτοῦ σύγκειται τὰ πάντα** Sir 43:26).[148] Just as the concept of the mediation of creation was applied to Christ by the Christian community, so too this latter concept was likewise applied. Christ upholds the universe "by his word of power" (**τῷ ῥήματι τῆς δυνάμεως αὐτοῦ**). Everything that is, is established in him alone, for he is the Lord, the head of the body.

■ **18** If the words "the church" (**τῆς ἐκκλησίας**) are

---

in M. Ant. 4.23.2 "All things come from you, subsist in you, go back to you" (ἐκ σοῦ πάντα, ἐν σοὶ πάντα, εἰς σὲ πάντα). The Paris magical papyrus has "for all things are from you, and in you, Eternal One, all things come to their end" (ἐκ σέο γὰρ πάντ' ἐστὶ καὶ εἰς <σ'>, αἰών[ι]ε, πάντα τελευτᾷ). Cf. p. 49, n. 120. For further parallels see Eltester, *Eikon im NT*, 145f.

138 In Jewish speculations about Wisdom there are no parallels for εἰς αὐτόν ("toward/to him"). Cf. Eltester, *Eikon im NT*, 142f; Schweizer, *Neotestamentica*, 296.

139 Cf. R. Jochanan (d. 279 A.D.), who said the world was only created "for the sake of the Messiah" (*b San.* 98b). Cf. Billerbeck 3, 626.

140 Cf. Käsemann, *Essays*, 157f, the words "created toward him" (εἰς αὐτὸν ἔκτισται v 16) "anticipate this eschatological orientation which then receives concrete expression in the soteriological statements of the second stanza." Cf. also Eltester, *Eikon im NT*, 146; Schweizer, *Neotestamentica*, 296.

141 Cf. Jn 8:58 "before Abraham was, I am" (πρὶν Ἀβραὰμ γενέσθαι ἐγὼ εἰμί).

142 The word πάντων is clearly to be taken as neuter, not masculine. Cf. Tertullian, *Marc.* 5.19 "For how is He before all beings, if He is not before *all things*? Again, how is He before all things, if He is not 'the first–born of creation'?" (*Quomodo enim ante omnes, si non ante omnia? Quomodo ante omnia, si non primogenitus conditionis?*).

143 Cf. Basil's *Adv. Eunom.* 4 (MPG 29, 701), "When the apostle says 'All things were created through him and for him,' he must (also) say 'he became before all things.' By saying 'he is before all things' he pointed out that the eternal one 'is,' but the creation 'became'." (ὁ ἀπόστολος εἰπών, πάντα δι' αὐτοῦ καὶ εἰς αὐτὸν ἔκτισται, ὤφειλεν εἰπεῖν καὶ αὐτὸς ἐγένετο πρὸ πάντων. Εἰπὼν δέ, καὶ αὐτός ἐστι πρὸ πάντων, ἔδειξε τὸν μὲν ἀεὶ ὄντα, τὴν δὲ κτίσιν γενομένην [Trans.]).

144 Cf. Plato, *Republic* 530a, ". . . that the artisan of heaven fashioned it and all that it contains" (οὕτω συνεστάναι τῷ τοῦ οὐρανοῦ δημιουργῷ αὐτόν τε καὶ τὰ ἐν αὐτῷ). [Note the many various English equivalents for this verb, as given in Liddell–Scott.]

145 This conviction is transferred to Isis in *P. Oxy.* 11, 1380, 183–85: "you became the discoverer of all things wet and dry and cold of which all things are composed" (πάντων ὑγρῶν καὶ ξηρῶν καὶ ψ[υχ]ρῶν· ἐξ ὧν ἅπαντα συνέστηκεν). For further examples see Josef Gewiess, *Christus und das Heil nach dem Kolosserbrief*, Unpub. Diss. (Breslau: 1932), 46.

146 Cf. Hegermann, *Schöpfungsmittler*, 95.

147 Cf. Philo, *Rer. Div. Her.* 23, "he is the bond of all things, the one who holds them together indissolubly and binds them fast, when in themselves they are dissoluble" (τῶν ὅλων δεσμὸς ἐστι συνέχων αὐτὰ ἄλυτα καὶ σφίγγων διαλυτὰ ὄντα ἐξ ἑαυτῶν). Cf. also *Fug.* 108ff.

148 What is true for the macrocosm pertains also to the microcosm, for only through God's care is man's body preserved. He would disintegrate if God did not hold his hand over him and protect him. Cf. Philo, *Rer. Div. Her.* 58, ". . . for this mass of clay

taken as a gloss—as was argued above on page 42f—then the concept "body" (σῶμα) in the context of the first strophe is to be understood in the cosmological sense.[149] The view that the whole cosmos can be compared to a body and that macrocosm and microcosm correspond to each other in their relationships is attested very early in ancient times; it appeared in manifold variations. Plato conceives of the cosmos as a living being with a soul and pervaded with reason (*Tim.* 31b; 32a,c; 39e; passim). The cosmos as a body is directed by the divine soul which it follows as it is led (*Tim.* 47c–48b).[150] In the syncretism of late antiquity Iranian concepts were connected with these Greek concepts. As the Pahlavi literature illustrates, the supreme God became pregnant and brought forth the entire creation: "And when it had been created, he bore it in his body. . . . he increased and everything became better and then one by one he created them out of his own body. First he created the sky out of his head . . . He created the earth from his feet, . . . He created water out of his tears. . . . He created plants out of his hair . . . He created fire out of his mind."[151] The cosmos is viewed as the body of the deity but the elements of the universe are viewed as the various parts of his body. In an Orphic fragment, Zeus is named as the deity who is the "head" (κεφαλή) of the cosmos and is the one who with his power pervades the universe, which rests in the body of the great deity (Fragment 168).[152] Other texts similarly describe the heaven as the head of the Pantocrator, the air as his body and the earth as his feet,[153] or again the heavenly world as the head of the All-Deity, the sea as his belly and the earth as his feet.[154] The Stoic view of nature takes this idea of the body of the All-Divinity and conceives of the whole cosmos as being filled by the deity. Men, however, are members of this world-encompassing body which binds all things

and blood, which in itself is dissoluble and dead, holds together and is quickened as into flame by the providence of God who is its protecting arm and shield . . ." (ὁ ἔναιμος ὄγκος ἐξ ἑαυτοῦ διαλυτὸς ὢν καὶ νεκρὸς συνέστηκε καὶ ζωπυρεῖται προνοίᾳ θεοῦ τοῦ τὴν χεῖρα ὑπερέχοντος καὶ ὑπερασπίζοντος).

149 Concerning the concept "body" (σῶμα), cf. Eduard Schweizer, *TWNT* 7, 1024–91. On p. 1024f there is a complete survey of the literature to which discussion of the concept of "body" should be referred.

150 Cf. Schweizer, *TWNT* 7, 1029; further examples are found there.

151 The Pahlavi *Riāvyat of the Dātāstan ī dēnīk*, ch. 46.3–5, 11, 13, 28. The lines are cited in Geo Widengren, *Die Religionen Irans*, Die Religionen der Menschheit 14 (Stuttgart: 1965), 9. The English translation is from H. W. Bailey, *Zoroastrian Problems in the Ninth-Century Books*, Ratanbai Katrak Lectures (Oxford: The Clarendon Press, 1943), 121. In Widengren, p. 10, the Indian All-Deity is described: "The fire is my mouth, the earth my feet, the sun and moon my eyes, the heaven my head, the firmament and the regions of the heaven my ears. The waters have originated from my perspiration. Space with its four world regions is my body, the wind is in my mind" (Mahabharata 3, 1296ff [Trans.]). For the connection of the Hellenistic concepts with those from Iran, cf. also Hegermann, *Schöpfungsmittler*, 60f.

152 *Orphicorum Fragmenta* (ed. O. Kern, 1922), 201f. "Zeus was the first, Zeus last, the lightning's Lord, Zeus head, Zeus center, all things are from Zeus . . . For in Zeus' mighty body these all lie . . . Such his immortal head, and such his thought. His radiant body, boundless, undisturbed, fearless in strength of mighty limbs was formed thus . . ." (Ζεὺς πρῶτος ἐγένετο, Ζεὺς ὕστατος ἀργικέραυνος, Ζεὺς κεφαλή, Ζεὺς μέσσα, Διὸς δ' ἐκ πάντα τέτυκται...πάντα γὰρ ἐν Ζηνὸς μεγάλωι τάδε σώματι κεῖται...ὧδε μὲν ἀθανάτην κεφαλὴν ἔχει ἠδὲ νόημα· σῶμα δέ οἱ περιφεγγές, ἀπείριτον, ἀστυφέλικτον, ἄτρομον, ὀβριμόγυιον, ὑπερμενὲς ὧδε τέτυκται Translation from Eusebius, *Evangelicae Praeparationis*, ed. and tr. by E. H. Gifford [Oxford: University Press, 1903], vol. 3, p. 109). Cf. also Heinrich Schlier, *TDNT* 3, 676; Dibelius–Greeven, p. 109, supplement 1. This Orphic fragment was known to the Hellenistic synagogue and transmitted by it. Cf. the presentation of the connections by Nikolaus Walter, *Der Thoraausleger Aristobulus: Untersuchungen zu seinen Fragmenten und zu pseudepigraphischen Resten der jüdisch-hellenistischen Literatur*, TU 86 (Berlin: 1964), 103–15, 202–61.

153 Magic Papyrus 12, 243 (equals Preis, *Zaub.* vol. 2, p. 74, cf. P. Leid. 2, p. 141); cf. also Magic Papyrus 13, 770ff (equals Preis. *Zaub.* vol. 2, p. 122); Magic Papyrus 21, 6ff (equals vol. 2, p. 146).

154 Macrob. *Sat.* 1.21.17: Serapis oracle concerning King Nicocreon of Cyprus, "Learn that the nature of my Godhead is such as I may tell thee: the firmament of heaven is my head; my belly the sea; the earth my feet"; (εἰμὶ θεὸς τοιόσδε μαθεῖν, οἷόν κ' ἐγὼ εἴπω· οὐράνιος κόσμος κεφαλή, γαστὴρ δὲ θάλασσα, γαῖα δέ μοι πόδες εἰσί Translation

together.[155] These conceptions also found entrance into Hellenistic Judaism[156] so that Philo of Alexandria speaks of the world of the heavens as a uniform body over which the Logos is set as the head (*Som.* 1.128).[157] The Logos encompasses all things, he fills and defines them to their extremities (*Quaest. in Ex.* 2.68).[158] Just as the body of man needs the direction and guidance given by the head (*Spec. Leg.* 3.184), so also the "body" (σῶμα) of the cosmos needs the eternal Logos of the eternal God, which is the head of the universe (*Quaest. in Ex.* 2.117)[159] and directs the whole body.[160] As the body is ruled by its head, so the cosmos is subject to the guidance of the divine Logos and thereby is directly under God's care.[161]

The statements of the Christian confession are summarized by the hymn in the words that Christ is the head of the body.[162] This mythological manner of conceptualization in which the cosmos appears as a body governed by its head provides the answer to man's search—man who is beset by worry and fear of the powers in the world and who asks how the world can be brought to its proper order: Christ is the "head" (κεφαλή) that governs the "body" (σῶμα) of the cosmos; the cosmos is

from *The Oxford Book of Greek Verse*, ed. Gilbert Murray *et al.* [Oxford: Clarendon Press, 1930], no. 482). Cf. Schlier, *TDNT* 3, 676.

155 Cf. Seneca, *Epist.* 92.30, "All this universe which encompasses us is one, and it is God; we are associates of God; we are his members." (*Totum hoc, quo continemur, et unum et deus: et socii sumus eius et membra*). For further examples see Hegermann, *Schöpfungsmittler*, pp. 63f; Schweizer, *TWNT* 7, 1036f.

156 Cf. (Pseudo) Philo, *De deo*, "Now the earth and water are like feet, the foundation of the world; and the air and the sky are its countenance, like a face. The forces of being are like their limbs extended from one end of the world to the other, and the forces of being protect the feet of the universe, its lower parts (which are the earth and water), and its face (that is, the air and sky) which includes those natures that tend to higher things, so that these be better preserved" (*Mundi vero basis sicut pedes sunt terra et aqua, facies autem quasi vultus, aer et caelum. Entis autem virtutes velut crura eorum ab orbe in orbem extensa; et universi pedes, inferiores nempe ipsius materiae partes, terram at aquam atque vultum, aera nimirum et caelum ad superiora tendentes naturas includentem ad melius conservandum protegunt.* [Trans.]). Cf. Hegermann, *Schöpfungsmittler*, 59.

157 In *Vit. Mos.* 2.117–35, Philo deals with the cosmic vesture of the high priest which is an image of the universe: the air, water, earth, fire, the heavens, the two hemispheres, and the zodiac. The "reason seat" (λογεῖον) of the high priest is an image of the divine Reason "which holds together and administers all things" (τοῦ συνέχοντος καὶ διοικοῦντος τὰ σύμπαντα 134). The priest, consecrated to the Father, must appear before him vested in the allegory of the world (133f). Concerning the cosmic vesture of the high priest, cf. also Wisd Sol 18:24.

158 Cf. Hegermann, *Schöpfungsmittler*, 59; further examples are found there, 59–67. Cf. also Weiss, *Untersuchungen zur Kosmologie*, 257–65.

159 Cf. Hegermann, *Schöpfungsmittler*, 58f; Carsten Colpe, "Zur Leib–Christi–Vorstellung um Epheserbrief," in *Judentum—Urchristentum—Kirche: Festschrift für Joachim Jeremias*, BZNW 26 (Berlin: 1960, ²1964), pp. 180f.

160 Philo's statements about the cosmos as a "body" (σῶμα) and the Logos as its "head" (κεφαλή) are to be distinguished from the Gnostic myth of the primeval man and must not be confused with it. Cf. Colpe, "Zur Leib–Christi–Vorstellung," 179–82; Hegermann, *Schöpfungsmittler*, 59–67; Schweizer, *TWNT* 7, 1051f; contra Heinrich Schlier, *TDNT* 3, 676–78.

161 In this way Philo answers the question which so greatly engaged late antiquity, that is, where and how is the universal body brought under its head and held together by it? Cf. Curtius Rufus, *Historiae Alexandri Magni Macedonensis* 10.9.1–4. In this work the empire of Alexander the Great is compared with a body (*corpus*) which, after his death, disintegrated into several members (*membra*). The application of this metaphor to the situation in the Roman Empire is then introduced: a new ruler sits on the throne and now the members which otherwise would tremble with discord are brought under their head (*cum sine capite membra trepidarent*). On this cf. Franz Mussner, *Christus, das All und die Kirche: Studien zur Theologie des Epheserbriefs*, Trierer Theologische Studien 5 (Trier: 1955), 155f; and Schweizer, TWNT 7, 1037, n. 185.

162 In the OT, the word "head" (κεφαλή/ראש) often designates the head of a community or tribe, or a ruler. E.g. Deut 28:13; Judg 10:18; 11:8f, 11, etc.; also Test Zeb 9:4; for further examples see Heinrich Schlier, *TDNT* 3, 675f. For Paul, "head" (κεφαλή) denotes the one to whom rule has been transferred (e.g., 1 Cor 11:3; also Col 2:10, 19; Eph 1:22; 4:15; 5:23). Cf. Stephen Bedale, "The Meaning of κεφαλή in the Pauline Epistles," *JTS*, NS 5 (1954): 211–15. Neither in the OT nor in the chief Pauline letters, however, is there any treatment of the relationship between the "head" and the "body." The statement of Col 1:18 is therefore to be explained from the Hellenistic conception concerning the cos-

ruled and held together by this head. The universe is founded and established through him alone, i.e. in him alone is salvation.[163]

The author of Col, however, proceeds to interpret this mythological statement in such a way that the concept "body" is defined by the "church" (ἐκκλησία) and is thereby understood as a historical entity.[164] Here and now the exalted Lord exercises his rule over all the world as the head of his body which is the church.[165] This definition, "his body, that is, the church," differs clearly from the comparison which was taken over from Stoic tradition and which is employed by Paul in Rom 12 and 1 Cor 12 in order to illustrate the many functions and services of the members.[166] One is rather reminded of the words about the one body into which we have all been baptized (1 Cor 12:13), in which we are all bound together as partakers of the Lord's supper (1 Cor 10:17), and which in its unity may not be divided (1 Cor 1:13). Even in these sentences of 1 Cor, however, the cosmic dimension is lacking and nothing is said of a head which is set over the body. Thus it is not sufficient to state that in its statements about the church Col goes beyond the chief Pauline letters; the understanding of the church in Col cannot be explained as a simple evolution from earlier beginnings within Pauline theology.[167] Rather, the understanding of the church expressed in Col must be determined by considering the religious presuppositions visible in the Hellenistic conception of the cosmic body. The author of the letter gives this cosmological train of thought a new direction by designating the church as the place where in the present Christ exercises his rule over the cosmos.[168] Christ is Lord over the universe (cf. 2:10, 19), his body, however, is the church. For this reason the worldwide rule of the Kyrios is proclaimed everywhere in the preaching of Christ among the nations (1:27), in the exhortation of every man and in the instruction of every man in all wisdom so that all may be presented as perfect in Christ (1:28).[169]

---

mic body and its head cited above, and not from the OT.

163 Cf. Schweizer, *Neotestamentica*, 296, "Christ is therefore the answer to the quest for the principle which rules the world and thereby binds it together in unity. For the Hellenists, this quest is the quest for salvation." Cf. also Schweizer, *TWNT* 7, 1072f.

164 Theodoret *ad loc.* characterizes the transition completed by the words "the church" (τῆς ἐκκλησίας) by saying, "he crosses over from knowledge of God into the economy of salvation" (ἀπὸ τῆς θεολογίας εἰς τὴν οἰκονομίαν μετέβη [Trans.]).

165 Cf. Lohse, "Christusherrschaft und Kirche," 205f.

166 In this comparison the "head" is not contrasted with the "body" but is rather cited as one member among the others which all belong to this one body. Cf. 1 Cor 12:21.

167 Isak Johannes du Plessis, *Christus as hoof van kerk en kosmos: 'N eksegeties-teologiese studie van Christus se hoofskap veral in Efesiërs en Kolossense* (Groningen: 1962), has again tried to relate the statements of Col and Paul in this way. Cf. the review by Georg Bertram in *ThLZ* 90 (1965): 116–18.

168 In doing so the author makes himself known as a Pauline theologian. A new concept, however, has been formulated by the connection of the notion of the "church" (ἐκκλησία) with the traditional cosmological statement: Christ is the head of the body. (The complicated hypothesis, that a cosmological misunderstanding of the talk about the body of Christ had arisen in the hymn and that this was "re-Paulinized" by the author of Col, is superfluous. Contra Gabathuler, *Jesus Christus, Haupt der Kirche*, p. 141, n. 809.)

169 Cf. Käsemann, *Essays*, 168 (adapted from ET), "The introduction of τῆς ἐκκλησίας in v 18 has dogmatic significance. It illustrates the condition of being 'translated' into the kingdom of the Son and changes the cosmological statement into an eschatological one. Christ is also the head of the powers and authorities. But they are not his body in the strict sense. They are 'in him,' inasmuch as he is their creator and has authority over them. The community is his body, inasmuch as it lives from the resurrection of the dead and wanders towards the resurrection of the dead. But that means, in the here and now, that it stands within the forgiveness of sins. It neither means, nor indeed can it mean, anything else at all. Because it stands within forgiveness, it is new creation, the cosmic powers have nothing more to say to it, to give to it, or to ask of it. There is no way to the creation other than the way which passes through, and continues in, forgiveness. Every immediate attempt to break through, every attempt, that is, which does not derive from eschatology, turns into cosmology, into apostasy from forgiveness, into renewed slavery to the cosmic tyrants, who then take on the aspect of demonic powers."

The second strophe, like the first one, begins with two predications for Christ. He is "the beginning" (ἀρχή)[170] and the "firstborn from the dead" (πρωτότοκος ἐκ[171] τῶν νεκρῶν). In Judaism both Wisdom and Logos were called "the beginning" (ἀρχή). Wisdom commends herself "In the beginning, before the ages, he established me" (πρὸ τοῦ αἰῶνος ἐθεμελίωσέν με ἐν ἀρχῇ LXX Pr 8:23). Philo characterizes Wisdom (σοφία) as " 'beginning' and 'image' and 'vision of God' " (ἀρχὴν καὶ εἰκόνα καὶ ὅρασιν θεοῦ *Leg. All.* 1.43).[172] However, when it is said of Christ that he is the "beginning," this does not mean that he is the "beginning of God's creation" (ἀρχὴ τῆς κτίσεως τοῦ θεοῦ Rev 3:14). Rather, he is the "beginning" as the one who is the "first–born from the dead" (πρωτότοκος ἐκ τῶν νεκρῶν) through whom the eschatological event has been initiated.[173] As the first one who has arisen from those who have fallen asleep, he is the first fruit (ἀπαρχή) who guarantees the future resurrection of the dead (1 Cor 15:20, 23). Thus he is the "Originator of Life" (ἀρχηγὸς τῆς ζωῆς Acts 3:15), the "first to rise from the dead" (πρῶτος ἐξ ἀναστάσεως νεκρῶν Acts 26:33) and the "firstborn of the dead and ruler of the kings on earth" (ὁ πρωτότοκος τῶν νεκρῶν καὶ ἄρχων τῶν βασιλέων τῆς γῆς Rev 1:5).[174]

Since Christ is the beginning and the first–born, he is therefore the first one in all things. In the purpose clause (ἵνα), the words "in all" (ἐν πᾶσιν) relate to the oft–repeated "all things" (τὰ πάντα) and thus these words of v 18 are to be taken as "in all things" in the neuter gender.[175] The words "be the first" (πρωτεύειν)[176] resume the twice–mentioned "first–born" (πρωτότοκος vss 15, 18b), and also the phrase of v 17a, "and he is before all things" (καὶ αὐτός ἐστιν πρὸ πάντων). The first place in the universe is properly his alone.[177]

■ **19** The reason for this follows, "for in him all the fullness was pleased to dwell" (ἐν αὐτῷ εὐδόκησεν πᾶν τὸ πλήρωμα κατοικῆσαι).[178] First of all, concerning the construction of the sentence, the Greek text permits that "God" (ὁ θεός) could be supplied as the subject; "all the fullness . . . to dwell" (πᾶν τὸ πλήρωμα κατοιῆσαι) in this case would have to be taken as an accusative with the infinitive: "God was pleased to let all the fullness dwell in him." This would achieve a smooth connection to the following participle "he (i.e. God) was making peace" (εἰρηνοποιήσας).[179] It is, however, also possible to take "all the fullness" (πᾶν τὸ πλήρωμα) as the sub-

170 The mss p^{46} B 1739 pc supply the article to read ἡ ἀρχή (*the* beginning).

171 The mss p^{46} ℵ* Ir delete ἐκ (from) to read "of the dead."

172 God's "first–born" (πρωτόγονος), "beginning" (ἀρχή), and "image" (εἰκών) are names also for the Logos, cf. Philo, *Conf. Ling.* 146. Cf. above, p. 47.

173 The words "first–born" and "beginning" occasionally appear together in order to describe the first–born as the founder of a people. Cf. LXX Gen 49:3 "Ruben, you are my first–born, my strength and the beginning of my children" (Ρουβην, πρωτότοκός μου σύ, ἰσχύς μου καὶ ἀρχὴ τῶν τέκνων μου). Cf. also LXX Deut 21:17.

174 The phrase "first–born from the dead" cannot be explained as coming from the Gnostic redeemer–myth. Cf. above, p. 45.

175 The gender is not masculine as a continuation of the preceding νεκροί (the dead); thus Heinrich Schlier, *Christus und die Kirche im Epheserbrief*, BHTh 6 (Tübingen: 1930), 55f, n. 1. Cf. Hegermann, *Schöpfungsmittler*, 103, "The words 'in all things' (ἐν πᾶσιν) accordingly are not to be explained from 'the dead' (νεκροί) but from the formula 'all things' (πάντα)."

176 The verb πρωτεύειν is a hapaxlegomenon in the NT; it also is rare in the LXX, e.g. Esth 5:11; 2 Macc 6:18, 13:15. But cf. Iamblichus, *Vit. Pyth.* 8.43 τῶν ἐν ἑκάστῳ τῷ γένει πεπρωτευκότων, which means "of the respective best in every generation" [Trans.]. Plutarch, *Lib. Educ.* 13 (9b): the fathers "in their eagerness that their children may the sooner rank first in everything" (σπεύδοντες γὰρ τοὺς παῖδας ἐν πᾶσι τάχιον πρωτεῦσαι). *P. Lips.* I, 40, 2, 16; 3, 6 has πρωτεύων meaning "head," "director." *P. Oxy.* XVI, 1983, 3. Further examples are in Wilhelm Michaelis, *TDNT* 6, 881f.

177 Cf. Chrysostom, *ad loc.* (before v 18), "For everywhere he is first; above first; in the Church first, for he is the Head; in the Resurrection first" (πανταχοῦ γάρ ἐστι πρῶτος· ἄνω πρῶτος, ἐν τῇ ἐκκλησίᾳ πρῶτος· κεφαλὴ γάρ ἐστιν· ἐν τῇ ἀναστάσει πρῶτος).

178 Cf. Gerhard Münderlein, "Die Erwählung durch das Pleroma, Bemerkungen zu Kol. I.19" *NTS* 8 (1961–62): 264–76.

179 For this reason many exegetes have favored this solution: Lightfoot; Erich Haupt, *Die Gefangenschaftbriefe*, KEK 8–9 (Göttingen: 1902); Lohmeyer, *ad loc.*; Gottlob Schrenk, *TDNT* 2, 741; Gerhard Delling, *TDNT* 6, 303f; Mussner, *Christus, das All*, 58, n. 89; Feuillet, "La Création," 228f.

ject to which the "making peace" (εἰρηνοποιήσας) is joined in a *constructio ad sensum*. Since this solution works without the addition of an unstated subject it is to be given preference over the other possibility.[180] The words "all the fullness" (πᾶν τὸ πλήρωμα) mean nothing else than the divine fullness in its totality and therefore in the following commentary on the hymn they are elucidated in 2:9 as "the whole fullness of deity" (πᾶν τὸ πλήρωμα τῆς θεότητος).

The concept "fullness"[181] or "pleroma" played a great role in the Christian Gnosticism of the second century.[182] The Valentinians meant by "pleroma" the fullness of the emanations which came forth from God. God himself is distinguished from these as "alone unbegotten, not subject to place or time" (μόνος ἀγέννητος, οὐ τόπον ἔχων, οὐ χρόνον Hippolytus, *Ref*. 6.29.5). In contrast to the "emptiness" of the divine (κένωμα Epiphanius, *Haer*. 31.16.1), "Pleroma" signifies the uppermost pneumatic world in immediate proximity to God which in turn is separated from the cosmos by a boundary. There exists "peace and harmony between all the Aeons within the Pleroma" (εἰρήνη καὶ συμφωνία πάντων τῶν ἐντὸς πληρώματος αἰώνων Hippolytus, *Ref*. 6,32,1 [trans. from ANF 5, 87]). The mature fruit of the "pleroma" which has been brought forth by all the Aeons together is Jesus (*Ref*. 6.32.1f; Irenaeus, *Adv. Haer*. 1.2.6), who descended from the divine fullness as the redeemer (*Ref*. 6.32.4). But the goal of the work of redemption is that all things which are of pneumatic origin be reassembled in the "pleroma," "in order that the Pleroma might be formed into an aggregate, according to a perfect number" (ἵν' ᾖ τὸ πλήρωμα ἐν ἀριθμῷ τελείῳ συνηθροισμένον *Ref*. 6.34.2 [trans. from ANF 5, 88]). Since, according to Valentinian teaching, the "pleroma" is indeed the heavenly fullness to which, however, God does not belong, this understanding of the word "pleroma" cannot contribute anything to the explanation of Col 1:19—for there can be no doubt that in the Christ-hymn, God himself is called "pleroma."

In the linguistic usages of the syncretism of late antiquity the concept "pleroma" was variously employed.[183] On the one hand God and the cosmos are distinguished, "for the cosmos is [the] pleroma of evil, but God is the pleroma of good" (ὁ γὰρ κόσμος πλήρωμά ἐστι τῆς κακίας, ὁ δὲ θεὸς τοῦ ἀγαθοῦ *Corp. Herm*. 6.4 [Trans.]); the cosmos, however, which is united intimately with God "is a pleroma of life" (πλήρωμά ἐστι τῆς ζωῆς *Corp. Herm*. 12.15 [Trans.]). On the other hand, thus the *Corpus Hermeticum* calls God "the Master and Maker and Father and Encompasser of All, and the One is all things and all things are the One," and then continues "for the pleroma of all things is one and in one, and one is not two but both are one being."[184] Since the All–One is not dual but rather is one and remains one, the All is thus not a second element alongside the One, so that God himself is thereby the "pleroma."[185] The term "pleroma" thus indicates the one God pervading the whole universe. "For he is incorrupt, the fullness of the aeons and their

180 Thus Abbott; H. von Soden, *Die Briefe an die Kolosser, Epheser, Philemon: die Pastoralbriefe* in Hand-Commentar zum Neuen Testament 3, 1 (Freiburg i.B. and Leipzig: ²1893); P. Ewald, *Die Briefe des Paulus an die Epheser, Kolosser und Philemon* in Kommentar zum Neuen Testament 10 (Leipzig: 1910); Masson; Dibelius–Greeven, *ad loc.*; Percy, *Probleme*, 76, n. 22; Käsemann, *Essays*, 157–59; Jervell, *Imago Dei*, 222, n. 191; Gerhard Münderlein, "Die Erwählung durch das Pleroma, Bemerkungen zu Kol. 1.19," *NTS* 8 (1961–62): 266; Schweizer, *Neotestamentica*, 294, n. 3.

181 Cf. Gerhard Delling, *TDNT* 6, 297–304 (with a thorough survey of the literature on p. 297). In addition, the following should be especially noted: Josef Gewiess, "Die Begriffe πληροῦν and πλήρωμα im Kolosser- und Epheserbrief," in *Vom Wort des Lebens, Festschrift für Max Meinertz*, NTAbh Suppl. 1 (Münster: 1951), 128–41; Sverre Aalen "Begrepet plaeroma i Kolosser- og Efeserbrevet," *TTK* 23 (1952): 49–67; Moule, *ad loc*. Concerning the concept of "pleroma" in Eph, special reference must be made to Mussner, *Christus das All*, 46–64, and Heinrich Schlier, *Der Brief an die Epheser* (Düsseldorf: ⁵1965), 96–99 (who has further listings of literature).

182 Cf. the examples given in Lightfoot's excursus on the concept "pleroma" (pp. 257–73), as well as Delling, *TDNT* 6, 299f.

183 Cf. Jervell, *Imago Dei*, 221f.

184 τῶν ὅλων δεσπότην καὶ ποιητὴν καὶ πατέρα καὶ περίβολον, καὶ πάντα ὄντα τὸν ἕνα, καὶ ἕνα ὄντα τὸν πάντα. . .τῶν πάντων γὰρ τὸ πλήρωμα ἕν ἐστι καὶ ἐν ἑνί, οὐ δευτεροῦντος τοῦ ἑνός, ἀλλ' ἀμφοτέρων ἑνὸς ὄντος *Corp. Herm*. 16.3 [Trans.].

185 Cf. Gerhard Delling, *TDNT* 6, 300: "Here the word is clearly meant to define a concept of God in which

father" (*Od.Sol.* 7.11[13]).[186]

The Christian community took up the word "pleroma" from the Hellenistic milieu[187] in order to speak of the fullness of God which decided to dwell in this One.[188] This, however, transferred the term from the context of cosmology into that of soteriology. The Greek verb **εὐδοκεῖν** (to be pleased) appears often in the LXX as an expression for the good pleasure of God. He takes pleasure in right actions and conduct, but not in evil or bad works (LXX Ps 43:4; 146:11; 149:4).[189] This verb is also used to designate divine election, and of those whom God has not chosen it is said that "the Lord took no pleasure in them" (**οὐκ εὐδόκησεν ἐν αὐτοῖς κύριος** LXX Ps 151:5). But God's voice rings out over the Chosen One with "You are my beloved Son, with you I am well pleased" (**σὺ εἶ ὁ υἱός μου ὁ ἀγαπητός, ἐν σοὶ εὐδόκησα** Mk 1:11; par.). A connection between God's choosing and his dwelling place is also expressed repeatedly. Zion is "the mountain on which it pleased God to dwell" (**τὸ ὄρος, ὃ εὐδόκησεν ὁ θεὸς κατοικεῖν ἐν αὐτῷ** LXX Ps 67:17). Similarly LXX Ps 131:13f: "for the Lord has elected Zion, he has chosen her for his dwelling. 'This is my resting place forever, here I will dwell for I have chosen her'" (**ὅτι ἐξελέξατο κύριος τὴν Σιων, ᾑρετίσατο αὐτὴν εἰς κατοικίαν αὐτῷ. Αὕτη ἡ κατάπαυσίς μου εἰς αἰῶνα αἰῶνος, ὧδε κατοικήσω, ὅτι ᾑρετισάμην αὐτήν**). The verb **ἐκλέγεσθαι** (to elect) has here replaced **εὐδοκεῖν** (cf. also LXX Isa 8:18; 49:20).[190] In Deuteronomy and in the Deuteronomic theology the sentence appears again and again that the God of Israel has chosen a place for himself where he wants his name to dwell.[191] This thought is also repeated in later writings: God has chosen a dwelling-place for himself in Israel; "since your good pleasure was in your glory amongst your people Israel, you sanctified this place" (**εὐδοκήσας τὴν δόξαν σοῦ ἐν τῷ λαῷ σοῦ Ἰσραηλ ἡγίασας τὸν τόπον τοῦτον** 3 Macc 2:16).[192]

As the hymn speaks of God's electing decree, it makes use of biblical language.[193] No reference is contained in this statement to any particular event, e.g., the incarnation,[194] the baptism or the transfiguration of Jesus,[195] rather, it relates to the Christ–event as a whole. "In him all the fullness was pleased to dwell," which means just that: "in him all the fullness of deity dwells (**κατοικεῖ**—present tense!) bodily" (2:9). In him and through him God accomplishes the work of reconciliation.[196]

God and the world merge into one another."

186 Translated from the German of Walter Bauer, in Hennecke–Schneemelcher 2, 585 (German ed.); cf. J. Rendel Harris, *The Odes and Psalms of Solomon*, (Cambridge: The University Press, [2]1911) for 7.13 on p. 99. Cf. also Rendel Harris and Alphonse Mingana, *The Odes and Psalms of Solomon* (Manchester: University Press; London: Longmans, Green & Co., 1920), vol. 2, The Translation, for 7.11 and 17.7, 19.5, 36.6, 41.13f. In the *Gospel of Truth* the dwelling place of the Father is described as the pleroma (16.35, 41.1, 43.15f); the same place can also be called the "rest of the Father" (23.29). Cf. Hans-Martin Schenke, *Die Herkunft des sogenannten Evangelium Veritatis* (Göttingen: 1959), 15f.

187 Aalen, "Begrepet," 57f, wants to understand "pleroma" to mean the same as שְׁכִינָה (abode). What misled him to this interpretation is the verb κατοικῆσαι (to dwell) which, however, does not correspond to the term "pleroma." Münderlein, "Die Erwählung," 275, is inclined to agree with this meaning. Against this Gerhard Delling makes the pertinent remark, "The statements in Col go much further than the Jewish statements" *TDNT* 6, 303. Cf. also the critical comments of Jervell, *Imago Dei*, 222, n. 191.

188 Cf. Schweizer, *Neotestamentica*, 294, n. 3, "thus it may be supposed that 'pleroma' was originally understood in the sense of the Hellenistic idea of the world–soul, but then for the community it meant the God who pervades the whole universe. Perhaps the Wisdom terminology which is otherwise present in the hymn is likewise in the background here, since it is the Sophia of God which pervades all things and penetrates them all (Wisd Sol 7.24; cf. 1.7 which for its part is dependent, of course, upon the Greek conceptions of the world–soul)." Yet this appealing supposition cannot be proven, for in the LXX, "pleroma" is found only with a spatial meaning (cf. Delling, *TDNT* 6, 299), and in Jewish Wisdom speculations the term is lacking.

189 Further examples in Gottlob Schrenk, *TDNT* 2, 738.

190 Hegermann, in *Schöpfungsmittler*, 107, goes too far with his supposition: "It can be assumed that the hymn makes a direct allusion to this passage."

191 E.g., LXX Deut 12:5, 11; 14:23; 16:2, 6, 11; 26:2; 3 Kg 6:13; 8:27; etc. Cf. here also the paraphrase in the Targum on 1 Kings 8:27, "Has it really pleased the Lord to cause his Sh[e]kina to dwell among men who live on the earth?" Similarly in the Targum on Ps 68:17, "It pleased the word of the Lord to let his Sh[e]kina dwell on it [Sinai]." Cf. Aalen, "Begrepet," 58; Münderlein, "Die Erwählung," 270; Feuillet, "La Création," 236–38.

192 Cf. also 2 Macc 14:35; Test Zeb 8:2; Test Joseph

■ **20** The last verse of the hymn deals with this work of reconciliation.[197] Although there has been no previous mention of it, it is presupposed here that unity and harmony of the cosmos have suffered a considerable disturbance, even a rupture. In order to restore the cosmic order reconciliation became necessary and was accomplished by the Christ–event. Through Christ, God himself achieved this reconciling.[198] The universe has been reconciled in that heaven and earth have been brought back into their divinely created and determined order[199] through the resurrection and exaltation of Christ.[200] Now the universe is again under its head[201] and thereby cosmic peace has returned.[202] This peace which God has established through Christ[203] binds the whole universe together again into unity and under-

10:2f; and Test Benj 6:4.

193 The words "in him" (ἐν αὐτῷ) which are given emphatic prominence must be connected with "to dwell" (κατοικῆσαι) and not with "was pleased" (εὐδόκησεν). Münderlein, who advocates this connection, seeks to support his interpretation with the unfounded supposition that one can assume a Semitic linguistic basis ("Die Erwählung," 268–70). In Col 2:9 the sentence of 1:19 is taken up by "in him the whole fullness of the deity dwells bodily" (ἐν αὐτῷ κατοικεῖ πᾶν τὸ πλήρωμα τῆς θεότητος σωματικῶς). Thus "in him" (ἐν αὐτῷ) is to be connected with "to dwell" (κατοικῆσαι).

194 This thought could be suggested by the comparable statement of the Johannine prologue, Jn 1:14.

195 Thus Münderlein, "Die Erwählung," 271, with reference to the heavenly voice's words "I am well pleased" (εὐδόκησα) in the stories of the baptism and transfiguration.

196 Genuine early Christian kerygma appears in this sentence. Cf. Augustine's words concerning the prologue of John: he had indeed also read in the books of the Neoplatonists that 'in the beginning was the Logos, and through the Logos all things were made.' "But that the Logos was made flesh and dwelt among us, I did not read there." (*Sed quia verbum caro factum est et habitaverit in nobis, non ibi legi. Conf.* 7.9 [Trans.]).

197 Cf. Johann Michl, "Die 'Versöhnung' (Kol 1,20)" *ThQ* 128 (1948): 442–62; B. N. Wambacq, " 'per eum reconciliare . . . quae in caelis sunt' (Col 1,20)," *RB* 55 (1948): 35–42; Wilhelm Michaelis, *Die Versöhnung des Alls* (Bern: 1950), 24f; Mussner, *Christus, das All*, 69–71; Lyonnet, "L'hymne christologique." Michl presents the history of the exegesis of this passage and gives v 20 the meaning of the renewed subordination of the angels under Christ after his *kenosis*. Wambacq understands "to reconcile" (ἀποκαταλλάξαι) as referring to the reconciliation of the angels of the Law which had been dethroned according to 2:15. Lyonnet wonders whether the Jewish New Year's festival should be recalled in connection with v 20 as well as in connection with Philo, *Spec. Leg.* 2.192. Cf. above p. 45, n. 94.

198 The verb ἀποκαταλλάσσειν (to reconcile) only appears in Christian literature. Cf. Friedrich Büchsel, *TDNT* 1, 258; Bauer, *s.v.* Paul uses καταλλάσσειν (to reconcile) in Rom 5:10; 1 Cor 7:11; and 2 Cor 5:18ff. The verb ἀποκαταλλάσσειν appears again only in Col 1:22 and Eph 2:16.

199 Cf. Ernst Käsemann, "Erwägungen zum Stichwort 'Versöhnungslehre im Neuen Testament' " in *Zeit und Geschichte, Festschrift für Rudolf Bultmann* (Tübingen: 1964), 48f, "We are dealing here with a tradition which originally was of a hymnic–liturgical character and which therefore derives from the 'doxologia' of the Hellenistic communities." [Trans.]

200 The second strophe is given its heading by the christological titles "the beginning" (ἀρχή) and "firstborn from the dead" (πρωτότοκος ἐκ τῶν νεκρῶν). Cf. Schweizer, *Neotestamentica*, 298.

201 The words εἰς αυτον (in him) are not to be read as εἰς αὑτόν (toward himself, i.e. to God) and thus be related to God (thus Moule, *ad loc.* with reference to 2 Cor 5:19). Rather, they correspond to the εἰς αὐτόν (in him, i.e. toward Christ) of v 16 and in connection with ἀποκαταλλάξαι (to reconcile) they signify "the conquering of the cosmic enmity through the rulership of Christ" (Dibelius–Greeven, *ad loc.*).

202 V 20 must not be interpreted by 1:22 in terms of the reconciliation of the world of men (thus Friedrich Büchsel, *TDNT* 1, 258), but rather, in pronouncing the word of reconciliation to the community, in 1:22 the author of Col utilizes the concept of a reconciliation which encompasses the whole of the universe.

203 The verb εἰρηνοποιεῖν (to make peace) is not used often, cf. Werner Foerster, *TDNT* 2, 418–20, and Bauer, *s.v.* In the LXX it occurs only in Pr 10:10. Isa 27:5 in the LXX reads ποιήσωμεν εἰρήνην (let us make peace); Aquila, Symmachus and Theodotion translate it with εἰρηνοποιήσει ("he shall make peace" in one Greek term). In the NT the

lines that the restored creation is reconciled with God.[204] Contrary to apocalyptic expectations, peace is not something which will come only at the end of time; rather, it has already appeared in all things and the cosmic work of redemption has been done (cf. Phil 2:10f).[205] As the one who reconciled the cosmos, Christ has entered his kingly rule. Because he is the mediator of reconciliation,[206] he is therefore also praised as the mediator of creation,[207] as Lord over the universe, over powers and principalities.[208]

At this point the author of the epistle to the Colossians has added an interpretive phrase: through the blood of his cross (διὰ τοῦ αἵματος τοῦ σταυροῦ αὐτοῦ);[209] this gives a new direction to the train of thought.[210] A "theology of glory," which might view the consummation as already achieved, is corrected by the "theology of the cross" (cf. 2:14f).[211] Peace has not been established in an other–worldly drama but rather in the death of Jesus Christ. In agreement with the direction of Pauline theology, this points to the cross as the place where the reconciliation occurred, which is proclaimed in the "word of the cross" (λόγος ὁ τοῦ σταυροῦ 1 Cor 1:18) or in the "word of reconciliation" (λόγος τῆς καταλλαγῆς 2 Cor 5:19). Since the Christ–event pertains to the whole world, the crucified and resurrected One must be heralded as the Lord in all lands (cf. 1:24–29). Whoever belongs to this Lord is "new creation; the old has passed away, behold, the new has come." (καινὴ κτίσις· τὰ ἀρχαῖα παρῆλθεν, ἰδοὺ γέγονεν καινά 2 Cor 5:17).

To be sure, the hymn emphasizes the universal sig-

---

word is used only here, yet cf. Mt 5:9 μακάριοι οἱ εἰρηνοποιοί (blessed are the peacemakers).

204 Concerning cosmic peace, cf. Asc Isa 11:23 "And I saw him and he was in the firmament . . . and all angels of the firmament and the Satan saw him and they worshipped him." In Jewish prayers the petition for peace "in his (God's) heights and among us and for all Israel" appears repeatedly (Qaddish prayer, cf. Willy Staerck, *Altjüdische liturgische Gebete*, KlT 58 [Berlin: ²1930], 29–32 [Trans.]). According to *b. Ber.* 16b, R. Saphra (ca. 300) used to pray, "May it be your will, Yahweh our God, that you grant peace to the upper family (world of angels) and to the lower family (Israel) and to the students who busy themselves with your Torah." [Trans.] Cf. Billerbeck 1, 420.

205 This conception of the cosmic reconciliation is to be clearly distinguished from Gnostic concepts, because the reconciliation of heaven and earth would be unthinkable for Gnosticism. Cf. Eduard Schweizer, *Neotestamentica*, 304, and also his article in *TWNT* 7, 1072, n. 474, "The reconciliation of the material world with the heavens would be the exact opposite of Gnostic hope." [Trans.]

206 For the interpretation of Lohmeyer, who would like to understand the reconciliation as well as the reference to the blood of the cross of Christ against the background of the Jewish Day of Atonement (Lohmeyer, 66–68), see the critical discussion of his thesis above, p. 45f. Cf. also Gabathuler, *Jesus Christus, Haupt der Kirche*, 132f.

207 Cf. Maurer, "Die Begründung der Herrschaft Christi," 89, "Thus the starting point for the connection of the Christ with creation is to be found in the understanding of the redeemer as the goal of all history. For Paul, Christ is the goal of all the ways and plans of God. Since, however, all things aim toward him, there is also, then, the disclosure which comes from him that, as the hidden goal, he was always there, even from the beginning of the ways." [Trans.]

208 The train of thought of the hymn aims at this: whoever belongs to this Lord is free from the enslaving (cosmic) powers and from the compelling force of fate. Cf. Tatian, *Or. Graec.* 9.2, "But we are superior to fate, and instead of the erring demons we have come to know one unerring master, and since we are not led by fate we reject the decrees of it." (ἡμεῖς δὲ καὶ εἱμαρμένης ἐσμὲν ἀνώτεροι καὶ ἀντὶ πλανητῶν δαιμόνων ἕνα τὸν ἀπλανῆ δεσπότην μεμαθήκαμεν καὶ οὐ καθ' εἱμαρμένην ἀγόμενοι τοὺς ταύτης νομοθέτας παρῃτήμεθα [Trans.]). Cf. also Eduard Schweizer, "Das hellenistische Weltbild as Produkt der Weltangst," in *Neotestamentica*, 15–27.

209 Cf. above, p. 43. By this formulation, the author joins with the common Christian parlance of the blood of Christ as a reference to the vicarious death of Christ, yet he gives it a Pauline interpretation by the addition of the phrase "of his cross" (τοῦ σταυροῦ).

210 Cf. the Pauline gloss at the end of the first strophe of the hymn of Phil 2:6–11: "even death on the cross" (θανάτου δὲ σταυροῦ 2:8).

211 This correction arrests all attempts to utilize the hymn for the purposes of a natural or cosmic theology; this must also be asserted over against a newly advocated "ecumenical" theology: Joseph Sittler, "Called to Unity," *The Ecumenical Review* 14 (1961–62): 177–87, does indeed establish first that "Against that error (i.e., among the Colossians) which, had it persisted, would have trapped Christ within terms of a purely moral and spiritual power and hope, Paul sets off a kind of chain–reaction from the central atom, and the staccato ring of *ta panta* is the

nificance of the Christ–event by exhibiting its cosmic dimensions and by speaking of salvation for the whole world, including the whole creation. This, however, does not ascribe any special dignity or eminence to the powers and principalities—as though salvation were their only aim from the beginning.[212] Rather, the reference to the powers and principalities is made in order to proclaim the message of Christ who has been installed as Head and Lord over all things. This means, however, that the right understanding of the cosmological statements of the first part of the hymn is disclosed only by the soteriological statements of the second strophe. The great drama, wherein the principalities are stripped of their power and the reconciliation of all things has taken place, is for the sake of man alone. To him comes the word of peace wrought by Christ. This peace now holds sway in the realm in which Christ rules, here and now, as the beloved Son of the Father—in the Church, in his body over which he is the Head.[213]

sounding of its reverberations into the farthest reaches of the human fact, event and thought. All is claimed for God, and all is Christic" (p. 178). But subsequently Sittler directly contradicts the theology of Col: "Creation is a work of God, who is light. And the light of the Creator–God falls upon and inheres within his creation. The world of nature can be the place of this light that 'came' by Jesus Christ because, despite the world's hostility to that light, it was never without the light of God" (p. 180). Otto Alexander Dilschneider, *Christus Pantokrator* (Berlin: 1962) develops his "fragments" of an ecumenical theology on the basis of the peculiar presupposition that the epistle to the Colossians is a case of "late Paulinism" (27f, *passim*) whose mythological terminology must be related and applied to the forms of the appearance of myth today by means of a "transmythical interpretation" (p. 57). For a critique of Sittler and Dilschneider, cf. also Gabathuler, *Jesus Christus, Haupt der Kirche*, 152–67, 177–81. Concerning the question of a cosmic Christology, cf. also Wilhelm Andersen, *Jesus Christus und der Kosmos* (Bad Salzuflen: 1963); Horst Bürkle, "Die Frage nach dem 'kosmischen Christus' als Beispiel einer ökumenisch orientierten Theologie" *KD* 11 (1965): 103–115.

212 Cf. Lohse, "Christusherrschaft und Kirche," 216.

213 By the previous vss 13 and 14, and by the following application of vss 21–23, the author of Col indicates in what sense he understands the hymn and in what sense he wants to utilize it in his argumentation with the "philosophy" (φιλοσοφία). In this connection it must be noted that the cosmological statements are not developed further. Rather, the concepts "head" (κεφαλή v 18; 2:10, 19), "body" (σῶμα v 18; 1:24; 2:9, 17, 19; 3:15) and "to reconcile" (ἀποκαταλλάσσειν v 20, 21f) are taken up again in order to describe the reconciliation as the reality which shapes the "church" (ἐκκλησία) which is the body under its head. The theme of "all"/"all things" (πᾶν/πάντα), going through the whole hymn, sounds continuously throughout the letter: "Christ is all and in all" (πάντα καὶ ἐν πᾶσιν Χριστός 3:11).

1 Assurance of the Reconciliation and Its Demand.

21 **You also, who once were alienated and of a hostile mind in evil deeds, 22/ he has now reconciled in his body of flesh through death, in order to present you holy, blameless and irreproachable before him, 23/ if indeed you continue in faith, firmly established and steadfast, and if you are never dissuaded from the hope of the gospel which you have heard, which is proclaimed to every creature under heaven, and of which I, Paul, became a minister.**

The words "and you" (*καὶ ὑμᾶς*) mark a new beginning in order to show the community that the message of reconciliation which pertains to the whole world applies to them. The catchword "to reconcile" (*ἀποκαταλλάξαι*) is taken up from the hymn (1:15–20) and is applied in the words "You also . . . he has now reconciled" (*καὶ ὑμᾶς . . . νυνὶ δὲ ἀποκατήλλαξεν* v 21f). The reconciliation has been wrought through Christ's death: "through the blood of his cross" (*διὰ τοῦ αἵματος τοῦ σταυροῦ αὐτοῦ* v 20); "in his body of flesh through death" (*ἐν τῷ σώματι τῆς σαρκὸς αὐτοῦ διὰ τοῦ θανάτου* v 22). According to the hymn, Christ's rule encompasses all things. Corresponding to this, it is said now that the proclamation of the good news is made to all the world. In Christ all things have been created (*ἐν αὐτῷ ἐκτίσθη τὰ πάντα* v 16); therefore the gospel must be preached to every creature under heaven (*ἐν πάσῃ κτίσει τῇ ὑπὸ τὸν οὐρανόν* v 23). The assurance of the reconciliation, however, also includes the demand to remain steadfast in faith and not to be dissuaded from the "hope of the gospel" (*ἐλπὶς τοῦ εὐαγγελίου* v 23).

■ **21** The *καί* (and) is connective, forming a transition to the exegesis which is now added to the hymn that was taken over from tradition.[1] The community is designated as the goal toward which the event encompassing heaven and earth is directed: to reconcile them, to draw those who were once alienated and at enmity with God and to place them on the firm ground of faith and hope. In his homiletic utilization of the hymn the author of Col avails himself in his interpretation of a contrast often employed in primitive Christian proclamation: "you were once—but now you are . . .".[2] The miracle of the salvation that was experienced is contrasted to the lostness from which God has freed them. Since, however, their lostness has been ended by God's wonderful act, this turn of events demands obedient loyalty.[3] What previously was, no longer has validity, but in order to measure the magnitude of what has occurred through God's mercy, the past is recalled.

"Once you were alienated"—this can be said only of former Gentiles and not of Jews, because the latter knew and know God's will and law. To be estranged from God means not to serve him, but to worship false gods and idols and thus to become enmeshed in idolatry and in slavery to sin.[4] Thus what is said of their Gentile past is that they existed in a persistent[5] state of alienation from God.[6] This estrangement, however, means that there was a conscious antagonism to the only true God, much like enemies (*ἐχθροί*) establishing themselves over against their avowed opponents.[7] The term "enemy"

---

1 Cf. the similar introductions with connective "and" in 2:13, "and you being dead" (*καὶ ὑμᾶς νεκροὺς ὄντας*); Eph 2:1 "And you who were dead" (*καὶ ὑμᾶς ὄντας νεκρούς*). Cf. also Lk 1:76, "And you, child, shall be called the prophet of the Most High" (*καὶ σὺ δέ, παιδίον, προφήτης ὑψίστου κληθήσῃ*).

2 Cf. Nils Alstrup Dahl, "Formgeschichtliche Beobachtungen zur Christusverkündigung in der Gemeindepredigt" in *Neutestamentliche Studien für Rudolf Bultmann*, BZNW 21 (Berlin: 1954, [2]1957), 5f. Also, Rudolf Bultmann, *Theology of the New Testament*, tr. Kendrick Grobel, vol. 1 (New York: Charles Scribner's Sons, 1951), 105f (=German edition, par. 10, pt. 4); Conzelmann, *Outline*, 88f; P. Tachau, "*Einst" und "Jetzt" im Neuen Testament*, Unpub. Diss. (Göttingen: 1968).

3 Cf. Gal 4:8f; 1 Cor 6:9–11; Rom 6:17–22, 7:5f, 11:30; Col 2:13f; Eph 2:1–10, 11–22; 1 Pt 1:14ff, 2:10; etc.

4 The passive form, *ἀπαλλοτριοῦσθαι* (to be alienated) appears again in the NT only in Eph 4:18, "darkened in their understanding they are alienated from the life of God" (*ἐσκωτισμένοι τῇ διανοίᾳ ὄντες, ἀπηλλοτριωμένοι τῆς ζωῆς τοῦ θεοῦ*). Eph 2:12 puts the estragement in terms of its relation to God's people: "alienated from the common-

(ἐχθροί) here is to be understood as an expression in the active sense.[8] Gentiles act in open enmity against God, both in their thinking as well as in their total conduct. The term "mind" (διάνοια) is neutral[9] and it is given a positive or negative meaning only when it is placed in a particular context. In the LXX διάνοια is usually the translation of לֵבָב (heart).[10] In the New Testament, διάνοια (mind) and καρδία (heart) are repeatedly used together to characterize the thinking and mentality of man.[11] Paul uses the word διάνοια nowhere else; but Eph employs it to describe the hostile position of the Gentiles toward God (Eph 2:3; 4:18). This thinking directed against God is said to have found its visible expression in "evil deeds" (ἐν τοῖς ἔργοις τοῖς πονηροῖς), for godlessness almost necessarily leads directly to the

wealth of Israel and strangers to the covenant of promise" (ἀπηλλοτριωμένοι τῆς πολιτείας τοῦ Ἰσραὴλ καὶ ξένοι τῶν διαθηκῶν τῆς ἐπαγγελίας). In the LXX the word is used in various ways. LXX Ps 57:4, "Sinners have become estranged from the womb" (ἀπηλλοτριώθησαν οἱ ἁμαρτωλοὶ ἀπὸ μήτρας); LXX Ps 68:9, "I have become a stranger to my brothers" (ἀπηλλοτριωμένος ἐγενήθην τοῖς ἀδελφοῖς μου); 3 Macc 1:3, "being alien as regards the ancestral ordinances" (τῶν πατρίων δογμάτων ἀπηλλοτριωμένος [Trans.]); Ps Sol 17:13 "Being an alien, the enemy acted proudly, And his heart was alien from our God" (ἐν ἀλλοτριότητι ὁ ἐχθρὸς ἐποίησεν ὑπερηφανίαν, καὶ ἡ καρδία αὐτοῦ ἀλλοτρία ἀπὸ τοῦ θεοῦ ἡμῶν, Charles, APOT 2, 648). For further examples see Friedrich Büchsel, *TDNT* 1, 265f, and Bauer, *s.v.*

5 In Greek, the word ἀπηλλοτριωμένους (were estranged) is emphasized by the participle ὄντας (being) "to express still more forcibly the persistence in the state of things now pertaining." (Blass–Debrunner, par. 352).

6 God alone is thus able to end the alienation. The members of the Qumran community were conscious of the fact that God had drawn them near to him, i.e., led them into the community (1 QS XI.13; also, 1 QH XIV.13f; XVI.12; etc.). The word קרב (to come near) almost became a technical term for acceptance into the community (1 QS VI.16, 19, 22; VII.21; VIII.18).

7 For a comparison, cf. the analogous formulations "So to the gods . . . the unjust man will be hateful, but the just man dear" Plato *Rep.* 352b. To the question, "Are you the Diogenes who does not believe in the existence of the gods?" Diogenes answered, "And how can that be? You I regard as hated by the gods." (καὶ πῶς . . . σὲ θεοῖς ἐχθρὸν νομίζω[ν] Epictetus, *Diss.* 3.22.91).

8 Cf. Rom 5:10 "While we were enemies we were reconciled to God" (ἐχθροὶ ὄντες κατηλλάγημεν τῷ θεῷ). In Rom 11:28 it is said of the unbelieving Jews that "as regards the gospel they are enemies of God, for your sake" (κατὰ μὲν τὸ εὐαγγέλιον ἐχθροὶ δι' ὑμᾶς). Also, Jas 4:4 has ". . . whoever wishes to be a friend of the world makes himself an enemy of God" (ὃς ἐὰν οὖν βουληθῇ φίλος εἶναι τοῦ κόσμου, ἐχθρὸς τοῦ θεοῦ καθίσταται). While the meaning "hated" is present in Rom 11:28 (cf. the "beloved" [ἀγαπητοί] in the same sentence), in the other passages, ἐχθρός is to be translated as "enemy." Cf. Werner Foerster, *TDNT* 2, 814.

9 Epictetus, in *Diss.* 3.22.20, calls "mind" (διάνοια) the "material" (ὕλη) to be formed: "From now on my mind is the material with which I have to work, as the carpenter has his timbers, the shoemaker his hides . . ." (νῦν ἐμοὶ ὕλη ἐστὶν ἡ ἐμὴ διάνοια, ὡς τῷ τέκτονι τὰ ξύλα, ὡς τῷ σκυτεῖ τὰ δέρματα).

10 Cf. LXX Gen 8:21; 17:17; 24:45; 27:41; 34:3, 45:26A; Ex 9:21; 28:3; etc. In the writings of Hellenistic Judaism, διάνοια (mind) is often interchangeable with καρδία (heart): e.g., Test Reuben 5:3, "women . . . in their *heart* they plot against men and by means of their adornment they deceive first their *minds*" (αἱ γυναῖκες . . . ἐν καρδίᾳ μηχανῶνται κατὰ τῶν ἀνθρώπων καὶ διὰ τῆς κοσμήσεως πλανῶσιν αὐτῶν πρῶτον τὰς διανοίας). For further examples see Johannes Behm, *TDNT* 4, 965. In the LXX, Deut 6:5 translates, "And you shall love the Lord your God with all your heart and with all your soul and with all your might" (καὶ ἀγαπήσεις κύριον τὸν θεόν σου ἐξ ὅλης τῆς καρδίας σου καὶ ἐξ ὅλης τῆς ψυχῆς σου καὶ ἐξ ὅλης τῆς δυνάμεώς σου). In Mk 12:30 the first two parts of the sequence follow the text of the LXX, but the last is expanded into a third and fourth which read "and with all your *mind* and with all your strength" (καὶ ἐξ ὅλης τῆς διανοίας σου καὶ ἐξ ὅλης τῆς ἰσχύος σου). Mt 22:37 on the contrary has three parts: heart, soul and *mind* (καρδία, ψυχή, διάνοια). Lk 10:27 reads heart, soul, strength and *mind* (καρδία, ψυχή, ἰσχύς, διάνοια).

11 Cf. Lk 1:51, "the proud in the 'mind' of their hearts"

result that men's actions and plans are evil.[12] Thus Judaism viewed all Gentiles as being enmeshed in moral corruption. Enmity toward God necessarily becomes effective in evil deeds (cf. Rom 1:18–32).[13] This negative view of the Gentile world is appropriated here[14] in order to point to a past that was nothing but estrangement from and enmity toward God.[15]

■ **22** Against the dark foil of the past there arises a present that is all the more gleaming: "now he has reconciled you" (*νυνὶ δὲ ἀποκατήλλαξεν*).[16] God's act has brought about the turning point, he has reconciled the community.[17] Therefore that which was has been crossed out; what matters now is only the present that is determined by the reconciliation (cf. Rom 3:21).[18] The reconciliation has been wrought through Christ's[19] death (cf. v 20) which he suffered "in his body of flesh" (*ἐν τῷ σώματι τῆς σαρκὸς αὐτοῦ*). By the addition of "of flesh" (*τῆς σαρκός*) the body is characterized as the physical body which is subject to suffering (cf. 2:11).[20] Thereby Christ's body that was given to death is clearly distinguished from the Church which is the body of the exalted Lord. Since he was a man as we are, he experienced in his body the bitterness of death in all its horror. Yet through this death God accomplished the reconciliation (cf. Rom 8:3); that which once was, has been abolished and the "now" (*νυνί*) has taken its place.[21]

The assurance of divine reconciliation includes a demand upon the life of the reconciled people. God accomplished the reconciliation with the goal "to present you holy, blameless and irreproachable before him" (*παρα-*

(*ὑπερηφάνους διανοίᾳ καρδίας αὐτῶν*). Heb 8:10, "I will put my laws into their minds, and write them on their hearts" (*διδοὺς νόμους μου εἰς τὴν διάνοιαν αὐτῶν, καὶ ἐπὶ καρδίας αὐτῶν ἐπιγράψω αὐτούς* =LXX Jer 38:33). Cf. Heb 10:16. For further examples see Johannes Behm, *TDNT* 4, 965f.

12 Cf. the Test Asher 6:5. The soul given to the evil spirit "served in lusts and evil works" (*ἐδούλευσεν ἐν ἐπιθυμίαις καὶ ἔργοις πονηροῖς*). Cf. also Test Zeb 9:7; Test Gad 3:1.

13 Cf. Jn 3:19; 7:7. The "works" (*ἔργα*) of the unbelieving "world" (*κόσμος*) are "evil" (*πονηρά*).

14 The expression "evil deeds" (*ἔργα πονηρά*) is otherwise not found in the Pauline letters.

15 The pre-Christian past of the community is described in phrases which remain general without making possible any closer knowledge of the particular circumstances.

16 This sentence does not go smoothly since the object of "he has reconciled" (*ἀποκατήλλαξεν*) has been placed at the beginning of v 21 (i.e., "you") in order to address the community directly. B Ephr (p[46] 33) have changed the verb to "you have been reconciled" (*ἀποκατηλλάγητε*) and the mss D * G it Ir[lat] alter this to "having been reconciled" (*ἀποκαταλλαγέντες*). Since the syntactic irregularity is even greater in this latter version of the text, Lightfoot and Lohmeyer, *ad loc.*, and C. Clare Oke, "A Hebraistic Construction in Colossians I. 19–22," *ExpT* 63 (1951–52): 155f, prefer to view this reading as the original text. The break in the sentence structure occasioned by "you have been reconciled" (*ἀποκατηλλάγητε*) Oke judges to be a Semitism. In fact, however, this reading very likely is an ancient alteration by which the direct address to the community was strengthened. Preference should be given to the best attested textual reading: "he has reconciled" (*ἀποκατήλλαξεν*) in ℵ A C K f vg sy, etc. Cf. also 2:13, "And you, who were dead . . . God made you alive together with him" (*καὶ ὑμᾶς νεκροὺς ὄντας . . . συνεζωοποίησεν ὑμᾶς σὺν αὐτῷ*).

17 The subject of the verb *ἀποκατήλλαξεν* (reconciled) is God, for the hymn spoke of his reconciling action (1:20).

18 Concerning "now" (*νυνί*), cf. Rom 5:9; 7:6; 11:30f; 16:26; Eph 2:13; 3:5; 2 Tim 1:10; etc. See also Gustav Stählin, *TDNT* 4, 1112f.

19 For further elucidation the mss ℵ A 1912 pm sy[p] Ir add "his" (*αὐτοῦ*) to "death" (*θανάτου*).

20 Cf. 1 QpHab IX.2, the wicked priest suffered "vengeance upon his body of flesh" (בגוית בשרו *ἐν τῷ σώματι τῆς σαρκὸς αὐτοῦ*). On this, cf. Karl Georg Kuhn, "New Light on Temptation, Sin, and Flesh in the New Testament" in *The Scrolls and the New Testament*, ed. Krister Stendahl (New York: Harper & Brothers, 1957), 107. Also Marc Philonenko, "Sur l'expression 'corps de chair' dans le Commentaire d'Habacuc," *Semitica* 5 (1955): 39f; Rudolf Meyer, *TWNT* 7, 109f; Herbert Braun, *Qumran und das Neue Testament*, vol. 1 (Tübingen: 1966), 227. The expression "body of flesh" (*σῶμα τῆς σαρκός*) occurs in the Greek of Sir 23:16–17, "An evil man in the body of his own flesh" (cf. RSV Apoc. and footnote *ad loc.* *ἄνθρωπος πόρνος ἐν τῷ σώματι σαρκὸς αὐτοῦ*). It also appears in 1 Enoch 102.5, "And be not grieved that your souls have gone down to Hades with grief, and the body of your flesh fared not in your life according to your holiness" (*μὴ λυπεῖσθε ὅτι κατέβησαν αἱ ψυχαὶ ὑμῶν εἰ<ς ᾅ>δου μετὰ λύπης καὶ οὐκ ἀπηντήθη τῷ σώματι τῆς σαρκὸς ὑμῶν ἐν τῇ ζωῇ ὑμῶν κατὰ τὴν ὁσιότητα ὑμῶν*. Text and trans. in Campbell Bonner, *The Last Chapters of Enoch in Greek*; Studies and Documents 8, ed. Kirsopp Lake and Silva Lake

στῆσαι ὑμᾶς ἁγίους καὶ ἀμώμους καὶ ἀνεγκλήτους κατενώπιον αὐτοῦ). In cultic language the words "holy" (*ἅγιος*) and "blameless" (*ἄμωμος*) serve to describe an unblemished animal set apart for God, to be sacrificed to him (cf. Heb 9:14; 1 Pt 1:19).[22] The verb *παραστῆσαι* (to present) can be used for the presentation of a sacrifice (cf. Rom 12:2).[23] Yet in this passage there is clearly no thought of a sacrifice,[24] for the adjective "irreproachable" (*ἀνέγκλητος*) that occurs side by side with "holy" (*ἅγιος*) and "blameless" (*ἄμωμος*) does not belong in the context of cultic statements. Rather, it means that someone is without "reproach" (*ἔγκλημα*) and that thus no one can bring an accusation against him.[25] Likewise, the verb *παραστῆσαι* (to present) is used often in legal language with the meaning "to bring another before the court."[26] The tribunal before which the sentence is passed is the divine court. All must appear before the judgment seat of God (Rom 14:10) in order that God may pass on us his valid judgment (Rom 8:33f). But it is the aim of God's work of reconciliation that those who have been reconciled by Christ's death will be irreproachable when they stand before him.[27] Besides "irreproachable" (*ἀνέγκλητος*), the words "holy" and "blameless" also indicate that no fault or stain shall be found on them (cf. Phil 2:15; Eph 5:27; Rev 14:5).[28] This full–sounding sentence draws upon formulations which have been shaped by liturgy.[29] Whereas Paul once expressed to the Corinthians the wish that the Kyrios "sustain you to the end, irreproachable on the day of our Lord Jesus Christ" (*βεβαιώσει ὑμᾶς ἕως τέλους ἀνεγκλήτους ἐν τῇ ἡμέρᾳ τοῦ κυρίου ἡμῶν Ἰησοῦ Χριστοῦ* 1 Cor 1:8), the words "before him" (*κατενώπιον αὐτοῦ*) in Col do not primarily refer to the future day of the Lord.[30] Rather, they express that the Christians' present lives are lived in God's presence. Therefore, to be holy, blameless, and irreproachable must characterize their conduct according to the will of God. God's act of reconciliation has already accomplished everything; perfection is thus not to be gained by one's own striving. Rather, perfection is there to be received as God's gift and to be verified in the life of the Christians. For this reason, the main point is to seek that which is above (cf. 3:1f) and to be obedient to the divine determination which alone is binding upon the community's life.

■ **23** A single condition, decisive for everything, must be

[London: Christophers, 1937], 106). Cf. Joachim Jeremias, "Beobachtungen zu neutestamentlichen Stellen anhand des neugefundenen griechischen Henoch–Textes," *ZNW* 38 (1939): 122f.

21 In this passage too Lohmeyer, *ad loc.*, wants to find an allusion to the Day of Atonement (Versöhnung = reconciliation). "No reconciliation was possible for Jewish faith which was not sealed through death. Thus this last stipulation, which owes its existence to Jewish thought on the festival of atonement, follows in turn." For a critique of this, cf. above, pp. 45f.

22 Cf. e.g. LXX Exod 29:37f "and the altar shall be most holy, everyone that touches the altar shall be hallowed. And these are the offerings which thou shall offer upon the altar: two unblemished lambs of a year old daily on the altar continually . . ." (*καὶ ἔσται τὸ θυσιαστήριον ἅγιον τοῦ ἁγίου· πᾶς ὁ ἁπτόμενος τοῦ θυσιαστηρίου ἁγιασθήσεται. καὶ ταῦτά ἐστιν, ἃ ποιήσεις ἐπὶ τοῦ θυσιαστηρίου· ἀμνοὺς ἐνιαυσίους ἀμώμους δύο τὴν ἡμέραν ἐπὶ τὸ θυσιαστήριον ἐνδελεχῶς*).

23 Cf. LXX Lev 16:7, "And he shall take the two goats and present them before the Lord" (*καὶ λήψεται τοὺς δύο χιμάρους καὶ στήσει αὐτοὺς ἔναντι κυρίου*). The verb *παρίστασθαι/παρεστηκέναι* (to stand near or by, to be present) often appears with the meaning of standing before God in priestly service. The commission given to the tribe of Levi was to "stand . . . before the Lord" (*παρεστάναι ἔναντι κυρίου* LXX Deut 10:8 and 18:5, 7). Cf. further LXX Num 16:9; 4 Kg 5:25; 2 Chr 6:3.

24 If the statement were determined by the idea of sacrifice, God would almost assume the role of an "examiner" (*μωμοσκόπος*), one who inspected the sacrifice to see if it was unblemished. Thus Lightfoot, *ad loc.*

25 Cf. Walter Grundmann, *TDNT* 1, 356.

26 Cf. 1 Cor 8:8; 2 Cor 4:14, 11:2; Rom 14:10; 2 Tim 2:15.

27 Cf. 1:28, "that we may present every man mature in Christ" (*ἵνα παραστήσωμεν πάντα ἄνθρωπον τέλειον ἐν Χριστῷ*).

28 The cultic concepts are thus used in a figurative sense. Cf. Eph 1:4, which simply uses "to be" (*εἶναι*) instead of "to stand before" (*παραστῆσαι*): "that we should *be* holy and blameless before him" (*εἶναι ἡμᾶς ἁγίους καὶ ἀμώμους κατενώπιον αὐτοῦ*).

29 Cf. Jude 24, "to present you without blemish before the presence of his glory with rejoicing" (*στῆσαι [ὑμᾶς] κατενώπιον τῆς δόξης αὐτοῦ ἀμώμους ἐν ἀγαλλιάσει*).

30 The word *κατενώπιον* (before, in the presence of) appears in the NT again only in Eph 1:4 and Jude 24.

fulfilled: to continue in the faith.[31] The verb "to continue" (*ἐπιμένειν*) is connected with the following noun (in the dative case), i.e. "faith," which indicates the basis upon which endurance must insist firmly and immovably.[32] Faith (*πίστις*) determines the beginning of being a Christian (cf. 1:14); to this one must adhere unperturbed. Then the life of the community will be established upon a firm foundation.[33] Just as a house is able to endure only if it has a foundation of rock (Mt 7:24–27; par.), so also the community as God's building is supported by a foundation which gives it unshakeable stability (1 Cor 3:10f; Eph 2:10; 2 Tim 2:19).[34] The word "established" (*τεθεμελιωμένοι*) is strengthened by "steadfast" (*ἑδραῖοι*).[35] These expressions pile up because traditional formulations are appropriated[36] which were constantly used in exhortation and in worship.[37] In an emphatic way, they serve to impress upon the community that they must not depart from faith and hope.[38] As was the case in the introductory thanksgiving, here "hope" (*ἐλπίς*) is named alongside "faith" (*πίστις*) as the real content of the good news (cf. 1:5).[39] Here too hope is understood as the anticipated blessing of which the gospel speaks. Christ, who is proclaimed everywhere, is the "hope of glory" (*ἐλπὶς τῆς δόξης* 1:27) so that "hope" (*ἐλπίς*) already fills the present time since it is present as the salvation that is proclaimed.

The salvation which the community heard in the word of the gospel (cf. 1:5f)[40] appears nowhere else than in the proclamation which is broadcast throughout the whole world.[41] Whereas 1:6 had "in the whole world" (*ἐν παντὶ τῷ κόσμῳ* cf. 1 Thess 1:8), here the area where the good news is sounded is described as every "creature" (*κτίσις*)[42] under heaven.[43] The cosmic scope of the Christ–event, as it was developed in the hymn, is thereby applied to the gospel that is directed to the whole world.[44] Since Christ is Lord over all things, the joyous message must be broadcast throughout the whole world.[45] If the charge is to carry out the mission "to

31 Concerning *εἴ γε* (if indeed), cf. Gal 3:4 *τοσαῦτα ἐπάθετε εἰκῆ; εἴ γε καὶ εἰκῆ* (Did you experience so many things in vain?—if indeed it was in vain); and 1 Cor 15:2 *ἐκτὸς εἰ μὴ εἰκῆ ἐπιστεύσατε* (except if you believed in vain); and also Eph 3:2 *εἴ γε ἠκούσατε* (if indeed you have heard).

32 For *ἐπιμένειν* (continue) with the following dative, cf. also Rom 6:1, *ἐπιμένωμεν τῇ ἁμαρτίᾳ*; (are we to continue in sin?); Rom 11:22, *ἐὰν ἐπιμένῃς τῇ χρηστότητι* (provided you continue in his kindness); 11:23, *ἐὰν μὴ ἐπιμένωσιν τῇ ἀπιστίᾳ* (if they do not persist in unbelief); Phil 1:24, *τὸ δὲ ἐπιμένειν τῇ σαρκί* (to remain in the flesh). Cf. also 1 Tim 4:16.

33 Concerning *θεμελιοῦν* (to found, to establish), cf. Karl Ludwig Schmidt, *TDNT* 3, 63. This word is used in the OT in two contexts of particular significance. One is that of God's establishing activity (LXX Ps 8:4; 23:2; 101:26; LXX Isa 48:13; 51:13, 16; etc.). The other is the founding of God's city on Mt. Zion (LXX Ps 47:9; LXX Isa 14:32; 44:28; LXX Hag 2:18; LXX Zech 4:9; 8:9; etc.). Cf. Lohmeyer, *ad loc.*

34 The image of the community as God's building was already much used in Judaism. Cf. 1 QS V.6; VII.17; VIII.7f; I.5f; 1 QH VI.25–27; VII.8f. For further examples see Otto Betz, "Felsenmann und Felsengemeinde (Eine Parallele zu Mt 16:17–19 in den Qumranpsalmen)" *ZNW* 48 (1957): 49–77. For the characterization of the Christian community as the holy building of God, cf. 1 Cor 3:10f, 17; 1 Tim 3:15; 1 Pt 2:4–10; Mt 16:17–19; etc.; and also Gerhard Delling, "Merkmale der Kirche nach dem Neuen Testament" *NTS* 13 (1966–67): 306.

35 For *ἑδραῖος* (steadfast), cf. Ethelbert Stauffer, *TDNT* 2, 362–64.

36 Cf. the participial style in Greek: *τεθεμελιωμένοι —μὴ μετακινούμενοι* (firmly established—not dissuaded). The connective *καί* ("and") is not found in p[46] 33.

37 Cf. 1 Cor 15:58, "be steadfast, immovable" (*ἑδραῖοι γίνεσθε, ἀμετακίνητοι*); Eph 3:17, "being rooted and grounded" (*ἐρριζωμένοι καὶ τεθεμελιωμένοι*); Ign *Eph* 10:2, "Be steadfast in the faith" (*ἑδραῖοι τῇ πίστει*); Ign *Pol* 3:1, "stand fast" (*στῆθι ἑδραῖος*); Pol *Phil* 10:1, "firm and unchangeable in faith" (*firmi in fide et immutabiles*).

38 The verb *μετακινοῦν* (to shift, to be dissuaded) appears nowhere else in the NT. Cf. Johannes Schneider, *TDNT* 3, 720.

39 Cf. Bornkamm, "Die Hoffnung" p. 58. Cf. also Eph 1:18 "the hope to which he has called you" (*ἡ ἐλπὶς τῆς κλήσεως αὐτοῦ*); 4:4 "to the one hope that belongs to your call" (*ἐν μιᾷ ἐλπίδι τῆς κλήσεως ὑμῶν*).

40 Cf. Gerhard Friedrich, *TDNT* 2, 732.

41 Cf. 1 Cor 1:23; 15:11f; Rom 10:8, 14f.

42 The Imperial (Koine) text adds the definite article *τῇ* to *κτίσει* ("the whole creation"). Cf. Mk 16:15 "the whole creation" (*πάσῃ τῇ κτίσει*).

43 The location where the preaching takes place is usually cited with the preposition *ἐν* (among, in). Cf. Gal 2:2 "among the Gentiles" (*ἐν τοῖς ἔθνεσιν*); Mt 24:14 "throughout the whole world" (*ἐν ὅλῃ τῇ*

every creature" (ἐν πάσῃ κτίσει cf. Mk 16:15f, see above p. 66, n. 45), then the meaning of "every creature" is all mankind[46] which is supposed to hear the proclaimed word.[47]

An additional relative clause notes that this message is the gospel taught by the apostle who is its minister. Instead of the "we" which appeared in the thanksgiving and intercession, there now appears an "I". This emphasizes that the reference is now to the office of the Apostle to the Nations which is *Paul's* commission alone. The characterization of the apostle as a "minister" (διάκονος)[48] is reminiscent of several comparable expressions in the chief Pauline letters. In the beginning of the letter to the Romans Paul presents himself as a slave of Christ Jesus and as "called to be an apostle, set apart for the gospel of God" (ἀπόστολος ἀφωρισμένος εἰς εὐαγγέλιον θεοῦ Rom 1:1). He continues by citing an old Jewish–Christian confession as the content of the gospel (Rom 1:3f). To the Corinthians Paul says that he and Apollos are "ministers" (διάκονοι) through whom they have come to faith—a statement that tells about the service which they, each in his own way, have provided to the community (1 Cor 3:5). As "ministers of God" (θεοῦ διάκονοι 1 Cor 6:4) or "ministers of Christ" (διάκονοι Χριστοῦ 2 Cor 11:23) the apostles are "ministers of a new covenant" (διάκονοι καινῆς διαθήκης 2 Cor 3:6). But neither the expression "minister of the gospel" (διάκονος τοῦ εὐαγγελίου) nor the characterization "minister of the church" (διάκονος τῆς ἐκκλησίας) occurs in the chief Pauline letters. By calling Paul "minister of the gospel" the apostolic office is emphasized as a basic function for the church.[49] Therefore "minister of the gospel" is interpreted by "minister of the church." At the beginning of the letter to the Romans, Paul was concerned to indicate the significance of the office of apostle by referring to the commission of proclaiming the gospel. Here the emphasis is that the gospel has binding validity because of its apostolic character.[50] This achieves a transition to the following section. The church lives from the apostolic word and is thereby bound to the apostolic office.[51]

οἰκουμένῃ); 26:13 "in the whole world" (ἐν ὅλῳ τῷ κόσμῳ). But cf. Mk 14:9 in Greek: εἰς ὅλον τὸν κόσμον (into the whole world). For further examples see Gerhard Friedrich, *TDNT* 3, 704f.

44 The expression "under heaven" (ὑπὸ τὸν οὐρανόν), which is otherwise not used in Paul, accords with OT language, cf. LXX Gen 1:9; 6:17; 7:19; LXX Exod 17:4; LXX Deut 2:25; 4:19; 9:14; 25:19; etc. Also, Bar 5:3; Ps Sol 2:32; Test Levi 18:4; Lk 17:24; Acts 2:5; 4:12.

45 The commission in Mk 16:15 reads "Go into all the world and preach the gospel to the whole creation" (πορευθέντες εἰς τὸν κόσμον ἅπαντα κηρύξατε τὸ εὐαγγέλιον πάσῃ τῇ κτίσει). Cf. also the hymn in 1 Tim 3:16, "preached among the nations, believed on in the world" (ἐκηρύχθη ἐν ἔθνεσιν, ἐπιστεύθη ἐν κόσμῳ).

46 The word κτίσις (creation, creature) in the sense of "mankind" corresponds to Jewish usage, as in *Ab.* 1:12, Hillel said, "Be . . . one that . . . loves the creatures" (הַבְּרִיּוֹת =mankind).

47 Concerning the concept of "mission" in Col, cf. Ferdinand Hahn, *Mission in the New Testament*, SBT 47 (London: S.C.M., 1965), 146–49. Also, Werner Bieder, *Das Mysterium Christi und die Mission: Ein Beitrag zur missionarischen Sakramentalgestalt der Kirche* (Zürich: 1964), esp. 44–53.

48 Cf. Hermann Wolfgang Beyer, *TDNT* 2, 89.

49 The alternate readings in the mss confirm that διάκονος (minister) was understood as a title of distinction, for ℵ* P have "herald and apostle" (κῆρυξ καὶ ἀπόστολος); A syh mg have "herald, apostle and minister" (κῆρυξ καὶ ἀπόστολος καὶ διάκονος); and 81 has "minister and apostle" (διάκονος καὶ ἀπόστολος).

50 Cf. 1 Tim 1:11 "in accordance with the glorious gospel of the blessed God with which I have been entrusted" (κατὰ τὸ εὐαγγέλιον τῆς δόξης τοῦ μακαρίου θεοῦ, ὃ ἐπιστεύθην ἐγώ); Eph 3:1f, "I, Paul, a prisoner for Christ Jesus on behalf of you Gentiles—assuming that you have heard of the stewardship of God's grace that was given to me for you . . ." (ἐγὼ Παῦλος ὁ δέσμιος τοῦ Χριστοῦ Ἰησοῦ ὑπὲρ ὑμῶν τῶν ἐθνῶν—εἴ γε ἠκούσατε τὴν οἰκονομίαν τῆς χάριτος τοῦ θεοῦ τῆς δοθείσης μοι εἰς ὑμᾶς).

51 Cf. Käsemann, *Essays*, 166f, ". . . the community is bound not only to its confession of faith, but, at the same time, to the apostolic office as guardian of the truth. The apostolate expounds the truth of the Gospel, as the confession of faith fixes it. We may justly doubt whether it is in fact Paul who is relating confession and apostolate in this way and thus making the apostolate in practice the explication of the confession. This is the voice of the sub-apostolic age."

1

Office and Commission of the Apostle

24 Now I rejoice in the sufferings for your
sake and in my flesh I complete what is
lacking in Christ's afflictions for the
sake of his body, that is, the church;
25/ of which I became a minister according to the divine office which was given
to me for you, in order to complete the
word of God, 26/ the mystery hidden
for ages and generations—but now
revealed to his saints, 27/ to whom God
wished to make known what is the
richness of the glory of this mystery
among the nations: Christ among you,
the hope of glory. 28/ Him we proclaim,
admonishing every man and teaching
every man, in all wisdom, that we may
present every man perfect in Christ.
29/ For this I also toil, working hard
according to his power which works
mightily in me.
1 For I want you to know how greatly I strive
for you and for those in Laodicea, and
for all who do not know me personally,
2/ that their hearts may be encouraged,
united in love and for all the riches of
the fullness of the insight, for the understanding of God's mystery, Christ, 3/ in
whom all the treasures of wisdom and
knowledge are hidden. 4/ I am saying
this in order that no one may delude you
by beguiling speech. 5/ For though I
am absent in body, I am yet with you in
the Spirit, rejoicing to see your order
and the firm stability of your faith in
Christ.

The comment that the apostle is the servant of the gospel (1:23) already produced the transition to this following section which now explains the significance of the apostle for the whole church and thus also for the community at Colossae. His suffering is beneficial for the body of Christ, i.e., the church, for which he performs the office given him by God (1:24f). The message entrusted to the office is the public proclamation of the now–revealed mystery, of Christ proclaimed among the nations (1:26f). Therefore the apostle seeks to admonish every man and to instruct him (1:28f); this catholic activity also applies, therefore, to the communities in Colossae and Laodicea (2:1–5). By virtue of his office, his authority is also valid for the community which does not know him; from this authority they receive instruction and strengthening in the faith.[1]

■ **24** "Now I rejoice" (Νῦν χαίρω)[2] are the words which begin this section.[3] The meaning is "now," when there is discussion of the universal saving act of reconciliation. All this discussion thus also pertains specifically to the community.[4] The suffering[5] of the apostle[6] by no means conflicts with the message which is to be pro-

1 A comparison with Romans suggests itself: Paul introduces himself to the community, personally unknown to him. However, while in the introduction to Romans the apostolic office is characterized by the commission to proclaim the gospel (Rom 1:1–7), Col certifies the gospel as the correct teaching by connecting it with the apostolic office. Cf. above, p. 67.

2 The words, "now I rejoice" (Νῦν χαίρω) indicate something of a new beginning, which admittedly has been prepared by the conclusion of 1:23. Cf. 2 Cor 7:9 and 1 Tim 1:12. The sharpness of the transition has been smoothed in D F G by placing a relative particle ὅς ("who") before Νῦν. This variant, however, is surely not to be regarded as the original text (thus Haupt and Lohmeyer, *ad loc.*) but rather

claimed to every creature under heaven (1:23). On the contrary, it fills the apostle with joy because he bears it "for your sake" (ὑπὲρ ὑμῶν). This phrase is more closely explained in the clarifying clause which follows the "and" (καί): "and in my flesh I complete what is lacking in Christ's afflictions for the sake of his body, that is, the church" (καὶ ἀνταναπληρῶ τὰ ὑστερήματα τῶν θλίψεων τοῦ Χριστοῦ ἐν τῇ σαρκί μου ὑπὲρ τοῦ σώματος αὐτοῦ, ὅ ἐστιν ἡ ἐκκλησία).

The expression, "what is lacking in Christ's afflictions" (τὰ ὑστερήματα τῶν θλίψεων τοῦ Χριστοῦ)[7] certainly cannot be taken to mean that there still might be something lacking in the vicarious sufferings of Christ which must be supplied by the apostle.[8] Paul and all other witnesses in the New Testament unanimously agree that the reconciliation was truly and validly accomplished in the death of Christ, and that no need exists for any supplementation.[9] Likewise, Col teaches that Christ removed all sins in his death and resurrection and that for the sake of his death on the cross all trespasses are forgiven (2:13f).[10] Again, the concept "Christ's afflictions" cannot describe a mystical union with Christ's passion which binds Christ and the community together so that unity with the Lord allows the whole body of Christ to benefit from the sufferings which they experienced.[11] Mysticism is not bound by the measure of time and it permits the mystic to become absorbed into his object. The apostle, however, understands himself as a "servant of Christ" (δοῦλος Χριστοῦ), as an obedient servant who must render service to his Lord. It also would remain incomprehensible how—in view of such an intimate communion of suffering—there could still be mention of a measure of afflictions which lacked something for its fulfillment.[12] What is indicated by this phrase is neither a mystical union of suffering nor a restriction

as an expansion due to dittography (διάκονος:ὅς).

3 Concerning 1:24, cf. W. R. G. Moir, "Colossians I.24" *ExpT* 42 (1930–31): 479f; Josef Schmid, "Kol. 1,24" *BZ* 21 (1933): 330–44; Gerhard Kittel, "Kol. 1,24" *ZSTh* 18 (1941): 186–91; B. N. Wambacq, "'Adimpleo ea quae desunt passionum Christi in carne mea . . .' (Col 1,24)" *VD* 27 (1949): 17–22; Maurice Carrez, "Souffrance et gloire dans les épîtres pauliniennes: Contribution à l'exégèse de Col. 1,24–27" *RHPR* 31 (1951): 343–53; M. Schmid, *Die Leidensaussage in Kol 1,24*, Unpub. Diss. (Vienna: 1956); Jacob Kremer, *Was an den Leiden Christi noch mangelt: Eine interpretationsgeschichtliche und exegetische Untersuchung zu Kol. 1,24b*, BBB 12 (Bonn: 1956); G. Le Grelle, "La plénitude de la parole dans la pauvreté de la chair d'après Col. I.24" *Nouvelle Revue Théologique* 81 (1959): 232–50; Michel Bouttier, "Remarques sur la conscience Apostolique de St. Paul" in *OIKONOMIA—Heilsgeschichte als Thema der Theologie, Festschrift für Oscar Cullmann* (Hamburg: 1967), 100–08.

4 The "now" (νῦν) does not refer to the time of Paul's imprisonment which does not appear until 4:3. Rather, it is to be explained from the immediate context.

5 The "sufferings" (παθήματα) of the apostle are also mentioned in 2 Cor 1:4–7 and Phil 3:10. Cf. Wilhelm Michaelis, *TDNT* 5, 930–35; also E. Kamlah, "Wie beurteilt Paulus sein Leiden? Ein Beitrag zur Untersuchung seiner Denkstruktur" *ZNW* 54 (1963): 217–32.

6 The mss. ℵ³ 81 al syʰ add "my" (μου) to "in [the] sufferings" (ἐν τοῖς παθήμασιν). Cf. *RSV*.

7 For the history of exegesis on this phrase, cf. the careful presentation in Kremer, *Leiden Christi*, 5–154.

8 *Contra* Hans Windisch, *Paulus und Christus: Ein biblisch–religionsgeschichtlicher Vergleich*, UNT 24 (Leipzig: 1934), 236–50. He remarks on Col 1:24 that Paul carried away the sufferings "which Christ could not carry away completely" (p. 244).

9 Cf. Lohse, *Märtyrer und Gottesknecht*, 200–03.

10 Staab, *ad loc.*, correctly points out that Christ's afflictions (θλίψεις τοῦ Χριστοῦ) cannot refer to the redemptive act of Christ, because for this in the Pauline letters the concepts "blood," "cross," "death," etc. are used; "however, the word 'afflictions' (θλίψεις) or the synonymous 'sufferings' (παθήματα cf. 2 Cor 1:5; Phil 3:10)" are never used to refer to the act of redemption.

11 Those interpreting this as a union with Christ's passion are Adolf Deissmann, *Paul: A Study in Social and Religious History*, tr. William E. Wilson (London: Hodder & Stoughton, Ltd, 1926), 162f, 181f, 202, *passim*; Otto Schmitz, *Die Christus–Gemeinschaft des Paulus im Lichte seines Genetivgebrauchs*, NTF 1, 2 (Gütersloh: 1924), 190–96; Johannes Schneider, *Die Passionsmystik des Paulus: Ihr Wesen, ihr Hintergrund und ihre Nachwirkungen*, UNT 15 (Leipzig: 1929). A more cautious position here is taken by Dibelius–Greeven, *ad loc.*

12 Cf. Lohmeyer, *ad loc.*; "Above all, the expression 'what is lacking in Christ's sufferings' remains unexplained, if one presupposes such a mysticism of suffering. In a 'mystical suffering in accordance

of the salvific significance of Christ's death.[13] What does, however, provide the background for the phrase "Christ's afflictions" (which appears only here in the New Testament) is the apocalyptic conception of the afflictions of the end time, the woes of the Messiah.[14]

Jewish apocalyptic often pictured the catastrophes and sufferings which must break in upon the earth according to God's definite design, and which must even fall upon believers. All this must transpire before God's new world dawns.[15] War, want, and plagues will befall mankind; the earth will withhold its produce, women will no longer bear children; the cosmic order will be so disturbed that the constellations will no longer follow their regular paths; and the pious shall experience persecution and bitter suffering. When, however, these horrors reach a zenith, the turn of events will come. For this reason the sufferings in the last days are also called woes of the Messiah, because they immediately precede the advent of the Anointed Ruler.[16] The Christian community's expectations for the end time were formed from these apocalyptic conceptions of Judaism. God has determined the measure and extent of these afflictions and thereby has limited them (Mk 13:19f, 24; par.). The final horrors can be compared with the labor pains which come upon a woman in childbirth (Mk 13:8; par.), because the coming turn of events is announced by pain and suffering.

In this context of the primitive Christian expectation of the end, the meaning of the apocalyptic concept of messianic woes has now been modified. That is, the hope of believers is not for an unknown envoy from God; rather, the Christ who is to appear as the Son of Man on the clouds of heaven is already known to the community as the crucified and risen Lord. The sorrows which must be endured in the last troubled times are understood as the forerunners of his glorious appearance for judgment over the world and for the liberation of his own (Mk 13:5–27; par.). Since entrance into the "kingdom of God" (*βασιλεία τοῦ θεοῦ*) is gained only through many "tribulations" (*θλίψεις* Acts 14:22),[17] these "tribulations" are characteristic of the situation of the community (1 Thess 3:3, 7). The believers can rejoice "in the tribulations" (*ἐν ταῖς θλίψεσιν* Rom 5:3), for no "tribulation" can separate them from the love of God in Christ Jesus (Rom 8:38f). Although the apostle must continually suffer "tribulations,"[18] he receives the wonderful strength of divine comfort exactly in the midst of tribulations: "in order that you receive comfort" (*ὑπὲρ τῆς ὑμῶν παρακλήσεως* 2 Cor 1:4–7).

The sufferings of the apostle which are mentioned in Col are far more significant than the "sufferings" (*παθήματα*) which all Christians share. In his sufferings, the apostle performs a vicarious service (cf. also 2 Cor 1:6), completing "what is lacking in Christ's afflictions" (*τὰ ὑστερήματα τῶν θλίψεων τοῦ Χριστοῦ*).[19] The

---

with Christ' either the entire suffering of Christ is present and 'what is lacking' is never perceptible, or else the personal suffering of faith remains separate from the exemplary sufferings of Christ. In the latter case the suffering would remain intrinsically incomplete as long as death or the parousia does not forbearingly adjust all these earthly deficiencies. And certainly one could not speak of 'completing' (the sufferings)". For a criticism of the mystical interpretation, cf. also Percy, *Probleme*, 128–34.

13 The attempt to explain the expression "Christ's suffering" from Gnostic presuppositions is beside the point. Walter Schmithals, *Die Gnosis in Korinth*, FRLANT 66 (Göttingen: ²1965), p. 63, maintains that in Christian–Gnostic circles the teaching was propounded "that the redemptive sufferings of Christ are only complete when the individual bearers of souls have suffered just as the Crucified One." Against this background Col 1:24 is then to be understood: "Paul's 'theology of suffering' is indeed a demythologized but clearly identifiable remnant of this basic mythical view." cf. also *idem*, *Das kirchliche Apostelamt: Eine historische Untersuchung*, FRLANT 79 (Göttingen: 1961), 39f, 200.

14 In the following verses there are further concepts which also have an apocalyptic source: "mystery — hidden / but now revealed" (*μυστήριον—ἀποκεκρυμμένον/νῦν δὲ ἐφανερώθη* v 26), "the riches of the glory of this mystery" (*τὸ πλοῦτος τῆς δόξης τοῦ μυστηρίου τούτου* v 27); "God's mystery" (*μυστήριον τοῦ θεοῦ* 2:2); "in whom all the treasures of wisdom and knowledge are hidden" (*ἐν ᾧ πάντες οἱ θησαυροὶ τῆς σοφίας καὶ γνώσεως ἀπόκρυφοι* 3:3). Cf. Lohse, "Christusherrschaft und Kirche," 212f.

15 Billerbeck 4, 977–86 has a wealth of examples.

16 Concerning the term "the travail of the Messiah" (חֶבְלוֹ שֶׁל מָשִׁיחַ), cf. *Mek. Ex* 16:25 (58b); 16:29 (59a); *b Shab* 118a; *b Pes* 118a; etc. Cf. Billerbeck 1, 950.

17 For the concept *θλῖψις* (tribulation), cf. Heinrich Schlier, *TDNT* 3, 139–48.

18 2 Cor 1:4, 8; 2:4; 4:17; 6:4; 7:4; 8:2, 13; Phil 1:17; 4:14.

19 Wilhelm Michaelis, *TDNT* 5, 933, wants to deny the presence of the idea of vicarious suffering in Col

word ὑστέρημα means what is lacking, a deficiency. This can express the absence of a person to whom one is consciously attached (1 Cor 16:17; Phil 2:30). However, it can also be a deficiency regarding a specific situation, as in 1 Thess 3:10, "what is lacking in your faith" (τὰ ὑστερήματα τῆς πίστεως ὑμῶν).[20] The concept of a definite measure for the last days[21] determines the phrase "what is lacking in Christ's afflictions."[22] Just as God has set a definite measure in time (cf. 4 Ezra 4:36f; Gal 4:4) and has determined the limitation of the tribulations at the end (cf. Mk 13:5–27; par.), so he has also decreed a definite measure for the sufferings which the righteous and the martyrs must endure (1 En 47:1–4; 2 Bar 30:2).[23] When this has been completed, the end is at hand; then the old aeon passes away and the wonderful new world dawns. For the present, however, this is not the case; something is still lacking in "Christ's afflictions." This lack is what the apostle through his sufferings is completing. The verb ἀνταναπληροῦν (to complete) occurs in the New Testament only in this passage;[24] it emphasizes that what is now being completed is a compensation which will be substituted for what is lacking.[25] The apostle, through the sufferings which he painfully bears in his own flesh,[26] contributes to foreshortening the eschatological afflictions. This, in turn, brings the dawning of the future glory all the closer.[27]

In the context of the epistle to the Colossians the afflictions of Christ are no longer understood as a part of the eager, imminent expectation of the end. The outlook

1:24; he refers to 2 Cor 1:6. However, the phrase "for your sake" (ὑπὲρ ὑμῶν) in Col 1:24 cannot be equated with "for your comfort" (ὑπὲρ τῆς ὑμῶν παρακλήσεως) of 2 Cor 1:6. It is also not the case that Col speaks of necessary sufferings because Jesus informed his disciples that persecution would have to come. *Contra* Kittel, "Kol 1,24" pp. 189f, who supposes that Paul was alluding to logia such as Mt 5:11; 10:22, 24ff; Jn 15:18ff.

20 Cf. also 2 Cor 8:14; 9:12; 11:9. Further examples in Kremer, *Leiden Christi*, 164–69.

21 The use of the definite article τά discloses that the phrase "what is lacking in Christ's afflictions" was taken to be familiar.

22 Moule, *ad loc.*, makes reference to the fact that in Gnosticism the word ὑστέρημα (deficiency) was the counter-concept to πλήρωμα (fullness). The Valentinians opposed πλήρωμα (fullness) with κένωμα (emptiness), cf. Epiphanius, *Haer.* 31.16.1. Yet for understanding the concept of "deficiency" in this passage, a Gnostic background is not relevant. As explained above, the statement of this verse is much better understood on the basis of apocalyptic presuppositions. For the concept "pleroma," cf. above, pp. 57f.

23 Cf. Lohse, *Märtyrer und Gottesknecht*, 197, n. 9.

24 Cf. Gerhard Delling, *TDNT* 6, 307. Paul indeed uses ἀναπληροῦν (to make complete, replace) in 1 Cor 16:17; Phil 2:30; etc.; or also προσαναπληροῦν (to supply) in 2 Cor 9:12; 11:9. But he never uses ἀνταναπληροῦν (to complete). Heinrich Julius Holtzmann, *Kritik der Epheser- und Kolosserbriefe* (Leipzig: 1872), p. 21, noted concerning this matter, "No one who is well versed in the world of Pauline ideas can read through 1:24 without taking offense (at such terms)" [Trans.].

25 Cf. Demosthenes, *Or.* 14.17. In dividing up the tax boards composed of sixty men each into five groups of twelve men each, the poorest men are to be balanced with the wealthy, i.e., so that the poor "fill up" (ἀνταναπληροῦντας) the measure of the wealthy. Dio Cassius, 44.48.2 states that no titles were spared Caesar. What any single title lacked as a complete expression of honor and authority was supplied (ἀνταναπληρωθῇ) by what the others contributed for mutual completion. Apollonius Dyscolus, *De syntaxi* 1.19 and 2.44 states that pronouns are responsible for completing (ἀνταναπληροῦσα or ἀνταναπληροῦσαι) that which it is impossible for the substantive to do. Concerning this concept, cf. further Gerhard Delling, *TDNT* 6, 307; also Kremer, *Leiden Christi*, 156–63. The supposition "that Paul probably seized upon and transformed one of the opponent's slogans with this compounding of πληροῦν (to make full)" (Kremer, p. 162) has no basis in the text.

26 Eduard Schweizer, *TWNT* 7, 136, states that σάρξ (flesh) here "refers to the corporeal reality of the apostle, beset with tribulations." Cf. "on my body" (ἐν τῷ σώματί μου Gal 6:17; 2 Cor 4:10).

27 Kremer, *Leiden Christi*, 190–95, explains this differently; he agrees with the explanation of Chrysostom: since the apostle, as the representative of Christ, stands in his stead, he can complete in his flesh whatever is still lacking of "Christ's afflictions." For a critique of this position, cf. also the review by Ernst Käsemann, *ThLZ* 82 (1957): 694f.

is not toward the future but rather to the present or to the past[28] which is characterized by the apostle's service of founding churches. The image of the apostle which was formed by the second Christian generation was essentially characterized by the exhibition of his sufferings,[29] much like the image which post-biblical Judaism developed of the prophets. Without exception they were pictured as persecuted and suffering, and martyrdom was the very reason they were raised to their position of honor.[30] According to Acts 9:16 it has been decreed from the beginning that Saul/Paul must suffer for the name of Christ. In Eph 3:1 Paul is called a prisoner of Christ Jesus on behalf of the Gentiles.[31] The Pastorals are presented as the testament which the imprisoned apostle entrusts to the church before his end (2 Tim 1:8, 16f; 2:9). Exactly in his sufferings did the apostle perform his office for the whole church. This particular concept is also that which matters for Col. The sufferings of the apostle belong to the unique dignity of his office. For this reason the emphatically contrasting "I" distinguishes Paul from all other members of the community.[32] He acts as a "minister of the gospel" (**διάκονος τοῦ εὐαγγελίου**) and thereby as a "minister of the church" (**διάκονος τῆς ἐκκλησίας**) in that he completes what is lacking of Christ's afflictions. The definition by which the body, over which Christ is the head, was interpreted as the worldwide "church" (**ἐκκλησία** 1:18) is repeated in this context: "for the sake of his body, that is, the church" (**ὑπὲρ τοῦ σώματος αὐτοῦ, ὅ ἐστιν ἡ ἐκκλησία**).

■ **25** Since this unique office has been entrusted to the apostle by God himself, his service is completely determined by this commission as its norm. Paul repeatedly speaks of the divine "grace" (**χάρις**) which has been granted to him.[33] It is God's grace that called him and shows itself to be active in his service. Concerning the office which was given him, Paul can also state that "I have been entrusted with an office" (**οἰκονομίαν πεπίστευμαι** 1 Cor 9:17).[34] He is not able to withdraw from it, but must fulfill it obediently; thus he desires that "this is how one should regard us, as servants of Christ and *stewards* of the mysteries of God" (**Οὕτως ἡμᾶς λογιζέσθω ἄνθρωπος ὡς ὑπηρέτας Χριστοῦ καὶ οἰκονόμους μυστηρίων θεοῦ** 1 Cor 4:1). It can naturally be expected of one who has been entrusted with the execution of an office (cf. Lk 16:2) "that he be found trustworthy" (**ἵνα πιστὸς εὑρηθῇ** 1 Cor 4:2).[35] The passage in Col does not refer to "the *grace* that was given me" (**τὴν χάριν τὴν δοθεῖσάν μοι** Gal 2:9). Rather the word **οἰκονομία** (commission or office)[36] is used instead of the word "grace" (**χάρις**) to describe the office of the apostle.[37] Of course, the concern is only with Paul's office, and no indication exists of a mention of the rest of the apostles, neither Peter nor the Twelve. Paul is, as *the* Apostle to the nations, the one and only Apostle. Thus

---

28 This also holds true for the apocalyptic terminology of the following verses. Cf. above, p. 70, n. 14, and Lohse, "Christusherrschaft und Kirche," 212f.

29 Cf. Lohse, "Christusherrschaft und Kirche," 213f.

30 Cf. H. A. Fischel, "Martyr und Prophet" *JQR* 37 (1946–47): 265–80; 363–86. Also Hans Joachim Schoeps, "Die jüdischen Prophetenmorde" in *Aus frühchristlicher Zeit: Religionsgeschichtliche Untersuchungen* (Tübingen: 1950), 126–43; and Lohse, *Märtyrer und Gottesknecht*, p. 66, n. 1.

31 Cf. further Eph 3:13, "over my afflictions for your sake" (*ἐν ταῖς θλίψεσίν μου ὑπὲρ ὑμῶν*). Also, G. H. P. Thompson, "Ephesians III.13 and 2 Timothy II.10 in the Light of Colossians I.24" *ExpT* 71 (1959–60): 187–89.

32 Cf. Lohmeyer, *ad loc.*; Käsemann, *ThLZ* 82 (1957), 695.

33 Cf. Gal 2:9; 1 Cor 3:10; 15:10; Rom 1:5; 12:3, 6; 15:15.

34 For the concept *οἰκονομία* cf. Otto Michel, *TDNT* 5, 151–53; and John Reumann, "OIKONOMIA = "Covenant"–Terms for *Heilsgeschichte* in Early Christian Usage," *Nov Test* 3 (1959): 282–92; *idem*, "*Οἰκονομία* as 'Ethical Accommodation' in the Fathers, and its Pagan Backgrounds," Studia Patristica, ed. F. L. Cross, TU 78 (Berlin: 1961), 370–79; *idem*, "OIKONOMIA-Terms in Paul in Comparison with Lucan *Heilsgeschichte*" *NTS* 13 (1966–67): 147–67.

35 Cf. John Reumann, " 'Stewards of God'—Pre-Christian Religious Application of OIKONOMOΣ in Greek" *JBL* 77 (1958): 339–49.

36 Concerning the connection of the norm with a qualifying genetive *οἰκονομία τοῦ θεοῦ* ("office of God" = divine office), cf. 1 Cor 15:10, *ἡ χάρις τοῦ θεοῦ* (the grace of God) and Eph 3:7, *τῆς χάριτος τοῦ θεοῦ τῆς δοθείσης μοι* (of God's grace which was given me).

37 In contrast Eph uses the word *οἰκονομία* to mean God's plan for the history of salvation which is to be completed in the fullness of time. *εἰς οἰκονομίαν τοῦ πληρώματος τῶν καιρῶν* (as a plan for the fullness of time Eph 1:10); *τίς ἡ οἰκονομία τοῦ μυστηρίου τοῦ ἀποκεκρυμμένου ἀπὸ τῶν αἰώνων ἐν τῷ θεῷ* (what is the plan of the mystery hidden for ages in God 3:9). The office of the apostle is also provided for in this divine plan of salvation: *τὴν οἰκονομίαν*

the church drawn from many nations is bound to that apostolic gospel which has been proclaimed to it by Paul and the co-workers installed by him.[38]

It is the commission of his office "to complete the word of God" (πληρῶσαι τὸν λόγον τοῦ θεοῦ). Just as a previously determined measure must be filled up to its limit, so also the apostle has to accomplish God's will and command.[39] Looking back upon his missionary work, Paul can say, "from Jerusalem and as far round as Illyricum I have brought (the preaching of) the gospel of Christ to completion" (ἀπὸ Ἰερουσαλὴμ καὶ κύκλῳ μέχρι τοῦ Ἰλλυρικοῦ πεπληρωκέναι τὸ εὐαγγέλιον τοῦ Χριστοῦ Rom 15:19). The word of God is brought to completion when it has been broadcast everywhere and proclaimed to every creature under the heaven (cf. v 23).[40] The commission to make the word of truth heard in an effective way has directed the apostle to the community in Colossae and assigned the community to him.

■ **26** The message with which the apostle was commissioned is more precisely designated as the "mystery" (μυστήριον). In Greek this sentence is broken off suddenly after a participial phrase; the words νῦν δὲ ἐφανερώθη (but now it is revealed) mark the beginning of a new sentence, and it is not until v 27 that the content of the mystery is stated: Christ proclaimed among the nations. As the structure of the sentence already shows, v 26 depends upon a traditional formulation for which there are several parallels in primitive Christian preaching: the mystery which was once hidden is now made manifest.[41] That which was present in God's decree from eternity and which neither angels nor men could ascertain is now proclaimed publicly (1 Cor 2:7f). God is praised for this "revelation" (ἀποκάλυψις) which is described as "the mystery which was kept secret for long ages but now is disclosed and through the prophetic writings is made known to all nations, according to the command of the eternal God to bring about obedience to the faith" (μυστηρίου χρόνοις αἰωνίοις σεσιγημένου,

τῆς χάριτος τοῦ θεοῦ τῆς δοθείσης μοι εἰς ὑμᾶς (the plan of God's grace that was given to me for you 3:2). Since χάρις (grace) is used here for the office of the apostle, it can be suggested that οἰκονομία should be understood in all three passages of Eph in the sense of the divine plan of salvation which is being realized. Cf. Schlier, *Epheser*, 147f on Eph 3:2; and Reumann, "OIKONOMIA-Terms," 164f. This understanding may not, however, be transferred from Eph to Col, *contra* Lohmeyer, *ad loc.*, "Thus it is God's plan of salvation which leads the history of the world from its very beginning to its predetermined goal. In order to accomplish this divine plan Paul has been given the office of 'ministry' " [Trans.]. Reumann, "OIKONOMIA-Terms," 162f, is inclined to adopt both, the meaning of "office" as well as a reference to the divine plan of salvation as being implied in the use of οἰκονομία in Col 1:25. In Reumann's opinion what is meant is "God's revealed plan or his plan and the execution thereof," because "Paul says, I am a minister 'according to the plan of God, the execution of which has been conferred upon me in that which concerns you' " (p. 163).

38 The "for you" (εἰς ὑμᾶς) must be connected with the preceding sentence. Cf. Eph 3:2 "the stewardship of God's grace that was given to me for you" (τὴν οἰκονομίαν τῆς χάριτος τοῦ θεοῦ τῆς δοθείσης μοι εἰς ὑμᾶς). Dibelius-Greeven, *ad loc.*, take "for you" to apply to what follows, on the grounds that the following verb πληρῶσαι (to complete) has extremely little effect if it is not connected with "for you." Comparable phrases (Rom 15:19 and the examples cited in the next following footnote) do not, however, require this connection.

39 Cf. Col 4:17, "take care that you fulfil the ministry which you have received in the Lord" (βλέπε τὴν διακονίαν ἣν παρέλαβες ἐν κυρίῳ, ἵνα αὐτὴν πληροῖς). Rev 3:2, "for I have not found your works perfect (fulfilled) in the sight of my God" (οὐ γὰρ εὕρηκά σου ἔργα πεπληρωμένα ἐνώπιον τοῦ θεοῦ μου). For another use, cf. Act 12:25, "they had fulfilled their mission" (πληρώσαντες τὴν διακονίαν). Cf. further, Acts 13:25; 14:26; etc. This expression occurs very often for the fulfilling of a promise announced in Scripture, e.g. Mk 14:49, par; Mt 1:22, 2:15, 13:35, 21:4, etc.; Lk 4:21, 24:44, etc.; Jn 13:18; 17:12; 19:24, 36. For further examples see Gerhard Delling, *TDNT* 6, 286–89.

40 Cf. Ragnar Asting, *Die Verkündigung des Wortes im Urchristentum* (Stuttgart: 1939), p. 138.

41 Cf. Dahl, "Formgeschtl. Beobachtungen," 41f. Dahl characterizes this description of the mystery as a revelation schema whose thematic phrases are "present from eternity"—"now revealed." Cf. also Bultmann, *Theology*, par. 10, sec. 4 (ET, 1, 105f). Dieter Lührmann, *Das Offenbarungsverständnis bei Paulus und in paulinischen Gemeinden*, WMANT 16 (Neukirchen: 1965), 113–40. Starting points for the development of this revelation schema can be recognized in 1 Cor 2:6–16. Clear expressions of it are to be found, however, in liturgical formulations such as appear in Rom 16:25–27 and in the deutero-Pauline letters. Cf. Conzelmann, *Outline*, 88.

φανερωθέντος δὲ νῦν διά τε γραφῶν προφητικῶν κατ' ἐπιταγὴν τοῦ αἰωνίου θεοῦ εἰς ὑπακοὴν πίστεως εἰς πάντα τὰ ἔθνη γνωρισθέντος Rom 16:25f).[42] Since the revelation concerns the whole world, the public announcement of the mystery is carried out in the proclamation of the good news to all nations (1 Tim 3:16).[43]

The concepts *μυστήριον* (mystery), *ἀποκρύπτειν* (to conceal, hide), *φανεροῦν* (to reveal, make known) have been taken into the primitive Christian language of preaching from apocalyptic tradition. The word *μυστήριον* (mystery)[44] corresponds to the Hebrew רָז (secret) which designates the secret of God's eschatological decree.[45] God discloses to the seers "what things must come to pass in the latter days" (*ὅσα δεῖ γενέσθαι ἐπ' ἐσχάτων τῶν ἡμερῶν*), for he alone is "he that reveals mysteries" (*ὁ ἀποκαλύπτων μυστήρια* LXX Dan 2:28f). His mysteries are "deep . . . and innumerable" (1 En 63:3), yet he grants to the pious a view of his plan. He makes known to them "the mystery of the times" and shows them "the advent of the periods" (2 Bar 81:4) as well as the "mysteries of the times" and "the end of the hours" (2 Esdr 14:5). According to the writing of Qumran, such a revelation was granted to the Teacher of Righteousness, for to him "God made known all the mysteries of the words of His servants, the prophets" (1 QpHab VII.4f).[46] Thus a prayer is thankfully raised to God, "You have given me to know your marvelous mysteries" (1 QH IV.27f).[47]

The primitive Christian proclamation gave witness to the revelation of a mystery that does not concern a future event which lies hidden in God's plan, but rather an act of God which has already become a reality. What has been kept secret for endless ages has now been revealed and is broadcast among all nations in the preached word (Rom 16:25f). The "mystery" was "hidden for ages and generations" (*ἀποκεκρυμμένον ἀπὸ τῶν αἰώνων καὶ ἀπὸ τῶν γενεῶν*). If the word *ἀπό* is translated as "from," the "ages" (*αἰῶνες*) and "generations" (*γενεαί*) must be taken to be powers and principalities to whom any insight into the mystery was denied.[48] It is, however, much more natural to take *ἀπό* in a temporal meaning.[49] This is also suggested by the following "but now" (*νῦν δέ*) which emphasizes the turn of events that has come about. That which was hidden from previous ages and generations[50] has now been disclosed[51] (cf. Eph 3:4f, 9f).[52] The saints who are mentioned as the recipi-

42 Col makes use of a revelation schema which had been developed in the tradition, so there is no need to suppose literary dependence on Rom 16:25–27, as does Ed Parish Sanders in "Literary Dependence in Colossians," *JBL* 85 (1966): 39f.

43 Cf. further Eph 3:4f, 9f; 2 Tim 1:9; Tit 1:2f; 1 Pt 1:20.

44 For the concept *μυστήριον* cf. Günther Bornkamm, *TDNT* 4, 802–28. Also, Arthur Darby Nock, " 'Mysterion'," *Harvard Studies in Classical Philology* 60 (1952): 201–04; E. Vogt, " 'Mysteria' in textibus Qumrān" *Biblica* 37 (1956): 247–57; B. Rigaux, "Révélation des Mystères et Perfection à Qumrân et dans le Nouveau Testament," *NTS* 4 (1957–58): 237–62; Raymond E. Brown, "The Semitic Background of the New Testament *mysterion*," *Biblica* 39 (1958): 426–48; 40 (1959): 70–87; reprinted in *The Semitic Background of the Term "Mystery" in the New Testament*, Facet Books, Biblical Series 21, John Reumann, ed. (Philadelphia: Fortress Press, 1968), 30–69; Helmut Krämer, "Zur Wortbedeutung 'Mysteria'," *Wort und Dienst*, NF 6 (1959), 121–25; J. Coppens, "Le 'mystère' dans la théologie paulinienne et ses parallèles qumrâniennes," *Littérature et Théologie Pauliniennes*, in Recherches Bibliques 5 (1960), 142–65.

45 In the mystery cults, to which Lührmann, *Offenbarungsverständnis*, 126–31, refers for comparison, the plural form *τὰ μυστήρια* is used consistently. Cf. Günther Bornkamm, *TDNT* 4, 803. In contrast to the apocalyptic texts, in which the plural form likewise appears most often, the examples from the mystery cults show no eschatological dimension of the concept of the "mystery" which must be presupposed in the revelation–schema. Concerning the contacts and essential differences between the apocalyptic language and that of the mystery cults and Gnosticism, cf. Bornkamm, *TDNT* 4, 816.

46 1 QpHab VII.4f כול רזי דברי עבדיו הנבאים.

47 1 QH IV.27f ברזי פלאכה. Cf. also 1 QH I.21.

48 Thus Dibelius–Greeven, *ad loc.*, "The *αἰῶνες* (ages) and *γενεαί* (generations) are then the *ἄρχοντες τοῦ αἰῶνος τούτου* (rulers of this age) from 1 Cor 2:7f, and the struggle in Colossae was about their importance."

49 Cf. 1 Cor 2:7 "before the ages" (*πρὸ τῶν αἰώνων*); Rom 16:25 "long ages" (*χρονοῖς αἰωνίοις*); also further Acts 3:21, 15:18 "from of old" (*ἀπ' αἰῶνος*); Mt 13:25, 25:34 "from the foundation of the world" (*ἀπὸ καταβολῆς κόσμου*).

50 Cf. 2 Esdr 14:5, "the secrets of the times"; 2 Bar 81:4, "the secrets of the times and the advent of the seasons"; 1 En 49:2, "all the secrets of righteousness"; 63:3, "from generation to generation." Cf.

ents of the revelation are neither angels,[53] nor a limited circle of charismatics,[54] but rather the believers,[55] the "saints . . . the faithful brothers in Christ" (ἅγιοι καὶ πιστοὶ ἀδελφοὶ ἐν Χριστῷ 1:2), who are "God's chosen ones, holy and beloved" (ἐκλεκτοὶ τοῦ θεοῦ ἅγιοι καὶ ἠγαπημένοι 3:12).[56] To them the "mystery" has been given in the word of truth. This mystery is not just shared by a few selected believers, but rather its content is made known in the apostolic proclamation in which the word is made complete (1:25) and Christ is preached among the nations (1:27).[57]

■ **27** God wanted to make known the mystery to the saints. The verb "to reveal" (φανεροῦν v 26; Rom 16:25f) is resumed in this verse by "to make known" (γνωρίζειν).[58] God wanted to make known "the richness of the glory[59] of this[60] mystery" (τὸ πλοῦτος τῆς δόξης τοῦ μυστηρίου τούτου).[61] The words "richness" (πλοῦτος) and "glory" (δόξα) make reference to the immense greatness of the "mystery."[62] But in what does the magnificent richness of the mystery consist, which God wanted to make known and have proclaimed among the nations[63] in the "word of God" (λόγος τοῦ θεοῦ)? The content of the "mystery" is stated succinctly as

also 1 En 84:2; 2 Bar 48:2f; 54:1, "You hasten the beginnings of the times, and you alone know the end of the seasons."

51 Cf. 1 En 46:3, "This is the Son of Man . . . who reveals all the treasures of that which is hidden." Cf. also 1 En 38:3; 48:7; 2 Esdr 12:39; etc.

52 Dahl, "Formgeschichtl. Beobachtungen," p. 5, appropriately emphasizes that the transition to a finite verb still testifies to a firm schema that was utilized here.

53 Thus Lohmeyer, *ad loc.*, with reference to 1 Thess 3:13 and 2 Thess 1:10. Likewise, Werner Bieder, *Der Kolosserbrief* in: Prophezei (Zürich: 1943), *ad loc.*, "superterrestrial creatures who now receive word of the mystery of God in Christ."

54 Thus Käsemann, *Leib Christi*, 146, n. 5, "The saints in Col 1:26 are charismatics, not merely believers." Thus also Ragnar Asting, *Die Heiligkeit im Urchristentum*, FRLANT 46 (Göttingen: 1930), 176f. Such a delimitation, however, is proposed only in the epistle to the Ephesians which defines the circle of saints as the apostles and thus narrowly restricts it (Eph 3:5). Bieder, *Mysterium Christi*, 46, wants to understand the saints as missionaries of Jewish origin sent to the Gentiles. Yet these assumptions are made without anything to go on in the text.

55 Dibelius–Greeven, *ad loc.*, foregoes a more exact definition, because the solemnity of the expression, colored by OT imagery, does not seem to allow such a subtle distinction between preachers of the gospel and all Christians. "It is sufficient to know that God has disclosed this mystery to his church." [Trans.].

56 Correctly noted by Günther Bornkamm, *TDNT* 4, 821; Hans Conzelmann, in Hermann W. Beyer, Paul Althaus, Hans Conzelmann, Gerhard Friedrich, Albrecht Oepke, *Die kleineren Briefe des Apostels Paulus*, NTD 8 (Göttingen: [10]1965), *ad loc.*; Lührmann, *Offenbarungsverständnis*, 132.

57 Cf. Rom 16:25f, εὐαγγέλιον—κήρυγμα (gospel—preaching); φανεροῦν—γνωρίζειν (to disclose—to make known). Also, Eph 3:8 εὐαγγελίζεσθαι (to preach).

58 Cf. Rom 16:26; Eph 1:9; 3:5, 10; 6:19. Also, cf. Rudolf Bultmann, *TDNT* 1, 718.

59 The ms p^{46} omits "of the glory" (τῆς δόξης).

60 Instead of "this" (τούτου) D* G it Ambst have "of God" (τοῦ θεοῦ), to read "the mystery of God." The ms ℵ* has only "the" (τοῦ).

61 Cf. Rom 9:23, "in order that he make known the riches of his glory" (ἵνα γνωρίσῃ τὸν πλοῦτον τῆς δόξης αὐτοῦ). Traditional phrases are used in Col 1:24 as well as in Rom 9:23 and thus it is not necessary to conjecture with Percy, *Probleme*, 50, that "here one could just possibly have to reckon with literary influence from the passage in Romans." Cf. also Sanders, "Literary Dependence," 39f.

62 Cf. Rom 9:23; Phil 4:19; Eph 1:18; 3:16; Rev 5:12. The word πλοῦτος (richness) is neuter here as in 2:2. The "richness" and "glory" of God are often mentioned together in the OT: cf. LXX Gen 31:16; 3 Kg 3:13; 1 Chr 29:28; Esth 1:4; 10:2; Ps 111:3; Pr 3:16; 8:18; 22:4; Sir 24:17; Ps Sol 1:4. Cf. Lohmeyer, *ad loc.*

63 The phrase ἐν τοῖς ἔθνεσιν means "among the nations." There is no emphasis upon the fact that the word is now *also* proclaimed to the *Gentiles*. This thought is, however, developed in Eph, where the mystery which is now disclosed consists of the Gentiles being "fellow heirs, members of the same body, and partakers of the promise in Christ Jesus through the gospel" (συγκληρονόμα καὶ σύσσωμα καὶ συμμέτοχα τῆς ἐπαγγελίας ἐν Χριστῷ Ἰησοῦ διὰ τοῦ εὐαγγελίου 3:3). But what Col stresses is that Christ, the Lord over all things, is proclaimed in all

"Christ among you" (Χριστὸς ἐν ὑμῖν).[64] Doubtless this does not mean the pneumatic indwelling of the Lord in the hearts of the believers,[65] but rather the Christ preached among the nations, the Lord proclaimed in the community's midst; cf. 2 Cor 1:19, "Christ Jesus, whom we preached among you" (Χριστὸς Ἰησοῦς, ὁ ἐν ὑμῖν δι' ἡμῶν κηρυχθείς).[66] Since the content of the mystery is nothing other than "Christ among you," it is no longer a matter of various mysteries concerning God's eschatological plan as in Jewish apocalyptic. Rather, the revelation of one mystery is proclaimed: Christ, the "hope of glory" (ἐλπὶς τῆς δόξης).[67] The hope is directed toward the "glory" which will become manifest in the consummation (cf. 3:4). Its basis and content is Christ alone so that also here the emphasis lies upon the content of the "hope" that shapes the present (cf. 1:5). This content God has made known through the worldwide proclamation of the message of Christ.

■ **28** Although the writer no longer uses the singular, the "we" can mean no one else than the apostle who is carrying out the commission given to him. The "we" includes the apostle's authorized messengers who brought the gospel to Colossae (cf. 1:7f), since he himself was not able to preach the gospel there. In v 29 the "I" (singular) of the Apostle is speaking again. This indicates that v 29 talks about the authority of the apostolic office by which the co-workers installed by the apostle are also certified to the community.

The verb "to proclaim" (καταγγέλειν)[68] indicates public announcing, or proclamation, and in the primitive

---

the world.

64 The original reading ὅς ἐστιν (who is) is to be found in ℵ C D E K L pm. The masculine relative ὅς (who) is used for the sake of the word Χριστός (Christ), cf. Blass-Debrunner, par. 132,2. The reading of a neuter relative ὅ ἐστιν (which is; cf. 3:14) is aimed at making a connection with πλοῦτος (richness) or μυστήριον (mystery) and is found in p[46] B A G al latt. The masculine form ὅς ἐστιν (who is) is thus the more difficult reading.

65 Cf. 2 Cor 13:5, "that Jesus Christ is in you" (ὅτι Ἰησοῦς Χριστὸς ἐν ὑμῖν); Rom 8:10, "But if Christ is in you" (εἰ δὲ Χριστὸς ἐν ὑμῖν); Eph 3:17, "Christ may dwell in your hearts through faith" (κατοικῆσαι τὸν Χριστὸν διὰ τῆς πίστεως ἐν ταῖς καρδίαις ὑμῶν). Many exegetes explain the passage in this sense; Günther Bornkamm, *TDNT* 4, 820, e.g., states: "In Col 1:27 the content of the μυστήριον is stated in the formula Χριστὸς ἐν ὑμῖν. That is to say, it consists in the indwelling of the exalted Christ 'in you' the Gentiles." Dibelius-Greeven, *ad loc.*: " 'Christ in you' characterizes the basis of Christian existence, e.g. Rom 8:10 where the word 'Christ' takes up again the expression πνεῦμα Χριστοῦ (the Spirit of Christ)." Bieder, *ad loc.*, asks how the phrase "Christ in you" can be used when, according to 3:1, Christ is enthroned at the right hand of God. He answers this with "Christ is in you only as the hope of glory." Wagenführer, *Die Bedeutung Christi*, 96, is beside the point when he states "The formula Χριστὸς ἐν ὑμῖν (Christ in you), which reverses the more frequently encountered ὑμεῖς (ἡμεῖς) ἐν Χριστῷ (you [we] in Christ), is used by Paul to express the inner union with Christ in which each individual Christian stands. This union also brings all into genuine community. Paul does not say Χριστὸς ἐν τῇ ἐκκλησίᾳ (Christ in the church) since he usually gives mystical statements a more personal note. According to his conception, each individual Christian embodies the "ecclesia" in a certain way, insofar as he stands in a mystical relation with Christ." Schmithals wants to interpret this phrase in a Gnostic sense (*Die Gnosis*, 63), "First of all, therefore, the mystery which previously was hidden from the Gentiles . . . but is now made known is spoken of in a purely Gnostic manner; and then the content of this gnosis is summarized in the catchword Χριστὸς ἐν ὑμῖν (Christ in you). The proclamation of Christ as the "Pneuma-Self," dwelling in men and guaranteeing redemption, is *the* content of the gnosis which is the background of Col."

66 The phrase "among the nations" (ἐν τοῖς ἔθνεσιν) is resumed by "among you" (ἐν ὑμῖν). Cf. Gewiess, *Christus und das Heil*, 12; and Dahl, "Formgeschtl. Beobachtungen," 5. Schweizer, *Neotestamentica*, 327, states: "The preaching of the gospel to the world, Christ among the gentiles, is according to the following verses, the mystery hidden for ages, now revealed. It is the eschatological fulfilment of God's plan of salvation (I.26f)." Cf. further, *ibid.*, p. 302; also, Lohse, "Christusherrschaft und Kirche," 213.

67 Cf. Ign. *Eph.* 21:2, "in Jesus Christ, our common hope" (ἐν Ἰησοῦ Χριστῷ, τῇ κοινῇ ἐλπίδι ἡμῶν); *Mag.* 11, "by Jesus Christ, our hope" (Ἰησοῦ Χριστοῦ, τῆς ἐλπίδος ἡμῶν); *Phil.* 5:2 "by Jesus Christ . . . of the common hope" (Ἰησοῦ Χριστοῦ . . . τῆς κοινῆς ἐλπίδος).

68 Cf. Julius Schniewind, *TDNT* 1, 70–73.

69 Cf. Schniewind, *TDNT* 1, 72, "This corresponds to the basic NT view. Teaching and tradition are taken up into the word which proclaims the *Kyrios Christos*. By its very nature, declaring the unique historical reality of Jesus, this word must also be instruction, admonition and tradition. But it is

Christian language it practically became a technical term for missionary preaching. The phrases "proclaim Christ" (**τὸν Χριστὸν καταγγέλλειν** Phil 1:17; cf. also Acts 17:3, 23) or "proclaim the gospel" (**τὸ εὐαγγέλιον καταγγέλλειν** 1 Cor 9:14), and "proclaim the word of God" (**τὸν λόγον τοῦ θεοῦ καταγγέλλειν** Acts 13:5; 17:13) are materially the same as "preach Christ" (**Χριστὸν κηρύσσειν** Phil 1:15; etc.) and "announce the good news" (**εὐαγγελίζεσθαι** Gal 1:16). The proclamation broadcast everywhere, that Christ is the Lord, is explained and developed in admonition and instruction.[69] The words **νουθετεῖν/νουθεσία** (to warn, admonish/admonition)[70] appear in the New Testament only in the exhortatory contexts of Pauline writings.[71] The apostle admonishes the Corinthians as his children (1 Cor 4:14) and the members of the community admonish one another and offer helpful counsel (1 Thess 5:12, 14; Rom 15:14; 2 Thess 3:14). The verb "to teach" (**διδάσκειν**) is added alongside "to admonish" in order to characterize the intensive teaching in pastoral care and instruction.[72] According to Col 3:16 the task of the whole community is to instruct and admonish. In this passage, however, the function of the apostle is described as effecting the proclamation of Christ through "warning" and "teaching." While it is true that Paul occasionally can speak of his teaching in all communities (1 Cor 4:17) and can also mention the gift of teaching among the charismata worked by the Spirit (Rom 12:7), it is also the case that in the Pauline letters the words "to teach" and "teaching" (**διδάσκειν/διδαχή**) are noticeably rare. In the Pastorals, however, the correct and sound teaching is emphatically contrasted with a false teaching (1 Tim 1:10; 2 Tim 4:3; Tit 1:9; 2:1; etc.) and the significance of the verb "to teach" is thereby underscored (1 Tim 2:12; 4:11; 2 Tim 2:2; Tit 1:11). This emphasis upon teaching begins to stand out more clearly in Col.[73] It is not only for all Christians to admonish and to instruct one another, but the whole community is directed to remain firm in the faith, "as you were taught" (**καθὼς ἐδιδάχθητε** 2:7), and they are therefore reminded that the correct teaching has been entrusted to them with the apostolic gospel (1:28). In fact, the apostle gave this instruction everywhere, since he was striving to make this teaching known to everyone. Three times "every man" (**πάντα ἄνθρωπον**) is referred to as the recipient of the apostolic admonition, in order to stress the truly ecumenical character of the apostolic message which is proclaimed in all the world.[74]

The apostolic proclamation takes place "in all wisdom" (**ἐν πάσῃ σοφίᾳ**) and is therefore not directed toward a speculative preoccupation with the knowledge of higher worlds. Rather, it aims at the practical verification of the insight gained with the message of Christ (cf. 1:9f); for correct "wisdom" (**σοφία**) and "understand-

teaching which participates in the eschatological and dramatic character of the message."

70 Concerning the concept **νουθετεῖν** cf. Johannes Behm, *TDNT* 4, 1019–22. This verb actually means to set the mind of someone into proper order, to correct him, to set him right. In the LXX it is used in the sense of "to reproach" or "to reprimand" (1 Kg 3:13), or "to admonish" (Job 4:3). It is used chiefly, however, to mean "to warn," "to set right" or "to instruct." Examples are found in Behm, *TDNT* 4, 1020.

71 Acts 20:31 has Paul saying, "to admonish every one with tears" (**μετὰ δακρύων νουθετῶν ἕνα ἕκαστον**).

72 Both verbs occur together quite often. Cf. Plato, *Prot.* 323D, "nobody is wroth with them or reproves them or lectures . . ." (**οὐδεὶς θυμοῦται οὐδὲ νουθετεῖ οὐδὲ διδάσκει**); *Rep.* 399B, "by teaching and admonition" (**ἢ διδαχῇ καὶ νουθετήσει**); *Laws* 845B "admonishing and instructing" (**νουθετήσαντα καὶ διδάξαντα**). Dio Chrysostom, *Or.* 32.27, "to those who admonish and instruct" (**τοῖς νουθετοῦσι καὶ διδάσκουσι**). Plutarch, *Aud.* 46B (15), "giving instruction or admonition" (**διδάσκοντος καὶ νουθετοῦντος**). Plutarch attributes to admonition (**νουθετεῖν**) the power to effect "repentance" (**μετάνοια**): in *Quomodo adulator* 68F (28) and *De virtute morali* 452C (12). Lightfoot and Lohmeyer, *ad loc.*, are employing Greek thought, however, when they assert that in Col 1:28 "warning" (**νουθετεῖν**) aims at "repentance" (**μετάνοια**) and "teaching" (**διδάσκειν**) at "faith" (**πίστις**). Cf. Behm, *TDNT* 4, 1021, n. 14.

73 Cf. Karl Heinrich Rengstorff, *TDNT* 2, 147, "It is only in the epistle to the Colossians that we find **διδάσκειν** mentioned with **νουθετεῖν** (1:28; 3:16) in a pastoral and ethical sense . . . Only in Col do we find this change, and in the Past. **διδάσκειν** and its derivations become prominent."

74 This sharply contradicts any attempt to limit the teaching of wisdom to only a small circle of initiates.

ing" (*σύνεσις*)[75] prove themselves exactly in this, that life is conducted "in wisdom" (*ἐν σοφίᾳ* 4:5) and that God's will is done (1:9f). The goal of the instruction is therefore "that we may present every man perfect in Christ" (*ἵνα παραστήσωμεν πάντα ἄνθρωπον τέλειον ἐν Χριστῷ*). So far, the intention of the divine reconciliation has been defined as "to present you holy, blameless and irreproachable before him" (*παραστῆσαι ὑμᾶς ἁγίους καὶ ἀμώμους καὶ ἀνεγκλήτους κατενώπιον αὐτοῦ*). Now it is further explained that God has this, his work, carried out by the apostle. God placed him in his apostolic office in order to realize his intention to present every man perfect in Christ. In the Hellenistic world, "someone who is perfect" (*τέλειος*)[76] often designated a man who was deemed worthy of special experiences of the divine by means of an appropriation of "spirit" (*πνεῦμα*) or by initiation into mysteries.[77] It is therefore conceivable that in the "philosophy" (*φιλοσοφία*) which the epistle to the Colossians has to oppose, those who had the experience of being filled with supernatural wisdom and divine power were regarded as "perfect" (*τέλειοι*).[78] To such a conception Col contrasts its own understanding of wisdom and perfection which is wholly directed toward obedient fulfillment of the divine will. The apostle and his co-workers therefore pray to God for the community that "you may stand forth perfect and be filled with everything that is God's will" (*ἵνα σταθῆτε τέλειοι καὶ πεπληροφορημένοι ἐν παντὶ θελήματι τοῦ θεοῦ* 4:12). This draws upon Old Testament and Jewish tradition[79] as it was appropriated and further developed in primitive Christian exhortation (e.g. Mt 5:48; Rom 12:2; Jas 1:4, 25; 3:2; etc.). What is necessary is to recognize and to examine "what is the will of God, what is good and acceptable and perfect" (*τί τὸ θέλημα τοῦ θεοῦ, τὸ ἀγαθὸν καὶ εὐάρεστον καὶ τέλειον* Rom 12:2). The demand to "be perfect, as your heavenly Father is perfect" (*ἔσεσθε οὖν ὑμεῖς τέλειοι ὡς ὁ πατὴρ ὑμῶν ὁ οὐράνιος τέλειός ἐστιν* Mt 5:48) is fulfilled where the will of God is done in obedience to the Lord.[80] Whoever belongs to the exalted Christ and follows his command will be "perfect in Christ" (*τέλειος ἐν Χριστῷ*).[81]

■ **29** The apostle exerts himself to deliver this message.[82] "I toil" (*κοπιῶ*) does not refer to the manual work which Paul performs to earn his own living (1 Thess 2:9; 1 Cor 4:12; 2 Thess 3:8). Rather, it signifies the difficult work of

---

75 For the concepts of wisdom and knowledge in the apocalyptic context, cf. 1 En 37:4; 48:7; 49:1, 3; 51:3; etc.

76 For the concept *τέλειος* (perfect), cf. Paul Johannes du Plessis, *Teleios, The Idea of Perfection in the New Testament* (Kampen: 1959); Gerhard Delling, *TWNT* 8, 68–79; and R. Newton Flew, *The Idea of Perfection in Christian Theology: An Historical Study of the Christian Ideal for the Present Life* (Oxford: The University Press; London: Humphrey Milford, 1934).

77 Iamblichus, *Myst.* 3.7 says that whoever is perfect (*τέλειος*) knows "what enthusiasm or divine possession really is and how it is developed" (*τίς ὁ ἐνθουσιασμός ἐστι καὶ ὅπως γίνεται.* Trans. from *Theurgia, or The Egyptian Mysteries*, tr. Alexander Wilder [London: William Rider & Son, Ltd.; New York: The Metaphysical Publishing Co., 1911], 117). Cf. also *Corp. Herm.* 4.4 "Now those who gave heed to the proclamation, and those who baptized themselves in the baptism of the mind, these men got a share of *gnosis* and then became perfect men, since they received the mind" (*ὅσοι μὲν οὖν συνῆκαν τοῦ κηρύγματος καὶ ἐβαπτίσαντο τοῦ νοός, οὗτοι μετέσχον τῆς γνώσεως καὶ τέλειοι ἐγένοντο ἄνθρωποι, τὸν νοῦν δεξάμενοι* [trans.]). Philo, *Som.* 2.234 has "Moses then describes the perfect man as neither God nor man, but, as I have said already, on the border line between the uncreated and the perishing form of being" (*τὸν μὲν οὖν τέλειον οὔτε θεὸν οὔτε ἄνθρωπον ἀναγράφει Μωυσῆς, ἀλλ', ὡς ἔφην, μεθόριον τῆς ἀγενήτου καὶ φθαρτῆς φύσεως*). In 1 Cor 2:6 Paul says "yet among the perfect (RSV: mature) we do impart wisdom" (*σοφίαν δὲ λαλοῦμεν ἐν τοῖς τελείοις*) and he uses *τέλειοι* to mean the same thing as *πνευματικοί* (spiritual; 1 Cor 3:1). Cf. Wilckens, *Weisheit*, 53–60, and the further examples there.

78 Cf. 4:12 where the word *τέλειοι* (perfect) stands alongside *πεπληροφορημένοι* (being filled)—which the author of Col, however, relates to the will of God. Cf. further Lightfoot, Dibelius–Greeven, *ad loc.*

79 Cf. LXX Deut 18:13; 3 Kg 8:61; 11:4, 10; 15:3, 14; 1 Chr 28:9; Wisd Sol 9:6; Sir 44:17; and also Lohmeyer, *ad loc.* The writings of the Qumran community continually emphasize that it is necessary "to walk perfectly in all the ways commanded by God" (להלכת תמים בכול דרכי אל 1 QS III.9f). Cf. further, 1 QS I.8; II.2; III.3; IV.22; VIII.1, 9f, 18, 20f; etc.; CD I.21; II.15; VII.5; etc.; also cf. Rigaux, "Révélation des Mystères," 237–62.

80 *παραστήσωμεν* (that we may present)—as *παραστῆσαι* (to present) in 1:22—is hardly to be understood in a futuristic–eschatological sense, related to the final judgment. Rather, the results of

the one who labors untiringly for the community's welfare.[83] Of course, others are engaged in faithful labor for the community (e.g., 1 Thess 5:12; 1 Cor 16:16; Rom 16:6; etc.), but this passage speaks only of the toiling of the apostle as he is performing missionary service in all the world.[84] Paul can say of himself, "I toiled harder than any of them" (**περισσότερον αὐτῶν πάντων ἐκοπίασα**); yet he also prevents any sort of misunderstanding, as though he would want to boast about himself, by adding "though it was not I, but the grace of God which is with me" (**οὐκ ἐγὼ δὲ ἀλλὰ ἡ χάρις τοῦ θεοῦ σὺν ἐμοί** 1 Cor 15:10). God's "power" (**δύναμις**) proves to be effective in the labor of its messenger. Paul says, "I can do all things in him who strengthens me" (**πάντα ἰσχύω ἐν τῷ ἐνδυναμοῦντί με** Phil 4:13), for God is "the one at work among you both to will and to work for his good pleasure" (**ὁ ἐνεργῶν ἐν ὑμῖν τὸ θέλειν καὶ τὸ ἐνεργεῖν ὑπὲρ τῆς εὐδοκίας** Phil 2:13).[85] His power[86] lifts up the weak and grants strength to endure.[87] Through this alone the apostle knows himself capable of accomplishing the exertion required of him.[88]

■ **2:1** Because Paul fulfills his apostolic commission in the worldwide proclamation of the gospel, the service rendered by the Apostle to the nations also pertains to the community at Colossae. Although Paul has never personally met the community, he has been active for them for a long time ("strife," **ἀγών**, 2:1, connects with "striving," **ἀγωνιζόμενος**, 1:29). Thus he can turn to them now in direct personal address.

Paul introduces important communications to the community by saying, "for I want you to know" (**θέλω γὰρ ὑμᾶς εἰδέναι** cf. 1 Cor 11:3) or "but I would not have you ignorant" (**οὐ θέλω δὲ ὑμᾶς ἀγνοεῖν** Rom 1:13).[89] After this phrase in Rom 1:13 Paul emphatically assures the community which he does not know personally that he had often undertaken to visit it, but had thus far been hindered in realizing his wish. In the same way this passage in Col is intended to establish the personal bond between Paul and the letter's recipients. For this reason it is explained that the striving[90] in which Paul engages in all places for the sake of the gospel and for the sake of the church also concerns the Christians in the cities of the Lycus valley. Thus a close bond between himself and the church has already been formed[91] and is now to be strengthened by the letter. The apostle knows that he is bound not only to the Christians in Colossae,[92]

the apostolic work should be visible in the conduct of the community. Therefore, it makes no sense to explain ἐν Χριστῷ (in Christ) as a forensic term and to paraphrase it as "So that through us (i.e. our proclamation) all men come before Christ as perfected" [Trans.]. This is the position of Hans-Ludolf Parisius, "Über die forensische Deutungsmöglichkeit des paulinischen ἐν Χριστῷ," *ZNW* 49 (1958): 287.

81 Concerning the formula-like expression "in Christ" in Col, cf. above, p. 10.

82 The words εἰς ὅ (for which) form a loose connection to the preceding.

83 Cf. Adolf v. Harnack, "Κόπος (Κοπιᾶν, Οἱ Κοπιῶντες) im frühchristlichen Sprachgebrauch," *ZNW* 27 (1928): 1–10; and Friedrich Hauck, *TDNT* 3, 827–30.

84 Cf. Gal 4:11; 1 Cor 3:8; 2 Cor 6:5; 11:23, 27; Phil 2:16.

85 For ἐνέργεια/ἐνεργεῖσθαι (the working power/to work effectively), cf. Georg Bertram, *TDNT* 2, 652–54.

86 Cf. 1 En 60:16, "according to the might of his strength."

87 Cf. Col 2:12, "through faith in the working power of God" (διὰ τῆς πίστεως τῆς ἐνεργείας τοῦ θεοῦ). Eph 1:19, "according to the working of his great might" (κατὰ τὴν ἐνέργειαν τοῦ κράτους τῆς ἰσχύος αὐτοῦ); and 3:7, "by the working of his power" (κατὰ τὴν ἐνέργειαν τῆς δυνάμεως αὐτοῦ).

88 The participle ἀγωνιζόμενος (striving) here does not mean a contest (1 Cor 9:25) but rather expresses the apostle's toil and exertion. Cf. Dibelius–Greeven, *ad loc.*, *contra* Ethelbert Stauffer, *TDNT* 1, 138f. In 4:12 this is said of Epaphras' activity on behalf of the Colossians: πάντοτε ἀγωνιζόμενος ὑπὲρ ὑμῶν ἐν ταῖς προσευχαῖς (constantly stands up for you in his prayers). Cf. Victor C. Pfitzner, *Paul and the Agon Motif: Traditional Athletic Imagery in the Pauline Literature*, Suppl. to *Nov Test* 16 (Leiden: 1967), 109f.

89 Cf. 1 Thess 4:13; 1 Cor 10:1; 12:1; 2 Cor 1:8; Rom 11:25.

90 The word ἀγών does not mean "martyrdom" (thus Lohmeyer, *ad loc.*) but rather connects with 1:29 and points to the apostle's engagement in his work.

91 Cf. Gal 2:5. Here Paul speaks of the effect of the previously achieved decision in Jerusalem upon the Galatian community, and he asserts that at that time the whole issue at stake was "that the truth of the gospel might be preserved for you" (ἵνα ἡ ἀλήθεια τοῦ εὐαγγελίου διαμείνῃ πρὸς ὑμᾶς).

92 In the mss ℜ D G al the word ὑπέρ (for) is replaced by the more common περί (concerning). Cf. Blass–Debrunner, par. 229, 231.

but also to their neighboring community in Laodicea.[93] Both communities are in close contact with one another and are therefore instructed to exchange between them the apostolic letter sent to them (4:16). The acute danger, against which the letter wants to warn the Colossians (2:6–23), clearly threatens not only this community, but all Christians in the whole area.[94] Since they are all expected to heed the apostolic teaching, they are first of all made aware of the apostle's genuine devotion to them. He not only strives for those Christians who are personally known to him, but particularly for those members of the Colossian and Laodicean communities who have not yet met him.[95] Although they have not yet seen each other face to face,[96] the apostle and the community are already bound together in mutual encouragement.

■ **2** The apostle strives for the communities "that their hearts may be encouraged" (ἵνα παρακληθῶσιν αἱ καρδίαι αὐτῶν). In the Hebraic manner of speech the heart is called the innermost part of man, his self,[97] and this is what receives the "encouragement" (παράκλησις cf. 4:8).[98] In the Pauline letters παρακαλεῖν can mean "admonish" as well as "encourage."[99] Here the concern is not with admonition but with the encouragement of their hearts which should result from the apostle's assurances which strengthen the community. In the following phrase, "united in love" (συμβιβασθέντες ἐν ἀγάπῃ),[100] the verb συμβιβάζειν could be understood in the sense of "to demonstrate" or "to instruct"[101] (cf. 1 Cor 2:16; Acts 9:22; 19:33). Then the words "in love" (ἐν ἀγάπῃ) would indicate how the instruction is given to the community, i.e., as loving admonition.[102] Indeed, the following terms "insight" (σύνεσις) and "knowledge" (ἐπίγνωσις) could also speak for this explanation. But this same verb is also used in 2:19 and there doubtless means "to bring together."[103] From its head the whole body is provided with sinews and ligaments, and "knit together . . . grows with a growth that is from God" (συμβιβαζόμενον αὔξει τὴν αὔξησιν τοῦ

93 A later report about the community in Laodicea appears in Rev 3:14–22.

94 Since 4:13 lists the community in nearby Hierapolis along with those in Colossae and Laodicea, several copyists (in 104 pc sy[h]) inserted "and for those in Hierapolis" (καὶ τῶν ἐν Ἱεραπόλει) in this passage.

95 The Greek phrasing, ὅσοι οὐχ ἑόρακαν τὸ πρόσωπόν μου ἐν σαρκί does not mean "all who have not yet seen me." Rather, it means "all who are among you and do not yet know me personally." Elsewhere the word ὅσοι (as many as = all who) usually introduces the conclusion which rounds off an enumeration. Cf. Acts 4:6, "Annas the high priest and Caiaphas and John and Alexander, and *all who* were of the high–priestly family" (Ἄννας ὁ ἀρχιερεὺς καὶ Καϊαφᾶς καὶ Ἰωάννης καὶ Ἀλέξανδρος καὶ ὅσοι ἦσαν ἐκ γένους ἀρχιερατικοῦ); Rev 18:17, "And all shipmasters and seafaring men, sailors and *all whose* trade is on the sea" (καὶ πᾶς κυβερνήτης καὶ πᾶς ὁ ἐπὶ τόπον πλέων καὶ ναῦται καὶ ὅσοι τὴν θάλασσαν ἐργάζονται).

96 Cf. 1 Thess 2:17, "we were bereft of you . . . in person not in heart" (ἀπορφανισθέντες ἀφ' ὑμῶν . . . προσώπῳ οὐ καρδίᾳ); 3:10, "that we may see you face to face" (εἰς τὸ ἰδεῖν ὑμῶν τὸ πρόσωπον); Gal 1:22, "not known by sight" (ἀγνοούμενος τῷ προσώπῳ). For πρόσωπον with the meaning of "personal presence," cf. Eduard Lohse, *TDNT* 6, 776. For the form ἑόρακαν cf. Blass–Debrunner, par. 83,1; Ludwig Radermacher, *Neutestamentliche Grammatik, Das Griechische des Neuen Testaments im Zusammenhang mit der Volkssprache*, HNT 1, 1 (Tübingen, [2]1925), 94, 96; and Moulton, *Prolegomena*, 52.

97 Cf. Johannes Behm, *TDNT* 3, 609–13.

98 Since the phrase "and for all who do not know me personally" (καὶ ὅσοι οὐχ ἑόρακαν) precedes this sentence, the following pronominal form is "their" (αὐτῶν) and not "your" (ὑμῶν) which could have been expected.

99 For παρακαλεῖν (to admonish, warn, etc.) cf. 1 Thess 4:1; 2 Cor 5:20; 10:1; Rom 12:1; Phil 4:2; etc. For its meaning as "to comfort," cf. 2 Cor 1:4, 6; 2:7; 7:6, 13; etc. Cf. also Otto Schmitz, *TDNT* 5, 793–99. Heinrich Schlier, "Vom Wesen der apostolischen Ermahnung" in *Die Zeit der Kirche* (Freiburg: 1956), 89, "The apostolic admonition is a concerned address which draws near to the brothers and at the same time contains requests, comfort and warning" [Trans.]. Cf. further, Carl J. Bjerkelund, *Parakalô: Form, Funktion und Sinn der parakalô–Sätze in den paulinischen Briefen*, Bibliotheca Theologica Norvegica (Oslo: 1967), 92.

100 In the mss 𝔎 pm the participle takes the genitive plural form συμβιβασθέντων to correspond to the previous plural genitive pronoun form αὐτῶν (their).

101 Iamblichus, *Vit. Pyth.* 13.60, "Pythagoras . . . taught that by learning all things are advantageous to those having intellect" (Πυθαγόρας . . . συμβιβάζων, ὡς διδασκαλίᾳ πάντα περιγίνεται τοῖς νοῦν ἔχουσιν [Trans.]). Cf. also Aristotle, *Topica* 7.5 (154A 35f); 8.3 (158B 27); 8.11 (161B 37). Also, Philo, *Rer. Div. Her.* 25 "You have taught me to say what should be said" (σὺ τὰ λεκτέα συνεβίβασας εἰπεῖν); and LXX Exod 4:12, 15; 18:16; Lev 10:11; Deut 4:9; etc. Further examples in Gerhard

θεοῦ cf. also Eph 4:16). In 3:4 love is called the "bond of perfection" (*σύνδεσμος τῆς τελειότητος*). Thus also in Col 2:1, *συμβιβάζειν* must mean "to bring together," "unite," and the words "in love" (*ἐν ἀγάπῃ*) show what will give stability to this "bringing together." The solidarity of the whole community is founded, maintained and strengthened by love, the bond of perfection.[104]

In this unity[105] the community should attain to "all the riches of the fullness of the insight, for the understanding of God's mystery, Christ" (*εἰς πᾶν πλοῦτος τῆς πληροφορίας τῆς συνέσεως, εἰς ἐπίγνωσιν τοῦ μυστηρίου τοῦ θεοῦ, Χριστοῦ*). This pleonastic phrase again stresses the significance of right "insight" (*σύνεσις*) and "understanding" (*ἐπίγνωσις*) for the life of the community (cf. 1:9f). The rich fullness[106] of insight and understanding is characterized by connecting the words "riches" (*πλοῦτος*)[107] and "fullness" (*πληροφορία*) with the term "insight" which follows them. The word *πληροφορία* (it is seldom used and does not appear in the LXX) means "complete fullness," but also "complete certainty."[108] Paul speaks of "full conviction" when he looks back on the beginnings of the Thessalonian community: "our gospel came to you not only in word, but also in power and in the Holy Spirit and with full conviction" (*τὸ εὐαγγέλιον ἡμῶν οὐκ ἐγενήθη εἰς ὑμᾶς ἐν λόγῳ μόνον, ἀλλὰ ἐν δυνάμει καὶ πνεύματι ἁγίῳ καὶ πληροφορίᾳ πολλῇ* 1 Thess 1:5).[109] In this passage of Col *πληροφορία* could also be translated as "certainty,"[110] yet the phrasing *πλοῦτος τῆς πληροφορίας* (riches of fullness) is better viewed as a tautology which aims at expressing the abounding fullness of understanding—indeed, "all" (*πᾶν*) stands in an emphatic position at the head of this word series! The life of the community should mature to this complete fullness of understanding. The object of this "insight" is expressed in the genitive which is attached to the parallel term "understanding" (*ἐπίγνωσις*). It is the mystery of God which he has made known in the proclamation of Christ among the nations (cf. 1:26f).[111]

The concise formulation, "God's mystery, Christ" (*τοῦ μυστηρίου τοῦ θεοῦ, Χριστοῦ*), which states that Christ proclaimed among the nations is the content of the divine mystery,[112] has given rise to manifold alterations. All of them can be explained as variants of the original text which is witnessed by p[46] B Hilary:[113]

Delling, *TWNT* 7, 763.

102 This is how the Vulgate understood it, "being instructed in charity" (*instructi in caritate*). Dibelius–Greeven, *ad loc.*, also take it in this sense; similarly, Spicq, *Agape*, 248–50. Cf. also Delling, *TWNT* 7, 764, n. 10.

103 For this meaning, known equally well from ancient times, cf. Herodotus, 1.74.3 (concerning the reconciliation of former foes): *οἱ δὲ συμβιβάσαντες αὐτούς* (those who brought them together; [Trans.]). Thucydides 2.29.6: *ξυνεβίβασε δὲ καὶ τὸν Περδίκκαν τοῖς Ἀθηναίοις*, i.e., he brought about a reconciliation between Perdiccas and the Athenians. Plato, *Prot.* 337E: *ὥσπερ ὑπὸ διαιτητῶν ἡμῶν συμβιβαζόντων εἰς τὸ μέσον* (as it were, under our arbitration, coming to terms).

104 Cf. Theodoret, *ad loc.*, "in order that they may guard the harmony according to Christ" (*ἵνα τὴν κατὰ Χριστὸν φυλάξωσιν συμφωνίαν* [trans.]). Also, Gerhard Delling, *TWNT* 7, 764; and Percy, *Probleme*, 427, and almost all exegetes, except those mentioned on p. 80, n. 102. The participle acquires an optative meaning in the context. Cf. Moulton, *Prolegomena*, 182.

105 In the mss D* Ambst the connective *καί* is missing.

106 The Greek *εἰς πᾶν πλοῦτος* (lit. =for all wealth) is changed by the mss A C pc to read *εἰς πᾶν τὸ πλοῦτος* (for the whole wealth [neuter]); and ℜ D pl changed it to read *πάντα* (D* adds *τὸν*) *πλοῦτον* (all [the] wealth [masc.]). Cf. above, p. 95, n. 62 on 1:27.

107 Cf. 1:27, "the richness of the glory of this mystery" (*τὸ πλοῦτος τῆς δόξης τοῦ μυστηρίου τούτου*).

108 Cf. Bauer, *s.v.*; Gerhard Delling, *TDNT* 6, 310f. In examples from non–Christian usage the meaning is always "certainty." Cf. *P. Giess.* 87.25f (2nd cent. A.D.) [*τ*]*ὴν πληροφο*[*ρίαν* . . .] *ἐπὶ τούτοις καί* (certainty in these things [Trans.]); and *Rhetores Graeci* (ed. Christian Walz [1833]), VII.108.3 *ἐπίρρημα βεβαιώσεως ὃν μετὰ πληροφορίας τὸ πάγιον ἐμφαίνει τῆς καταλήψεως* (being a byword of surety, [that which is clear] shows with certainty that which is firm in the concept. [Trans.]).

109 Cf. also Heb 6:11 "in full assurance of hope" (*πρὸς τὴν πληροφορίαν τῆς ἐλπίδος*).

110 Cf. James Hope Moulton, *A Grammar of New Testament Greek*, vol. 3, *Syntax* by Nigel Turner (Edinburgh: T. &. T. Clark, 1963), 211, "conviction which is the result of insight (or intelligence)."

111 The understanding of the divine mystery belongs with the recognition of the divine will (1:9), for whoever has recognized Christ as the content of the mystery owes him obedience as his Lord.

112 Lohmeyer, *ad loc.*, takes the word *Χριστοῦ* (Christ) to be a marginal gloss which intruded into the text quite early. But the manuscript tradition offers no support for this supposition.

1.

Abbreviations of the original text want to make it more understandable:

τοῦ μυστηρίου τοῦ θεοῦ
H P 69 pc "of the mystery of God"
τοῦ μυστηρίου Χριστοῦ
1739 "of the mystery of Christ"
τοῦ μυστηρίου τοῦ Χριστοῦ
1462 pc "of the mystery of the Christ"

2.

The insertion of *ὅ ἐστιν* (which is) after "mystery of God" clearly separates *Χριστοῦ* (Christ) from the preceding and characterizes it as an explanation: *τοῦ μυστηρίου τοῦ θεοῦ, ὅ ἐστιν Χριστός* D* Aug (*De trin* 13.2.4) d c Vigilius of Thapsus "of the mystery of God, which is Christ."

3.

One or several words are inserted between "God" and "Christ" to achieve a smoother text:

τοῦ μυστηρίου τοῦ θεοῦ καὶ Χριστοῦ Cyril Alex
"of the mystery of God *and* Christ"
τοῦ μυστηρίου τοῦ θεοῦ πατρὸς τοῦ Χριστοῦ ℵ* (without *τοῦ*) A C pc
"of the mystery of God, *the Father of* Christ"
τοῦ μυστηρίου τοῦ θεοῦ καὶ πατρὸς τοῦ Χριστοῦ ℵ^3 Ψ sy^h
"of the mystery of God *and of the Father of* Christ"
τοῦ μυστηρίου τοῦ θεοῦ πατρὸς καὶ τοῦ Χριστοῦ 0208 442 sy^p
"of the mystery of God, *of the Father and of* Christ"
τοῦ μυστηρίου τοῦ θεοῦ καὶ πατρὸς καὶ τοῦ Χριστοῦ 𝔎
"of the mystery of God *both of the Father and of* Christ"

4.

The genitive, *Χριστοῦ* (of Christ) is altered into the prepositional dative to read *ἐν Χριστῷ* (in Christ):
τοῦ μυστηρίου τοῦ θεοῦ ἐν Χριστῷ 33 (+ *τοῦ* before *ἐν Χριστῷ*) ClemAlex:
"the mystery of God in Christ" or "the mystery of God, which is in Christ."

■ **3** The concept "Christ alone," which has just been stated, is reinforced by the relative clause. Just as the right understanding of the community is dependent upon Christ alone, so also "wisdom" (*σοφία*) and "knowledge" (*γνῶσις*) have their ground only in him. The modifier, "all" (*πάντες*), bans all exceptions, so that all attempts to search out other sources of knowledge besides Christ are both vain and false. "Wisdom" (*σοφία*) and "knowledge" (*γνῶσις*) are almost combined into a single entity by the use of one definite article for both terms; they are frequently juxtaposed in Jewish tradition.[114] They occur together also in the praise which Paul raises to the marvel of God's governance: "O the depth of the riches and wisdom and knowledge of God" (*ὦ βάθος πλούτου καὶ σοφίας καὶ γνώσεως θεοῦ* Rom 11:33). All the treasures of wisdom and knowledge are contained[115] in Christ, but they are "hidden" (*ἀπόκρυφοι*).[116] The image here is that of a hidden treasure for which there are hints that entice the searcher to wager everything on finding it. Thus this sentence implies challenge to search out the only place where the treasures of wisdom and knowledge are to be found.[117] Jewish apocalyptic often speaks of a hidden treasure in order to create interest in its invitations to right knowledge, since under the guise of the mystery lies the gift which God through revelation has allotted to the elect.[118] In the same way Col mentions the concealment of the treasures

113 Cf. Bruce M. Metzger, *The Text of the New Testament: Its Transmission, Corruption, and Restoration* (New York and Oxford: Oxford University Press, ^{2}1968), 236–38.

114 LXX Eccl 1:16–18; 2:26; 7:12; 9:10; Sir 21:13; also 1 QS IV.3, 22; 1 QH I.18f; CD II.3.

115 In the Greek sentence, *εἰσίν* (they are) means the existence of the treasures, whereas *ἀπόκρυφοι* (hidden) indicates the manner of their existence. Cf. 1 En 49:3, "and in him (i.e. the Son of Man) dwells the spirit of wisdom, and the spirit which gives insight, and the spirit of understanding and of might, and the spirit of those who have fallen asleep in righteousness."

116 For *ἀπόκρυφος* (hidden), cf. Albrecht Oepke, *TDNT* 3, 961.

117 The text neither contains an OT quote nor is any allusion to an OT passage intended. Cf. LXX Isa 45:3, *καὶ δώσω σοι θησαυροὺς σκοτεινούς, ἀποκρύφους ἀοράτους ἀνοίξω σοι* (And I shall give to you dark treasures; hidden and invisible things I shall disclose to you); Sir 1:25, *ἐν θησαυροῖς σοφίας* (in the treasures of wisdom); also, Pr 2:3f.

118 E.g. 1 En 46:3, "This is the Son of Man who has righteousness, with whom dwells righteousness, and who reveals all the treasures of that which is hid-

in order to mark the location where they are to be found. The mystery which was hidden for ages and generations is now revealed to the saints of God (1:26) and it is announced in the proclamation of Christ among the nations (1:27). Therefore, in him alone exists the right "insight," "understanding," "wisdom," and "knowledge."

■ **4** Now, however, the warning is sounded: all this has been said[119] so that the community does not unwarily heed the splendid, high–sounding words of the deceivers. *πιθανολογία* is the art of persuading[120] which is clearly given a negative meaning here: they are attempting to deceive others by false pretenses. This kind of fraudulent activity is called *παραλογίζεσθαι* (to delude).[121] The community is warned not to be drawn onto thin ice by means of charming speech.[122] The genuine messenger of the gospel can be recognized by his spreading of the word "not in plausible words of wisdom, but in demonstration of the Spirit and power" (*οὐκ ἐν πειθοῖς σοφίας λόγοις, ἀλλ' ἐν ἀποδείξει πνεύματος καὶ δυνάμεως* 1 Cor 2:4).

■ **5** Indeed, the danger at hand is not to be underestimated,[123] because the Apostle is distant and cannot be on hand to speak directly to the community. Even if he is not present in body,[124] he is, however,[125] present with it in spirit. Although *πνεῦμα* (spirit) means the individual self as distinguished from the body of a person, this self is connected with the divine Spirit which grants strength to the apostle to unite with the community in common action, despite the distance.[126] Since he is united with the community in this way, he is pleased that the commu-

den."

119 The words, "I am saying this" (*τούτο λέγω*), relate to what was just said, and not to what follows (as is often the case for Paul; cf. Gal 3:17; 1 Cor 1:12). The reason here is that a purpose clause, introduced by "in order that" (*ἵνα*), follows. Cf. Jn 5:34, "But I say this in order that you may be saved" (*ταῦτα λέγω ἵνα ὑμεῖς σωθῆτε*). Concerning the *ἵνα* cf. Moulton–Turner, 102: "In Col. 2:4 *ἵνα* may be final: *I say this in order that* . . ., but equally possible is an imperatival sense: "Let us owe . . .." Since Paul otherwise likes to use "*but* I say this" (*τούτο δὲ λέγω*), the mss C ℜ D pl ClemAlex have added a *δέ* here.

120 Cf. Plato, *Theaet.* 162E: "So you . . . had better consider whether you will accept arguments founded on persuasion and probabilities in such important matters" (*σκοπεῖτε οὖν . . . εἰ ἀποδέξεσθε πιθανολογίᾳ τε καὶ εἰκόσι περὶ τηλικούτων λεγομένους λόγους* [Trans.]); Aristotle, *Eth. Nic.* 1.3 (1094B). *P. Lips.* I.40.3.7: "they sought to keep the booty by employing the art of persuasion" (*διὰ πιθανολογίας τὰ ἁρπαγέντα ζητοῦσι κατέχειν*). The word is not used in the LXX and does not reappear in the NT. Cf. Bauer, *s.v.*

121 In the NT the verb *παραλογίζεσθαι* (to delude, deceive) reappears only in Jas 1:22, which speaks of the self–deception of those who are only hearers and not doers of the word (*παραλογιζόμενοι ἑαυτούς*). The word is widely attested outside the NT. Cf. Dio Chrysostom, *Or.* 11.108, "Athena disguised as him" (*'Αθηνᾶν παραλογίσασθαι αὐτόν* [Trans.]); Epictetus, *Diss.* 2.20.7, "deceiving you and leading you astray" (*ἐξαπατῶσιν ὑμᾶς καὶ παραλογίζονται*); *P. Amh.* 2.35.12f, "and deceived our farmers" (*παραλογισάμενος τοὺς περὶ ἡμῶν γεωργούς* [Trans.]); and *P. Magd.* 29.5, "he has deceived me" (*παραλελόγισταί με*). Also LXX Gen 29:25; 31:41; Josh 9:22; Judg 16:10, 13, 15A; etc.; Bel 7, "let no one deceive you" (*μηδείς σε παραλογιζέσθω*). Cf. Bauer, *s.v.*

122 The mss ℜ pm ClemAlex[pt] have *μή τις* instead of *μηδείς*.

123 The particle "for" (*γάρ*) makes the connection to the preceding. Dibelius–Greeven, *ad loc.*, state that it "gives Paul a basis for speaking such words to the Colossians even though he is unknown to them and not present with them."

124 The meaning of *σάρξ* (flesh), in this instance, is the same as *σῶμα* (body), i.e., bodily existence. Cf. 1 Cor 5:3 "absent in body . . . present in spirit" (*ἀπὼν τῷ σώματι, παρὼν δὲ τῷ πνεύματι*). The same thought with different words is in 1 Thess 2:17, "we were bereft of you . . . in person not in heart" (*ἀπορφανισθέντες ἀφ' ὑμῶν . . . προσώπῳ οὐ καρδίᾳ*). Concerning the formulaic character of the phrase "absent in body, present in spirit," cf. Gustav Karlson, "Formelhaftes in den Paulusbriefen" *Eranos* 54 (1956): 138–41, who also lists further examples from ancient epistolary literature.

125 The word *ἀλλά* (yet) introduces the second part of this sentence. Cf. 1 Cor 9:2; 2 Cor 4:16; Rom 6:5; etc.; and Blass–Debrunner, par. 448,5.

126 Cf. Eduard Schweizer, *TDNT* 6, 436 on 1 Cor 5:3 and Col 2:5, "Here and in Col 2:5 the *πνεῦμα* of the apostle is to be regarded as the gift of the Spirit of God which has been given to him, which denotes his authority, and which also exerts an influence beyond his physical presence." Cf. also Bultmann, *Theology*, par. 18,3 (ET 1, 208); Conzelmann, *Outline*, 176f, 180.

nity is faring quite well. Both the participles χαίρων καὶ βλέπων are to be taken together as one expression, "rejoicing to see."[127] What sort of picture does the community offer to the apostle's view?

The words τάξις (order) and στερέωμα (firmness, solid part) can appear in a military context. Then "order" indicates the positions, the posts which the soldiers occupy;[128] "firmness" is the bulwark or fortification.[129] But it is not probable that the thought here is based on a military image, so that the community would be in rank and file order as though prepared for battle.[130] The "order" and "bulwark" of an army would of course be requisites for the activity of soldiers, but hardly a cause for praise and joy.[131] But also the context does not suggest in any way that the position of troops prepared for battle is described here.[132] Thus both concepts are employed in a more general sense. The well-ordered condition which, according to the apostle's exhortation, should characterize the community is what "order" (τάξις) means:[133] "all things should be done decently and in order" (πάντα δὲ εὐσχημόνως καὶ κατὰ τάξιν γινέσθω 1 Cor 14:40). The firm strength which supports the faith of the community is what "firmness" (στερέωμα) means.[134] The word "your" (ὑμῶν) before "order" shows that it means the correct order of the community, and "firmness" is followed by the words "of your faith in Christ" (τῆς εἰς Χριστὸν πίστεως ὑμῶν) in order to bring the section to an effective conclusion. The faith of the community is firmly founded because it is oriented toward Christ alone.[135] If the community holds to him resolutely, no temptation can really endanger it, but it will persevere, strong and steadfast in faith.[136]

The praise given the community does not contain a description of a particular situation which is known more clearly by the letter's author (cf. 1:3–8). Rather, generalizing phrases are used and the words of praise present a typical image of a community which preserves the apostolic message faithfully and persists in it unwaveringly—even when a new teaching is enticingly presented. In order to unmask and fend off such teaching, this community needs insight in the right gospel, as it was spread by the apostle in the proclamation of Christ among the nations. This furnishes the basis for carrying out a controversy with false preaching, for the apostolic gospel establishes the norm against which every other message is to be measured.

The Language and Style of Colossians

The language and style of Colossians[137] demonstrate numerous similarities to the other Pauline letters. These connections involve phrases and clauses which are conditioned by the formal structure of the Pauline letter, such as introduction and conclusion,[138] the beginning of the thanksgiving prayer,[139] connecting phrases and words introducing instruc-

127 Cf. Blass–Debrunner, par. 471,5.

128 Cf. Xenophon, *An.* 1.2.18: "was filled with admiration at beholding the brilliant appearance and *order* of the [Greek] army" (ἰδοῦσα τὴν λαμπρότητα καὶ τὴν τάξιν τοῦ στρατεύματος ἐθαύμασε). Also Plutarch, *De vita Pyrrh.* 16 "and when he had observed their *order*, the appointment of their watches, their good behavior, and the general arrangement of their camp, he was amazed" (κατιδὼν τάξιν τε καὶ φυλακὰς καὶ κόσμον αὐτῶν καὶ τὸ σχῆμα τῆς στρατοπεδείας ἐθαύμασε [Trans.]).

129 Cf. 1 Macc 9:14, "Judas saw that Bacchides and the *solid strength* of the ranks were on the right" (καὶ εἶδεν Ἰούδας ὅτι Βακχίδης καὶ τὸ στερέωμα τῆς παρεμβολῆς ἐν τοῖς δεξιοῖς [Trans.]). For further examples see Georg Bertram, *TWNT* 7, 609–14.

130 With others, Lohmeyer takes this view, *ad loc.*, "The apostle is 'with them' as a field commander standing before his troops and arranging the ranks for battle once more."

131 Cf. Dibelius–Greeven, *ad loc.*

132 Cf. Abbott, *ad loc.*, who correctly points out that τάξις and στερέωμα do not necessarily have a military meaning, but only assume one from their respective contexts.

133 Cf. Bauer, *s.v.*

134 Cf. Bauer, *s.v.* The word στερέωμα can also mean the firmament of heaven. Thus, e.g., LXX Gen 1:6–10; Ezek 1:22–26; also 1 En 18:2; Philo, *Op. Mund.* 36; Test Naph 3:4.

135 Cf. Phlm 5, "the faith which you have toward the Lord Jesus" (τὴν πίστιν ἣν ἔχεις πρὸς τὸν κυρίον Ἰησοῦν).

136 Cf. 1 Pt 5:9: "resist him, firm in your faith" (ἀντίστητε στερεοὶ τῇ πίστει); Acts 16:5: "So the churches were strengthened in the faith" (αἱ μὲν οὖν ἐκκλησίαι ἐστερεοῦντο τῇ πίστει).

137 Cf. Ernst Theodor Mayerhoff, *Der Brief an die Colosser, mit vornehmlicher Berücksichtigung der drei Pastoralbriefe kritisch geprüft* (Berlin, 1838); Holtzmann, *Kritik*, esp. 104–21; and Percy, *Probleme*, esp. 16–66; *idem*, "Zu den Problemen der Kolosser- und Epheserbriefe," *ZNW* 43 (1950–51): 178–93. Also cf. the various NT Introductions.

138 As seen in Παῦλος ἀπόστολος κτλ (Paul, an apostle, etc.); χάρις ὑμῖν καὶ εἰρήνη κτλ (grace to you

tional expositions and hortatory conclusions,[140] and listing of messages and greetings.[141] But this is not all, for the contacts extend into the theological terminology, such as the formulaic expressions "in Christ" (ἐν Χριστῷ) in 1:2, 4, 28; or "in the Lord" (ἐν κυρίῳ) in 3:18, 20; 4:7, 17; or "with Christ" (σὺν Χριστῷ) in 2:12, 20; 3:1, 3; expositions about belonging to Christ through baptism in 1:13, 2:11–15; statements concerning the freedom from the compulsive power of the regulations (2:14, 20f); about the opposition between the old and the new man (3:5–17); and also concerning the relation between the indicative and the imperative in the exhortations (*ibid.*). Many expressions used in Col present decidedly Pauline peculiarities of style,[142] as seen in the superfluous use of καί after διὰ τοῦτο (1:9; cf. 1 Thess 2:13; 3:5; Rom 13:6; etc.); in phrases like οἱ ἅγιοι αὐτοῦ (his saints, 1:26; cf. 1 Thess 3:13; 2 Thess 1:10) and ἐν μέρει (in regard to, 2:16; cf. 2 Cor 3:10; 9:3);[143] and in verbs such as χαρίζεσθαι, meaning "to forgive" (2:13; 3:13; cf. 2 Cor 2:7, 10; 12:13).

These similarities which Col has to other Pauline letters do not, however, do away with the differences which are worthy of attention. Altogether in Col there are thirty–four hapaxlegomena, words which appear nowhere else in the New Testament writings:

προακούειν (1:5)	to hear before
ἀρέσκεια (1:10)	good pleasure
ὁρατός (1:16)	visible
πρωτεύειν (1:18)	to be the first
εἰρηνοποιεῖν (1:20)	to make peace
μετακινεῖν (1:23)	to be dissuaded, moved
ἀνταναπληροῦν (1:24)	to complete
πιθανολογία (2:4)	beguiling speech
στερέωμα (2:5)	firm stability
συλαγωγεῖν (2:8)	to snare
φιλοσοφία (2:8)	philosophy
θεότης (2:9)	deity
σωματικῶς (2:9)	bodily
ἀπέκδυσις (2:11)	putting off
χειρόγραφον (2:14)	certificate
προσηλοῦν (2:14)	to nail
ἀπεκδύεσθαι (2:15; 3:9)	to strip
νεομηνία (2:16)	new moon
καταβραβεύειν (2:18)	to condemn
ἐμβατεύειν (2:18)	to enter into mystery rites
δογματίζειν (2:20)	to have regulations imposed
ἀπόχρησις (2:22)	use
ἐθελοθρησκία (2:23)	self–chosen worship
ἀφειδία (2:23)	severity
πλησμονή (2:23)	indulgence
αἰσχρολογία (3:8)	abusive language
Σκύθης (3:11)	Scythian
μομφή (3: 13)	complaint
βραβεύειν (3:15)	to hold sway
εὐχάριστος (3:15)	thankful
ἀθυμεῖν (3:21)	to become timid
ἀνταπόδοσις (3:24)	reward
ἀνεψιός (4:10)	cousin
παρηγορία (4:11)	comfort

There are twenty–eight words which do reappear in the New Testament, but not in the other Pauline letters:[144]

ἀποκεῖσθαι (1:5)	to lie prepared
σύνδουλος (1:7; 4:7)	fellow servant
δυναμοῦν (1:11)	to strengthen
κλῆρος (1:12)	lot
θρόνος (1:16)	throne
συνεστηκέναι (1:17)	to be established
ἀπόκρυφος (2:3)	hidden

and peace, etc.; 1:1–2); and in ἡ χάρις μεθ' ὑμῶν (grace be with you; 4:18).

139 E.g., 1:3, Εὐχαριστοῦμεν τῷ θεῷ πατρὶ τοῦ κυρίου ἡμῶν Ἰησοῦ Χριστοῦ πάντοτε περὶ ὑμῶν προσευχόμενοι (We thank God, the Father of our Lord Jesus Christ, always when we pray for you.).

140 As seen in θέλω γὰρ ὑμᾶς εἰδέναι (For I want you to know 2:1) and in the uses of οὖν (therefore) in 2:6, 16; 3:1, 5 and elsewhere.

141 These appear in 4:8, ὃν ἔπεμψα πρὸς ὑμᾶς (I am sending him to you); in 4:10, 12, ἀσπάζεται ὑμᾶς (greets you); in 4:15, ἀσπάσασθε (greet . . .) and elsewhere.

142 Cf. Kümmel, *Introduction*, 241, and also the thorough discussion of the linguistic and stylistic relations to the genuine Pauline epistles in Percy, *Probleme*, 36–66.

143 Kümmel, *Introduction*, 241, also cites πᾶν ἔργον ἀγαθόν (all good works, 1:10; cf. 2 Cor 9:8 and 2 Thess 2:17). But in this case the reference has to do with an expression picked up from Jewish tradition. Concerning the phrase, οἱ ἅγιοι (his saints), it must be realized that there are differing meanings for 1:26 on the one hand, and for 1 Thess 3:13 and 2 Thess 1:10 on the other. Cf. above, pp. 74f on 1:26.

144 Those letters whose authenticity is disputed (i.e., 2 Thess and the Pastorals) are not taken into consideration at this point or later. The comparison with Eph is made separately in each instance.

παραλογίζεσθαι (2:4) to delude
ἐξαλείφειν (2:14) to destroy utterly
ὑπεναντίος (2:14) standing against
δειγματίζειν (2:15) to put on display
ἑορτή (2:16) festival
σκία (2:17) shadow
θρησκεία (2:18) worship
κρατεῖν (2:19) to adhere steadfastly
γεύεσθαι (2:21) to taste
θιγγάνειν (2:21) to touch
ἔνταλμα (2:22) regulation
τὰ ἄνω(3:1) that which is above
κρύπτειν (3:3) to hide
τελειότης (3:14) perfection
πλουσίως (3:16) abundantly
πικραίνειν (3:19) to make bitter
ἅλας (4:6) salt
ἀρτύειν (4:6) to season
ἀποκρίνεσθαι (4:6) to answer
πόνος (4:13) work
ἰατρός (4:14) physician

There are ten words which Col has in common only with Eph:

ἀποκαταλλάσσειν (1:20, 22) to reconcile
ἀπαλλοτριοῦσθαι (1:21) to be alienated
ῥιζοῦσθαι (2:7) to be rooted
συνεγείρειν (2:12) to raise together
συζωοποιεῖν (2:13) to make alive together
ἁφή (2:19) sinew
αὔξησις (2:19) growth
ὕμνος (3:16) hymn
ὀφθαλμοδουλία (3:22) eye–service
ἀνθρωπάρεσκος (3:22) pleaser of men

Finally, there are fifteen words used in Col and Eph as well as in the rest of the New Testament, but not in the other Pauline letters:

αἰτεῖσθαι (1:9) to ask
κράτος (1:11) might
ἄφεσις (1:14) forgiveness
κυριότης (1:16) dominion
κατοικεῖν (1:19; 2:9) to dwell
διάνοια (1:21) mind
κατενώπιον (1:22) before
θεμελιοῦν (1:23) to be firmly established
ἀπάτη (2:8) deceit
δόγμα (2:14) regulaton
σύνδεσμος (2:19; 3:14) ligament, bond
αὔξειν (intrans.) (2:19) to grow
βλασφημία (3:8) slander
ᾠδή (3:16) song
ᾄδειν (3:16) to sing

In order to judge correctly the number of words which do not appear in the clearly authentic Pauline letters, it must be kept in mind that a good part of the terms just cited either appear in the hymn (1:15–20) which was taken from tradition, or they appear in the argumentation with the false teaching which threatened the community (2:6–23). It is hardly surprising that in these sections many expressions occur which were either taken from quotations or which played a part in the polemic. With respect to the hapaxlegomena and other terms rarely used elsewhere, it must be noted on the other hand, that eleven words appear only in Col and in the other Pauline letters, and nowhere else in the New Testament.

ἱκανοῦν (1:12) to authorize
ἑδραῖος (1:23) steadfast
ἀπεῖναι (2:5) to be absent
συνθάπτεσθαι (2:12) to be buried with
θριαμβεύειν (2:15) to triumph
εἰκῇ (2:18) without reason
φυσιοῦσθαι (2:18) to be puffed up
πάθος (3:5) passion
ἐρεθίζειν (3:21) to provoke
ἰσότης (4:1) fairness
συναιχμάλωτος (4:10) fellow–prisoner

Compounds of more than two parts in Col, ἀποκαταλλάσσειν (1:20, 22), ἀνταναπληροῦν (1:24), ἀπεκδύεσθαι (2:15; 3:9) and ἀνταπόδοσις (3:24), must be compared with similar compounds found in 2 Cor, προσαναπληροῦν (9:12; 11:9), in Gal, συμπαραλαμβάνειν (2:1), in Rom ἀποκαραδοκία (8:19) and in Phil ἐξανάστασις (3:11).[145] Finally, it must not be overlooked that hapaxlegomena and unusual expressions appear in considerable numbers in the other Pauline letters.[146] In view of these results the relation of the language of Col to the chief Pauline letters cannot simply be determined according to statistics, that is, merely by determining how many new terms appear. Consideration must rather be given to determining what significance in subject matter should be assigned to the differences which are indicated in the comparison of the vocabulary of Col with that of other Pauline letters.

Attention should be given first of all to the fact that a group of specific Pauline terms, which are otherwise quite common, is missing in Col, such as,

ἁμαρτία (in the sing.) sin
ἀποκάλυψις revelation

145 Otherwise Paul writes καταλλάσσειν (1 Cor 7:11; 2 Cor 5:18–20; Rom 5:10). Likewise, he uses ἀναπληροῦν in Phil 2:30 and elsewhere; the verb ἐκδύεσθαι in 2 Cor 5:4; and uses ἀποδιδόναι (with various shades of meaning) in 1 Cor 7:3; Rom 2:6; 12:17 and 13:7.

146 Cf. Percy, *Probleme*, 17f. Zahn, *Introduction*, 521f, collected the material concerning Gal for compari-

δικαιοσύνη, δικαιοῦν, δικαίωμα, δικαίωσις	righteousness, and related words
δοκιμάζειν, δοκιμή, δόκιμος	to examine, and related words
ἐλευθερία, ἐλευθεροῦν	freedom, to free
ἐπαγγελία, ἐπαγγέλλεσθαι	promise, to promise
κατεργάζεσθαι	to achieve
καυχᾶσθαι, καύχημα	to boast, boast
κοινός, κοινωνία	communal; community
λοιπός	other, and related meanings
νόμος	law
πιστεύειν	to believe
πείθειν, πεποίθησις	to convince, confidence
σῴζειν, σωτηρία	to save, salvation
ὑπακοή	obedience

Yet it is true that in other Pauline letters occasionally one or another of these words listed fails to appear or is strikingly infrequent. Thus in 1 Thess and Phil, the word ἀποκάλυψις (revelation) is not used. The word δικαιοσύνη (righteousness) appears in 1 Cor only in 1:30 and not at all in 1 Thess. Neither is the verb δικαιοῦν (to justify) used in 1 Thess, in Phil, or in 2 Cor. The word νόμος (law) is not used in 2 Cor, and this letter uses πιστεύειν (to believe) only in 4:13 in an Old Testament quotation. Likewise, the word σωτηρία (salvation) does not appear in Gal or in 1 Cor, and ὑπακοή (obedience) is not used in 1 Thess, Gal, Phil or 1 Cor. To be sure, the non-appearance of one or another word or concept may be occasioned by chance or by the different topic of a specific letter. But the epistle to the Colossians is engaged in a controversy with a legalistic doctrine, and it is quite peculiar that the very terms which actually could be expected to occur in such a confrontation are exactly the ones which are missing: ἁμαρτία (sin; in the sing.), δικαιοσύνη (righteousness), δικαιοῦν (to justify), νόμος (law), πιστεύειν (to believe).

It is true, on the one hand, that the use of the theological terminology is conditioned by the theme dealt with in a particular instance and by the author's shaping of that theme. On the other hand, however, the use of such words—which are not a part of the theological vocabulary—hardly depends upon the conscious consideration of the author. For this reason, linguistic differences in this area of vocabulary are of particular importance. In his letters, Paul likes to address his hearers as "brothers" (ἀδελφοί) or as "my brothers" (ἀδελφοί μου). This is true even for the Roman community which was personally unknown to him. Yet this address does not appear in Col or in Eph or in the Pastorals.[147] Furthermore, a whole group of connective words, which Paul otherwise likes to use, are missing in Col:[148] μᾶλλον, εἰ μή, οὐδέ, οὔτε, εἴ τις, εἰ καί, εἴπως, εἴπερ, μόνον, οὐ μόνον δὲ—ἀλλὰ καί, ἔτι, οὐκέτι, μηκέτι, τε. This is also the case with the inferential particles διό, διότι, ἄρα, ἄρα οὖν. It is possible, however, to make similar observations in other letters: Phil does not use ἄρα and both Corinthians do not use ἄρα οὖν. Also, Gal has only one διό, in 4:31. In 1 Cor, only 15:9 has διότι, while 2 Cor lacks it.

The investigation of the vocabulary demonstrates, therefore, that Col contains several peculiarities. But the differences which show up in comparisons with other Pauline letters are balanced by many similarities, and divergencies are paralleled in other letters. These findings, thus, do not allow a judgment about the facts of the case which have been stated thus far. Not until an investigation of the stylistic peculiarities is made and coordinated with the in-

son, and Gal has the following hapaxlegomena: ἀλληγορεῖν, βασκαίνειν, δάκνειν, ἐθνικῶς, εἴκειν, ἐκπτύειν, ἐπιδιατάσσειν, εὐπροσωπεῖν, ἰουδαΐζειν, ἰουδαϊκῶς, Ἰουδαϊσμός, ἱστορεῖν, κατασκοπεῖν, κενόδοξος, μορφοῦν, μυκτηρίζειν, ὀρθοποδεῖν, πατρικός, παρείσακτος, πεισμονή, προευαγγελίζεσθαι, προθεσμία, προκαλεῖν, προκυροῦν, προσανατίθεσθαι, στίγμα, συνηλικιώτης, συνυποκρίνεσθαι, συστοιχεῖν, φθονεῖν, φρεναπατᾶν. Furthermore, the following words appear in the NT but not in any other letter of the Pauline corpus: ἀκυροῦν, ἀναλίσκειν, ἀναστατοῦν, ἀνατίθεσθαι, ἀνέρχεσθαι, ἄνωθεν, ἀποκόπτειν, διαμένειν, ἐγκράτεια, ἐκλύεσθαι, ἐνέχειν, ἐνευλογεῖν, ἐνιαυτός, ἐξαιρεῖν, ἐξαποστέλλειν, ἐξορύττειν, ἐπίτροπος, εὐθέως, Ἱεροσόλυμα, καταγιγνώσκειν, κατάρα, κρέμασθαι, μετατιθέναι, μεταστρέφειν, μήν, ὅμοιος, παιδίσκη, παρατηρεῖν, πηλίκος, πορθεῖν, προϊδεῖν, προστιθέναι, συμπαραλαμβάνειν, ταράσσειν, ὑποστέλλειν, ὑποστρέφειν, φαρμακεία, φορτίον, ὠδίνειν. Only in disputed letters is there a reappearance of these words: ἀναστροφή, ἐξαγοράζειν, ζυγός, μεσίτης, οἰκεῖος, παρέχειν, στοιχεῖα τοῦ κόσμου, στύλος.

147 Cf. Eduard Schweizer, "Zur Frage der Echtheit des Kolosser- und Epheserbriefs" *ZNW* 47 (1956): 287; reprinted in *Neotestamentica*, 429.

148 Cf. Holtzmann, *Kritik*, 107.

vestigation of the terminology of Col, can an accurate picture of the language and style of Col emerge.[149]

The style of the letter is marked by a series of characteristic features. Quite frequently, expressions are combined which belong to the same stem:

1:11 ἐν πάσῃ δυνάμει δυναμούμενοι
strengthened with all *power*

1:29 κατὰ τὴν ἐνέργειαν αὐτοῦ τὴν ἐνεργουμένην
according to his *power* which *works*

2:11 περιετμήθητε περιτομῇ ἀχειροποιήτῳ
circumcised with a *circumcision* not made by hands

2:19 αὔξει τὴν αὔξησιν τοῦ θεοῦ
grows with the *growth* of God

Admittedly similar usages can be cited from the chief Pauline letters:

1 Cor 7:20 ἐν τῇ κλήσει ᾗ ἐκλήθη
in the *calling* in which he was *called*

1 Cor 10:16 τὸ ποτήριον τῆς εὐλογίας ὃ εὐλογοῦμεν
the cup of *blessing* which we *bless*

1 Cor 11:2 καθὼς παρέδωκα ὑμῖν τὰς παραδόσεις[150]
the *traditions* just as I *delivered* them to you

Again, frequently Col piles synonyms together:

1:9 προσευχόμενοι καὶ αἰτούμενοι
to *pray* . . . and to *ask*

1:11 πᾶσαν ὑπομονὴν καὶ μακροθυμίαν
all *endurance* and *patience*

1:22 ἁγίους καὶ ἀμώμους καὶ ἀνεγκλήτους
holy, *blameless* and *irreproachable*

1:23 τεθεμελιωμένοι καὶ ἑδραῖοι
firmly *established* and *steadfast*

1:26 ἀπὸ τῶν αἰώνων καὶ ἀπὸ τῶν γενεῶν
for *ages* and *generations*

2:7 ἐρριζωμένοι καὶ ἐποικοδομούμενοι
rooted and *built up*

3:8 ὀργήν, θυμόν
anger, wrath

3:16 (cf. 1:28) διδάσκοντες καὶ νουθετοῦντες
teach and *admonish*

3:16 ψαλμοῖς, ὕμνοις, ᾠδαῖς πνευματικαῖς
psalms, *hymns*, and *songs* prompted by the Spirit

4:12 τέλειοι καὶ πεπληροφορημένοι[151]
perfect and *filled*

Yet the major Pauline letters also employ similar phrases:

Rom 1:18 πᾶσαν ἀσέβειαν καὶ ἀδικίαν

Rom 1:21 ἐδόξασαν καὶ ηὐχαρίστησαν

Rom 1:25 ἐσεβάσθησαν καὶ ἐλάτρευσαν

Rom 1:29 ἀδικίᾳ, πονηρίᾳ[152]

What is particularly striking is that Col heaps up series of dependent genitives:

1:5 ἐν τῷ λόγῳ τῆς ἀληθείας τοῦ εὐαγγελίου

1:12 εἰς τὴν μερίδα τοῦ κλήρου τῶν ἁγίων

1:13 εἰς τὴν βασιλείαν τοῦ υἱοῦ τῆς ἀγάπης αὐτοῦ

1:20 διὰ τοῦ αἵματος τοῦ σταυροῦ αὐτοῦ

1:24 τὰ ὑστερήματα τῶν θλίψεων τοῦ Χριστοῦ

1:27 τὸ πλοῦτος τῆς δόξης τοῦ μυστηρίου τούτου

2:2 εἰς πᾶν πλοῦτος τῆς πληροφορίας τῆς συνέσεως

2:2 εἰς ἐπίγνωσιν τοῦ μυστηρίου τοῦ θεοῦ

2:11 ἐν τῇ ἀπεκδύσει τοῦ σώματος τῆς σαρκός

2:12 διὰ τῆς πίστεως τῆς ἐνεργείας τοῦ θεοῦ

The major Pauline letters may also do that:

Rom 2:5 ἐν ἡμέρᾳ ὀργῆς καὶ ἀποκαλύψεως δικαιοκρισίας τοῦ θεοῦ

Rom 4:11 σφραγῖδα τῆς δικαιοσύνης τῆς πίστεως ἐν τῇ ἀκροβυστίᾳ

1 Cor 2:6 σοφίαν . . . τῶν ἀρχόντων τοῦ αἰῶνος τούτου[153]

Of course such series of genitives are not by any means as common as they are in Col. Another point of interest here is that Col repeatedly attaches nouns to phrases by the preposition ἐν (in):

1:6 τὴν χάριν τοῦ θεοῦ ἐν ἀληθείᾳ

1:8 τὴν ὑμῶν ἀγάπην ἐν πνεύματι

1:12 εἰς τὴν μερίδα τοῦ κλήρου τῶν ἁγίων ἐν τῷ φωτί

1:29 κατὰ τὴν ἐνέργειαν αὐτοῦ τὴν ἐνεργουμένην ἐν ἐμοὶ ἐν δυνάμει

149 Cf. Percy, *Probleme*, 18: "Thus the real problems concerning the form of the letter are lying completely within the area of style."

150 Further examples are in Percy, *Probleme*, 32.

151 This heaping up of synonyms, and especially in genitive connections, is also documented repeatedly in the writings of Qumran. E.g., 1 QS XI.19f; 1 QH XVIII.8; IV.32 has בכוח גבורתו (the might of his power); and 1 QH VII.17 has להעיז בכוח (to make strong through power). Further passages are found in K. G. Kuhn, "Der Epheserbrief im Lichte der Qumrantexte," *NTS* 7 (1960–61): 335f. For an evaluation of the parallels found in Qumran writings, cf. below, p. 181, n. 11.

152 For further examples see Percy, *Probleme*, 20.

153 *Ibid.*, p. 27.

Cf. also 2:4, 15 and 3:4.[154] This connective device is particularly frequent in Col[155] even though other chief letters of Paul contain the phrases:

Rom 14:17 δικαιοσύνη καὶ εἰρήνη καὶ χαρὰ ἐν πνεύματι
Rom 15:13 ἐν τῇ ἐλπίδι ἐν δυνάμει πνεύματος ἁγίου

In order to introduce an explanation, Col occasionally uses the formulaic phrase, ὅ ἐστιν (which is). This is retained unaltered even when the gender of the word which is to be explained does not fit the ὅ (which):

1:24 ὑπὲρ τοῦ σώματος αὐτοῦ, ὅ ἐστιν ἡ ἐκκλησία
3:14 ἐπὶ πᾶσιν δὲ τούτοις τὴν ἀγάπην, ὅ ἐστιν σύνδεσμος τῆς τελειότητος

and also cf. 2:10, 17.[156] Other Pauline letters never employ this device for making connections.[157] Col often makes use of a loosely joined infinitive construction with either a purpose or a result as the intended meaning:

1:10 περιπατῆσαι ἀξίως τοῦ κυρίου (to conduct)
1:22 παραστῆσαι ὑμᾶς ἁγίους κτλ (in order to present)
1:25 πληρῶσαι τὸν λόγον τοῦ θεοῦ (in order to complete)
4:3 λαλῆσαι τὸ μυστήριον τοῦ Χριστοῦ (to announce)
4:6 εἰδέναι πῶς δεῖ ὑμᾶς ἑνὶ ἑκάστῳ ἀποκρίνεσθαι (so that you may know)

In Paul's chief letters similar cases are much rarer but some are found in Rom 1:28, ποιεῖν τὰ μὴ καθήκοντα and 2 Cor 11:2, παραστῆσαι τῷ Χριστῷ.[158]

When comparing Col with other Pauline letters, what is most striking is the peculiarity of the sentence structure and sequence. In the major Pauline letters the train of thought is most often developed in an argumentative style comparable to the Cynic and Stoic diatribes or to the discussion of Jewish scribes.

Col, however, is marked by a liturgical–hymnic style. In its long sentences, in which parts are occasionally interlocked with each other, a seemingly endless chain of verbose expression is arranged into a pleonastic unit.[159] An example is the thanksgiving, starting at 1:3 with "we give thanks" (εὐχαριστοῦμεν) and not coming to its proper conclusion until v 23. This sentence is divided into smaller sections only twice, by "therefore" (διὰ τοῦτο) at 1:9 and by "and you" (καὶ ὑμᾶς) at 1:21. Relative clauses, inserted causal phrases, participial phrases and secondary notes inflate the sentence to a degree that its form almost collapses. Again in the second chapter of Col one statement after another is loosely joined to the preceding one so that an unwieldy structure emerges in 2:8 to 15. Of course there are several heavily–laden sentences in the chief Pauline letters which are almost incomprehensible (e.g. Gal 2:3–5, 6–9; Rom 1:1–7, 2:5–10, 14–16; 3:23–26). Yet the style of Col differs from the other letters by its liturgical–hymnic character, which results in a pleonastic manner of speaking, in long word–connections and in the stringing together of sentence after sentence. This liturgical style is caused to a great degree by the influence of tradition, since not only in the first chapter (1:12–14, 15–20) but also in other sections, the letter assimilates any number of formulated pieces from the tradition (e.g., 2:9–15). Furthermore, the confrontation with false teaching doubtless created a situation which influenced the language and style of the letter. In spite of all this, however, it is hardly possible to say that

154 There are linguistic parallels in the Qumran texts, e.g., 1 QS XI.2, has תום דרכי עם ישור לבבי (the perfection of my way and the uprightness of my heart); and 1 QS V.2 has ליחד בתורה (a community in the Law). Cf. also 1 QS IV.7f, 13; IX.7, and also Karl Georg Kuhn, "Der Epheserbrief im Lichte der Qumrantexte," *NTS* 7 (1960–61), 337.

155 Cf. Percy, *Probleme*, 27–31.

156 The manuscript evidence is not uniform in either passage. Cf. the comments *ad loc.* in this commentary and also Percy, *Probleme*, pp. 33f. For 1:27, see above, p. 76.

157 Cf. Moulton–Turner, 317, concerning Col 3:14, "Such a solecism appears nowhere else in the Paulines."

158 Infinitive phrases added in a loose fashion are quite numerous in Qumran texts. E.g., 1 QS I.1, לדרוש אל (to seek God); I.2, לעשות הטוב (and do what is good); I.3, ולאהוב (and to love); I.4, ולשנוא (and to hate) and, לרחוק (to depart); I.5, ולדבוק (to cling) and, לעשות (to practice); I.6, ולוא ללכת (and to walk no more); I.7, לעשות (to commit) and, ולהבי (to cause), and לעשות (to practice); I.8, להוחד (to be united) and, ולהתהלך (and to behave); I.9, ולאהוב (that they may love); and I.10, ולשנוא (that they may hate). This is also seen in 1 QS V.1 לשוב (to be converted) and ולהחזיק (to cling) and, להבדל (to separate); and V.2, להיות (to become).

159 For this loose connecting of clauses, the style of the Qumran texts must be compared continuously. Cf. Kuhn, "Epheserbrief," 335f.

the stylistic peculiarities of Col are completely conditioned by its particular content and therefore ought not give rise to doubts about Pauline authorship.[160] What justifies the cause for critical consideration is exactly the letter's intimate dependence upon traditional formulations which so strongly influence its formal structure as well as the organization of its content.

Ernst Theodor Mayerhoff was the first to dispute the Pauline authorship of Col; he proposed the thesis that Col was composed on the model of the equally post–Pauline Eph.[161] Ferdinand Christian Baur and his followers did not ascribe Col to Paul, dating its composition in the second century.[162] Heinrich Julius Holtzmann undertook a thoroughgoing investigation of the problem and advocated a complicated hypothesis to solve it.[163] He suggests that Paul indeed wrote a letter to the community in Colossae, but that it was much shorter than the writing that has come down to us. To this original letter Holtzmann ascribes only these parts: 1:9b–12, 14–24, 26–28; 2:2b–3, 7a, 9–11, 15, 17–19, 22f; 3:1, 2, 4–11, 14–16, 18–25; 4:1, 9, 15–17. This original letter would have been used by another author who also gave Col its present form by reworking and expanding it. Thus Col and Eph would stand in a reciprocal relationship of mutual literary interdependence. Hermann von Soden suggested that the interpolations were of a narrower scope; initially he considered only 1:15–20; 2:10, 15 and 18 as later insertions in the letter.[164] Later, however, he viewed only 1:16b, 17 as a secondary addition.[165] These artifices, however, were rightly opposed by Adolf Jülicher with this fundamental objection, "that the suspicion of such an interpolation into this epistle, which runs on in an even flow without obstacle or gap, would never have arisen but for the presence of the epistle to the Ephesians beside it."[166]

Nevertheless, Charles Masson renewed this hypothesis in a modified form, suggesting that a shorter letter to Colossae had been written by Paul himself, but that this letter was then later expanded by the author of Eph.[167] The original letter consisted of 1:1–4, 7f; 2:6, 8f, 11a, 12a, 16, 20f; 3:3f, 12, 13a, 18–22a, 25; 4:1–3a, b, 5–8a, 9–12a, 14, (15), 17f. This short letter was supposedly then supplemented by the author of Eph in order that these expansions of a "Pauline" letter might assure his own work (i.e. Eph) of greater authority. This analysis by Masson is, however, rather arbitrary. It sunders related sentences without sufficiently proving whether (and to what extent) material formulated by tradition was taken up and employed by Col. It is therefore appropriate that the hypothesis which sees Col as an editorially expanded Pauline letter has not found support.[168] Col has a thoroughly unified structure from the point of view of form as well as that of content.

The question as to what the relation is between the language and style of Col and that of the major Pauline letters is still unanswered today, after more than a century of scholarly discussion. It is generally conceded that the liturgical–hymnic style points to considerable differences from the speech and manner of expression used in the chief Pauline letters. Attempts to explain these differences, however, have generally referred to the peculiar situation necessitating the letter,[169] or they have assumed that the Pauline style changed over the years. This explanation would have Col demonstrate marks of prolonged imprisonment and the apostle's declining power to compose.[170] Those who are not satisfied with these explanations have taken into consideration the possibility that a secretary of Paul

160 Percy, *Probleme*, 43, states "that the stylistic peculiarity of Col, compared with the rest of the Pauline letters, has its basis entirely in the peculiarity of the letter's content. This content, for its part, is clearly connected with the peculiarity of the situation which necessitated the letter."

161 Cf. Mayerhoff, *Der Brief an die Colosser*.

162 Cf. the survey and presentation in Heinrich Julius Holtzmann, *Lehrbuch der historisch-kritischen Einleitung in das Neue Testament* (Freiburg: [2]1886), 280–83.

163 Cf. Holtzmann, *Kritik*, 104–21.

164 Hermann von Soden, "Der Kolosserbrief" *JPTh* 11 (1885): 320–68, 497–542, 672–702.

165 Cf. von Soden's commentary on Col, *ad loc.*

166 Adolf Jülicher, *An Introduction to the New Testament*, tr. Janet Penrose Ward (New York: G. P. Putnam's Sons; London: Smith, Elder Co., 1904), 137f; 7th German edition with Erich Fascher, 1931.

167 Masson attempted to carry out this view in detail in his commentary. P. N. Harrison, "Onesimus and Philemon," *ATR* 32 (1950): 271–74, 281f, states a supposition for which he does not give any further evidence, i.e., that during his Ephesian imprisonment Paul wrote a letter to Colossae, but one which was later reworked by the writer of Eph which would account for the expansions in Col 1:15–20, and 2:4, 8–23.

168 Cf. Werner Bieder's review of Masson's commentary in *ThZ* 8 (1952): 137–43; Michaelis, *Einleitung*, 214; and Kümmel, *Introduction*, 240, 244.

169 Thus Percy, *Probleme*, 43 (cf. above, n. 159). This is similar to Kümmel, *Introduction*, 240–44.

170 Thus Karl Staab, *Die Gefangenschaftsbriefe*, in Regensburger Neuen Testament 7 (Regensburg: [3]1959), 67, "The aged apostle has become calmer, his speech milder, more clarified, more wordy, more winsome,

could have composed this letter under Paul's direction. This would explain the connections with the Pauline letter style as well as the considerable departures. The situation is expressed in Isaac's words to Jacob that the voice is Jacob's voice but the hands are the hands of Esau (Gen 27:22). The voice perceived in Col would be that of Paul, but the hands which wrote out the words were not his.[171] But if one reckons with the possibility that a hand other than Paul's gave shape to Col,[172] then is it not far more probable that the author was a theologian decisively influenced by Paul? Rather than being his secretary, could he not have written Col as one who acted and decided for himself? Yet on the basis of the observations made about the language and style of the letter, no final decision can yet be reached on the question of Pauline or non-Pauline authorship of the letter. To answer this question, the theology of this letter must first be contrasted to that of the major Pauline letters and the mutual relation of these theologies must be thoroughly examined.[173]

even though the old fiery spirit is ever yet visible as soon as he senses a danger to his communities (cf. Col 2:8, 16–23; Phil 3:2). The enforced rest of the long imprisonment of Paul also his greater self-possession which has resulted from his more mature years have directed his view now more than previously toward the depth and breadth of the mystery of Christ." In a similar manner, Paul Feine and Johannes Behm, *Einleitung in das Neue Testament* (Heidelberg: [9]1950), 191, wish to reckon with the "influence which a long imprisonment had upon the apostle's spirit and his ability to compose." They assert "the language and style of Col cannot be called un-Pauline for historical and psychological reasons."

171 Cf. Pierre Benoit, "Rapports littéraires entre les épîtres aux Colossiens et Éphésiens," in *Neutestamentliche Aufsätze, Festschrift für Joseph Schmid* (Regensburg, 1963), 71f, who says that the secretary who composed Col stood more directly under Paul's influence than did the one who wrote Eph. This latter one relied more on earlier writings, especially Col.

172 For a critique of the secretary–hypothesis, cf. above, p. 7, n. 13 on 1:1.

173 Cf. below, pp. 177–83.

2 Christ Jesus the Lord

6 As, then, you have accepted Christ Jesus
the Lord, so conduct yourselves in him,
7/ rooted and built up in him and es-
tablished in the faith, as you were
taught, abounding in thanksgiving. 8/ Be
on your guard that no one snares you
by philosophy and empty deceit accord-
ing to the tradition of men, according
to the elements of the universe and not
according to Christ. 9/ For in him the
entire fullness of deity dwells bodily,
10/ and you have been filled in him, who
is the head of every power and princi-
pality; 11/ in him you were also circum-
cised with a circumcision not made by
hands, by putting off the body of flesh,
by the circumcision of Christ; 12/ with
him you were also buried in baptism;
in him you were also raised with him by
faith in the power of God, who raised
him from the dead. 13/ Also you, who
were dead in your sins and in the uncir-
cumcision of your flesh—he made you
alive together with him,
who forgave us all our trespasses
14 who wiped out the certificate of indebted-
ness which was made out against us,
which—because of the regulations—was
against us;
and he removed it,
nailed it to the cross;
15 who stripped the powers and principalities
and put them on public display,
who triumphed over them in him.

A community that realizes that it is rooted in the apostolic gospel will know how to distinguish right tradition from false teaching. Therefore, before the author states his warning with respect to "philosophy" (*φιλοσοφία*), he once again admonishes them to persevere in the teaching they received and to remain unshakeable in their faith (2:6f). But once this has been said, the community is confronted with the alternative that demands of them a clear and unequivocal decision: "according to the elements of the universe" (*κατὰ τὰ στοιχεῖα τοῦ κόσμου*) means "not according to Christ" (*οὐ κατὰ Χριστόν* 2:8). Referring back to the hymn of 1:15–20, Christ is proclaimed as Lord over all powers and principalities (2:9f). In the two sentences introduced by "in him" (*ἐν ᾧ*) which show that baptism is the basis of belonging to Christ, the author says that the community committed itself to Christ long ago; the decision has been made (2:11f). The subject of the sentence changes in v 13: the text now treats of God's deed which allows those who are baptized to participate in Christ's victory (2:13–15). The piling up of participial clauses shows that in these verses the author takes up formulations that were already at hand and incorporates them into his argument. The exegesis sections will delimit these formulations more exactly and show how the author has reworked them.

■ **6** The connective particle "then" (*οὖν*) marks the transition to this new section. The author briefly refers to the preceding remarks about the reception of the gospel and the community's good standing. Then he engages in a concentrated attack against the false teaching. The community must remain steadfast in the proclamation as it had received it. Paul reminded the Corinthians: he had transmitted to them what he had previously received (1 Cor 15:1–5),[1] and he quotes as the content of this "tradition" (*παράδοσις*) the Good News of Jesus Christ. In a similar way he also demanded of his other communities that they not accept any other so-called gospel "beyond that which you received" (*παρ' ὃ παρελάβετε*

Gal 1:9), and he admonished them to conduct their lives "according to what you received from us" (καθὼς παρελάβετε παρ' ἡμῶν 1 Thess 4:1; cf. 2:13; 1 Cor 11:2; 2 Thess 3:6). "What you have learned, and received and heard and seen in me, do" (ἃ καὶ ἐμάθετε καὶ παρελάβετε καὶ ἠκούσατε καὶ εἴδετε ἐν ἐμοί, ταῦτα πράσσετε Phil 4:9). The content of that which had been communicated to the community in the apostolic tradition[2] is described in Col with the words "Christ Jesus the Lord" (τὸν Χριστὸν Ἰησοῦν τὸν κύριον). These words should surely not be construed as an allusion to sayings of Jesus, which had been communicated to the community as admonitions for right conduct.[3] For Col never cites a saying of the Lord or refers to Jesus' preaching. Rather the reference is to the confession which was recited and preached everywhere in the Hellenistic communities: "Jesus Christ is Lord" (κύριος Ἰησοῦς Χριστός Phil 2:11; cf. 1 Cor 12:3; Rom 10:9). In this confession, "Christ" was no longer understood as a title, but was joined to "Jesus" to form a double name.[4] Christ Jesus is the Lord: that means that he is not a lord alongside other lords, but is the Kyrios in an absolute sense (cf. 1 Cor 8:5f).[5] The community had accepted this proclamation[6] and therefore is bound to be obedient to the Lord. Thus, the community is again summoned to prove that it has truly understood the divine will as its conduct and actions fulfill the request "to lead a life worthy of the Lord" (περιπατῆσαι ἀξίως τοῦ κυρίου 1:10).[7]

■ **7** The conduct of the community is described in more detail by four participial clauses. The first participle appears in the perfect tense and indicates that the Christians have been firmly "rooted" (ἐρριζωμένοι) in Christ, so that they will continue—and this is the point of the following three present tense participles—to conduct their lives in accordance with this beginning. Upon the image of being rooted follows that of being built up (cf. on 1:23).[8] Both images, however, were rather frequently joined together to describe a solid foundation upon which men could base their lives. Thus, Paul tells the Corinthians: "You are God's field, God's building" (θεοῦ γεώργιον, θεοῦ οἰκοδομή ἐστε 1 Cor 3:9). To the image of planting and growth—"I planted, Apollos watered, but God gave the growth" (ἐγὼ ἐφύτευσα, Ἀπολλῶς ἐπότισεν, ἀλλὰ ὁ θεὸς ηὔξανεν 1 Cor 3:6)—he joins the image of the building which has been erected upon the only foundation able to support it: "who is Jesus

1 The verbs "to receive," "to accept" (παραλαμβάνειν) and "to transmit" (παραδιδόναι cf. 1 Cor 11:23; Gal 1:12) corresponds to the Rabbinic concepts קִבֵּל and מָסַר which were used to describe the reception and transmission of tradition: "Moses received Torah from Sinai and delivered it to Joshua, and Joshua to the Elders, and the Elders to the Prophets, and the Prophets delivered it to the men of the Great Synagogue" (*Ab.* 1:1, R. H. Charles, *APOT*.) Cf. Joachim Jeremias, *The Eucharistic Words of Jesus*, tr. Norman Perrin (New York: Charles Scribner's Sons, ³1966), 101–103. Primitive Christian tradition, however, is not connected with the authority of the names of famous teachers. But Paul cites the source from which alone all Christian teaching derives its authority: "from the Lord" (ἀπὸ τοῦ κυρίου 1 Cor 11:23).

2 Cf. Leonhard Goppelt, "Tradition nach Paulus," *KD* 4 (1958): 213–233, esp. 215; Klaus Wegenast, *Das Verständnis der Tradition bei Paulus und in den Deuteropaulinen*. WMANT 8 (Neukirchen: 1962), esp. 121–130.

3 This is the position of Oscar Cullmann, "The Tradition: The Exegetical, Historical and Theological Problem" in *The Early Church*, ed. and tr. A. J. B. Higgins (London: SCM Press Ltd., 1956), 64.

4 Moulton–Turner, 167, maintain: "In Col. 2, 6 the author reverts to the earlier designation of Χριστός as a title = Messiah." Since, however, "the Lord" (τὸν κύριον) follows as a title of honor, "Christ" (Χριστός) is no longer used in a titular sense even in this passage.

5 Cf. 2 Cor 4:5: "For we do not preach ourselves but Christ Jesus as Lord" (οὐ γὰρ ἑαυτοὺς κηρύσσομεν ἀλλὰ Χριστὸν Ἰησοῦν κύριον) further, Eph 3:11: "In Christ Jesus our Lord" (ἐν τῷ Χριστῷ Ἰησοῦ τῷ κυρίῳ ἡμῶν).

6 The verb "to receive," "to accept" (παραλαμβάνειν) in Col also refers to the reception of the apostolic tradition (contrary to Wegenast, *Verständnis*, 128).

7 Thus, Christology and ethics are intimately conjoined. The second part of the letter (3:1–4:6) follows upon the first part (1:9–2:23) as its necessary consequence.

8 The verb "to be rooted" (ῥιζοῦσθαι), which by its position next to "to be built up" (ἐποικοδομεῖσθαι) loses most of its original figurative meaning, is repeatedly used in ancient literature in reference to buildings. Cf. e.g., Sophocles, *Oed. Col.* 1591: "the threshold (to Hades) rooted in the earth with bronze steps" (ὀδὸν χαλκοῖς βάθροισι γῆθεν ἐρριζωμένον). Further evidence may be found in Christian Maurer, *TDNT* 6, 990.

Christ" (ὅς ἐστιν Ἰησοῦς Χριστός 1 Cor 3:10f).[9] And Eph 3:17 says of the life of the community: "rooted and grounded in love" (ἐν ἀγάπῃ ἐρριζωμένοι καὶ τεθεμελιωμένοι). The participles "rooted and built up" (ἐρριζωμένοι καὶ ἐποικοδομούμενοι) are thus closely joined together and are both connected with the "in him" (ἐν αὐτῷ) that follows. Only Christ Jesus, the Lord, is the firm foundation. Whoever stands on this foundation will not waver.

The words "and established" (καὶ βεβαιούμενοι) continue the notion of the consolidation of the community's life. The Lord "will establish you" (βεβαιώσει ὑμᾶς 1 Cor 1:8).[10] The community will have a solid foundation in the true faith[11] which it was taught. "Faith" (πίστις) in this passage is "the faith which is the object of believing" (*fides quae creditur*) which was presented as the content of the teachings. The importance of instruction is thereby stressed emphatically. For only the faith that corresponds to the apostolic teaching provides the stability that can defy all attacks (see the commentary to 1:28). Finally, to conduct one's life in the Lord means that the community abounds "in thanksgiving" (ἐν εὐχαριστίᾳ).[12] "Thanksgiving" not only means to express gratitude, but also to praise the Lord in hymnic confessions (cf. the commentary to 1:12). Jubilant and thankful song must be part of the Christian's obedient conduct (cf. 3:16f), in order that everyone can see how the community praises its Lord in order to conduct its life in the Lord whom it has accepted.[13]

■ **8** An urgent warning cry is intended to rouse the community to a state of watchful attention: Pay attention, be on your guard! Paul often introduces polemical statements with the admonition: "beware" (βλέπετε).[14] What is at stake is to watch carefully, to weigh matters soberly.[15] Be on your guard lest anyone snare you![16] The verb "to snare" (συλαγωγεῖν)[17]—a rare word, that is used in the NT nowhere else—means the capture and carrying off of booty.[18] Therefore, a word has been chosen that not only indicates seduction but also points to the evil intent of those who are trying to gain influence over the community. These people are not named. Only the indefinite "someone" (τις) draws attention to the dangerous situation (cf. 2:16).[19] It is said clearly, however, by what means these people intend to carry through their plan to ensnare the community: "through philosophy" (διὰ τῆς φιλοσοφίας).

In Hellenistic language usage the word "philosophy" (φιλοσοφία) was used to describe all sorts of groups, tendencies and points of view and thus had become a rather broad term. Hellenistic Judaism, e.g., wants to be viewed by its non-Jewish contemporaries as a "philosophy."[20] Josephus, in his description of the sects of the Pharisees, Sadducees and Essenes, told his readers that they were three philosophical schools that existed

9 Cf. further the *Odes of Solomon* 38:16–18: "And I was established and lived and was redeemed, and my foundations were laid by the Lord. For he planted me. For He set the root and watered it and fixed it and blessed it; and its fruits will be for ever" (tr. from *The Odes and Psalms of Solomon*, re-edited by Rendel Harris and Alphonse Mingana, vol. 2: The Translation (Manchester: The University Press, 1920) p. 392. Cf. Walter Bauer in the German ed. of Hennecke-Schneemelcher II, p. 619. The two images are also repeatedly used in Mandaean texts. Cf. Marc Lidzbarski, *Ginza. Der Schatz oder Das grosse Buch der Mandäer* (Göttingen: 1925), pp. 495, 12; 500, 9; 536, 1f.

10 Concerning "to establish" (βεβαιοῦν) cf. Heinrich Schlier, *TDNT* 1, 600–03.

11 Instead of τῇ πίστει (BD* 33 al lat) ACI al read: ἐν πίστει, whereas ℵ 𝔎 al Clem Alex have: ἐν τῇ πίστει.

12 B 𝔎 pm insert "in it" (ἐν αὐτῇ namely in the "faith"); ℵ[3] D* it vg[cl] insert "in him" (ἐν αὐτῷ, namely, in Christ).

13 On the connection between thanksgiving and exhortation, cf. above, pp. 14f on 1:3 and Schubert, *Pauline Thanksgivings*, 89: "All Pauline thanksgivings have either explicitly or implicitly paraenetic function."

14 Cf. Gal 5:15; 1 Cor 8:9; 10:12, 18; Phil 3:2, etc.

15 The future indicative follows the verb "beware lest" (βλέπετε μή) to indicate the danger about which one is warned. For "lest" (μή) followed by the future cf. Blass–Debrunner, par. 369, 2; Moulton, *Prolegomena*, 178, 192f; Radermacher, *Grammatik*, 173, 178. On the warning "beware" cf. further Mk 13:5 par.; 13:9, 33.

16 The word order ὑμᾶς ἔσται is inverted by the witnesses ℵ AD ClemAlex[pt].

17 The connection of an attributive participle with the article—"someone *who is* snaring" (ὁ συλαγωγῶν) —corresponds to common Hellenistic language usage. Cf. Blass–Debrunner, par. 412, 4; 474, 5; Radermacher, *Grammatik*, 117.

18 Cf. Heliodorus 10:35 (307): A priest says of the alleged kidnapper of his daughter: "This is the one that carried my daughter off" (οὗτός ἐστιν ὁ τὴν ἐμὴν θυγατέρα συλαγωγήσας [Trans.]); Aris-

side by side within Judaism (*Bell.* 2:119; *Ant.* 18:11). Other religious groups also tried to convey the image that they were imparting philosophy.[21] Even those who through spells and magic knew how to unleash hidden powers called themselves sages and philosophers. A prophet endowed with the special power of knowledge works "in order that philosophy and magic might nourish the soul" (**ἵνα φιλοσοφία μὲν καὶ μαγεία ψυχὴν τρέφῃ** Stobaeus, *fragm.* 23.68). Initiations that unlocked the doors to the hidden sources of being were likewise considered gateways to philosophy so that "one might say that philosophy is the rite of genuine initiation and the handing on of those mysteries which are genuine mysteries" (**τὴν φιλοσοφίαν μύησιν φαίη τις ἂν ἀληθοῦς τελετῆς καὶ ὄντων ὡς ἀληθῶς μυστηρίων παράδοσιν** Theon of Smyrna, *Expositio rerum mathematicarum* (ed. Edvard Hiller, 1878), p. 14 [Trans.]). Just as philosophy step by step paves the way to higher knowledge, so too initiation into the mysteries gives insight into the ultimate connections of being. Thus, philosophy is understood as the knowledge of the divine ground of being of the universe—a knowledge attained by secret revelation. It is obviously in this meaning that the word was used by people who wanted to gain recognition for their teaching. What they offered as "philosophy" had nothing in common with the critical thinking and discerning knowledge of Greek philosophy, except the name. In an ironic parody of their claims the author says that their philosophy is empty, without content, in truth nothing but "empty deceit" (**κενὴ ἀπάτη**).[21a]

Philosophical knowledge was transmitted as teaching.[22] The tradition,[23] which stemmed from the earlier philosophers, must be thought through anew.[24] The "philosophy," about which the mysteries spoke, was also protected by a sacred tradition. The initiation rites communicated to the devotee of the mysteries the "sacred word" (**ἱερὸς λόγος**) which as sacred "tradition" (**παράδοσις**) conveyed tidings of divine revelation.[25] And

taenetus, *Epist.* 2:22: "He is trying to rob us of our home" (ἐγχειροῦντα συλαγωγῆσαι τὸν ἡμέτερον οἶκον [Trans.]). Cf. Bauer, *s.v.*

19 Cf. also 1 Cor 3:17; 4:18; 11:16; 15:12.

20 Cf. 4 Macc 5:11; Philo, *Leg. ad Gaium* 156: "the ancestral philosophy" (τὴν πάτριον φιλοσοφίαν); cf. *De mut. nom.* 223.

21 Cf. Bornkamm, *Aufsätze* 1, p. 143, n. 12; *idem*, *TDNT* 4, 808–10.

21a For a negative evaluation of this so-called "Philosophy," cf. 4 Macc 5:11 where King Antiochus calls Judaism a "foolish philosophy" (φλύαρος φιλοσοφία Charles, *APOT*). Eph 5:6 puts it this way: "Let no one lead you astray with empty words" (μηδεὶς ὑμᾶς ἀπατάτω κενοῖς λόγοις).

22 Cf. Gerhard Delling, *TDNT* 4, 11f; Wegenast, *Verständnis*, 123–26.

23 Cf. Plato, *Theaetetus*, 198b: "And we say that when anyone transmits them he teaches, and when anyone receives them he learns" (καὶ καλοῦμέν γε παραδιδόντα μὲν διδάσκειν, παραλαμβάνοντα δὲ μανθάνειν).

24 Cf. Aristotle, *An* 2:2 (p. 412a): "The theories of the soul handed down by our predecessors have been sufficiently discussed" (τὰ μὲν δὴ ὑπὸ τῶν πρότερον παραδεδομένα περὶ ψυχῆς εἰρήσθω); *Phys.* 4:10 (p. 218a): "But what time really is and under what category it falls, is likewise not revealed by anything that has come down to us from earlier thinkers" (τί δ' ἐστὶν ὁ χρόνος καὶ τίς αὐτοῦ ἡ φύσις, ὁμοίως ἔκ τε τῶν παραδεδομένων ἄδηλόν ἐστιν).

25 Cf. Athenaeus, *The Deipnosophists* 2.40d: "Further, we call by the name of 'mystic rites' those festivals which are still more important and are accompanied *by certain traditional mysteries*, deriving the name from the large sums expended upon them" (τελετάς τε καλοῦμεν τὰς ἔτι μείζους καὶ μετά τινος μυστικῆς παραδόσεως ἑορτὰς τῶν εἰς αὐτὰς δαπανημάτων ἕνεκα); Plutarch, *De Iside et Osiride* 2 (p. 351f); "For Isis is a Greek word, and so also is Typhon, her enemy, who is conceited, as his name implies, because of his ignorance and self-deception. He tears to pieces and scatters to the winds the 'sacred word,' which the goddess collects and puts together and *gives into the keeping of those that are initiated into the holy rites* (by) divinization" (Ἑλληνικὸν γὰρ ἡ Ἶσίς ἐστιν καὶ ὁ Τυφὼν πολέμιος ὢν τῇ θεῷ καὶ δι' ἄγνοιαν καὶ ἀπάτην τετυφωμένος καὶ διασπῶν καὶ ἀφανίζων τὸν ἱερὸν λόγον, ὃν ἡ θεὸς συνάγει καὶ συντίθησι καὶ παραδίδωσι τοῖς τελουμένοις διὰ θειώσεως [Trans.]); Plutarch, *De Demetrio* 26:1 (p. 200e): "He wished to be initiated into the mysteries as soon as he arrived, and *to receive all the grades* in the ceremony, from the lowest to the highest (the 'epoptics')" (βούλεται παραγενόμενος εὐθὺς μυηθῆναι καὶ τὴν τελετὴν ἅπασαν ἀπὸ τῶν μικρῶν ἄχρι τῶν ἐποπτικῶν παραλαβεῖν [Trans.]); Ditt. *Syll.*³ 704 E 12: "He entered into the tradition of the mysteries" (εἰσαγαγὼν τὴν τῶν μυστηρίων παράδοσιν [Trans.]); Cicero, *Tusc. Disput.* 1:13, 29: "Recall, since you have been initiated, the lore *imparted* to you in the mysteries" (Reminiscere, quoniam es initiatus, quae *tradantur* mysteriis);

through the tradition, which Gnostic teaching claimed, great pains were taken that the origin of the teachings be protected and the source of the revelation not be obscured.[26] Tradition, which was distinguished by its antiquity, was universally considered as a proof of the dignity and sacredness of the communicated knowledge. It made no difference whether this tradition was now handed on through instruction or through secret rites. Obviously the proponents of that "philosophy" which had been introduced into the Asia Minor communities spared no effort to clothe their teaching with the aura of wisdom transmitted from of old. They did this by appealing to the "tradition" (**παράδοσις**) which would guarantee the unimpaired transmission of the divine revelation.

As a result tradition stands against tradition, claim against claim: here the apostolic tradition, which the community had accepted (2:6f), there the "tradition" of "philosophy." Even though the proponents insisted that their "philosophy" rested upon venerable tradition, in reality it was nothing other than "the tradition of men" (**παράδοσις τῶν ἀνθρώπων**). Just as the Pharisaic–Rabbinic teaching of the law had been rejected as being "the tradition of men" (**παράδοσις τῶν ἀνθρώπων** cf. Mk 7:8), so too in the controversy with the "philosophy" the point was urged that its tradition was a human fabrication and was not based on divine revelation. With respect to its content the author remarks tersely: "according to the elements of the universe and not according to Christ" (**κατὰ τὰ στοιχεῖα τοῦ κόσμου καὶ οὐ κατὰ Χριστόν**).

"The Elements of the Universe" (Στοιχεῖα τοῦ κόσμου)[27]

The word "element" (στοιχεῖν) is related to "series" (στοῖχος) and describes first of all a member of a series or list of things. Examples of this meaning of the word are quite old: "elements" (στοιχεῖα) are the letters of the alphabet as they follow one another in order.[28] Then "elements" can also mean the fundamental principles which provide the basis for everything that is to be built upon it. For example, Xenophon writes: "Shall we consider it, beginning with the elementary question of food" (βούλει σκοπῶμεν ἀρξάμενοι ἀπὸ τῆς τροφῆς ὥσπερ ἀπὸ τῶν στοιχείων *Memor*. 2, 1, 1). And Heb draws attention to the fundamental principles of Christian teaching, which the community already knows, with the words: "You need someone to teach you again the first principles of God's words" (πάλιν χρείαν ἔχετε τοῦ διδάσκειν ὑμᾶς τινα τὰ στοιχεῖα τῆς ἀρχῆς τῶν λογίων τοῦ θεοῦ Heb 5:12).

"Element" is a common word in the language of the philosophers when they treat of the matter or the elements out of which everything is formed. Plato speaks of the "primary elements of which we and all else are composed" (στοιχεῖα, ἐξ ὧν ἡμεῖς

Apuleius, *Metamorph*. 11:21: "*The taking of* such orders was like to a voluntary death and a difficult recovery to health" (*Traditionem* ad instar voluntariae mortis et precariae salutis celebrari). Further examples may be found in Gerhard Delling, *TDNT* 4, 12; Wegenast, *Verständnis*, 123 n. 1.

26 Cf. *Corp. Herm*. 1:26: "as one who has received everything" (ὡς πάντα παραλαβών [Trans.]). Christian Gnostics claimed apostolic origin for their teachings. Cf. Ptolemy *To Flora* 5:10 (Epiphanius, *Panarion Haer*. 33:7): "If you are deemed worthy of knowing the apostolic tradition which we too have received from a succession together with the confirmation of all our words by the teaching of the Saviour" (ἀξιουμένη τῆς ἀποστολικῆς παραδόσεως, ἣν ἐκ διαδοχῆς καὶ ἡμεῖς παρειλήφαμεν μετὰ καὶ τοῦ κανονίσαι πάντας τοὺς λόγους τῇ τοῦ σωτῆρος ἡμῶν διδασκαλίᾳ) (modified trans. from Robert M. Grant, *Second-Century Christianity: A Collection of Fragments* (London: SPCK, 1946), p. 36.) Cf. further Hippolytus, *Refut*. 5, 7, 1; 7, 20, 1; Clem. Alex., *Strom*. 7, 106, 4. Further evidence may be found in Odo Casel, "Zur Kultsprache des heiligen Paulus," *Archiv für Liturgiewissenschaft* 1 (1950): 38f; Hans von Campenhausen, "Lehrerreihen und Bischofsreihen im 2. Jahrhundert" in *In Memoriam Ernst Lohmeyer* (Stuttgart: 1951), 240–49; *idem*, *Ecclesiastical Authority and Spiritual Power in the Church of the First Three Centuries*, tr. J. A. Baker (Stanford, Calif.: Stanford University Press, 1969), 157–61; Wegenast, *Verständnis*, 124 n. 1.

27 Concerning the term "element" (στοιχεῖον) cf. esp. Dibelius–Greeven, 27–29; Bauer, *s.v.* and Gerhard Delling, *TWNT* 7, 670–87 (on p. 670 Delling has an extensive survey of the literature). Cf. further Josef Blinzler, "Lexikalisches zu dem Terminus τὰ στοιχεῖα τοῦ κόσμου bei Paulus" in *Studiorum Paulinorum Congressus Internationalis Catholicus* 1961 2, Analecta Biblica 18 (Rome: 1963), 429–43.

28 Cf. Dionys. Thrax (=*Grammatici Graeci* 1:3, ed. Hilgard [1901]), p. 197:17ff: "And therefore, they (scil. the letters) are said to be component parts of a series, because they are in a row and are ordered to one another. It follows then that they are elements. Whenever they are not written in order, they are called letters and no longer elements" (καὶ διὰ

τε συγκείμεθα καὶ τἆλλα *Theaetetus* 201e).[29] And Zeno defines the term "element" in this way: "An element is defined as that from which particular things first come to be at their birth and into which they are finally resolved" (ἔστι δὲ στοιχεῖον ἐξ οὗ πρώτου γίνεται τὰ γινόμενα καὶ εἰς ὃ ἔσχατον ἀναλύεται). "Earth" (ὕλη), "fire" (πῦρ), "water" (ὕδωρ), and "air" (ἀήρ) are then cited as the four elements which constitute everything (Diogenes Laertius 7:136f). This meaning of "element," which was widely disseminated by Hellenistic philosophical schools, was also current in Hellenistic Judaism.[30] In Jewish texts where the terminological connection "elements of the universe" (στοιχεῖα τοῦ κόσμου) occurs, what is meant is prime matter, the elements from which the universe was shaped. Philo says that just as the seasons of the year periodically follow one another, so too is the case with the "elements of the universe": these elements seem to perish as they change, yet in truth are imperishable as they change: earth is liquified and becomes water, water vaporizes into air, air rarefies into fire (*De aetern. mundi* 109f). Air, fire, water, and earth are also the "sensible elements of the sensible world" (στοιχεῖα αἰσθητὰ αἰσθητοῦ κόσμου *Rer. div. her.* 134), the "four elements of the world" τέτταρα τοῦ κόσμου στοιχεῖα *ibid.*, 140).[31]

In Hellenistic syncretism the teaching about the elements was mythologized, so that the "elements" were described as animated spirits.[32] In the Orphic hymns it says: "Eminent fire, the world's best element" (ὑψιφανὴς Αἰθέρ, κόσμου στοιχεῖον ἄριστον 5:4) and "[Vulcan], workman, destiny of the world, pure element" (["Ηφαιστ'] ἐργαστήρ, κόσμοιο μέρος, στοιχεῖον ἀμεμφές 66:4 [Trans.]). At a later period, in the *Testament of Solomon*, the "elements" are described as beings who appear to be persons. Solomon sees seven spirits coming and asks them who they are. He receives the answer: "We are the elements, the cosmic rulers of darkness" (ἡμεῖς ἐσμεν στοιχεῖα κοσμοκράτορες τοῦ σκότους 8:2). A group of thirty–six spirits likewise introduces itself with the words: "We are the thirty–six elements, the world–rulers of the darkness of this age" (ἡμεῖς ἐσμεν τὰ τριάκοντα ἓξ στοιχεῖα, οἱ κοσμοκράτορες τοῦ σκότους τοῦ αἰῶνος τούτου 18:2 [Trans.]). The term στοιχεῖα not only designates the elements of the universe but also the stars[33] which consist of the elements, and whose constellations control the order of the entire universe as well as men's fate. Consequently, the twelve signs of the zodiac are called "the twelve elements" (τὰ δώδεκα στοιχεῖα Diogenes Laertius 6:102). Whoever knows how to discern and chart the course of

---

τοῦτο λέγει αὐτὰ [scil. τὰ γράμματα] εἶναι στοιχεῖα, διὰ τὸ ἔχειν αὐτὰ <στοῖχόν τινα καὶ> τάξιν πρὸς ἄλληλα· τότε γὰρ καὶ στοιχεῖά ἐστιν· ὅταν δὲ μὴ κατὰ τάξιν γράφωνται, γράμματα μὲν λέγονται, οὐκέτι δὲ στοιχεῖα [Trans.]).

29 Also cf. *Soph.* 252b: "And further, all who teach that things combine at one time and separate at another, whether infinite elements combine in unity and are derived from unity or finite elements separate and then unite . . ." (καὶ μὴν καὶ ὅσοι τότε μὲν συντιθέασι τὰ πάντα, τότε δὲ διαιροῦσιν, εἴτε εἰς ἓν καὶ ἐξ ἑνὸς ἄπειρα εἴτε εἰς πέρας ἔχοντα στοιχεῖα διαιρούμενοι καὶ ἐκ τούτων συντιθέντες).

30 Cf. 4 Macc 12:13: All men are "made from the same elements" (ἐκ τῶν αὐτῶν γεγονότας στοιχείων [Charles, *APOT*]); Wisd Sol 7:17: "operation of the elements" (ἐνέργειαν στοιχείων); 19:18: "the elements changed places with one another" (τὰ στοιχεῖα μεθαρμοζόμενα); Philo, *De Cher.* 127: "the four elements" (τὰ τέσσαρα στοιχεῖα) are the "material" (ὕλη) from which God fashioned the universe; Josephus, *Ant.* 3:183: "The tapestries woven of four materials denote the natural elements" (τά τε φάρση ἐκ τεσσάρων ὑφανθέντα τὴν τῶν στοιχείων φύσιν δηλοῖ).

31 According to *Sibyl.* 3:80f, part of the apocalyptic woes was that "then the elements of the world one and all shall be widowed" (τότε δὴ στοιχεῖα πρόπαντα χηρεύσει κόσμου [Charles, *APOT*]). Cf. also *Sibyl.* 2:206f; 8:337f. 2 Pt 3:10, 12 speaks of the dissolution of the "elements" through the annihilating fire on the last day.

32 Cf. Dibelius–Greeven, p. 27. When according to the Hermetic fragment Κόρη Κόσμου of Hermes Trismegistos (= *Fragments of Stobaeus* 23:53–61) the elements fire, air, water, and earth complain to God about man, it is a question of a personification of the elements for dramatic effect. Cf. Heinrich Schlier, *Der Brief an die Galater*, KEK 7 (Göttingen: [12]1962), p. 191 n. 3; Gerhard Delling, *TWNT* 7, 676 n. 45; Hans Dieter Betz, "Schöpfung und Erlösung im hermetischen Fragment 'Kore Kosmu'," *ZThK* 63 (1966): 180–83.

33 Cf. Ps–Callisthenes 1, 12, 1: "Nectanebos, who has measured the heavenly courses of the stars exactly . . . and who has utterly confounded the cosmic elements by employing his magical art, . . . who has ascertained the heavenly courses of the cosmic elements" (ὁ Νεκτανεβὼς καταμετρήσας τοὺς οὐρανίους τῶν ἀστέρων δρόμους . . . καὶ συγκλονήσας τὰ κοσμικὰ στοιχεῖα τῇ μαγικῇ τέχνῃ χρώμενος . . . κατανοήσας τοὺς οὐρανίους δρόμους τῶν κοσμικῶν στοιχείων [Trans.]).

the stars gains powerful knowledge. It is told of the Egyptian king Nectanebos that he had magical power at his disposal, "for all the elements of the universe were subject to his word" (τὰ γὰρ κοσμικὰ στοιχεῖα λόγῳ πάντα αὐτῷ ὑπετάσσετο Ps.–Callisthenes 1, 1, 3 [Trans.]). And in the *Paris Magical Papyrus* 4, 1303 the constellation of Ursa Major, which never sets, is called: "beautiful–shining goddess, incorruptible element" (καλλιφεγγὴ<s> θεά, στοιχεῖον ἄφθαρτον *PreisZaub* 1, p. 116 [Trans.]). With the help of magical knowledge a person can harness for his own purposes the power of the "elements" and release supermundane forces.

Interwoven with the syncretistic embroidery of notions about the "elements of the universe" are also strands of Jewish speculations about how the universe hung together. To be sure, in Judaism no divine dignity is ascribed to the stars. They are, however, related to the angels, be it that the angels ruled over the stars, or be it that the stars themselves were thought of as a distinct class of angels.[34] In apocalyptic vision the order of the stars was revealed to the seer: "And I saw other lightnings and the stars of heaven, and I saw how He called them all by their names and [how] they hearkened unto Him. And I saw . . . their revolution according to the number of the angels, and [how] they keep faith with each other" (1 En 43:1f). Just as God gave his orders to the angels, so too he prescribed the course that the stars should take (1 En 60:11f; 69:20–25, etc.). Full of reverential awe, the seer beholds the established relationships of the cosmic order: "And there I saw seven bands of angels, very bright and very glorious, and their faces shining more than the sun's shining . . . And these make the orders, and learn the goings of the stars, and the alteration of the moon, . . . and the good government of the world. And when they see evil–doing, they make commandments and instruction, and sweet and loud singing, and all songs of praise. These are the archangels . . . and the angels who are appointed over seasons and years, and the angels who are over rivers and sea, and the angels who are over the fruits of the earth, and the angels who are over every grass, giving food to all, and the angels of all the souls of men" (2 En 19:1–4 [Charles, *APOT* modified]). Angels are "the elders and rulers of the stellar orders." They have power over "the stars and the composition of heaven" (2 En 4:1 [Charles, *APOT* modified]).

While in Judaism worship and reverence were alone offered to the one God, in the world of syncretism the cosmic powers were worshipped as divine powers: "And this is said with regard to those gods who rule over the elements, those who preside over all the elements" (καὶ πρὸς τοὺς στοιχειοκράτορας λέγεται θεούς, τοὺς τῶν ὅλων στοιχείων ἐπιβεβηκότας Simplicius, *Comm. in IV libros Aristotelis de caelo* 1, 3 [Trans.]). From ancient times the stars and powers which determine and preserve the universe received offerings and were worshipped. Herodotus narrates of the Persians: "They sacrifice also to the sun and moon and earth and fire and water and winds" (θύουσιν δὲ ἡλίῳ τε καὶ σελήνῃ καὶ γῇ καὶ πυρὶ καὶ ὕδατι καὶ ἀνέμοισι 1, 131). In Hellenistic times this reverence was explained by the assertion that man is formed out of the same elements from which the entire cosmos had been fashioned.[35] This correlation of microcosm and macrocosm implies that "just as light is apprehended by the luciform sense of sight, and sound by the aeriform sense of hearing, so also the nature of all things ought to be apprehended by its kindred reason" (καὶ ὡς τὸ μὲν φῶς ὑπὸ τῆς φωτοειδοῦς ὄψεως καταλαμβάνεται, ἡ δὲ φωνὴ ὑπὸ τῆς ἀεροειδοῦς ἀκοῆς, οὕτω καὶ ἡ τῶν ὅλων φύσις ὑπὸ συγγενοῦς ὀφείλει καταλαμβάνεσθαι τοῦ λόγου Sextus Empiricus, *Adv. math.* 1:93). Where faith in God and gods had grown weak, magical fear of sinister forces often supplanted it. Either a person strove to do justice to all the gods, to those of the heavenly world as well as to those of the underworld and to those of the realm in between, and to implore them all together;[36] or a person adhered to the stars and elements and swore by them: "I adjure you by the sun and the moon and by the courses of the five planets, by nature and providence and the four elements" (ὁρκίζω σε Ἥλιον καὶ Σελήνην καὶ τῶν πέντε ἀστέρων τοὺς δρόμους φύσιν τε καὶ πρόνοιαν καὶ τὰ τέσσαρα στοιχεῖα Vettius Valens 7, 5 [p. 293, 27]) [Trans.].[37] Man's cry to God went upward through the elements: "You are god. This is what the man who belongs to you cries through fire, through air, through earth, through water, through spirit, through your creatures" (σὺ εἶ ὁ θεός. ὁ σὸς ἄνθρωπος ταῦτα βοᾷ διὰ πυρός, δι' ἀέρος, διὰ γῆς, διὰ ὕδατος, διὰ πνεύματος, διὰ τῶν κτισμάτων σου *Corp. Herm.* 13:20 [Trans.]). Thus it is necessary not only to possess knowledge about the elements, the movements of the stars, and the powers of the cosmos; man must also become part of the cosmic order insofar as he proffers the powers and principalities the requisite reverence and submits to the laws and prescriptions they impose upon his life.

34 Cf. Schlier, *Galater*, 192f, and the plentiful evidence cited there.

35 Cf. Philo, *Spec. leg.* 1:266. Further evidence may be found in Dibelius–Greeven, 28.

36 Cf. *P.Leiden* 2, p. 25: "During the initiation rite I implore and pray: O heavenly gods. O gods under the earth. O gods who dwell in the middle realm" (ἐπικαλοῦμαι καὶ εὔχομαι τὴν τελετὴν ὦ θεοὶ οὐρά-

This meaning of the term "elements of the universe" which is determined by syncretistic concepts is doubtless present in the sharply formulated antithesis: "according to the elements of the universe and not according to Christ."[38] Consequently, "elements of the universe" cannot be taken as an expression that the author of Col has chosen to discredit that philosophy as a man–made tradition which was concerned merely with the elements—inadequate supports of man's being.[39] Rather "elements of the universe" must have played a special role in the teaching of the "philosophers." The confrontation of the elements and Christ already indicates that they are conceived of as personal powers.[40] Furthermore, the context as a whole shows that the elements of the universe are precisely those demonic principalities who want to exercise their tyranny over men (2:10, 15).[41] Against this teaching about the "elements of the universe," which control men's lives and which bring demands men must satisfy (cf. 2:16–23),[42] the clear antithesis stands: there is only one authority that can rightfully claim to be Lord over everything and thus to be the only Lord over the life and conduct of the community—Christ. The community must not be led astray to acknowledge other authorities beside him. For the community's course must be solely under the command of the Lord, who alone gives it direction and purpose: "according to Christ" (*κατὰ Χριστόν*).

■ **9** In this verse the author more precisely substantiates the summons to recognize the danger of false teaching and to follow Christ unwaveringly. He does this by resuming the phrase "in him" (cf. v 7) and repeating it as a motif in the following verses. "In him" (*ἐν αὐτῷ*) the entire fullness of deity dwells bodily (v 9); "in him" (*ἐν αὐτῷ*) you have been filled (v 10); "in whom" (*ἐν ᾧ*) you have been circumcised (v 11); with him you have been buried, "in whom" (*ἐν ᾧ*) you also have been raised with him (v 12); God has made you alive "with him" (*σὺν αὐτῷ* v 13); he has led the powers and principalities in triumphal procession "in him" (*ἐν αὐτῷ* v 15).[43]

This train of thought is introduced by: "for in him the entire fulness of deity dwells bodily" (*ὅτι ἐν αὐτῷ κατοικεῖ πᾶν τὸ πλήρωμα τῆς θεότητος σωματικῶς*). This sentence is clearly an explanatory repetition of 1:19: "for in him all the fulness was pleased to dwell" (*ὅτι ἐν*

νιοι· ὦ θεοὶ ὑπὸ γῆν· ὦ θεοὶ ἐν μέσῳ μέρει κυκλούμενοι [Trans.]).

37 Cf. Gerhard Delling, *TWNT* 7, 681f.

38 Cf. Lohmeyer, Dibelius–Greeven, Conzelman *ad loc.*; Bornkamm, *Aufsätze* 1, 143f; Schenke, "Widerstreit," 396f.

39 Thus Gerhard Delling, *TWNT* 7, 685f. Similarly Moule *ad loc.*: " 'elementary teaching'—teaching by Judaistic or pagan ritualists, a 'materialistic' teaching bound up with 'this world' alone, and contrary to the freedom of the Spirit." Percy, *Probleme*, 156–67, likewise explains "the elements of the universe" as a term of Paul's critical vocabulary, but he understands the term as referring to spiritual powers that were the elements of pre–Christian worship. Masson *ad loc.* holds a similar opinion. Blinzler, "Lexikalisches," 442 takes "the elements of the universe" as an expression of a negative criticism which refers to those elements which gave the decisively characteristic marks to pre– and non–Christian existence: "Flesh" (*σάρξ*), "sin" (*ἁμαρτία*), and "death" (*θάνατος*).

40 A comparison with Gal 4:3, 9 is instructive. Here "the elements of the universe" are also conceived of as angelic powers. They are (1) compared to "guardians" (*ἐπίτροποι*) and "trustees" (*οἰκονόμοι* Gal 4:2); (2) described as "not being gods by nature" (*φύσει μὴ ὄντες θεοί* Gal 4:8); (3) thought of as "lords" (*κύριοι*) who demand special services from their devotees, Gal 4:3. Cf. Schlier, *Galater*, 191.

41 This explanation of the concept "elements of the universe" is demanded by the context, and it cannot be objected that the meaning "stars," "elementary spirits," or "spirits of the stars" is not attested in any non–Christian text that can be dated with certainty in pre–Pauline times (thus Blinzler, "Lexikalisches," 432–39). It is quite legitimate to make conclusions about earlier traditions on the basis of later witnesses, especially in view of the fact that the combination of angels and heavenly powers is already present in Jewish apocalyptic texts (cf. also Gal 4!), and that the context of Col 2 compellingly demands the identification "elements of the universe" (*στοιχεῖα τοῦ κόσμου*) = "powers and principalities" (*ἀρχαὶ καὶ ἐξουσίαι*) = "angels" (*ἄγγελοι*).

42 The preposition "according to" (*κατά*) refers to this life–determining authority.

43 Schille, *Frühchristliche Hymnen*, 31–37, maintains without sufficient evidence that a redeemer or baptismal hymn underlies Col 2:9–15. This hymn would have consisted of vss 9, 10b, 11b, 13b–15. The author of Col would have adopted this hymn and commented on it. To be sure, it is incontestable that traditional material has been used in this passage. Nevertheless, more exact distinctions must be made. Vss 9, 10b are surely not the beginning of a hymn.

αὐτῷ εὐδόκησεν πᾶν τὸ πλήρωμα κατοικῆσαι). In both verses the term "fulness" (πλήρωμα) is reinforced by "entire, all" (πᾶν). However, the genitive "of deity" (τῆς θεότητος) more exactly determines "fulness" in this verse. The term "deity" (θεότης) should be distinguished from "divine nature" (θειότης). The term "divine nature" (θειότης) describes the character of God, divinity.[44] The term "deity" (θεότης) describes the quality of being divine.[45] Since the words "fulness" and "to be filled" (πληροῦσθαι) are stressed so emphatically, they must have been key concepts in the "philosophy." Where is the fulness to be found? And how does man attain and participate in it so that he is suffused by divine power? Col answers these questions with the polemical assertion: The entire fulness of deity dwells in Christ. Therefore, only that person can be filled who belongs to this Lord—only he who is in him, who has died with him, and has been raised to new life "with Christ" (σὺν Χριστῷ). Under no circumstances whatsoever can entrance to the "fulness" be attained by submissive worship of the "elements of the universe" and fearful observance of their "regulations" (δόγματα).

The adverb "bodily" (σωματικῶς),[46] which is placed at the end of the sentence, lends special emphasis to the statement.[47] While the aorist "was pleased to dwell" (εὐδόκησεν κατοικῆσαι) occurs in 1:19, here the present tense "dwells" (κατοικεῖ) is used to refer to the present reality. The word "bodily" indicated that the divine indwelling is real.[48] Since the author chose the word "bodily" to express this thought, a relationship to the

Rather it is a question here of an explanatory resumption of 1:15–20. Verse 11b is motivated by the argument about the term "circumcision" (περιτομή). It also remains to be demonstrated to what extent adopted material underlies v 13b–15. Cf. below on v 13 (p. 106). For a critique of Schille's thesis cf. also Deichgräber, *Gotteshymnus und Christushymnus*, 167f.

44 Cf. Rom 1:20: "his eternal power and divinity" (ἡ ἀΐδιος αὐτοῦ δύναμις καὶ θειότης). Cf. also Hermann Kleinknecht, *TDNT* 3, 123.

45 The word "deity," which is only used here in the NT, is frequently attested in Hellenistic literature. Cf., e.g., Plutarch, *Def. orac.* 10 (p. 415b, c): "Even so from men into heroes and from heroes into demigods better souls obtain their transmutation. But from the demigods a few souls still, in the long reach of time, because of supreme excellence, come, after being purified, to share completely in deity" (οὕτως ἐκ μὲν ἀνθρώπων εἰς ἥρωας, ἐκ δὲ ἡρώων εἰς δαίμονας αἱ βελτίονες ψυχαὶ τὴν μεταβολὴν λαμβάνουσιν. ἐκ δὲ δαιμόνων ὀλίγαι μὲν ἔτι χρόνῳ πολλῷ δι' ἀρετῆς καθαρθεῖσαι παντάπασι θεότητος μετέσχον [Loeb modified]). Further evidence may be found in Ethelbert Stauffer, *TDNT* 3, 119, and Bauer, *s.v.*

46 The adverb "bodily" (σωματικῶς) in Hellenistic Greek indicates corporeal reality, the state in which one is affected as a person. Cf. Bauer, *s.v.*; Preisigke, *Wört.* 2, col. 567f. By way of example the following may be cited: Ditt.*Or.* 2, 664, 17f: "They will be punished either by fine or corporeally" (ἢ ἀργυρικῶς ἢ σωματικῶς κολασθήσεται [Trans.]); Preisigke, *Sammelbuch* 5, 8748, 15: "not to take it upon oneself corporeally" (μὴ ἄγεσθαι σωματικῶς [Trans.]); further 8900, 17; Vettius Valens 5, 10 (p. 231, 2); 7, 2 (p. 269, 28); Plutarch, *Def. orac.* 26 (p. 424e).

47 Concerning the different interpretations of "bodily" that scholars have championed, cf. Moule *ad loc.* The problem had already been a concern among the Church Fathers. Jerome takes it in the sense of "completely:" "not partially as in the rest of the Saints" (nequaquam per partes ut in ceteris sanctis *Comm. in Is* 11:1 [*MPL* 24, col. 144] [Trans.]). Augustine understood "bodily" (corporaliter) as "really, as opposed to shadowy" (*Epist.* 149, 25 [W. Parsons]). Hilary explained it as meaning "essentially:" "But if, what is more likely, the God who dwells in Him bodily refers to the truth of the nature in Him of God from God. . . ." (Si vero, quod est potius, corporaliter in eo manens divinitas naturae in eo Dei ex Deo significat veritatem. . . . *De trin.* 8, 54 [S. McKenna]). The Greek Fathers without exception understand "bodily" as "in essence" (οὐσιωδῶς). The evidence may be found in Lightfoot, *ad loc.*

48 Cf. Dibelius–Greeven, *ad loc.*; Eduard Schweizer, *TWNT* 7, 1075: " 'bodily' here has the meaning of the corporeality in which God encounters man in the world in which he lives. It is thus an exact description of the complete humanity of Jesus—not a humanity which was a mere external wrapping for the deity." Jervell, *Imago Dei*, 223f, wants to explain "bodily" on the basis of 2:17. His argument runs: Since "body" (σῶμα) in 2:17 is synonymous with "image" (εἰκών), it is legitimate to translate "bodily" of 2:9 by "in the form of an image" (εἰκονικῶς). "Thus it indicates the highest level of reality" (p. 224). This last point is obviously correct. It is worth noting, however, that the author of Col does not use the term "image" (εἰκών) either in 2:17 or in 2:9. Rather he employs the term "body" (σῶμα), obviously because he wants to emphasize this term.

statements about the "body" is no doubt intended.[49] Since in Christ the entire fulness of deity dwells "bodily," he is the "head of every principality and power" (κεφαλὴ πάσης ἀρχῆς καὶ ἐξουσίας 2:10), the "head of the body" (κεφαλὴ τοῦ σώματος 1:18). This body of his is the "church" (ἐκκλησία) over which he already in the present exercises his universal rule. Therefore, whoever has been transferred into the domain of his kingdom is free from the powers which rule in the cosmos and which want to force their enslaving yoke upon men.

■ **10** From this the conclusion follows directly: And you have been filled in him—and only in him! Since the reception of salvation is here described as being filled, this verse contains more than a play on words which refers back to the preceding term "fulness."[50] It also affirms an emphatic contrast to the teaching of the "philosophy": not by groveling before "the elements of the universe," but in Christ alone have you been "filled" (πεπληρωμένοι).[51] While Paul otherwise would say that he desires and prays that the community might be filled with divine gifts,[52] here the presence of salvation is affirmed: you have been filled in him![53] The rule of Christ over the powers, which according to apocalyptic presuppositions is not inaugurated until the end of this aeon (cf. Rev 19:11–16, etc.), is here proclaimed as an accomplished fact.[54] He is "the head of every principality and power" (ἡ κεφαλὴ πάσης ἀρχῆς καὶ ἐξουσίας).[55] This verse is another example of a flashback to the Christ hymn. Just as all things have been created in Christ—"whether thrones or dominions, principalities or powers" (εἴτε θρόνοι εἴτε κυριότητες εἴτε ἀρχαὶ εἴτε ἐξουσίαι 1:16) —so too in him all things have their existence (1:17). God has revealed that Christ is "head" (κεφαλή) over the principalities and powers[56] by overthrowing the "principalities" (ἐξουσίαι) and "powers" (ἀρχαί) on the cross of Christ (cf. 2:15).[57]

■ **11** The author continues: for a long time now you have been joined to Christ by baptism. Baptism is called circumcision here, but a distinction is introduced immediately: "a circumcision not made by hands" (περιτομὴ ἀχειροποίητος). Since baptism and circumcision are nowhere else in the NT compared with one another and since the comparison is distinctly delimited, there are sufficient grounds for the assumption that the author of Col adopted the term "circumcision" (περιτομή) from

49 Cf. Lohse, "Christusherrschaft und Kirche," 206f.

50 Thus Gerhard Delling, *TDNT* 6, 292.

51 Cf. Jacques Dupont, *Gnosis: La connaissance réligieuse dans les épîtres de Saint Paul*, UCL 2, 40 (Louvain and Paris: ²1960), 422: "It is in him that we participate in the *pleroma*."

52 Cf. Rom 15:13: "May the God of hope fill you with all joy and peace" (ὁ δὲ θεὸς τῆς ἐλπίδος πληρώσαι ὑμᾶς πάσης χαρᾶς καὶ εἰρήνης); Phil 1:10f: "So that you may be pure and blameless for the day of Christ, filled with the fruit of righteousness which comes through Jesus Christ" (ἵνα ἦτε εἰλικρινεῖς καὶ ἀπρόσκοποι εἰς ἡμέραν Χριστοῦ πεπληρωμένοι καρπὸν δικαιοσύνης τὸν διὰ Ἰησοῦ Χριστοῦ); 4:19: "And my God will supply every need of yours according to his riches in glory in Christ Jesus" (ὁ δὲ θεός μου πληρώσει πᾶσαν χρείαν ὑμῶν κατὰ τὸ πλοῦτος αὐτοῦ ἐν δόξῃ ἐν Χριστῷ Ἰησοῦ).

53 Cf. Jn. 1:16: "And from his fulness have we all received, grace upon grace" (ἐκ τοῦ πληρώματος αὐτοῦ ἡμεῖς πάντες ἐλάβομεν, καὶ χάριν ἀντὶ χάριτος); Eph 1:23; 3:19; 4:13.

54 The reading ὅς ἐστιν (he who is) is to be considered as the original text, for the relative clause deals with Christ. The neuter relative ὅ (which, p[46] BDG), on the other hand, is an assimilation to the common expression ὅ ἐστιν (which is, 1:24; 3:14).

55 For the meaning of the concepts "principality" (ἐξουσία), "power" (ἀρχή), and "head" (κεφαλή), cf. above, pp. 51, 53–55 on 1:16 and 1:18 respectively.

56 The author of Col avoids the term "body" (σῶμα) here because he wants it to be understood in an ecclesiological sense (cf. 1:18, 24).

57 Since Christ is called on the one hand "head of every principality and power" (2:10) and on the other hand "head of the body, the church" (κεφαλὴ τοῦ σώματος, τῆς ἐκκλησίας 1:18), Oscar Cullmann has concluded that the reign of Christ has a double character. Cf. his "The Kingship of Christ and the Church in the New Testament" in *The Early Church: Studies in Early Christian History and Theology*, ed. A. J. B. Higgins and tr. S. Godman (Philadelphia: The Westminster Press, 1956), 101–37, and his *The Christology of the New Testament*, tr. S. C. Guthrie and C. A. M. Hall (Philadelphia: The Westminster Press, ²1963), 224–32. The church is taken to form the inner circle of his Lordship while the world or state forms the outer, because the "principalities" are also said to be subject to Christ. This thesis, however, can in no way be based on Rom 13:1–7. Cf. Ernst Käsemann, "Römer 13:1–7 in unserer Generation," *ZThK* 56 (1959): 353–61. Nor can statements of Col be used to support Cullmann's position. For Col does not say a single word about the state. Christ is Lord over the powers and principalities; this, his Lordship, however, is a present reality in the

the "philosophy."[58] There is no indication, however, in this passage that, as in the communities in Galatia, circumcision was considered a sign of the covenant which required obedience to the OT law and effected entrance into fellowship with Israel's patriarchs. "Circumcision" is rather understood as a sacramental rite by which a person entered the community and gained access to salvation. The reference to the phrase "putting off the body of flesh" (**ἀπέκδυσις τοῦ σώματος τῆς σαρκός**) suggests the practices of mystery cults. In the initiation rites the devotee had to lay aside what previously had served him as clothing so that he could be filled with divine power. Jewish terminology, in this case, would clearly function as a means of giving greater authority and appeal to the sacramental rite of initiation.[59]

The phrase "body of flesh" (**σῶμα τῆς σαρκός**) characterizes the human body in its earthly frailty wherein it is subject to suffering, death, and dissolution (cf. on 1:22). It must be stripped off if the devotee wants to experience the divinizing vision and be filled with divine power. Before the initiation rites the initiand must remove his clothes and take a purificatory bath. After fasting during the period of preparation before the deity's feast, he is clothed with sacred garments (Apuleius, *Metamorph.* 11, 23f). In this act his soul experiences rebirth, i.e. transformation by divine power. Even in those Hellenistic syncretistic circles where no specific initiation rites were practiced, it was a matter of course that the body, which had been formed from perishable material, must remain on earth when the soul rose to God.[60] Wherever "circumcision" was understood as the "putting off the body of flesh" it is clear that one was far removed from the Jewish interpretation of circumcision and that the cultic act had assumed a meaning that by all means corresponded to the Gnostic way of viewing the world. For precisely that is what is of concern: to flee the world, to discard the husk that binds one to the earth, and to open up the way to the heavenly homeland.[61]

Against this background the statements about Christian baptism take on a more distinct meaning: the circumcision, with which you have been circumcised, is not made by hands. Since the phrase "made by hands" (**χειροποίητα**) is used in the OT for the graven images and idols the pagans made for themselves,[62] it has fundamentally negative connotations. Contrariwise, something not made by hands is that which God himself creates.[63] Thus, in the saying of Jesus the temple made with hands is contrasted with the temple "not made with hands" which Jesus will erect within three days (Mk 14:58 par). And Paul talks about a "building from God" (**οἰκοδομὴ ἐκ θεοῦ**), which he describes as "a house not made with hands, eternal, in the heavens" (**οἰκίαν ἀχειροποίητον αἰώνιον ἐν τοῖς οὐρανοῖς** 2 Cor 5:1). When the circumcision, which has been performed on those who were

church over which he is head since he is "head of the body." For a critique of Cullmann's use of Col, cf. also Gabathuler, *Jesus Christus, Haupt der Kirche*, 170–73.

58 On the fringes of Diaspora Judaism there are divers syncretistic phenomena, e.g., the "association of the Sabbatists" (*ἑταιρεία τῶν Σαββατιστῶν*), a community of those who kept the Sabbath and also worshipped the god Sabazios. From the syncretistic circles of Diaspora Judaism also stems the sect of "Hypsistarians" who worshipped "the highest god," observed the Sabbath, abided by food regulations, but rejected circumcision. The evidence and further material can be found in Eduard Lohse, *TWNT* 7, 8 n. 44.

59 It is no longer clear whether "circumcision" was merely a name for the sacramental rite or whether circumcision was actually practiced. The *Gospel of Thomas* shows how "circumcision" could be understood symbolically in Gnostic circles: "His disciples said to Him: Is circumcision profitable or not? He said to them: If it were profitable, their father would beget them circumcised from their mother. But the true circumcision in Spirit has become profitable in every way" (Logion 53 [A. Guillaumont]).

60 Cf. Philo, *Leg. all.* 2, 55: "The soul that loves God, having disrobed itself of the body and the objects dear to the body and fled abroad far away from these, gains a fixed and assured settlement in the perfect ordinances of virtue" (*ἡ φιλόθεος ψυχὴ ἐκδῦσα τὸ σῶμα καὶ τὰ τούτῳ φίλα καὶ μακρὰν ἔξω φυγοῦσα ἀπὸ τούτων πῆξιν καὶ βεβαίωσιν καὶ ἵδρυσιν ἐν τοῖς τελείοις ἀρετῆς δόγμασι λαμβάνει*).

61 Cf. Bornkamm, *Aufsätze* 1, 145. On the mutual relationship between the Mysteries and Gnosticism cf. Hans Dieter Betz, *Nachfolge und Nachahmung Jesu Christi im Neuen Testament*, BHTh 37 (Tübingen: 1967), 171f.

62 Cf. LXX Lev 26:1, 30; Is 2:18; 21:9, etc.

63 The word "not made by hands" (*ἀχειροποίητος*) indeed does not occur in the LXX, but is attested in Greek since Herodotus. Cf. Bauer, *s.v.*

64 The fact that baptism is compared with circumcision provides no clues for answering the question whether the early Christians baptized children. For a different view, see Joachim Jeremias, *Infant Bap-*

baptized, is characterized as "not made with hands," the author points to the work of God which they experienced in baptism.[64] Consequently, in this and the following sentences, passive verb forms are chosen in order to indicate that God himself accomplished the decisive change from the old to the new life. The old life, in which "flesh" determined the conduct of the "body,"[65] has been put aside. Putting off[66] the body of flesh, however,—and the author of Col makes this point clear—does not mean contempt for earthly life. Rather it means being active in this life in obedience to the Lord: "put off the old man with his practices, and put on the new man, who is being renewed in knowledge according to the image of his creator" (**ἀπεκδυσάμενοι τὸν παλαιὸν ἄνθρωπον σὺν ταῖς πράξεσιν αὐτοῦ καὶ ἐνδυσάμενοι τὸν νέον τὸν ἀνακαινούμενον εἰς ἐπίγνωσιν κατ' εἰκόνα τοῦ κτίσαντος αὐτόν** 3:9f). This true circumcision, which is fundamentally different not only from the practices of the "philosophers" but also from the Jewish rite,[67] is the "circumcision of Christ" (**περιτομὴ τοῦ Χριστοῦ**).[68]

■ **12** The circumcision of Christ which every member of the community has experienced is nothing other than being baptized into the death and resurrection of Christ. The formulation of the sentence depends on expressions used in the primitive Christian teaching on baptism. Such expressions also underlie Rom 6:4f. Christianity believes and acknowledges that Christ died for our sins, that he was buried and that God raised him from the dead (1 Cor 15:3–5). We have been joined to this event by an indissoluble bond; for we have died with him in baptism and have been laid into the grave so that the old life is put aside. In Rom 6 Paul's concern is to demonstrate that it is therefore impossible for us still to live under the dominion of "sin" (**ἁμαρτία**). The old man has indeed been crucified with Christ (Rom 6:6). Just as the reference in the kerygma to the grave underscores the reality of the death of Jesus Christ (1 Cor 15:4), it is also stressed in Rom 6 that in baptism a real death has occurred. For "we were buried therefore with him by baptism into death" (**συνετάφημεν οὖν αὐτῷ διὰ τοῦ βαπτίσματος εἰς τὸν θάνατον** Rom 6:4). In many circles of Hellenistic Christianity baptism was thought to convey divine powers of life by means of which the baptized person experienced in himself the resurrection of Christ.[69] Paul also says that in baptism we have been joined to the death and resurrection of Christ. Yet Paul characteristically gives a new turn to this thought. Life in Christ is lived in faith: "If we died with Christ, we believe that we will also live with him" (**εἰ δὲ ἀπεθάνομεν σὺν Χριστῷ, πιστεύομεν ὅτι καὶ συζήσομεν αὐτῷ** Rom 6:8). Against an enthusiastic evaluation of baptism which would conceive of it as a pledge of accomplished ressurection (cf. 2 Tim 2:18), Paul objects that our resurrection is still ahead of us (Rom 6:5). Accordingly, Paul concludes the sentence that began with "we were buried with him" (**συνετάφημεν**) with the admonition: "so that as Christ was raised from the dead by the glory of the Father, we too might conduct ourselves in newness of life" (**ἵνα ὥσπερ ἠγέρθη Χριστὸς ἐκ νεκρῶν διὰ τῆς δόξης τοῦ πατρός, οὕτως καὶ ἡμεῖς ἐν καινότητι ζωῆς περιπατήσωμεν** Rom 6:4). Victory over sin, law, and death,

---

tism in the First Four Centuries, tr. David Cairns, The Library of History and Doctrine (Philadelphia: The Westminster Press, 1961), 39f.

65 The Koine text secondarily inserts "of sins" (τῶν ἁμαρτιῶν) after "the body" (τοῦ σώματος).

66 The word "putting off" (ἀπέκδυσις) occurs nowhere else in the NT and is also very rare outside the NT. Cf. Albrecht Oepke, *TDNT* 2, 321, and Bauer, *s.v.* The word first occurs in post-Pauline times in Eusthatius Thessalonicensis, *Commentarii in Homeri Iliadem* 91, 28.

67 On the practice and understanding of "circumcision" cf. Rudolf Meyer, *TDNT* 6, 72–84. For the figurative uses of the word "circumcision" compare the prophetic words about the circumcision of the heart (Jer 4:4; 6:10; 9:25) which are appropriated by the writings of the Qumran community (1 QS V, 4f, 26; 1 QpHab XI, 13) as well as by Paul (Rom 2:28f).

68 Moule, *ad loc.*, would understand "circumcision of Christ" (περιτομὴ τοῦ Χριστοῦ) as Christ's circumcision, i.e. as his death (cf. 1:2; Rom 7:4). He himself, however, realizes the difficulty which thwarts this interpretation: the phrase "in putting off the body of flesh" cannot refer to the death of Christ unless this were indicated by the addition of a possessive "his" (αὐτοῦ). Harald Sahlin, "Die Beschneidung Christi," *Symbolae Biblicae Upsalienses* 12 (1950): 5–22 interprets the entire passage Eph 2:11–22 on the basis of the concept of Christ's circumcision.

69 Concerning Paul's argument against this enthusiastic understanding of the sacrament, cf. Eduard Lohse, "Taufe und Rechtfertigung bei Paulus" *KD* 11 (1965): 308–24; also Ernst Käsemann, *The Testament of Jesus: A Study of the Gospel of John in the Light*

accomplished once and for all time in Christ's death and resurrection, determines Christian existence. This existence takes place under the sign of the resurrection of the dead which still lies in the future.

Like Rom 6, Col also says that in baptism we have died with Christ. But in contrast to Rom 6 this statement is just a cursory remark in the development of thought. The participle is used instead of the finite verb; the words "into death" (εἰς τὸν θάνατον) do not occur.[70] The full emphasis falls on the following verse: you have been raised with him![71] In contrast to Rom 6:4f it is said:[72] the resurrection has actually already happened in baptism.[73] In Col, what is still to come in the future is not called the resurrection of the dead. Instead, the future event is described as the revelation of that life which was received in baptism and is now still hidden "with Christ in God" (σὺν τῷ Χριστῷ ἐν τῷ θεῷ 3:3).[74]

The phrase "with Christ" (σὺν Χριστῷ)[75] occurs in the Pauline letters much less frequently than the formulaic expression "in Christ" (ἐν Χριστῷ). As a result there is no uniform usage. Rather Paul employs the phrase "with Christ" in different contexts to describe the closest possible union with Christ.[76] After the resurrection of the dead the triumphant community will go to meet its Lord to receive future glory: "And so we shall always be with the Lord" (**καὶ οὕτως πάντοτε σὺν κυρίῳ ἐσόμεθα** 1 Thess 4:17). Consequently, to be "with Christ" signifies the perfection which is to come.[77] However, Paul can also say that close union with Christ is already a present reality. For it is already founded in baptism in

---

of Chapter 17, tr. Gerhard Krodel (Philadelphia: Fortress Press, 1968), 15.

70 Col 2:12f presupposes the expositions of Rom 6:1–11, but modifies them in the light of the common Christian understanding of baptism. Cf. Sanders, "Literary Dependence," 40–42.

71 Rom 6:4 says: "through baptism into death" (διὰ τοῦ βαπτίσματος εἰς τὸν θάνατον). Col 2:12 simply says: "in baptism" (ἐν τῷ βαπτίσματι). In place of ἐν τῷ βαπτίσματι (in baptism) p[46] B D* G pc read ἐν τῷ βαπτισμῷ (in washing) without thereby changing the meaning. The word "washing" (βαπτισμός) is somewhat rare (cf. Josephus, *Ant.* 18, 117; Mk 7:4; Heb 6:2; 9:10).

72 The difference is inadmissibly harmonized if Col 2 is taken as an authentic commentary on Rom 6. Thus, Albrecht Oepke, "Urchristentum und Kindertaufe," *ZNW* 29 (1930): 104. For a critique of Oepke, cf. Erich Grässer, "Kol. 3, 1–4 als Interpretation secundum homines recipientes," *ZThK* 64 (1967): 150. Percy, *Probleme*, 110, tries to diminish the contrast with Rom 6 by taking the future tenses of Rom 6:4, 5, 8 as logical future tenses. Against this interpretation cf. Robert C. Tannehill, *Dying and Rising with Christ: A Study in Pauline Theology*, BZNW 32 (Berlin: 1967), 47–54.

73 Since ἐν ᾧ συνηγέρθητε is directly connected with ἐν τῷ βαπτίσματι, it might seem natural to link ἐν ᾧ with βάπτισμα (in which baptism you were raised). Cf. Abbott, Haupt *ad loc.*, also Albrecht Oepke, *TDNT* 1, 545, and Jervell, *Imago Dei*, 233 n. 226. Nevertheless, since "in him" (ἐν ᾧ), which frequently occurs in the context, almost always refers to Christ, the same connection must also be assumed here. Cf. the parallel clause in v 11: "in him you were also circumcised" (ἐν ᾧ καὶ περιετμήθητε). Eph 2:6 places "with" and "in Christ" (σύν and ἐν Χριστῷ) next to each other in the same way: "and raised us up with him and made us sit with him in the heavenly places in Christ Jesus" (καὶ συνήγειρεν καὶ συνεκάθισεν ἐν τοῖς ἐπουρανίοις ἐν Χριστῷ Ἰησοῦ).

74 Erich Klaar, "Die Taufe nach paulinischem Verständnis," *Theologische Existenz heute* NF 93 (München: 1961), wrongly denies that baptism in Paul has a sacramental character. His remarks on Col 2 completely miss the mark: "As a matter of fact, Paul's argument in Col 2 is altogether tactical and filled with very bitter sarcasm against the illusions of the mystery cults. Against them Paul says that the effects of grace which are equal to the resurrection from the dead are communicated 'through faith' from the power of God which alone is real and life-producing without any sacramental communication." (p. 22) Against this view cf. Rudolf Schnackenburg, *Baptism in the Thought of St. Paul: A Study in Pauline Theology*, tr. G. R. Beasley-Murray (New York: Herder and Herder, 1964), 67–72, and Gerhard Delling, *Die Taufe im Neuen Testament* (Berlin: 1963), 122–25.

75 On the meaning of "with Christ" (σὺν Χριστῷ) in Paul cf. Walter Grundmann, *TWNT* 7, 780–86, and the bibliography on p. 766.

76 Ernst Lohmeyer, "ΣΥΝ ΧΡΙΣΤΩΙ" in *Festgabe für A. Deissmann* (Tübingen: 1927), 218–57, wanted to take "with Christ" as a firmly established and traditional formula which went back to a Son of Man Christology which Paul and John had in common. Against this view Pierre Bonnard, "Mourir et vivre avec Jésus-Christ selon Saint Paul," *RHPR* 36 (1956): 101–12, held the opinion that "with Christ" is a formula derived from the liturgies of the Hellenistic mystery cults. Of course, in an assessment of the "with Christ" passages that deal with the parousia,

which the Christian is taken up into the death and resurrection of Christ. On the one hand, Rom 6 says: "We were buried with him" (v 4), "we have been united with him in a death like his" (v 5), "our old self has been crucified" (v 6): **συνετάφημεν αὐτῷ** (v 4), **σύμφυτοι γεγόναμεν τῷ ὁμοιώματι τοῦ θανάτου αὐτοῦ** (v 5), **ὁ παλαιὸς ἡμῶν ἄνθρωπος συνεσταυρώθη** (v 6). On the other hand, Rom 6 strictly maintains that resurrection in Christ is an event of the future: "We will live with him" (**συζήσομεν αὐτῷ** v 8).[78] In baptism our "body" is taken out of the dominion of "sin" (**ἁμαρτία**) and placed under the rule of the Kyrios (Rom 6:6; 1 Cor 6:13). But God has raised the Kyrios and will also raise us "through his power" (**διὰ τῆς δυνάμεως αὐτοῦ** 1 Cor 6:14). Finally, Paul also talks about a union with Christ that comes to be known through suffering, a union that the Christian experiences in suffering together with his Lord (Rom 8:17). The Christian endures this suffering in view of the future glory, since he is certain "that we may also be glorified with him" (**ἵνα καὶ συνδοξασθῶμεν** *ibid.*).[79]

Col repeatedly uses the phrase "with Christ." With the exception of 3:4 this phrase uniformly speaks about death and resurrection with Christ as having already taken place in baptism. The passages are: "You were buried with him—you were raised together with him" (2:12), "he made you alive together with him" (2:13), "with Christ you died" (2:20), "if therefore you have been raised with Christ" (3:1), "your life is hidden with Christ in God" (3:3): **συνταφέντες—συνηγέρθητε** (2:12), **συνεζωοποίησεν ὑμᾶς σὺν αὐτῷ** (2:13), **ἀπεθάνετε σὺν Χριστῷ** (2:20), **εἰ οὖν συνηγέρθητε τῷ Χριστῷ** (3:1), **ἡ ζωὴ ὑμῶν κέκρυπται σὺν τῷ Χριστῷ ἐν τῷ θεῷ** (3:3). Since this letter's statements about union "with Christ" refer to such an extent to the present fellowship with Christ, the phrase "with Christ" takes on almost the same meaning as the formula "in Christ." For both expressions are used to describe the appropriation of the new life which the Christian received in baptism. Therefore, the train of thought begun by "in him" (2:9f) and "in whom" (2:11f) can be continued by "with him" (2:13) without any difference in meaning. "Life" (**ζωή**) is already present, but still hidden with Christ in God (3:3). Nevertheless, "when Christ, our life, is revealed, then you also will be revealed with him in glory" (**ὅταν ὁ Χριστὸς φανερωθῇ, ἡ ζωὴ ἡμῶν, τότε καὶ ὑμεῖς σὺν αὐτῷ φανερωθήσεσθε ἐν δόξῃ** 3:4).

Col is still far removed from falling into a fanatic enthusiasm of which the catchword is found in 2 Tim 2:18: "the resurrection has already occurred" (**ἀνάστασιν ἤδη γεγονέναι**).[80] For to be raised with Christ means nothing else than to have forgiveness of sins (1:13f; 2:13).[81] Resurrection with Christ is a reality only "by faith in the power of God, who raised him from the dead" (**διὰ τῆς πίστεως τῆς ἐνεργείας τοῦ θεοῦ τοῦ ἐγείραν-**

apocalyptic presuppositions should be compared. Likewise, in an exegesis of "with Christ" where it occurs in sacramental contexts, the concepts of the mystery religions should be explored. (Cf. Jacques Dupont, ΣΥΝ ΧΡΙΣΤΩΙ: *L'union avec le Christ suivant Saint Paul* (Bruges, Louvain and Paris: 1952), 100–10 ["Avec le Christ" dans la vie future]; Otto Kuss, Excursus "Mit Christus" in *Der Römerbrief* (Regensburg: ²1963), 319–81; Walter Grundmann, *TWNT* 7, 781 n. 79). Nevertheless, the mutual relationship between the passages on the future union with Christ and the sacramental statements cannot be defined in such a way that the sacramental usage is derived from apocalyptic concepts (thus Eduard Schweizer, "Die 'Mystik' des Sterbens und Auferstehens mit Christus bei Paulus," *EvTheol* 26 (1966): 239–57; *idem*, "Dying and Rising with Christ," *NTS* 14 (1967–68): 1–14). Rather, in view of the diverse history of religions background which must be referred to in the different "with Christ" passages, it seems best to conclude that "with Christ" is no fixed formula. Cf. Tannehill, *Dying and Rising*, 87f.

77 Cf. 2 Cor 4:14; 13:4; Phil 1:23; 3:20f.

78 Cf. also Rom 6:5: "We will be [united with him] in a resurrection [like his]" ([σύμφυτοι τῷ ὁμοιώματι] τῆς ἀναστάσεως ἐσόμεθα); in addition cf. 2 Tim 2.11: "For if we have died with him, we shall also live with him" (εἰ γὰρ συναπεθάνομεν, καὶ συζήσομεν).

79 Cf. Tannehill, *Dying and Rising*, *passim*, who organizes the passages about dying and rising with Christ in relationship to Pauline theology and interprets them from that base.

80 Cf. Hans Conzelmann, RGG³ 1, col. 695: "The expectation of a future resurrection" in Col "is not abolished in Gnostic fashion."

81 Amid the differences between Rom 6 and Col 2 the common elements should not be overlooked. Cf. Bornkamm, "Baptism and New Life in Paul," in *Early Christian Experience*, 77: "Of course, Col. 2.12 also speaks—unlike Rom. 6—of the latter (*scil.* being raised with Christ) as an event already completed in baptism. But otherwise it says in essence what Rom. 6.5 also says: 'if we have been united with him in a death like his . . .' "

τος αὐτὸν ἐκ[82] ***νεκρῶν*** 2:12). Faith, however, relies on the message: God has raised Christ from the dead.[83] God's "working" (***ἐνέργεια***), which raised him from the dead, is the "glory of the Father" (***δόξα τοῦ πατρός*** Rom 6:4), is his "power" (***δύναμις*** 1 Cor 6:14).[84] Where there is openness to the power of God, which is operative in the Gospel (cf. 1 Cor 1:18; Rom 1:16f), there it creates new life. And Col describes this new life as being raised with Christ, summoning its readers to put aside the old man and to put on the new man who lives according to the will of his creator (3:9f).

■ **13** Verse 13 marks a change in this section, as is already indicated in the switch in the subject of the sentences from "you" to "he."[85] God has made you, who were dead, alive with him. This sentence is couched in the traditional style of preaching which contrasts the past with the present, a present made possible by God's action. In v 13c the confessing community speaks using the first person plural: "he forgave us all our trespasses" (***χαρισάμενος ἡμῖν πάντα τὰ παραπτώματα***). The piling up of the participles "having forgiven," "having utterly destroyed," "having nailed," "having stripped," "having triumphed" (***χαρισάμενος, ἐξαλείψας, προσηλώσας, ἀπεκδυσάμενος, θριαμβεύσας***) indicates that traditional expressions underlie vss 13c–15. The remarkably large number of uncommon words and expressions corroborate the assumption that the author adopted traditional formulations. Words that occur nowhere else in the NT are: "certificate of indebtedness" (***χειρόγραφον*** v 14), "to nail" (***προσηλοῦν*** v 14), "to strip" (***ἀπεκδύεσθαι*** v 15; cf. 3:9). The words "to destroy utterly" (***ἐξαλείφειν*** v 14; cf. Acts 3:19; Rev 3:5; 7:17), "against" (***ὑπεναντίος*** v 14; cf. Heb 10:27), "to put on public display" (***δειγματίζειν*** v 15; cf. Mt 1:19) occur only here in the Pauline letters; "to triumph" (***θριαμβεύειν***) only one other time, in 2 Cor 2:14. Forgiveness of sins is described in terms that correspond to the primitive community's theology, not to the Pauline concept of sin (cf. 1:14). The term "regulation" (***δόγμα***), which occurs again only at Eph 2:15 in the Pauline Corpus, was significant for the controversy with the "philosophy," as the question "why do you want to have regulations imposed . . .?" (***τί . . . δογματίζεσθε*** 2:20) points out. Thus, the term was probably inserted into the traditional material for polemical purposes. The phrase "in him" concludes the section. Once again it takes up the theme of the entire passage (cf. "in him" or "in whom" in vss 9, 10, 11, 12): In Christ, God has triumphed over the powers and principalities.

Verses 13c–15 can be arranged in this way:

13c who forgave us all our trespasses,
14 who utterly destroyed the certificate
of indebtedness which stood against us which
[because of the regulations] was against us,
and he removed it,
he nailed it to the cross,
15 who stripped the principalities and powers
and put them on public display,
who triumphed over them in him.

13c ***χαρισάμενος ἡμῖν πάντα τὰ παραπτώματα,***
14 ***ἐξαλείψας τὸ καθ' ἡμῶν χειρόγραφον [τοῖς***
δόγμασιν] ὃ ἦν ὑπεναντίον ἡμῖν,
καὶ αὐτὸ ἦρκεν ἐκ τοῦ μέσου,
προσηλώσας αὐτὸ τῷ σταυρῷ,
15 ***ἀπεκδυσάμενος τὰς ἀρχὰς καὶ τὰς ἐξουσίας***
ἐδειγμάτισεν ἐν παρρησίᾳ,
θριαμβεύσας αὐτοὺς ἐν αὐτῷ.

The confession of forgiveness of sins is thematic and stands at the beginning. Verse 14 describes the destruction of the "certificate of indebtedness" (***χειρόγραφον***), v 15 the triumph over the powers and principalities. In both verses a finite verb occurs in the middle, bracketed by two participles. On the basis of the above observations on the vocabulary and style of the passage, a high degree of probability exists for the assumption that a fragment of a confession formulated in hymnic phrases underlies vss 14–15. The author of Col appropriated this confession because it clearly expressed what was for him the essen-

82 Manuscripts B ℜ DG pc expand by adding the Greek definite article *τῶν* before *νεκρῶν*.

83 Cf. 1 Thess 4:14; 1 Cor 15:3–5; 2 Cor 5:15; Rom 1:3f; 4:24f; 10:9f, etc.

84 Cf. Eph 1:19f: "According to the working of his great might which he accomplished in Christ when he raised him from the dead" (*κατὰ τὴν ἐνέργειαν τοῦ κράτους τῆς ἰσχύος αὐτοῦ, ἣν ἐνήργηκεν ἐν τῷ Χριστῷ ἐγείρας αὐτὸν ἐκ νεκρῶν*).

85 God, not Christ, is the subject of this and the following statements. God forgives sins and effects the resurrection with Christ. Cf. also Eph 2:4f; "But God . . . even when we were dead through our trespasses made us alive together with Christ" (*ὁ δὲ θεὸς . . . καὶ ὄντας ἡμᾶς νεκροὺς τοῖς παραπτώμασιν συνεζωοποίησεν τῷ Χριστῷ*).

tial connection between forgiveness of sins and victory over the powers and principalities.[86] Therefore, he placed what was, in his mind, the crucial statement of the confession (cf. 1:14; 2:13a; 3:13) at the beginning. The words "because of the regulations" (τοῖς δόγμασιν) might have been inserted by him into v 14 to emphasize that with the forgiveness of sins each and every claim of the "elements of the universe" (στοιχεῖα τοῦ κόσμου) was nullified. This stresses even more forcefully that both affirmations form an indissoluble pair: on the cross of Christ the certificate of indebtedness is erased; on the cross of Christ the powers and principalities are disempowered. Consequently, where there is forgiveness of sins, there is freedom from the "powers" and "principalities," there is life and salvation!

And you, who were dead, he made alive together with him! This address[87] to the community, like the previous section, points to the resurrection "with him" which occurred in baptism. But death no longer means: having died with Christ. Rather the entire pre-Christian period is considered as being under the dominion of death.[88] The word "dead" is thus used in a figurative sense.[89] This state of being lost had been caused "by trespasses[90] and the uncircumcision of your flesh" (τοῖς παραπτώμασιν καὶ τῇ ἀκροβυστίᾳ τῆς σαρκὸς ὑμῶν). "Trespass" (παράπτωμα)[91] is that act by which man violates God's command. This is the term Paul uses (Rom 5:15–18, 20) to describe Adam's disobedience, by which "sin" (ἁμαρτία) entered the world and gained dominion (Rom 5:12). Likewise, he describes as "trespasses" (παραπτώματα) the transgressions for which man is culpable and by which all men rebel against God (Gal 6:1; 2 Cor 5:17; Rom 5:16). Primitive Christian preaching says that Christ was handed over "on account of our trespasses" (διὰ τὰ παραπτώματα ἡμῶν Rom 4:25), but also that he died "for our sins" (ὑπερ τῶν ἁμαρτιῶν ἡμῶν 1 Cor 15:3). Accordingly, there is no difference in meaning between "trespasses" (παραπτώματα) and "sins" (ἁμαρτίαι). Rebellion against God which takes place in permanent disobedience characterizes the life of those who are without Christ. They live in the uncircumcision[92] of their flesh, i.e., they are heathens and godless. When "flesh" (σάρξ) governs life, only sin and death can result.[93]

However, that which once was is now no longer valid. The "uncircumcision" of which the Gentile Christians

86 On Schille's thesis (cf. his *Frühchristliche Hymnen*, 31–37) that a baptismal hymn underlies vss 9–15, cf. above p. 99, n. 43 and the critique of Deichgräber, *Gotteshymnus und Christushymnus*, 167f. Deichgräber, nevertheless, leaves open the possibility that hymnic material may underlie vss 13c–15. Cf. further Wengst, *Formeln*, 181–89, who assumes that vss 13–15 are based on a continuous traditional piece which began with "and when we [not: you] were dead" (καὶ ὄντας ἡμᾶς [not: ὑμᾶς] νεκροὺς) and which consisted of three verses, each containing three lines (vss 13, 14, 15).

87 On the introductory "and you" (καὶ ὑμᾶς), which reflects preaching style, cf. 1:21: "And you, who once were estranged and hostile-minded" (καὶ ὑμᾶς ποτε ὄντας ἀπηλλοτριωμένους καὶ ἐχθροὺς). On the contrast between "then" and "now" cf. p. 62.

88 On the concept "dead" (νεκρός) cf. Rudolf Bultmann, *TDNT* 4, 892–94 and André Feuillet, "Mort du Christ et mort du chrétien d'après les épîtres pauliniennes," *RB* 66 (1959): 481–513.

89 Cf. Lk 15:24, 32: "This my son was dead and is alive again" (οὗτος ὁ υἱός μου νεκρὸς ἦν καὶ ἀνέζησεν); that means "he was lost, and is found" (ἦν ἀπολωλὼς καὶ εὑρέθη). On the usage of "dead" in a figurative meaning, cf. also Rev 3:1: "You have the name of being alive, and you are dead" (ὄνομα ἔχεις ὅτι ζῇς καὶ νεκρὸς εἶ); cf. further Jas 2:17–26: "Faith" (πίστις) which has no "works" (ἔργα) is "dead" (νεκρά).

90 This is a causal dative; cf. Blass–Debrunner, par. 196. Before "trespasses" (τοῖς παραπτώμασιν) p[46] AC ℜ DG pm insert "in" (ἐν); D*G it insert "in" (ἐν) before "uncircumcision" (τῇ ἀκροβυστίᾳ).

91 Cf. Wilhelm Michaelis, *TDNT* 6, 170–73.

92 Paul often uses "uncircumcision" (ἀκροβυστία) to designate pagans. Cf. Gal 2:7; 5:6; 6:15; 1 Cor 7:18f; Rom 2;25–27; 3:30; 4:9–12; and further Eph 2:11. Cf. Karl Ludwig Schmidt, *TDNT* 1, 225f.

93 Cf. Theodore of Mopsuestia, *ad loc.*: "He does not refer here to the uncircumcision of the body. Rather just as he called circumcision the putting off of mortality, so too he says here that uncircumcision is the continued wearing of mortality" (ἀκροβυστίαν ἐνταῦθα οὐ τὴν τοῦ σώματος λέγει, ἀλλ' ὥσπερ περιτομὴν τὴν ἀφαίρεσιν ἐκάλεσεν τῆς θνητότητος, οὕτως ἀκροβυστίαν τὸ περικεῖσθαι ἔτι τὴν θνητότητα [Trans.]).

are reminded, has been removed by the "circumcision not made by hands" (2:11). In baptism the passage from death to life has taken place. God has made you[94] alive together with him (cf. 2:13).[95] The phrase "with him" is again strongly emphasized:[96] you have been joined with Christ, made alive with him.[97] Therefore, death has been vanquished and life attained, but attained only—though here in rich fulness—where fellowship with Christ exists.

This has come about, as the community confesses, because he forgave us all our sins.[98] The "trespasses," which had changed life before and without Christ into death, have been forgiven without exception.[99] God has removed the debt[100] and destroyed the document on which it was recorded.

■ **14** The debtor issues a certificate of indebtedness in his own hand as an acknowledgement of his outstanding debts.[101] In Judaism the relationship between man and God was often described as that between a debtor and his creditor. For example, Rabbi Akiba used to compare God to a shopkeeper who would lend money and goods and record all the amounts on a ledger. Whosoever wished to borrow would come and borrow. Just as the shopkeeper got back what was his due through collectors, so too God, through the angels, demands of men what they owe him. Just judgment is rendered according to the record kept on the ledger (*Ab.* 3:20). Therefore, in the prayer Abinu Malkenu God is addressed: "Our Father, our King, in your great mercy cancel all our debts."[102] God's response is the promise: "I, I am he who blots out your transgressions, and I will not remember your sins" (*ἐγώ εἰμι ἐγώ εἰμι ὁ ἐξαλείφων τὰς ἀνομίας σου καὶ οὐ μὴ μνησθήσομαι* LXX Is 43:25 [Trans.]).

This image derived from legal practice about debts is presupposed by the reference to the "certificate of indebtedness" (*χειρόγραφον*). There is no allusion here to a myth wherein the handwritten certificate of indebtedness is the document of a pact which a man makes with the devil and according to which he commits himself to a life of sin and death in exchange for the benefits Satan grants him.[103] This verse mentions neither the devil nor a pact that a man concluded with him. Rather the "certificate of indebtedness" tells about man's condition of indebtedness before God. It accuses us, as both "which stood against us" (*τὸ καθ' ἡμῶν*) and "which was against us" (*ὃ ἦν ὑπεναντίον ἡμῖν*) expressly

---

94 Since the manuscripts p^{46} B 1 69 had already written "us" (*ἡμᾶς*) here, they assimilate to "we" in v 13c, 14a.

95 In Paul's usage, the verbal compounds in "with" (*σύν*) govern the dative, but the preposition "with" is not repeated. Cf. Rom 6:4: *συνετάφημεν οὖν αὐτῷ*; 6:5: *σύμφυτοι γεγόναμεν τῷ ὁμοιώματι*; 6:8: *συζήσομεν αὐτῷ*. Cf. also Col 2:12: *συνταφέντες αὐτῷ*. In this passage (2:13), however, "with" is repeated: *συνεζωοποίησεν ὑμᾶς σὺν αὐτῷ*.

96 Eph 2:5 changes the phrase into a confessional statement: "Even when we were dead through our trespasses, he made us alive together with Christ" (*καὶ ὄντας ἡμᾶς νεκροὺς τοῖς παραπτώμασιν συνεζωοποίησεν τῷ Χριστῷ*).

97 The verb "to make alive with" (*συζωοποιεῖν*) occurs only here and at Eph 2:5. Elsewhere in the Pauline epistles the verb "to make alive" (*ζωοποιεῖν*) is always used: Gal 3:21; 1 Cor 15:22, 36, 45; 2 Cor 3:6; Rom 4:17; 8:11.

98 The manuscripts LP 69 al f vg alter the "us" (*ἡμῖν*) of the confession to "you" (*ὑμῖν*) to conform to the address of v 13a.

99 The verb *χαρίζεσθαι* here as in 3:13 means "to forgive." Cf. 2 Cor 2:7, 10; 12:13: "forgive me this wrong" (*χαρίσασθέ μοι τὴν ἀδικίαν ταύτην*). It does not mean "to give freely" (cf. Gal 3:18; 1 Cor 2:12; Rom 8:32; Phil 1:29; 2:9). Cf. Bauer, *s.v.* The phrase "to forgive trespasses" (*χαρίζεσθαι τὰ παραπτώματα*) never occurs elsewhere in the Pauline letters.

100 On the use of "to forgive" (*χαρίζεσθαι*) in the meaning of "to remit" cf. Philo, *Spec. leg.* 2, 39 about the remission of debts in the seventh year "in cancelling loans to their fellow–nationals, this also in the seventh year" (*τὰ δάνεια ἑβδόμῳ ἔτει τοῖς ὁμοφύλοις χαριζομένων*). Cf. also Lk 7:42: "When they could not pay, he forgave them both their debts" (*μὴ ἐχόντων αὐτῶν ἀποδοῦναι ἀμφοτέροις ἐχαρίσατο*); 7:43: "to whom he forgave more" (*ᾧ τὸ πλεῖον ἐχαρίσατο*).

101 Cf. Polybius 30, 8, 4: "For convicted as they were to their faces by their own handwriting" (*ἐλεγχόμενοι γὰρ κατὰ πρόσωπον ὑπὸ τῶν ἰδίων χειρογράφων*); *Ditt. Syll.*[3] 2, 742, 50f: ". . . and those who lent the money borrowed on bottomry according to the certificates of indebtedness and the deposits." (*καὶ οἱ δεδανεικότες τὰ σύμβολα τά τε ναυτικὰ καὶ κατὰ χειρόγραφα καὶ παραθήκας* [Trans.]). In the LXX "certificate of indebtedness" (*χειρόγραφον*) occurs only at Tob 5:3; 9:5: "And he gave him the certificate of indebtedness" (*καὶ ἔδωκεν αὐτῷ τὸ χειρόγραφον*). More examples can be found in Bauer, *s.v.*, and in Deissmann, *LAE*, 332–34.

102 Cf. Willy Staerk, *Altjüdische liturgische Gebete*, KlT 58 (Berlin: [2]1930), 28. Cf. also *Tanḥuma Midrash*

state.[104] The words "because of the regulations" (**τοῖς δόγμασιν**) occur unconnectedly in the middle of the sentence.[105] The word "regulations" (**δόγματα**) does not mean the stipulations of an edict of grace,[106] but binding statutes. Thus, the words "because of the regulations" (**τοῖς δόγμασιν**) indicate why the "certificate of indebtedness" has a case against us.[107] It is, therefore, not impossible to connect "because of the regulations" directly with "certificate of indebtedness" and to supply a supposed participle "written" (**γεγραμμένον**).[108] Since this participle, however, does not occur in the text, other exegetes have construed "because of the regulations" with "which stood against us."[109] But one can also connect "because of the regulations" with the following relative clause.[110] In this case, the relative clause states the reason why the "certificate of indebtedness" could make its enmity against us effective. The words "because of the regulations" stand first in a position of emphasis in order to call special attention to the legal basis for the certificate's witness against us.[111] However, if it can be assumed—as was explained above (p. 106, on 2:13)—that a fragment of a traditional confession underlies the sentence, then the author of Col is responsible for the reference to the "regulations." The phrase "because of the regulations" is his comment which he adds to the traditional material in the middle of the sentence in order

---

צו (140b): Rabbi (217?) said: "When a man sins, God writes down the debt of death. If the man repents, the debt is cancelled (i.e., declared invalid). If he does not repent, what is recorded remains genuine (valid)." For further Rabbinic parallels cf. Billerbeck 3, p. 628.

103 A few Church Fathers discuss this myth in their exegesis of this passage. The evidence can be found in Georg Megas, "Das χειρόγραφον Adams. Ein Beitrag zu Kol 2:13–15," *ZNW* 27 (1928): 305–20, who says that "certificate of indebtedness" could refer to a pact with the devil. Lohmeyer and Bieder, *ad loc.*, hold the same opinion. Franz Joseph Dölger, *Die Sonne der Gerechtigkeit und der Schwarze. Eine religionsgeschichtliche Studie zum Taufgelöbnis*, Liturgiegeschichtliche Forschungen 2 (Münster i. W.: 1918), 129–41, assumes that the cross is represented as the "trophy" (τρόπαιον) onto which, as a sign of victory over the enemy (= the devil), his weapons (= χειρόγραφον as the document about the pact) were fastened. But "this is a combination of hypotheses, which is uncertain and thus carries no conviction." (Dibelius–Greeven, *ad loc.*). Lohmeyer, *ad loc.*, tries to bolster his exegesis by the following interpretation: he puts a period after "regulations" (τοῖς δόγμασιν) and begins a new sentence with "which" (ὅ): "What was hostile to us, that he has removed, that he has nailed to the cross." As a result the verse is supposed to deal in "obscure and ambiguous terms" with an enemy of mankind. God has crucified Christ and with him the most hated enemy of mankind. The word "which" (ὅ), however, refers to "certificate of indebtedness" (χειρόγραφον) and cannot at all be construed as the beginning of a new sentence.

104 The twice-repeated stress on the hostile character of "certificate of indebtedness" overloads the sentence. The phrase "which was against us" (ὃ ἦν ὑπεναντίον ἡμῖν) is appended to the expression "the certificate of indebtedness which stood against us" (τὸ καθ' ἡμῶν χειρόγραφον) as an interpretative clarification. (Cf. also Schille, *Frühchristliche Hymnen*, 33: "The phrase 'which stood against us' in v 14 seems to be a gloss.") Nevertheless, the entire sentence—including the relative clause "which was against us"—must have belonged to the material used by the author of Col, since he, in turn, supplies a new accentuation with the words "because of the regulations" (τοῖς δόγμασιν). Cf. above p. 106; on "against" (ὑπεναντίος) cf. below p. 110, n. 119.

105 Moule, *ad loc.*, correctly says: "The dative τοῖς δόγμασιν is problematic." For the history of exegesis of this passage cf. Ernest Best, *A Historical Study of the Exegesis of Col 2, 14*, Unpub. Diss. Gregoriana (Rome: 1956). Cf. further the survey in Masson, *ad loc.*

106 Thus, Bengel, *Gnomon*, *ad loc.*: "decrees of grace" (decreta gratiae).

107 Eph 2:15 is formulated more clearly than Col 2:14: "by abolishing the law of commandments and regulations" (τὸν νόμον τῶν ἐντολῶν ἐν δόγμασιν καταργήσας).

108 This is the view of Lightfoot, Abbott, Haupt, *ad loc.*; its most recent proponent is Larsson, *Christus*, 85.

109 Thus, e.g., Dibelius–Greeven, *ad loc.*, on the grounds that "which stood against us" needs something to define its content.

110 For the basis of this interpretation, cf. Percy, *Probleme*, 88f.

111 For an example of a noun in proleptic position before the next verse, cf. Col 4:16: "Make sure . . . that you also read the letter from Laodicea" (ποιήσατε . . . καὶ τὴν [*scil.* ἐπιστολὴν] ἐκ Λαοδικείας ἵνα καὶ ὑμεῖς ἀναγνῶτε). Further examples may be found in Percy, *Probleme*, p. 88 n. 43.

to state:[112] it is because of the regulations that the "certificate of indebtedness" is against us.[113]

In Hellenistic Judaism the commandments of God are also called "regulations"[114] (*δόγματα*).[115] The teaching of the "philosophers" also demanded of its adherents (cf. 2:20f) that they observe the "regulations" which, as legal ordinances, minutely governed the lives and conduct of men.[116] These regulations, however—this is stressed against this teaching—are things of the past which God definitely nullified. Actually, these "regulations" supplied the legal grounds for our entanglement in a debt which we were unable to pay off.[117] According to the view of Judaism, God cancels a debt only when the scales of merits and debts balance.[118] The Christian community, however, confesses that God has forgiven all sins and blotted out[119] the certificate of indebtedness that stood against us, so that it can no longer accuse us.[120] He has not only utterly destroyed the debt, but has also removed the "certificate of indebtedness."[121] Whatever has been removed is no longer valid.[122] The total destruction of the "certificate of indebtedness" was accomplished when God nailed it onto the cross.[123] The image

112 Cf. Rom 3:24–26: Paul adopts a Jewish Christian confessional sentence and interprets it, by means of the emphatic insertion "by faith" (*διὰ πίστεως*) which he places between the two closely connected concepts "expiation" and "by his blood" (*ἱλαστήριον* and *ἐν τῷ αὐτοῦ αἵματι*). Cf. Lohse, *Märtyrer und Gottesknecht*, 149–54.

113 Masson, *ad loc.*, also understands "because of the regulations" as an insertion, but ascribes it to the author of Eph, who supposedly reworked a more primitive, shorter letter to the Colossians. Concerning this hypothesis cf. above p. 90.

114 Cf. 3 Macc 1:3: "the ancestral commandments" (*τῶν πατρίων δογμάτων*) [Trans.]; Josephus, *Contra Apionem* 1, 42 says of the OT: "It is an instinct with every Jew, from the day of his birth, to regard them as the decrees of God, to abide by them, and, if need be, cheerfully to die for them" (*πᾶσι δὲ σύμφυτόν ἐστι εὐθὺς ἐκ πρώτης γενέσεως Ἰουδαίοις τὸ νομίζειν αὐτὰ θεοῦ δόγματα καὶ τούτοις ἐμμένειν καὶ ὑπὲρ αὐτῶν, εἰ δέοι, θνήσκειν ἡδέως*); Philo, *De gig.* 52: "Mark you that not even the high–priest Reason, though he has the power to dwell in unbroken leisure amid the sacred doctrines, has received free license to resort to them at every season" (*ὁρᾶς ὅτι οὐδὲ ὁ ἀρχιερεὺς λόγος ἐνδιατρίβειν ἀεὶ καὶ ἐνσχολάζειν τοῖς ἁγίοις δόγμασι δυνάμενος ἄδειαν ἔσχηκεν ἀνὰ πάντα καιρὸν πρὸς αὐτὰ φοιτᾶν*). Cf. further 4 Macc 10:2; Josephus, *Ant.* 15, 136; Philo, *Leg. all.* 1, 54f.

115 Concerning the term *δόγμα* ("regulation") which occurs in the NT only here and in Eph 2:15 as well as Lk 2:1; Acts 16:4; 17:7, cf. Gerhard Kittel, *TDNT* 2, 230–32.

116 Paul and the deutero–Paulines almost never mention "regulations" (Eph 2:15 is dependent on Col 2:14). Since the question "Why do you want to have regulations imposed . . .?" (*τί . . . δογματίζεσθε* 2:20) alludes to the tenets of the "philosophy," the term "regulations" seems to be derived from the controversy with the false teaching.

117 The word "against" (*ὑπεναντίος*) occurs in the NT only once more, at Heb 10:27. In the LXX it occurs often as a designation for enemies: Gen 22:17; 24:60; Ex 1:10; 15:7; 23:27, etc.

118 In this case "God quickly removes a certificate of debt from the scale loaded with trespasses so that the merits tip the scales" and thus predominate (*j. Peah* 1, 16b, 37). Cf. Billerbeck 3, p. 78f.

119 Cf. Acts 3:19: "that your sins may be blotted out" (*πρὸς τὸ ἐξαλειφθῆναι ὑμῶν τὰς ἁμαρτίας*). In Rev 3:5 "to blot out" (*ἐξαλείφειν*) refers to the removal of a name, so that a legal claim no longer exists; Rev 7:17; 21:4 talk about the wiping away of tears, so that there is no more sadness.

120 Cf. Lohse, *Märtyrer und Gottesknecht*, 156–58.

121 The verb "to remove" (*αἴρειν ἐκ μέσου*) is not to be taken as a Latinism (*de medio tollere*); cf. Blass–Debrunner, par. 5, 3b. Rather, it was quite common in Greek. Cf. e.g., BGU 2, 388, 2, 23: "remove these [*scil.* vessels]" (*ἆρον ταῦτα* [*scil.* vessels] *ἐκ τοῦ μ*[*έ*]*σ*[*ου*]); Plutarch, *De curiositate* 9 (p. 519d): "men remove the matter from the discussion and conceal it" (*αἴρουσιν ἐκ μέσου καὶ ἀποκρύπτουσιν* [Loeb modified]); Epictetus, *Diss.* 3, 15: "Out of the way with it! = Away with it!" (*αἶρε ἐκ μέσου = ἀπόβαλε*).

122 Cf. 1 Cor 5:2: "so that he may be removed from among you" (*ἵνα ἀρθῇ ἐκ μέσου ὑμῶν*); 1 QS II, 16: "he shall be cut off from the midst of all the sons of light" (ונכרת מתוך כול בני אור [Vermes]); 2 Thess 2:7: "only he who now restrains it will do so until he is out of the way" (*μόνον ὁ κατέχων ἄρτι ἕως ἐκ μέσου γένηται*); Mt 13:49: "the angels . . . will separate the evil from the righteous (*οἱ ἄγγελοι . . . ἀφοριοῦσιν τοὺς πονηροὺς ἐκ μέσου τῶν δικαίων*).

123 Deissmann, *LAE*, 332f, thought that the participle "nailed" (*προσηλώσας*) referred to a custom that is unknown to us. According to this custom it was common "to cancel a bond (or other document) by crossing it out with the Greek cross–letter Chi (X)." There is, however, no mention of the crossing out of the "certificate of indebtedness." In the verse at hand the image drawn from legal stipulations re-

of indebtedness is not pursued further. Instead, words from the primitive Christian confession are used.[124] God canceled the certificate by nailing it onto the cross. Because Christ was nailed to the cross in our stead, the debt is forgiven once and for all.[125] And thus the preceding confessional statement "who forgave us all our trespasses" (χαρισάμενος ἡμῖν πάντα τὰ παραπτώματα) is explained: for the sake of Christ God has forgiven all our sins.

■ **15** On the cross of Christ God not only destroyed the "certificate of indebtedness," but also triumphed over the "principalities" (ἐξουσίαι) and "powers" (ἀρχαί). The rarely used middle verb ἀπεκδύεσθαι[126] means "to take off," "to put aside" (with the accusative of the object as in 3:9: "put off the old man" [ἀπεκδυσάμενοι τὸν παλαιὸν ἄνθρωπον]). The middle, however, can also be used in an active sense. Then it means "to strip."[127] The question which of the two possibilities applies here, is answered by determining the implied subject of ἀπεκδυσάμενος. The opinion that Christ is the subject of the sentence was widespread in the early church[128] and has also been propounded in recent times by many exegetes. To be sure, the Latin Fathers in their explanation presupposed a supplement or alteration in the text: Christ put aside the flesh.[129] The Greek Fathers, for their part, maintained the transmitted text and said that Christ had divested the powers and principalities of evil.[130] It is a peculiarity of this latter explanation that it assumes that Christ once must have been clothed with the "principalities" (ἐξουσίαι) and "powers" (ἀρχαί). This would have been a clothing in an alien garment, namely the powers of evil.[131] At his ascension he stripped off this clothing and thus emerged victorious over the powers. This thought would come close to the concepts of the Gnostic myth in which the redeemer strips off the clothing of the body at his ascension and leads the way to heaven for his own.[132] However, this interpretation faces the difficulty that there is no change of subject from v 14

garding indebtedness is presently abandoned and has ceased to be determinative for the meaning of "nailed" (προσηλώσας).

124 On αἴρειν in the meaning of "to remove," "to carry away," cf. Joachim Jeremias, *TDNT* 1, 186. For instances of this primitive Christian confession cf. Jn 1:29, 36; 1 Jn 3:5; 1 Pt 2:24; Ign. *Eph.* 9:1; Ign. *Tr.* 11:2; *Barn.* 9:8; 12:1.

125 The statement of the kerygma that Christ died "for our sins" (ὑπὲρ τῶν ἁμαρτιῶν ἡμῶν 1 Cor 15:3) can be intensified by Paul to: Christ became "a curse for us" (ὑπὲρ ἡμῶν κατάρα Gal 3:13) and to: God "for our sake made him to be sin who knew no sin, so that in him we might become the righteousness of God" (τὸν μὴ γνόντα ἁμαρτίαν ὑπὲρ ἡμῶν ἁμαρτίαν ἐποίησεν, ἵνα ἡμεῖς γενώμεθα δικαιοσύνη θεοῦ ἐν αὐτῷ 2 Cor 5:21). It is, however, not possible to conclude on the basis of these passages that Col 2:14 identifies the "certificate of indebtedness" with Christ, cf. Moule, *ad loc.*: "for the body of Christ, nailed to the cross, does in some sense represent humanity's guilt." Cf. also Oliva A. Blanchette, "Does the Cheirographon of Col 2, 14 represent Christ himself?" *CBQ* 23 (1961): 306–12. Rather there seems to be reference to the custom "of affixing to the cross the 'inscription' (τίτλος) bearing the crime of the wrongdoer (Mk 15:26)," Dibelius–Greeven, *ad loc.*

126 Cf. Albrecht Oepke, *TDNT* 2, 318f; Bauer, *s.v.*

127 Cf. Blass–Debrunner, par. 316, 1.

128 The references may be found in Lightfoot and Lohmeyer, *ad loc.*

129 ΤΑΣ ΑΡΧΑΣ→ΤΗΝ ΣΑΡΚΑ (the powers→the flesh).

130 The evidence may be found in Lightfoot, *ad loc.*

131 This garment may be compared to the robe, which was dipped into the blood of the centaur Nessus whom Heracles had killed; the robe poisoned by the blood was presented to Heracles. This is Lightfoot's explanation *ad loc.*: "The powers of evil, which had clung like a Nessus robe about his humanity, were torn off and cast aside for ever." Also cf. Moule, *ad loc.*

132 Käsemann, *Leib Christi*, 139–44 (see also *Essays*, 161–63), is the main proponent who explains this verse by reference to the Gnostic Redeemer myth: the redeemer during his ascension has laid aside the powers and principalities, namely, "the Adamic body tyrannized over by the demonic rulers of this aeon" (*Essays*, p. 162). Just as he has stripped himself of the "flesh" (σάρξ), so too those who are his own should follow him and undertake the "putting off the body of flesh" (ἀπέκδυσις τοῦ σώματος τῆς σαρκός) (*Leib Christi*, p. 139f). But apart from the highly intricate complex of problems surrounding the origin and date of the Gnostic Redeemer myth (cf. Carsten Colpe, *Die religionsgeschichtliche Schule: Darstellung und Kritik ihres Bildes vom gnostischen Erlösermythus*, FRLANT 78 [Göttingen: 1961]), one question is paramount: does Col 2:15 really say that Christ is clohted with the "powers" and "principalities"? It is neither hinted at nor to be inferred that these beings are identical with the "body of flesh" (σῶμα τῆς σαρκός).

to v 15.[133] Therefore, most exegetes rightly maintain that God is the subject of the entire section.[134] It is he who has destroyed powers and principalities on the cross of Christ. The word **ἀπεκδυσάμενος**, which thus must be taken in an active sense, means that he stripped them[135] and completely divested them of their power.[136] In hymnic words Christianity praises the victory over the "powers" and "principalities."[137] Though they brought Christ to the cross, God has exposed them on the cross in their powerlessness (cf. 1 Cor 2:6–8).[138] God has proclaimed publicly that he has divested them of their usurped majesty by putting them on public display and exposing them to ridicule.[139] As their devastating defeat is shown to the whole world, the infinite superiority of Christ is demonstrated.[140]

The powers and principalities have been conquered and therefore can no longer have any power over those who belong to the victor.[141] In a triumphal procession God parades[142] the powerless "powers" and "principalities" to manifest to all the magnitude of the victory.[143] They are powerless figures who can neither help man nor demand homage and obeisance from him. Since their period of rule is finished, they have no choice but to worship the victor.[144]

By the words "in him" (**ἐν αὐτῷ**) at the end of this section it is stressed once more: in him God has triumphed over the powers and principalities, in him victory is seized, triumph obtained.[145] And thus the train of thought returns to that decisive question which was put to the community: whether alongside or outside of Christ

133 Cf. Dibelius–Greeven, *ad loc.* and Larsson, *Christus*, 90 n. 1. If Christ is taken as the subject, the concluding phrase "in him" (ἐν αὐτῷ) must be construed either with "the cross" (τῷ σταυρῷ) [thus Lightfoot, *ad loc.* with a reference to Eph 2:16: "through the cross" (διὰ τοῦ σταυροῦ); and Moule, *ad loc.*] or must be read as "in himself" (ἐν αὐτῷ). Since this phrase "in him" has been repeatedly used in the previous verses, its occurrence at the end of v 15 cannot be explained differently than its use in vss 9–12.

134 Cf. Lohmeyer, Dibelius–Greeven, Masson, Conzelmann *ad loc.*; Rudolf Bultmann, "New Testament and Mythology" in *Kerygma and Myth: A Theological Debate* 1, ed. Hans Werner Bartsch, tr. Reginald H. Fuller (London: SPCK, 1953), 36.

135 Albrecht Oepke, *TDNT* 2, 319, and Bauer, *s.v.*, propose the translation "disarm." It is not necessary, however, to think of weapons. The powers and principalities are stripped and thus exposed to ridicule. Cf. Lohmeyer, *ad loc.*; Heinrich Schlier, *TDNT* 2, 31 n. 2.

136 Cf. *Evangelium Nicodemi* 2, 7 (= *Acta Pilati* B, 23; ed. Carl von Tischendorf [1853] p. 329): Hades asks Satan: "Through what necessity did you contrive that the King of glory should be crucified, so that he should come here and strip us naked?" (διὰ ποίαν ἀνάγκην ᾠκονόμησας σταυρωθῆναι τὸν βασιλέα τῆς δόξης εἰς τὸ ἐλθεῖν ὧδε καὶ ἐκδῦσαι ἡμᾶς [F. Scheidweiler, *Hennecke–Schneemelcher* 1, 474]).

137 Cf. Phil 2:9–11; 1 Tim 3:16; Heb 1:9–14. Cf. further *OdSol* 22:3–5: "He who scattered my enemies and my adversaries; He who gave me authority over bonds that I might loose them; He that overthrew by my hands the dragon with seven heads" [Harris–Mingana]. Cf. W. Bauer, *Hennecke–Schneemelcher* 2, (German ed.), 602.

138 The manuscripts p^{46} B introduce a connective "and" (καί) before "he put on public display" (ἐδειγμάτισεν). Supposing that "and" (καί) is the original reading—and this is conceivable on the basis of its strong attestation—then the sentence structure would correspond exactly to that of v 14b: "and he removed it" (καὶ αὐτὸ ἦρκεν).

139 The word δειγματίζειν is rarely used, in the NT only here and in Mt 1:19 in the meaning of "to expose." Cf. further *AscIs* 3:13: "For Beliar harbored great wrath against Isaiah on account of the vision and of the exposure with which he had exposed Sammael" (ἦν γὰρ ὁ Βελιὰρ ἐν θυμῷ πολλῷ [ἐ]πὶ Ἠσαίαν ἀπὸ τῆς [ὁρά]σεως καὶ ἀπὸ το[ῦ δει]γματισμοῦ ὅτι [ἐ]δειγμάτισεν τὸν [Σ]αμαήλ) [*Hennecke–Schneemelcher* 2, p. 647]. Further examples may be found in Heinrich Schlier, *TDNT* 2, 31f; Bauer, *s.v.*

140 Cf. Heinrich Schlier, *TDNT* 5, 883f.

141 Cf. Severian of Gabala *ad loc.*: "And how are they displayed? As rendered weaker than men, as tread upon, as ridiculed by them in the name of the Lord" (καὶ τίς τούτων ὁ δειγματισμός; ὅτι ἀσθενέστεροι τῶν ἀνθρώπων γεγόνασιν, ὅτι πατοῦνται, ὅτι ὑπ' αὐτῶν ἐμπαίζονται ἐν τῷ ὀνόματι τοῦ κυρίου [Trans.]).

142 The word θριαμβεύειν here and in 2 Cor 2:14—the only two places in the NT where it occurs—means "to triumph over, to lead in a triumphal procession." Cf. Gerhard Delling, *TDNT* 3, 159f; Bauer, *s.v.* In 2 Cor 2:14 God is also the subject of the sentence: in his triumphal procession he carries the apostle along.

143 Cf. Horace, *Epist.* 1, 17, 33: "to display captive foemen to one's fellow citizens" (*captos ostendere civibus hostes*).

144 Cf. Bornkamm, "Baptism and New Life in Paul,"

there is any other possibility of participating in divine fulness. Worship the "elements of the universe," submit to the powers and principalities—so say "the philosophers." Col opposes these demands with the assertion *solus Christus*, "Christ alone." In him dwells the entire fulness of deity bodily—in him you have been filled—in him you were circumcised with a circumcision not made by hands—in him you were raised together with him through faith in the power of God, who raised him from the dead. The decision has already been made. For in baptism those who were baptized have been placed into the domain of the beloved Son of God. Therefore, the powers and principalities are no longer their concern. What matters for them is Christ alone—and nobody and nothing outside of or alongside him![146]

Early Christian Experience, 80: "Colossians, too, does not say that the powers are done away, but that they are disarmed, incorporated as the vanquished in the triumphal procession of Christ (Col. 2.15). As in a triumphal procession in which the subjugated follow behind the victor, all still are visible and must proclaim the greatness of the victory that has been achieved through the very might of their appearance. So the 'rulers' and 'powers' are still there, but for believers they no longer bear any weapons and thereby they glorify the victory of Christ."

145 The words "in him" cannot be connected with "certificate of indebtedness" (thus von Soden, *ad loc.*), for according to v 14 it has been destroyed. Nor can "in him" be taken with "the cross" (τῷ σταυρῷ) [thus Lightfoot, Haupt, Masson, Moule, *ad loc.*]. Rather it refers to Christ; this is the position of many exegetes: Lohmeyer, Dibelius–Greeven, Conzelmann, *ad loc.*; Bultmann, "Neues Testament und Mythologie," p. 42 [the English translation has missed the German: ". . . in ihm (in Christus). . ."].

146 Cf. Käsemann, "Römer 13:1–7," 359: "The letter itself answers the question at hand in terms of 'Christ alone.' The powers cannot establish a connection with Christ, nor can they separate from him. All that can be said about them is that they who were once rulers of the world have been disempowered by the Christ, who alone as the eschatological ruler of the All [κοσμοκράτωρ] holds in his hands the governance of the world and the salvation of his own."

2 The End of the Regulations

16 Therefore, let no one pass judgment on
you in matters of eating and drinking
or with regard to a festival or a new
moon or a sabbath; 17/ these are only a
shadow of what is to come, but the
body belongs to Christ. 18/ Let no one
condemn you, who takes pleasure in
readiness to serve and in worship of
angels, as he has had visions of them
during the mystery rites, puffed up
without reason by his earthly mind,
19/ and who does not adhere steadfastly
to the head, from which the whole
body, supported and knit together by
sinews and ligaments, grows with a
growth that is from God.
20 If, therefore, with Christ you died to the
elements of the universe, why do you
want to have regulations imposed on
you as if you still lived in the world:
21/ Do not handle, do not taste, do not
touch—22/ all of this is destined to
perish through use!—according to
regulations and doctrines of men?
23/ These things indeed have the reputa-
tion of wisdom in self-chosen worship,
readiness to serve, and severe treatment
of the body, but they have nothing to
do with honor and only serve to satiate
the flesh.

Since victory over the powers and principalities has been gained on the cross of Christ, and since he is head over all powers and principalities, all who belong to him are free from the constraint of the "elements of the universe" (*στοιχεῖα τοῦ κόσμου*) who demand submission in the "worship of the angels" (*θρησκεία τῶν ἀγγέλων*). Therefore, they should not be impressed by those who boast to them of their experiences and arrogantly pass disparaging judgments (vss 16–19). On the contrary, he who has died with Christ has died to the elements of the universe. Thus, for him the "regulations" (*δόγματα*) and their ordinances do not concern him any more. He does not have to pay heed to rules that forbid this and that. Rather the things of the world have been given to him from God, to be used without restrictions (vss 20–23).

This section is written in a pointed polemical style and is filled with allusions to the teaching and to catchwords of the "philosophy" (*φιλοσοφία*). Therefore, the sentences are not easily comprehensible. For it cannot always be determined with certainty what words in each single instance are taken from the opponents and used in the polemic against them and what phrases have been formulated by the author himself. Point by point, the presumptuous claim which the "philosophers" tried to validate in the community is rejected. Using their own terms, the author lays bare the vacuity of their "philosophy."

■ **16** No one has the right arrogantly to constitute himself as judge over other persons because they do not follow certain regulations. Again the indefinite "someone" (*τις*) points to the danger that threatens the community (cf. v 8). Thus, "someone" refers to anybody who tries to carry through his viewpoint in the community and claims that only his own conduct corresponds to knowledge. Such a person does not scruple to consider himself superior to the others. And when they fail to recognize appropriately the necessity for the "regulations" (*δόγματα*), he levels sarcastic criticism at them.[1] The judg-

1 Cf. Rom 14:3: "Let not him who abstains pass judgment on him who eats" (*ὁ δὲ μὴ ἐσθίων τὸν ἐσθίοντα μὴ κρινέτω*).

2 Instead of the "and" (*καί*) which manuscripts p^{46} B 1739 sy^{p} have, manuscripts ℌ ℜ DG al read "or" (*ἤ*).

ment that arises out of his conviction of superiority first of all refers to *βρῶσις*[2] and *πόσις*,[3] eating and drinking.[4] It follows from the demand of "severe treatment of the body" (*ἀφειδία τοῦ σώματος* v 23) that abstinence from certain food is required (cf. v 21; 1 Tim 4:3: "to abstain from food" *ἀπέχεσθαι βρωμάτων*).

In the ancient world the view was widespread that by asceticism and fasting man served the deity, came closer to him, or could prepare himself to receive a divine revelation.[5] Thus a person often abstained from meat and ate only those foods which the earth produced.[6] He also abstained from wine and strong drink.[7] The reasons for such an ascetic way of life were very diverse. The belief in the transmigration of souls might forbid a person to eat meat; other people might follow certain ideas of what constituted purity; and again many others shared a dualistic world view which led them to asceticism. The regulations to which the "philosophy" of Col demanded obedience concerned taboos and observance of sacred times. They are thus related to the obedient submission to the "elements of the universe" (*στοιχεῖα τοῦ κόσμου*).

It was according to their regulations that man had to live; consequently he had to conduct himself with regard to[8] the holy days they prescribed. Since these sacred times are referred to as "festival, new moon, sabbath"[9] (*ἑορτή, νεομηνία, σάββατα*), the author enumerates three terms which often occur in the OT in this combination and describe special days dedicated to God.[10] In the context of Col, however, the command to keep festival, new moon, and sabbath is not based on the Torah according to which Israel received the sabbath as a sign of her election from among the nations. Rather the sacred days must be kept for the sake of "the elements of the universe," who direct the course of the stars and thus also prescribe minutely the order of the calendar.[11] By birth and fate man is subjected to the elements of the universe and must serve them by meticulous conformity to food

---

3 Cf. Rom 14:17: "For the kingdom of God does not consist of eating and drinking" (*οὐ γάρ ἐστιν ἡ βασιλεία τοῦ θεοῦ βρῶσις καὶ πόσις*); 1 Cor 8:4: "hence, as to the eating of food offered to idols" (*περὶ τῆς βρώσεως οὖν τῶν εἰδωλοθύτων*).

4 The words "eating" (*βρῶσις*) and "drinking" (*πόσις*) are to be distinguished from "food" (*βρῶμα* cf. 1 Cor 3:3; 6:13; 8:8, 13; 10:3; Rom 14:15) and "drink" (*πόμα* cf. 1 Cor 10:4). On "food/eating" (*βρῶμα/βρῶσις*) cf. Johannes Behm, *TDNT* 1, 642–45; on "drink/drinking" (*πόμα/πόσις*) cf. Leonhard Goppelt, *TDNT* 6, 145–48.

5 References can be found in Lietzmann, *Römer*, 114f; Günther Bornkamm, *TDNT* 4, 65–67; Johannes Behm, *TDNT* 4, 924–35.

6 Cf. Apuleius, *Metamorph.* 11, 28: "abstain from all animal meats" (*inanimis contentus cibis*); Philostratus, *Vita Apollonii* 1, 8: "He declined to live upon a meat diet, on the ground that it was unclean, and also that it made the mind gross; he partook only of dried fruits and vegetables, for he said that all the fruits of the earth are clean" (*τὰς μὲν ἐμψύχους βρώσεις ὡς οὔτε καθαρὰς καὶ τὸν νοῦν παχυνούσας παρῃτήσατο, τραγήματα δὲ καὶ λάχανα ἐσιτεῖτο, καθαρὰ εἶναι φάσκων, ὁπόσα ἡ γῆ αὐτὴ δίδωσι*).

7 Cf. Philostratus, *ibid.*; Eusebius, *Hist. eccl.* 2, 23, 5 says of James, the brother of the Lord: "He drank no wine or strong drink, nor did he eat meat" (*οἶνον καὶ σίκερα οὐκ ἔπιεν οὐδὲ ἔμψυχον ἔφαγεν*).

8 The Greek phrase *ἐν μέρει* has a technical meaning: "in the matter of," "with regard to." Cf., e.g., Plutarch, *Consolatio ad Apollonium* 4 (p. 102e): "in the matter of advice" (*ἐν ὑποθήκης μέρει*) [Trans.]; Philo, *Det. pot. ins. sol.* 5: "in the matter of the principle" (*ἐν μέρει λόγου*) [Trans.]; cf. also 2 Cor 3:10: "with regard to this" (*ἐν τούτῳ τῷ μέρει*); 9:3: "with regard to this" (*ἐν τῷ μέρει τούτῳ*). Further examples may be found in Bauer, *s.v.*

9 The plural *τὰ σάββατα* is very frequently used to designate the singular. Cf. Eduard Lohse, *TWNT* 7, 7, 20

10 Cf. LXX Hos 2:13; Ezek 45:17; 1 Chr 23:31; 2 Chr 2:3; 31:3; cf. also Jub 1:14; *Tos. Ber.* 3:11; Justin, *Dial.* 8:4.

11 Apocalypticism and the Qumran community also speculated about the relationship between the angels and the powers of the stars on the one hand, and sacred times on the other. The evidence can be found in Schlier, *Galater*, 204–06. Nevertheless, in Judaism the observance of sacred times continued to be an expression of obedience to the law of God who was the Lord of the universe. In the syncretistic "philosophy," however, observance of days and seasons had an essentially different character. They were expressions of the worship of the elements of the universe. A Jew would find it impossible to participate in such worship. Thus, it does not prove true, if one wants to consider the "philosophy" an offshoot of the teaching of the Qumran community. This is the view of W. D. Davies, "Paul and the Dead Sea Scrolls: Flesh and Spirit" in: *The Scrolls and the New Testament*, ed. Krister Stendahl (New York: Harper & Brothers, 1957), 167f, who maintains that clear allusions to various passages from the Qumran

laws and special times.[12] The "philosophy" made use of terms which stemmed from Jewish tradition, but which had been transformed in the crucible of syncretism to be subject to the service of "the elements of the universe." It is this service which they are now supposed to express.[13] Since the angelic powers are in charge of the order of the cosmos and the course of the stars, their sacred seasons and times must be observed and the regulations, codified in a list of taboos, must be followed.[14]

■ **17** All these[15]—the argument now turns on the "regulations" (*δόγματα*) which had been represented as a *sine qua non* for salvation—are only the "shadow of what is to come" (*σκιὰ τῶν μελλόντων*), not the reality itself. The opposition between outer appearance and the real essence, as it was taught in Platonic philosophy,[16] was a theme repeatedly considered and described in Hellenistic times. True being belongs to ideas and not to the shadows they cast in this world, which are perceived by our senses. The concepts most frequently used to describe this contrast are: *σκιά* (shadow) and *εἰκών* (form, image).[17] At times, however, "body" (*σῶμα*) is used instead of "form" (*εἰκών*) to describe the true reality as distinguished from mere appearance. Philo, for example, discussing the allegorical method of interpretation, explains that the words of the divine oracle are like "the shadows of the bodies" (*σκιάς τινας ὡσανεὶ σωμάτων*) and that the meanings revealed in the latter are "the things that really and truly exist" (*τὰ ὑφεστῶτα ἀληθείᾳ πράγματα De conf. ling.* 190). "Shadow" (*σκιά*) is related to "body" (*σῶμα*) as the "copy" (*μίμημα*) to the "original" (*ἀρχέτυπος De migr. Abr.* 12). Josephus narrates how Archelaus, the son of Herod the Great, was trying to obtain Augustus' confirmation of the kingship bequeathed him by his father. In doing so, Archelaus met with the reproach that he had not really waited for Caesar's decision. For in reality he had already begun to rule as King and now appeared in Rome "begging for the shadow of royalty, of which he had already appropriated the body" (*σκιὰν αἰτησόμενος βασιλείας, ἧς ἥρπασεν ἑαυτῷ τὸ σῶμα Bell.* 2, 28). The shadow is mere appearance; "body" (*σῶμα*), however, is the reality.[18]

This relationship between copy and original probably also played a role in the teaching of the Colossian "philosophy." It is possible that the proponents of the philosophy reasoned something like this: the "worship of angels" (*θρησκεία τῶν ἀγγέλων*) and observance of the "regulations" (*δόγματα*) represent the copy; the "fulness" (*πλήρωμα*) is the original. A person can gain access to the pleroma only via the copy which implies obedience to the "elements of the universe."[19] In Col the contrast between "shadow" and "body" is turned into a polemical argument against the "philosophy." The author of Col understands the contrast as an antithesis

---

writings can be recognized in the ascetic rules as well as in the worship of the powers and principalities. Similarly, Pierre Benoit, "Qumran et le Nouveau Testament," *NTS* 7 (1960–61): 287 = *Exégèse et théologie* 3 (Paris: 1968), 387, is of the opinion that circumcision, exact observance of food laws and of the festal calendar as well as speculation about the angelic powers, tally completely with the views of the pious Jews who lived on the shore of the Dead Sea. The "philosophy," however, does not reveal any signs of the kind of radical understanding of the law that is advocated by the Qumran community. The term "law" (*νόμος*) is absent anyway from the controversy in which Col is engaged. Cf. also Braun, *Qumran* 1, pp. 228–32 and below p. 129.

12 Cf. Eduard Lohse, *TWNT* 7, 31

13 Cf. Eduard Lohse, "Christologie und Ethik," 157f.

14 Cf. the teaching of Elchasai, who directed his followers to keep the Sabbath because the Sabbath was one of the days which, because of the course of the stars, had to be observed carefully, with scrupulous awe (Hippolytus, *Refut.* 9, 16, 2f). Cf. also Eduard Lohse, *TWNT* 7, 34.

15 The Greek neuter plural relative pronoun "these" (ἅ) should be read with the majority of manuscripts; the Greek neuter singular relative pronoun "this" (ὅ) [BG it Marcion] must be considered an assimilation to "this is" (ὅ ἐστιν) in 1:24; 3:14.

16 Cf. the famous image of the cave in Plato's *Republic* 514a–518b.

17 Thus, e.g., Heb 10:1: "For since the law has but a shadow of the good things to come instead of the true form of these realities" (*Σκιὰν γὰρ ἔχων ὁ νόμος τῶν μελλόντων ἀγαθῶν, οὐκ αὐτὴν τὴν εἰκόνα τῶν πραγμάτων*); cf. also 8:5.

18 Cf. further Philo, *de post. Caini* 112: " 'Sella' means 'a shadow,' and is a figure of bodily and external goods, which in reality differ not a whit from a shadow" (*Σελλὰ τοίνυν ἑρμηνεύεται σκιά, τῶν περὶ σῶμα καὶ ἐκτὸς ἀγαθῶν, ἃ τῷ ὄντι σκιᾶς οὐδὲν διαφέρει, σύμβολον*); *De decal.* 82; *De plantatione* 27: "not shadows but the actual archetype" (*οὐ σκιὰς ἀλλὰ τὰς ἀρχετύπους*); further *de somn.* 1, 206; *leg. all.* 3, 96: "shadow . . . the image" (*σκιὰν . . . ἡ εἰκών*); further 3, 99–103. Cf. also Siegfried Schulz, *TWNT* 7, 398f.

characterized by the turning of the ages. The commands spelled out in the "regulations" (δόγματα) are nothing but the "shadow of what is to come" (σκιὰ τῶν μελλόντων). Just as Adam was "a type of the one who was to come" (τύπος τοῦ μέλλοντος Rom 5:14) and just as the law had only the shadow "of the good things to come" (τῶν μελλόντων ἀγαθῶν Heb 10:1), so it becomes apparent under the sign of the fulfillment in Christ that the regulations are merely shadows of things to come, i.e. "the body that belongs to Christ" (τὸ δὲ σῶμα τοῦ Χριστοῦ). Since reality is with Christ alone, the shadowy appearances have lost all right to exist.[20] Since the only true reality, before which the shadows must disperse, is described here not by εἰκών (form) but by σῶμα (body), the author of Col obviously wants to emphasize this term "body" once again: Christ is "head of the body, i.e., of the church" (κεφαλὴ τοῦ σώματος, τῆς ἐκκλησίας). The reality which exists solely with Christ is shared only by those who, as members of the body of Christ, adhere to the head (2:19).[21] Therefore, for them the shadows have become completely meaningless, and the "regulations," to which the arrogant exponents of the "philosophy" refer, have lost all binding force.[22]

■ 18 Again, in different words, the author refutes one of the claims the opponents voiced in the community: "let no one condemn you" (μηδεὶς ὑμᾶς καταβραβευέτω). The compound Greek verb translated with "to condemn" καταβραβεύειν, which is used here instead of "to pass judgment" (κρίνειν v 16), is rarely found in Greek literature.[23] If the simple verb βραβεύειν means to award a prize won in a contest,[24] then the compound verb καταβραβεύειν means "to award a prize unjustly" (τὸ ἀδίκως βραβεύειν),[25] i.e., to decide against a person and rob him of a prize, to convict him, to condemn him.[26] In the dependent participial clauses the grounds are briefly indicated on which these people base such judgments. The words "puffed up without reason, etc." (εἰκῇ φυσιούμενος κτλ) surely contain a negative evaluation of these people. However, the clause that immediately follows the principal verb still indicates on what basis they bolster their position and haughtily boast of it. Therefore, the reference to "readiness to serve" (ταπεινοφροσύνη) and in "worship of angels" (θρησκεία τῶν ἀγγέλων) as well as the relative clause "as he has had visions of them during the mystery rites" (ἃ ἑόρακεν ἐμβατεύων) are quotes[27] from the catchwords

19 Cf. Conzelmann, *ad loc.*: "Obviously the opponents think that their liturgical celebrations are an image of what is eternal which is present in earthly things."

20 Cf. Severian of Gabala, *ad loc.*: "Therefore, when the substance has come, the shadow is superfluous" (ἐλθόντος οὖν τοῦ σώματος περιττὴ ἡ σκιά [Trans.]).

21 The term "body" (σῶμα), therefore, refers to Christ as the Lord and to the Church as the domain of his lordship. Moule, *ad loc.*, correctly remarks that a reference to the church is also contained in the word "body." He goes too far, however, when he also finds in it a reference to the sacrificial body of Christ.

22 It is not the case that the regulations have at least some conditional authority, since as "shadow of what is to come" (σκιὰ τῶν μελλόντων) they have as it were, the quality of a promise. Rather what is demonstrated is the definitive end of the regulations, since, as shadows, they must disappear once the substance has appeared. Wide of the mark is the proposal of I. A. Moir in his review of *The Bible Societies' Greek New Testament*, *NTS* 14 (1967–1968): 142: "Since there appears no satisfactory explanation of the σκιά/σῶμα antithesis at Col II. 17, perhaps we could repunctuate with the stop after μελλόντων and link the σῶμα with the following verb?"

23 Cf. Bauer, *s.v.*

24 Cf. the discussion of 3:15 below and consult Ethelbert Stauffer, *TDNT* 1, 637f.

25 Cf. Theodoret, *ad loc.*

26 Cf. Demosthenes, *Orat.* 21, 93: "Strato was victimized by Meidias" (Στράτωνα ὑπὸ Μειδίου καταβραβευθέντα); Vettius Valens 9, 7 (p. 344, 28–30): "As we observe, the earth itself seems to have power over all things as the originator and can condemn the rest" (δοκεῖ δὲ καθὼς ὁρῶμεν ἡ γῆ καταβραβεύειν τῶν λοιπῶν ἐπέχουσα αὐτὴ τὰ πάντα ὡς πρόγονος) [Trans.]; Preisigke *Sammelbuch* 4512 B, 57: καταβεβραβευμένοι = "condemned" (cf. Preisigke *Wört.* 1, col. 744).

27 Percy, *Probleme*, 169, contrariwise would understand the entire clause as a critical remark: "Let no one rob you of salvation. Those people take pleasure in something so vile as self-abasement and worship of angels—that is all the piety of the false teachers amounts to." This explanation, however, flounders on the term ταπεινοφροσύνη (readiness to serve). Cf. below p. 118, n. 32.

of the proponents of the "philosophy."[28]

No one should presume to exalt himself above the community "taking pleasure in readiness to serve and in worship of angels" (θέλων ἐν ταπεινοφροσύνῃ καὶ θρησκείᾳ τῶν ἀγγέλων). The phrase θέλων ἐν is to be understood as "to take pleasure in" and corresponds to the Hebrew חָפֵץ בְּ.[29] The verse continues by referring to the things in which the devotees of the "philosophy" took great pride and pleasure. Since the word θρησκεία (worship) again occurs in the term mentioned in v 23 ἐθελοθρησκία and there designates a self-chosen worship, θέλων here refers to a choice that is freely made to adhere to the teaching and praxis of the "philosophy."[30] A person condemns the others because he takes pleasure in "readiness to serve" (ταπεινοφροσύνη) and in "worship of angels" (θρησκεία τῶν ἀγγέλων).[31] Both concepts take up the opponents' catchwords. Consequently, ταπεινοφροσύνη here cannot mean humility, which in 3:12 is mentioned along with the other virtues of the Christians (cf. also Phil 2:3; Eph 4:2). Rather it means the fulfillment of specific cultic regulations, to which v 23 also refers with the words ἐν ἐθελοθρησκίᾳ καὶ ταπεινοφροσύνῃ (in self-chosen worship and readiness to serve).[32] Since both here and there the term "readiness to serve" occurs next to "worship," it does not describe a disposition. Rather, it is talking about cultic conduct. Of course, ταπεινοφροσύνη can, like the Hebrew תַּעֲנִית, mean fasting.[33] The word, however, must in no way be restricted to this meaning. It describes the eagerness and docility with which a person fulfills the cultic ordinances.[34] For the "worship of the angels" demands this. The angels determine the course of the cosmos and consequently man's life as well.[35] Man submits to them insofar as he performs the prescribed cultic acts and fulfills the regulations laid down for him.[36]

The short relative clause "as he has had visions of them during the mystery rites" (ἃ ἑόρακεν ἐμβατεύων) also deals with the cult which embraces "readiness to serve"

---

28 After a thorough consideration of the exegetical discussion, F. O. Francis, "Humility and Angelic Worship in Col 2:18," *ST* 16 (1962): 109–34 opts for the background of ascetic–mystical piety as the explanatory matrix for the sentence. His investigation will be given special consideration in the following discussion.

29 The phrase "to take pleasure in" (θέλειν ἐν) often corresponds to the Hebrew חָפֵץ בְּ. Cf. 1 Sam 18:22; 2 Sam 15:26; 1 Kings 10:9; 1 Chr 28:4; Ps 111:1; 146:10; TestAsher 1:6: "therefore if the soul take pleasure in the good [inclination]" (ἐὰν οὖν ἡ ψυχὴ θέλῃ ἐν καλῷ) [Charles, *APOT*]. Cf. Lightfoot, Haupt, Lohmeyer, Moule *ad loc.*; Gottlob Schrenk, *TDNT* 3, 45 n. 13; Percy, *Probleme*, 145–47; Bauer, *s.v.*; Francis, "Humility," 113f. Ivar Heikel, "Kol. 2, 16–18," *Theologische Studien und Kritiken* 107 (1936), 464f, without any convincing evidence, alters "taking pleasure in" to "of gods" (ΘΕΛΩΝ becomes ΘΕΙΩΝ).

30 Dibelius–Greeven, *ad loc.*, take θέλων adverbially in the meaning of "willfully" and connect it with "let no one condemn you" (καταβραβευέτω): "Let no one willfully condemn you." On θέλων = "intentionally," "deliberately" cf. also Anton Fridrichsen, "ΘΕΛΩΝ Col 2:18," *ZNW* 21 (1922): 135–37; Harald Riesenfeld, "Zum Gebrauch von ΘΕΛΩ im Neuen Testament," *Arbeiten und Mitteilungen aus dem neutestamentlichen Seminar zu Uppsala* 1 (Uppsala: 1936), 1–8; Blass–Debrunner, par. 148, 2.

31 The preposition "in" (ἐν) is omitted by א *. There is no reason to make conjectures like "in self-abasement" (ἐν ἐθελοταπεινοφροσύνῃ) [Hort] or to change θέλων (taking pleasure in) to ἐλθών (entering into). Cf. Abbott, *ad loc.*

32 This meaning certainly is not implied in 3:12. Consequently, in 2:18, 23 the term has been taken from the teaching of the "philosophy." Contra Percy, *Probleme*, 169. Cf. above p. 117, n. 27.

33 Cf. Hermas, *Vis.* 3, 10, 6; *Sim.* 5, 3, 7; Tertullian, *De jujun.* 12. Cf. Percy, *Probleme*, 147–49. Francis, "Humility," 113–19 places great emphasis on this meaning and then interprets the passage: by "fasting" a person prepares himself for ecstatic–mystic experiences. This explanation, however, reads something into the text of Col 2:18 which is not there.

34 A person fulfills these so much the more eagerly when God himself appears to be inaccessibly distant. Cf. Theodoret, *ad loc.*: "They practice humility, I suppose, saying that since the God of all things is invisible, inaccessible and incomprehensible, it is fitting to work at the divine favor through the angels" (ταπεινοφροσύνῃ δῆθεν κεχρημένοι, καὶ λέγοντες ὡς ἀόρατος ὁ τῶν ὅλων θεός, ἀνέφικτός τε καὶ ἀκατάληπτος, καὶ προσήκει διὰ τῶν ἀγγέλων τὴν θείαν εὐμένειαν πραγματεύεσθαι [Trans.]).

35 The word "worship" (θρησκεία cf. Acts 26:5; Jas 1:26f) can be used in either a positive or negative sense, to be ascertained from the particular context. Cf. Karl Ludwig Schmidt, *TDNT* 3, 157f.

36 Because of its position next to "readiness to serve," "worship of angels" must also designate cultic behavior. Therefore, the context convincingly demands the explanation given by almost all exegetes

and "worship of angels." These few words, to be sure, are so difficult to understand in their brevity that scholars have proposed various ways of altering the text. Since it did not seem proper for the adherents of that teaching to have had real visionary experiences, many manuscripts introduce a negation. In reality the adherents had seen nothing at all.[37] Col, however, does not base its polemic on the untenable presupposition that it was impossible for pagans and heretics to experience ecstasies and visions. Supposing that the transmitted text could not possibly be correct, many exegetes have made ingenious conjectures.[38] Yet all of these proposals are based on the idea that the short relative clause must be a polemic directed against the "philosophy." Actually, however, the clause is not polemical; it is a quotation. Therefore, there is no reason to depart from the transmitted text. **ἃ ἑόρακεν ἐμβατεύων** (as he has had visions of them during the mystery rites).[39]

The verb **ἐμβατεύειν**[40] means "to enter into," "to set foot upon"—a place, a city, a sanctuary or a country.[41] This verb **ἐμβατεύειν** can then also mean "to approach something to investigate it."[42] If this is the meaning in this passage too, then it could be explained: "What he had seen, he sought to investigate." Questioning, he strives to fathom what he has seen during ecstasy.[43] This translation, however, is somewhat flat; it gains meaning only if one implies in the explanation the quest for knowledge as the motive which dominates the adherents of the "philosophy." It is noteworthy, however, that the same verb, **ἐμβατεύειν**, is found in the language of the mysteries. It describes the act of entering into the sanctuary in order to participate in the completion of the initiation rites and to experience the mysteries.[44] In the excavations of the sanctuary of Apollo at Klaros a series of inscriptions was found that told how embassies came to the temple, underwent an initiation rite, and then received the oracle they had requested. In this description the word **ἐμβατεύειν** occurs often: "having been ini-

that "of angels" is an objective genitive. Against them Francis, "Humility," 126–30—as earlier Zahn, *Introduction* 1, p. 246f—champions an interpretation in terms of the subjective genitive: the initiate is enraptured and participates in the heavenly worship of angels. Francis is correct in asserting that worship of angels is unthinkable within Judaism (cf. Percy, *Probleme*, 149–55). It should be noted, however, that the syncretistic character of the "philosophy" would not necessarily exclude the possibility of a cult of angels. (Cf. Gerhard Kittel, *TDNT* 1, 86; Wilhelm Bousset and Hans Gressmann, *Die Religion des Judentums im späthellenistischen Zeitalter*, HNT 21 [Tübingen: ^{4}1966], 330f). Francis' interpretation fails because of v 23 where "self-chosen worship" (ἐθελοθρησκία) specifically characterizes the concept "worship" (θρησκεία) as performed by men.

37 The manuscripts C𝔎 (G) pl lat sy insert the negative μή after the relative pronoun; G inserts the negative οὐκ.

38 Lightfoot, *ad loc.* offers the conjecture: αἰώρᾳ κενεμβατεύων = "treading on a rope suspended in empty air," "indulging in vain speculations." Other conjectures are: ἃ ἑώρα κενεμβατεύων ("treading on the air" Blass–Debrunner, par. 154; later rejected); ἀέρα κενεμβατεύων ("walking, as it were, on the wind" Taylor, Westcott, Hort); τὰ μετέωρα κενεμβατεύων ("walking in mid-air" Hitzig). Cf. J. Rendel Harris, *Sidelights on New Testament Research: Seven Lectures Delivered in 1908, at Regents' Park College, London* (London: The Kingsgate Press, n.d.), 198f; J. H. Moulton and W. F. Howard, *A Grammar of New Testament Greek* vol. 2, *Accidence and Word-Formation* (Edinburgh: T. & T. Clark, 1919–29), 273f. All of these proposals are based on the Greek verb κενεμβατεύειν ("to walk on emptiness," "to tread the air," "to be full of empty boasts") and maintain that the followers of the false teaching were reproached for having made a false step.

39 This is found in manuscripts p^{46} ℌ D* 69 pc Marcion.

40 Cf. Herbert Preisker, *TDNT* 2, 535f; Bauer, *s.v.*

41 For the evidence cf. Preisker, *TDNT* 2, 535.

42 Cf. 2 Macc 2:30: "To enter into details and general discussion and elaborate researches is the business of the original historian" (τὸ μὲν ἐμβατεύειν καὶ περίπατον ποιεῖσθαι λόγων καὶ πολυπραγμονεῖν ἐν τοῖς κατὰ μέρος τῷ τῆς ἱστορίας ἀρχηγενέτῃ καθήκει); Philo, *De plantatione* 80: "those, who make more than ordinary progress in various kinds of knowledge, and go deeper [*v. l.*: research] into them than most of us" (οἱ προσωτέρω χωροῦντες τῶν ἐπιστημῶν καὶ ἐπὶ πλέον ἐμβαθύνοντες [*v. l.*: ἐμβατεύοντες] [Loeb modified].

43 Cf. Lohmeyer, *ad loc.*; Preisker, *TDNT* 2, 535f.

44 Martin Dibelius, "Die Isisweihe des Apulejus und verwandte Initiations-Riten," SAH 1917 = *Aufsätze* 2, pp. 30–79, esp. pp. 55–65, drew attention to the relevant evidence and made full use of it interpreting Col 2:18. Cf. also Dibelius–Greeven, *ad loc.*

tiated, they entered" or "having received the mysteries, he entered" (μυηθέντες ἐνεβάτευσαν or παραλ[αβ]ὼν τὰ μυστήρι[α] ἐνεβάτευσεν).[45] First the initiation takes place; only afterward is entrance into the inner sanctuary permitted[46] and the message from the god received: "having been initiated and having entered, they consulted the oracle" (μυηθέντες καὶ ἐνβατεύσαντες ἐχρήσαντο). The word ἐμβατεύειν, "to enter into the sanctuary," accordingly describes one portion of the entire rite which, as a whole, is called: "to complete the mysteries" (ἐπιτελεῖν μυστήρια). Since the verb ἐμβατεύειν is frequently used in the inscriptions, it obviously is a fixed term in the language of the mysteries.[47] In the circle of the "philosophy," so we must assume, cultic rites were performed,[48] and the expression ἃ ἑόρακεν ἐμβατεύων must have referred to such rites.[49] Since the catchword of the philosophy is quoted in a very curtailed form, it it not really clear to what the vision (ἑόρακεν) refers[50] and whether ecstasy played a role in these mystery–like performances.[51] Nevertheless, ἑόρακεν (he has had visions) probably indicates that the initiand, upon whom the initiation rites were performed, experienced the vision of cosmic correlations. With his senses, therefore, he experienced and performed the worship of the "elements of

45 These inscriptions have been rendered by the translator. The texts of the inscriptions, which probably stem from the second century A.D., can be found in Dibelius, *Aufsätze* 2, p. 59f, as well as in Dibelius–Greeven, *ad loc.* Cf. also Ditt. *Or.* 530, 15.

46 Cf. Apuleius, *Metamorph.* 9, 23: "I approached near unto hell, even to the gates of Proserpine, and after that I was ravished throughout all the elements" (accessi confinium mortis et calcato Proserpinae limine per omnia vectus elementa remeavi).

47 Again the inscriptions have been rendered by the translator. The interpretation first proposed by Dibelius has not gone unchallenged. It has been objected that ἐμβατεύειν has this meaning only in conjunction with other terms of the language of the mysteries, and could only refer to a procedure in a sanctuary, of which Col 2:18 says nothing (Lohmeyer, *ad loc.*; Preisker, *TDNT* 2, 535f). The objection, however, loses its force when it is recognized that ἃ ἑόρακεν ἐμβατεύων (as he has had visions of them during the mystery rites) is a quotation. For when a catchword–like phrase is quoted, it is not surprising that no other terms of the language of the mysteries appear in the context and that a sanctuary is not mentioned specifically. Furthermore, reference must be made to the word "worship" (vss 16, 23); and it should be recalled that the use of the concept "circumcision" in v 11 justifies the conclusion that initiation and admission rites were performed in the circle of the "philosophy." Percy, *Probleme*, 170–74 severely criticizes Dibelius. However, he is not in a position to offer a useful counterproposal to interpret the term, and retreats to Lightfoot's conjecture: "treading the air." Masson, *ad loc.*, remains indecisive: "None of the interpretations proposed is satisfactory."

48 Cf. S. Eitrem, "EMBATEYΩ. Note sur Col. 2, 18," *ST* 2 (1948): 93, "'Ἐμβατεύειν, 'the solemn entrance,' refers to the rite of consulting the oracle after initiation." Cf. further Casel, "Kultsprache," 40–44; Bauer, *s.v.* Stanislas Lyonnet, "L'Épître aux Colossiens (Col 2, 18) et les mystères d'Apollon Clarien," *Biblica* 43 (1962): 417–35 takes ἐμβατεύειν as an expression that was used in the mysteries, but assumes that Paul used the word polemically against the false teachers in the meaning of "to examine thoroughly."

49 Francis, "Humility," 119–26 has a different interpretation. He appeals to an observation of Wilhelm Bousset ("Die Himmelsreise der Seele," *Archiv für Religionswissenschaft* 4 (1901, p. 273 = Darmstadt: 1960, p. 83) who wants to interpret Col 2:18 against the background of the soul's journey to heaven: through fasting the soul prepares for ecstatic experiences and enters the heavenly spheres to participate in the angels' worship of God. Cf. also Arthur Darby Nock, "The Vocabulary of the New Testament," *JBL* 52 (1933): 132f on ἐμβατεύειν: "It may indicate some claim to special knowledge obtained on a visionary entry into heaven." True, Francis can refer to a whole battery of evidence from apocalyptic literature which deals with the seer's being raptured up to heaven (pp. 119–26). Yet ἐμβατεύειν occurs in none of the passages he lists. Moreover, in Col 2:18 there is no allusion that one ought to imagine a soul being raptured up to heaven.

50 Grammatically speaking, "as he has had visions of them" (ἃ ἑόρακεν) is connected with "readiness to serve" (ταπεινοφροσύνη) and "worship" (θρησκεία) — without prejudice to the different grammatical gender of the relative. Cf. 3:6: "on account of such deeds (i.e., the vices enumerated in v 5) the wrath of God is coming" (δι' ἃ ἔρχεται ἡ ὀργὴ τοῦ θεοῦ). Fridrichsen, "ΘΕΛΩΝ," 137 takes a different tack and links it with the next phrase: "vainly conceited . . . over what he beheld at his initiation." Cf. also Blass–Debrunner, par. 154.

51 In an earlier publication (*Aufsätze* 2, p. 62f) Dibelius defended the position that ἃ ἑόρακεν ("what he had seen") was the object of ἐμβατεύων ("entering into"): "entering into that which he had seen." He assumed that the sacred symbols were first shown

the universe."[52] Despite the terse, abrupt way in which the words "readiness to serve," "worship of angels," and "as he has had visions of them during the mystery rites" follow one another, it is, nevertheless, evident that not only was a distinct teaching propagated, but also that cultic rites were actually performed in order to worship the "angels" and "elements of the universe."[53]

Because of their teaching and cultic praxis the followers of the "philosophy" are boastful and think they are superior to the community. The author polemically characterizes this arrogance as "to be puffed up, be conceited" (φυσιοῦσθαι). "Knowledge puffs up" (ἡ γνῶσις φυσιοῖ 1 Cor 8:1), and its proponents "are puffed up" (πεφυσιωμένοι 1 Cor 5:2; cf. further 4:18f; 2 Cor 12:20), because one exalts himself above another (cf. 1 Cor 4:6). The cause of this conceit is "the mind of the flesh" (νοῦς τῆς σαρκός).[54] Thought and action are completely under the control of the "flesh." What is proudly termed "fulness" is in reality nothing but a conceited emptiness and an entirely unfounded feeling of exalted exuberance.[55]

■ **19** The alternatives "according to the elements of the universe" (κατὰ τὰ στοιχεῖα τοῦ κόσμου) or "according to Christ" (κατὰ Χριστόν 2:8) do not admit of a compromise. Whoever espoused the "philosophy" cannot at the same time adhere to Christ as the "head" (κεφαλή) over the powers and principalities.[56] And every Christian who is of the opinion that he should become a devotee of that teaching must clearly realize that at that very moment he severs his relationship with the head, who is the Lord alone.[57] Therefore, the author's stress comes down clearly on the fact that the Christians must adhere steadfastly to the "head."[58] For only from the head does the entire body receive strength and life.[59] From the head the body is supported and held together by sinews and ligaments. The image that is used here corresponds to ancient physiology: **ἁφαί** are the sinews, σύνδεσμοι the ligaments[60] which knit together[61] and

to the initiate or that he had a preparatory vision. Afterward he entered into what he had seen (cf. Apuleius, *Metamorph.* 11, 27). Dibelius, however, later correctly chose the interpretation proposed above. The present tense of the participle ἐμβατεύων ("entering") is another argument for this interpretation: "The formal parallelism with 2:16 also suggests that the relative clause be construed here, just as there, with the previously mentioned praxis of the false teachers: in our case with 'humility' and 'angel worship'." (Dibelius–Greeven, *ad loc.*)

52 Cf. Apuleius, *Metamorph.* 11, 23: "And after that I was ravished throughout all the elements, I returned to my proper place: about midnight I saw the sun brightly shine, I saw likewise the gods celestial and the gods infernal, before whom I presented myself and worshipped them" (Per omnia vectus elementa remeavi, nocte media vidi solem candido coruscantem lumine, deos inferos et deos superos accessi coram et adoravi de proxumo).

53 Cf. further Lucien Cerfaux, "L'influence des 'Mystères' sur les épîtres de S. Paul aux Colossiens et aux Éphésiens" in *Sacra Pagina* 2, Bibliotheca Ephemeridum Theologicorum Lovaniensum 13 (Paris and Gembloux: 1959), 373–79.

54 Cf. Rom 8:7: "the mind that is set on the flesh" (τὸ φρόνημα τῆς σαρκός).

55 Cf. Bornkamm, *Aufsätze* 1, 144 n. 14.

56 On the use of καὶ οὐ here instead of the regular καὶ μή with a participle, cf. Blass–Debrunner, par. 430, 3; Moulton, *Prolegomena*, 231.

57 On the verb κρατεῖν in the meaning of "to hold fast to something" cf. Mk 7:3: "holding fast to the tradition of the elders" (κρατοῦντες τὴν παράδοσιν τῶν πρεσβυτέρων); Rev 2:13: "you hold fast to my name" (κρατεῖς τὸ ὄνομά μου); 2:14f: "holding fast to the teaching of Balaam . . . holding fast to the teaching of the Nicolaitans" (κρατοῦντας τὴν διδαχὴν Βαλαάμ . . . κρατοῦντας τὴν διδαχὴν τῶν Νικολαϊτῶν). Further examples can be found in Wilhelm Michaelis, *TDNT* 3, 910–12; Bauer, *s.v.* The verb "to let go" (ἀφιέναι) is the antithesis: LXX Cant 3:4: "I held fast to him and would not let him go" (ἐκράτησα αὐτὸν καὶ οὐκ ἀφήσω αὐτόν).

58 On the concept "head" cf. the discussion of 1:18 and 2:20 and Heinrich Schlier, *TDNT* 3, 680f.

59 The prepositional phrase "from whom" (ἐξ οὗ) instead of "from it, *scil.* the head" (ἐξ ἧς) is a construction based on the sense and not on the grammar, since it is obviously Christ who is thought of as the head. The manuscripts D* sy^h introduce "Christ" after "the head."

60 Cf. Bauer, *s.v.* On "ligaments" (σύνδεσμοι) cf. also Gottfried Fitzer, *TWNT* 7, 854–57. The evidence from ancient medical writings is collected in Lightfoot, *ad loc.* Wide of the mark is Lightfoot's opinion, *ad loc.*, that Paul probably adopted the physiological image from Luke the physician (cf. Col 4:14). This opinion has again cropped up in the literature: Sebastianus Tromp, " 'Caput influit sensum et motum'. Col 2, 19 and Eph 4, 16 in luce traditionis," *Gregorianum* 39 (1958): 353–66.

61 On the verb "to knit together, unite" (συμβιβάζειν)

support[62] the members. The "body" is totally dependent on the "head." Under the head's guidance it is accomplishing "the growth[63] that is from God."[64]

The decisive point of comparison in this image is the relationship between "head" and "body."[65] Christ is the "head of the body" (1:18). Since he is the head of the powers and principalities (2:10), it is under him as their head that all things find the destination which was assigned to them through God's creation.[66] But the author of Col is not content with this statement. Rather he specifies that the "body" over which Christ is the "head" is the "church" (1:18, 24). To be sure, Christ is head over the universe. His body, however, which receives life and growth from the head, is the church.[67] This means that a person can only adhere to the head insofar as he belongs, as a member of Christ's body, to the "church" which is the domain of his present lordship.[68]

■ **20** Since the presupposition is certainly correct that everyone who has died with Christ has also died to the "elements of the universe," it is downright absurd to accept the imposition of regulations. For in baptism the Christian has been handed over to death with Christ (cf. on 2:12).[69] Consequently, he now belongs entirely to his head. Therefore, anything else that might put forward a claim to lordship has lost its authority over him. Indeed, the elements of the universe still exist, but they can and should no longer concern the Christian (cf. on 2:8). The Christian has died to them and is forever separated from them.[70] Col asks: how then can you conduct your lives "as if you still lived in the world" (*ὡς ζῶντες ἐν*

---

cf. above pp. 80f on 2:2. (In 2:2 the sense of the passage is better rendered by "to unite" rather than by "knit together" [Trans.])

62 On the verb "to support" (*ἐπιχορηγεῖν*) cf. Bauer, *s.v.* This word occurs often in marriage and divorce contracts in the meaning of "to provide for," "to support." For example, cf. *P.Oxyrh.* 2, 282, 6–8: "I for my part provided for my wife in a manner that exceeded my resources" (*[ἐ]γὼ μὲν οὖν ἐπεχορήγησα αὐτῇ τὰ ἑξῆς καὶ ὑπὲρ δύναμιν* [Greenfell–Hunt]); 6, 905, 10f: "And the husband shall supply the wife with necessaries in proportion to his means" (*[καὶ ὁ γαμῶν ἐπι]χορηγείτω τῇ γαμουμένῃ τὰ δέοντα κατὰ δύναμιν [τοῦ βίου]* [Greenfell–Hunt]); BGU 3, 717, 18: "I will supply her with all the necessities" (*[ἐπιχορηγή]σω αὐτῇ τὰ δέ[ο]ντα πάντα*) [Trans.]. Cf. further *P.Oxyrh.* 6, 905, 6; BGU 1, 183, 6f; *P.Rainer* 1, 27, 12.

63 The phrase "the growth that is from God" (*τὴν αὔξησιν τοῦ θεοῦ*) is an accusative of content. Cf. e.g., Eph 2:4: "On account of the great love with which he loved us" (*διὰ τὴν πολλὴν ἀγάπην αὐτοῦ ἣν ἠγάπησεν ἡμᾶς*) and consult Blass–Debrunner, par. 153, 1. The Greek verb *αὔξειν/αὐξάνειν* means "to cause to grow," but in Hellenistic Greek it was also used in the intransitive meaning of "to grow, increase." Cf. Jn 3:30: "he must increase" (*ἐκεῖνον δεῖ αὐξάνειν*); Acts 6:7: "the word of God increased" (*ὁ λόγος τοῦ θεοῦ ηὔξανεν*); Eph 4:15: "let us grow into him in every way" (*αὐξήσωμεν εἰς αὐτὸν τὰ πάντα*). Cf. Blass–Debrunner, par. 309, 2 and Bauer, *s.v.*

64 Cf. *P.Leid.* 2, 27: "You are the Lord who brings forth, conserves, and increases everything" (*Σὺ εἶ κύριος, ὁ γεννῶν καὶ τρέφων καὶ αὔξων τὰ πάντα*) [Trans.]); 2, 141: "You are the ocean, the one who brings forth good things and conserves the universe" (*Σὺ ῖ (= εἶ) ὁ ὠκεανώς (= ὠκεανός), ὁ γεννôν (= γεννῶν) ἀγαθὰ καὶ τρωφôν (= τροφῶν* or *τρέφων) τὴν οἰκουμένην*) [Trans.]. Cf. also *Mithrasliturgie* (ed. Albrecht Dieterich, 3d ed. 1923) 14, 31f: "Lord, since I have come into existence again, I will again begin to grow up and when I have grown up, I will die" (*κύριε, πάλιν γενόμενος ἀπογίγνομαι αὐξόμενος καὶ αὐξηθεὶς τελευτῶ*) [Trans.]; *Act. Phil.* 144: "You are the one who purifies, multiplies and increases and gives life to all your very own servants" (*σὺ εἶ ὁ καθαρίζων καὶ πληθύνων καὶ αὐξάνων καὶ ζωοποιῶν πάντας τοὺς ἰδίους δούλους σου*) [Trans.]. Cf. further Schlier, *Epheser*, 206, n. 1.

65 Theodoret, *ad loc.* allegorizes: "As to the joints in the body, that refers to the apostles and prophets and teachers in the constitution of the church" (*Ὅπερ δέ εἰσιν ἐν τῷ σώματι σύνδεσμοι, τοῦτο ἀπόστολοι καὶ προφῆται καὶ διδάσκαλοι ἐν τῷ τῆς ἐκκλησίας συστήματι*) [Trans.].

66 Concerning the idea that the universe grows, cf. Philo, *Quaest. in Ex.* 2, 117: "The head of all things is the eternal Logos of the eternal God, under which, as if it were his feet or other limbs, is placed the whole world" (Verbum est sempiternum sempiterni dei caput universorum; sub quo pedum instar aut reliquorum quoque membrorum subiectum iacet universus mundus). Cf. also above pp. 53f on 1:18.

67 Cf. Eduard Schweizer, *TWNT* 7, 1074: "Christ is also head over the world; but only the church is his body into which flows all the power of growth that comes from him."

68 Cf. Lohse, "Christusherrschaft und Kirche," 206f. The relationship between "body—head" is elaborated further in Eph 4:16: "The head, Christ, from whom the whole body, joined and knit together by every joint with which it is supplied, when each part is working properly, makes bodily growth and up-

κόσμῳ)? This phrase refers to a situation in which the world completely determines a person's life so that one remains in the old way of life to which one has died. For otherwise, one could not possibly submit to regulations as they are demanded by the "elements of the universe" which are no longer the Christian's concern.[71] Clearly the "philosophy," which had been introduced into the community, had so strongly influenced many Christians that they were ready to acknowledge the binding power of the "regulations." If that should come true—the author addresses the waverers, those who hesitate, and those who have already fallen victim to the false teaching—nothing would be accomplished but a reversion into the slavery once experienced in their pagan past (cf. Gal 4:3, 8f).

■ **21** The "regulations" include strong prohibitions that admit of no exception. Three examples of such directives are cited. In the form in which they are cited here, the imperatives have no object which might more exactly indicate what each prohibits; thus they appear to be an intense caricature of the legalistic commands.[72] Nevertheless, the apodictic form seems to agree with the character of those commands. It is hardly possible to distinguish the difference in meaning between the two verbs *ἅπτεσθαι* and *θιγγάνειν*.[73] While *θιγγάνειν* means "to touch,"[74] *ἅπτεσθαι* can be somewhat stronger: "to take hold of something with a view to possessing it."[75] Of course, the proponents of the "philosophy" did not think that a person should absolutely not touch anything.[76] Rather, we must assume that their "regulations" included distinct taboos which referred to contact with objects that had been declared unclean or with forbidden foods.[77] To taste such food and drink is

builds itself in love" (*ἡ κεφαλή, Χριστός, ἐξ οὗ πᾶν τὸ σῶμα συναρμολογούμενον καὶ συμβιβαζόμενον διὰ πάσης ἁφῆς καὶ ἐπιχορηγίας κατ' ἐνέργειαν ἐν μέτρῳ ἑνὸς ἑκάστου μέρους τὴν αὔξησιν τοῦ σώματος ποιεῖται εἰς οἰκοδομὴν ἑαυτοῦ ἐν ἀγάπῃ*).

69 On the phrase "with Christ" (*σὺν Χριστῷ*) cf. above pp. 104f on 2:12. Here, too, the accent is on the believers' union "with Christ" which is already present.

70 Paul usually construes "to die" (*ἀποθνήσκειν*) with the dative. Cf. Gal 2:19: "For I through the law died to the law" (*ἐγὼ γὰρ διὰ νόμου νόμῳ ἀπέθανον*); Rom 6:2: "We died to sin" (*ἀπεθάνομεν τῇ ἁμαρτίᾳ*). The same verb with the preposition "from" (*ἀπό*) emphasizes the definitive separation caused by death. Cf. Rom 7:6: "But now we are separated from the law, dead to that which held us captive" (*νυνὶ δὲ κατηργήθημεν ἀπὸ τοῦ νόμου ἀποθανόντες ἐν ᾧ κατειχόμεθα*).

71 The verb *δογματίζειν* means "to represent and affirm an opinion or tenet," "to establish or publish a decree," "to proclaim an edict" (LXX Dan 2:13; Esth 3:9; 2 Macc 10:8). Cf. Bauer, *s.v.*; Gerhard Kittel, *TDNT* 2, 230–32. The passive has the meaning "to submit to regulations." Cf. Blass–Debrunner par. 314 and consult 1 Cor 6:7: *ἀδικεῖσθαι* = "to let yourselves be wronged"; further: *βαπτίζεσθαι* = "to submit to baptism."

72 Cf. Chrysostom, *ad loc.*: "Mark how he makes sport of them, *handle not*, *touch not*, *taste not*, as though they were keeping themselves clear of some great matters" (*ὅρα πῶς αὐτοὺς κωμῳδεῖ, Μὴ θίγῃς, μὴ ἅψῃ, μὴ γεύσῃ, ὡς μεγάλων τινῶν ἀπεχόμενος*) [trans. from NPNF 13, 289].

73 Cf. LXX Ex 19:12: "Take heed to yourselves that you do not go up to the mountain, nor touch any part of it. Everyone who touches the mountain shall surely die" (*Προσέχετε ἑαυτοῖς τοῦ ἀναβῆναι εἰς τὸ ὄρος καὶ θιγεῖν τι αὐτοῦ. πᾶς ὁ ἁψάμενος τοῦ ὄρους θανάτῳ τελευτήσει*).

74 Cf. also Heb 11:28; 12:20.

75 Cf. 1 Cor 7:1: "not to touch a woman" (*γυναικὸς μὴ ἅπτεσθαι*). Col 2:21, however, does not indicate that sexual questions played a role in the "philosophy," as Robert Leaney, "Colossians II. 21–23. (The use of *πρός*)" *ExpT* 64 (1952–53): 92 proposes. On the prohibition of marriage by Gnostic teachers cf. 1 Tim 4:3: "who forbid marriage and enjoin abstinence from foods" (*κωλυόντων γαμεῖν, ἀπέχεσθαι βρωμάτων*).

76 Bauer, *s.v.*, considers the possibility of translating *ἅπτεσθαι* with "to handle," "to eat something;" in this case the three prohibitions could form an anticlimax: do not eat, do not taste, do not touch! However, no object is mentioned; thus it remains quite problematic to restrict the general verb *ἅπτεσθαι* to the meaning "to eat."

77 Lucian of Samosata in *De Syr. dea* 54 tells a story about people for whom doves as opposed to other kinds of birds were taboo; "and if they unwittingly touch them, they are unclean that day" (*καὶ ἢν ἀέκοντες ἅψωνται, ἐναγέες ἐκείνην τὴν ἡμέρην εἰσίν*) [Trans.]. An inadvertent touch also caused defilement. Cf. Betz, *Lukian*, 32. Similar reg-

strictly prohibited.[78] Such ascetic taboo regulations describe in minute detail what is to be eaten and what not.[79] The fence that is erected by "Do not" restricts the ascetic's area of action.[80] Therefore, he must scrupulously observe the "Do not trespass" signs set up for him: Do not handle—also do not taste—do not even touch!

■ **22** The things, however—this is the message of the short critical note that follows—whose touching or tasting is forbidden by the taboos are things destined to be used by man. God has decreed that all of them without exception ("all"—*πάντα*!) be consumed through man's use.[81] Consequently, it is only right that man use[82] and consume them,[83] instead of failing to recognize God's good gifts because of a false legalism.

Those teachers want to burden men with something that in reality is nothing but man-made commandments and teachings. The correspondence of this polemical phrase with LXX Is 29:13 should not be overlooked: "In vain do they worship me teaching the commandments and doctrines of men" (*μάτην δὲ σέβονταί με διδάσκοντες ἐντάλματα ἀνθρώπων καὶ διδασκαλίας*). This Scripture passage is also cited in Mk 7:7 (par. Mt 15:9) in the argument against the legalism of the Pharisees and was obviously quoted often in disputes with proponents of a legalistic type of piety. The author of Col takes this argument from the tradition[84] without introducing it as a quotation from Scripture and brings it to bear against the legalistic praxis as taught and enjoined by that "philosophy." Although the opponents claim that they are passing on traditions hallowed by antiquity, what they really offer are regulations and doctrines fabricated by men (2:8: "according to the tradition of men" [*κατὰ τὴν παράδοσιν τῶν ἀνθρώπων*]).

■ **23** How must one evaluate the regulations and teaching of the "philosophy"? The word "which" (*ἅτινα*)[85] refers to the "regulations" which the author wants to characterize once more in conclusion. Catchwords from the false teaching and a polemic directed against them are entwined most closely. Many exegetes believe that the verse is so confused that it is no longer possible to discern its structure.[86] Other exegetes tried to account for the difficulties that the verse presents by assuming that the text must have been corrupted very early,[87] and that through conjectures and additions a comprehensible wording of the probable original text must be reconstructed.[88] Nevertheless, none of these attempts can base

---

ulations, which forbid contact under penalty of defilement, are also not foreign to Judaism. Cf. e.g., *Tamid* 1, 4: "They said to the priest who was to clear the ashes from the altar in the morning: 'Take heed that you touch not the vessel before you have sanctified your hands and feet in the laver' " [Danby]. Further examples can be found in Billerbeck 3, p. 629. Also cf. 2 Cor 6:17: "And do not touch anything unclean" (*καὶ ἀκαθάρτου μὴ ἅπτεσθε*).

78 On the verb "to taste" (*γεύεσθαι*) cf. Johannes Behm, *TDNT* 1, 675–77.

79 Cf. Jewish food laws and especially the regulations of the Nazirites who were to abstain from wine and strong drink (Num 6:3). As *Makkoth* 3, 7f says: "If a Nazirite drank wine throughout the day he is liable (for scourging) only on one count. If they said to him (as often as he proposes to drink), 'Do not drink! Do not drink!' and he drank (nevertheless), he is liable on each count. If he contracted uncleanness because of the dead throughout the day, he is liable (for scourging) only on one count. If they say to him, 'Do not contract uncleanness! Do not contract uncleanness!', and he (nevertheless) contracted uncleanness, he is liable on each count" [Danby]. Cf. Billerbeck 3, p. 629.

80 The concept "severe treatment of the body" (*ἀφειδία σώματος* v 23) also refers to ascetic practices. Cf. Hans von Campenhausen, "Early Christian Asceticism" in *Tradition and Life in the Church: Essays and Lectures in Church History*, tr. A. V. Littledale (Philadelphia: Fortress Press, 1968), 104.

81 The phrase *εἶναι εἰς* means "to be destined for." Cf. Acts 8:20: "May your silver be destined to perish with you" (*τὸ ἀργύριόν σου σὺν σοὶ εἴη εἰς ἀπώλειαν*); 2 Pt 2:12: "like irrational animals, creatures of instinct, destined to be caught and killed" (*ὡς ἄλογα ζῷα γεγεννημένα φυσικὰ εἰς ἅλωσιν καὶ φθοράν*). Also cf. Blass–Debrunner par. 145, 1.

82 The word "perish through use" (*ἀπόχρησις*) does not imply abuse, but normal use. Cf. Plutarch, *Quaestiones Romanae* 18 (p. 267e): "and pleased by such a way of using up" (*χαίρειν ταῖς τοιαύταις ἀποχρήσεσι*); Dionysius of Halicarnassus, *Ant. Rom.* 1, 58, 5; *P.Strassb.* 1, 35, 6. Cf. Bauer, *s.v.*

83 Cf. Theodoret, *ad loc.*: "For everything is changed to excrement" (*Εἰς κόπρον γὰρ ἅπαντα μεταβάλλεται*) [Trans.].

84 Cf. also Tit 1:14: "not giving heed to Jewish myths or to commands of men" (*μὴ προσέχοντες Ἰουδαϊκοῖς μύθοις καὶ ἐντολαῖς ἀνθρώπων*).

85 Cf. Gal 4:24; 5:19; Phil 3:7.

86 Cf. Conzelmann, *ad loc.*, who describes the entire section vss 16–23 this way: "This section cannot be translated. A person can only just sample the mean-

its case on a witness from the manuscript tradition. Rather the manuscript tradition has almost unanimously retained the obscurity of the sequence of words.[89] One must not try to lessen the burdens of exegesis by patching up a text so that it has fewer difficulties. How then does one determine the structure of this seemingly mysterious sentence?

Dibelius–Greeven hold that Paul originally wanted to write: *ἅ ἐστιν πάντα εἰς φθορὰν τῇ ἀποχρήσει, οὐκ ἐν τιμῇ τινι πρὸς πλησμονὴν τῆς σαρκός* (all of which are destined to perish through use, and not to be given honor for the satisfaction of earthly pleasures).[90] Then, it is assumed, Paul split the sentence by inserting a rather lengthy parenthesis in v 22b, 23a, which added a criticism to the question: *τί δογματίζεσθε* (Why do you submit to regulations?). This, however, results in a very ill constructed train of thought; the parenthesis would be separated from v 20f and the sentence Paul intended to write (22a, 23b) would be split far apart. Bo Reicke tries to divide the sentence differently. He construes "which are" (*ἅτινά ἐστιν*) together with the conclusion "for indulgence of the flesh" (*πρὸς πλησμονὴν τῆς σαρκός*) and places in a parenthesis everything that occurs in between: *ἅτινά ἐστιν—λόγον μὲν ἔχοντα σοφίας ἐν ἐθελοθρησκίᾳ καὶ ταπεινοφροσύνῃ καὶ ἀφειδίᾳ σώματος, οὐκ ἐν τιμῇ τινι—πρὸς πλησμονὴν τῆς σαρκός* (These [human commandments and teachings]—which have only a reputation of wisdom, consisting in quasi–piety and asceticism and bodily chastening, [but] not in any sort of [Christian] consideration for others—lead to satiating the flesh]).[91] In this way, however, the words "which are—they indeed have the reputation etc." (*ἅτινά ἐστιν—λόγον μὲν ἔχοντα κτλ.*) are separated from one another and no convincing grounds are given why the author added something in parenthesis. C. F. D. Moule understands *οὐκ ἐν τιμῇ τινι πρὸς πλησμονὴν τῆς σαρκός* in the sense of "but are of no value in combating sensual indulgence." Still he admits: "This verse is by common consent regarded as hopelessly obscure—either owing to corruption or because we have lost the clue."[92] After Ernst Lohmeyer had observed that catchwords of the opponents were listed in this verse and that Paul's ironic response was contrasted to them in formulaic expressions,[93] Günther Bornkamm pointed out that enumerations of five concepts occur often in Col. The members of the old man are "fornication" (*πορνεία*), "impurity" (*ἀκαθαρσία*), "passion" (*πάθος*), "evil desire" (*ἐπιθυμία κακή*), "covetousness" (*πλεονεξία*) [3:5] and "anger" (*ὀργή*), "wrath" (*θυμός*), "malice" (*κακία*), "slander" (*βλασφημία*), "abusive language" (*αἰσχρολογία*) [3:8]. The members of the new man are "merciful compassion" (*σπλάγχνα οἰκτιρμοῦ*), "kindness" (*χρηστότης*), "humility" (*ταπεινοφροσύνη*), "meekness" (*πραΰτης*),

---

ing of the passage and then try to reproduce it to some extent with reference to the Greek text."

87 Cf. Haupt, *ad loc.*: "The verse is an impenetrable fortress which defies any attempt to conquer its meaning, so that one can only conclude that a very ancient corruption of the text stands behind the verse."

88 Cf. the conjectures mentioned in the apparatus of the Nestle Greek text: Eberhard Nestle would change the dative "in severe treatment" (*ἀφειδίᾳ*) into the nominative and thus read: "and severe treatment of the body is of no value in checking the indulgence of the flesh" (*ἀφειδία σώματος οὐκ ἐν τιμῇ τινι πρὸς πλησμονὴν τῆς σαρκός*). Ernst von Dobschütz (cf. Nestle's apparatus) would also like to begin a new sentence with "severe treatment": "severe treatment of the body is of no value for someone who wants to check indulgence of the flesh" (*ἀφειδία σώματος οὐκ ἐντίμῃ τινὶ πρὸς πλησμονὴν τῆς σαρκός*). B. G. Hall, "Colossians II.23," *ExpT* 36 (1924–25): 285 thinks that "forgetting" (*ἐπιλησμοσύνην*) was original; asceticism "is of no value to the forgetting of the flesh." P. L. Hedley, "Ad Colossenses 2:20–3:4," *ZNW* 27 (1928): 211–16 would add a line that probably dropped out of the text: "[Therefore, use them, but] not as having value. . . ." ([*Χρῆσθε οὖν αὐτοῖς, ἀλλ'*] *οὐκ ἐν τιμῇ* . . .). Nevertheless, if a smooth sentence such as the ones produced by the conjectures were really the original text, it is still unexplained how the entire manuscript tradition arrived at the present wording.

89 After "readiness to serve" (*ταπεινοφροσύνῃ*) G it sy^h introduce "of mind" (*τοῦ νοός*). The manuscripts p^{46} B 1739 m Ambst omit the "and" (*καί*) before "severe treatment" (*ἀφειδίᾳ*).

90 Consult Dibelius–Greeven, *ad loc.*

91 Cf. Bo Reicke, "Zum sprachlichen Verständnis von Kol 2, 23," *ST* 6 (1952): 39–53.

92 Cf. Moule, *ad loc.*

93 Cf. Lohmeyer, *ad loc.*

"patience" (*μακροθυμία*) [3:12]. Consequently, it is possible that a list of five concepts also underlies verse 23: "self–chosen worship, readiness to serve, severe treatment of the body, honor, indulgence of the flesh" (*ἐθελοθρησκία, ταπεινοφροσύνη, ἀφειδία σώματος, τιμή, πλησμονὴ τῆς σαρκός*) which originally had their place in the teaching of the "philosophy."[94] The words "to the satiation of the flesh" (*πρὸς πλησμονὴν τῆς σαρκός*) doubtless contain a polemical thrust which was perhaps directed at the "philosophy's" important concept of "being filled." Only the first three members of the list are clearly recognizable as slogans of the false teachers. No doubt "honor, value" (*τιμή*) was also a slogan, but the author's negation of it has changed it into its opposite. Thus, the sentence moves from quoting the opponents' concepts to polemically turning them upside down. At the end of the sentence the argument against the false teaching turns into a full–scale attack with sharp criticisms. A sober view of reality is contrasted with the opponents' pompous contentions.[95]

What is presented as "philosophy" has the reputation[96] that it is based on "wisdom" (*σοφία*) [cf. 1:9, 28; 2:3; 3:16].[97] But this wisdom is only a façade.[98] In reality it is empty and barren.[99] Its proponents try to convince people that the teaching conveys wisdom and knowledge, and they demand a distinct way of life as a consequence of this teaching. The first concept *ἐθελοθρησκία* (self–chosen worship)[100] refers back to *θρησκεία τῶν ἀγγέλων* (worship of angels) as it was performed in the circle of the "philosophy." The prefix *ἐθελο–* could express the fact that this worship was self–made and produced by one's own whims.[101] In this case, we would have polemical recasting of one of the words which the "philosophers" understood differently.[102] It is more probable, however, that just like the next two words *ταπεινοφροσύνη* (readiness to serve) and *ἀφειδία σώματος* (severe treatment of the body), *ἐθελοθρησκία* also describes an expression used by the opponents.[103] They proudly boasted that they had freely chosen the cult in which they participated.[104] They performed this freely–chosen worship in "readiness to serve" (*ταπεινοφροσύνη* cf. on 2:18). The proponents of the "philosophy" describe the way of life they preach with the seldomly used word *ἀφειδία*. This term describes a severe and austere way of life,[105] and in conjunction with "body" (*σῶμα*) refers to the ascetic severity demanded by the

94 Cf. Bornkamm, *Aufsätze* 1, p. 151f. Concerning the history–of–religions problem of the list of five items, cf. p. 137 below on 3:5.

95 Cf. Lohmeyer, *ad loc.*: The opponents' positions are rejected "by irony and sarcasm which repudiate more tellingly as they seem to agree more exactly with their propagated formulations."

96 On *λόγον ἔχειν* = "to have the reputation of," "to be considered as" cf. e.g., Demosthenes, *Orat.* 31, 11: *καὶ γὰρ οὐδὲ λόγον τὸ πρᾶγμ' ἔχον ἐστίν* (The assumption is not even worth being considered) [Trans.]; Ps-Plato, *Epinomis* 987b: *ὁ μὲν γὰρ ἑωσφόρος ἕσπερός τε ὢν αὑτὸς Ἀφροδίτης εἶναι σχεδὸν ἔχει λόγον* (Thus, that Lucifer, or Hesperus [which is the same], should almost belong to Aphrodite, deserves consideration) [Trans.].

97 Lucian, *Peregrinus* 11ff depicts the teaching of the Christians as "wondrous lore" (*θαυμαστὴ σοφία*). Cf. Betz, *Lukian*, 7f.

98 In this verse no "on the other hand" (*δέ*) follows "on the one hand" (*μέν*). Cf. Blass–Debrunner par. 447, 2. An exact correlative is found, however, in "have nothing to do with honor" (*οὐκ ἐν τιμῇ τινι*).

99 Cf. Theodoret, *ad loc.*: "He pointed out that they dealt with external form, not truth" (*ἔδειξε σχῆμα περικειμένους, οὐκ ἀλήθειαν*) [Trans.].

100 Cf. Karl Ludwig Schmidt, *TDNT* 3, 159; Bauer, *s.v.*

101 The word *ἐθελοθρησκία* (self–chosen worship), which does not occur in Greek before Paul, can be compared to constructions like *ἐθελοδιδάσκαλος* (self–appointed teacher), *ἐθελόδουλος* (one who wills to be a slave), and *ἐθελοκακεῖν* (to let oneself be beaten). Cf. Blass–Debrunner, par. 118, 2.

102 Cf. Lohmeyer, *ad loc.*: "constructed according to a Colossian slogan like "angel worship" (*ἀγγελοθρησκεία*), in order to deprecate this service as man's work and not as a command of God" = "arbitrary service." Bauer, *s.v.*, translates: "self–made religion." Reicke, "Verständnis," 46 writes: "A critical, deprecatory expression is indeed expected after the previous word 'reputation' (*λόγον*)."

103 Cf. Dibelius–Greeven, *ad loc.*; Bornkamm, *Aufsätze* 1, p. 144 n. 15.

104 Cf. Apuleius, *Metamorph.* 11, 21: "like to a voluntary death" (ad instar voluntariae mortis); *Corp. Herm.* 13, 7: "Will it, and it comes to be" (*θέλησον καὶ γίνεται*) [Trans.].

105 Cf. Ps-Plato, *Definitiones* 412d: "severity in the use of and in the acquisition of possessions" (*ἀφειδία ἐν χρήσει καὶ ἐν κτήσει οὐσίας*) [Trans.]; Lucian, *Anacharsis* 24: "unmindful of their bodies" (*τῶν σωμάτων ἀφειδεῖν*); cf. further Plutarch, *Amatorius* 18 (p. 762e); Bauer, *s.v.*

106 Cf. 1 Tim 4:3: "who forbid marriage and enjoin

"regulations."[106] Through fasting and abstinence one endeavors to dispose himself for the reception of divine fulness. Nevertheless, all this taken together effects nothing more than a mere appearance of "wisdom" (σοφία).

Moreover, the "honor" (τιμή), which they claim for themselves, cannot be conferred on them. In the mystery religions τιμή signifies the divine election and deification which the initiate experiences.[107] But precisely that claim is contested: What they are promoting can never merit the title "honor." On the contrary, it has nothing whatsoever to do with honor.[108] Even though a legalistic way of life demands asceticism (and perhaps precisely because it does), it leads finally only "to the satiation of the flesh" (πρὸς πλησμονὴν τῆς σαρκός).[109] Behind this critical observation there is obviously hidden the philosophers' slogan "fulness," which indicates the aim and goal of every effort to worship the "elements of the universe." The actual result, however, of all these efforts[110]—so the author says polemically—is nothing but the satiation[111] of the flesh. Therefore, once more the antithesis is sharply put.[112] While this "philosophy" claims that through "worship of angels," "readiness to serve" and asceticism man will attain the goal of being filled with divine power, in reality the man who pursues this plan of legal piety and way of life turns in upon himself, becomes a prisoner of the "flesh," "puffed up without reason by his earthly mind" (εἰκῇ φυσιούμενος ὑπὸ τοῦ νοὸς τῆς σαρκὸς αὐτοῦ 2:18).

The Teaching of the "Philosophy"[113]

From the short quotations and catchwords which the author of Col cites in the context of his instruction to the community, the main features of the teaching which threatened to engulf the community can be reconstructed with some certainty. The "philosophy," which claimed to be based on venerable tradition (2:8), was supposed to impart true

abstinence from foods" (κωλυόντων γαμεῖν, ἀπέχεσθαι βρωμάτων).

107 Cf. e.g., Apuleius, *Metamorph.* 11, 21: "the clear and evident dignity of the great goddess" (perspicua evidentique magni numinis dignatione) [Trans.]; 22: "Thou are most happy and blessed, whom the divine goddess doth so greatly accept with mercy" (te felicem, te beatum, quem propitia voluntate numen augustum tantopere dignatur) [Loeb]. Cf. R. Reitzenstein, *Die hellenistischen Mysterienreligionen* (Leipzig and Berlin: ³1927), 252–54; Bornkamm, *Aufsätze* 1, p. 151f; Johannes Schneider, *TWNT* 8, 178. Reicke, "Verständnis," 47–51, on the contrary, wants to understand τιμή as "honor to be rendered," i.e., "respect" (cf. 1 Thess 4:4; 1 Cor 12:23f; Rom 12:10; 13:7). This interpretation, however, does not give proper emphasis to the polemic which forges its weapons from the concepts used by the opponents.

108 Cf. Lohmeyer, *ad loc.*: "The little word 'a certain' also reduces all worth and honor the philosophy claimed to triviality and the ridiculous; it is only 'some kind of,' no special honor."

109 This combination of words surely represents a polemical expression coined by the letter's author. While the quoted catchwords are introduced without the definite article, e.g., ἀφειδία σώματος (severe treatment of the body), the article is used here to bind together the two nouns: "to the satiation of the flesh."

110 Concerning the phrase "to be unto," "to serve to" (εἶναι πρός) cf. Jn 11:4: "This illness is not unto death" (αὕτη ἡ ἀσθένεια οὐκ ἔστιν πρὸς θάνατον).

111 On the word "satiation, satiety" (πλησμονή) cf. Antiphanes in Athenaeus, *Deipnosophistae* 1, 28f: "For Love dwells where satiety is, but among those who are hard up Aphrodite will not stay" (ἐν πλησμονῇ γὰρ Κύπρις, ἐν δὲ τοῖς κακῶς πράσσουσιν οὐκ ἔνεστιν Ἀφροδίτη βροτοῖς [Loeb modified]). Further examples may be found in Bauer, *s.v.*, who says: "satiety," Col 2:23: "for the satiation of the fleshly mind."

112 The question, how to interpret "to the satiation of the flesh" already vexed the early church's exegetes. Cf. Theodore of Mopsuestia, *ad loc.*: "It is indeed obscure" (ἀσαφὲς μέν ἐστιν) [Trans.]. On the early church's interpretation cf. Gerhard Delling, *TDNT* 6, 133: generally speaking, the opinion was that "flesh = body" (σάρξ = σῶμα), and "indulgence" were taken as the quieting of man's natural (not sinful) appetites. The sense of the passage then would be: the followers of the "philosophy" did not grant the body the honor that was its due according to God's will. This interpretation, however, fails to come to grips with the fact that "flesh" is not synonymous with "body," but is used in a negative sense.

113 Cf. the excursus or introductions of the commentaries, especially Lightfoot, 71–111; Dibelius–Greeven, 38–40. Cf. further Martin Dibelius, "Die Isisweihe bei Apulejus und verwandte Initiations–Riten," SAH 1917 = *Aufsätze* 2, pp. 30–79; Percy, *Probleme*, 137–78; Günther Bornkamm, "Die Häresie des Kolosserbriefes," *ThLZ* 73 (1948): 11–20 = *Aufsätze*

knowledge and insight.[114] Such knowledge is concerned with the "elements of the universe" (2:8, 20) which are conceived as angelic powers (2:18) and cosmic principalities (2:10, 15). One has to establish the right relationship to them through obedient worship; only thus is it possible to gain entry to the "pleroma" (2:9) and participate in the divine fulness (2:10). The relationship between the "elements of the universe" and the "fulness" is not entirely clear; the powers could be understood as representatives of the divine fulness or as dangerous principalities who block the way to the "fulness" and allow free passage only after they have received due reverence.[115] In any case, man can be suffused with the divine "fulness" only after he proves himself subservient to the angels and powers in the "worship of angels." He voluntarily declares himself prepared (self–chosen worship 2:23) to "be ready to serve" (2:23) as he pays homage to the angels in cultic worship (2:18) and as he promises to obey what they enjoin upon him. Through his asceticism he withdraws from the world (putting off the body of flesh 2:11; severe treatment of the body 2:23), observes the special sacred days and seasons (2:16), and adheres to the regulations which prohibit him from either tasting or touching certain foods and beverages (2:16, 21). Thus he orders his whole life according to the laws, which as the ordering principles of the macrocosm also prescribe the regulations that obtain in the microcosm of human life; he submits himself to them in humble readiness to serve.

This teaching, in which knowledge and legal observance are closely joined, is clearly syncretistic. Since the cosmic powers control the fate of men, they are worshipped. Above the All is enthroned the one deity who, as the "fulness," contains the fulness in himself. Insofar as the "philosophy" demands in strict legal terms the observance of special days and the keeping of food prohibitions, an important contribution to this philosophy has also been made by the Jewish tradition.[116] The "regulations," however, were not thought of as a sign of allegiance to the God of Israel, who had chosen his people from among all other nations as the community of his covenant. Rather they are thought of as expressing

---

1, pp. 139–56; Werner Bieder, *Die kolossische Irrlehre und die Kirche von heute*, Theologische Studien 33 (Zürich: 1952); Stanislas Lyonnet, "L'étude du milieu littéraire et l'exégèse du Nouveau Testament. §4. Les adversaires de Paul à Colosses," *Biblica* 37 (1956): 27–38; *idem*, "St. Paul et le gnosticisme: la lettre aux Colossiens" in: *Le Origini dello Gnosticismo*, ed. Ugo Bianchi (Leiden: 1967), 538–61; Hegermann, *Schöpfungsmittler*, 158–99; Josef Gewiess, "Die apologetische Methode des Apostels Paulus im Kampf gegen die Irrlehre in Kolossä," *Bibel und Leben* 3 (1962): 258–70; Hans–Martin Schenke, "Der Widerstreit gnostischer und kirchlicher Christologie im Spiegel des Kolosserbriefes," *ZThK* 61 (1964): 391–403; Werner Foerster, "Die Irrlehrer des Kolosserbriefes," in *Studia Biblica et Semitica, Festschrift für Th. Vriezen* (Wageningen: 1966), 71–80.

114 Cf. the terms *σοφία* (wisdom 1:9, 28; 2:3, 23; 3:16; 4:5), *σύνεσις* (insight 1:9; 2:2), *γνῶσις* (knowledge 2:3), *ἐπίγνωσις/ἐπιγνώσκειν* (knowledge/to know 1:6, 9, 10; 2:2; 3:10).

115 Cf. Ernst Käsemann, *RGG*³ 3, col. 1728: "Any conclusion drawn about the viewpoints of the heretics must remain fragmentary. Were the powers worshipped because they were considered dangerous or because they represented the heavenly fulness?" Schenke, "Widerstreit," 392–99 tries to demonstrate that the worship of the angels was a cult of hostile powers, since he wants to find a basis for his view that the "philosophy" was Gnostic in character. Nevertheless, the possibility that the "elements of the universe" were considered representatives of the "fulness" cannot be excluded. Thus, Bornkamm (*Aufsätze* 1, 140, cf. p. 146) thinks that the "elements" were taken to be divine principalities: "Apparently the heretical teaching held that in the 'elements of the universe' the 'fulness' of the deity dwells. This is clear from the manifestly polemical and antithetically formulated clause in Col 2:9: 'because in him dwells the entire fulness of deity bodily' (*ὅτι ἐν αὐτῷ κατοικεῖ πᾶν τὸ πλήρωμα τῆς θεότητος σωματικῶς* cf. 1:19)." In no way is it possible to follow Schenke ("Widerstreit," 397f) in his identification of the "elements of the universe" with the archons of Gnosticism.

116 Since in Asia Minor and especially in the cities of the Lycus Valley there was a strong Jewish settlement (cf. above p. 9), we must assume that the Jewish element in the syncretistic "philosophy" came from this source. The Magical Papyri, for their part, give evidence of the extent to which the syncretism of late antiquity adopted Jewish names and terms. Also in the Christian Gnosticism of the second century, heterodox Jewish concepts became effective on a large scale. Qumran texts that have recently come to light show that syncretistic influences did not stop at the boundaries of Judaism (cf. above p. 102, n. 58 on 2:11). The fragment 4 QCry indicates that in the Qumran community the view existed that the constellation in whose sign a man was born determined his physical appearance—strong or frail—and what portion of light and darkness he would possess. Cf. John M. Allegro, "An

man's submission to the "angels," "powers," and "principalities," under whose control man has come through origin and fate. Consequently the adherents of the "philosophy" cannot be considered Essenes,[117] members of the Qumran community[118] or proponents of heretical Jewish propaganda.[119] Rather their teaching is one made up of diverse elements which, because of the emphasis placed on knowledge as well as its world–negating character, can be termed Gnostic or, if a more cautious designation is desired, pre–Gnostic.[120] A Gnostic understanding of the world is also exhibited in the desire to be filled with divine power as well as in the boastful arrogance of those who think they have experienced such fulness and possess wisdom and knowledge.

The cult, as it was performed by the adherents of the "philosophy," probably took the form of a mys-

---

Astrological Cryptic Document from Qumran," *Journal of Semitic Studies* 9 (1964): 291–94; Jean Starcky, "Un texte messianique araméen de la Grotte 4 de Qumrân," in: *Mémorial du Cinquantenaire de l'École des langues orientales anciennes de l'Institut Catholique de Paris* (Paris: 1964), 51–66; Jean Carmignac, "Les Horoscopes de Qumrân," *Revue de Qumrân* 5 (1965–66): 199–217; J. Licht, "שוקיים סימן לבחירה (צד חדש בתורתם של אנשי כת מדבר יהודה)" *Tarbiz* 35 (1965–66): 18–26; Mathias Delcor, "Recherches sur un horoscope en langue hébraïque provenant de Qumrân," *Revue de Qumrân* 5 (1965–66): 521–42. Thus, some circles of Judaism held that the course of a man's life was already predetermined by the stars before birth. On the problem of syncretism in Judaism cf. further the important reference found in Morton Smith, "Goodenough's Jewish Symbols in Retrospect," *JBL* 86 (1967): 60f: "Margalioth's recovery of 'Sefer ha Razim' (The Hebrew edition is now in the press in Israel), however, has given us a Hebrew text, written by a man steeped in the OT and the poetry of the synagogue, which yet contains prescriptions for making images and prayers to pagan deities, including Helios, who are conceived as gods subordinate to Yahweh." Cf. Mordecai Margalioth, *Sefer ha Razim* (Jerusalem: 1966).

117 In his learned treatise Lightfoot referred to the Essenes, but he did not in fact claim that there must have been a direct dependence: "But indeed throughout this investigation, when I speak of the Judaism in the Colossian Church as Essene, I do not assume a precise identity of origin, but only an essential affinity of type, with the Essenes of the mother country" (p. 92f).

118 Ever since the Qumran texts were discovered, a connection between the teaching of the Qumran community and the "philosophy" of Col has been frequently suggested. Beside the articles of W. D. Davies and Pierre Benoit cited above (p. 115, n. 11) cf. A. R. C. Leaney, " 'Conformed to the Image of His Son' (Rom. VIII.29)," *NTS* 10 (1963–64): 478: "It is striking that the tradition of men, which is according to this–worldly elements, is coupled with 'philosophy' (II.8) and the elements of it are such as found at Qumran (II.16–18)." Lyonnet, "Colossiens," 429–32 also reckons with strong Jewish influences, possibly from Qumran. Cf. further S. Zedda, "Il carattere gnostico e guidaico dell' errore colossese nella luce dei manoscritti del Mar Morto," *Rivista Biblica* 5 (1957): 31–56; Edwin M. Yamauchi, "Sectarian Parallels: Qumran and Colossae," *Bibliotheca Sacra* 121 (1964): 141–52; Frank Moore Cross, *The Ancient Library of Qumran and Modern Biblical Studies* (New York: Doubleday & Co. Anchor Books, rev. ed. 1961), 201–02. Against such suppositions, however, one must maintain that at Qumran it is exclusively the rigoristic demand of undivided obedience to the law which determines the strict interpretation and observance of the purificatory and food laws as well as the scrupulous keeping of the calendar and of the days of rest laid down in the Torah. The elements of the "philosophy" taken from Jewish tradition are not impregnated with the idea of radical legalism as is the case at Qumran, but they are subordinated to the service of the elements of the universe. Cf. Lohse, "Christologie und Ethik," 157f; Braun, *Qumran* 1, pp. 228–32.

119 Hegermann, *Schöpfungsmittler*, 162, thinks "it is a question of heretical Jewish propaganda." That is hardly the case. The concept "law" (*νόμος*) is absent in Col, and the polemic against the "philosophy" takes a completely different tack than that against the Judaizers in Gal.

120 Cf. Dibelius–Greeven, 38–40, and Bornkamm, *Aufsätze* 1, p. 147: "Col leaves no doubt that in the Colossian heresy we are confronted with a variant of Jewish Gnosticism." Cf. also Leonard Goppelt, "Christentum und Judentum im ersten und zweiten Jahrhundert," *Beiträge zur Förderung christlicher Theologie* 2, 55 (Gütersloh: 1954), 137–40: "Gnostic Judaism" (p. 140). Percy, *Probleme*, 176–78, however, denies that there is a connection between the Colossian false teaching and Gnosticism. Yet he admits: "On the other hand, however, the Colossian false teaching clearly has this in common with Gnosticism, that it represents a kind of syncretism of Christianity and non–Christian late–Hellenistic piety of a speculative bent" (p. 178). Likewise, Hegermann, *Schöpfungsmittler*, 163, wants to doubt the Gnostic character of the "philosophy." Nevertheless, he admits that pre–Gnostic influences could be at work. Stanislas Lyonnet, "St. Paul et le gnosti-

tery.[121] This is not only indicated in the expressions which Col quotes: "as he had visions of them during the mystery rites" (2:18), "self-chosen cult" and "honor" (2:23), but through the reference to "circumcision." This seemed to point to a decisive act of initiation (2:11) through which a person was accepted into the community of those who in right wisdom and knowledge served the "elements of the universe." The particulars of this act—whether circumcision was actually performed or whether the act of initiation only bore this Jewish name which was understood figuratively as the "putting off the body of flesh," i.e. ascetic withdrawal from the world—can no longer be discerned. In any case, one sought to make the sacramental initiation more attractive and more appealing by dressing it up in a Jewish term.[122]

Since it was the commonly accepted opinion of the time that one could undergo several initiations and be a member of different mystery-cult communities at the same time, those who were attracted to this teaching[123] probably assumed that it was advisable also for a Christian not to refuse the knowledge offered and not to disdain the perfecting power that this "philosophy" made available. Of course, while adhering to this philosophy, these Christians did not want to surrender their faith in Christ. One probably desired rather to bolster it with additional protection. For the forgiveness of sins conferred in baptism did not seem to provide adequate security against the cosmic principalities and the powers of fate. To be sure, the polemic of Col does not give a clear picture of how these Christians tried to define the relationship of the powers and principalities to Christ. Undoubtedly, however, they endeavored to find a place for Christ through a synthesis that accorded with the syncretistic character of the "philosophy"—perhaps this way: only through submissive worship of the angelic powers is the way opened to Christ who is enthroned beyond the powers and principalities.[124] Whoever pays homage to them and observes their laws and prescriptions is protected from the pernicious effects produced by the "powers" and "principalities." In this way alone is entry to the divine fulness assured. The knowledge about the synthesis between faith in Christ and worship of the elements of the universe, thus achieved, filled adherents with the feeling that they had attained the true insight and were superior to other Christians.[125]

To this community into which the "philosophy" was trying to make inroads, the author of Colossians states with unequivocal clarity that a synthesis of this kind is absolutely impossible. Whoever joins the "philosophy" turns his back on Christ. One must make a decision: either "according to the elements

cisme: la lettre aux Colossiens" in *Le Origini dello Gnosticismo*, ed. U. Bianchi (Leiden: 1967), 538–61 also emphasizes that the term Gnosticism must be used with great caution.

121 Cf. Franz Cumont, *The Oriental Religions in Roman Paganism*, authorized trans. (Chicago: The Open Court Publishing Co., ^{2}1911), 205: "All the Oriental religions assumed the form of mysteries."

122 Cf. Bornkamm, *Aufsätze* 1, pp. 145–47; Lohse, "Christologie und Ethik," 158. On the other hand, Eduard Meyer, *Ursprung und Anfänge des Christentums* 3 (Stuttgart and Berlin: 1923 = Darmstadt: 1962), 488f has put forward a daring but equally unfounded proposal about the origin of the "Judaistic movement in Colossae;" the evangelist Philip, mentioned in Acts, and his daughters settled in Hierapolis—as Papias of Hierapolis says (Eusebius, *Hist. eccl.* 3, 39, 9). Thus "the supposition can be made that his appearance in Hierapolis, which then also included the neighboring cities, is connected with the Judaistic movement in Colossae; the appeal to revelations corresponds quite well with the prophetic abilities of his daughters."

123 Following Dibelius-Greeven, 38, one should distinguish "between those leaders of the 'philosophy' (2:8), i.e. the cult of the elements, who are not members of the Christian community at Colossae and those members of the Christian community who were won over by their propaganda." Cf. also Dibelius, *Aufsätze* 2, p. 56; further Foerster, "Irrlehrer," 72f who maintains, however, that the opponents were Jews who espoused tendencies related to those of the Essenes and "are found outside of the community" (p. 72).

124 Cf. Bornkamm, *Aufsätze* 1, p. 140f, who maintains: "The mythological and Christological expression of this teaching must have been that the opponents understood the 'elements of the universe' themselves as the 'body' of Christ or as its members, and Christ as the embodiment of the elements of the universe" (p. 141). Schenke, "Widerstreit," 398, judges the case this way: "The Gnostics attacked in Col, of course, also worshipped Christ, and indeed as Savior. This is not said in the letter, because it was entirely taken for granted." The text, however, lends no secure support to such an unequivocal statement. Only cautious conjectures can be made about the kind of faith in Christ that the adherents of the "philosophy" held.

125 Sectarian groups, who like the "philosophy" of Col advocated the worship of a highest divine being and service determined by legal regulations, still existed in Asia Minor in the fourth Christian century. On the sect of the so-called Hypsistarians, cf. Bornkamm, *Aufsätze* 1, pp. 153–56.

126 Cf. Bultmann, *Theology* par. 59, 2 = Vol. 2, p. 205.

of the universe" or "according to Christ" (2:8). Whoever declares his humble readiness to bow before the elements of the universe has thereby separated himself from the Head, who alone gives life and power to the body (2:11)—no matter how much such an adherent of the "philosophy" thinks that his newly acquired knowledge makes him superior to the others, and no matter how much he proudly boasts and haughtily passes judgment on others. In truth, what fills him and makes him proud is nothing other than "his earthly mind" (2:18). What he considers fulness will soon be revealed to be emptiness and inner shallowness. He is a slave to the shadows, which long since had to give way, for the light which floods everything dispersed them.

In Christ and nowhere else dwells "the entire fulness of deity bodily" (2:9). In him alone is fulness, for he is the "head of all powers and principalities" (2:10). He presently exercises his lordship as head of his body, the "church." Only by belonging to the church as the body of Christ can a person adhere to Christ the head. He who has been baptized into him, he who has died and has been raised with him (2:11f, 20), has thereby also died once and for all to the "elements of the universe." He is no longer petrified by the powers of fate, and the elements of the universe have lost all possible claims on him (2:20f). He is freed from the compulsion to view the things of the world in anxious awe and regulate his use of them according to certain taboos. For food and drink are created to be used and should be gratefully accepted as God's good gifts.

The answer to the "philosophy's" dualistic understanding of the world is not stated in terms of a Christian metaphysic. Rather, the author of Col confronts the "philosophy" with an antithesis that is historically grounded: the crucified, resurrected and exalted Christ is the Lord, and beside him there can be no other. While the "philosophy" conveys its esoteric tradition only to initiates and to those who possess understanding, the proclamation of the Lord is directed to the entire world and to everyone. Christ is preached among the nations. On his cross the certificate of indebtedness that stood against us was destroyed (2:14). God has forgiven us all our sins (2:13). To have forgiveness of sins, however, also means to be free from the powers and principalities, who on the cross of Christ were subjected to ridicule and shame (2:15). Whoever is baptized into Christ is placed under the dominion of the beloved Son of God, who as Lord holds in his hands authority over the whole world as well as the salvation of those who belong to him—freed for the new life of obedience that confesses his rule. This is what matters now: "If, therefore, you have been raised with Christ, seek that which is above, where Christ is, sitting at the right hand of God. Consider that which is above, not that which is on earth" (*Εἰ οὖν συνηγέρθητε τῷ Χριστῷ, τὰ ἄνω ζητεῖτε, οὗ ὁ Χριστός ἐστιν ἐν δεξιᾷ τοῦ θεοῦ καθήμενος· τὰ ἄνω φρονεῖτε, μὴ τὰ ἐπὶ τῆς γῆς* 3:1f).[126]

II. The Hortatory Section: The Rule of Christ in the Life of the Believers

Colossians 3:1–4

3

Seek What Is Above!

1 If, therefore, you have been raised with Christ, seek that which is above, where Christ is, sitting at the right hand of God. 2/ Consider that which is above, not that which is on earth. 3/ For you have died, and your life is hidden with Christ in God. 4/ When Christ, our life, is revealed, then you also will be revealed with him in glory.

The hortatory section of the letter begins by stating a conclusion which refers back to the preceding verses: "If, therefore, you have been raised" (*εἰ οὖν συνηγέρθητε* v 1) refers back to "you were raised" (*συνηγέρθητε* 2:12); "for you have died" (*ἀπεθάνετε γάρ* v 3) refers back to "you were buried with him" (*συνταφέντες αὐτῷ* 2:12) and to "you died" (*ἀπεθάνετε* 2:20). Although Col is no longer dealing with the slogans of false doctrine, it is probable that the material content of such controversy is still very much in view. Previously, Col has explained that belonging to the resurrected and glorified Christ meant freedom from the compulsion of the powers and principalities. Beginning in Col 3:1 the new life of the believer who has been raised with Christ is described as obedient conduct of life within the realm of the Lord's rule. This unfolds what was already mentioned briefly in various ways in the two preceding chapters: genuine wisdom and understanding are manifest in the fulfillment of the divine will (1:9–11). To be transferred to the "rule of his beloved Son" (*βασιλεία τοῦ υἱοῦ τῆς ἀγάπης αὐτοῦ*) means to have become subject to him who is the Lord over all things (1:12–20). The reconciliation which has been received must be appropriated and maintained "through perseverance in faith" (*ἐπιμένειν τῇ πίστει*) and in holding steadfastly to the "hope of the gospel" (*ἐλπὶς τοῦ εὐαγγελίου* 1:21–23). "As, therefore, you received Christ Jesus the Lord, so conduct yourselves in him" (*Ὡς οὖν παρελάβετε τὸν Χριστὸν Ἰησοῦν τὸν κύριον, ἐν αὐτῷ περιπατεῖτε* 2:6). This demand is made more tangible in the hortatory expositions. The first two chapters of this letter are thus intimately bound to the following two chapters by their subject matter. Accordingly, in the introduction to the exhortation the author points to baptism as the basis of the new life, and thus a Christological foundation for ethics precedes the detailed instructions. Life with Christ is actualized when one belongs to the Kyrios and follows his command.

■ **1** The transition to the exhortation[1] is indicated by "therefore" (*οὖν* cf. Rom 12:1; Eph 4:1). In this way what follows is connected to the train of thought previously developed: you have been raised with Christ for the new life![2] God's eschatological act has already taken place; he has called man from death to life. To be sure, this life is not conveyed to man as the divine fulness and power of immortality. Rather, it is the summons to obedient appropriation which results from having acquired salvation: "Seek that which is above" (*τὰ ἄνω*[3] *ζητεῖτε*). The phrase "that which is above" (*τά ἄνω*), which does not appear in the Pauline letters, refers to the heavenly world. It is the location of "the Jerusalem which is above" (*ἡ ἄνω Ἰερουσαλήμ* Gal 4:26), and from there the "upward call" (*ἄνω κλῆσις* Phil 3:14) comes.[4] As it has been said already that "hope" (*ἐλπίς*) is already prepared in heaven for the believers (1:5), spatial con-

1 For section 3:1–4 I refer to P. Th. Camelot, "Ressuscités avec le Christ," *La Vie Spirituelle* 84 (1951): 353–63; F. W. Grosheide, "Kol 3, 1–4; 1 Petr 1, 3–5; 1 Jo 3, 1–2," *Gereformeerd Theologische Tijdschrift* 54 (1954): 139–47; F. J. Schierse, "'Suchet, was droben ist!'" *Geist und Leben* 31 (1958): 86–90; Erich Grässer, "Kol 3, 1–4 als Beispiel einer Interpretation secundum homines recipientes," *ZThK* 64 (1967): 139–68.

2 It has already been shown for 2:12 (pp. 103–105) that this sentence goes beyond the Pauline statements of Rom 6. Cf. Reitzenstein, *Mysterienreligionen*, 269; Grässer, "Kol 3, 1–4," 148 and see below p. 134, n. 16.

3 For the use of the definite article before *ἄνω* cf. Moulton–Turner, 14.

4 Cf. further Jn 8:23: "You are from below, I am from above" (*ὑμεῖς ἐκ τῶν κάτω ἐστέ, ἐγὼ ἐκ τῶν

cepts are also employed here.[5] Christians are to look upward in order to receive clear direction for their conduct. In this way the goal for their striving is manifest, the path for their "seeking" (ζητεῖν)[6] is indicated—it is upward, that is, toward the place where Christ is, exalted and enthroned at God's right hand.[7] In the participial construction a statement of a creedal character is incorporated which has been formulated with reference to Ps 110:1.[8] The messianic promise that God would give the anointed one the place of honor at his right hand has been fulfilled by the resurrection and enthronement of Christ.[9] The community, as it looks to that which is above, confesses Jesus as the Christ whom God has installed in his office of government. So it is that in the midst of this world his own people are already linked to the heavenly world. Because the head is above, his own people cling to him, knowing that they are freed from everything that might wish to draw them downward.

■ **2** The summons is issued for a second time by the words "consider that which is above" (τὰ ἄνω φρονεῖτε), with "to consider" (φρονεῖν) replacing "to seek" (ζητεῖν). The verb "to consider" (φρονεῖν) connotes the thought and the aspirations[10] which determine actions. Thus Paul also exhorts that one ought "not to consider oneself too highly" (μὴ ὑπερφρονεῖν παρ' ὃ δεῖ φρονεῖν Rom 12:3) and to that end constrains the community: "in order that you may consider the same thing" (ἵνα τὸ αὐτὸ φρονῆτε Phil 2:2), i.e., "consider among yourselves what you are in Christ Jesus" (τοῦτο φρονεῖτε ἐν ὑμῖν ὃ καὶ ἐν Χριστῷ Ἰησοῦ Phil 2:5). Because "to consider" demands sobriety, every kind of reckless enthusiasm is rejected. The right understanding of God wants to be actualized in the relevant probing of that which applies here and now as his command.[11] This "considering" is accompanied by the "renewal of the mind" (ἀνακαίνωσις τοῦ νοός Rom 12:2) and is determined by that which is above. The mind should be oriented in that direction, for the home of the believers is above (Phil 3:20f). The phrase "that which is above" (τὰ ἄνω) is more precisely defined through the negative "not that which is on earth" (μὴ τὰ ἐπὶ τῆς γῆς). This by no means implies that the Christians have been removed from this world.[12] It is precisely in considering "that which is above" that they mold everyday life accordingly, in obedience to the Lord. For that reason, their "seeking" (ζητεῖν) and their "considering" (φρονεῖν) are directed upward and may not be drawn down by some heavy burden, as it were, to the level where man is held prisoner in his disobedient thoughts and activities (cf. v 5ff).

■ **3** What was once, no longer applies. The old life has been put aside forever through the death which they died together with Christ. It is only that life which has been bestowed by God's creative power which has decisive reality. This life exists in the present, for God "made you alive together with him" (συνεζωοποίησεν ὑμᾶς σὺν αὐτῷ 2:13). Yet this "life" (ζωή) is a reality only where it is received and directed "by faith" (διὰ τῆς πίστεως 2:12). This clearly averts the spiritualistic idea of salvation in which one conceives of salvation as something that is visibly present in its fulness, and of death as already vanished, and of the resurrection of the dead as already

ἄνω εἰμί); Friedrich Büchsel, *TDNT* 1, 376–78. For the contrast of the upper and lower worlds in Rabbinic writings, cf. the citations in Billerbeck 1, pp. 395, 977; 2, pp. 116, 133, 430f.

5 For the Hellenistic presuppositions concerning the opposition of the earthly and heavenly worlds, above and below, cf. Schweizer, *Erniedrigung*, 145–55.

6 Cf. Heinrich Greeven, *TDNT* 2, 894–96.

7 The verb "is" (ἐστίν) is not to be connected with "sitting" (καθήμενος) as a *conjugatio periphrastica*, but is to be separated from the participle by a comma.

8 By citing the creedal formulation, the author indicates that he wishes to use the phrase "seek that which is above" to state what is contained in the Christian creed: Christ has been exalted above the powers and is enthroned at God's right hand. Whoever belongs to him is thereby freed for new life. Cf. also Grässer, "Kol 3, 1–4," 155–58.

9 Cf. Mk 12:36 par; 14:62 par; Acts 2:34; 1 Cor 15:25; Rom 8:34; Eph 1:20; Heb 1:3, 13; 8:1; 10:12f; 13:2.

10 Cf. Bauer, *s.v.*

11 Cf. Bornkamm, "Faith and Reason in Paul," *Early Christian Experience*, 41: True understanding "means simultaneously the right intelligence with regard to the situation of man before God and the sensible, rational examination of what is 'good and acceptable and perfect' (Rom. 12.2) before God and neighbour."

12 Gnosis on the other hand teaches that the true self of man ascends into the heavenly world, lays aside evil in its ascent through the spheres, and thus attains its own proper destination. Cf. *Corp. Herm.* 1, 25f.

accomplished (2 Tim 2:18).[13] The old life has come to an end with the death which was died together with Christ, and thus the past can lay no more claims. The "life" (ζωή), moreover, which God created in the resurrection with Christ, is and remains totally bound to Christ and is not at man's disposal.[14] Man has life only in that situation where he lives with Christ, obeys his Lord, and puts his trust in him.[15] The expression "you have died" (ἀπεθάνετε) in this context takes the place of "you have been raised" (συνηγέρθητε v 1); thus the author makes clear that the consummation is not yet attained but lies in the future.[16] Life is hidden with Christ in God, removed from the view of men, and it cannot be tangibly exhibited. Rather it is received by faith as an eschatological gift and is retained by setting the mind on what is above.[17]

■ **4** That which is now secretly present shall become manifest at some future time,[18] when Christ shall appear. The verb "to be revealed" (φανερωθῆναι) in this context does not refer to the appearance that has already taken place as in 1:26.[19] Rather it refers to the parousia in which the veil will be drawn back so that whatever is veiled from our eyes shines in bright light.[20] The parousia of Christ, which Col does not otherwise mention, is referred to with a traditional phrase[21] to which a short confession is joined: "when Christ, our life, will be revealed" (ὅταν ὁ Χριστὸς φανερωθῇ, ἡ ζωὴ ἡμῶν). Indeed, the mss p⁴⁶ 𝔖 D* G pm lat provide very strong evidence in favor of the variant reading "your life" (ἡ ζωὴ ὑμῶν). Nevertheless, the reading "our life" (ἡ ζωὴ ἡμῶν), which manuscripts B 𝔎 sy and several minuscules offer, is to be considered the original text, which was altered very early and made to conform to the second person style of this section of the letter. Christ is our life.[22] Whoever belongs to Christ has already passed from death to life.[23] When, however, Christ who is now enthroned at God's right hand appears at the end of days, then it will also become manifest that his own are with him[24] in

13 Paul never says that Christians are already raised with Christ. The Christian has died with Christ and looks forward to the future resurrection; only then he will be with the Lord always. Thus Pauline exhortation is not defined by the upward view but calls for obedience in anticipation of the one who is coming. Helmut Koester, "The Purpose of the Polemic of a Pauline Fragment (Philippians III)," *NTS* 8 (1961–62): 329 points out the contrast to Col in a sharply formulated antithesis: "This fundamental exhortation (i.e., Col 3:1f) refers to the theological presupposition 'if you are risen with Christ' (III.1) —a presupposition which would have been as unacceptable to Paul as the exhortation itself." Nevertheless, Col remains bound to Pauline theology insofar as it excludes a spiritualistic explanation of "you were raised with Christ" (συνηγέρθητε τῷ Χριστῷ). For "your life is hidden with Christ in God" (ἡ ζωὴ ὑμῶν κέκρυπται σὺν τῷ Χριστῷ ἐν τῷ θεῷ). Cf. also Tannehill, *Dying and Rising*, 47–54.

14 The concept "life," which simply means the gift of salvation, is interpreted here by the expressions "you were raised" and "you have died." "Life" as a present reality, as it is understood in this context, is very close to the Johannine concept of "life." Yet the explicit reservation that this life is still hidden with Christ in God is Pauline. Only when Christ, "our life," is manifest, "then also will you be revealed with him in glory" (τότε καὶ ὑμεῖς σὺν αὐτῷ φανερωθήσεσθε ἐν δόξῃ v 4). Cf. also Grässer, "Kol 3, 1–4," 160–66.

15 This state of affairs cannot be described as mysticism. Against Dibelius–Greeven, *ad loc.*: "The new life, the powers of which the mystic already senses, is only latently available at present."

16 "But it is characteristic that our author indeed does not speak apocalyptically about the resurrection of the dead as Paul does. Rather he speaks unconditionally about 'life' as the eschatological gift as such" (Grässer, "Kol 3, 1–4," 161).

17 Cf. Bornkamm, *Aufsätze* 1, p. 46: "Only in Christ do the believers have the new life which is granted to them . . . 'This life does not have the experience of itself, but has faith' (Haec vita non habet experientiam sui, sed fidem [Luther]); the man who is baptized is nothing else than the someone who believes and hopes."

18 Cf. Rudolf Bultmann, *TDNT* 2, 866.

19 Cf. also Rom 3:21; 16:26; 1 Tim 3:16; 1 Pt 1:20.

20 Cf. also 2 Cor 5:10: "For we must all appear before the judgment seat of Christ" (τοὺς γὰρ πάντας ἡμᾶς φανερωθῆναι δεῖ ἔμπροσθεν τοῦ βήματος τοῦ Χριστοῦ).

21 Cf. 1 Jn 2:28; 3:2: "when he appears" (ἐὰν φανερωθῇ). Primitive Christian eschatology lies behind the sentence "when Christ appears" (ὅταν ὁ Χριστὸς φανερωθῇ). Cf. Günther Bornkamm, "Hoffnung," 61.

22 For further references to the formulation "Christ, our life:" cf. Phil 1:21: "For me to live is Christ" (ἐμοὶ γὰρ τὸ ζῆν Χριστός); 1 Jn 5:12: "he who has the Son has life" (ὁ ἔχων τὸν υἱὸν ἔχει τὴν ζωήν); Ign. *Eph.* 7:2: Christ "true life in death" (ἐν θανάτῳ ζωὴ ἀληθινή); Ign*Eph* 3:2: "Jesus Christ,

life. Communion "with Christ" (*σὺν τῷ Χριστῷ*), which has been established through baptism and which fills the life of Christians, will then reach its fulfillment, "in glory" (*ἐν δόξῃ*) which is unending.

Although the reference to the parousia, which was taken from primitive Christian tradition, functions as a means to distinguish the present from the future in which the revelation will be visible, the emphasis of this statement is upon existence "with Christ," in which the life of Christians is grounded. To be sure, while Christ is in heaven, those who belong to him exist on earth. Since they have died and risen with Christ, they are already joined to the heavenly Lord in an indissoluble communion. Since they are his very own, the decision about the direction and the goal of their lives has already been made: "seek the things above—consider the things above." Yet the life of those who have been raised together with Christ is still hidden. Therefore, they still have need of admonitions and encouragement which will strengthen them in their holding fast to the gospel and will urge them to authenticate their Christian existence in their conduct. The spatial distinction between "the things above" and "the things on earth" thus functions to point up the either/or of the decision that continually determines obedient conduct. In dying and rising "with Christ" this decision has already been made with binding force. Therefore, in their conduct the believers have nothing else to do than to put off the old man, who has already died with Christ, and to put on the new man, whom God has created and called into life in the resurrection with Christ.[25]

our inseparable life" (Ἰησοῦς Χριστός, *τὸ ἀδιάκριτον ἡμῶν ζῆν*); Ign. *Smyrn.* 4:1: "Jesus Christ who is our true life" (Ἰησοῦς Χριστός, *τὸ ἀληθινὸν ἡμῶν ζῆν*); Ign. *Magn.* 1:2: "Jesus Christ who is our everlasting life" (Ἰησοῦ Χριστοῦ, *τοῦ διὰ παντὸς ἡμῶν ζῆν*).

23 Cf. Jn 5:24f; 11:25f, etc.

24 Manuscript Λ omits "with him" (*σὺν αὐτῷ*).

25 Christian ethics, consequently, is "an ethics that in one's own conduct of life draws the conclusions from the gracious acts of God" (Wolfgang Nauck, "Das *οὖν*–paräneticum," *ZNW* 49 [1958]: 134f).

3 Put on the New Man!

5 Therefore, put to death the earthly members, fornication, impurity, passion,
evil desire, and covetousness which is
idolatry; 6/ on account of such deeds
the wrath of God is coming. 7/ You, too,
once conducted your lives in these
things when you lived in them. 8/ But
now put away also all these: wrath,
anger, malice, slander, and abusive
language from your mouth. 9/ Do not lie
to one another; put off the old man
with his practices, 10/ and put on the
new man, who is being renewed in
knowledge according to the image of his
creator, 11/ where there is no longer
Greek and Jew, circumcision and uncircumcision, barbarian, Scythian, slave,
and free, but Christ is all and in all.
12 Put on, then, as God's chosen ones, holy
and beloved, merciful compassion, kindness, humility, meekness, patience;
13/ bear with one another and forgive if
someone has a complaint against another; as the Lord has forgiven you, so
you also must forgive. 14/ In addition
to all these, love, which is the bond of
perfection. 15/ And let the peace of
Christ rule in your hearts, to which you
were also called in the one body. And
be thankful. 16/ Let the word of Christ
dwell abundantly among you, in all
wisdom teach and admonish one another; with psalms, hymns, and songs
that are prompted by the Spirit sing—
since you stand in the grace—to God in
your hearts. 17/ And whatever you do
in word or deed, do everything in the
name of the Lord Jesus; give thanks to
God the Father through him!

The demand "to seek the things above—to set your minds on things that are above" (*τὰ ἄνω ζητεῖτε—τὰ ἄνω φρονεῖτε*) is further developed in the following imperatives: "put to death" (*νεκρώσατε* v 5), "put away" (*ἀπόθεσθε* v 8), "do not lie" (*μὴ ψεύδεσθε* v 9), and "put off" (*ἀπεκδυσάμενοι* v 9). They delimit Christian life negatively. The positive definition of Christian life is juxtaposed later on in v 10 with "and put on . . ." (*καὶ ἐνδυσάμενοι . . .*). The exhortations follow traditional forms and sequences of enumeration and do not at all refer to specific problems in the community. However, references and flashbacks to the theme of the whole letter are used to interpret this traditional exhortatory material. For example, because the believers have died with Christ in baptism (2:12f; 3:3), the demand is laid upon them: "put to death" (*νεκρώσατε* v 5). The "putting off the body of flesh" (*ἀπέκδυσις τοῦ σώματος τῆς σαρκός* 2:11) is accomplished in "the putting off" (*ἀπεκδύεσθαι* v 9) of the old man. To this, however, corresponds the putting on of the new man, who is being renewed "in knowledge according to the image of his creator" (*εἰς ἐπίγνωσιν κατ᾽ εἰκόνα τοῦ κτίσαντος αὐτόν* v 10).

The exhortatory section moves into positive terms with the command "to put on" the new man (*ἐνδυσάμενοι* v 10—*ἐνδύσασθε* v 12). Accordingly, two catalogs of vices of v 5, 8, are followed by a catalog of virtues. The injunctions "bear with one another and forgive one another" (*ἀνεχόμενοι ἀλλήλων καὶ χαριζόμενοι ἑαυτοῖς* v 13) interpret the catalog of virtues. In love the life of the community attains its perfection (v 14). Life, as it unfolds itself in the community as the place of Christ's lordship, is then described as peace (v 15), thanksgiving (v 15b), acceptance and witness of the Word in teaching and song (v 16) as well as in deeds in the name of the Lord Jesus (v 17). The concept "to give thanks" (*εὐχάριστοι* v 15, *ἐν χάριτι* v 16, and *εὐχαριστοῦντες* v 17) binds these last three verses together. Everything that those who are gathered together "in one body" (*ἐν ἑνὶ σώματι*) do, is a song of thankful praise to God.

■ **5** Put to death. That means: let the old man, who has already died in baptism, be dead: "So you also must consider yourselves dead to sin and alive to God in Christ Jesus" (*οὕτως καὶ ὑμεῖς λογίζεσθε ἑαυτοὺς εἶναι νεκροὺς μὲν τῇ ἁμαρτίᾳ ζῶντας δὲ τῷ θεῷ ἐν Χριστῷ Ἰησοῦ* Rom 6:11); "Put yourselves at God's disposal as men who have been brought from death to life" (*παραστήσατε ἑαυτοὺς τῷ θεῷ ὡσεὶ ἐκ νεκρῶν ζῶντας* Rom 6:13; cf. also Rom 8:10). The dying with Christ,[1] undergone in baptism, should be appropriated now by putting to death "the earthly members" (*μέλη τὰ ἐπὶ τῆς γῆς*). Man conducts his life with his members by yielding them either to "sin" (*ἁμαρτία*) as "instruments of wickedness" (*ὅπλα ἀδικίας*) or "to God as instruments of righteousness" (*ὅπλα δικαιοσύνης τῷ θεῷ* Rom 6:13). Depending on whom man acknowledges as his Lord, his members are either slaves of "impurity" (*ἀκαθαρσία*) and "iniquity" (*ἀνομία*) or obedient servants of "righteousness" (*δικαιοσύνη* Rom 6:19). However, in the admonition to put to death "the earthly members" (*μέλη*[2] *τὰ ἐπὶ τῆς γῆς*) in which five different vices are mentioned as the members, it is scarcely possible to interpret "members" as man's bodily members.[3] Rather, this is apparently a reference to a traditional manner of expression. According to Iranian concepts, man's members are his good or bad deeds, out of which his heavenly self is constituted and thus his other-worldly fate is decided.[4] Five good and five evil deeds are mentioned in every instance in the Iranian tradition. In Col both the two catalogs of vices (3:5, 8) and the list of virtues (3:12) are based on a fivefold enumeration. It is quite likely that this is derived from the Iranian "pentaschema" of anthropology in which man's deeds are said to be his members and are enumerated according to this schema of fives.[5] In using this schema, the author of Col hardly had in mind the myth of the two cosmic "men" (*ἄνθρωποι*) who each had five members.[6] He was probably not at all conscious of the history-of-religions connections, but just took over a traditional manner of speaking about false and true conduct and adopted the existing fivefold schema in order to spell out, in the exhortations, the type of life demanded of the Christian.[7] The words "not that which is on earth" ([*μὴ*] *τὰ ἐπὶ τῆς γῆς* 3:2) are repeated because now a summons is issued to put to death "the earthly members." Man cannot distance himself from his actions; he is so intimately bound up with them that his actions are a part of himself. Only through the death in which the old self dies, can the way to new life be opened. The following list of five vices specifies what is involved in the decision to put to death the earthly members.

The catalog of vices is not occasioned by the situation in which the community addressed finds itself. Rather

1 Paul otherwise never uses the verb "to put to death" (*νεκροῦν*) in such a context. The verb "to extirpate" (*θανατοῦν*) occurs at Rom 8:13: "But if by the Spirit you extirpate the deeds of the body" (*εἰ δὲ πνεύματι τὰς πράξεις τοῦ σώματος θανατοῦτε*). Nevertheless, the Pauline use of the adjective "dead" (*νεκρός*) in reference to baptism is surely reflected in the verb "to put to death" (*νεκροῦν*). Cf. Rudolf Bultmann, *TDNT* 4, 892–94.

2 Manuscripts A ℜ D G pl latt Ir add "your" (*ὑμῶν*) and thus imitate Pauline usage. Cf. Rom 6:13, 19: "your members" (*τὰ μέλη ὑμῶν*).

3 Along with others Johannes Horst, *TDNT* 4, 565 wants to interpret: "here again the reference is to the members which constitute active and concrete corporeality under sin." Masson, *ad loc.*, on the other hand, appeals to Blass–Debrunner, par. 147, 2 and proposes that "the members" be understood as a vocative and refer to the Christians as members of Christ's body. This interpretation, however, would "be possible only if the context were to develop explicitly the image head–body–members" (Dibelius–Greeven, *ad loc.*).

4 Cf. Richard Reitzenstein, *Das iranische Erlösungsmysterium* (Bonn: 1921), 152–63; *idem*, *Mysterienreligionen*, 265–75; Dibelius–Greeven, Conzelmann, *ad loc.*

5 Cf. Bornkamm, *Aufsätze* 1, p. 151.

6 Against Käsemann, *Leib Christi*, 150.

7 Cf. Dibelius–Greeven, *ad loc.*: "The appearance of another list in 3:8 which also has five vices and actually competes with the first list" indicates "that Paul is really only employing a schema and is not concerned with the . . . full-blown myth of two cosmic men who each" are supposed to have "five members, namely, the virtues or vices."

it is already given in the tradition.[8] Sexual sins, covetousness, and idolatry are cited, because these were vices for which the Jews especially reproached the pagans.[9] Illegitimate sexual intercourse (πορνεία) is mentioned first. It is always emphatically forbidden.[10] Similarly, Gal 5:19 lists "fornication" (πορνεία) as the first of the "works of the flesh" (ἔργα τῆς σαρκός). 1 Thess 4:3 enjoins: "that you abstain from fornication" (ἀπέχεσθαι ὑμᾶς ἀπὸ τῆς πορνείας). And 1 Cor 6:18 resolutely admonishes: "shun fornication" (φεύγετε τὴν πορνείαν). For no "sexually immoral person" (πόρνος) will inherit the "kingdom of God" (βασιλεία τοῦ θεοῦ 1 Cor 6:9; cf. 5:9–11; Eph 5:5). In contradistinction to the loose living which was almost universal in the Hellenistic world, Christian teaching demands unconditional obedience to the prohibition on "fornication."[11] The addition of "impurity" (ἀκαθαρσία) underlines this admonition.[12] "Impurity" occurs frequently together with "fornication" and indicates moral impurity, i.e. immoral sexual conduct.[13] Just like "fornication," "impurity" is a "work of the flesh" (ἔργον τῆς σαρκός Gal 5:19) and is incompatible with life in the Spirit.[14]

In the third position "passion" (πάθος), a specifically Greek term, occurs. The Stoics would use it to describe the fundamental failure of the man who lets himself be dominated by his emotions and thus is incapable of attaining "tranquillity" (ἀπάθεια).[15] In primitive Christian exhortation, however, "passion" (πάθος) is not used in this Stoic sense. Rather it designates that shameful passion (cf. 1 Thess 4:5; Rom 1:26) which leads to sexual excesses.[16] The next word, "desire" (ἐπιθυμία)[17] is further characterized negatively by means of the adjective "evil" (κακή)[18] as the evil desire; it is the wicked concupiscence; the "desire of flesh" (ἐπιθυμία σαρκός Gal 5:16), which leads men in their disobedience to God.[19] The fifth member of the list is set off a little from the previous vices by "and" (καί) and the definite article which refers to the following relative clause.[20] Along with sexual sins and evil desires, "covetousness" (πλεονεξία) is characterized as an especially gross sin.[21] Again and again in the NT this forceful warning—also in catalog-like enumerations (cf. Mk 7:22; Rom 1:29; Eph 5:3)—is issued: "beware of all covetousness" (φυλάσσεσθε ἀπὸ πάσης πλεονεξίας Lk 12:15). Covetousness and greed seize the heart of man, lead it away from God, and imprison it in idolatry: "The love of money

8 Cf. Burton Scott Easton, "New Testament Ethical Lists," *JBL* 51 (1932): 1–12; Anton Vögtle, *Die Tugend- und Lasterkataloge im Neuen Testament: Exegetisch, religions- und formgeschichtlich untersucht*, NTAbh 16, 4.5 (Münster i.W.: 1936); Siegfried Wibbing, *Die Tugend- und Lasterkataloge im Neuen Testament und ihre Traditionsgeschichte unter besonderer Berücksichtigung der Qumran-Texte*, BZNW 25 (Berlin: 1959). Rich comparative material for the NT catalogs of vices is also available in the writings of Lucian of Samosata. Cf. Betz, *Lukian*, 185–94. When treating Col 3:5, Wibbing, *Tugend- und Lasterkataloge*, 112f refers to CD IV, 17–19: "fornication" (הזנות = πορνεία); "covetousness" (ההון = πλεονεξία); "impurity" (טמא [המקדש] = ἀκαθαρσία); "idolatry" (הלכו אחרי צו = εἰδωλολατρία). The context accentuates sexual sins, covetousness and idolatry. CD IV, 17–19, however, has neither a fivefold schema nor an exact correspondence with Col 3:5—"passion" (πάθος) is absent. Cf. also Braun, *Qumran* 1, p. 232.

9 Jewish polemic argued: the pagans are idolaters and therefore entangled in every vice (cf. Wisd Sol 13–14). Easton, "Ethical Lists," has highlighted the presuppositions of the Hellenistic-Jewish apologetics which are visible in the NT catalogs of vices and virtues.

10 Cf. 1 Thess 4:3; Gal 5:19–21; 1 Cor 5:10f; 6:9f; 2 Cor 12:21; Eph 5:3; 1 Tim 1:9f.

11 Cf. Vögtle, *Tugend- und Lasterkataloge*, 223–25; Friedrich Hauck and Siegfried Schulz, *TDNT* 6, 593f.

12 The Jews considered the Gentiles unclean. And in the Jewish point of view the Gentiles' immorality stemmed from this uncleanness. The Jew proudly referred to the sexual purity which was preserved in Judaism. Cf. the evidence in Billerbeck 3, pp. 62–74.

13 Cf. 1 Thess 4:7; Gal 5:19; 2 Cor 12:21; Rom 1:24; Eph 5:3, 5. Also cf. Friedrich Hauck, *TDNT* 3, 427–29.

14 P. Joüon, "Note sur Colossiens III, 5–11," *Recherches de Science Religieuse* 26 (1936): 185–89 has called special attention to the points of contact that exist between Col 3:5–11 and Gal 5:19–21.

15 Cf. Vögtle, *Tugend- und Lasterkataloge*, 208–10; Wilhelm Michaelis, *TDNT* 5, 926–30.

16 This is the Jewish use of this word. Cf. Ps-Phocylides 194: "For Eros is not God, and passion is destructive of absolutely everything" (οὐ γὰρ ἔρως θεός ἐστι, πάθος δ᾽ ἀΐδηλον ἁπάντων [Trans.]).

17 The noun "desire" (ἐπιθυμία) can also be used occasionally in a positive sense, e.g., Lk 22:15; 1 Thess 2:17; Phil 1:23. Likewise, the verb "to desire" (ἐπιθυμεῖν) can be used in a positive sense, e.g., Mt 13:17; Lk 17:22; 1 Tim 3:1; Heb 6:11; 1 Pt 1:12. Cf. Friedrich Büchsel, *TDNT* 3, 168–71.

leads to idolatry; because, when led astray through money, men name as gods those who are not gods" (ἡ φιλαργυρία πρὸς εἴδωλα ὁδηγεῖ, ὅτι ἐν πλάνῃ δι' ἀργυρίου τοὺς μὴ ὄντας θεοὺς ὀνομάζουσι TestJudah 19:1).[22] The critical judgment, leveled against "covetousness" already in Jewish exhortation,[23] is evident also in the short relative clause, which refers to what "covetousness" invariably brings in its train: "which is idolatry" (ἥτις ἐστιν ἡ εἰδωλολατρία). Man can only serve one lord—God or Mammon (Mt 6:24 par; Lk 16:13).[24] If he sets his heart on wealth, he adores false gods and abandons the one true God. Therefore a "covetous person" (πλεονέκτης) is an "idolater" (εἰδωλολάτρης Eph 5:5). Although there is no further mention of opposition to pagan vices in the context of Col, the traditional warning against "idolatry" (εἰδωλολατρία) is firmly maintained.[25] Sexual aberrations and evil will may estrange man from God and drive him to the worship of false gods. But the danger of "covetousness" is stressed very emphatically because it is so closely bound up with "idolatry."[26]

■ 6 God will punish all that[27] and deliver the judgment it deserves. At the conclusion of a catalog of vices reference is frequently made to the future judgment.[28] This is also the case here in the reminder that God's wrath is coming because of the evil deeds of men. The concept "wrath" (ὀργή) does not indicate an emotion of God—in view of the many abominable deeds of men, fits of wrath should have seized him long ago! Rather ὀργή is God's judgment of wrath (cf. 1 Thess 1:10; 2:16),[29] which befalls all sinful and evil actions of men and summons both Jews and Gentiles before its court (Rom 1:18–3:20).[30]

18 The adjective "evil" (κακήν) is absent in manuscripts p[46] G.

19 Cf. also Gal 5:24; Rom 1:24; 6:12; 7:7f; 13:14. The words "passion" and "desire" also occur together in 1 Thess 4:5: "not in the passion of desire like heathen who do not know God" (μὴ ἐν πάθει ἐπιθυμίας καθάπερ καὶ τὰ ἔθνη τὰ μὴ εἰδότα τὸν θεόν).

20 Cf. Blass–Debrunner, par. 258, 1: "The addition of the relative clause "which . . ." (ἥτις . . .) occasions the use of the article by making the preceding noun definite."

21 Cf. Gerhard Delling, *TDNT* 6, 266–74.

22 Cf. the negative evaluation placed on "possessions, wealth" (הון) in the writings of the Qumran community. The godless, the Kittim and the evil priest, strive after "possessions, wealth" (הון) with violence and deceit (1 QpHab VI, 1; VIII, 11f; IX, 5f; 1QS X, 19: XI, 2, etc.). The members of the community, however, renounce their own property and contribute their goods to the "common fund" (הון) which is used for the entire community (1QS I, 12f; III, 2; V, 2f; VI, 17–19, 22, etc.).

23 Cf. also the sharp censure of covetousness found in Philo, *Spec. leg.* 1, 23–27; further examples from the writings of Philo can be found in Gerhard Delling, *TDNT* 6, 270.

24 Direct dependence on a saying of Jesus, as proposed among others by Delling, *TDNT* 6, 271, can hardly be assumed. The critique of "covetousness" is based on a value judgment common to Judaism and primitive Christianity. Cf. the evidence in Billerbeck 2, p. 190; 3, p. 606f.

25 Easton, "Ethical Lists," p. 6, maintains that the catalog originally consisted of six members; "idolatry" was the sixth. Since the Colossians, however, did not have to be admonished with respect to idolatry, Paul mentioned idolatry only in a relative clause. The proposal, however, that the list was originally made up of six members is improbable (cf. above p. 137 on the fivefold schema). Yet it is certain that the train of thought explicated in the relative clause ("covetousness" and "idolatry" are intimately connected) was adopted from the tradition.

26 Cf. also Pol. *Phil.* 11:2: "If any man does not abstain from avarice, he will be defiled by idolatry and shall be judged as if he were among the Gentiles who 'know not the judgment of God' " (Si quis non se abstinuerit ab avaritia, ab idolatria coinquinabitur et tamquam inter gentes judicabitur, qui ignorant judicium domini). The term "idolatry" frequently occurs in catalogs of vices. Cf. Gal 5:20; 1 Cor 5:10f; 6:9; 10:7, 14; Eph 5:5; 1 Pt 4:3; Rev 21:8; 22:15 and consult Friedrich Büchsel, *TDNT* 2, 380.

27 The prepositional phrase "on account of that" (δι' ἅ) refers to the vices listed in v 5. The variant reading of D* G, "on account of this" (δι' ὅ), is clearly secondary.

28 Cf. 1 Thess 4:3–6; 1 Cor 5:10f; 6:9; Rom 1:18–32.

29 Cf. Gustav Stählin, *TDNT* 5, 419–47.

30 In dependence on Eph 5:6 the manuscripts 𝔊 𝔎 G pl lat sy add: "upon the sons of disobedience" (ἐπὶ τοὺς υἱοὺς τῆς ἀπειθείας). Nevertheless, the "shorter reading," attested to by p[46] B d sa ClemAlex Ephr Ambst, certainly offers the original text.

■ **7** The believers also once lived in such vices.[31] The words "and you" (*καὶ ὑμεῖς*) apply the traditional list of vices to the readers[32] and recall their pre–Christian past. They conducted their lives[33] in evil actions, lived in shameful doings[34] and were dead in their sins (cf. 2:13; Eph 2:1f). Nevertheless, what once was is now definitively erased and removed by the death which was experienced with Christ in baptism. Therefore, the past is replaced by the present which from now on has sole validity.

■ **8** Consequently, what the Christian life must be now is contrasted to what it once was (cf. 1:21f)[35]: to put aside everything which once was done in the evil will and wicked action of the old man.[36] The imperative "put away" (*ἀπόθεσθε*) corresponds to Pauline baptismal exhortation: "let us therefore put away the works of darkness" (*ἀποθώμεθα οὖν τὰ ἔργα τοῦ σκότους* Rom 13:12; cf. Eph 4:22; 1 Pt 2:1).

The vices that have to be put away are again listed in a five–member catalog which originated in the tradition. The readers are once more addressed by "and you" (*καὶ ὑμεῖς*) and shown what they have to do now in contrast to their past. The sins that should be put off have to do with angry passion, evil mind, and slander which poison and destroy the relationships between men. Whoever is angry with his brother "shall be liable to judgment" (*ἔνοχος ἔσται τῇ κρίσει* Mt 5:22).[37] Therefore, "wrath" (*ὀργή*) must be done away with.[38] Together with wrath, vehement rage, "anger" (*θυμός*), should disappear (cf. Eph 4:31). There is no material difference between "wrath" and "vehement rage, anger."[39] A rage of anger belongs to the "works of the flesh" (*ἔργα τῆς σαρκός* Gal 5:19f), which must be found no more in the community of Jesus Christ (2 Cor 12:20). Along with them every type of "malice" must vanish, since it ruins social intercourse.[40] A wicked disposition expresses itself in evil speech. The word *βλασφημία*, which often occurs in catalogs of vices, means "slander," the conscious telling of falsehood.[41] Under no circumstances must the Christian do this. Therefore, the command states: "not to tell lies about anybody" (*μηδένα βλασφημεῖν* Tit 3:2). Consequently, *αἰσχρολογία*,[42] every kind of abusive language from man's mouth, is also forbidden.[43] Since what was once had to yield in baptism to the now of Christian existence, this prior decision should and must be made reality in obedience. Consequently: also you must put away all these things!

■ **9** "Do not lie[44] to one another" (*μὴ ψεύδεσθε εἰς ἀλλήλους*) continues the series of imperatives and is connected most immediately with the previously mentioned concepts "slander" and "abusive language." Within the Christian community, truth alone is allowed to speak.[45] The phrase "to one another" (*εἰς ἀλλήλους*)

---

31 The prepositional phrase "in which" (*ἐν οἷς*) is used of the vices mentioned in v 5. If, however, one reads "upon the sons of disobedience" (*ἐπὶ τοὺς υἱοὺς τῆς ἀπειθείας*) at the end of v 6, then *ἐν οἷς* (among them) would refer to the "sons of disobedience."

32 Cf. Vögtle, *Tugend– und Lasterkataloge*, 19; Jervell, *Imago Dei*, 235.

33 Concerning "to conduct oneself" (*περιπατεῖν* = הלך) cf. above p. 27 on 1:10.

34 Allusion is again made to the vices by "in these things" (*ἐν τούτοις*). Manuscripts 𝔎 G pm read: "in them" (*ἐν αὐτοῖς*).

35 In Greek vss 7, 8a are arranged in chiastic order: (a) *ἐν οἷς* (b) *καὶ ὑμεῖς* (c) *περιεπατήσατέ* (d) *ποτε.* (d) *νυνὶ δέ* (c) *ἀπόθεσθε* (b) *καὶ ὑμεῖς* (a) *τὰ πάντα* [(a) in which (b) you also (c) conducted your lives (d) once. (d) but now (c) put off (b) you also (a) all these]. Cf. P. Tachau, *'Einst' und 'Jetzt' im Neuen Testament*, Unpub. Diss. (Göttingen: 1968), 126.

36 Heb 12:1; Jas 1:21; 1 Pt 2:1 also link the verb "to put away, off" (*ἀποτίθεσθαι*) with "all" (*πᾶς/πᾶν*). Cf. E. Kamlah, *Die Form der katalogischen Paränese im Neuen Testament*, WUNT 7 (Tübingen: 1964), 183: "The object of the putting off is always designated as a totality. It is the entire sinful nature that is thus described."

37 The vice "wrath" (*ὀργή*) corresponds to קצור אפים in the catalog of vices in 1 QS IV, 10. Cf. Wibbing, *Tugend– und Lasterkataloge*, 94.

38 On the negative appraisal of human wrath in the NT cf. Stählin, *TDNT* 5, 420f.

39 Cf. Friedrich Büchsel, *TDNT* 3, 167f.

40 Cf. 1 Cor 5:8; 14:20; Rom 1:29; Eph 4:31. Cf. further Walther Grundmann, *TDNT* 3, 482–84. The word "malice" (*κακία*) corresponds to רוע in the catalog of vices in 1 QS IV, 11. Cf. Wibbing, *Tugend– und Lasterkataloge*, 94.

41 Cf. Mk 7:22 par; Eph 4:31; 1 Tim 6:4; 2 Tim 3:2. Cf. further Hermann Wolfgang Beyer *TDNT* 1, 621–25. On "slander" (*βλασφημία*) compare the Hebrew לשון גדופים of 1 QS IV, 11; CD V, 12. Cf. Wibbing, *Tugend– und Lasterkataloge*, 93.

42 This word only occurs here in the NT. Cf. Bauer, *s.v.* Its meaning is spelled out in the catalog of sins of

should in no way be taken to mean that Christians could take the question of truth less seriously when speaking to non-Christians. Rather the author is concerned primarily with the immediate life situation in which the Christian exists and must prove himself. Here, in daily contact with the brothers, he must live up to the command of unconditional veracity.

The verb forms "put off" (**ἀπεκδυσάμενοι**) and "put on" (**ἐνδυσάμενοι**) emphatically stress the relationship to baptism.[46] Since both participles are aorists, they could describe the past event of baptism, which should be determinative of the present; thus they would be construed as genuine participles.[47] Nevertheless, it is far more plausible to understand these verb forms as imperatives continuing a sequence of admonitions. The imperative "do not lie" (*μὴ ψεύδεσθε*) precedes them (v 9) and the command "put on" (**ἐνδύσασθε** v 12) follows.[48] The parallel Eph 4:24 clearly supports translating them as imperatives: "put on[49] the new man, created after the likeness of God" (**ἐνδύσασθαι τὸν καινὸν ἄνθρωπον τὸν κατὰ θεὸν κτισθέντα**), which agrees with the use of "to put on" (**ἐνδύεσθαι**) in the context of baptismal exhortation: "put on the Lord Jesus" (**ἐνδύσασθε τὸν κύριον Ἰησοῦν** Rom 13:14); "let us put on the armor of light" (**ἐνδυσώμεθα δὲ τὰ ὅπλα τοῦ φωτός** Rom 13:12).[50] The doubly composite verb "to put off" (**ἀπεκδύεσθαι**) occurs only in Col (cf. 2:15) where it recalls the phrase "putting off the body of the flesh" (**ἀπέκδυσις τοῦ σώματος τῆς σαρκός** 2:11).[51] In other instances the verb **ἀποτίθεσθαι** ("to take off") which is put in contrast with "to put on" (**ἐνδύεσθαι**) appears more frequently in exhortatory contexts.[52]

The image of putting off and putting on a garment was widespread in the ancient world and was used in the mystery religions in order to interpret the action of initiation. The account, e.g., that Apuleius gives in the *Metamorphoses* of Isis' rites describes how the initiate was clothed in twelve robes during the initiation ceremony and received a garment adorned with images of animals.[53] The putting on of the garment consecrated him, i.e. he was filled with the powers of the cosmos and experienced within himself a physical–substantial transformation by which he received a share of the divine power of life.[54] Gnostic texts understand the image of putting on or receiving the garment as expressing that the redemption had come true, a redemption which is accomplished while man is taken up into the divine world and suffused with its light and power.[55] When Paul employs the image of putting off and putting on, he describes neither an ontological transformation of man nor the release of a divine kernel so as to allow it to develop fully and to let man possess salvation. Rather, the image illustrates the change of rule that has taken place in baptism. The baptized have been transferred into the domain of Christ's rule and

the tongue which Jas 3:1–12 lists.

43 Manuscripts G aeg Ambst add the words: "let not proceed" (*μὴ ἐκπορευέσθω*).

44 Manuscript p^{46} places the subjunctive (*ψεύδησθε*) after "not" (*μή*). Cf. Blass–Debrunner, par. 364, 3.

45 God cannot lie (cf. Heb 6:18). Therefore, the Christian too must not lie (cf. Gal 1:20; 2 Cor 11:31; Rom 9:1; 1 Tim 2:7, etc.)

46 On 3:9–11 special reference should be made to Käsemann, *Leib Christi*, 147–50; Eltester, *Eikon im NT*, 156–64; Jervell, *Imago Dei*, 231–56.

47 This is the opinion of Abbott, Masson, *ad loc.*; Christian Maurer, *TDNT* 6, 644 n. 5; Jervell, *Imago Dei*, 236; Otto Merk, *Handeln aus Glauben: Die Motivierungen der paulinischen Ethik*, Marburger Theologische Studien 5 (Marburg: 1968), 205. Joüon, "Colossiens III, 5–11," 186f, takes "put off" (**ἀπεκδυσάμενοι**) and "put on" (**ἐνδυσάμενοι**) as dependent on the imperative "put away" (**ἀπόθεσθε** v 8), so that they actually have a present meaning. Putting off and putting on is an act that lasts throughout one's life.

48 On the use of the participle in an imperatival sense, cf. above p. 32, n. 1 on 1:12. Cf. further the explanation in Lightfoot, *ad loc.*, and Larsson, *Christus*, 197f, who, however, wants to construe the participles as subjunctive–participles.

49 Whether one reads the infinitive or the imperative (**ἐνδύσασθε**) which is found in p^{46} B* ℵ K 69 al lat sy ClemAlex^{pt}.

50 Cf. further 1 Thess 5:8: "put on the breastplate of faith and love" (**ἐνδυσάμενοι θώρακα πίστεως καὶ ἀγάπης**); Eph 6:11: "put on the whole armor of God" (**ἐνδύσασθε τὴν πανοπλίαν τοῦ θεοῦ**); Eph 6:14: "having put on the breastplate of righteousness" (**ἐνδυσάμενοι τὸν θώρακα τῆς δικαιοσύνης**).

51 Eph 4:22 has: "Put off the old man" (**ἀποθέσθαι ὑμᾶς . . . τὸν παλαιὸν ἄνθρωπον**).

52 Cf. 1 Thess 5:8; Gal 3:27; Rom 13:12, 14; Eph 4:24; 6:11, 14.

53 Cf. Lohse, "Taufe," 316f.

54 Apuleius, *Metamorph.* 11, 24.

55 The evidence can be found in Käsemann, *Leib Christi*, 87–94; Eltester, *Eikon im NT*, 160; Albrecht Oepke, *Der Brief des Paulus an die Galater* in Theologischer Handkommentar zum NT 9 (Berlin: ^{2}1957), 89f; *idem*, *TDNT* 2, 318–21; Schlier, *Galater*, 173f. Gnos-

are called to conduct their lives in obedience. Therefore, they need words of exhortatory encouragement and of comforting support on their way. Consequently, to the statement "for as many of you as were baptized into Christ have put on Christ" (ὅσοι γὰρ εἰς Χριστὸν ἐβαπτίσθητε, Χριστὸν ἐνεδύσασθε Gal 3:27) the admonition must be added: "but put on the Lord Jesus Christ" (ἀλλὰ ἐνδύσασθε τὸν κύριον Ἰησοῦν Χριστόν Rom 13:14). This admonition demands of the Christian that he actualize what has already happened, that he accept what God has done for him, and that, in obedience, he enter into the new life given him in baptism.[56]

What must be put aside is the old man, who—and here the image almost breaks down—not only adheres to man like a garment, but who is man himself. He must hand himself over to death because "our old self has been crucified" (ὁ παλαιὸς ἡμῶν ἄνθρωπος συνεσταυρώθη Rom 6:6).[57] Since he has already died, he must now be laid to rest[58] "with his practices"[59] (σὺν ταῖς πράξεσιν αὐτοῦ), with his manner of conduct and action (cf. Rom 8:13) as it had been described in the catalog of vices.

■ **10** The "new man" (νέος ἄνθρωπος) must be put on in place of the old man.[60] The Greek word **νέος** (new), here in contrast to **παλαιός** (old), means the same thing as the Greek word **καινός** (new).[61] If anyone is "in Christ" (ἐν Χριστῷ), he is a "new creation" (καινὴ κτίσις Gal 6:15; 2 Cor 5:17). God's eschatological new creation is described here with reference to Gen 1:26f. To be sure, this reference does not consist of an explicit Scripture citation, but originated in the adopted catechetical tradition which in turn relied on Gen 1:26f.[62] Col does not speak of putting on Christ like Gal 3:27 and Rom 13:14. Rather it exhorts to put on the "new man," who is formed according to the Creator's "image" (εἰκών)[63] which, in fact, is Christ (cf. 1:15), and who must be renewed "in knowledge" (εἰς ἐπίγνωσιν). The new creation accomplished in baptism is thus realized in constant "renewal" (ἀνακαίνωσις): "our inner [*scil.* man] is being renewed daily" (ὁ ἔσω ἡμῶν [*scil.* ἄνθρωπος] ἀνακαινοῦται ἡμέρᾳ καὶ ἡμέρᾳ 2 Cor 4:16).[64] The new man is being created "according to the image of his creator" (κατ' εἰκόνα τοῦ κτίσαντος αὐτόν).[65] While Rom 8:29 talks about a future fulfillment: "those whom he foreknew he also predestined to be conformed to the image of his Son" (οὓς προέγνω, καὶ προώρισεν

ticism, however, cannot speak of the putting off of the old man and the putting on of the new man. For it deals with the release of the Pneuma–Ego, which must be awakened from prison and sleep and brought to its realization.

56 Cf. Bornkamm, "Baptism and New Life," *Early Christian Experience*, 71–86.

57 On Paul's use of the concept "old" (παλαιός) cf. Heinrich Seesemann, *TDNT* 5, 719f.

58 Cf. 1 Cor 5:7: Since the eschatological feast of passover has already begun with Christ's expiatory death, it is high time to cleanse out "the old leaven" (τὴν παλαιὰν ζύμην).

59 On the term "practice" (πρᾶξις) cf. Christian Maurer, *TDNT* 6, 642–44.

60 It is important "to be able to state that no parallel to this unique concept has been found in non-Christian sources" (Jervell, *Imago Dei*, 240). The image cannot be derived from Gnosticism (cf. Käsemann, *Leib Christi*, 147f). For in Gnostic texts "there is no idea of, nor can there be any idea of an old and a new man. For the inner man, the Spirit–Image (Pneuma–Eikon) in man, is the Anthropos himself" (Jervell, *Imago Dei*, 241). Judaism knew of the expectation that at the end of days splendor and glory, which had been lost through Adam's fall, would be restored (evidence in Billerbeck 1, p. 11), but it did not know the antithesis between the old and the new man. Cf. also Robin Scroggs, *The Last Adam: A Study in Pauline Anthropology* (Philadelphia: Fortress Press, 1966), 29–32; 54–58. Kamlah, *Form*, 204 refers to Philo's treatment of the ideal and the earthly man. This concept, however, is surely not a possible direct source for the Pauline contrast between the old and new man, mainly because in Philo there is not the least trace of an eschatological referent. Cf. also Merk, *Handeln*, 206.

61 Cf. Eph 4:24: "put on the new man" (ἐνδύσασθαι τὸν καινὸν ἄνθρωπον). When Col 3:10 has νέος (new) instead of καινός (new), the reason is probably stylistic, for the participle τὸν ἀνακαινούμενον (being renewed) follows immediately. Cf. also 1 Cor 5:7 where "new lump" (νέον φύραμα) is set over against the "old leaven" (παλαιὰ ζύμη). On the concept "new man" (νέος ἄνθρωπος) cf. Joachim Jeremias, *TDNT* 1, 365f; Johannes Behm, *TDNT* 4, 898–901; Roy A. Harrisville, "The Concept of Newness in the New Testament," *JBL* 74 (1955): 69–79.

62 Cf. Jervell, *Imago Dei*, 232.

63 Concerning the concept "image" (εἰκών) cf. above pp. 46–48 on 1:15.

64 It is not the old man or primeval man that is being renewed, but the new man created in baptism.

συμμόρφους εἶναι τῆς εἰκόνος τοῦ υἱοῦ αὐτοῦ); here, conformity to the image is described as something that is already present reality. Nevertheless, this image of God has not been given as a secure piece of property to the person baptized into Christ. Rather it places him under the imperative to prove in his conduct his confession of Christ as the "image of God" (*εἰκὼν τοῦ θεοῦ*).[66] The participle "being renewed" (*τὸν ἀνακαινούμενον*) lays stress on the exhortation. Just as the old man together with his practices has to be removed, so too must the new man be renewed in fulfillment of the duty of obedience laid upon him. The "knowledge" (*ἐπίγνωσις*)[67] which the new man has attained means the ability to recognize God's will and command (cf. 1:9).[68] The old man did not possess this knowledge.[69] The new man, however, should conduct his life in conformity to the creator's will.

■ 11 What separates men from one another in the world—which of course still exists—has been abolished in the community of Jesus Christ. Among those who belong to Christ "there is neither Jew nor Greek; there is neither slave nor free, there is neither male nor female; for you are all one in Jesus Christ" (*οὐκ ἔνι Ἰουδαῖος οὐδὲ Ἕλλην, οὐκ ἔνι δοῦλος οὐδὲ ἐλεύθερος, οὐκ ἔνι ἄρσεν καὶ θῆλυ· πάντες γὰρ ὑμεῖς εἷς ἐστε ἐν Χριστῷ Ἰησοῦ* Gal 3:28). For "we were all baptized into one body—Jews or Greeks, slaves or free" (*ἡμεῖς πάντες εἰς ἓν σῶμα ἐβαπτίσθημεν, εἴτε Ἰουδαῖοι εἴτε Ἕλληνες, εἴτε δοῦλοι εἴτε ἐλεύθεροι* 1 Cor 12:13). Also the series introduced here deals with the unity in Christ which is grounded in baptism. That Greeks and Jews are the first ones mentioned in this series corresponds to tradition,[70] even though, in distinction to Gal 3:28 and 1 Cor 12:13, "Greek" (*Ἕλλην*) comes first.[71] The Jew knew that as a member of the chosen people of God he was separated from the Gentiles, whose outstanding representatives were the Greeks. The Gospel, however, is addressed to all, "to the Jew first and also to the Greek"

Jervell, *Imago Dei*, 244f, correctly rejects Käsemann's interpretation: "The sense of 'renewal' becomes clear when one realizes that the image (eikon) is indeed the fallen primeval man. In so far as the primeval man is at the same time redeemer, he is renewed to become the true image (eikon) of God and now has knowledge of God and of himself as 'inner man,' who is likewise the Christ who fills all in all" (Käsemann, *Leib Christi*, 148). Neither grammatically nor materially can the participle "being renewed" (*ἀνακαινούμενον*) be connected with "the old man" (*τὸν παλαιὸν ἄνθρωπον*). Cf. Jervell, *Imago Dei*, 244, n. 254.

65 The description of God—for God, not Christ, is meant (cf. Jervell, *Imago Dei*, 249; Larsson, *Christus*, 205f)—as "the creator" (*ὁ κτίσας*) corresponds to a traditional way of speaking (1 Cor 11:9; Rom 1:25; Eph 2:10; 3:9; 1 Tim 4:3, etc.). Cf. Gerhard Delling, "Partizipiale Gottesprädikationen in den Briefen des Neuen Testaments," *ST* 17 (1963): 25. The reference here, however, is not to the first creation (thus Werner Georg Kümmel, *Man in the New Testament* tr. John J. Vincent [Philadelphia: Westminster, rev. and enlarged ed.: 1963], 67f, n. 78; Merk, *Handeln*, 207), but to the creation of the new man.

66 Cf. Jervell, *Imago Dei*, 248–50; Johannes Behm, *TDNT* 3, 453: "The Christian is to become a new man as Christ is the new man."

67 The phrase "in knowledge" (*εἰς ἐπίγνωσιν*) occurs here in an absolute sense as in Phil 1:9: "That your love may abound more and more with knowledge and all discernment" (*ἵνα ἡ ἀγάπη ὑμῶν ἔτι μᾶλλον καὶ μᾶλλον περισσεύῃ ἐν ἐπιγνώσει καὶ πάσῃ αἰσθήσει*).

68 The "knowledge" can neither be defined as "morality" (Dibelius-Greeven, *ad loc.*) nor be identified with "conformity to the image." Rather, as a consequence of both (cf. Jervell, *Imago Dei*, 255f), it is "knowledge of his will" (*ἐπίγνωσις τοῦ θελήματος αὐτοῦ* 1:9). Eltester, *Eikon*, 162 correctly observes that the connection between conformity to the image and ethics is best understood on the basis of Jewish presuppositions.

69 Cf. Eph 4:17f; "You must no longer live as the Gentiles do, in the futility of their minds; they are darkened in their understanding, alienated from the life of God because of the ignorance that is in them" (*μηκέτι ὑμᾶς περιπατεῖν καθὼς καὶ τὰ ἔθνη περιπατεῖ ἐν ματαιότητι τοῦ νοὸς αὐτῶν, ἐσκοτισμένοι τῇ διανοίᾳ ὄντες ἀπηλλοτριωμένοι τῆς ζωῆς τοῦ θεοῦ, διὰ τὴν ἄγνοιαν τὴν οὖσαν ἐν αὐτοῖς*).

70 Except for this verse the distinction between Greeks and Jews is of no concern to Col. On "circumcision/uncircumcision" (*περιτομή/ἀκροβυστία*) cf. 2:11, 13. The mention of barbarians and Scythians likewise has no connection with the train of thought developed in the letter. On "slave/free" (*δοῦλος/ἐλεύθερος*) compare the admonition directed to the slaves in 3:22–25. The series undoubtedly has been adopted from the tradition. Cf. also Günther Klein, *Die Zwölf Apostel: Ursprung und Gehalt einer Idee*, FRLANT 77 (Göttingen: 1961), 195.

71 The recipients of the letter are, as is also indicated here (cf. 1:21f; 2:13), Gentile Christians.

(Ἰουδαίῳ τε πρῶτον καὶ Ἕλληνι Rom 1:16).[72] For in Christ there is no longer any validity either to the boundaries between different nations or to the distinction between Israel and the Gentiles.[73] Consequently, even "circumcision" (περιτομή) and "uncircumcision" (ἀκροβυστία) have lost their meaning;[74] "for neither circumcision counts for anything, nor uncircumcision, but a new creation" (οὔτε γὰρ περιτομή τί ἐστιν οὔτε ἀκροβυστία, ἀλλὰ καινὴ κτίσις Gal 6:15).[75] The words "barbarian" (βάρβαρος) and "Scythian" (Σκύθης), which follow in the series, are no longer juxtaposed to one another antithetically but are an enumerative continuation of the series. The "barbarian" (βάρβαρος) is the non–Greek.[76] This opposition, however, between Greeks and barbarians has been abolished in the Christian community.[77] The Scythians are cited as an especially strange kind of barbarian. It was said of them: "they are little better than wild beasts" (βραχὺ τῶν θηρίων διαφέροντες Josephus, *Ap.* 2, 269).[78] Besides overcoming the differences that distinguish men from one another in the world, the Christian community has also cut through distinctions of social position. Whether slave or[79] free—this is emphasized with great force—the only thing that matters in the Christian community is the "new creation" in Christ. "For he who was called in the Lord as a slave is a freedman of the Lord. Likewise he who was free when called is a slave of Christ" (ὁ γὰρ ἐν κυρίῳ κληθεὶς δοῦλος ἀπελεύθερος κυρίου ἐστίν· ὁμοίως ὁ ἐλεύθερος κληθεὶς δοῦλός ἐστιν Χριστοῦ 1 Cor 7:22).[80] The author is not talking about the natural equality of all men[81] nor about a morality that is binding on all men.[82] Rather, he speaks about men of completely diverse origins who have been gathered together in unity in Christ through allegiance to one Lord. True, they also continue to live in the roles that the world assigns to them as Greeks or Jews, slaves or free. But where the Body of Christ exists and where his members are joined together into a fellowship, there the differences which separate

72 Cf. further 1 Cor 1:22–24; 10:32; Rom 2:9f; 3:9; 10–12; Acts 14:1; 18:4; 19:10, 17; 20:21. Manuscripts D* G it vg[s] put "male and female" (ἄρσεν καὶ θῆλυ cf. Gal 3:28) at the beginning of the series.

73 On the concept "Greek" (Ἕλλην) in Paul, cf. Hans Windisch, *TDNT* 2, 512–16; on the concept "Jew" (Ἰουδαῖος) in Paul, cf. Walter Gutbrod, *TDNT* 3, 380–82.

74 On "uncircumcision" (ἀκροβυστία) cf. Karl Ludwig Schmidt, *TDNT* 1, 225f; on "circumcision" (περιτομή) cf. Rudolf Meyer, *TDNT* 6, 82f.

75 Cf. further Gal 5:6; 1 Cor 7:19; Rom 2:25–29; 4:9–12. The antithesis "circumcision/uncircumcision" is certainly traditional and in any case is not exploited in the immediate context. Cf. Klein, *Die Zwölf Apostel*, 195; contrary to Jervell, *Imago Dei*, 251: "The author took up the formula, but employed it for his special purposes."

76 Cf. Hans Windisch, *TDNT* 1, 546–53. Theodor Hermann, "Barbar und Skythe. Ein Erklärungsversuch zu Kol 3, 11," *Theologische Blätter* 9 (1930): 106f, cites evidence that the word "Barbaria" (Βαρβαρία) is occasionally used to describe the Somali coast and a part of Ethiopia. Hence the contrast here would be between southern and northern peoples, or even between whites and blacks. It is unlikely, however, that "barbarian," following after "Greek," could indicate a particular nation or race rather than "non–Greek" in general. Cf. Windisch, *TDNT* 1, 552f.

77 Cf. Rom 1:14: "I am under obligation to both Greeks and barbarians" (Ἕλλησίν τε καὶ βαρβάροις . . . ὀφειλέτης εἰμί). The designation "barbarian" also occurs in 1 Cor 14:11; Acts 28:2, 4.

78 The Scythians are not mentioned again in the NT. But consult 2 Macc 4:47; 3 Macc 7:5, and cf. Otto Michel, *TWNT* 7, 448–51. The mention of the name "Scythian" is surely not "motivated by some special situation in Colossae" (thus Michel, *ibid.*, 450). Rather it belongs to the series adopted from the tradition.

79 Manuscripts A D* G pc put "and" (καί) between "slave" (δοῦλος) and "free" (ἐλεύθερος) to accentuate the contrast: cf. "Greek and Jew; circumcision and uncircumcision."

80 Cf. Karl Heinrich Rengstorf, *TDNT* 2, 274–76; Heinrich Schlier, *TDNT* 2, 501.

81 On the Stoic concept of the natural equality of all mankind, cf. Seneca, *Epist.* 31, 11: "The soul . . . upright, good, great . . . may descend into a Roman knight just as well as into a freedman's son or a slave. For what is a Roman knight, or a freedman's son, or a slave? They are mere titles, born of ambition or of wrong." (Animus . . . rectus, bonus, magnus . . . tam in equitem Romanum quam in libertinum quam in servum potest cadere. Quid est eques Romanus aut libertinus aut servus? Nomina ex ambitione aut iniuria nata). In the heavenly city described by Lucian, *Hermotimus* 24, complete equality exists for all its inhabitants: "inferior or superior, noble or common, bond or free, simply did not exist and were not mentioned in the city" (τὸ δὲ χείρων ἢ κρείττων ἢ εὐπατρίδης ἢ ἀγεννὴς ἢ δοῦλος ἢ ἐλεύθερος οὐδὲ ὅλως εἶναι ἢ λέγεσθαι ἐν τῇ πόλει).

men from one another are abolished.

The words "but Christ is all and in all" (ἀλλὰ[83] πάντα καὶ ἐν πᾶσιν Χριστός) contrast the new reality that obtains in Christ with that which divides men in the world. It is not said that the fulness of salvation will be inaugurated only by the future consummation in which God will be everything to everyone (1 Cor 15:28). Rather, the present rule of Christ already inaugurates the fulness of salvation so that Christ is all in all.[84] His rule embraces everything (cf. 1:15–20). Thus the unity of the new humanity is grounded in him, for "all" (πάντες) have been baptized "into one body" (εἰς ἓν σῶμα 1 Cor 12:13) and therefore are "one in Christ Jesus" (εἷς ἐν Χριστῷ Ἰησοῦ Gal 3:28).[85]

The fact that the imperative in Col's exhortation is based on and developed out of the indicative agrees completely with Pauline theology.[86] On the one hand, indicative statements refer to salvation as already appropriated: "you have been raised with Christ" (3:1); "you have died" (3:3); God has created the new man (3:10); in the new creation there is no distinction between "Greek and Jew, circumcision and uncircumcision, barbarian, Scythian, slave, free, but Christ is all and in all" (3:11).[87] Since this is the case, the Christians are admonished to fulfill what God has already accomplished: "seek that which is above" (3:1); "consider that which is above, not that which is on earth" (3:2); "therefore, put to death your earthly members" (3:5); "put away" (3:8); "do not lie to one another" (3:9); "put off the old man . . . and put on the new man" (3:9f); "put on then" (3:12). While the indicative sentences refer back to the passing from death to life already effected in baptism, the imperatival admonitions point ahead, into the actualization of the new life of those who have been raised with Christ. But whereas Paul in Romans says that we have died to sin in baptism "so that we should no longer be enslaved to sin" (τοῦ μηκέτι δουλεύειν ἡμᾶς τῇ ἁμαρτίᾳ Rom 6:6), Col states: "with Christ you have died to the elements of the universe" (ἀπεθάνετε σὺν Χριστῷ ἀπὸ τῶν στοιχείων τοῦ κόσμου 2:20). There is no mention of the enslaving power of "sin" (ἁμαρτία) from whose lordship

Cf. Betz, *Lukian*, 95f.

82 *Seder Eliyyahu Rabba* 10 (ed. Friedmann, Wien: 1902)—to be sure, as late as the tenth century A.D. (cf. Hermann L. Strack, *Introduction to the Talmud and Midrash*, Authorized Translation [Philadelphia: Jewish Publication Society of America, 1931], 227f)—says: "I call heaven and earth to witness that both Gentiles and Israelites, men and women, slave and maidservant can attain possession of the Holy Spirit through ethical conduct." Cf. G. Klein, *Der älteste christliche Katechismus und die jüdische Propaganda–Literatur* (Berlin: 1909), 73; Dibelius–Greeven, *ad loc.*

83 Manuscripts B ℜ D G pl put the article τά (the) before πάντα (all).

84 Cf. 1 Cor 15:28: "that God may be everything to every one" (ἵνα ᾖ ὁ θεὸς πάντα ἐν πᾶσιν); Eph 1:23: "the fulness of him who fills all in all" (τὸ πλήρωμα τοῦ τὰ πάντα ἐν πᾶσιν πληρουμένου). The question whether "in all" (ἐν πᾶσιν) is masculine or neuter is unanswerable. The passage 1:15–20 supports its understanding as neuter. The immediate context, however, could justify construing it as masculine: Christ is in all the people who are "in Christ" —wherever they come from. With this pleonastic expression the author of Col wants to draw attention to the Lordship of Christ which embraces all things. Thus he is not concerned with the distinction between masculine or neuter, people or things. Similar formulae from the Hellenistic world are cited above, pp. 51f on 1:16.

85 Alfred Wikenhauser, *Die Kirche als der mystische Leib Christi nach dem Apostel Paulus*, (Freiburg i.B.: [2]1940), 163, wants to speak of a mystical unity formed by the believers and Christ: "The formula 'Christ is all and in all' (Col 3:11) almost identifies the Christians with Christ. . . . Christ is 'all' (τὰ πάντα) insofar as he as the mystical Christ embraces all the redeemed within himself. And he is 'in all' insofar as he, as their inner man, as the 'essence of God' in them, represents their new life–principle." Despite all the stress on unity in Christ, the difference between the believers and their Lord is strictly maintained. Therefore, the concept of mysticism fails to capture the real message of the passage. Cf. above p. 134, n. 15 on 3:3.

86 Cf. Bornkamm, "Baptism and New Life," *Early Christian Experience*, 71–86. The section 3:5–11 shows contacts with different Pauline baptismal passages; thus, it presupposes Pauline tradition. Sanders, "Literary Dependence," p. 42f, opts for literary dependence on the letters to the Romans, the Corinthians, and the Galatians. Cf. on this p. 182 below.

87 Cf. also 3:13: "forgive one another . . . as the Lord has forgiven you, so you also must forgive" (χαρι-

we have been snatched through baptism.[88] In Romans and 1 Corinthians Paul connects conformity to God's image with the future resurrection (1 Cor 15:49; Rom 8:29). Colossians, on the contrary, says that in baptism the new man has been created "according to the image of his creator" (**κατ' εἰκόνα τοῦ κτίσαντος αὐτόν** 3:10).[89] Resurrection with Christ has already taken place. Life "with Christ" is already present—obviously not as one's very own property, but as God's new creation which must constantly be renewed in order to discern and fulfill obediently God's will. Therefore, to put on the new man means: "Put on, then, as God's chosen ones, holy and beloved, merciful compassion, kindness, humility, meekness, patience" (3:12).

■ **12** The word "then, therefore" (**οὖν**) indicates that the exhortation "put on" (**ἐνδύσασθε**) is seen as a consequence of the preceding series of admonitions, from which it is somewhat set off by means of direct address. The phrase "as God's chosen ones" (**ὡς ἐκλεκτοὶ τοῦ**[90] **θεοῦ**) is not meant as a comparison, as if Christians try to become equals of the heavenly elect.[91] Rather, the community is addressed as the chosen, holy and beloved people of God. Just as Israel had been singled out by God as his possession (Dt 4:37; 7:7; Ps 33:12, etc.) and the Qumran community understood itself to be the assembly of the chosen ones,[92] so too it now is said of the Christian community: "But you are a chosen race, a royal priesthood, a holy nation, God's own people" (**ὑμεῖς δὲ γένος ἐκλεκτόν, βασίλειον ἱεράτευμα, ἔθνος ἅγιον, λαὸς εἰς περιποίησιν** 1 Pt 2:9). The believers, who through baptism belong to the Lord, are "God's elect" (**ἐκλεκτοὶ θεοῦ** Rom 8:33).[93] The parallel concepts "holy" (**ἅγιοι**) and[94] "beloved" (**ἠγαπημένοι**) are added to "elect" (**ἐκλεκτοί**) as attributives.[95] Those who have been sanctified[96] by God are called to "holiness" (**ἁγιασμός** 1 Thess 4:3). They have experienced God's love as his act of election[97] and therefore should deal with other men in terms of "love" (**ἀγάπη**).[98] In vss 5 and 8 above, two lists were quoted, each naming five vices that must disappear with the old man. Now five virtues, which should be put on, are enumerated in a catalog–like series. In this list, the accent is not placed on a certain disposition,[99] but on the action through which the new man reveals his identity. To be sure, were it only out of his own resources, he would be incapable of such actions. He owes his new capabilities to the elec-

---

ζόμενοι ἑαυτοῖς . . . καθὼς καὶ ὁ κύριος ἐχαρίσατο ὑμῖν οὕτως καὶ ὑμεῖς).

88 Moreover, Col makes no mention of the role of the "Spirit" (πνεῦμα) in determining Christian conduct. The term "Spirit" (πνεῦμα) occurs only at 1:8; 2:25; "spiritual" (πνευματικός) only at 1:9; 3:16. There is no reference to "to conduct your life in the Spirit" or "according to the Spirit" (περιπατεῖν ἐν πνεύματι or κατὰ πνεῦμα). This must be contrasted with Gal 5:25: "If we live by the Spirit, let us also walk by the Spirit" (εἰ ζῶμεν πνεύματι, πνεύματι καὶ στοιχῶμεν).

89 Cf. Jervell, *Imago Dei*, 236, n. 232.

90 The article is absent in manuscripts A D* G pc.

91 Thus according to Lohmeyer, *ad loc.*, who wants to refer "elect" (ἐκλεκτοί) to the heavenly "communion of saints" (communio sanctorum) and thus to the "angels" (ἄγγελοι). The word "as" (ὡς), however, does not indicate separation or comparison, but identity.

92 Cf. 1 QpHab X, 13: "God's elect;" V, 4: "his elect;" 1 QH XIV, 15: "your elect;" 4 QpPs 37 II, 5: "the community of his elect."

93 Cf. further Mk 13:20, 22, 27 par; Mt 20:16 *v. l.*; 22:14; Lk 18:7; Rom 16:13; 2 Tim 2:10; Tit 1:1; 1 Pt 1:1 and consult Gottlob Schrenk, *TDNT* 4, 181–92; Delling, "Merkmale der Kirche," 305.

94 The connective "and" (καί) is absent in manuscripts B pc.

95 Cf. Otto Procksch, *TDNT* 1, 107.

96 Concerning the concept "holy" (ἅγιος) cf. above p. 7f on 1:2.

97 In Rom 1:7 "God's beloved" and "called to be saints" (ἀγαπητοῖς θεοῦ, κλητοῖς ἁγίοις) occur next to one another. Cf. further Eph 1:4f: "He *chose* us in him before the foundation of the world, that we should be *holy* and blameless before him. He destined us in love to be his sons through Jesus Christ" (ἐξελέξατο ἡμᾶς ἐν αὐτῷ πρὸ καταβολῆς κόσμου, εἶναι ἡμᾶς ἁγίους καὶ ἀμώμους κατενώπιον αὐτοῦ, ἐν ἀγάπῃ προορίσας ἡμᾶς εἰς υἱοθεσίαν διὰ Ἰησοῦ Χριστοῦ εἰς αὐτόν). The verb form, "having been loved" (ἠγαπημένοι) is found only here and in 1 Thess 1:4; 2 Thess 2:13; Jude 1. In other instances, "beloved" (ἀγαπητοί) always occurs.

98 Cf. Ethelbert Stauffer, *TDNT* 1, 49.

99 The proper mind–set or disposition, which is creditable in itself and apart from any concrete realization in action, is stressed in similar Stoic catalogues. Cf. Epictetus, *Diss.* 2, 22, 36: "He will be . . . always straightforward to one who is like himself, while to one who is unlike he will be tolerant, gentle, kindly, forgiving, as to one who is ignorant or is making a mistake in things of greatest importance; he will

tion, sanctification, and love which God has imparted to him. All of the five terms that describe the new man's conduct are used in other passages to designate acts of God or of Christ.[100] In Rom 12:1 and 2 Cor 1:3 "mercies" (*οἰκτιρμοί*) describes God's compassion. Rom 2:4; 11:22; Eph 2:7; Tit 3:4 speak of God's "kindness" (*χρηστότης*). Phil 2:8 says: Christ "humbled himself" (*ἐταπείνωσεν ἑαυτόν*). In 2 Cor 10:1 the Apostle refers to the "meekness of Christ" (*πραΰτης τοῦ Χριστοῦ*).[101] In his dealings with men God practices "patience" (*μακροθυμία* Rom 2:4; 9:22, etc.). All these virtues are the fruit of the Spirit. And in putting them on, the renewal comes to light which the new man, created by God, both experiences and realizes.

"Merciful compassion"[102] is mentioned first.[103] The "kindness" (*χρηστότης*) which a man extends to his fellow man is cited second.[104] The virtue "humility"[105] (*ταπεινοφροσύνη*) follows, by which a person looks up to others and in which no one is concerned with his own interests, but each one is concerned with the interests of others (cf. Phil 2:3f). Through "meekness" (*πραΰτης*)[106] a Christian helps his brother to get back on the straight and narrow path (cf. Gal 6:1).[107] "Patience" (*μακροθυμία*)[108] enables one to wait quietly for a long time and to exercise forbearance.[109] All five concepts show how a Christian should deal with his fellow man. He should stop making himself and his interests the center of his life, and should completely put himself at the service of his neighbor who needs his sympathetic readiness and helping hand.

■ **13** The dependent participles "bear with" (*ἀνεχόμενοι*) and "forgive" (*χαριζόμενοι*) continue the series of imperatives,[110] and underline once more the importance of the right action of the Christians. There is no

not be harsh with anybody" (*ἔσται . . . τῷ μὲν ὁμοίῳ παντὶ ἁπλῶς, τοῦ δ' ἀνομοίου ἀνεκτικός, πρᾷος πρὸς αὐτόν, ἥμερος, συγγνωμικὸς ὡς πρὸς ἀγνοοῦντα, ὡς πρὸς διαπίπτοντα περὶ τῶν μεγίστων· οὐδενὶ χαλεπός*). Cynic–Stoic tradition is also adopted in the catalogues of virtues that Lucian of Samosata cites in his writings. Cf. Betz, *Lukian*, 206–11.

100 Cf. Lohmeyer, *ad loc.*; Jervell, *Imago Dei*, 252f; Larsson, *Christus*, 210–20. Merk, *Handeln*, 210, rightly draws attention to the fact that one should "not read the ideas of imitation or of the example of God or Christ for the believers" into the statement of 3:12. Rather, the verse is concerned with the new domain of life opened by God's act, in which the believer should conduct his life.

101 Cf. also Mt 11:29: "I am meek and humble of heart" (*πραΰς εἰμι καὶ ταπεινὸς τῇ καρδίᾳ*).

102 On "compassion" (*οἰκτιρμός*), cf. Rudolf Bultmann, *TDNT* 5, 159–61.

103 Cf. Phil 2:1: "if there is any affection and compassion" (*εἴ τις σπλάγχνα καὶ οἰκτιρμοί*). Helmut Köster, *TWNT* 7, 557, proposes with regard to Col 3:12: "This formulation could scarcely have arisen without literary dependence on the "affection and compassion" (*σπλάγχνα καὶ οἰκτιρμοί*) of Phil 2:1." It is also possible, however, to explain "merciful compassion" (*σπλάγχνα οἰκτιρμοῦ*) as an expression formulated in parallel to "affection of mercy" (*σπλάγχνα ἐλέους* TestZeb 7:3); cf. Köster, *ibid.*, 557, n. 51. The phrase "abundant mercy" (רוב רחמים) in the catalogue of virtues of 1 QS IV, 3 should be compared (cf. Wibbing, *Tugend- und Lasterkataloge*, 105). Cf. the adjective "merciful" (*εὔσπλαγχνος*) in the catalogues of Eph 4:32 and 1 Pt 3:8.

104 Cf. Gal 5:22; 2 Cor 6:6; Eph 2:7. Cf. further Eph 4:32: "be kind to one another" (*γίνεσθε δὲ εἰς ἀλλήλους χρηστοί*). On the concept "kindness" (*χρηστότης*), cf. L. R. Stachowiak, *Chrestotes: Ihre biblisch-theologische Entwicklung und Eigenart*, Studia Friburgensia NF 17 (Freiburg, Switzerland: 1957), esp. 91f, 98–102.

105 Cf. Walter Grundmann, *TWNT* 8, 22–4. On "humility" (*ταπεινοφροσύνη*) and "meekness" (*πραΰτης*), cf. "spirit of lowliness" (רוח ענוה 1 QS IV, 3). The catalogue of virtues in 1 QS IV, 3, however, is not an exact parallel; cf. Wibbing, *Tugend- und Lasterkataloge*, 104. There is not only a difference in the sequence of the virtues, but 1 QS IV, 3 also lacks the image of putting on the new man. "The parallel arises from the fact that the content of late Jewish exhortation is generally the same; the parallel dispenses with the typical" (Braun, *Qumran* 1, p. 233).

106 Cf. Friedrich Hauck and Siegfried Schulz, *TDNT* 6, 645–51.

107 Cf. further Gal 5:23; 1 Cor 4:21; Eph 4:2; 2 Tim 2:25; Tit 3:2.

108 Cf. Johannes Horst, *TDNT* 4, 374–87.

109 Cf. further Gal 5:22; 2 Cor 6:6; Eph 4:2; 2 Tim 3:10; 4:2. Cf. also "forbearance" (ארך אפים 1 QS IV, 3); Wibbing, *Tugend- und Lasterkataloge*, 104.

110 On the imperatival force of the participles, cf. above p. 141 on "put off" (v 9) and "put on" (v 10).

reference to a specific situation in the community.[111] Rather, the admonition expresses something that is universally valid for the community's life together: to bear with[112] one another[113] and to forgive if one has a complaint against another.[114] For as the Lord has forgiven you, so should you also forgive one another. The sentence introduced by "as" (καθώς) takes up a phrase from the community instruction,[115] and refers to the Lord's action which gives the believers basis and direction for their conduct.[116] The Lord is Christ,[117] not God. There is no reference, however, to Jesus' earthly activity during which he sought out the lost and forgave their sins. Rather the Kyrios is the exalted Lord in his dealings with his people.[118] Forgiveness of sins has been conveyed through baptism (2:13). The forgiveness received in baptism gives the community freedom and readiness not to bear and not to foster a grudge against another even though there may be grounds for complaint and grievance.

■ **14** "Love" (ἀγάπη) surpasses everything else that the new man has to put on and to do (cf. 1 Cor 13; Rom 13:8, 10). Therefore,[119] love is called the bond of perfection. The word "bond" (σύνδεσμος) means the fastening together of separate items which are thus brought together into a unity.[120] Consequently, one could interpret love as the perfect bond[121] which joins all the other virtues to form an organic unity.[122] This idea, however, is nowhere found in the context of NT statements about love[123] and it is unlikely that it is intended in this verse.[124] Since the term "perfection" (τελειότης) has

111 The author of Col thus does not have in mind the controversy which had been introduced in the community because of the "philosophy." Chapter 2 shows that the false teaching should be rejected, not patiently endured.

112 Concerning "to bear with" (ἀνέχεσθαι), cf. Heinrich Schlier, *TDNT* 1, 359f.

113 On the interchange of the expressions "one another" (ἀλλήλων) and "each other" (ἑαυτοῖς), cf. Xenophon, *Mem.* 3, 5, 16: "Instead of working with each other for the general good, they are more envious and bitter against one another than against the rest of the world . . . and would rather thus make profit of one another than aid each other" (ἀντὶ μὲν τοῦ συνεργεῖν ἑαυτοῖς τὰ συμφέροντα, ἐπηρεάζουσιν ἀλλήλοις καὶ φθονοῦσιν ἑαυτοῖς μᾶλλον ἢ πρὸς ἄλλοις ἀνθρώποις . . . καὶ προαιροῦνται μᾶλλον οὕτω κερδαίνειν ἀπ' ἀλλήλων ἢ συνωφελοῦντες αὐτούς [Loeb modified]); Lk 23:12: "with one another . . . with each other" (μετ' ἀλλήλων . . . πρὸς αὐτούς). Also consult Blass–Debrunner par. 287.

114 The word "blame, cause for complaint" (μομφή) (cf. Walter Grundmann, *TDNT* 4, 571–74) occurs rarely and only in poetry. Cf. Aristophanes, *Pax* 664: "Listen, spectators, why she blames you so" (ἀκούσαθ' ὑμεῖς ὧν ἕνεκα μομφὴν ἔχει); Euripides, *Or.* 1069: "First, one reproach have I for thee" (ἓν μὲν πρῶτά σοι μομφὴν ἔχω). It is not found in the LXX, and in the NT only in this passage. Instead of it, manuscript D* puts "reason for complaint" (μέμψιν), G has "wrath" (ὀργήν).

115 Cf. Dahl, "Formgeschtl. Beobachtungen," 6f.

116 Cf. Rom 15:7: "Welcome one another, therefore, as Christ has welcomed us" (Διὸ προσλαμβάνεσθε ἀλλήλους, καθὼς καὶ ὁ Χριστὸς προσελάβετο ἡμᾶς). Cf. further Eph 4:32; 5:2, 25, 29.

117 The witnesses C ℜ pl sy ClemAlex are materially correct in clarifying the passage by the addition of "Christ." Witness ℵ* on the contrary, adds "God." Witnesses 33 arm Aug have "God in Christ" (cf. Eph 4:32). Merk, *Handeln*, 211, is of the opinion that one must think not of Christ, but of God. This understanding, however, cannot appeal to 1:10 as its basis, for "Lord" there likewise refers to Christ.

118 Cf. Jervell, *Imago Dei*, 252f.

119 The phrase "(love) which is" (ὅ ἐστιν) is used without reference to the gender of the word explained. On Col's distinctive use of this phrase (cf. 1:24, 27; 2:10, 17), cf. above p. 89 and Blass–Debrunner par. 132, 2. Witnesses ℵ* D* alter the reading to "who" (ὅς); ℜ pl to "that" (ἥτις). Eph 5:5 and Ignatius use the phrase "which is" (ὅ ἐστιν) in a way similar to Col. Cf. Ign. *Rom.* 7:3: "I desire the 'bread of God', which is the flesh of Jesus Christ . . . his blood, which is incorruptible love" (ἄρτον θεοῦ θέλω, ὅ ἐστιν σὰρξ Ἰησοῦ Χριστοῦ . . . τὸ αἷμα αὐτοῦ, ὅ ἐστιν ἀγάπη ἄφθαρτος); Ign. *Tr.* 8:1: "Be renewed in faith, which is the flesh of the Lord, and in love, which is the blood of Jesus Christ" (ἀνακτίσασθε ἑαυτοὺς ἐν πίστει, ὅ ἐστιν σὰρξ τοῦ κυρίου, καὶ ἐν ἀγάπῃ, ὅ ἐστιν αἷμα Ἰησοῦ Χριστοῦ); Ign. *Mag.* 10:2: "Turn to the new leaven, which is Jesus Christ" (μεταβάλεσθε εἰς νέαν ζύμην, ὅ ἐστιν Ἰησοῦς Χριστός); Ign. *Eph.* 17:2: "having received knowledge of God, that is, Jesus Christ" (λαβόντες θεοῦ γνῶσιν, ὅ ἐστιν Ἰησοῦς Χριστός).

120 Cf. above pp. 181f on 2:19 and Gottfried Fitzer, *TWNT* 7, 854–57.

121 Cf. Simplicius, *Commentarius in Epicteti Enchiridion* 30 (in *Theophrasti Characteres* ed. F. Dübner, 1840, 89, 16f): The Pythagoreans regarded "friendship" (φιλία) as the highest of the virtues "and used to say that it was the bond of all the virtues" (καὶ σύνδεσμον αὐτὴν πασῶν τῶν ἀρετῶν ἔλεγον) [Trans.].

the definite article, the genitive is to be understood not as qualitative, but as final. It indicates result or purpose.[125] Thus love is understood as the bond that leads to perfection.[126] It binds together the members of the community who live in the unity of the "body of Christ" (σῶμα Χριστοῦ)[127] and thus produces "perfection" in the community of the one body.[128]

■ 15 The exhortation flows into the prayer for peace which is often voiced in the Pauline letters with the confidence that God will hear the prayer and that the "peace of God, which surpasses all understanding, will keep your hearts and your minds in Christ Jesus" (**εἰρήνη τοῦ θεοῦ ἡ ὑπερέχουσα πάντα νοῦν φρουρήσει τὰς καρδίας ὑμῶν καὶ τὰ νοήματα ὑμῶν ἐν Χριστῷ Ἰησοῦ** Phil 4:7).[129] This peace is here described with the peculiar expression "the peace of Christ" (**ἡ εἰρήνη τοῦ Χριστοῦ**).[130] A few similar phrases can be adduced. For example, the Johannine Christ says to the disciples: "Peace I leave with you, my peace I give to you" (**Εἰρήνην ἀφίημι ὑμῖν, εἰρήνην τὴν ἐμὴν δίδωμι ὑμῖν** Jn 14:27). Eph 2:14 states: "For he is our peace" (**Αὐτὸς γάρ ἐστιν ἡ εἰρήνη ἡμῶν**). He is the "Lord of peace" (**κύριος τῆς εἰρήνης**) who bestows peace on the believers (2 Thess 3:16). His peace should fill those who belong to him. The verb **βραβεύειν** only occurs here in the NT and means "to rule," "to hold sway."[131] The "peace of Christ" should rule in the hearts of the Christians. This does not refer to some inner peace of soul or disposition of the heart. Rather this Hebraized way of speaking singles out the "heart" (**καρδία**) as the innermost part of man,

---

Plato, *Polit.* 310a says of the true idea of the right, the beautiful and the good: "this bond which unites unlike and divergent parts of virtue is more divine" (*τοῦτον θειότερον εἶναι τὸν σύνδεσμον ἀρετῆς μερῶν φύσεως ἀνομοίων καὶ ἐπὶ τὰ ἐναντία φερομένων*).

122 Likewise, in the Iranian system of thought, referred to above p. 137 on 3:5, a sixth virtue which represents the entire self can be added to the five virtues. Cf. Reitzenstein, *Erlösungsmysterium*, 160f.

123 In 1 Cor 13 love is not understood as the embodiment of the charismata or virtues, but as surpassing all of them. In the so-called hymn on love the Apostle depicts the "still more excellent way" (*καθ' ὑπερβολὴν ὁδόν* 1 Cor 12:31).

124 Cf. Gerhard Delling, *TWNT* 8, 79f.

125 Cf. Gunnar Rudberg, "Parallela. 2. Syndesmos (Col 3, 14)," *Coniectanea Neotestamentica* 3 (1939): 19–21; Anton Fridrichsen, "Charité et perfection. Observation sur Col. 3, 14," *Symbolae Osloenses* 19 (1939): 41–45; Percy, *Probleme*, 407; Dibelius–Greeven, *ad loc.*; Blass–Debrunner, par. 163; Henry Chadwick, " 'All things to All Men' (I Cor. IX.22)," *NTS* 1 (1954–55): 273; Moulton–Turner, 212: "the bond producing perfection;" Gerhard Delling, *TWNT* 8, 79f; Larsson, *Christus*, 221.

126 Cf. Plutarch, *Numa* 63e: Numa should "be a bond of goodwill and friendship . . . in . . . her native city and the whole Sabine nation" (*τῇ . . . πατρίδι καὶ παντὶ τῷ Σαβίνων ἔθνει σύνδεσμος εὐνοίας καὶ φιλίας . . . γενέσθαι*). More evidence can be found in Rudberg, "Parallela" and Fridrichsen, "Charité." As a material parallel Dibelius–Greeven, *ad loc.* cite Plutarch, *Aqua an ignis utilior* 7 (p. 957a), where it is said of the Sea: "This element [namely, the Sea], therefore, when our life was savage and unsociable, linked it together and made it complete, redressing defects by mutual assistance and exchange and so bringing about co-operation and friendship" (*ἄγριον οὖν ἡμῶν ὄντα καὶ ἀσύμβολον τὸν βίον τοῦτο τὸ στοιχεῖον* [namely, the Sea] *συνῆψε καὶ τέλειον ἐποίησε, διορθούμενον ταῖς παρ' ἀλλήλων ἐπικουρίαις καὶ ἀντιδόσεσι, κοινωνίαν δ' ἐργαζόμενον καὶ φιλίαν*).

127 The textual variant "of unity" (*τῆς ἑνότητος* D* G it) stresses the idea of oneness. This variant, however, is secondary and slipped into the text transmission from Eph 4:13.

128 Käsemann, *Leib Christi*, 151, holds that "love" is the Aion that unites the virtues. Against this view Dibelius–Greeven, *ad loc.* rightly say: this explanation "cannot be based on the fact that 'love' is still dependent on 'put on' and thus should also be 'put on' just as Christ himself is put on. Surely the same would have to hold for 'compassion, kindness, etc.' Käsemann, however, does not ascribe the same importance to these other virtues."

129 Cf. further 1 Thess 5:23; Gal 6:16; 2 Cor 13:11; Rom 16:20; Phil 4:9; 2 Thess 3:16.

130 The Imperial text assimilates to Phil 4:7: "the peace of God" (*ἡ εἰρήνη τοῦ θεοῦ*).

131 The verb "to rule, to hold sway" (*βραβεύειν*) refers originally to the activity of the referee and is evidenced from the time of Euripides. The LXX uses the word only once in Wisd Sol 10:12 where wisdom is the umpire. Our passage does not say that peace "settles all strifes" (thus Ethelbert Stauffer, *TDNT* 1, 638), but that it rules in the hearts of the believers. In the meaning of "to judge," "to lead," *βραβεύειν* occurs in Philo, *Vit. Mos.* 1, 163: "So having received the authority which they willingly gave him, with God leading and approving" (*'Επειδὴ τοίνυν παρ' ἑκόντων ἔλαβε τὴν ἀρχήν, βραβεύοντος καὶ ἐπινεύοντος τοῦ θεοῦ*) [Loeb modified]. When Philo,

the seat of his emotions, thought, and will.[132] Therefore, the peace of Christ embraces the entire man,[133] so that "peace of Christ" actually describes the sphere in which man as the new man exists. The call, which came to the believers in the word of the Gospel, introduced them into this realm of peace. They live "in one body" (ἐν ἑνὶ[134] σώματι) in the church, which as the body of Christ is the domain of the exalted Lord's present rule (cf. 1:18, 24).[135]

The admonition "and be thankful" (καὶ εὐχάριστοι[136] γίνεσθε.) does not merely mean that men should have a thankful disposition and voice it in prayer to God. Rather the community should give thanks by acknowledging in its praise and glorification[137] that God has freed them from the power of darkness and transferred them into the domain of his beloved Son's rule (1:12f). In the domain of the one "body," that is, in the "church," thanksgiving should sound forth in hymnic praise in which Christ is glorified as the "image of the invisible God" (εἰκὼν τοῦ θεοῦ τοῦ ἀοράτου) and the Lord over everything (1:15–20).[138]

■ **16** Appropriate thanksgiving, which v 15b encourages, occurs in the hearing of and reflection upon the word and in the songs sung by the community to glorify God. Instead of "the word" (ὁ λόγος 4:3), "the word of God" (ὁ λόγος τοῦ θεοῦ 1:25) or "word of the Lord" (λόγος κυρίου 1 Thess 4:15; 2 Thess 3:1),[139] "the word of Christ" (ὁ λόγος τοῦ Χριστοῦ) occurs here. It corresponds to the expression used in v 15: "the peace of Christ" (ἡ εἰρήνη τοῦ Χριστοῦ). This word is the "Gospel of Christ" (εὐαγγέλιον τοῦ Χριστοῦ Gal 1:7; 1 Cor 9:12; 2 Cor 2:12, etc.), which "in the word of truth, i.e. of the gospel" (ἐν τῷ λόγῳ τῆς ἀληθείας τοῦ εὐαγγελίου) came to the community, where it gained ground (1:5f). This message should dwell among them. As Wisdom found a dwelling place in Israel (Sir 24:8) and the Spirit of God dwells in the believers (1 Cor 3:16; Rom 8:9, 11),[140] so should the "word of Christ" reside within the community in rich abundance and produce its effects. The conduct of the community ought to correspond to this power of the word which is sustained by the Spirit; this will come about when the community reflects upon and interprets the word in its teaching and admonition.[141] The functions of "teaching" (διδάσκειν) and "admonishing" (νουθετεῖν),[142] which in 1:28 were mentioned as functions of the Apostle, are not bound

Rer. div. her. 95 speaks of the "judgment–bar of truth" (ἀλήθεια βραβεύουσα) [Loeb], he is talking about the judiciary function of truth. Cf. further *P. Masp* 2, 67151, 221–23 (sixth century A.D.): "the righteous co[ve]na[nt] . . . ruled and [guarded] [by] J(esu)s our L(or)d a(nd) G(o)d" (δικαία δ [ιαθ] ήκ[η] . . . [ὑπὸ] Ἰ(ησο)ῦ τοῦ κ(υρί)ου κ(αὶ) θ(ε)οῦ ἡμῶν βραβευομένη καὶ [φυλαττομένη]) [Trans.].

132 Cf. Johannes Behm, *TDNT* 3, 611–13.

133 The phrase "in your hearts" (ἐν ταῖς καρδίαις ὑμῶν) is continued in v 16 by "in you" (ἐν ὑμῖν). Cf. Werner Foerster, *TDNT* 2, 414: Peace appears in Col 3:15 "as a power . . . that rules in men, . . . as a kingdom, in which the believer is protected" [Bromiley modified].

134 The adjective "one" (ἑνί) is missing in manuscripts p[46] B 1739.

135 Also cf. above pp. 100f, 122 on 2:9, 19.

136 The adjective "thankful" (εὐχάριστος) is rare: in LXX only in Prov. 11:16: "a graceful woman" (γυνὴ εὐχάριστος), in NT only here. Cf. Bauer, *s.v.*

137 Cf. Schlier, *Epheser*, 249: "καὶ εὐχάριστοι γίνεσθε here not only means: be thankful, but be the ones who give thanks."

138 Cf. Robinson, "Hodajot–Formel," 225: "Col 3:16 is prefaced with a type of heading in v 15b: 'and be thankful' (καὶ εὐχάριστοι γίνεσθε) which echoes 1 Thess 5:18, and is concluded in v 17b with: 'give thanks to God the Father through him' (εὐχαριστοῦντες τῷ θεῷ πατρὶ δι' αὐτοῦ). On the basis of the pattern in 1:12: 'give thanks to the Father' (εὐχαριστοῦντες τῷ πατρί) this conclusion is to be seen as an allusion to a variant of the Hodajot–formula which was current in this community. Thus, on the basis of the terms used to describe thanksgiving one can connect the singing of 3:16 with 1:12ff and place it in the stream of thanksgiving in early Christianity."

139 Cf. the survey in Gerhard Kittel, *TDNT* 4, 114f. The textual variants are assimilations to the more current expressions: "the word of the Lord" (ὁ λόγος τοῦ κυρίου ℵ* I ClemAlex); "the word of God" (ὁ λόγος τοῦ θεοῦ A C* 33 al).

140 Cf. also the expression "sin which dwells in me" (ἡ ἐνοικοῦσα ἐν ἐμοὶ ἁμαρτία Rom 7:17), and consult Otto Michel, *TDNT* 5, 135f.

141 The dependent participles again occur here with imperatival force. Cf. above p. 32, n. 1 on 1:12 and p. 141, n. 48 and p. 147, n. 110 on 3:9f and 3:13 respectively.

142 On both these terms cf. above p. 77 on 1:28.

143 Cf. Sir 19:20: "And wisdom is entirely constituted by the fulfilling of the Law" (καὶ ἐν πάσῃ σοφίᾳ ποίησις νόμου) [Jerusalem Bible].

to a distinct office, but were exercised by members of the community because of the gifts of the Spirit bestowed upon them (1 Cor 12:28; 14:26). The words "in all wisdom" (ἐν πάσῃ σοφίᾳ) are to be construed with the participles "teach and admonish" (διδάσκοντες καὶ νουθετοῦντες). The participles stress anew that wisdom requires sobriety and must be authenticated in concrete actions.[143] In the power of this "wisdom" (σοφία) which is produced by the Spirit, the community understands what God's will is (1:9f). It knows that in Christ are "hid all the treasures of wisdom and knowledge" (πάντες οἱ θησαυροὶ τῆς σοφίας καὶ γνώσεως ἀπόκρυφοι 2:3) and it knows how to unmask those things that only have "semblance of wisdom" (λόγον σοφίας 2:23); it realizes what right conduct is (4:5). The community responds to the preaching and interpretation of the word in the songs which it sings.[144] "Psalms" (ψαλμοί) often designates the OT psalms.[145] The gift of the Spirit is active in the community and prompts its members to express their thankful rejoicing in newly coined songs of praise which can also be called "psalm" (ψαλμός) 1 Cor 14:26. "Hymn" (ὕμνος) is the festive hymn of praise.[146] "Song" (ᾠδή) is the song in which God's acts are praised and glorified.[147] It is impossible to differentiate exactly[148] between these three terms "psalms," "hymns," and "songs."[149] Taken together, they describe the full range of singing[150] which the Spirit prompts.[151] It is said of these songs presented to God[152] that they should be sung "in your hearts" (ἐν ταῖς καρδίαις ὑμῶν).[153] As in v 15, a Semitic expression is used here. Man should not only praise God with his lips. The entire man should be filled with songs of praise.[154] The words ἐν τῇ χάριτι cannot be translated "with gracefulness" as if they were further

144 Eph 5:19 connects both parts of our verse by linking "addressing" (λαλοῦντες) directly with the singing: "addressing one another in psalms and hymns and songs that are prompted by the Spirit, singing and making melody to the Lord in your heart" (λαλοῦντες ἑαυτοῖς ψαλμοῖς καὶ ὕμνοις καὶ ᾠδαῖς πνευματικαῖς, ᾄδοντες καὶ ψάλλοντες τῇ καρδίᾳ ὑμῶν τῷ κυρίῳ).

145 Cf. Lk 20:42; 24:44; Acts 1:20; 13:33.

146 Cf. LXX Is 42:10; 1 Macc 13:51; Acts 16:25; Heb 2:12.

147 Cf. Rev 5:9; 14:3; 15:3 and Schlier, *Epheser*, 247.

148 Efforts to distinguish more exactly among the three concepts have often been made. Cf. e.g., Gregory of Nyssa, *In Psalm.* 2, 3: "For a psalm is a melody produced by a musical instrument, a song is a melody sung with words—a hymn is a song of praise sung to God for the good things he has given us" (ψαλμὸς μὲν γάρ ἐστιν ἡ διὰ τοῦ ὀργάνου τοῦ μουσικοῦ μελῳδία, ᾠδὴ δὲ ἡ διά στόματος γινομένη τοῦ μέλους μετὰ τῶν ῥημάτων ἐκφώνησις . . . ὕμνος δὲ ἡ ἐπὶ τοῖς ὑπάρχουσιν ἡμῖν ἀγαθοῖς ἀνατιθεμένη τῷ θεῷ εὐφημία) [Trans.]. Also consult Lightfoot, *ad loc.* Nevertheless, a sure differentiation between the three ideas is not possible. Cf. Joseph Kroll, *Die christliche Hymnodik bis zu Klemens von Alexandria* in: Verzeichnis der Vorlesungen an der Akademie zu Braunsberg im Sommer 1921, p. 4f: "What does a person understand by a Christian hymn? This question in itself raises immediate difficulties. In the letter to the Colossians Paul, in a well-known passage, speaks of 'psalms,' 'hymns,' and 'songs prompted by the Spirit,' words which Eph afterwards repeats. How should 'hymn' be interpreted here next to the two other terms? How should the three be distinguished from one another? That is a bone of contention. From the time of Jerome up till our own day this question has been debated time and again without any definitive solution emerging. We are at a loss concerning these terms which stand side by side." Cf. Robinson, "Hodajot–Formel," 224; further Gerhard Delling, *TWNT* 8, 502: "It is impossible to discern whether 'psalm' and 'hymn' refer to two types of song which can be distinguished with respect to their genre."

149 Manuscripts (A) 𝔎 pm connect each of these three words together with "and" (καί).

150 Hymnic texts like Phil 2:6–11; Col 1:15–20; 1 Tim 3:16 offer examples of such songs. Cf. Gerhard Delling, *Der Gottesdienst im Neuen Testament* (Berlin and Göttingen: 1952), 81–88.

151 The adjectival expression "prompted by the Spirit" (πνευματικαῖς) refers materially to all three terms.

152 Col 3:16 is not yet speaking of "song sung to Christ, as to a god" (carmina Christo quasi deo). Cf. Pliny the Younger, *Epist.* 10, 96, 7. The Byzantine text (𝔎 pm) in accordance with Eph 5:19 alters the text to "to the Lord" (τῷ κυρίῳ); p[46] probably agrees with the Egyptian witnesses which read "to God" (τῷ θεῷ).

153 Witnesses I 𝔎 pm ClemAlex modify to the singular "in your heart" (ἐν τῇ καρδίᾳ ὑμῶν).

154 Cf. Theodoret, *ad loc.*, "The expression 'with the hearts' is used instead of 'not only with the mouth' "

defining the preceding terms;[155] for the songs are hardly to be evaluated according to the canons of aesthetics. More probable is the proposal that sees ἐν τῇ χάριτι as a reference to the spirit of thankfulness[156] which permeates the community's singing. Nevertheless, this translation cannot account for the definite article which specifies χάρις as God's bestowal of grace which gives life to the believers.[157] The phrase ἐν τῇ χάριτι reminds the readers of *sola gratia* (by grace alone) which is the sole basis of existence and creates the realm in which Christian life can exist and develop.[158] That is the reason why God is praised. He has empowered believers to share in the inheritance of the saints in light (1:12).

■ 17 This section is concluded with an admonition that sums up everything else. The phrase "whatsoever" (πᾶν ὅ τι ἐάν, a Semitizing expression),[159] introduces the section and is taken up again later by "everything" (πάντα). Thus it is forcefully stressed that absolutely everything that believers do must be done[160] "in the name of the Lord Jesus" (ἐν ὀνόματι κυρίου 'Ιησοῦ).[161] With this phrase[162] which originates in primitive Christianity, the Christians' entire life is placed under obe-

(Τὸ δὲ 'ἐν ταῖς καρδίαις' ἀντὶ τοῦ 'μὴ μόνον τῷ στόματι'). [Trans.]

155 This is the way Luther translates "in geistlichen lieblichen Liedern" (in pleasing spiritual songs). If one reads ἐν χάριτι (gracefully) without the article on the basis of witnesses 𝔊 𝔎 pm, then this translation could be taken into consideration. The reading ἐν τῇ χάριτι, attested to by p^{46} B D* G al Clem-Alex, must, however, be regarded as the original text.

156 Cf. Moule, *ad loc.*, "On the whole, the easiest sense, at any rate, is 'gratefully singing' . . ." On χάρις in the meaning of "thanks, gratitude," cf. Bauer, *s.v.*

157 Cf. Gillis P:son Wetter, *Charis: Ein Beitrag zur Geschichte des ältesten Christentums*. Untersuchungen zum Neuen Testament 5 (Leipzig: 1913), 77f; Dibelius–Greeven, *ad loc.*

158 On the absolute use of "grace" (χάρις), cf. Col 4:18: "Grace be with you" (ἡ χάρις μεθ' ὑμῶν); Gal 5:4: "You have fallen away from grace" (τῆς χάριτος ἐξεπέσατε); cf. further 2 Cor 4:15.

159 Cf. Karl Beyer, *Semitische Syntax im Neuen Testament* 1, 1. Studien zur Umwelt des Neuen Testaments 1 (Göttingen: 1962), 169; cf. also Blass–Debrunner par. 466, 3.

160 Cf. what Sir 47:8 says of David: "In all that he did he gave thanks to the Holy One, the Most High, with ascriptions of glory" (ἐν παντὶ ἔργῳ αὐτοῦ ἔδωκεν ἐξομολόγησιν ἁγίῳ ὑψίστῳ ῥήματι δόξης). Cf. also *Ab.* 2, 16: "R. Jose [the Priest, c. 100 A.D.] said . . . let all your actions be in the name of God [lit: in the name of heaven לְשֵׁם שָׁמַיִם], that is, referring them to God or doing them for the sake of God" (Charles, *APOT*, and Billerbeck 3, p. 631). The pious Jew said a blessing daily in every situation that presented an occasion for thanking God. With this blessing he acknowledged the God of Israel in praising him.

161 "Lord Jesus" (κύριος 'Ιησοῦς) also occurs in 1 Cor 5:4; 11:23; 12:3; Rom 10:9. At other places "Lord Jesus Christ" (κύριος 'Ιησοῦς Χριστός) occurs, e.g., Phil 2:11; Rom 13:14. Instead of "Lord Jesus" (κυρίου 'Ιησοῦ) manuscripts ℵ* pc vg^{cl} have "Lord Jesus Christ" (κυρίου 'Ιησοῦ Χριστοῦ); A C D* G have "Jesus Christ" ('Ιησοῦ Χριστοῦ).

162 Cf. 1 Cor 5:40; 6:11; Phil 2:10; etc.

163 The phrase "in the name of the Lord Jesus [Christ]" (ἐν ὀνόματι κυρίου 'Ιησοῦ [Χριστοῦ]) is indeed occasionally used in reference to the assembly of worship in 1 Cor 5:4 or to baptism in 1 Cor 6:11, but its occurence in no way necessarily indicates a "cult situation" (Schlier, *Epheser*, 248). Rather, as the word "everything" (πάντα) indicates, Col applies it to the entire life of the Christians. Cf. also Hans Bietenhard, *TDNT* 5, 274: "The whole life of the Christian stands under the name of Jesus."

164 Wilhelm Heitmüller, "*Im Namen Jesu*"*: Eine sprach- und religionsgeschichtliche Untersuchung zum Neuen Testament, speziell zur altchristlichen Taufe*. FRLANT 2 (Göttingen: 1903), 68, comments: "in everything that a Christian does, in every life-situation, the Christian should call upon and invoke the name of the Lord Jesus." This invocation which accompanies the actions can occur in prayer (cf. *ibid.*, p. 70), but also in proclamation or confession. "In everything they say and do Christians should also somehow use, call upon the name of the Lord Jesus. According to the immediate context we must define this invocation more precisely as an expression of gratitude, as a thankful, joyous invocation, proclamation or even confession." (*ibid.*, p. 260). Gerhard Delling, *Die Zueignung des Heils in der Taufe* (Berlin: 1961), 54: "The phrase 'in the name' used in Col 3:17 does not differ very much materially from the Hebrew l^{e}shem [in the name]: everything that the Christian does is referred to the Lordship of Jesus (who attained his position of Lordship precisely through the salvation event of cross and resurrection.)"

165 This is the opinion of Wilhelm Bousset, *Kyrios Christos: Geschichte des Christusglaubens von den Anfängen des Christentums bis Irenaeus*. FRLANT 21 (Göttingen: ^{2}1921 = ^{5}1965), 86f; L. G. Champion, *Benedictions and Doxologies in the Epistles of Paul*. Unpub. Diss. (Heidelberg: 1934), 38–40. Schlier, *Epheser*, 249,

dience to the Lord.[163] They must always acknowledge their Lord in their words and actions.[164] "In word or deed" (*ἐν λόγῳ ἢ ἐν ἔργῳ*) interprets the introductory word *πᾶν* (all). Thus the primary reference is obviously not to worship.[165] Rather, it is precisely in the Christian's everyday life, where he toils and sweats, that he is placed under the command to prove his allegiance to the Lord.[166] Amid the activities of the world he must render "spiritual worship" (*λογικὴ λατρεία* cf. Rom 12:1f). He has to make the praise of God resound by listening to and spreading the word, in song and prayer, but especially in his daily life and dealings with his fellow man.[167] This praise is offered to God the Father[168] "through him" (*δι' αὐτοῦ*), i.e., "through Christ."[169] For Christ is the Lord who provides the basis and sets the goal for the life of believers.[170] Therefore, they can express their grateful praise of the Father in no other way than by confessing Christ as the Lord.[171]

wants to refer "word" (*λόγος*) and "deed" (*ἔργον*) to "every cultic word and every cultic 'work' " and proposes: "The 'in deed' (*ἐν ἔργῳ*) refers to the performance of the Lord's Supper during which the Eucharistia takes place." This passage, however, makes no allusion to the celebration of the Eucharist as it is presupposed in Ign. *Phld.* 4; Ign. *Mag.* 6:1 (cf. Dibelius–Greeven, *ad loc.*).

166 Cf. Chrysostom, *ad loc.*: "If you eat, if you drink, if you marry, if you travel, do all in the Name of God, that is, calling Him to aid you" (*ἐὰν ἐσθίῃς, ἐὰν πίνῃς, ἐὰν γαμῇς, ἐὰν ἀποδημῇς, πάντα ἐν ὀνόματι τοῦ θεοῦ πρᾶττε· τουτέστιν, αὐτὸν καλῶν βοηθόν* [modified from NPNF 13, 302]).

167 Cf. Rom 12:1f and Ernst Käsemann, "Worship in Everyday Life: a Note on Romans 12" in *New Testament Questions of Today*, tr. W. J. Montague (Philadelphia: Fortress Press, 1969), 188–95.

168 On the designation "God the Father" (*θεὸς πατήρ*), which is used especially in liturgical phrases, cf. above pp. 14f and p. 34 on 1:3 and 1:12 respectively. Witnesses I ℜ D G pl Clem Alex add "and" (*καί*) to read "to God and the Father" (*τῷ θεῷ καὶ πατρί* cf. Eph 5:20).

169 Heitmüller, "*Im Namen Jesu*," 260–62 wanted to take "through him" as expressing opposition to "through the angels:" "Jesus Christ is thought of as the one who mediates thanks to God" (p. 261). Theodoret, *ad loc.*, had already given a similar interpretation: "And send up the thanksgiving to God the Father through him, it says, not through the angels" (*καὶ τῷ θεῷ καὶ πατρὶ τὴν εὐχαριστίαν δι' αὐτοῦ, φησίν, ἀναπέμπετε, μὴ διὰ τῶν ἀγγέλων* [Trans]). Surely, however, there is no polemic here against the "worship of angels" (*θρησκεία τῶν ἀγγέλων*) propounded by the "philosophy." The primary argument, however, against such an interpretation is "that the formula 'through Christ' is never linked with verbs of asking" (Albrecht Oepke, *TDNT* 2, 68f). Rather, the phrase "through Christ" gives "pregnant expression to the constitutive significance of Christ for the whole of the Christian life" (*ibid.*, p. 69). Cf. also W. Thüsing, *Per Christum in Deum*, Neutestamentliche Abhandlungen NF 1 (Münster: 1965), 164–237, where, however, only passages from the major Pauline epistles are investigated, not those in Col and Eph.

170 The phrase "through Christ" has no mystical overtones (against Dibelius–Greeven, *ad loc.*).

171 "Through Christ" resumes "in the name of the Lord Jesus." Cf. Eph 5:20: "Always and for everything giving thanks in the name of our Lord Jesus Christ (Col 3:17: through him) to God the Father" (*εὐχαριστοῦντες πάντοτε ὑπὲρ πάντων ἐν ὀνόματι τοῦ κυρίου ἡμῶν Ἰησοῦ Χριστοῦ* [Col 3:17: *δι' αὐτοῦ*] *τῷ θεῷ καὶ πατρί*).

3

Rules for the Household

18 **Wives, be subject to your husbands, as it is
proper in the Lord. 19/ Husbands, love
your wives and do not be embittered
against them. 20/ Children, be obedient
to your parents in all things; for that is
pleasing in the Lord. 21/ Fathers, do not
provoke your children, lest they become
timid. 22/ Slaves, obey your earthly
masters in all things, not with eyeservice in order to please men, but with
singleness of heart in the fear of the
Lord. 23/ Whatever you do, do it from
your heart as for the Lord and not for
men; 24/ realize that from the Lord you
will receive the inheritance as a reward.
Serve the Lord Christ. 25/ For whoever
engages in wrongdoing will receive the
reward for the wrong he has done;
and there is no partiality. 4:1/ Masters,
treat your slaves justly and fairly; realize
that you too have a Master in heaven.**

The Rules for the Household[1]

The admonitions addressed successively to wives and husbands, children and fathers, slaves and masters, are introduced without any connective transition. They form a self-contained and clearly delimited section within the letter.[2] Parallels are found in Eph 5:22–6:9; 1 Tim 2:8–15; 6:1–2; Tit 2:1–10; 1 Pt 2:13–3:7 and in the writings of the Apostolic Fathers.[3] It is quite obvious that an exhortatory tradition has been utilized in these sentences—a tradition which had played an important part in the teaching of the communities. In the second and third Christian generation, answers had to be given to the many questions that pressed upon Christians in their everyday lives. In answering these questions, Christians did not renounce the world and flee it, but faced it head-on and tried to learn from the rules of life which had been formulated and practiced in Hellenistic popular philosophy. Christians took over many directives which had attained wide circulation as successful guidelines to life and its problems, and made use of them in the community's preaching and instruction. Just as Hellenistic or Jewish traditions were often drawn upon for exhortatory material, so too traditional patterns for rules of conduct which presented tried and true examples of ethical instruction were used, in particular for the development of the so-called *Haustafeln* (rules for the household).[4]

In the instruction of contemporary popular philosophy, a fixed schema listed the duties which a conscientious man had to fulfill. For example, Polybius depicts the exemplary conduct of Attalus within the circle of his family and says: "he lived ever most virtuous and austere as husband and father, never breaking his faith to his friends and allies" (*σωφρονέστατα μὲν ἐβίωσε καὶ σεμνότατα πρὸς γυναῖκα*

1 Cf. the commentaries on 3:18–4:1, especially Dibelius–Greeven. Cf. further: Karl Weidinger, *Die Haustafeln: Ein Stück urchristlicher Paränese*. Untersuchungen zum Neuen Testament 14 (Leipzig: 1928); Heinz Dietrich Wendland, "Zur sozialethischen Bedeutung der neutestamentlichen Haustafeln," in *Die Leibhaftigkeit des Wortes, Festschrift für Adolf Köberle* (Hamburg: 1958), 34–46 (= *Die Botschaft an die soziale Welt* [Hamburg: 1959], 104–14); D. Schroeder, *Die Haustafeln des Neuen Testaments: Ihre Herkunft und ihr theologischer Sinn*. Unpub. Diss. (Hamburg: 1959); Merk, *Handeln*, 214–24.

2 Verse 4:2: "be watchful . . . with thanksgiving" (*γρηγοροῦντες . . . ἐν εὐχαριστίᾳ*) would connect smoothly with 3:17: "give thanks to God" (*εὐχαριστοῦντες τῷ θεῷ*).

3 Cf. Did 4:9–11; Barn 19:5–7; 1 Clem 21:6–9; Pol. *Phil.* 4:2–6:3.

4 These rules for the household are not, insofar as their content is considered, "a genuinely Christian creation" and thus they cannot, without further ado, be considered to be "applied kerygma" (this is the position of Karl Heinrich Rengstorf, "Die neutestamentlichen Mahnungen an die Frau, sich dem Manne unterzuordnen" in *Verbum Dei manet in aeternum, Festschrift für Otto Schmitz*, ed. Werner Foerster

καὶ τέκνα, διεφύλαξε δὲ τὴν πρὸς πάντας τοὺς συμμάχους καὶ φίλους πίστιν 18, 41, 8f). The excerpts of Hierocles in Stobaeus contain a detailed catalog of ethical teachings: on conduct toward the gods, fatherland, parents, brothers, relatives, work, marriage and children.[5] With various modifications this schema recurs in the common moral teaching of the Stoics.[6] Thus Epictetus teaches that a true student would say to him: "I want also, as a god–fearing man, a philosopher, and a diligent student, to know what is my duty toward the gods, toward parents, toward brothers, toward my country, toward strangers" (*θέλω δ' ὡς εὐσεβὴς καὶ φιλόσοφος καὶ ἐπιμελὴς εἰδέναι τί μοι πρὸς θεούς ἐστι καθῆκον, τί πρὸς γονεῖς, τί πρὸς ἀδελφούς, τί πρὸς τὴν πατρίδα, τί πρὸς ξένους Diss.* 2, 17, 31). The purpose of the ethical instruction is to spell out those things that should be done at any given time as one's "duty" (*καθῆκον*) toward the gods, parents, friends, fatherland, and strangers: "Befitting acts are all those which reason prevails upon us to do; and this is the case with honoring one's parents, brothers and country, and intercourse with friends" (*καθήκοντα μὲν οὖν εἶναι ὅσα λόγος αἱρεῖ ποιεῖν, ὡς ἔχει τὸ γονεῖς τιμᾶν, ἀδελφούς, πατρίδα, συμπεριφέρεσθαι φίλοις* Diogenes Laertius 7, 108). In Stoic "tranquillity" (*ἀταραξία*) man will know how to discern what is right and to do it: "maintaining with his associates both the natural and the acquired relationships, those namely of son, father, brother, citizen, wife, neighbour, fellow–traveller, ruler, and subject" (*μετὰ τῶν κοινωνῶν τηροῦντα τὰς σχέσεις τάς τε φυσικὰς καὶ ἐπιθέτους, τὸν υἱόν, τὸν πατέρα, τὸν ἀδελφόν, τὸν πολίτην, τὸν ἄνδρα, τὴν γυναῖκα, τὸν γείτονα, τὸν σύνοδον, τὸν ἄρχοντα, τὸν ἀρχόμενον* Epictetus, *Diss.* 2, 14, 8). Everyone has to consider what task is allotted to him in his situation. He will receive correct guidance on that task from philosophy, "which supplies precepts appropriate to the individual case, instead of framing them for mankind at large—which, for instance, advises how a husband should conduct himself toward his wife, or a father should bring up his children, or how a master should rule his slaves" (quae dat propria cuique personae praecepta nec in universum componit hominem, sed marito suadet quomodo se gerat adversum uxorem, patri quomodo educet liberos, domino quomodo servos regat. Seneca, *Epist.* 94, 1).[7]

Hellenistic Judaism borrowed this schema of ethical instruction from the popular philosophy of antiquity and, with slight modifications, used it in its synagogue teaching.[8] Instead of worship of the gods, stress was now laid on obedience to the one God, whose commandments had to be kept. The didactic poem of Ps–Phocylides lists, one after another, the duties that had to be fulfilled in marriage, in the procreation and rearing of children, in relationships with friends and relatives, and in the treatment of slaves (175–227). From the commandment on honoring parents Philo of Alexandria derives a number of concomitant commandments, namely, "the [laws] drawn up to deal with the relations of old to young, rulers to subjects, benefactors to benefited, slaves to masters" (*τοὺς ἐπὶ πρεσβύταις καὶ νέοις ἀναγραφέντας* [*scil.* *νόμους*], *τοὺς ἐπ' ἄρχουσι καὶ ὑπηκόοις, τοὺς ἐπ' εὐεργέταις καὶ εὖ πεπονθόσι, τοὺς ἐπὶ δούλοις καὶ δεσπόταις De decal.* 165). For the parents belong to the superior class, that of rulers, benefactors, and masters. On the other hand, the children occupy the lower class together with juniors, subjects, receivers of benefits, and slaves. The lower class should honor and respect the superior class while the superior class should care for the

(Witten: 1953), 136, 141 n. 24; *idem*, "Mann und Frau im Urchristentum" in *Arbeitsgemeinschaft für Forschung des Landes Nordrhein–Westfalen* 12 (Köln and Opladen: 1954), 24f, 32. Rather a distinction must be drawn between the ethical directives which were developed in the cultural environment and their adoption and new justification by the Christian community. Schroeder, *Die Haustafeln*, 79–107, wants to explain the NT house rules as a genuinely Christian construction which had its roots in the adoption of a form developed in the OT and Judaism, namely, that of divine law. For a critique of this view cf. below p. 157, n. 15 and Merk, *Handeln*, 215f.

5 Cf. the brief analysis of these excerpts found in Weidinger, *Die Haustafeln*, 27–33.

6 Cf. the material assembled in Dibelius–Greeven, 48–50 and Weidinger, *Die Haustafeln*, 34–39.

7 Concerning ethical teaching in Hellenistic popular philosophy, cf. further Albrecht Dihle, *Die goldene Regel: Eine Einführung in die Geschichte der antiken und frühchristlichen Vulgärethik*, Studienhefte zur Altertumswissenschaft 7 (Göttingen: 1962).

8 In Palestinian Judaism and especially in Rabbinic literature there are no "rules for the household." Under the heading "Haustafeln" David Daube, *The New Testament and Rabbinic Judaism*. Jordan Lectures in Comparative Religion 2, 1952 (London: Univ. of London, Athlone, 1956), 90–105 deals with the meaning of the participle used with imperatival force (cf. thereto above p. 32, n. 1)—not, however, with the contents and construction of the NT "rules for the household" which undoubtedly were adopted from the Hellenistic cultural milieu.

lower class (*De decal.* 165–67).[9] In *Ap.* 2, 198–210 Josephus gives a list of Jewish laws and prohibitions. Beginning with the worship of God, he then mentions proper conduct in marriage, in the rearing of children, the burial of the dead, and love of parents. He concludes with the duties to be fulfilled in one's relationships with friends and with strangers.

In the ethics of Hellenistic popular philosophy, which was probably transmitted to the Christian communities via the Hellenistic synagogues, there was a rich collection of material from which a person could ascertain what was generally considered proper conduct. Just as in Judaism, naturally no mention was made of the cultic duties owed the gods. But there was also silence concerning the homeland and political duties. Of course, here and there, brief instructions about right conduct toward political authorities were transmitted.[10] In general, however, the ethical admonitions concentrated on the type of conduct that was fitting in one's immediate life–situation, namely, in one's dealings with members of the family, slaves and masters. There was no attempt to develop a program to fashion the world according to Christian blueprints. Rather, Christians acknowledged those things which were everywhere adjudged right and reasonable. Remember that Paul had instructed the community: "Whatever is true, whatever is honorable, whatever is just, whatever is pure, whatever is lovely, whatever is gracious, if there is any excellence, if there is anything worthy of praise, think about these things" (ὅσα ἐστὶν ἀληθῆ, ὅσα σεμνά, ὅσα δίκαια, ὅσα ἁγνά, ὅσα προσφιλῆ, ὅσα εὔφημα, εἴ τις ἀρετὴ καὶ εἴ τις ἔπαινος, ταῦτα λογίζεσθε Phil 4:8). There is no attempt to change the world and reorganize it on a new basis. Rather, there was sober recognition of the fact that the Christian in his life–situation had to do what could be expected of a human being who tried to act in a morally responsible way. A completely new meaning, however, was given to these instructions, which had been adopted from contemporary culture, for their fulfillment was understood as obedience due to the Kyrios.[11]

In Col 3:18–4:1—the oldest Christian "rule for the household"—it is clearly discernible how the ethical teaching was adopted and Christianized. Not only the individual admonitions, but also the reference to what is fitting and generally valid correspond to Hellenistic moral teaching: "as is proper" (ὡς ἀνῆκεν 3:18); "pleasing" (εὐάρεστον 3:20); "justly and fairly" (τὸ δίκαιον καὶ τὴν ἰσότητα 4:1). The commands, however, are furnished with a completely new motivation through the phrase "in the Lord" (ἐν κυρίῳ) and now read: "as is proper in the Lord" (ὡς ἀνῆκεν ἐν κυρίῳ 3:18); "for this is pleasing in the Lord" (τοῦτο γὰρ εὐάρεστόν ἐστιν ἐν κυρίῳ 3:20); the author reminds of the fear of God (3:22); conduct is considered as done "for the Lord" (ὡς τῷ κυρίῳ 3:23); reference is made to the Lord's rewarding judgment (3:24f; 4:1), and the admonition is given: "serve the Lord Christ" (τῷ κυρίῳ Χριστῷ δουλεύετε 3:24). It is true that the content of the directives was taken from the cultural environment. The phrase "in the Lord," however, which introduces the new motivation, is not a mere formal element whose only function is to Christianize the traditional material.[12] Rather the entire life, thought and conduct of believers is subordinated to the lordship of the Kyrios. At the same time the words "in the Lord" set forth a critical principle which makes it possible to determine which ethical admonitions were considered binding for the community. Man's relationships with his fellow men are the field upon which the Christian proves

9 Further examples from Philo's writings can be found in Weidinger, *Die Haustafeln*, 25f.

10 Cf. Rom 13:1–7; 1 Tim 2:2; Tit 3:1; 1 Pt 2:13–17.

11 Cf. Wolfgang Schrage, *Die konkreten Einzelgebote in der paulinischen Paränese* (Gütersloh: 1961), p. 222: "It is just this subordination within the 'house' (οἶκος) and the fulfillment of the tasks and duties proper to each worldly 'state of life' which is pleasing to the Lord (Col 3:20) and corresponds to the 'in–the–Lord'–existence of the Christian (Col 3:18). Obedience to the heavenly Lord is shown and takes place, for example, in 'obedience' (ὑπακούειν) to parents or earthly masters (Col 3:20 and 3:22) and therefore within the earthly schemata of authority and subordination."

12 This is the position of Weidinger, *Die Haustafeln*, 51. Cf. against it Schroeder, *Die Haustafeln*, 154f; Schrage, *Einzelgebote*, 202.

13 Eph 5:22–6:9 speaks of wives, husbands, children, fathers, slaves and masters in the same sequence as Col 3:18–4:1. To the admonitions, however, it adds a detailed Christological motivation (Eph 5:25–33) and a reference to Scripture (Eph 6:2f).

14 Cf. Conzelmann, 153: "These rules do not offer a timeless, 'Christian' ethics. They presuppose the current social structures and viewpoints. Their validity lies rather in the presuppositions which justified the adoption of these middle class statements. Whoever would want to transport these directives mechanically into today's social order, would in reality completely alter them both in meaning and content. Moreover, he would grossly misunderstand their theological, namely eschatological basis. This is seen right away in the first admonition, the subordination of wives. This admonition at that time simply meant the observation of an obvious social

his obedience to the Lord insofar as he conducts his life in "love" (ἀγάπη).[13] The content of the individual sentences is conditioned by the situations of that time. They do not offer timelessly valid laws, nor do they endow a particular social order with ageless dignity. As times change, so does the general estimation of what is fitting and proper. Christian exhortation, however, must constantly impress on new generations the admonition to be obedient to the Kyrios. How this obedience is to be expressed concretely at any given time, will always have to be tested and determined anew.[14]

First of all, wives and husbands are addressed, then children and fathers, and finally slaves and masters. In each pairing the sudordinated party is mentioned first and admonished "to be subject" (ὑποτάσσεσθαι) or "to be obedient" (ὑπακούειν). Then the superior party is reminded of its responsibilities which have to be verified toward the people who are entrusted to him. Therefore, the command that subordinates should be subject can and should not be misunderstood or even misused. If the one group is obliged to be obedient, then the other is urged to imagine itself in the position of the subordinates and to let its entire life be guided by the command of love.[15]

■ **18** Wives[16] should be subject to their husbands.[17] In this admonition they are commanded to conduct their lives in accord with the prevalent social order.[18] They are not given a specifically Christian directive,[19] nor are they called upon to make a free decision in the matter.[20] Rather, wives should submit to their husbands,[21] because

position, the observation of what was fitting."

15 The admonitions are couched in the form of imperatives. Hence there can be no question here of apodictic laws (against Schroeder, *Die Haustafeln*, 95). Likewise, Schroeder cannot substantiate his position by appealing (p. 92f) to the citation of the Decalogue in Eph 6:2f. For the rules for the household of Eph are an expansion of the shorter ones in Col. They do not refer to sentences of holy law found in the OT and Jewish tradition.

16 In the LXX the arthrous Semitic vocative is reproduced by the nominative with the article. Cf. Martin Johannessohn, *Der Gebrauch der Kasus und der Präpositionen in der Septuaginta* 1, Unpub. Diss. (Berlin: 1910), 14f. Still it is also entirely possible in Greek to express the address in the nominative with the article. Cf. Blass–Debrunner, par. 147, 3.

17 Witnesses L pm add "your own" (ἰδίοις) before "husbands" (ἀνδράσιν) [cf. Eph 5:22]. Manuscripts D* G it sy append "your" (ὑμῶν).

18 Cf. Plutarch, *Conjugalia praecepta* 33 (p. 142e): "If they [the wives] subordinate themselves to their husbands, they are commended, but if they want to have control, they cut a sorrier figure than the subjects of their control" (ὑποτάττουσαι [scil. αἱ γυναῖκες] μὲν γὰρ ἑαυτὰς τοῖς ἀνδράσιν ἐπαινοῦνται, κρατεῖν δὲ βουλόμεναι μᾶλλον τῶν κρατουμένων ἀσχημονοῦσι); Ps–Callisthenes 1, 22, 4: "For it is proper for the wife to be subject to her husband" (πρέπον γάρ ἐστιν τὴν γυναῖκα τῷ ἀνδρὶ ὑποτάσσεσθαι [Trans.]).

19 This is the opinion of Rengstorf, "Mahnungen an die Frau," 132.

20 Else Kähler, *Die Frau in den paulinischen Briefen, unter besonderer Berücksichtigung des Begriffes der Unterordnung* (Zürich and Frankfurt a.M.: 1960) wants to understand "to be subject" (ὑποτάσσεσθαι) as "the free act of acknowledging the order which is established through the word of God in Jesus Christ" (p. 156). He assumes that, on the basis of a profound insight, the act "of being subject" is carried out voluntarily. "Whenever 'to be subject' occurs, there is no trace of compulsion" (p. 179). "Man as husband or wife, child, slave or citizen is constantly called upon to renew his decision with respect to subordination" (p. 201f). But, in these admonitions "to be subject," there is in fact no mention of a decision, nor of voluntary action. Rather what is demanded is acknowledgement of the existing order.

21 Cf. 1 Cor 14:34; Eph 5:22–24; Tit 2:5; 1 Pt 3:1. This directive must not be misinterpreted as if it implied the downgrading of the dignity of a woman. The verb "to be subject" is the general designation of the relationship that exists between those in authority and those who are subordinated: "Let every person be subject to the governing authorities" (Πᾶσα ψυχὴ ἐξουσίαις ὑπερεχούσαις ὑποτασσέσθω Rom 13:1). Christ will be subject to God who is his "head" (κεφαλή 1 Cor 11:3); "The Son himself will also be subjected to him who put all things under him" (αὐτὸς ὁ υἱὸς ὑποταγήσεται τῷ ὑποτάξαντι αὐτῷ τὰ πάντα 1 Cor 15:28). Although Paul demands the "subjection" of wives to their husbands (1 Cor 14:34), he still knows of the unity of all in

it is proper.[22] Custom and tradition determine what is fitting.[23] The binding motivation of the command "to be subject" is only given in the appended words "in the Lord." It is obvious that the content of the admonition is based on a universally acknowledged rule of conduct. But now the members of the community are told that it is an expression of their confession of Christ as Lord, if they observe a social order which has been recognized as right and just. For there is no corner of human life in which they could live without their Lord.[24]

■ **19** The wives have been admonished "to be subject" to their husbands. The husbands now are directed to love their wives.[25] They are forbidden to behave in an overbearing manner or to imagine that they belong to a superior species. They are responsible for their wives and must live together with them in "love" which is the only true manner of conduct.[26] This command needs no justification,[27] for the commandment of "love" is absolutely valid.[28] Put negatively, it means this: "do not be embittered against them" (**μὴ πικραίνεσθε πρὸς αὐτάς**).[29] Any reasonable man would surely follow the advice that he should not be irritable or angry[30] with his wife.[31] This verse, however, is not just giving sage advice. Rather the admonition "do not be embittered" is an exemplification of the commandment of love which determines Christian conduct.[32]

■ **20** Children[33] are commanded to be obedient to their parents in all things. Obedience is to be shown to father and mother in the subordination due to them (cf. 3:22; Eph 6:1, 5).[34] The motivation given is that this is "pleas-

---

Christ: "There is neither Jew nor Greek, there is neither slave nor free, there is neither male nor female; for you are all one in Christ Jesus" (*οὐκ ἔνι Ἰουδαῖος οὐδὲ Ἕλλην, οὐκ ἔνι δοῦλος οὐδὲ ἐλεύθερος, οὐκ ἔνι ἄρσεν καὶ θῆλυ· πάντες γὰρ ὑμεῖς εἷς ἐστε ἐν Χριστῷ Ἰησοῦ* Gal 3:28).

22 Cf. Gerhard Delling, *TWNT* 8, 44; John Foster, "St. Paul and Women," *ExpT* 62 (1950–51): 376–78; Heinrich Baltensweiler, *Die Ehe im Neuen Testament: Exegetische Untersuchungen über Ehe, Ehelosigkeit, und Ehescheidung*, AThANT 52 (Zürich: 1967), 210–17.

23 The phrase *τὸ ἀνῆκον* indicates what is proper, one's duty. Cf. Bauer, *s.v.*; Heinrich Schlier, *TDNT* 1, 360. The expression gained entry into Christian exhortation from Hellenistic popular philosophy as mediated through the Hellenistic synagogue. Cf. Arist. 227: "the fitting" (*τὸ καθῆκον*); Ps-Phocylides 80: "it is fitting" (*καθῆκει*); cf. also Heinrich Schlier, *TDNT* 3, 437–40; Eph 5:4: "which are not fitting" (*ἃ οὐκ ἀνῆκεν*). The imperfect form "it is fitting" (*ἀνῆκεν*) is used instead of the customary present tense of classical Greek and refers to that which is considered to be fitting. Cf. Blass–Debrunner, par. 358, 2; Moulton–Turner, 90.

24 The "subordination" of wives was sanctioned at that time by custom and usage. This directive, however, which presupposes the social order of antiquity, and likewise the directive about the relationship between slaves and masters, cannot be taken as expressions of timelessly valid law. It is surely more to the point to notice how the structures of human relationships change from time to time and to discover new ways in which the Christian must render obedience to the Kyrios in the world's social structures (cf. above p. 157).

25 Witnesses D* G it vg^cl add "your" (*ὑμῶν*).

26 In the rules for the household, "love" is not demanded of the wives; they are always admonished "to be subject." Tit 2:4, however, says: the young wives should be urged "to love their husbands" (*φιλάνδρους εἶναι*).

27 Eph 5:25–33 adds a detailed Christological argument to the short directive to love one's wife.

28 Pre-Christian antiquity indeed knew of the terms "to love/love" (*ἀγαπᾶν/ἀγάπη*) [cf. Merk, *Handeln*, 216 n. 114], but in the Hellenistic world these terms do not occur in the rules for the household.

29 The verb "to make bitter, embitter" (*πικραίνεσθαι*) occurs in an ethical context only here in the NT. It frequently occurs, however, in this meaning in Greek literature since the time of Plato. Cf. Bauer, *s.v.* Cf. the other occurrences of the word in Rev 8:11; 10:9f and Wilhelm Michaelis, *TDNT* 6, 122–25.

30 Cf. *b. B.M.* 59a: "Rab [†247] said: one should always be heedful of wronging his wife, for since her tears are coming (quickly) the revenge of her insult is close at hand" (cf. Billerbeck 3, p. 631); Plutarch, *De cohibenda ira* 8 (p. 457a): "they rage bitterly against women" (*πρὸς γύναια διαπικραίνοντα*); Hermas, *Mand.* 10, 2, 3: "to become bitter" (*πικραίνεσθαι*) as an effect of "ill temper" (*ὀξυχολία*).

31 The construction of the preposition "against" (*πρός*) after "to be embittered" (*πικραίνεσθαι*), which is not attested in LXX or Philo, "perhaps suggests that what is also, or especially, in view is the 'bitterness' [*πικρία*] vented on the wife though not caused by her" (Michaelis, *TDNT* 6, 125 n. 16).

32 Cf. Schrage, *Einzelgebote*, 260: "All relationships and orders of the world provide room and give scope for the Christian's loving conduct and often enough undergo a thoroughgoing transformation because of this subordination to the law of Christ."

33 The word *τέκνον* signifies "the child from the

ing" (εὐάρεστον) which originally must have referred to that which all men considered proper.[35] "In the Lord," however, again points out how the concept of what is pleasing is to be understood in the community.[36] The Lord commands, and his command is to be followed without any objection.[37]

■ **21** To be sure, the children have to obey both parents, but the fathers have a special responsibility toward them. They have to be on their guard not to irritate or provoke[38] their children lest they become discouraged and timid.[39] It is not said in which respects they might become discouraged. The obvious reference, however, is to the common life of children and parents which should not be marred by the father's thoughtless or undisciplined conduct.[40]

■ **22** The first four sentences were of the utmost conciseness. Now, however, a more protracted message is directed to the Christian slaves.[41] The question had to be answered: what is the relationship between the freedom granted in Christ and the "slavery" (δουλεία) in which the slaves must continue to serve their earthly masters

---

standpoint of origin" (Albrecht Oepke, *TDNT* 5, 638) and can also indicate the child that has grown up. The evidence for this latter interpretation may be found in Gerhard Delling, "Nun aber sind sie heilig" in *Gott und die Götter, Festgabe für Erich Fascher* (Berlin: 1958), 84–93; *idem*, "Lexikalisches zu τέκνον. Ein Nachtrag zur Exegese von I. Kor. 7, 14" in "... *und fragten nach Jesus,*" *Festschrift für Ernst Barnikol* (Berlin: 1964), 35–44. The reference here, however, is surely to children who are growing up and still subject to their parents; cf. Eph 6:4: "bring them [*scil.* the children] up" (ἐκτρέφετε αὐτά [*scil.* τὰ τέκνα]).

34 The verb "to be obedient" (ὑπακούειν) corresponds to "to be subject" (ὑποτάσσεσθαι) and helps to express the command of absolute subordination. Cf. 1 Pt 3:5f: "The holy women ... *were subject* to their husbands, as Sarah *obeyed* Abraham" (αἱ ἅγιαι γυναῖκες ... ὑποτασσόμεναι τοῖς ἰδίοις ἀνδράσιν, ὡς Σάρρα ὑπήκουσεν τῷ Ἀβραάμ). The wives were told: "be subject" (v 18); the children and slaves are admonished "to be obedient" (vss 20, 22). Cf. Gerhard Kittel, *TDNT* 1, 223f.

35 Cf. Dibelius–Greeven, *ad loc.*: "pleasing" (εὐάρεστον) points "clearly to an established social value."

36 The dative phrase "to the Lord" (τῷ κυρίῳ) [cf. Moulton–Turner, 263] really would have been expected here and witnesses 81 al ClemAlex (cf. Eph 5:10) actually have that reading. The reason why "in the Lord" (ἐν κυρίῳ) occurs here is that a Christian transformation of a generally used phrase has taken place. Cf. Weidinger, *Die Haustafeln*, 51; Dibelius–Greeven, *ad loc.* On εὐάρεστος meaning "what is acceptable to God," cf. 2 Cor 5:9; Rom 12:1; 14:18; Phil 4:18; Eph 5:10: "pleasing to the Lord" (εὐάρεστον τῷ κυρίῳ).

37 Eph 6:2f gives as motivation a reference to the divine commandment to honor father and mother.

38 The only other occurrence of the verb ἐρεθίζειν in the NT is at 2 Cor 9:2 where it is used in a positive sense of the encouraging example. Cf. Bauer, *s.v.* On ἐρεθίζειν in the meaning of "to provoke," "to irritate," cf. Epictetus, *Enchiridion* 20: "therefore, when someone irritates you" (ὅταν οὖν ἐρεθίσῃ σέ τις) refers to the previous sentence "the man who reviles or strikes you" (ὁ λοιδορῶν ἢ ὁ τύπτων). Instead of "provoke" (ἐρεθίζετε) manuscripts 𝔖 D* G K L pm in dependence on Eph 6:4 have: "make angry" (παροργίζετε).

39 The verb "to be discouraged, become timid" (ἀθυμεῖν) occurs only here in the NT. It occurs frequently in LXX (e.g., Dt 28:65; 1 Kings 1:6f; 15:11; 2 Kings 6:8) and is attested since Aeschylus. Cf. Bauer, *s.v.* On the Hellenistic uage cf. *P.Amh.* 2, 37, 7: "do not be discouraged" (μὴ ἀθυμεῖ); *P.Giessen* 1, 79, 3, 11: "nob[od]y is timid in selling property" (οὐδ[εὶ]ς ἀθυμεῖ πωλεῖν κτῆμα); 14f: "they will be discouraged" (ἀθυμή[σουσι]) [Trans.].

40 There is no positive directive like the one in Eph 6:4 that follows the negative admonition. The absence of this directive is not to be explained "by the expectation of an imminent end" (Dibelius–Greeven, *ad loc.*). It is conditioned rather by the terse formulation of the sentence. On the duties which were impressed on fathers by the Hellenistic moral teaching, cf. the chapter heading in Stobaeus, *Anthol.* 4, 26: "The things that are expected of fathers in their dealings with their children, and that a certain physical relationship binds both together" (ὁποίους τινας χρὴ εἶναι τοὺς πατέρας περὶ τὰ τέκνα, καὶ ὅτι φυσική τις ἀνάγκη ἀμφοτέρους εἰς διάθεσιν ἄγει) [Trans.]. Jewish texts explicitly state the prohibition against exposing children: Ps–Phocylides 185; Philo, *Spec. leg.* 3, 110; Josephus, *Ap.* 2, 202; and *Barn.* 19:5 as a Christian example of this prohibition.

41 Almost without exception the commentators link this extended exhortation to the slaves with the case of Onesimus. To be sure, Col 4:9 mentions the name of Onesimus. No word, however, is spent describing his fate. Therefore, there is no justification for directly combining Col 3:22–25 with Phlm. It is true, however, that Phlm is a graphic example of the urgent need of the Christian communities for a special message for slaves.

(cf. 1 Cor 7:21–24)?[42] Consequently, the exhortation to the slaves could not simply draw upon admonitions from traditional moral teaching, but had to be newly formulated as specifically Christian instruction. The slaves, who have become Christians, are told to acknowledge their earthly slavery as the social position assigned them and to obey their earthly lords in all things.[43] As "earthly kyrioi" (οἱ κατὰ σάρκα κύριοι) they are distinguished from the one Kyrios to whom the slaves belong as members of the community. The obedience the slaves must render to their earthly masters should be genuine and not mere "eyeservice" (ἐν ὀφθαλμοδουλίαις).[44] This word, which is not attested outside the NT, means a service done not for its own sake or to please God, but performed for the sole purpose of attracting attention.[45] "Those who want to please men" (ἀνθρωπάρεσκοι)[46] only take into account men and their authority, not God.[47] The Christian slaves should guard themselves against such insincere conduct and serve their masters "with singleness of heart" (ἐν ἁπλότητι καρδίας).[48] As the innermost part of man, the heart which determines his thought and conduct[49] should be simple and sincere. If this is the case, everything that a man does will not be guided by false, ulterior motives, but will be done in the fear of God. The OT phrase "to fear God" (φοβεῖσθαι τὸν θεόν)[50] is also frequently used in the NT.[51] But the words "fearing the Lord" (φοβούμενοι τὸν κύριον)[52] here do not refer to God as in the OT[53] and Rev 15:4, but to Christ. He is the Lord, and his word must be obeyed. "To fear the Lord" is mentioned as the guiding principle of Christian conduct[54] which must be followed by all. It especially points out to the slaves how they can willingly perform their daily service and use it to worship the heavenly Lord.

■ **23** Hence the general directive that whatever is done in word or deed should be done in the name of the Kyrios Jesus (3:17), can now be applied to the conduct demanded of slaves.[55] They should do with their whole

42 Cf. further Eph 6:5–8; 1 Pt 2:18–25.

43 The phrase "in all things" (κατὰ πάντα) is absent in witnesses p[46] 81 pc.

44 In most manuscripts the noun occurs in the plural, but also the singular, ὀφθαλμοδουλία, has strong attestation (p[46] B A D G al); however, it should be taken as an assimilation to the singular used at Eph 6:6. [The English translation would be the same: "eyeservice."—Trans.]

45 Cf. Karl Henrich Rengstorf, *TDNT* 2, 280; Blass–Debrunner, par. 115, 1; Bauer, *s.v.* Cf. also Theodoret on Eph 6:6f (*MPG* 82, col. 552): "He calls eyeservice that type of service that does not issue from a sincere heart, but is content in mere external appearance" (ὀφθαλμοδουλείαν δὲ καλεῖ τὴν οὐκ ἐξ εἰλικρινοῦς καρδίας προσφερομένην θεραπείαν, ἀλλὰ τῷ σχήματι κεχρωσμένην) [Trans.].

46 The word "men-pleaser" (ἀνθρωπάρεσκος) is found in LXX Ps 52:6; PsSol 4:7, 8, 19; in the NT again only in Eph 6:6; further in *2 Clem.* 13:1. Cf. Bauer, *s.v.*

47 Cf. Werner Foerster, *TDNT* 1, 456.

48 Cf. Diodorus Siculus 5, 66, 4: "singleness of soul" (τὴν ἁπλότητα τῆς ψυχῆς); Test Reuben 4:1; Test Simeon 4:5: "in singleness of soul" (ἐν ἁπλότητι ψυχῆς); 1 Chr 29:17; Wisd Sol 1:1: "in singleness of heart" (ἐν ἁπλότητι καρδίας); Test Levi 13:1: "with the whole heart . . . in singleness" (ἐξ ὅλης τῆς καρδίας...ἐν ἁπλότητι) [Trans.]. Cf. Otto Bauernfeind, *TDNT* 1, 386f; Ceslaus Spicq, "La vertu de simplicité dans l'Ancien et le Nouveau Testament," *Revue des Sciences Philosophiques et Théologiques* 22 (1933): 1–26; Bauer, *s.v.*

49 On "heart" (καρδία) cf. above p. 149f on 3:15.

50 Cf. LXX Ex 1:17, 21; Lev 19:14, 32; 25:17; Ps 54:20; etc.

51 Cf. Lk 18:2, 4; Acts 10:2, 22, 35; 13:16, 26; 1 Pt 2:17; Rev 11:18; 14:7; 19:5.

52 Witnesses p[46] 𝔎 pm d vg[cl] follow the familiar biblical expression and write "God" (θεόν) instead of "Lord" (κύριον).

53 Cf. LXX Lev 14:31; 19:14; Ps 14:4; 21:24; etc.

54 Cf. Bultmann, *Theology*, sec. 59, 3 = II, p. 214.

55 The Koine text attempts a more exact assimilation to 3:17 by beginning the verse in the same way with "and whatever" (καὶ πᾶν ὅ τι).

56 The Greek phrase ἐκ ψυχῆς (from the soul, cf. Eph 6:6) corresponds to ἐκ καρδίας (from the heart). Cf. Mk 12:30 par: "And you shall love the Lord your God with all your heart and with all your soul, etc." (καὶ ἀγαπήσεις κύριον τὸν θεόν σου ἐξ ὅλης τῆς καρδίας σου καὶ ἐξ ὅλης τῆς ψυχῆς σου κτλ.). In the OT and Jewish exhortation similar phrases are found in many places, e.g., LXX Prov 11:17: "A man who is merciful does good to his own soul" (τῇ ψυχῇ αὐτοῦ ἀγαθὸν ποιεῖ ἀνὴρ ἐλεήμων); Sir 6:26: "with all your soul" (ἐν πάσῃ ψυχῇ σου); 7:29: "with your entire soul" (ἐν ὅλῃ ψυχῇ σου) [Trans.]; cf. further 14:4; 19:16; 37:12; etc.

57 The particle "as" (ὡς) frequently occurs with the participle to indicate the reason or motivation why something happens. "This same ὡς occurs also in elliptical constructions from which the participle is dropped: e.g. C 3:23" (Blass–Debrunner, par.

heart[56] whatever is assigned to them and be conscious that they are serving the Lord[57] and not men.[58]

■ **24** For the Kyrios will render judgment on every deed. Therefore, the slaves should also not forget that they will receive judgment and recompense from the Kyrios.[59] The term translated by "reward" (**ἀνταπόδοσις**), which occurs only here in the NT, is used most often in a bad sense, as is also the case with the related term "repayment" (**ἀνταπόδομα**).[60] Here, however, it does not refer to divine retribution, but to the reward which the "inheritance" (**κληρονομία**) constitutes.[61] The eternal inheritance[62] is already prepared in the heavens (cf. 1:5, 27; 3:1–4). No one would want to forfeit this precious gift through disobedience. Whoever obediently performs his task will receive the "inheritance." Therefore: "serve the Lord Christ" (**τῷ κυρίῳ Χριστῷ δουλεύετε**). This brief sentence should not be taken to be a statement clause;[63] it is an admonition which resumes the imperative "do" (**ἐργάζεσθε** of v 23).[64] Christ is the Kyrios.[65] When the slave faithfully serves his earthly lord, he is also thereby obedient to the one Kyrios, who is Lord over all.

■ **25** In case someone might take this directive in a light vein, he is reminded of the inviolable law: whoever does wrong[66] will receive the reward his deed deserves. For he will receive the punishment that exactly fits his transgression.[67] To whom, however, is this absolutely valid principle addressed? It would be possible to take it as referring to the master of the slave. The master would be warned against wrongdoing. And if the master had acted unjustly toward his slave, the slave would be comforted.[68] Since the "masters" (**κύριοι**) are not addressed until 4:1, it is more probable that v 25 still refers to the slaves.[69] If they trespass against their masters, they will have to give an account of themselves to God. They should not suppose that since they are miserable slaves they would not be held responsible for their actions or would be granted indulgence because of extenuating circumstances.

425, 4).

58 In dependence on Eph 6:7 manuscripts A al Clem Alex add the participle "serving" (δουλεύοντες) after "the Lord" (τῷ κυρίῳ). Witnesses p[46] B 1739 omit the connective "and" (καί).

59 Although ἀπὸ κυρίου (from the Lord) does not have the article, there can be no doubt that the one Lord is meant who will judge and give recompense.

60 The word "recompense," "reward" (ἀνταπόδοσις) is attested since Thucydides. Cf. Friedrich Büchsel, *TDNT* 2, 169; Bauer, *s.v.* On "repayment" (ἀνταπόδομα) cf. Rom 11:9; Lk 14:12.

61 Cf. Bauer, *s.v.*

62 On the word group "to inherit/inheritance" (κληρονομεῖν/κληρονομία) in the NT, cf. Werner Foerster, *TDNT* 3, 781–85, and Paul Hammer, "A Comparison of KLERONOMIA in Paul and Ephesians," *JBL* 79 (1960): 267–72.

63 The indicative meaning, whose chief proponent is Lightfoot, *ad loc.*, and which is also taken into consideration by Dibelius–Greeven and Conzelmann, *ad loc.*, would surely be correct if "for" (γάρ) were added in accordance with the Byzantine text and the sentence were construed as the motivation for the preceding clause. Witnesses (D) G (it Ambst) also try to produce a smoothflowing train of thought: "the inheritance of our Lord Jesus Christ whom you serve" (τῆς κληρονομίας τοῦ κυρίου ἡμῶν Ἰησοῦ Χριστῷ, ᾧ δουλεύετε). Nevertheless, the asyndetic connection of the sentence "serve the Lord Christ" certainly represents the original text.

64 Cf. also Rom 12:11: "serve the Lord" (τῷ κυρίῳ δουλεύοντες)—an imperatival participle.

65 Except for this passage the combination "Lord Christ" (κύριος Χριστός) never occurs in the Pauline epistles. Cf. Kramer, *Christ, Lord, Son of God*, par. 65, p. 214: "Paul speaks of *the Lord Jesus Christ*, of *our Lord Jesus Christ*, and of *the Lord Jesus*, but not of the *Lord Christ*. . . . In all these instances *Lord* and *Christ* never stand immediately side by side. . . . Moreover, if we take into consideration that *Lord* is a title and that *Christ*, as a translation of 'Messiah,' originally ranked as a title, it is natural that the two titles were not made to follow immediately upon one another." In this passage "Christ" is obviously added to "the Lord" to make clear which Lord is alone deserving of "service."

66 "To do wrong" (ἀδικεῖν) is the violation of law, illegal conduct. Cf. Gustav Schrenk, *TDNT* 1, 157–61; Bauer, *s.v.*

67 This principle is in exact agreement with the *jus talionis*. Cf. Ernst Käsemann, "Sentences of Holy Law in the New Testament" in *New Testament Questions of Today*, tr. W. J. Montague (Philadelphia: Fortress Press, 1969), 66–81.

68 In Eph 6:9 the "masters" (κύριοι) are admonished to treat their slaves decently, "knowing that he, who is both their Master and yours is in heaven, and that there is no partiality with him" (εἰδότες ὅτι καὶ αὐτῶν καὶ ὑμῶν ὁ κύριός ἐστιν ἐν οὐρανοῖς, καὶ προσωπολημψία οὐκ ἔστιν παρ' αὐτῷ).

69 Cf. Schrenk, *TDNT* 1, 160 n. 11. Masson, *ad loc.* and Lightfoot, *ad loc.* think—hardly correctly—that v 25 is directed to both slaves and masters.

Before God's judgment there is no partiality:[70] no favor is shown the masters, nor are the slaves permitted to transgress God's commandment with impunity.[71] Slaves and masters must appear before God's judgment seat and be recompensed by his righteous judgment according to their deeds.[72]

■ 4:1 Only a brief message is directed to the masters. At that time probably very few Christians had large holdings and owned slaves. Hence there is no need to expand on the conduct of the "masters." They are not commanded to free their slaves;[73] they are, however, ordered to fulfill their duties toward their "slaves" conscientiously. Each and every misuse of their authority is forbidden. They are commanded to treat their slaves justly and fairly. The mutual relationship between "justness" (**δίκαιον**) and "fairness" (**ἰσότης**) was a constant theme in the moral teaching and instruction of popular philosophy.[74] Hence everyone knew what was meant by this norm of ethical conduct. For Christians, however, the fundamental principle of justness and fairness had an entirely new meaning. For they had to give account of their conduct to their Kyrios. Consequently, the masters are accountable to the Lord for the way they treat their slaves. For also above them stands the Lord in heaven.[75] Thus the relationship between masters and slaves has undergone a fundamental change. If both realize that they owe obedience to the one Lord, so both have in hand the true standard for their conduct toward one another.[76]

The series of sober admonitions, which are assembled in the rules for the household, points out to the community how each Christian must prove his obedience to his Kyrios in the position in which he was when the "call" (**κλῆσις**) came to him (cf. 1 Cor 7:20–24). Since they are all one in Christ (cf. 3:11) and since there is therefore no distinction in the community between Jew and Greek, slave and free, man or woman (cf. Gal 3:28; 1 Cor 12:13), they are bound to one another and concerned for one

70 The substantive "partiality" (προσωπολημψία) was formed from the OT phrase "to raise the face" (πρόσωπον λαμβάνειν). Indeed the first occurrence is in the NT, but it was probably in use already in Hellenistic Judaism. Cf. Eduard Lohse, *TDNT* 6, 779f.

71 In dependence on Eph 6:9 manuscripts G I it vg [cl] add "with God" (παρὰ τῷ θεῷ) to "partiality."

72 Cf. *Ab.* 2, 18: "R. Eleazar [b. Arach, c. 90 A.D.] said: Know before whom you toil, and who is master of your work"; 2, 20: "R. Tarphon [c. 110 A.D.] said: The master of your work is faithful who will pay you the hire of your labor. And know that the giving of the reward of the righteous is for the time to come" [Charles, *APOT* modified].

73 It is evidence of unhistorical thinking to fault Paul and primitive Christianity on this point. Thus Gerhard Kehnscherper, *Die Stellung der Bibel und der alten christlichen Kirche zur Sklaverei* (Halle: 1957). Cf. the critical reviews of this book by: Hans von Campenhausen, *Zeitschrift für Kirchengeschichte* 69 (1958): 328f and Erich Fascher, *ThLZ* 85 (1960): 521–24. On the entire problem cf. Heinz–Dietrich Wendland, "Sklaverei und Christentum," *RGG*³ 6, col. 101–04; Hennecke Gülzow, *Kirche und Sklaverei in den ersten Jahrhunderten*, Unpub. Diss. (Kiel: 1966). 1:12, 3:9f, 13, 16 respectively.

74 Aristotle, *Topica* 6, 5 (p. 143a) defines "justice" (δικαιοσύνη) as "a state productive of equality or distributive of what is equal" (ἕξιν ἰσότητος ποιητικὴν ἢ διανεμητικὴν τοῦ ἴσου). Lysias, *Orat.* 2, 77 says of death: "For it neither disdains the wicked nor admires the virtuous, but is even-handed with all" (οὔτε γὰρ τοὺς πονηροὺς ὑπερορᾷ, οὔτε τοὺς ἀγαθοὺς θαυμάζει, ἄλλ' ἴσον ἑαυτὸν παρέχει πᾶσιν). Plutarch, *Quaestiones convivales* 8, 2, 2 (p. 719b) discusses the relationship between "justice" (δικαιοσύνη) and "fairness" (ἰσότης). Philo gives a detailed exposition on "fairness" (ἰσότης) *Rer. div. her.* 141–206 and describes it as the "mother of justice" (μήτηρ δικαιοσύνης) *De spec. leg.* 4, 231. On "justness, justice, what is right" (δίκαιον) cf. Gottlob Schrenk, *TDNT* 2, 187f; on "fairness" (ἰσότης) cf. Gustav Stählin, *TDNT* 3, 354f.

75 The author again expresses himself in spatial terms. The Lord is above and sees what happens on earth. Witnesses ℜ D G pm it read the plural "heavens" (οὐρανοῖς); cf. 1:5: "in the heavens" (ἐν τοῖς οὐρανοῖς).

76 Cf. Schrage, *Einzelgebote*, 266: "Love waives what it should justly receive, but it does not waive justice itself. The Christian himself will deal justly and fairly with all (Col 4:1), but for himself he will always set love over justice. It is indeed true that the existing social structures and legal order are not annulled. At the same time, however, neither are they sanctioned as rigidly established institutions. Rather it is from the perspective of love that they are critically tested, transformed, put right and set in motion. And where they do not help to foster the realization and practice of love, they are renounced. Thus love again shows itself to be superior even to the norms which are in accord with creation; indeed it is the absolutely highest norm of Christian conduct."

another because of love, which is the "bond of perfection." But this unity which is grounded in Christ must not be misunderstood to mean that all the distinctions which now and as always exist and are valid in the world should be transcended or levelled in a frenzy of enthusiasm. Rather the Christian must follow the commandment of the Lord and conduct his life according to it, precisely in that position he holds in society. No program for a new social order is drawn up. Rather, the transforming power of love should determine men's relationships with one another. While guiding its life by "love," the community must act in the real circumstances of everyday life in a manner worthy of the Lord and do everything it does in the name of the Lord Jesus—for the praise and glory of God.

4

Final Admonitions

2 **Persevere in prayer, be watchful in it with thanksgiving; 3/ pray at the same time also for us that God may open to us a door for the word, to announce the mystery of Christ, on account of which I am in bonds, 4/ that I may make it known, as I ought to speak. 5/ Conduct yourselves in wisdom toward outsiders; make the most of the time. 6/ Your speech should always be full of graciousness, seasoned with salt, so that you may know how you ought to answer every one.**

A loose sequence of a few additional admonitions follows, again addressed to the entire community. The beginning of this sequence resumes the context which had been interrupted by the rules for the household. 3:17 ended with the words "give thanks to God the Father through him" (εὐχαριστοῦντες τῷ θεῷ πατρὶ δι' αὐτοῦ). Now the directive to pray faithfully is renewed with "be watchful in it [*scil.* in prayer] with thanksgiving" (γρηγοροῦντες ἐν αὐτῇ ἐν εὐχαριστίᾳ 4:2). When the community prays, it should remember the imprisoned Apostle and offer petitions for him so that he may be able to reveal the "mystery of Christ" (μυστήριον τοῦ Χριστοῦ v 3f). Thus, vss 2–4 contain encouragements for prayer, thanksgiving, and petition. The last two verses give directives on the relationships toward outsiders: to conduct one's life in wisdom, to make the most of the time (v 5), and to give a judicious answer to anyone who addresses a question to the community (v 6).

It is probable that a schema handed down in tradition is behind this sequence of thoughts; this schema is also visible in Mk 4:11 par: To the disciples has been given the "mystery of the kingdom of God, but for those outside everything is in parables" (μυστήριον τῆς βασιλείας τοῦ θεοῦ, ἐκείνοις δὲ τοῖς ἔξω ἐν παραβολαῖς τὰ πάντα γίνεται). In its content the term "mystery" (μυστήριον) is here completely determined by the Christology: Christ must be preached as the mystery which has been revealed (cf. 1:26f). It is consonant with the missionary idea, which Col wants to underline, that Col does not stop with the statement that the "mystery" is hidden from those "outside" (ἔξω). Rather in its daily life the community should show consideration for those who are outside. Thus the outsiders will be won over by the "wise" (ἐν σοφίᾳ) conduct of the believers and by the right response which Christians give to questions directed to them.

■ **2** The community is called to constant prayer. This admonition has a fixed place in the community instruction and therefore is repeatedly stressed in the exhortation.[1] God wants to be called upon with unceasing perseverance (cf. Lk 18:1–8).[2] Engaged in that type of prayer,[3] the community will be on its guard. The participle γρηγοροῦντες (be watchful) follows as an independent command.[4] Prayer is the right way to exercise watchfulness.[5] The command "to be watchful" (γρηγορεῖν) is not motivated here by a reference to the day

1 Cf. Rom 12:12; Acts 1:14; 2:42, 46; 6:4; etc. The verb "to persevere in, busy oneself with" (προσκαρτερεῖν) takes the dative of the object. Cf. *P.Amh.* 2, 65, 1, 2f: "to busy themselves with their own cultivation" (τῇ ἑαυτῶν γεωργίᾳ προσκαρτερεῖν) [Trans.]; *P.London* 3, 904, 24–27: "in order that . . . they may busy them[selves] with the cultivation which c[on]cerns them" (ἵν[α] . . . τῇ προσ[ηκού]σῃ αὐτοῖς γεωργίαι προσκαρτερήσω[σιν]) [Loeb]). Cf. Walther Grundmann, *TDNT* 3, 618f; Bauer, *s.v.*

2 Cf. Heinrich Greeven, *TDNT* 2, 807f.

3 Cf. Moulton–Turner, 265: "ἐν =occupied in."

4 Again the participle must be taken in an imperatival sense. Cf. above p. 32, n. 1, p. 141, n. 48, p. 147, n. 110, p. 150, n. 141 on 1:12, 3:9f, 13, 16 respectively. Witnesses I 33 69 $vg^{codd\ pe}$ Or have the participial form also for "persevering in" (προσκαρτεροῦντες) instead of the imperative form "persevere in" (προσκαρτερεῖτε).

5 Cf. Haupt, *ad loc.*

6 Cf. 1 Thess 5:6; Mk 13:34f par; Mt 25:13; etc. Cf. also Albrecht Oepke, *TDNT* 2, 338f.

7 The words "with thanksgiving" (ἐν εὐχαριστίᾳ) have been omitted by manuscripts D* Ambst.

8 The participle προσευχόμενοι (pray) is likewise to be taken in the imperatival sense. Cf. above note 4.

of the Lord which will occur suddenly and unexpectedly.[6] Rather, it simply describes the believers' general stance. They should be watchful and pray at all times. Their prayer should also constantly be filled with thanksgiving and praise as they extol and glorify God (cf. 1:2; 2:7; 3:15, 17).[7]

■ **3** Whenever the community calls upon God, it should not forget to pray for the Apostle.[8] He is praying unceasingly for them (1:3, 9). Therefore they should also raise their hands to God for him. As in 1 Thess 5:25, a request is made to pray "for us" (περὶ ἡμῶν). The "we" refers to the common commission to preach which has been given to the Apostle and to the other messengers of the Gospel. Since in the following clauses the author returns to the singular ("on account of which I am in bonds; that I may make known" [δι' ὃ δέδεμαι; ἵνα φανερώσω]), also "for us" here means no other than the Apostle for whom God should open a "door for the word" (θύρα τοῦ λόγου). In 1 Cor 16:9 and 2 Cor 2:12 Paul speaks of the door that has been opened to him by which he wants to say that his preaching had met with listeners who had a ready disposition (cf. also Acts 14:27). In Col, on the other hand, the meaning is that the imprisoned Apostle might, after all, be given another opportunity to preach.[9] The "mystery of Christ"[10] is named as the content of Paul's preaching. Thus, "mystery" is actually understood as a technical term for the Christian message of salvation (cf. 1:26; 2:2).[11] For its sake[12] the Apostle must endure suffering and imprisonment as is the lot of the ambassadors of Jesus Christ (cf. Eph 6:19f). God, however, knows how the door for the unhindered course of the word can be pushed open despite imprisonment and affliction.

■ **4** May God then decree that the Apostle continue to reveal the mystery of Christ as he ought to speak about it. As God's compelling command this duty is laid upon him and obligates him to spread the word (cf. 1 Cor 9:16). The words employed in other passages to describe this proclamation are not found here: "to announce" (καταγγέλλειν 1 Cor 2:1); "to impart" (λαλεῖν 1 Cor 2:7); "to preach" (εὐαγγελίζεσθαι Eph 3:8). The usage here is: "to make known, reveal the mystery" (φανεροῦν μυστήριον). Indeed, other passages often state that the mystery has been made manifest (1:26; Rom 16:26; 1 Tim 3:16), referring thereby to God's revelation. Nowhere else, however, does Paul use "to make known, reveal" (φανεροῦν) to describe his preaching. When the apostolic preaching is described here in these words, its unique significance of being the proclamation of divine revelation is emphasized. Through his suffering and through his service for the word the Apostle labors for the entire church (1:24f). Both, suffering and service, are equally necessary for the church. Consequently, no word is wasted bemoaning his imprisonment. The community, however, should pray that God may clear an unimpeded path for the apostolic word. No matter what the circumstances may be, this word must be preached (cf. 1:26–28). And the community should be conscious of the fact that it is co-responsible for the success of this apostolic commission.

The Imprisonment of Paul

Since the days of the ancient Church no efforts have been spared to answer the question: where was Paul when the letter to the Colossians was written? The letter says nothing more than that Paul was in bonds for the sake of the mystery of Christ (4:3), that Aristarchus, Paul's fellow prisoner, was with him (4:10),

The adverb ἅμα here has the meaning of "at the same time"; cf. Blass–Debrunner, par. 425, 2.

9 Haupt, *ad loc.*; Joachim Jeremias, *TDNT* 3, 174. Rabbinic evidence for the use of the door image to signify that opportunity is knocking can be found in Billerbeck 3, p. 631. Manuscript A adds: "with boldness" (ἐν παρρησίᾳ), cf. Eph 6:19: "with boldness."

10 Witnesses B* L pc alter "of Christ" to "of God"; cf. 2:2: "of God's mystery, Christ."

11 "Mystery" is used in this meaning especially in the deutero-Pauline letters. Cf. Eph 6:19: "so that utterance may be given to me in opening my mouth boldly to proclaim the mystery of the gospel" (ἵνα μοι δοθῇ λόγος ἐν ἀνοίξει τοῦ στόματός μου, ἐν παρρησίᾳ γνωρίσαι τὸ μυστήριον τοῦ εὐαγγελίου); 1 Tim 3:9: "the mystery of the faith" (τὸ μυστήριον τῆς πίστεως); 3:16: "the mystery of religion" (τὸ τῆς εὐσεβείας μυστήριον). Cf. Günther Bornkamm, *TDNT* 4, 821f.

12 Manuscripts B G read "on account of him" (δι' ὅν) and understand the relative pronoun as referring to "of Christ" instead of "the mystery."

and that the community should remember his imprisonment (4:18). These verses, however, contain no mention of where Paul was imprisoned.

The "subscript" which was added to the epistle at a later date asserts: "written from Rome by Tychicus and Onesimus" (ἐγράφη ἀπὸ Ῥώμης διὰ Τυχίκου καὶ Ὀνησίμου) [K L al]. According to this Paul would have dictated the writing to the Colossians and had it dispatched to the community during the Roman imprisonment. To be sure, Rome is a great distance from Colossae, but not so far away that a messenger could not have travelled to the community and re-established communication between it and the Apostle.

Along with Rome, Ephesus is also named as the city in which Paul was in prison when he wrote to the community at Colossae. The Marcionite prologue to Col reads: "The Apostle already in fetters writes to them from Ephesus" (Apostolus iam ligatus scribit eis ab Epheso).[13] It is indeed true that there is no explicit mention either in the Pauline epistles or in the Acts of the Apostles of an Ephesian imprisonment. Yet Paul points out to the Corinthians that he had to suffer imprisonment often (2 Cor 11:23) and that during his long stay in Ephesus he experienced great hardship (1 Cor 15:32). Therefore, it must be considered highly probable that Paul was thrown into prison for a shorter time also in Ephesus.[14] If Col were written in Ephesus, it must have been composed before 2 Cor and Rom, perhaps also before 1 Cor. But such an early date for the epistle must be positively excluded, for Col, because of its theology, must unquestionably be placed after the major Pauline epistles.[15]

Some exegetes have proposed Caesarea as the place where Col was composed.[16] This hypothesis, however, does not stand up under closer examination. It is true that according to this dating Col would have been written after Paul's major epistles to communities. But references in Col can in no way be reconciled with the account given in Acts. In the final section of Col, Tychicus, Onesimus, Aristarchus, Mark, Jesus Justus, Epaphras, Luke, and Demas are mentioned as the companions who are at the Apostle's side (4:7–14). None of these names occurs in the chapters in Acts that describe Paul's imprisonment in Caesarea (Acts 23:23–26:32). In addition, it can hardly be imagined that there would have been enough room in the small harbor city of Caesarea for the missionary work of such a large staff of Paul's co-workers.[17] Therefore, neither Ephesus nor Caesarea can be considered as the places where Col was written. But Rome could be the city where Paul, toward the end of his life, composed Col.[18]

Nevertheless, this traditional opinion, which is espoused by many exegetes,[19] does not solve all existing problems. In Col's section on messages and greetings almost all the same names are mentioned as in the letter to Philemon. Would this short writing also have been composed in Rome? The runaway slave Onesimus must have undertaken a long and dangerous journey to Rome before he found refuge there with Paul. In Phlm 22 Paul requests that quarters be readied for a visit that he would make to Philemon after his release from prison. In Rom

13 Cf. Erwin Preuschen, *Analecta: Kürzere Texte zur Geschichte der Alten Kirche und des Kanons* II, Sammlung ausgewählter kirchen- und dogmengeschichtlicher Quellenschriften 1, 8 (Tübingen: [2]1920), p. 87. [The subscript and the prologue have been rendered by the translator.]

14 Cf. especially Adolf Deissmann, "Zur ephesinischen Gefangenschaft des Apostels Paulus" in *Anatolian Studies presented to Sir W. M. Ramsay* (Manchester: Manchester Univ. Press, 1923). 121–27; *idem*, *LAE*, 237f; *idem*, *Paul: A Study in Social and Religious History*, tr. William E. Wilson (London: Hodder and Stoughton, 1926), p. 17f; Wilhelm Michaelis, *Die Gefangenschaft des Paulus in Ephesus und das Itinerar des Timotheus*, *Untersuchungen zur Chronologie des Paulus und der Paulusbriefe*. Neutestamentliche Forschungen 1, 3 (Gütersloh: 1925); *idem*, *Einleitung*, 215–18 (on p. 218 more proponents of this position are named); and George S. Duncan, *St. Paul's Ephesian Ministry: A Reconstruction with Special Reference to the Ephesian Origin of the Imprisonment Epistles* (New York: Charles Scribner's Sons, 1930).

15 Cf. Kümmel, *Introduction*, 244.

16 The main exponents of this thesis are: Haupt, 4–6; Lohmeyer, 14f; Dibelius–Greeven, 52; Martin Dibelius and Werner Georg Kümmel, *Paul*, tr. Frank Clarke (Philadelphia: Westminster Press, [1]1953), 138, 146.

17 Cf. Kümmel, *Introduction*, 245.

18 If Pauline authorship is accepted, then Col must have been written during the Roman imprisonment. Cf. Ernst Käsemann, "Kolosserbrief," *RGG*[3] 3, col. 1728: "The dating of the epistle presents two alternatives: If genuine, then because of content and style as late as possible; if not genuine, then as early as conceivable."

19 Cf. Percy, *Probleme*, 467–74; Moule, 21–25; Kümmel, *Introduction*, 245f (where the names of more exponents of this view are mentioned).

20 On this, cf. the more detailed discussion below, p. 186.

21 On this point cf. all the evidence assembled in the excursus "Colossians and Pauline Theology," pp. 177–83.

15:24, 28, however, Paul writes that he plans to travel to Spain from Rome. Now Paul could have changed his plans during his imprisonment. Still, the question whether Phlm was actually written in Rome is justifiably raised. As far as its theology is concerned, there are absolutely no grounds for putting it at the end of the Pauline epistles. There are strong reasons to make the assumption that it was written during an Ephesian imprisonment. Onesimus could reach Ephesus within a few days' journey. And from there Paul could have his request quickly delivered to the master of the slave, that he receive Onesimus back as a brother in Christ. On the one hand, it is advisable to consider Ephesus as the place where Phlm was composed.[20] Col, on the other hand, for the previously mentioned reasons can in no way be assigned to such an early date. There is no reasonable doubt that Paul is the author of Phlm. But a list of weighty reasons exists that makes the Pauline authorship of Col appear doubtful.[21] The agreements in the greetings of both letters would then be attributed to the fact that the author of Col knew and used Phlm.[22] Consequently, a comparison with Phlm cannot yield an answer to the question about where Col was written. The circumstances that produced the two letters, and their relationship, must instead be discussed independently of one another.

Although the imprisonment of Paul is mentioned three times in Col (4:3, 10, 18), there is no allusion that can be used to get a clear idea of where Paul was. The letter simply says that the Apostle is suffering and in bonds. Paul had written the letters to Philemon and to the Philippians in prison. In post–Pauline times this situation was generalized, and the Apostle was represented as constantly suffering. While he was imprisoned, he communicated with his communities and fellow workers through epistles. This typical picture is already sketched with a few strokes in Col and lies behind both Ephesians (3:1) and the Pastoral Epistles (2 Tim 1:8, 16f; 2:9). Thus the suffering Apostle is represented as the witness to the Gospel who is made perfect through suffering.[23] As revealer of the mystery of Christ, he exhibits in his suffering the sign of its incontestable verification.[24]

■ **5** The members of the community should conduct themselves "in wisdom" (*ἐν σοφίᾳ*). This admonition once more emphasizes an understanding of wisdom which is geared toward practical authentication. The right kind of perception enables the Christian to know what God's will is and to fulfill it faithfully (cf. 1:9f, 28; 2:3; 3:16). Whoever conducts his life in this type of "wisdom," which is fundamentally different from everything that has only the outward appearance of wisdom (2:23), will not withdraw into a narrow, closed clique, as the adherents of speculative wisdom do. On the contrary, he will know that in all his actions and in his way of life the "mystery of Christ," revealed by God, is publicly witnessed. The outsiders have a critical eye on the community to see whether or not its conduct is authentic. Those who are not Christians are called "outsiders" (*οἱ ἔξω*) [cf. 1 Thess 4:12; 1 Cor 5:12f; Mk 4:11].[25] How will they judge the community's conduct?[26] The Christians must remember this question and must be conscious of their great responsibility: "Give no offense to Jews or to Greeks or to the Church of God" (*ἀπρόσκοποι καὶ Ἰουδαίοις γίνεσθε καὶ Ἕλλησιν καὶ τῇ ἐκκλησίᾳ τοῦ θεοῦ* 1 Cor 10:32).[27]

Make the most of the time—so runs the next command which is not directly connected with the previous in-

22 For the detailed argumentation for this position cf. below, pp. 175–77.

23 On the exegesis of 1:24 cf. above pp. 68–72.

24 If the authorship of Col is not ascribed to Paul but to a later Pauline student who wrote at a later date, there is no justification for holding that it was written in Rome. Rather, it is highly probable that the author of the letter is to be sought in the Ephesian circle of Pauline theologians. Cf. below pp. 180–83.

25 This expression corresponds to the Rabbinic concept הַחִיצוֹנִים = "those who are outside;" i.e. those who belong to another religious community. The evidence can be found in Billerbeck 3, p. 362. Also cf. Johannes Behm, *TDNT* 2, 575f, and W. C. van Unnik, "Die Rücksicht auf die Reaktion der Nicht–Christen als Motiv in der altchristlichen Paränese" in *Judentum—Urchristentum—Kirche, Festschrift für Joachim Jeremias*. BZNW 26 (Berlin: 1960 = [2]1964), 221–34.

26 Cf. Theodoret, *ad loc.*: "Give them, he says, no grounds for censure; plan for their salvation in all ways" (*μηδεμίαν, φησίν, αὐτοῖς πρόφασιν δίδοτε βλάβης, πάντα ὑπὲρ τῆς αὐτῶν μηχανᾶσθε σωτηρίας*) [Trans.].

27 Cf. Eph 5:15: "Look carefully then how you walk, not as unwise men but as wise" (*Βλέπετε οὖν ἀκρι-*

struction.[28] The word "time" (*καιρός*) here does not mean a specific point in time.[29] Rather it means each and every opportunity offered by time. The Christians must always seize these opportunities. "Time" (*καιρός*) does not refer to a particular period of time in the plan of salvation,[30] nor to the paucity of time that is at one's disposal.[31] Rather, it expresses a rule of life that is absolutely valid:[32] accept each day that God gives with joy and thanksgiving,[33] do not idle away the time that has been given you.[34]

■ **6** In conclusion the Christians are admonished that their speech should always be *ἐν χάριτι*. The word *χάρις* could have the meaning here of "grace" (cf. 3:16). Then it would mean that divine grace, as it were, is directly given to the hearers in the information that the Christians give to outsiders about their faith.[35] Since, however, the words "seasoned with salt" (*ἅλατι ἠρτυμένος*) follow *ἐν χάριτι*, the formulation of the sentence must be based upon an idiomatic expression that was generally current at that time.[36] In this case, *ἐν χάριτι* means that the Christians' speech should be gracious,[37] seasoned with salt[38] (cf. Mk 9:49f; Mt 5:13). This tradi-

---

βῶς πῶς περιπατεῖτε, μὴ ὡς ἄσοφοι ἀλλ' ὡς σοφοί). Cf. further Sent. 16 of *The Sentences of Sextus* (ed. Henry Chadwick, *The Sentences of Sextus*. Texts and Studies 5 [Cambridge: Cambridge University Press, 1959), p. 14]: "In your conduct do not give the world an opportunity to censure you" (*σεαυτὸν ἐπιλήψιμον μὴ πάρεχε τῷ κόσμῳ*). Cf. Gerhard Delling, "Zur Hellenisierung des Christentums in den 'Sprüchen des Sextus' " in *Studien zum Neuen Testament und zur Patristik, Festschrift für Erich Klostermann*. TU 77 (Berlin: 1961), p. 215f.

28 Once more the participle is used with the force of the imperative. Cf. above p. 164, n. 4.

29 Thus, e.g., Gal 6:9: "For in due season we shall reap, if we do not lose heart" (*καιρῷ γὰρ ἰδίῳ θερίσομεν μὴ ἐκλυόμενοι*); 1 Pt 1:5: "in the last time" (*ἐν καιρῷ ἐσχάτῳ*); 5:6: "in due time" (*ἐν καιρῷ*). Cf. Gerhard Delling, *TDNT* 3, 455–64.

30 This view is taken against that of Oscar Cullmann, *Christ and Time: The Primitive Conception of Time and History*, tr. F. V. Filson (Philadelphia: Westminster Press, ³1964), 42, 225.

31 This is the case in 1 Cor 7:29: "the appointed time has grown very short" (*ὁ καιρὸς συνεσταλμένος ἐστίν*); also in Gal 6:10: "as we have opportunity, let us do good" (*ὡς καιρὸν ἔχομεν, ἐργαζώμεθα τὸ ἀγαθόν*).

32 Cf. Seneca, *Epist*. 1, 1: "gather and save your time" (Tempus . . . collige et serva).

33 Concerning this formulation cf. LXX Dan 2:8: "you are buying the time" (*καιρὸν ὑμεῖς ἐξαγοράζετε*); this expression obviously means: you are trying to gain time. Cf. Friedrich Büchsel, *TDNT* 1, 128. The verb *ἐξαγοράζειν* here has the meaning of "an intensive buying, a buying which exhausts the possibilities available" (Büchsel, *ibid*.). It does not, however, mean "to redeem" or "to deliver" or "to satisfy," as if the evil "time" would occasion "severe demands (1 Cor 7:29–32) which have to be satisfied" (Bauer, 5th German ed., col. 537).

34 Eph 5:16 also has the admonition "make the most of the time" (*ἐξαγοραζόμενοι τὸν καιρόν*), but adds a motivating clause to it: "because the days are evil" (*ὅτι αἱ ἡμέραι πονηραί εἰσιν*). The use of the word "time" in Col 4:5 and Eph 5:16 corresponds to the imagery that results when a different set of eschatological concepts is employed. Cf. above pp. 17, 103–06, 132–35 on 1:5; 2:12; 3:1–4 respectively. The expectation of an imminent end has receded; spatial, not temporal, concepts are used.

35 This is the opinion of Haupt, *ad loc*.

36 Cf. Dibelius–Greeven, *ad loc*.

37 Concerning *ἐν χάριτι* in the meaning of "gracious" cf. *The Acts of Paul*, *P.Hamb*. (ed. C. Schmidt [1936]) p. 3, 13: "A youth entered who was very handsome and gracious" (*εἰσῆλθεν παῖς λείαν εὐειδὴς ἐν χάριτι*) [Trans.].

38 Cf. Friedrich Hauck, *TDNT* 1, 288f.

39 There is both Hellenistic and Rabbinic evidence for this usage. Cf. Plutarch, *De garrulitate* 23 (p. 514f): "They seek to ingratiate themselves with each other by seasoning with the salt of conversation the pastime or business in which they happen to be engaged" (*χάριν τινὰ παρασκευάζοντες ἀλλήλοις ὥσπερ ἁλσὶ τοῖς λόγοις ἐφηδύνουσι τὴν διατριβὴν καὶ τὴν πρᾶξιν*). This passage obviously does not talk about seasoning words with salt. Rather it says that men try to season with the salt of conversation the occupations in which they are presently engaged; cf. Moule, *ad loc*. Cf. Plutarch, *Quaestiones convivales* 5, 10, 2 (p. 685a): "For wit is probably the tastiest condiment of all. Therefore, some call it 'graciousness' because it makes the necessary chore of eating pleasant" (*κινδυνεύουσι γὰρ οἱ ἅλες τῶν ἄλλων ὄψων ὄψον εἶναι καὶ ἥδυσμα, διὸ καὶ 'χάριτας' ἔνιοι προσαγορεύουσιν αὐτούς, ὅτι τῆς τροφῆς τὸ ἀναγκαῖον ἡδὺ ποιοῦσιν*) [Trans.]; consult also *Quaestiones convivales* 5, 10, 4 (p. 685 e, f). The following may be mentioned from the Rabbinic literature: *b. Ber*. 34a Bar.: "Our Rabbis taught: If one is asked to pass before the Ark, he ought to refuse, and if he does not refuse he resembles a dish without salt; but if he persists too much in refusing he resembles

tional bit of wisdom about choosing the right word[39] is now applied to the "speech" (λόγος) of the Christians, and given a specifically Christian twist: in responding to those who approach the community with questions, the Christians should be capable of answering to the point (cf. 1 Pt 3:15).[40] Hence, the speech of the Christians must not be dull, but interesting and judiciously chosen.[41] Then the "wisdom," which should characterize the believers' conduct "toward outsiders" (πρὸς τοὺς ἔξω), will also find suitable expression in their speech.[42]

a dish which is oversalted" [Epstein]; *Sopherim* 15:8: "The Torah is like salt." Further examples in Billerbeck 1, pp. 232–36; 2, pp. 21–23; 3, p. 631.

40 Cf. *Ab.* 2, 18: "R. Eleazar (b. Arach, c. 90 A.D.) said: Be alert to learn Torah, and know what you shall answer to an Epicurean, i.e., a free-thinker" [Charles, *APOT* modified]. Cf. Billerbeck 3, p. 765; further examples will be found there.

41 Cf. Mk 9:50: "Have salt in yourselves" (ἔχετε ἐν ἑαυτοῖς ἅλα); Ign. *Mag.* 10:2: "be salted in him, *scil* Christ" (ἁλίσθητε ἐν αὐτῷ [*scil.* Χριστῷ]).

42 Cf. Photius of Constantinople, *ad loc.*: "Therefore, just as fleshly nourishment is scarcely absorbed by the body unless it is seasoned with salt and well flavored, so too the word of instruction which nourishes the soul, unless it is well seasoned with graciousness, will neither nourish nor be absorbed" (ὥσπερ οὖν οὐδὲν τῶν σῶμα τρεφόντων σχεδὸν χωρὶς ἅλατος ἡδύνει καὶ εἰς τροφὴν εὔχυμον ἀναδίδοται, οὕτως ὁ διδασκαλικὸς λόγος ὁ τὴν ψυχὴν τρέφων, ἂν μὴ ᾖ χάριτι ἠρτυμένος, οὔτε θρέψει οὔτε ἀναδοθήσεται) [Trans.].

4 Messages and Greetings

7 Tychicus, the beloved brother and faithful
minister and fellow servant in the Lord,
will tell you how I am doing; 8/ I am
sending him to you for that very pur-
pose, that you may learn how we are
and that he may comfort your hearts,
9/ together with Onesimus, the faithful
and beloved brother, who is one of
you; they will tell you how everything
is here.
10 Aristarchus, my fellow prisoner, greets
you, and so does Mark, the cousin of
Barnabas,—concerning whom you have
already received instructions; if he
comes to you, receive him—11/ and
Jesus, who is called Justus; these are
the only ones among my fellow workers
for the kingdom of God who came from
the circumcision; they have been a
comfort to me. 12/ Epaphras greets you,
who is one of you, a servant of Christ
Jesus, who constantly stands up for you
in his prayers that you may stand forth
perfect and be filled with everything
that is God's will. 13/ For I bear him wit-
ness that he worked tirelessly for you
and for those in Laodicea and Hierapolis.
14/Luke, the beloved physician, and
Demas greet you. 15/ Greet the brethren
in Laodicea for me and Nympha and the
community in her house. 16/ And when
this letter has been read among you,
make sure that it is also read in the
community of the Laodiceans, and that
you also read the letter from Laodicea.
17/ And say to Archippus: take care that
you fulfill the ministry which you have
received in the Lord.
18 I, Paul, write this greeting in my own hand.
Remember my bonds. The grace be
with you!

As in all Pauline letters, the end of the letter is taken up with messages (vss 7–9), greetings (vss 10–15), and brief instructions (vss 16–17). The final greeting written in Paul's own hand, the request to remember the Apostle's bonds, and the wish for grace (v 18) conclude the letter.

■ **7** There is no mention of how the Apostle is faring personally. The messengers who are traveling to the community will report about Paul's condition.[1] The phrase **τὰ κατ' ἐμέ** refers (as in Phil 1:12; Eph 6:21, etc.) to Paul's personal situation.[2] It is again taken up in the following verses by "how we are" (**τὰ περὶ ἡμῶν** v 8)[3] and "how everything is here" (**τὰ ὧδε** v 9). Tychicus,[4] who is expected to set out for Colossae, is mentioned in Acts 20:4 as one of the Asians who accompanied Paul

1 The verb "he will tell" (γνωρίσει) is taken up again in v 9 by "they will tell" (γνωρίσουσιν). This verb is used to refer to important messages (cf. Gal 1:11; 1 Cor 12:3; 15:1; 2 Cor 8:1; etc.).

2 The phrase τὰ κατ' ἐμέ is a common expression for describing the situation in which a person is. Cf. e.g., Herodotus 7, 148: "their own part" (τὰ κατ' ἑωυτούς); Diodorus Siculus 1, 10, 6: "even in our day" (ἐν τοῖς καθ' ἡμᾶς ἔτι χρόνοις); 1 Esdr 9:17: "the cases of the men" (τὰ κατὰ τοὺς ἄνδρας); Tob 10:9: "how things are with you" (τὰ κατὰ σέ); Acts 24:22: "your case" (τὰ καθ' ὑμᾶς); 25:14: "Paul's case" (τὰ κατὰ τὸν Παῦλον). Cf. Moulton–Turner, 15; Schlier, *Epheser*, 306.

3 Despite the plural only the personal situation of the Apostle is in view.

on his journey to Jerusalem with the collection. In Eph 6:21 he is commended to the community in the same words that are used here. 2 Tim 4:12 and Tit 3:12 also name him as a messenger of the Apostle. He is not only described as "beloved brother" (**ἀγαπητὸς ἀδελφός**) like all the members of the community (cf. 1:2), but also as "faithful minister" (**πιστὸς διάκονος**). The "minister" (**διάκονος**) is not the holder of a fixed office in the community, but anyone who discharges a specific ministry. It is not said whether Tychicus rendered this service to the communities or to Paul.[5] It is pointed out, however, that he had proven himself to be a faithful and reliable[6] "minister" (cf. 1 Thess 3:2). His ministry is not concerned with some subordinate tasks. In the final analysis, he does the same thing as the Apostle. Consequently, Paul treats both Epaphras (cf. 1:7) and him as "fellow servants" (**σύνδουλοι**). The phrase "in the Lord" (**ἐν κυρίῳ**), which is to be connected materially with both "brother" and "minister," refers to the fact that he performs his task as a Christian.

■ **8** The Apostle is sending[7] him to the community for the purpose of giving a report about him.[8] For the community wants to know how Paul is doing.[9] But Tychicus is not only to convey information. As the Apostle's fellow servant he is instead to impress the apostolic teaching on the community by encouraging[10] and admonishing "their hearts," i.e. "them" (cf. 2:2).[11]

■ **9** Tychicus will be accompanied by Onesimus,[12] who is described as a faithful and beloved brother (cf. 1:2), not however as "minister" and "fellow servant." It is simply said of him, that he comes from Colossae.[13] There is no indication that the slave Onesimus had run away from his master and was being sent back to him by Paul (cf. Phlm 10–12). Since the names, which are mentioned in the last section of Col show close contacts with Phlm, it must be supposed that one and the same Onesimus is meant.[14] However, the events connected with his flight and how Paul persuaded him to return home are of no interest here.[15] Both Tychicus and Onesimus are coming to the community to discharge their common mission.

---

4 The name Tychicus is variously attested on inscriptions. Cf. Bauer, *s.v.*

5 Cf. Acts 19:20: "two of his helpers" (*δύο τῶν διακονούντων αὐτῷ*).

6 On *πιστός* in the meaning of "faithful," "reliable" cf. above pp. 9, 22f on 1:2 and 1:7 respectively.

7 The verb "I am sending" (*ἔπεμψα*) is an epistolary aorist. Cf. Phlm 12.

8 The phrase "for that very purpose" (*εἰς αὐτὸ τὸ τοῦτο*) thus refers to "he will tell" (v 7).

9 Tychicus is supposed to bring news to the community, not obtain news from it. The variant "that he may know how you are" (*ἵνα γνῷ τὰ περὶ ὑμῶν*) [p[46] C 𝔎 pm f vg sy], therefore, changes the meaning of the sentence into its opposite. Eph 6:22 says exactly the same thing: "that you may know how we are, and that he may encourage your hearts" (*ἵνα γνῶτε τὰ περὶ ἡμῶν καὶ παρακαλέσῃ τὰς καρδίας ὑμῶν*).

10 Cf. Bjerkelund, *Parakalô*, 92.

11 The Greek phrase *τὰς καρδίας ὑμῶν* (your hearts) is a Hebraizing expression (cf. above p. 149 on 3:15f). Cf. 2:2: "that their hearts may be encouraged" (*ἵνα παρακληθῶσιν αἱ καρδίαι αὐτῶν*).

12 The name Onesimus is frequently found on inscriptions, often also as the name of a slave. Thus, e.g., Galen, *De optima doctrina* liber 1: "Onesimus, the slave of Plutarch" (*Ὀνήσιμος ὁ Πλουτάρχου δοῦλος*) [Trans.]. Further examples may be found in Bauer, *s.v.*

13 Concerning the phrase "who is one of you" (*ὁ ἐξ ὑμῶν*) cf. 4:12: "Epaphras, who is one of you" (*Ἐπαφρᾶς ὁ ἐξ ὑμῶν*); Rom 16:10f: "those who belong to the family of Aristobulus . . . those who belong to the family of Narcissus" (*τοὺς ἐκ τῶν Ἀριστοβούλου . . . τοὺς ἐκ τῶν Ναρκίσσου*); Phil 4:22: "those of Caesar's household" (*οἱ ἐκ τῆς Καίσαρος οἰκίας*).

14 Calvin, *ad loc.*, has doubts about this view: "For it is scarcely credible that this is the slave of Philemon, for the name of a thief and a fugitive would have been liable to reproach" (Vix est credibile hunc esse servum illum Philemonis, quia furis et fugitivi nomen dedecori subiectum fuisset) trans. from *Calvin's Commentaries: the Epistles of Paul the Apostle to the Galatians, Ephesians, Philippians and Colossians*, trans. T. H. L. Parker, eds. David W. Torrance and Thomas F. Torrance, (Edinburgh and London: Oliver and Boyd, 1965), p. 359. It is completely uncertain whether the Onesimus who is mentioned here could be identical with the Bishop Onesimus in Ephesus mentioned by Ignatius (Ign. *Eph.* 1:3; 2:1; 6:2). Cf. also p. 184, n. 2.

15 It was not necessarily tact that prevented the author

They will bring them the message of the Apostle and relate how he is.[16]

The list of greetings can only be compared in its scope with Rom 16.[17] The long list of names clearly serves the purpose of establishing closer ties with the community. First, particular men from Paul's company are named, who are already known to the community (vss 10–14). Then the Apostle extends his own greetings (vss 15–17). In contradistinction to Rom 16 Paul's fellow workers are more in the foreground.

■ **10** In the Greek text three names follow the verb "greets" (ἀσπάζεται), the first word of the verse. The first is that of Aristarchus,[18] who also appears in Phlm 24 and is mentioned in Acts as a companion of Paul on the trip to Jerusalem for the collection (19:29; 20:4) and on the journey to Rome (27:2). As a fellow prisoner[19] he is in Paul's company.[20] Second occurs the name of Mark, the cousin[21] of Barnabas.[22] The name presumably refers to John Mark, who was from Jerusalem (Acts 12:12, 25), journeyed with Barnabas and Paul, then separated from Paul (Acts 13:13; 15:37, 39), later, however, was again Paul's fellow worker (Phlm 24; 2 Tim 4:11) and then Peter's also (1 Pt 5:13). The community is supposed to have already received instructions concerning him. If he comes, he should be extended a hearty welcome. It is not said who gave those "instructions" (ἐντολαί). The Apostle probably did not give them since he would hardly have needed to repeat them; they must have come from someone else. The recommendation given to Mark now serves to corroborate those instructions.[23]

■ **11** Jesus, who is also called Justus, is mentioned third. In the Hellenistic Roman world he did not use the Jewish name "Jesus" (Ἰησοῦς),[24] but called himself Justus.[25] There is no further information given about him.[26] It is noted about these three men that they are the only Jewish Christians who have remained faithful to the Apostle as fellow workers for the kingdom of God. The phrase "kingdom of God" (βασιλεία τοῦ θεοῦ) is a formal expression that has lost its full original meaning so that the eschatological character of the concept is no longer in the foreground.[27] In this short sentence there are some faint allusions to bitter battles that Paul had to wage concerning the Law, which had been abolished in Christ as a way to salvation (cf. Rom 10:4). Although many have deserted the Apostle, these three Jewish Christians have persevered with him and stand together with him in

---

of Col from describing these events (thus Dibelius–Greeven, *ad loc.*). Only the name of Onesimus, so it seems, was important to the author of Col—not his life's history. For him the only point that had significance was that Onesimus came from Colossae, so that his name could help to strengthen the relationship with the community.

16 Perhaps in dependence on the Latin tradition, witness G expands "how everything is here" (τὰ ὧδε) by adding "transpiring" (πραττόμενα).

17 It is disputed whether Rom 16 was an integral part of the epistle sent to Rome. Cf. Kümmel, *Introduction*, 222–26 (with extensive bibliography and meticulous examination of the different viewpoints). Nevertheless, even if Rom 16 were originally addressed to Ephesus and were brought to the community together with a copy of Rom 1–15, in any case the list of greetings belongs to the Epistle to the Romans which was known and studied in Ephesus.

18 "Aristarchus" (Ἀρίσταρχος) was a common name. Cf. Bauer, *s.v.*

19 Phlm 23 does not name Aristarchus, but Epaphras as a "fellow prisoner" (συναιχμάλωτος).

20 The word "fellow prisoner" (συναιχμάλωτος) describes anyone who shares one's imprisonment (cf. Rom 16:7; Phlm 23). The word, of course, could also be used in a figurative sense: one who, like Paul, is a prisoner of Christ. Cf. Gerhard Kittel, *TDNT* 1, 196f. Since "fellow prisoner," however, occurs without any further qualification ("of Christ" or something similar), it is most probable to take the word in its literal meaning.

21 The word ἀνεψιός means "cousin," not "nephew." Cf. Bauer, *s.v.*

22 It is taken for granted that the community is acquainted with the name of Barnabas. Cf. Gal 2:1, 9, 13; 1 Cor 9:6; Acts 4:36; 9:27; 11:22, 30; etc. Concerning the names "Mark" (Μᾶρκος) and "Barnabas" (Βαρναβᾶς), cf. Bauer, *s.vv.*

23 Acts 18:27 should be compared on this type of recommendation.

24 On the name "Jesus" cf. Werner Foerster, *TDNT* 3, 284–93.

25 At that time many Jews also took a Hellenistic Roman name that was similar to their Hebrew or Aramaic name. Cf. above p. 6 on 1:1. The name "Justus" was frequently taken by Jews. Cf. Acts 1:23; 18:7 and consult Bauer, *s.v.*

26 If one follows the attractive conjecture of Zahn, *Introduction*, 451, also at Phlm 23 the name "Jesus" (Ἰησοῦς) would have to be read instead of "of Jesus" (Ἰησοῦ). Cf. also Foerster, *TDNT* 3, 286 n. 18 and p. 207, n. 16 below.

27 Cf. Karl Ludwig Schmidt, *TDNT* 1, 587, who draws

the same ministry.[28] Hence they have become a genuine comfort to him.[29]

■ **12** Epaphras sends a special greeting to the community. He has been associated with them from the beginning (cf. 1:7f) and still belongs to them. In the introductory thanksgiving of the letter he was described by the Apostle as "our beloved fellow servant" (ἀγαπητὸς σύνδουλος ἡμῶν 1:7). Here he is given the predicate of honor "a servant of Christ Jesus" (δοῦλος Χριστοῦ Ἰησοῦ cf. Phil 1:1). He is in his Lord's ministry as his obedient servant. Even though miles separate them, he constantly exercises this ministry for the community by standing up for it in prayer (cf. 2:1).[30] His prayer is that the community may stand forth perfect (cf. 1:23; 2:7; 1 Cor 15:58) and be filled with everything that is God's will.[31] Perfection here is also understood as obedience to God's commandment (cf. 1:28).[32] The rare verb πληροφορεῖσθαι[33] could have the meaning of "to be fully convinced, certain." Then it would mean that the community might attain full certainty about everything that is God's will (cf. Rom 4:21; 14:5).[34] It is more probable, however, that πληροφορεῖσθαι here takes the place of the more frequently used verb "to be filled" (πληροῦσθαι cf. 1:9, 19; 2:9, 10). In that case the formulation of the prayer addressed to God once again recalls the polemic against the "philosophy." Man does not attain entry to the "fulness" (πλήρωμα) through speculative knowledge about cosmic relationships, secret initiation rites and worship of the elements of the universe. Rather by adhering to Christ as head over the powers and principalities, the believers have "their fulness in him" (ἐν αὐτῷ πεπληρωμένοι 2:9f) and know what God's will is (1:9f). Consequently, they can stand firmly as "perfect" (τέλειοι) only if they have been entirely and completely filled "with everything that is God's will" (ἐν παντὶ θελήματι τοῦ θεοῦ).[35]

■ **13** Epaphras receives an explicit testimony that he works tirelessly for the community.[36] Why he has to

attention to the fact that in spite of the expression "fellow workers" (συνεργοί) there is no concept of synergism. Phlm 24 merely says: "my fellow workers" (οἱ συνεργοί μου). On "fellow worker" cf. 1 Cor 3:9; 2 Cor 1:24; 8:23; Rom 16:3, 21; Phil 2:25; 4:3; Phlm 1, and Georg Bertram *TWNT* 7, 869–75.

28 The formulation of this sentence did not come off too well. One has the impression that the original intention was to write "my Jewish Christian fellow workers" (οἱ ὄντες ἐκ περιτομῆς συνεργοί) and then "these only" (οὗτοι μόνοι) was added. Cf. Haupt, Dibelius–Greeven, *ad loc.* In any case, the words "these only" (οὗτοι μόνοι) now receive a strong emphasis: they have remained with me, the others have not.

29 This is the only occurrence of "comfort" (παρηγορία) in the NT. But check 4 Macc 5:12: "benevolent comfort" (τὴν φιλάνθρωπον παρηγορίαν) [Trans.]; 6:1: "to the comforts of the tyrant" (ταῖς τοῦ τυράννου παρηγορίαις) [Trans.]; Plutarch, *De exilio* 1 (p. 599b): "The language addressed to us by friends and real helpers should comfort us, not vindicate what distresses us" (δεῖ δὲ τὸν παρὰ τῶν φίλων καὶ τῶν βοηθούντων λόγον παρηγορίαν εἶναι μὴ συνηγορίαν τοῦ λυποῦντος) [Loeb modified]. The word "comfort" often occurs on funeral inscriptions, e.g., *Epigr. Graec.* 204, 12: "as I have you as a comfort even among the dead" (ὡς δὲ παρηγορίην κἀν φθιμένοισιν ἔχω) [Trans.]; further 261, 19; 502, 4; *P.Oxyrh.* 1, 115, 11: "therefore comfort one another" (παρηγορεῖτε οὖν ἑαυτούς) [Trans.]. Further examples may be found in Bauer, *s.v.*

30 As at 2:1, ἀγωνιζόμενος does not refer to a contest or fight, but to the strain and effort exerted for the sake of the community. Cf. above pp. 78f on 1:29; 2:1.

31 Instead of the surely original aorist passive subjunctive σταθῆτε (you may stand) [p⁴⁶ B ℵ* 1912 pc], witnesses A C 𝔎 D G pm read the aorist active subjunctive στῆτε (you may stand) and I 327 al have ἦτε (you may be). Witnesses p⁴⁶ 𝔎 pm replace "be filled" (πεπληροφορημένοι) with the more common "be completed" (πεπληρωμένοι).

32 For the interpretation of the term "perfect" (τέλειος), cf. above p. 78 on 1:28.

33 Cf. Gerhard Delling, *TDNT* 6, 309f. On the noun "fulness" (πληροφορία) cf. above p. 81 on 2:2.

34 Cf. Dibelius–Greeven, Moule, *ad loc.*

35 On the preposition ἐν after πεπληροφορημένοι in in the meaning of "be filled *with*" cf. Blass–Debrunner, par. 172.

36 The word "labor, work" (πόνον) [="he worked" in the translation] is found in the Egyptian witnesses and should surely be acknowledged as the original reading. Instead of this word which never again turns up in the Pauline Corpus, the variants have more frequent expressions: D* G: "toil" (κόπον); 104 1912 pc: "longing" (πόθον); 33 pc (𝔎 sy): "zeal" (ζῆλον); 6 1739: "effort" (ἀγῶνα).

"work so hard" (πολὺν πόνον) for the community is not indicated. Were there difficulties that forced him to get away for a rather prolonged period of time? Could it be that the controversies with the "philosophy" were the reason why he had to withdraw? Nothing is said, however; only a superb testimony is given which accredits Epaphras as the plenipotentiary representative of the Apostle also in the neighboring communities[37] of Laodicea and Hierapolis[38] (cf. 1:7f). Epaphras had clearly worked in all three communities. Also in the future he will stand up for the entire church in the Lycus Valley, especially since the danger which the "philosophy" presents affects not only a few communities, but Christians of the whole area.

■ **14** Luke and Demas add their greetings. Luke[39] is also mentioned in Phlm 24 and 2 Tim 4:11 as Paul's fellow worker. Only here, however, is he called "the beloved physician" (ὁ ἰατρὸς ὁ ἀγαπητός).[40] Yet, no emphasis whatsoever is put on this designation. Consequently, there is no reason to believe that Luke gave medical assistance to the Apostle nor is it possible to draw any conclusions from this mention of Luke about the place of Paul's stay.[41] Demas (cf. Phlm 24)[42] is the last one to send greetings to the community.[43]

■ **15** Only now does the Apostle extend his own greetings, first to the community at Laodicea (cf. v 13), even though it has a special letter coming, then to Nympha and the community that has assembled at her house. It cannot be decided with certainty whether the greeting to Νυμφαν (Nympha) refers to a man with the name of Νυμφᾶς (Nymphas) or to a woman whose name was Νύμφα (Nympha). If one reads "her" (αὐτῆς) with witnesses B 6 1739 sy^h, then a woman is meant. The Byzantine text and Western witnesses (𝔎 D G pm) consider the person to be a man since they read "his" (αὐτοῦ).[44] It could be that the mention of a woman was considered extraordinary, and hence the name of the woman was changed into that of a man by altering "her" to "his." Earliest Christianity did not own special buildings. They gathered together for worship, instruction, and the celebration of the Lord's Supper in the houses of individual members of the community (cf. 1 Cor 16:15; Rom 16:5; Phlm 2).[45]

■ **16** The content of the letter should be made known to the assembled community. When that has been done, there should be[46] an exchange of letters with the com-

37 On the relative location of the three neighboring communities cf. above pp. 8f on 1:2.

38 On the question whether Hierapolis is a genuine compound noun and should be declined accordingly cf. Blass–Debrunner, par. 115, 2.

39 On the name "Luke" (Λουκᾶς) cf. Bauer, *s.v.*

40 The adjective "beloved" (ὁ ἀγαπητός) is missing only in a few minuscules (33 pc).

41 Luke did not serve as a kind of personal physician to Paul. From the mention of Luke's name it can in no way be concluded that Paul must have been in Caesarea, since according to the account of Acts Luke (=the author of Acts) could be supposed to have been with Paul in Caesarea. Lohmeyer weaves together an opinion from invisible thread when he remarks, *ad loc.*: "Luke accompanied Paul on his last journey to Jerusalem and two years later on his journey to Rome. Thus, he also must have shared his imprisonment in Caesarea."

42 On the name "Demas" (Δημᾶς), perhaps a shortened form of "Demetrius" (Δημήτριος), cf. Blass–Debrunner, par. 125, 1 and Bauer, *s.v.*

43 In 2 Tim 4:10 Demas is mentioned once more: "For Demas, in love with this present world, has deserted me" (Δημᾶς γάρ με ἐγκατέλιπεν ἀγαπήσας τὸν νῦν αἰῶνα).

44 The Egyptian text (𝔖 1912 al) reads "their" (αὐτῶν). In this case, the reference would be either to Nymphas and his wife or to Nymphas and his friends. Lightfoot, *ad loc.*, considers this reading to be the original text; the plural "their," however, is more easily explained as resulting from efforts to reconcile the readings "her" and "his." On this text-critical problem cf. also Moule, 28 n. 1, who is of the opinion that Nymphas and "his" should be read. In any case, the problem whether the name stands for a man or a woman cannot be done away with, as Mussner, *ad loc.* does, when he explains that the reference is probably to a married couple in whose house the Christian community or a part of it assembled for worship.

45 Cf. Gerhard Delling, "Zur Taufe von 'Häusern' im Urchristentum," *NovTest* 7 (1965): 285–311, especially 306f.

46 On ποιεῖν ἵνα (to cause that) cf. Jn 11:37; Rev 13:15.

47 The phrase "the letter from Laodicea" (τὴν ἐκ Λαοδικείας) does not mean a letter that the community in Laodicea has sent to Paul, but a letter that the Apostle had dispatched there. The preposition "from" (ἐκ) is used because this letter should be brought from Laodicea to Colossae. Cf. Blass–Debrunner, par. 437. Charles P. Anderson, "Who Wrote 'The Epistle from Laodicea'?," *JBL* 85

munity at Laodicea to which a writing was also dispatched.[47] The Laodicean letter should be read aloud to the community.[48] From this admonition one can get an idea of how the Pauline letters were already disseminated and collected at an early date. Col should be sent to Laodicea, so that this neighboring community can be put on the alert against the dangers of the "philosophy."
■ **17** A special directive should be addressed to Archippus.[49] In Phlm 2 Archippus is called "our fellow soldier" (ὁ συστρατιώτης ἡμῶν). There is no longer any way of ascertaining what was meant by the "ministry" (διακονία) that he had undertaken and which he ought to fulfill faithfully. There is no indication that his ministry was that of a deacon,[50] nor that he was to make a collection,[51] nor is there any hint that it had anything to do with the affair of the runaway slave Onesimus.[52]

The Lists of Greetings in Philemon and Colossians

Almost all the names that appear in the last section of Col are also mentioned in Phlm:[53]

	Philemon:		Col 4:
2	And to Archippus our fellow soldier	17	To Archippus
10f	Onesimus who formerly was useless to you but now he is indeed useful to you and to me	9	with Onesimus the faithful and beloved brother, who is one of you
23	Greets you Epaphras my fellow prisoner	12	Greets you Epaphras who is one of you, a servant of Christ Jesus
	(of?) Jesus	11	Jesus who is called Justus
24	Mark	10	Mark the cousin of Barnabas
	Aristarchus		Aristarchus my fellow prisoner
	Demas		Demas
	Luke	14	Luke the beloved physician
	my fellow workers	11	fellow workers for the kingdom of God

(1966): 436–40 sketches a picture that is drawn purely with the pencil of conjecture. He assumes that the Laodicean Epistle presupposes a situation in the community similar to that which existed in the Colossian community since the communities are directed to exchange letters. But if Paul charged the Colossians to give his greetings to the Christians at Laodicea (Col 4:15), he himself would not have written a letter to the Laodiceans at the same time. In addition, Epaphras was probably the author of the Laodicean Epistle.

48 There is no trace of the Epistle to the Laodiceans. Even though in Eph the words "in Ephesus" (ἐν Ἐφέσῳ 1:1) were only added at a later date, no stock can be put in considering Eph as that letter to the Laodiceans. In order to fill this lacuna, someone later compiled an Epistle to the Laodiceans from sentences gleaned from other Pauline epistles. Cf. the extensive excursus in Lightfoot, 272–98; Hennecke–Schneemelcher, 2, pp. 128–32; Werner Foerster, "Laodicenerbrief," *RGG*[3] 4, col. 231.

49 "Archippus" (Ἄρχιππος) is widely attested as a proper name. Cf. Bauer, *s.v.*

50 The concept "ministry" (διακονία) describes the discharge of service, not the exercise of the office of deacon. Cf. Hermann Wolfgang Beyer, *TDNT* 2, 88.

51 This is contrary to the view of Michaelis, *Einleitung*, 152–54, whose dating of Col is untenable. Cf. above p. 166.

52 This view is taken in opposition to John Knox, *Philemon Among the Letters of Paul, A New View of its Place and Importance* (New York and Nashville: Abingdon Press, [2]1959), who is of the opinion that Phlm was a writing addressed to Archippus. "Ministry," then, would refer to the request which Paul makes in Phlm. Cf. below p. 186.

53 Both Phlm 1 and Col 1:1 name Timothy as cooperating with Paul in sending the epistle.

Philemon:		Col 4:	
2	καὶ Ἀρχίππῳ τῷ συστρατιώτῃ ἡμῶν	17	Ἀρχίππῳ
10f	Ὀνήσιμον τόν ποτέ σοι ἄχρηστον νυνὶ δὲ καὶ σοὶ καὶ ἐμοὶ εὔχρηστον	9	σὺν Ὀνησίμῳ τῷ πιστῷ καὶ ἀγαπητῷ ἀδελφῷ, ὅς ἐστιν ἐξ ὑμῶν
23	Ἀσπάζεταί σε Ἐπαφρᾶς ὁ συναιχμάλωτός μου	12	Ἀσπάζεται ὑμᾶς Ἐπαφρᾶς ὁ ἐξ ὑμῶν, δοῦλος Χριστοῦ Ἰησοῦ
	Ἰησοῦ(s?)	11	Ἰησοῦς ὁ λεγόμενος Ἰοῦστος
24	Μᾶρκος	10	Μᾶρκος ὁ ἀνεψιὸς Βαρναβᾶ
	Ἀρίσταρχος	10	Ἀρίσταρχος ὁ συναιχμάλωτός μου
	Δημᾶς	14	Δημᾶς
	Λουκᾶς	14	Λουκᾶς ὁ ἰατρὸς ὁ ἀγαπητός
	οἱ συνεργοί μου	11	συνεργοὶ εἰς τὴν βασιλείαν τοῦ θεοῦ

Both in Phlm and in Col Archippus and Onesimus are mentioned outside the list of greetings proper. Onesimus is to accompany Tychicus to Colossae (4:9). In Phlm Archippus is designated as co-recipient of the letter and as "fellow soldier" (συστρατιώτης). In Col, however, his name occurs at the end: he should be admonished to fulfill faithfully the "ministry" which he has received in the Lord (4:17). The names that are found in the list of greetings in Phlm 23f reoccur without exception in Col 4:10–14.[54] But whereas, in Phlm, Epaphras is described as a "fellow prisoner" (συναιχμάλωτος), according to Col 4:10 Aristarchus is the Apostle's fellow prisoner.[55] As far as other particulars go, Phlm 23f merely mentions the names, saying of all of them that they are "fellow workers" (συνεργοί) of Paul. Col 4:10–14, on the other hand, comments on each name (except Demas): Epaphras is a member of the Colossian community and a servant of Christ Jesus (4:12f); Jesus is also called Justus (4:11); Mark is the cousin of Barnabas (4:11); Luke is the beloved physician (4:14). It is also said of Aristarchus, Mark and Jesus Justus that they were the only Jewish Christians who remained faithful as "my fellow workers for the kingdom of God" (συνεργοὶ εἰς τὴν βασιλείαν τοῦ θεοῦ 4:11).

Since such thoroughgoing agreements are found between both lists of greetings, the two letters must be closely related to one another. This close relationship could be quickly explained if both writings originated at the same time. While Phlm, however, was certainly written by Paul, there are strong reasons to doubt the Pauline authorship of Col.[56] Hence, if Col was composed by a student of Paul's, he must have known and used Phlm.[57] In any case, a comparison of both lists of greetings shows that Phlm must have been written before Col.[58] Col considerably expands Phlm's concise list of greetings by enriching it with information and notes about the circle of the Apostle's fellow workers. While Paul in Rom 16 produces a long list of names of individual members of the community and extends greetings to them, mentioning a few greetings from other men only in conclusion (Rom 16:21–23), in the last chapter of Col it is the Apostle's helpers who send greetings to the community. Only after that are the Apostle's own greetings given (Col 4:15–18). The Apostle's fellow workers have to continue his work. Therefore, they are written about more fully and are recommended to the community by the Apostle as the Lord's legitimate ministers. Tychicus is not only a beloved brother, but also a "faithful minister and fellow servant in the Lord" (πιστὸς διάκονος

54 The correspondence would be perfectly complete, if one agreed with Zahn's conjecture to read at Phlm 23 "Jesus" (Ἰησοῦς) instead of "of Jesus" (Ἰησοῦ). Cf. above p. 172, n. 26 on 4:11. The only names that are without parallel in Phlm are those of Tychicus (4:7f) and of Nympha (4:15).

55 This variation could mean that different fellow workers successively shared the Apostle's imprisonment. If "fellow prisoner," however, is taken in a figurative sense, it could be that now this one, now that one was described as a fellow prisoner (of Christ?). However, cf. above p. 172, n. 20 on 4:10.

56 Cf. below, pp. 181–83.

57 If both letters were actually written at the same time, why then does not Phlm call attention to the danger posed by the "philosophy"? It is far more probable that when Phlm was composed this problem was not yet pressing.

58 Cf. the approved rule that the shorter text is to be considered the older text.

59 Consequently, the list of greetings and the news notes cannot be used as a proof of the epistle's Pauline authorship. For another view, cf. Gottfried Schille, *Die urchristliche Kollegialmission*. AThANT 48 (Zürich: 1967), 52–54. For it would be very advantageous for an author who wrote at a later date

καὶ σύνδουλος ἐν κυρίῳ 4:7), accompanied by Onesimus, "the faithful and beloved brother" (τῷ πιστῷ καὶ ἀγαπητῷ ἀδελφῷ 4:9). Aristarchus is "my fellow prisoner" (ὁ συναιχμάλωτός μου 4:10). The "instructions" (ἐντολαί), which have been issued concerning Mark, are explicitly confirmed (4:10). Aristarchus, Mark, and Jesus are faithful "fellow workers for the kingdom of God" (συνεργοὶ εἰς τὴν βασιλείαν τοῦ θεοῦ 4:11). Epaphras as a "servant of Christ Jesus" (δοῦλος Χριστοῦ Ἰησοῦ) has always labored tirelessly for the communities (4:12f). And Archippus is once more reminded to be diligent in his "ministry" (διακονία 4:17).

Thus for the author of Col the messages and greetings as well as the particulars about individual fellow workers of the Apostle connected with these greetings serve to prove that his writing is an apostolic message; at the same time, they serve to recommend to the communities the men explicitly named as faithful ministers and helpers of the Apolste.[59] In using Phlm's list of greetings and making it more vivid, he ensures that his letter will gain a hearing as a message from Paul. Therefore, to the greetings he joins the directive that the letters be exchanged with the community in Laodicea (4:16). In this way his teaching would quickly pass into circulation as an apostolic message and be disseminated among the communities.[60]

■ 18 The conclusion of the letter only contains a few words. It was common custom to write in one's own hand the last words of a letter that had been dictated (cf. Rom 16:22).[61] Hence, it says here as in Gal 6:11; 1 Cor 16:21 and 2 Thess 3:17 that the final greeting has been written by Paul himself. Once again the community is called upon to remember the Apostle's bonds (cf. 4:3). This admonition "to remember" (μνημονεύειν cf. 1 Thess 2:9; 2 Thess 2:5) refers to the total work of the Apostle, to his preaching and his suffering on behalf of the entire church (cf. 1:24f). The community should be conscious of what Paul has done for it, so that it may acknowledge[62] him and therefore recognize his authority (cf. Phlm 9).[63] The wish for grace, which again takes up the introductory greeting (1:2), is expressed with formal conciseness.[64] It is shorter in Col than in all the other Pauline epistles with the exception of the Pastorals.[65] Only God's grace (χάρις) sustains the community. Thus the last word of the letter is a reference to the "by grace alone," *sola gratia*.[66]

The Letter to the Colossians and Pauline Theology

This letter is directed to a community that is bound to its confession of faith. The author of Col takes great pains to point out what that confession means for the belief and teaching of the church as well as for the life and conduct of the believers. Therefore, at the very beginning of his letter he places the

to bolster the authority of his writing by statements about individual persons and by more detailed information. On the problem, cf. Dibelius–Conzelmann, *The Pastoral Epistles*. Hermeneia (Philadelphia: Fortress Press, 1972), Excursus on 2 Tim 4:19–21.

60 The so-called Letter to the Laodiceans is introduced into circulation by a similar demand: "And see that this epistle is read to the Colossians and that of the Colossians among you" (Et facite legi Colosensibus et Colosensium vobis v 20) [Hennecke–Schneemelcher 2, p. 132].

61 Cf. Deissmann, *LAE*, 171f.

62 The verb μνημονεύειν means not only "to remember," but also conveys the immediate overtone of "to acknowledge." Cf. Otto Michel, *TDNT* 4, 682f.

63 Cf. Moule, *ad loc.*: "The reference to 'bonds' is not chiefly a matter of pathos but of authority."

64 Later copyists added "Amen" (ἀμήν) [𝔎 D pl lat sy]. Witnesses K L al remark in a concluding subscript: "Written from Rome by Tychicus and Onesimus" (ἐγράφη ἀπὸ Ῥώμης διὰ Τυχίκου καὶ Ὀνησίμου).

65 Cf. 1 Tim 6:21; 2 Tim 4:22; Tit 3:15; also Heb 13:25.

66 Cf. Photius of Constantinople, *ad loc.*: "They need grace to be saved. For what could man do without grace?" (χάριτος εἰς τὸ σωθῆναι δέονται. τί γὰρ ἂν ποιήσοι ἄνθρωπος ἄνευ χάριτος; [Trans.]).

Christ–hymn with which the community is acquainted. Then he draws the conclusions which follow from this confession for a community that wants to remain faithful to the apostolic word, that wants to distinguish between true and false teaching, between pretended and genuine wisdom, and that wants to remain obedient to the commandment of its Lord. Instructing the community in the truth of the Gospel, the author draws to a large extent upon traditional phrases and sentences in order to base his instruction on the tradition. The adherents of the so-called "philosophy" (φιλοσοφία) espoused speculative wisdom and knowledge. Opposing this "philosophy," Col champions the understanding of "wisdom" (σοφία) and "knowledge" (ἐπίγνωσις) that comes from Palestinian tradition and is aimed at practical application. Thus, he corrects the search for knowledge of the higher worlds by connecting knowledge with the will of God (1:9f; 2:8, 23; 3:10, 16). Instead of the initiation rites modelled on the ceremonies of the mystery religions, the church practices the common Christian rite of baptism which is understood as dying and rising with Christ (2:11–13). Col shows how the Christian should actualize the new life to which he has been raised with Christ. This is demonstrated by contrasting the catalogues of vices and virtues (3:5, 8, 12) which demand that one put off the old man and put on the new man (3:10). The rules for the household, the contents of which are taken largely from Hellenistic popular philosophy, then illustrate how life "in the Lord" (ἐν κυρίῳ) is to be conducted in active daily obedience (3:18–4:1). The material which the author of Col adopts and uses in many places is stamped with the leitmotif that runs throughout the letter from beginning to end: Christ is Lord over everything—over powers and principalities, but also over the Christian's daily life.

The major Pauline epistles also often appeal to the common Christian confessions and refer to traditional formulations. In the beginning of Rom, e.g., Paul refers to the Gospel, which he has been called as an apostle to preach (Rom 1:3–4); he concludes his extensive proof from scripture for justification by faith with a reference to the confession of the atoning death and resurrection of Christ (Rom 4:25); and at the beginning of his controversy about the resurrection of the dead he reminds the Corinthians of the common faith in the crucified and resurrected Christ (1 Cor 15:3–5). It is true, Paul can exegete scripture passages in detail to expound the truth of his preaching of the Gospel, and he can have recourse to statements of common Christian confession in order to show the communities that he has delivered to them nothing other than the Good News that is preached to and believed by all Christians. But when he wants to state the meaning of this preaching, he always develops his thoughts in his own language and his own terminology. This enables him to express the content of the Gospel in a fresh way. Col on the other hand, lacks a great many characteristic terms of Pauline theology, e.g., "sin" (ἁμαρτία) [singular], "law" (νόμος), "promise" (ἐπαγγελία), "righteousness" (δικαιοσύνη), "to believe" (πιστεύειν), etc. In their place appears a way of speaking that is stamped by tradition to a much greater extent, a mode in which traditionally coined words and phrases are used in order to establish and to explain the validity of the confession.[1]

Col develops its *Christology* on the basis of the Christ–hymn: Christ is the first–born of all creatures, in whom all things have been created and have their existence; and he is the first–born of the dead; whose blood on the cross has brought about cosmic reconciliation (1:15–20). Nothing is said about Christ's victory over the constraining power of sin, law, and death. The stress is on Christ's triumph over the cosmic principalities. On the cross God rendered the "principalities" (ἐξουσίαι) and "powers" (ἀρχαί) powerless, publicly displayed and paraded them in his triumphal procession (2:15). The exalted Christ is head over all powers and principalities (2:10) and is preached among the Nations as Lord over everything (1:27). The believers have already been placed in the domain of his rule (1:13). These verses delineate the world-wide significance of the Christ–event. The other Pauline letters also contain the common Christian confession that God has exalted Christ and given him a name which is above every other name, that in the name of Jesus every knee should bend—of those who are in heaven, on earth and under the earth—and every tongue should confess: Jesus Christ is Lord—to the glory of God the Father (Phil 2:9–11). Although there may be many so–called gods and lords in heaven and on earth, "yet for us there is one God, the Father, from whom are all things and for whom we exist, and one Lord, Jesus Christ, through whom are all things and through whom we exist" (ἀλλ' ἡμῖν εἷς ὁ θεὸς ὁ πατήρ, ἐξ οὗ τὰ πάντα καὶ ἡμεῖς εἰς αὐτόν, καὶ εἷς κύριος Ἰησοῦς Χριστός, δι' οὗ τὰ πάντα καὶ ἡμεῖς δι' αὐτοῦ 1 Cor 8:6). Paul quotes these

1 It is characteristic for Paul that "in writing his letters he, so to speak, always lets his theological thoughts take shape before his readers and listeners, while Col from the very beginning operates with previously coined and fixed views and concepts" (Bornkamm, "Die Hoffnung," 63).

sentences to proclaim to his community Christ as the Lord who has freed them from the coercion of the law and calls them to the service of mutual love. Because God is for us, nothing—not even angelic powers or cosmic principalities—can separate us from the love of God in Christ Jesus, our Lord (Rom 8:31–39). Col goes beyond these statements by teaching that in Christ the entire fulness of deity dwells "bodily" (σωματικῶς 2:9) and that he is the "head of every principality and power" (κεφαλὴ πάσης ἀρχῆς καὶ ἐξουσίας 2:10). The exalted Lord already exercises authority as Lord over all, not just at the end of the apocalyptic events (1:15–20; 2:9f; 3:1f, 11). And it is precisely for that reason that the Apostle to the Nations has been charged with a worldwide mission. Because Christ is enthroned at the right hand of God (3:1), he must be proclaimed as the Kyrios so that every man may be instructed in all wisdom and be presented perfect in Christ (1:27f).

Col's *ecclesiology* is most intimately connected with its Christology: Christ is the "head of the body" (κεφαλὴ τοῦ σώματος), that is, "of the church" (τῆς ἐκκλησίας 1:18). Christ is Lord over all, but the exalted Lord exercises his rule over the entire world as the head of his body, which is the church (1:24). This statement is not dependent on the Stoic image of a living organism with its multiple and different members; neither does it, like Rom 12 and 1 Cor 12, compare the individual community with a body and the diversity of its members. The author of Col gives a new twist to the cosmological statement that Christ is the "head of the body" (κεφαλὴ τοῦ σώματος) by describing the church as the place where Christ here and now realizes his worldwide lordship.[2] Consequently, the "church" (ἐκκλησία) is the people of God all over the world, whom God has delivered from the dominion of darkness and transferred to the "rule of his beloved Son" (βασιλεία τοῦ υἱοῦ τῆς ἀγάπης αὐτοῦ 1:13). At the same time, however, the local community, indeed even the small house community, is designated by the same word "church" (ἐκκλησία 4:15f). For the worldwide body of Christ becomes visible as the domain of the rule of Christ wherever the saints and the believing brothers in Christ are (1:2), who are joined together by love, the bond of perfection (3:14), who sing praise to God in the assembly of worship (3:16), hold fast to Christ as they have received him in the apostolic tradition (2:6f), and conduct their lives in wisdom (4:5). Thus Col places the primitive Christian concept of the church, which Paul adopted in his letters, into the context of a truly ecumenical theology[3] by designating the church as the world-embracing body of Christ, which as "body" (σῶμα) is subordinated to its "head" (κεφαλή).[4]

The "minister" (διάκονος) of the worldwide "church" (ἐκκλησία) is the *Apostle*, who in suffering and in the preaching of the Gospel "to every creature under heaven" (ἐν πάσῃ κτίσει τῇ ὑπὸ τὸν οὐρανόν 1:23) fulfills the office God assigned to him (1:24). By preaching Christ among the Nations (1:26f; 4:3f), he must proclaim in the entire world the mystery revealed by God. Jerusalem and the twelve are not mentioned; Paul is the only apostle, the Apostle of the Nations. There is no mention at all of any other office beside his apostolic "ministry" (διακονία). Preaching and instructing are not restricted to a group of officeholders. Rather the members of the community are to admonish and teach one another (3:16). In this view of things Col concurs with the major Pauline epistles, which occasionally also mention teachers, prophets, and ministers of the word along with the apostle, but at the same time describe teaching as the entire community's duty which every Christian, by virtue of the charisma bestowed on him, may and should fulfill. The Pastoral Epistles, on the other hand, presuppose a fixed order of the offices of "bishops" (ἐπίσκοποι), "presbyters" (πρεσβύτεροι), and "deacons" (διάκονοι). And Ephesians lists apostles, prophets and evangelists, shepherds and teachers as those to whom Christ has entrusted the preaching of the word for the sake of preparing the saints for service and of building up the body of Christ (Eph 4:11f). In Col, however, the community is not tied to a definite order of offices or officeholders,[5] but simply to the apostolic word through which the Apostle fulfills his ministry. This word has been brought to the communities by the accredited messengers of the Gospel as the true teaching, and it took root among them (1:5–8). The community should unswervingly hold fast to this message (2:6f). For the apostolic tradition gives the community a firm criterion for warding off false teaching and deceitful seduction. Therefore, the community is pledged to the transmitted word, in the form in which it has been entrusted to the apostolic office and is preached by it. Thus confession and apostol-

2 Cf. above p. 54f on 1:18.

3 Cf. Eduard Schweizer, *Church Order in the New Testament*, tr. Frank Clarke. SBT 32 (London: SCM Press, 1961), 105–107 (8a–c).

4 Cf. Lohse, "Christusherrschaft und Kirche," 204–07.

5 Cf. Schweizer, *Church Order*, 107 (8c): "The dangers

ate are coordinated with each other; one cannot be conceived of without the other.[6]

The fact that *eschatology* in Col has receded into the background corresponds to this emphasis upon the apostolic teaching. The expectation that the Lord would soon come has disappeared. True, it is said that Christ will appear at some future day (3:4) and that hope is the content of preaching and belief (1:5, 23, 27). "Hope" (ἐλπίς), however, now means the object of hope which already lies prepared in heaven for believers (1:5). A spatially determined mode of thought replaces the expectation which eagerly longs for the future fulfillment of the divine promise. The Kairos is no longer the point of time for which the believers yearn with eager expectation, but the time that offers opportunities that must be used (4:5). Just as the concept of "faith" (πίστις) is taken in the sense of "faith that is believed in" (*fides quae creditur*) [2:7; cf. also 1:23], so too is "hope" (ἐλπίς) understood as "hope that is hoped for" (*spes quae speratur*). While Paul grounds hope on faith (cf. Rom 4:18), in Col "hope" (ἐλπίς) has actually become the content of the Gospel which is to be preached throughout the world.[7]

Since eschatology has receded into the background, the understanding of *baptism* has undergone an essential transformation. In the epistle to the Romans Paul says that in baptism we died to sin once and for all so that we no longer have to serve it. The baptized Christian lives by faith in the resurrected Lord and is filled with hope for the resurrection of the dead (Rom 6:11). Col, however, not only says that in baptism we have died with Christ and been buried with him, but adds: you have risen with Christ (2:12); God made you alive together with him (2:13); you have been raised with Christ (3:1). The resurrection to new life has already happened, so that the future event is no longer called the resurrection of the dead, but the revelation of life in which the Christians already participate and which is still hidden "with Christ in God" (σὺν Χριστῷ ἐν τῷ θεῷ 3:3). Consequently, the meanings of the formula-like phrases "in Christ" (ἐν Χριστῷ) and "with Christ" (σὺν Χριστῷ) almost merge. For "with Christ" (σὺν Χριστῷ) refers to the new life with Christ appropriated in baptism, a new life which is demonstrated in conduct "in Christ" (ἐν Χριστῷ). The exhortation calls upon the Christian to put off the old man and put on the new man "who is being renewed in knowledge according to the image of his creator" (τὸν ἀνακαινούμενον εἰς ἐπίγνωσιν κατ' εἰκόνα τοῦ κτίσαντος αὐτόν 3:10). Accordingly, the imperative is closely related to the indicative in order to describe the actualization of the "life" (ζωή) of those who were raised with Christ. However, while Paul, in the epistle to the Romans, states that we have died to sin "so that we might no longer be enslaved to sin" (τοῦ μηκέτι δουλεύειν ἡμᾶς τῇ ἁμαρτίᾳ Rom 6:6), Col says: "with Christ you died to the elements of the universe" (ἀπεθάνετε σὺν Χριστῷ ἀπὸ τῶν στοιχείων τοῦ κόσμου Col 2:20). While Paul directs the conduct of believers toward the future resurrection of the dead, Col consistently develops its exhortation by referring back to baptism. Resurrection with Christ has already taken place; life "with Christ" is a present reality. Consequently, "if, therefore, you have been raised with Christ, seek that which is above—consider that which is above" (εἰ οὖν συνηγέρθητε τῷ Χριστῷ, τὰ ἄνω ζητεῖτε—τὰ ἄνω φρονεῖτε 3:1).[8]

It is true that the thought of Col certainly exhibits Pauline features. The differences, however, that exist between Col and the theology of the major Pauline epistles must not be overlooked. They are not at all limited to the passages that argue against the "philosophy," but also occur in sections that are free of polemic. Consequently, the appearance of non-Pauline concepts and expressions cannot be explained simply by saying that they were coined by the specific circumstances of this controversy. Rather Pauline theology has undergone a profound change in Col, which is evident in every section of the letter and has produced new formulations in Christology,

that have arisen in Colossae are met on the facts of the case, not by recourse to offices and order." Cf. also Lohse, "Christusherrschaft und Kirche," 215.

6 Cf. Käsemann, *Essays*, 166f.

7 Cf. Bornkamm, "Die Hoffnung," 56–64, esp. 64; Conzelmann, *Outline*, 341f.

8 Cf. Koester, "The Purpose," 329 n. 2: "There is not a single instance in the genuine epistles of Paul in which the resurrection of the Christians in the past or present is referred to as the basis of the imperative. On the contrary, the resurrection of the believer remains a future expectation, or it is contained in the imperative itself, that is, it is only present in the dialectical demand to walk in the newness of life."

9 The problem posed by these facts is not resolved, but only camouflaged, when Col is described as a work of the aging Paul who had developed his theology further and now, in Col, ponders the mystery of the divine plan of salvation. This is the opinion of Alfred Wikenhauser, *New Testament Introduction*, tr. Joseph Cunningham (New York: Herder & Herder, [2]1958), 417; Lucien Cerfaux, *Christ in the Theology of St. Paul*, tr. Geoffrey Webb and Adrian Walker (New York: Herder & Herder, 1959), 418: "The epistles of the captivity mark, both in liturgy and theology, a deepening of the element of revelation and knowl-

ecclesiology, the concept of the apostle, eschatology, and the understanding of baptism.[9] Therefore, Paul cannot be considered to be the direct or indirect author of Col.[10] Rather a theologian schooled in Pauline thought composed the letter with the intention of bringing the Apostle's word to bear on the situation that had arisen in the Asia Minor communities because of the "philosophers." Just as Paul maintained his ties with his communities through letters, so also for his students the letter was the opportune form to be used in order to make binding positions and statements known to the communities. The legacy of the Apostle was at hand in the letters which the circle of his students preserved and carefully studied. By frequently referring to correct teaching and tradition (1:5–8, 23, 28; 2:6f; 3:16; etc.) and often adopting traditional phrases and liturgical formulations,[11] Col presupposes a Pauline school tradition. It is likely that this school tradition was based in Ephesus as the center of the Pauline mission in Asia Minor, and that it was cultivated and further developed in the circle of the Apostle's students.[12]

The form for this letter was given in the other Pauline letters. And the author of Col found a ready-made list of names and information in Phlm which he could adopt and expand with news from the circle of the Apostle's fellow workers.[13] Since the recipient of Phlm most likely lived in Colossae, it is probable that the pattern of Phlm also determined the choice of the addressees. In the small city of Colossae there would have been only a tiny community. The earthquake catastrophe of 60–61 A.D. caused considerable damage in the Lycus Valley. And it is uncertain whether Colossae was rebuilt at all after that earthquake, or whether a community still remained there.[14] In any case, the author of Col had in mind not only the goings-on of a small community. Rather, his concern was to paint a typical picture of the life of a Christian community. Therefore, his letter is aimed at a larger circle of readers with the intention of teaching Christians in Asia Minor how they should conduct themselves in true obedience to their Lord, in the face of the menace of syncretism.

In the Pauline communities and in the circle of

---

edge in the Johannine manner." Cf. also *idem*, "En faveur de l'authenticité des épîtres de la captivité. Homogénité doctrinale entre Éphésiens et les grandes épîtres" in: *Littérature et Théologie Pauliniennes*, *Recherches Bibliques* 5 (1960): 60–71; *idem*, *The Christian in the Theology of St. Paul*, tr. Lilian Soiron (London: Geoffrey Chapman, 1967), 515–40: Col and Eph present the final phase of Pauline theology and at the same time give a resume of its themes. The theology of both epistles "is like the end of a journey which has already begun in the major epistles . . . There is a progressive enrichment of the theme of revelation, with its two focal points, the mystery of the wisdom of God, and the Christian's knowledge of this mystery" (p. 538). Although Heinrich Schlier at first held the position that Col and Eph differ "essentially from the Pauline epistles" (*Christus*, p. 39 n. 1), he now thinks that Eph can be explained as a mature work of the Apostle, written by Paul towards the end of his life (*Epheser*, p. 27f). Cf. on this viewpoint the criticism of Käsemann, *Exegetische Versuche und Besinnungen, Aufsätze* 2 (Göttingen: 1960), p. 255f: "It is disappointing to see Schlier use the cheap argument that the wisdom of old age caused such modifications (*scil.* the movement from Pauline theology to that of Col and Eph). For in this way, to put the matter succinctly, decisive elements in the original message and theology of Paul are curtailed and devaluated."

10 Only embarrassment can have caused the proposal that Paul instructed one of his secretaries to compose the letter. Thus, the divergencies in vocabulary and style as well as in essential argumentation of points would have to be ascribed to the secretary. This is the opinion of Benoit, "Rapports littéraires," 21f. = *Exégèse et théologie* 3, p. 333f. Cf. also above p. 91.

11 Consult the excursus "Language and Style of Colossians," pp. 84–91. The fact that a list of noteworthy parallels to the vocabulary and style of the Qumran texts can be uncovered in Col (cf. above pp. 88f) is of special importance here. Hymnic prose, liturgical phrases and instructional formulations depend in both instances on a school tradition which preceded the fixing of the tradition in writing. Surely one should not think that Col is directly dependent on the writings of Qumran. But the Hellenistic synagogue could represent the connecting link both for the adoption of certain ideas (cf. above p. 38, n. 48) and for the influence that is visible in comparable features of language and style.

12 Concerning the problem of a Pauline school tradition, cf. Hans Conzelmann, "Paulus und die Weisheit," *NTS* 12 (1965–66): 231–44, esp. p. 233f. The rise of deutero-Pauline writings presupposes such a school tradition. It is another question (which will not be discussed here), however, whether it is also possible already to detect in the undoubtedly authentic letters—as Conzelmann leads one to suspect—traces of a Pauline school.

13 Cf. above pp. 175–77.

14 Cf. above pp. 8f. The community of Colossae is not mentioned in the letters of the Revelation of John. Since, however, only seven communities are enumerated (Rev. 1:11; 2–3), it is impossible to draw

the Apostle's students, Paul's letters were read and studied again and again, above all the letter to the Romans. In many passages Col clearly exhibits the degree to which the letter to the Romans influenced the Pauline school tradition.[15] Both Rom and Col follow the same clear epistolary construction in which an exhortatory section comes after an instructional one (Rom 1–11; 12–15 [16]; Col 1–2; 3–4; cf. also Eph 1–3; 4–6). Both writings are addressed to readers with whom the Apostle is not personally acquainted. The Christians in Rome are addressed as "God's beloved, who are called to be saints" (ἀγαπητοὶ θεοῦ, κλητοὶ ἅγιοι Rom 1:7), not as "church" (ἐκκλησία); the Colossians are called "saints, the faithful brothers" (ἅγιοι καὶ πιστοὶ ἀδελφοί Col 1:2). A Jewish–Christian confession occurs at the beginning of Rom (Rom 1:3f), a hymnic confession of Christ occurs at the beginning of Col (Col 1:15–20). As in Rom 1:8–15, Col also emphatically refers to the apostolic commission to preach the Gospel among the Nations (Col 1:5–8, 24–29), and thereby at the same time shows why the Apostle is the duly qualified authority even for a community he does not know personally. Both Rom 6:1–11 and Col 2:11–13 take up the theme of the Christian's union with the death and resurrection of Jesus Christ as grounded in baptism. The imperative of ethical demand is related to the indicative of the affirmation of salvation (Rom 6:1–11; Col 3:5–11). Both letters lean heavily on traditional material for the contents of their exhortation (Rom 12–13; Col 3:1–4:6). Finally, the list of greetings at the end of the letter serves to establish ties with the community (Rom 16; Col 4:7–18).

Just as in the case of the letter to the Romans, there are also various connections between Col and the other Pauline letters. The letter to the Galatians says that the Christian who belongs to his Lord can and should not submit to the "weak and beggarly elements" (ἀσθενῆ καὶ πτωχὰ στοιχεῖα Gal 4:9; cf. Col 2:8, 20). Since Christ has freed us from the curse of the law (Gal 3:13), the decrees of the law can no longer have constraining power over Christians (Gal 4:8–10, etc.; cf. Col 2:20f). In the First Epistle to the Corinthians, the wisdom of this world is contrasted with the foolishness of the preaching of the cross in order to proclaim Christ as the Wisdom of God (1 Cor 1:18–31; cf. Col 2:3, etc.). The Second Epistle to the Corinthians highlights the task of the Apostle and the "sufferings of Christ" (παθήματα τοῦ Χριστοῦ) which he bears for the sake of the community (2 Cor 1:3–7; cf. Col 1:24). A number of sentences that are similar to statements in Col are found also in the letter to the Philippians. In both letters the Apostle is in prison (Phil 1:7, 13, 17; cf. Col 4:3, 10, 17), the community is called upon to be joyful (Phil 3:1; 4:4, etc.; cf. Col 1:11), admonished to genuine wisdom and knowledge (Phil 1:9; cf. Col 1:9, etc.), reminded of the hymnic praise of Christ's work (Phil 2:6–11; Col 1:15–20), and pledged to the tradition which was entrusted to them by the word of the Apostle (Phil 4:9; cf. Col 2:6).

It is adundantly clear from the examples cited above[16] that the author of Col was thoroughly acquainted with the principal themes of Pauline theology. He acquired this familiarity by an exacting study of the Pauline school tradition. He is, no doubt, well versed in the epistles of Paul. But in writing Col, he did not use them constantly as if to produce a patchwork of individual passages from other epistles. Rather, he responds to the challenge that the "philosophy" presented by applying Pauline theology to this new problem. Only in the case of the letter to Philemon is literary dependence obvious, for Phlm's list of greetings was used and expanded in Col.

The Pauline tradition is linked in Col with various elements of tradition from Hellenistic Christianity. Adopted elements were confessions, hymns of praise, and catechetical instruction (1:12–14, 15–20; 2:9f, 14f; 3:18–4:1; etc.). In many passages of the letter, however, these traditional elements are interpreted along Pauline lines by connecting them with the cross of Christ where God has established reconciliation (1:20) and nailed up the certificate of indebtedness (2:14). As a result of this blending of Pauline teaching and common Christian tradition many specifically Pauline concepts are omitted or played in low key, while others undergo substantial transformation, e.g., the disappearance of an imminent expectation of the parousia; the reformulation of the understanding of baptism; the close connection of apostolate and confession, right teaching and apostolic instruction. In the changed situation which

---

any certain conclusion from this fact.

15 Sanders, "Literary Dependence," 28–45, has correctly drawn attention to connections with the major Pauline epistles. Sanders, however, too onesidedly wants to explain the connections by means of literary dependence.

16 The list of similar expressions—as the parallels mentioned in the commentary indicate—could be considerably expanded without difficulty.

17 It is certain that Col was written earlier than Eph and no doubt also before the Pastorals. Therefore, its date of composition should not be placed too long after the death of Paul. A date around 80 A.D. could be considered. Ephesus has highest probability as the city where Col was composed, since it was the center of the Pauline school tradition.

obtained for some time after Paul's death[17] the author of Col affirms to the communities the message of the Apostle in a powerful new formulation.[18] As Paul made clear to the Galatians that the Christian had died to the law, so it is now stated that the Christian in baptism has died to the "elements of the universe." He belongs to Christ, who is Lord over everything, so that the powers and principalities no longer concern him. By disclosing to the community the broad horizon of the reality of salvation which is spanned by the confession in Christ, the author of Col binds it to the obligating power of its confession.[19] Wherever Christ is believed in and confessed as Lord, wherever he grants forgiveness of sins, there is life and blessedness.[20] For the Christ who is preached throughout the world is not only the "hope of glory" (ἐλπὶς τῆς δόξης 1:27), but also "our life" (ἡ ζωὴ ἡμῶν 3:4).[21]

18 Cf. also Peter Stuhlmacher, "Christliche Verantwortung bei Paulus und seinen Schülern," *EvTheol* 28 (1968): 165–86, esp. pp. 174–81.

19 Cf. Bornkamm, *Aufsätze* 2, p. 200.

20 The emphasis on present "life" (ζωή) as a matter of fact has a certain affinity with Johannine theology. Cf. above, p. 134, n. 14.

21 In the literature of the ancient church Col is first attested for certain in Irenaeus: "And again in the Epistle to the Colossians he says: 'Luke, the beloved physician, greets you' " (Et iterum in epistola quae est ad Colossenses ait: 'Salutat vos Lucas medicus dilectus' *Adv. haer.* 3, 14, 1) [Trans.]. For the time after Irenaeus, cf. Clement of Alexandria, *Strom.* 1, 15, 5; Origen, *Contra Celsum* 5, 8. In the Muratorian Canon, Col is listed among the Pauline epistles: "the fourth epistle was addressed to the Colossians" (ad Colossenses quarta) [Trans.]. It cannot be proved for certain that any of the allusions to Col that occur in the writings of the Apostolic Fathers or in Justin are actual citations: these contacts with Col are entirely limited to formula-like phrases. Cf. Ign.*Tr.* 5:2: "things seen and unseen" (ὁρατά τε καὶ ἀόρατα) cf. Col 1:16; Ign.*Rom.* 5:3: "of things seen or unseen" (τῶν ὁρατῶν καὶ ἀοράτων) cf. *ibid.*; Ign.*Sm.* 6:1: "things in heaven . . . visible and invisible" (τὰ ἐπουράνια . . . ὁρατοί τε καὶ ἀόρατοι), cf. *ibid.*; Ign.*Eph.* 10:2: "steadfast in faith" (ἑδραῖοι τῇ πίστει), cf. Col 1:23; Pol.*Phil.* 10:1: "firm and unchangeable in faith" (firmi in fide et immutabiles), cf. *ibid.*; *Barn.* 12:7: "for all things are in him and for him" (ὅτι ἐν αὐτῷ πάντα καὶ εἰς αὐτόν), cf. Col 1:16. Cf. further, Justin, *Dial.* 84:2: "the First–born of all creatures" (τὸν πρωτότοκον τῶν πάντων ποιημάτων), cf. Col 1:15; cf. also *Dial.* 85:2; 100:2; 125:3; 138:2: "Now, since Christ was the First–born of every creature" (ὁ γὰρ Χριστὸς πρωτότοκος πάσης κτίσεως ὤν) [trans. T. B. Falls, *Writings of Saint Justin Martyr*, The Fathers of the Church Series (New York: Christian Heritage, Inc., 1948)].

Philemon

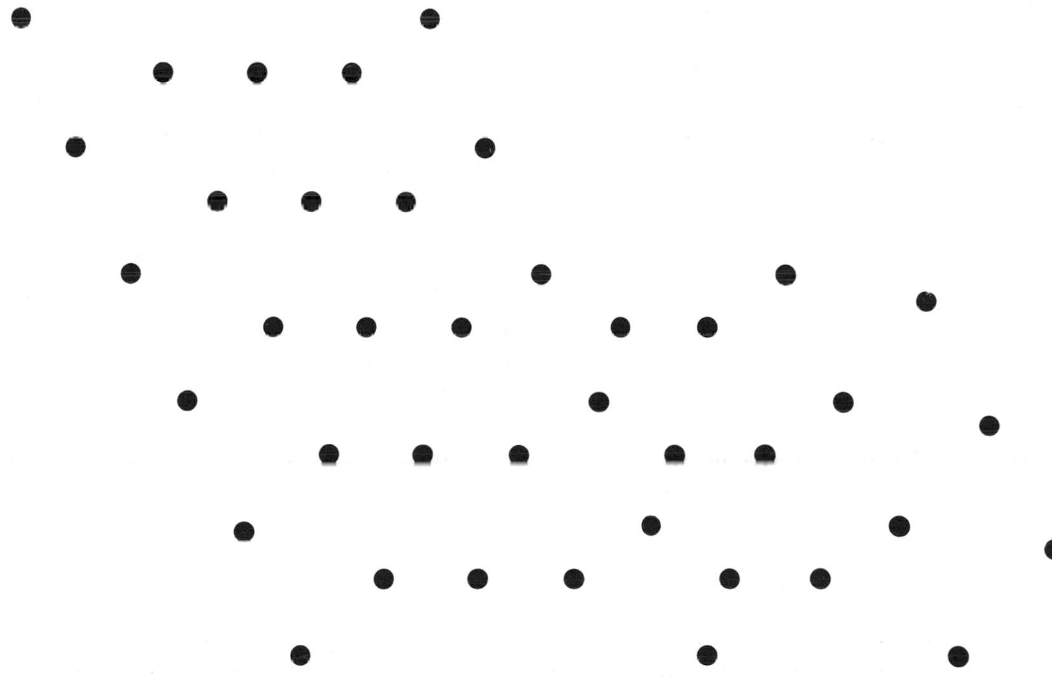

1. The recipient of the letter

Paul addressed this letter to Philemon, whom he calls his beloved fellow worker. Additional addressees are the sister Apphia, the fellow soldier Archippus, and the community assembled in Philemon's house. Since Col expressly mentions that Onesimus (Col 4:9) and Archippus (Col 4:17) belong to the community at Colossae, it can also be assumed that Philemon, from whose house the slave Onesimus fled, lived in Colossae. Philemon was obviously well-to-do and had become a Christian through encountering Paul (v 19)—possibly in Ephesus. He had placed his house at the disposal of the community for its meetings (v 2) and had given concrete expression to his love for the saints (vss 5, 7). Perhaps Apphia, whose name is mentioned alongside his, was his wife. It is unclear how Archippus was related to him.

According to John Knox,[1] the master of Onesimus should be Archippus, not Philemon. Consequently, Archippus would be the recipient of the letter. Knox arrives at this position by presupposing that Phlm and Col were written at the same time. Since he thinks it highly unlikely that the letter from Laodicea, mentioned in Col 4:16, would be lost, he assumes that the letter meant by that designation is none other than Phlm. Onesimus came from Colossae (Col 4:9); the same is true of Archippus whom the community should tell to fulfill his "ministry" (διακονία Col 4:17). According to Col 4:16 the letter from Laodicea should be conveyed to the community at Colossae. Therefore Philemon, whose name occurs at the beginning of the letter, is supposed to have been a distinguished member of the community at Laodicea. Paul would have sent the letter first to him, so that he might pass it on to Colossae and exert his authority on Archippus, urging him to fulfill the apostolic request. The "ministry" (διακονία) that Archippus is admonished to fulfill in Col 4:17 was none other than the service Paul requests of him with regard to Onesimus.[2]

Knox establishes his case by arbitrarily harmonizing statements in Col and Phlm. There is not the slightest basis in Phlm for linking it to the letter from Laodicea mentioned in Col 4:16. Moreover, it is not possible to construe Col 4:17 in such a way that Archippus' "ministry" is discharged in his relationship to Onesimus. The beginning of Phlm lends no support to the thesis that Archippus, not Philemon, was the master of the runaway slave Onesimus. Although Apphia, Archippus and the "house community" are mentioned along with Philemon as the addressees of the letter, there is no doubt that when the Apostle later addresses the letter's recipient in the singular (vss 2, 4),[3] he has only Philemon in mind. Knox's

1 John Knox, *Philemon Among the Letters of Paul: A New View of its Place and Importance* (Chicago: University of Chicago Press, 1935; rev. ed.: New York and Nashville: Abingdon Press, 1959); *idem*, "Philemon and the Authenticity of Colossians," *Journal of Religion* 18 (1938): 144–60; cf. the earlier work of J. Pommier, "Autour du billet à Philémon," *RHPR* 8 (1928): 180f. For a critique of Knox cf. P. N. Harrison, "Onesimus," 268–94; Heinrich Greeven, "Prüfung der Thesen von J. Knox zum Philemonbrief," "*ThLZ* 79 (1954): 373–78: Werner Schmauch, *Evangelisches Kirchenlexikon* 3, col. 183; Kümmel, *Introduction*, 246.

2 To this description of the origins of the letter to Philemon Knox joins a further hypothesis which he establishes by linking together highly uncertain suppositions. Cf. his *Philemon*, 91–108, "The Historical Importance of Philemon:" Onesimus was responsible for preserving Paul's brief letter to Philemon. He later became bishop of Ephesus and there started to collect the letters of Paul. At this point Knox builds on the hypothesis of Goodspeed, who held that Ephesians was placed at the beginning of the collection of Pauline letters (Edgar J. Goodspeed, *The Meaning of Ephesians* [Chicago: University of Chicago Press, 1933]; *idem*, *The Key to Ephesians* [Chicago: University of Chicago Press, 1956]). Onesimus, bishop of Ephesus, would have been responsible for putting Ephesians in this prominent place in the sequence of the Apostle's letters. (Harrison, "Onesimus," 290–94, concurs to a large extent with this hypothesis of Knox.) It must remain entirely uncertain, however, whether the bishop Onesimus, mentioned by Ignatius (Ign.*Eph.* 1:3; 2:1; 6:2), is the same Onesimus referred to in Phlm. The references to Phlm that Knox finds in Ign.*Eph.* 1–6 (*Philemon*, pp. 99–103) are nothing more than reminiscences or common Christian phrases. They can in no way prove that Ignatius is citing Phlm in order to call attention to the fact that the bishop of Ephesus is that Onesimus who decades ago fled from his master and for whom Paul interceded. For a further critique of Knox's position cf. Moule, pp. 14–18.

3 Cf. below on Phlm 2.

hypothesis collapses when one enforces the methodological rule of first trying to understand a writing in the light of its own statements before drawing on other documents for purposes of comparison.[4] The letter to Philemon itself offers no basis whatsoever for the position that Archippus, not Philemon, was the recipient of the letter.

2. The occasion for the letter

Paul writes to Philemon to intercede for his slave Onesimus. It is not said what caused Onesimus to flee. A slave who emancipated himself could take asylum in a sanctuary.[5] He could also disappear in a large city and there eke out an existence by begging and thievery. If he were captured, he had to be taken back to his master. Then the least he could expect was to be enslaved again. A far worse fate, however, might be in store for him. The master could punish him at his discretion. He could put him up for sale. If he wanted to, he could even kill him. Onesimus had taken refuge with the imprisoned Apostle. He had certainly not been apprehended by the police and been thrown into prison. If that were the case, it would have been the duty of the authorities to take him back to his master.[6] Perhaps he had heard the Apostle's name mentioned in the house of his Christian master and had now hastened to him for help in his perplexity. Paul took an interest in him, converted him to the Christian faith (v 10), developed great affection for him, and benefited from his dedicated service (v 13). Nevertheless, he could not retain him and had no authority to do so. Therefore, he sent him back to Philemon with an accompanying letter. Through this letter Paul used his influence on Philemon so that he would receive Onesimus as a beloved brother (v 16), indeed that he welcome him as he would the Apostle himself (v 17). Paul refrained from giving Philemon any command and from urging a distinct demand such as: give Onesimus his freedom. Rather he puts the matter in Philemon's hands. The decision is his. Paul's sole injunction to him is the commandment of love as the norm for his conduct.

3. The structure of the letter

The introductory greeting (vss 1–3) is followed by the thanksgiving (vss 4–7) which leads into (v 7) the principal part of the letter where the Apostle develops his plea for Onesimus (vss 8–20). A few sentences, greetings and the prayer for grace, form the letter's conclusion (vss 21–25).

In his letter to Philemon the Apostle makes use of the structure he employs in all his letters. Paul associates Timothy with himself as a sender of the letter. The recipients are not only Philemon, to whom the import of the letter is directed, but also Apphia, Archippus, and the "house community." The greeting at the beginning (v 3) and end (v 25) of the letter is extended to all of these people. For this reason Phlm is not a mere private letter[7] —not to speak of the fact that the length of the letter exceeds the customary length of a private letter.[8] Rather it is a binding message from the Apostle. Although Paul foregoes mentioning his official titles, he trusts that his word will be respected and obeyed (v 21). Therefore, he addresses not only Philemon, but also the persons mentioned along with him, so that the entire community will be aware of the Apostle's word and will take care that Onesimus on his return is received into the community of brothers which is sustained by love.[9]

4 This principle must be maintained under all circumstances, no matter how one answers the question whether Col is Pauline or deutero-Pauline. If one opts for the latter position, all the presuppositions on which Knox builds his case crumble away.

5 About this situation, as it existed by virtue of the law, cf. Erwin R. Goodenough, "Paul and Onesimus," *HTR* 22 (1929): 181–83; cf. further P. J. Verdam, "St. Paul et un serf fugitif. Étude sur l'épître à Philémon et le droit" in *Symbolae ad Jus et Historiam Antiquitatis Pertinentes, J. C. van Oven dedicatae* (Leiden: 1946), 211–30. On the law of asylum cf. Hennecke Gülzow, "Kirche und Sklaverei in den ersten zwei Jahrhunderten." Unpub. Diss. (Kiel: 1966), 204–09.

6 Cf. Théo Preiss, *Life in Christ*, tr. Harold Knight. SBT 13 (London: SCM Press, 1954), 35.

7 This is the view of J. Müller-Bardorff, *RGG*³ 5, col. 331f.

8 Phlm is more than half again as long as the comparable letter of Pliny the Younger to Sabinianus. On this letter cf. below pp. 196f.

9 Cf. Ulrich Wickert, "Der Philemonbrief—Privatbrief oder apostolisches Schreiben?" *ZNW* 52 (1961): 230–38; cf. further Preiss, *Life in Christ*, p. 34: ". . . in the Body of Christ personal affairs are

4. The time and origin of the letter

Paul is in prison (vss 1, 9f, 13, 22f),[10] but hopes to be freed in the near future. The letter gives no hint about the place where the Apostle is detained. Many exegetes espouse the traditional view that Paul was in Rome.[11] Others hold that Paul wrote from Caesarea.[12] Both cities, however, are such a considerable distance from Colossae that it is difficult to imagine how a runaway slave could have travelled so far without being detected. Furthermore, if Paul were imprisoned in Rome or Caesarea, he would scarcely have held out a prospect of a visit to Colossae in the near future. Consequently, one must assume that Ephesus was the city in which Paul was imprisoned when he met Onesimus. It is from Ephesus that Paul wrote Phlm in the mid-fifties.[13]

The letter to Philemon was recognized as a Pauline letter from the beginning. It appears already in Marcion's canon[14] and is also listed in the Muratorian Canon. The ancient church did not lavish much attention on this letter because it was taken up with questions about life in this world and "the gospel is not concerned with trivia" (de minimis non curat evangelium).[15] However, since the Pauline authorship of the letter was uncontested, it retained its place in the Pauline corpus. Of course, Ferdinand Christian Baur and the Tübingen "tendency criticism" called its Pauline authorship into question. The purpose of Phlm, it was assumed, was to illustrate in a novelistic fashion how the Christian communities in the post–Pauline period handled the question of slavery.[16] For good reasons this view has found no acceptance and today is no longer held by anyone.[17] The letter to Philemon is neither the disguise of a general idea nor the promulgation of a generally valid rule about the question of slavery. It is the intercession of the Apostle in a concrete situation in which "love" (ἀγάπη) must be promoted by decision and deed.

"This epistle gives us a masterful and tender illustration of Christian love. For here we see how St. Paul takes the part of poor Onesimus and, to the best of his ability, advocates his cause with his master. He acts exactly as if he were himself Onesimus, who had done wrong. Yet he does this not with force or compulsion, as lay within his rights; but he empties himself of his rights in order to compel Philemon also to waive his rights. What Christ has done for us with God the Father, that St. Paul does also for Onesimus with Philemon. For Christ emptied himself of his rights (Phil. 2:7) and overcame the Father with love and humility, so that the Father had to put away his wrath and rights, and receive us into favor for the sake of Christ, who so earnestly advocates our cause and so heartily takes our part. For we are all his Onesimus's if we believe."[18]

---

no longer private."

10 On the opinion of those exegetes who interpret "prisoner of Christ Jesus" (δέσμιος Χριστοῦ Ἰησοῦ) in a figurative sense, cf. p. 189, n. 3 below.

11 This is the opinion of: Lightfoot, 310f; Marvin R. Vincent, *The Epistles to the Philippians and to Philemon. ICC* (Edinburgh: T. & T. Clark, 1897, [5]1955), 161f; Werner Bieder, *Der Philemonbrief* in: Prophezei (Zürich: 1944), 5; Percy, *Probleme*, 467–74; Moule, 24f.

12 This is the viewpoint of: Haupt, 5; Dibelius–Greeven, 52, 102; Lohmeyer, 172.

13 Cf. pp. 165–67 above on Col 4:4 and the works of Deissmann ("Zur ephesinischen Gefangenschaft") and Michaelis (*Gefangenschaft* and *idem*, *Einleitung*) cited on p. 166, n. 14. Cf. further Friedrich, "Philemonbrief," p. 189; L. Kh. Jang, *Der Philemonbrief im Zusammenhang mit dem theologischen Denken des Apostels Paulus*. Unpub. Diss. (Bonn: 1964), 7, and Harrison, "Onesimus," 271–74. Concerning the opinion on the origin of Col that Harrison champions in this context, cf. p. 90, n. 167 above.

14 Cf. Tertullian, *Adv. Marc.* 5:21: "To this epistle alone did its brevity avail to protect it against the falsifying hands of Marcion" (Soli huic epistolae brevitas sua profuit, ut falsarias manus Marcionis evaderet. [Ante–Nicene Fathers].

15 Cf. Lightfoot, 314f. In parts of the Syrian Church Phlm was ignored as un–Pauline, or rejected. Cf. Kümmel, *Introduction*, 353.

16 Cf. Kümmel, *Introduction*, 246.

17 Heinrich Julius Holtzmann, "Der Brief an den Philemon, kritisch untersucht," *Zeitschrift für wissenschaftliche Theologie* 16 (1873): 428–41 advocates an opinion similar to the one he proposed with regard to the origin of Col (cf. p. 90 above): the redactor of Col later revised a letter to Philemon written by Paul and added vss 4–6.

18 Martin Luther, "Preface to the Epistle of Saint Paul to Philemon, 1546 (1522)" in *Luther's Works*, American Edition vol. 35, ed. E. Theodore Bachmann (Philadelphia: Fortress Press, 1960), 390. The German text in: *D. Martin Luthers Werke, Kritische Gesamtausgabe*, Deutsche Bibel 7 (Weimar: 1931), 252.

Introductory greeting

1 **Paul, a prisoner of Christ Jesus, and Timothy, the brother, to Philemon, our beloved and fellow worker, 2/ and Apphia, our sister, and Archippus, our fellow soldier, and the community in your house: 3/ grace be with you and peace from God our Father and the Lord Jesus Christ.**

The introduction follows the pattern found in the Pauline letters:[1] after the sender and his associate are mentioned, the addressee and his fellow recipients are referred to. Greetings and the wish for grace are extended to all of them.

■ **1** Paul does not add any title of authority to his name. He calls himself neither "apostle" (ἀπόστολος) nor "the servant of Christ" (δοῦλος Χριστοῦ). He designates himself simply as "a prisoner of Christ Jesus" (δέσμιος Χριστοῦ Ἰησοῦ).[2] Thus at the very beginning of the writing, reference is made to the situation of the Apostle. Paul is "in prison for the Gospel" (ἐν τοῖς δεσμοῖς τοῦ εὐαγγελίου v 13) and he considers his imprisonment as the fate that is in store for the messenger of the gospel—that is, part and parcel of the commission given to him.[3] The messenger of the Kyrios must suffer like his master to whom he owes obedience. For this reason, it is not, after all, the external circumstances but Christ Jesus alone, in whose triumphal victory parade the Apostle is carried along (2 Cor 2:14), who determines the way Paul has to go. The sufferings, however, which he must endure in the service of his Lord, allow him to speak to the community with greater authority.[4] Although he foregoes any display of his apostolic authority, the words "a prisoner of Christ Jesus" already indicate that this writing should not be taken to be a mere private letter. It conveys a message that obligates its recipients to obey the apostolic word.[5] The fact that an associate is mentioned also calls attention to the authoritative character of the letter. Timothy is at the Apostle's side as a trustworthy Christian brother (cf. 2 Cor 1:1). The associate, however, plays no role in the formulation of the letter.[6] The writing is Paul's alone. Accordingly, beginning in v 4 he speaks in the singular; in vss 9 and 19 he mentions his own name without that of Timothy.

The name of the recipient of the letter is Philemon.[7] First of all, he is characterized as "beloved" (ἀγαπητός). Although Paul uses this word in other situations to characterize addressees (Rom 1:7) or to address the community,[8] here it bears special significance. Philemon is reminded at the very beginning of the letter that he belongs to a community of mutual love (cf. vss 5, 7, 9, 16). As a Christian he lives in "love" (ἀγάπη) and manifests it in his deeds. Thus, he cannot deny that love to a slave whom the Apostle calls "beloved brother" (ἀδελφὸν ἀγαπητόν v 16).[9] Moreover, Philemon is called the

1 Cf. above on Col 1:1.

2 Minuscules 322 and 605 assimilate to the titles of the other Pauline letters by reading "servant" (δοῦλος); D* assimilates by reading "apostle" (ἀπόστολος).

3 Reitzenstein, *Mysterienreligionen*, 214, tries to shed light on the phrase "a prisoner of Christ Jesus" (δέσμιος Χριστοῦ Ἰησοῦ) from the language used in the mystery religions. Before initiation the initiand subjected himself to an imprisonment (κατοχή cf. κατέχειν [to detain] which is used in Phlm 13) in which he became the prisoner of the cult deity. Paul is thus assumed to understand his prison experience as that of a "prisoner" (δέσμιος) of his Lord who is waiting to be united with him (cf. Phil 1:23). The hypothesis that the terminology of the mysteries comes into play here is substantiated neither by the term "prisoner" nor by the context. Cf. Dibelius–Greeven, *ad loc.*, and Gerhard Kittel, *TDNT* 2, 43.

4 Cf. Eph 3:1: "I, Paul, a prisoner for Christ Jesus on behalf of you Gentiles" (ἐγὼ Παῦλος ὁ δέσμιος τοῦ Χριστοῦ Ἰησοῦ ὑπὲρ τῶν ἐθνῶν); 4:1 "I, a prisoner for the Lord" (ἐγὼ ὁ δέσμιος ἐν κυρίῳ); 2 Tim 1:8: "do not be ashamed then . . . of me, his (*scil.* the Lord's) prisoner" (μὴ οὖν ἐπαισχυνθῇς . . . ἐμὲ τὸν δέσμιον αὐτοῦ [*scil.* τοῦ κυρίου]).

5 Cf. Wickert, "Philemonbrief," 230–38.

6 Cf. above on Col 1:1.

7 On the same Philemon cf. Ovid, *Metamorphoses* 8.631; further examples may be found in Lightfoot, 303f and in Zahn, *Introduction*, p. 458.

8 Cf. 1 Cor 10:14; 15:58; 2 Cor 7:1; 12:19; Phil 2:12; 4:1.

9 Manuscripts D* Ambst add "brother" (ἀδελφῷ) to "beloved" (τῷ ἀγαπητῷ). The adjective "beloved" already singles out Philemon as the addressee of the letter, on whom the Apostle will use his in-

Apostle's fellow worker.[10] Just like the men mentioned in the letter's list of greetings (v 24), he shares, as an active member of the community, in the common work of testifying to the gospel in word and in active love.

■ **2** Apphia, Archippus, and the entire "house community" are named along with Philemon as recipients of the letter. Their names are mentioned because the matter that the Apostle is dealing with is not just a personal affair that concerns Philemon alone. Rather the decision that must be arrived at is a concern of the entire community. Apphia is called "sister" (ἀδελφή)[11] and, like Philemon, is a Christian.[12] Since her name follows immediately after Philemon's, one can assume that she is his wife.[13] The lady of the house had to deal daily with the slaves. Therefore, she also had to give her opinion when the question of taking back a runaway slave was raised. It is said of Archippus, whose name[14] follows Apphia's, that he is a "fellow soldier" (συστρατιώτης) of the Apostle. If Paul calls him his comrade–in–arms, he is using that term in a figurative sense to refer to the fact that he is a fellow worker.[15] But this term does not mean that Archippus is the leader of the Christian community in Colossae.[16] Nor does it indicate that Archippus, not Philemon, is Onesimus' master who should now welcome him as his Christian brother.[17] Rather, this term means that since Archippus as a fellow combatant of the Apostle bears responsibility for the life of the community, he should also be informed of what Paul expects of Philemon.[18]

The list of addressees[19] concludes with the mention of

fluence for the sake of the runaway slave Onesimus. For the critique of Knox's hypothesis which interprets these facts differently, cf. pp. 186f above.

10 On *συνεργός* as a name for the fellow workers of the Apostle, cf. further 1 Thess 3:2; 2 Cor 8:23; Rom 16:3, 9, 21; Phil 2:25; 4:3; Col 4:11.

11 The Byzantine text assimilates to Philemon's designation and reads "beloved" (ἀγαπητῇ) [𝔎 pl sy^{p}]. Both readings are joined together by manuscripts vg^{cl} sy^{h} Ambst to form "beloved sister" (ἀδελφῇ ἀγαπητῇ).

12 The name "Apphia" (Ἀπφία) is frequently attested; cf. Lightfoot, *ad loc.*; Zahn, *Introduction*, p. 458. It also occurs on an ancient tomb inscription for an Apphia from Colossae. Cf. Dibelius–Greeven, 111, Appendix 6: "Hermas in [memor]y to A[p]phia his wife, daughter of Tryphon, from Colossae" (Ἑρμᾶς Ἀ[π]φιάδι, τῇ ἰδίᾳ γυναικί, τῇ Τρύφωνος θυγατρί, γένει Κολοσσηνῇ, [μνήμ]ης ἕνεκα). *CIG* 3, 4380 k^{3}. [Trans.]

13 Cf. Theodoret, *ad loc.*: "Paul . . . adds the name of the wife . . . to that of the husband" (Paulus . . . marito . . . jungit uxorem) [Trans.].

14 On the name "Archippus" (Ἄρχιππος) cf. p. 175, n. 49 above on Col. 4:17.

15 Cf. Bauer, *s.v.* The word "fellow soldier" (συστρατιώτης), however, cannot be read to mean that Paul during his Jewish period "could have incited and honored people with the predicate 'fellow soldier' " and that "later on he was not able to eliminate completely this 'Zealotic' expression from his vocabulary" (Otto Bauernfeind, *TWNT* 7, 711 n. 37). The word *συστρατιώτης* refers to the fellow worker. This meaning is clearly brought out in the characterization of Epaphroditus as "my brother and fellow worker and fellow soldier" (τὸν ἀδελφὸν καὶ συνεργὸν καὶ συστρατιώτην μου Phil 2:25).

16 This is the opinion of Lohmeyer, *ad loc.*, who without basis in the text holds that Archippus had replaced Epaphras as leader of the community in Colossae.

17 On the hypothesis of Knox that Archippus was the real recipient of the letter, cf. p. 186 above.

18 The opinion that Archippus was the son of Philemon and Apphia (cf. Lightfoot, 308f) was already held by Theodore of Mopsuestia, *ad loc.*: "he addresses his son, that is, the son of Philemon and Apphia" (υἱῷ αὐτοῦ λέγει, τόν τε Φιλήμονος καὶ τῆς Ἀπφίας). "Speculation," however, "about Archippus' position in Philemon's household is idle." (Dibelius–Greeven, *ad loc.*).

19 Later tradition makes the persons named in Phlm bishops of various communities: *Const. Ap.* 7.46. 12f: "(Bishop) of Laodicea in Phrygia, Archippus. Of Colossae, Philemon. Of Beroea in Macedonia, Onesimus, once the servant of Philemon" (τῆς δὲ ἐν Φρυγίᾳ Λαοδικείας [*scil.* ἐπίσκοπος] Ἄρχιππος, Κολασσαέων δὲ Φιλήμων· Βεροίας δὲ τῆς κατὰ Μακεδονίαν Ὀνήσιμος ὁ Φιλήμονος) [trans. from ANF, 7, 478].

20 On the primitive Christian "house communities" cf. above on Col 4:15.

21 Cf. *BGU* 1.33.16–19: "Gr[ee]t your sister and your brother and the little girl and all those living in the house" (Ἀσπ[άζο]υ τὴν ἀδελφὴν σου καὶ τὸν ἀδελφόν σου καὶ τὴν μικρὰν καὶ τοὺς ἐν οἴκῳ πάντες [sic]); 1.261.32–34: "Herois greets you and all those living in the house by n(a)me" (ἀσπάζεταί σε Ἡροὶς καὶ οἱ ἐν οἴκῳ πάντες κατ' ὄ(νο)μα) [Trans.].

22 In ancient letters occasionally additional names are listed alongside that of the recipient, even though the message of the letter was directed only to the first person mentioned. The proem of a letter that Hi-

the community that gathers in Philemon's house.[20] Ancient letters sometimes mention the acquaintances that exist between the different households.[21] Accordingly, in this case, the community is mentioned and becomes the witness[22] to what the Apostle has to say to Philemon.[23]

■ **3** The greeting is formulated in words that Paul always uses in the prescript of a letter to wish the community grace and peace.[24] This greeting is extended not only to Philemon, but also to the entire community that should take the message of the Apostle to heart.

larion, an Egyptian laborer, wrote to Alis, his wife, is a good example of this custom (1 B.C.): "Hilarion to Alis his sister, many greetings, and to my lady Berous and Apollonarin" (Ἱλαρίων Ἄλιτι τῆι ἀδελφῆι πλεῖστα χαίρειν καὶ Βερoῦτι τῇ κυρίᾳ μου καὶ Ἀπολλωνάριν [Trans.]). The letter then proceeds in the singular: "know that" (γίνωσκε) [*Pap.Oxyrh.* 4.744]. Cf. Deissmann, *LAE*, 167.

23 The singular possessive adjective "your" (σου) in the phrase "the community in your house" (τῇ κατ' οἶκόν σου ἐκκλησίᾳ) also refers to Philemon as the recipient of the letter.

24 Cf. pp. 10f above on Col 1:2.

Thanksgiving and Petition

4 **I thank my God always when I remember you in my prayers; 5/ for I hear of your love and your faith in the Lord Jesus and for all the saints. 6/ May your sharing in the faith become effective in the knowledge of all the good that is in us for the glory of Christ. 7/ For I have derived much joy and comfort from your love because the hearts of the saints have been refreshed by you, brother.**

At the beginning of the letter Paul prays to God in thanksgiving and introduces his prayer with: "I thank my God" (εὐχαριστῶ τῷ θεῷ μου). To this he adds the temporal adverb "always" (πάντοτε) which is explained by "when I remember you in my prayers" (μνείαν σου ποιούμενος ἐπὶ τῶν προσευχῶν). A second participial clause gives the reason which motivates the Apostle's prayer of thanksgiving; he has received a good report about the faith and love of the recipient (v 4: "for I hear, etc." [ἀκούων κτλ]). These verses, therefore, present the more extensive form of the thanksgiving which also occurs in other letters of the Apostle.[1]

Its structure is very clearly recognizable because of the concise formulation of the verse.[2]

The petition, which is always closely linked with the prayer of thanksgiving, begins with the sentence of v 6 which is introduced by the Greek word ὅπως. It is true that in the Greek text no verb introduces the petition.[3] However, from a comparison with the outline of the thanksgiving in the other Pauline letters it is clear that ὅπως marks the beginning of the petition.[4] Paul prays that Philemon's faith might continue to show itself as an active faith. Verse 7 once more refers, full of praise, to the love that Philemon has shown toward the saints.[5] This latter sentence is, at the same time, the transition to the content proper of the letter.

■ **4** Like the petitioners in the OT psalms (cf. LXX 3:8; 5:3; 21:2, etc.) Paul prays "my God" (cf. Phil 1:3). Thanks is given to God, not to a human being, that Philemon has conducted himself as a genuine Christian.[6] Since God has effected love and faith, to him alone all thanks are due. The Apostle renders thanks πάντοτε, that is, "always," when at prayer he thinks of Philemon. To assure an addressee that one thought of him faithfully correponds to the style of the Hellenistic letter.[7] By mentioning their names before God, Paul knows that he is intimately linked with the communities and their individual members.[8] In prayer each act of remembering

1 Cf. 1 Thess 1:2–5; Phil 1:3–11; Col 1:3–8; etc. Cf. further p. 13 above on Col 1:3.

2 Cf. Schubert, *Pauline Thanksgivings*, 12.

3 A verb like "praying" (προσευχόμενος) might be expected. Cf. Phil 1:9; Col 1:3, 9; etc.

4 Cf. Dibelius–Greeven, *ad loc.*: Paul would have "sensed that a phrase like 'I pray' (προσεύχομαι) was contained in 'when I remember you in my prayers' (μνείαν ποιούμενος ἐπὶ τῶν προσευχῶν). The ὅπως–clause is dependent on that phrase."

5 Not only the word "love" (ἀγάπη) [cf. vss 5, 7, 9, 16], but a series of additional terms that are used in the thanksgiving recur in the following verses: "prayers" (προσευχῶν) [v 4, v 22]; "sharing, partnership" (κοινωνία) [v 6, v 17]; "the good deed" (ἀγαθόν) [v 6, v 14]; "hearts" (τὰ σπλάγχνα) [v 7, vss 12, 20]; "has refreshed" (ἀναπέπαυται) [v 7, v 20]; "brother" (ἀδελφέ) [v 7, v 20]. In this way the thanksgiving and the body of the letter are closely joined to one another. Cf. Knox, *Philemon*, p. 22.

6 On the thanksgiving in the introduction of Hellenistic letters, cf. p. 12 above on Col 1:3.

7 Cf. e.g., *BGU* 2.632.3–6, which may be found in Deissmann, *LAE*, p. 184: The soldier Apion writes to his sister Sabina (second century A.D.): "Before all things I pray that thou art in health, for I myself also am in health. Making mention of thee before the gods [he]re . . ." (πρὸ μὲν πάντων εὔχομαί σε ὑγιαίνειν, καὶ 'γὼ γὰρ αὐτὸς ὑγιαίν[ω]. Μνίαν σου ποιούμενος παρὰ τοῖς [ἐν]θάδε θεοῖς . . .) [Deissmann trans.].

8 Cf. Otto Michel, *TDNT* 4, 678.

9 Dibelius–Greeven, *ad loc.*, point out that instances where " 'I hear' (ἀκούων) or a similar verb expresses the motivation for thanks to God . . ." occur "elsewhere only in those letters of Paul addressed to communities which are unknown to him." (Col 1:4; Eph 1:15; cf. further Rom 1:8). Paul had not travelled to Colossae where Philemon and his "house community" lived. Philemon, however, must have met the Apostle in some other place, perhaps in Ephesus, since it was Paul through whom Philemon was converted to the Christian faith (v 19). Therefore, one cannot conclude from the use of the word "to hear"

becomes thanksgiving and petition.

■ **5** Paul has received a good report about the conduct of the addressee. This news gives him reason to give thanks to God.[9] The substance of what Paul had learned is described briefly as the "love" (ἀγάπη) and "faith" (πίστις) of Philemon. Although in other Pauline passages faith, from which love springs, is mentioned first,[10] here "love" (ἀγάπη) occurs before "faith" (πίστις).[11] Paul says about faith that its content is the acknowledgement of Jesus as Lord (cf. Rom 10:9).[12] The formula–like statement about faith, however, is enclosed by the words about the love that Philemon has shown "for all the saints" (εἰς πάντας τοὺς ἁγίους).[13] Thus a chiastic structure results from placing "love" first, in an accentuated position.[14] Together with "faith," its foundation and object, "love" is mentioned; only the latter refers to "all the saints" to whom Philemon had extended his love.[15] In this way the reference to "love" gains special emphasis.[16] Since "love" is at the front and center of the stage, hope is not mentioned along with love and faith. Because it is not a question of the verification of "hope" (ἐλπίς), but of the "love" which is rendered to all the saints, that is, to all Christians,[17] not only to those with whom one lives at home, but to all the members of the people of God.

■ **6** The thanksgiving leads directly into the petition:[18] that the κοινωνία "of the faith" of Philemon might also be effective in the future. The Greek word κοινωνία, therefore, does not mean fellowship here, but participation.[19] Philemon shares in the common faith.[20] This

(ἀκούειν) that Philemon was not personally acquainted with the Apostle. Greeven, "Prüfung der Thesen von J. Knox zum Philemonbrief," col. 376 interprets this verse differently: "Thus the 'I hear' (ἀκούων) of Phlm 5 also points to the fact that until the writing of this letter no personal bond existed between Paul and the actual addressee of the letter."

10 Cf. p. 16 above on Col 1:4.

11 Manuscripts D 69 1739 al syᵖ alter the sequence of words to the usual order: "faith and love" (τὴν πίστιν καὶ ἀγάπην).

12 On the title of dignity "Lord" (κύριος), cf. p. 15, n. 21 above on Col 1:3. Here the object of "faith" is not construed in the usual way with the Greek preposition εἰς (in), but with πρός (in). Cf. 1 Thess 1:8: ἡ πίστις ὑμῶν ἡ πρὸς τὸν θεόν (your faith in God). εἰς (in, for), however, is used to refer to the persons upon whom Philemon has bestowed his "love."

13 On "love for" (ἀγάπη εἰς) cf. 2 Cor 2:8; Rom 5:8; 2 Thess 1:3; Col 1:4; Eph 1:15. The change of prepositions occurs "for mere stylistic variation" (Moulton–Turner, 256). Within a sentence Paul likes to vary his prepositions in order to lend more color and emphasis to a statement. Cf. e.g., Rom 3:30: "on the ground of faith—through faith" (ἐκ πίστεως—διὰ τῆς πίστεως); Gal 2:16: "through faith in Christ Jesus—by faith in Christ" (διὰ πίστεως Χριστοῦ Ἰησοῦ—ἐκ πίστεως Χριστοῦ).

14 On the chiastic structure of this sentence, which Haupt, *ad loc.* would surely contest, cf. especially Lightfoot, Vincent, Lohmeyer, Moule, Friedrich, *ad loc.* Cf. further Rudolf Bultmann, *TDNT* 6, 212 n. 277; Blass–Debrunner, par. 477. Spicq, *Agape* 2, pp. 302–06 doubts that there is a chiasm present and argues: " 'Faith' and 'charity' are inseparable in Pauline theology. . . . Faith and charity are addressed to Christ as to their proper object . . . but their joint effort 'leads' to one's neighbor." (p. 303f) [Trans. adjusted].

15 Therefore, the words "for all the saints" are no longer to be connected with "faith." Otherwise, "faith" would have to be understood in the sense of "faithfulness." Paul can indeed occasionally use πίστις to refer to God's faithfulness (cf., e.g. Rom 3:3). In conjunction with "love," however, πίστις always means "faith."

16 The sentence which is phrased chiastically is to be resolved in the following way: "the love which you have for all the saints, and the faith which you have in the Lord Jesus" (τὴν ἀγάπην, ἣν ἔχεις εἰς πάντας τοὺς ἁγίους, καὶ τὴν πίστιν, ἣν ἔχεις πρὸς τὸν κύριον Ἰησοῦν). Cf. Lohmeyer, *ad loc.*

17 On "saint" (ἅγιος) as a self–designation of the Christians, cf. pp. 7f above on Col 1:2.

18 On the organization of this section of the letter, cf. p. 192 above. Verse 6 (the ὅπως– clause) depends on neither "when I remember" (μνείαν ποιούμενος) [according to Lightfoot, *ad loc.*] nor on "which you have" (ἣν ἔχεις) [thus Haupt, *ad loc.*]. Rather it states the content of the petition.

19 Cf. Heinrich Seesemann, *Der Begriff* ΚΟΙΝΩΝΙΑ *im Neuen Testament*, BZNW 14 (Giessen: 1933), 79–83; Friedrich Hauck, *TDNT* 3, 805. On κοινωνία in the meaning of "sharing, participation" cf. 1 Cor 10:16: "participation in the body" (κοινωνία τοῦ σώματος); 10:17: "we partake of the one bread" (ἐκ ἑνὸς ἄρτου μετέχομεν); cf. further 10:18, 20f.

20 Cf. Phil 1:5: "for your sharing in the gospel" (ἐπὶ τῇ κοινωνίᾳ ὑμῶν εἰς τὸ εὐαγγέλιον).

share of faith he possesses should be active as the "faith working through love" (πίστις δι' ἀγάπης ἐνεργουμένη Gal 5:6) insofar as he realizes that the blessing bestowed on the believer should now appear in concrete acts of love.[21] In this context, reference is made first to the "knowledge" (ἐπίγνωσις)[22] which spurs faith to action. Then the object of the knowledge is given in the words "of all the good that is in us" (παντὸς ἀγαθοῦ τοῦ ἐν ἡμῖν).[23] These words contain a seemingly universal statement: all the good that is in us, that is, which God has given us. "The good" ([τὰ] ἀγαθά) is the salvation that has been offered in preaching (Rom 10:15). The Apostle writes that God himself has begun a "good work in you" (ἐν ὑμῖν ἔργον ἀγαθόν) which he will also bring to perfection (Phil 1:6; cf. Rom 8:28). Not only God's good gifts are designated as "the good;" so also is his will, which commands to do what is plainly good.[24] Thus the admonition is given: "always seek to do the good to one another" (πάντοτε τὸ ἀγαθὸν διώκετε εἰς ἀλλήλους 1 Thess 5:15), or "let us do the good to all men, and especially to those who are of the household of faith" (ἐργαζώμεθα τὸ ἀγαθὸν πρὸς πάντας, μάλιστα δὲ πρὸς τοὺς οἰκείους τῆς πίστεως Gal 6:10). In the community each one should "please his neighbor for that which is good" (τῷ πλησίον ἀρεσκείτω εἰς τὸ ἀγαθὸν Rom 15:2).[25] Therefore, if Philemon recognizes "the good" that God has given to us and that consequently is "in us" (ἐν ἡμῖν), he will also comprehend the will of God and heed the admonition of the Apostle: "so that your good deed might not stem from compulsion, but from your own free will" (ἵνα μὴ ὡς κατὰ ἀνάγκην τὸ ἀγαθόν σου ᾖ ἀλλὰ κατὰ ἑκούσιον v 14).[26]

The verse ends with the words εἰς Χριστόν (which has been translated here "for the glory of Christ").[27] This phrase is neither attached to "in the knowledge" (ἐν ἐπιγνώσει) nor to "of all the good that is in you" (παντὸς ἀγαθοῦ τοῦ ἐν ἡμῖν).[28] Its purpose is to emphasize in conclusion that all active working of the faith—a faith

21 Cf. Rudolf Bultmann, *TDNT* 1, 708; Chrysostom, *ad loc.*: "If you are a partaker, he says, with respect to the faith, you ought to share also with respect to other things" (εἰ κοινωνὸς εἶ, φησί, κατὰ τὴν πίστιν, καὶ κατὰ τὰ ἄλλα ὀφείλεις κοινωνεῖν).

22 On the concept "knowledge" (ἐπίγνωσις) cf. pp. 25f above on Col 1:9.

23 This phrase is difficult to understand and has been altered much in the manuscript tradition. Manuscripts G al vg[el] insert "work" (ἔργου) after "all" (παντός) [cf. Col 1:10: "in every good work" (ἐν παντὶ ἔργῳ ἀγαθῷ)]. Manuscripts A C omit "the" (τοῦ). Manuscripts p[61] ℵ G P 33 69 pm lat sy replace "us" (ἡμῖν) with "you" (ὑμῖν) in order here also to retain the form of address. The "us" (ἡμῖν), however, attested by A C ℜ D is to be taken as original since it is not in accordance with the address of the context and is chosen by Paul because he recognizes that he is bound to the recipients by one and the same "knowledge" (ἐπίγνωσις).

24 According to Jewish understanding, knowledge of the good means knowledge of the divine will. Cf. 1 QS IV.26: "that they may know good [and evil]" (לדעת טוב [ורע]) ; 1 QSa I.10f: "when [she] knows [good] and evil" (בדעתו [טוב] ורע); cf. further 1 QS I.2: "[and] do what is good" ([ל]עשות הטוב).

25 On "the good" in Paul, cf. further Gal 6:6; 2 Cor 5:10; Rom 2:10; 5:7; 7:13, 19; 9:11; 12:2, 9, 21; 13:3; 14:16.

26 Cf. Col 1:9: "the knowledge of his will" (τὴν ἐπίγνωσιν τοῦ θελήματος αὐτοῦ).

27 Manuscripts P ℜ D G pl lat sy add "Jesus" (Ἰησοῦν).

28 If this were the case, one would expect the Greek definite article τῇ or τοῦ before εἰς Χριστόν. Since the formulation of this "most obscure verse in this letter" (Moule, *ad loc.*) is extremely terse and difficult to understand, all exegetes try to approximate its meaning by paraphrase. Lohmeyer's rendition, however, is put too generally: "to Christ. He is the embodiment of all glory, to whom all knowledge and activity of faith remain directed as long as it is still active in time and space." Dibelius–Greeven, *ad loc.*, explain: "The fellowship of faith with Christ (1 Cor 1:9) which Philemon has already received is hoped to lead, through a continuing ethical growth, to an ever closer union with Christ (εἰς Χριστόν)." Percy, *Probleme*, 125, opts for taking εἰς Χριστόν with the immediately preceding words, and translates: "the knowledge of all the good among us and in relationship to Christ." In this case the meaning of εἰς Χριστόν would be identical with that of "in Christ" (ἐν Χριστῷ) and the faith of Philemon would become effectual in such a way that his knowledge of what he possesses as a believer in Christ will be deepened. Yet, it is not a convincing argument that Paul, because of the preceding ἐν ἡμῖν (in us), wrote εἰς Χριστόν (for the glory of Christ) instead of ἐν Χριστῷ (in Christ) in order to introduce some stylistic variation into the sentence.

29 Cf. 2 Cor 1:21: "who establishes us with you for Christ" (ὁ δὲ βεβαιῶν ἡμᾶς σὺν ὑμῖν εἰς Χριστόν); 11:3: "from a sincere [and pure] devotion for Christ" (τῆς ἁπλότητος καὶ τῆς ἁγνότητος τῆς εἰς Χρι-

which acts according to the knowledge of the good which God has bestowed upon us—should be for the glory of Christ.[29] This is scarcely a reference to Christ as the judge before whom all of us must one day appear.[30] For just as v 5 speaks only of "love" and "faith," but not of "hope," so too v 6 does not look toward future consummation or the judgment. There is only one concern: that Christian faith must manifest itself in love.

■ **7** To this point Paul has spoken of Philemon's conduct in words that could be applied to every true Christian. Now, however, he indicates that he has learned of one particular deed by which Philemon has helped the community. From this report he derived [31] "much joy and comfort" (*χαρὰν*[32] *πολλὴν καὶ παράκλησιν*). Paul writes in similar terms to the Corinthians about the joy (2 Cor 7:4) and the comfort (2 Cor 7:7) he has experienced: "and besides our own comfort we rejoiced still more at the joy of Titus, because his mind has been set at rest" (*ἐπὶ δὲ τῇ παρακλήσει ἡμῶν περισσοτέρως μᾶλλον ἐχάρημεν ἐπὶ τῇ χαρᾷ Τίτου, ὅτι ἀναπέπαυται τὸ πνεῦμα αὐτοῦ* 2 Cor 7:13). Also Philemon's deeds of love have been a rich source of[33] joy and "comfort"[34] to the Apostle. Paul does not detail Philemon's deeds of love. He merely says that through Philemon "the hearts of the saints have been refreshed" (*τὰ σπλάγχνα τῶν ἁγίων ἀναπέπαυται*). With the words "the hearts" (*τὰ σπλάγχνα*) Paul designates the whole person of the Christian insofar as he makes effective and experiences the affection and love between human beings.[35] By using the expression "the hearts" (*τὰ σπλάγχνα*) Paul indicates that the "saints" (*ἅγιοι*) have been refreshed in their innermost feelings.[36] By the gift of his love Philemon has strengthened the community of brothers. Therefore, he is once more referred to as a brother. Since he has filled the hearts of the other Christians with deep joy by his own personal efforts, he will not refuse the request of the Apostle who intercedes for Onesimus as "my heart" (*τὰ ἐμὰ σπλάγχνα*): "refresh my heart in Christ" (*ἀνάπαυσόν μου τὰ σπλάγχνα ἐν Χριστῷ* v 20).[37]

στόν); Rom 16:5: "the first convert in Asia for Christ" (*ἀπαρχὴ τῆς Ἀσίας εἰς Χριστόν*). In all instances "for Christ" means "for the glory of Christ." [Trans.]

30 This is the view of Wickert, "Philemonbrief," 231: "Therefore, with *εἰς Χριστόν* Phlm 6 also seems to reflect the concept of Christ as judge.

31 Manuscripts D* pc have the plural "we derived" (*ἔσχομεν*) instead of "I derived" (*ἔσχον*); manuscripts 𝔎 al sy have "we derive" (*ἔχομεν*).

32 Manuscripts P 𝔎 al change *χαράν* (joy) to *χάριν* (grace).

33 On the preposition *ἐπί* in the meaning of "on account of," "from," cf. Bauer, *s.v.*

34 On "comfort" (*παράκλησις*) cf. Otto Schmitz, *TDNT* 5, 797 and Schlier, "Vom Wesen der apostolischen Ermahnung," p. 75: "The noun *παράκλησις* conveys more the meaning of comfort and encouragement, than of admonition and request."

35 Cf. 2 Cor 6:12; 7:15; Phil 1:8; 2:1. Cf. further Helmut Köster, *TWNT* 7, 555.

36 Cf. Köster, *ibid.* On "to refresh" (*ἀναπαύειν*) in Paul cf. 1 Cor 16:18: "for they refreshed my spirit as well as yours" (*ἀνέπαυσαν γὰρ τὸ ἐμὸν πνεῦμα καὶ τὸ ὑμῶν*).

37 Köster, *ibid.*, correctly observes: "The frequent occurrence of this term (*scil.* 'the heart') in this brief letter reveals the personal interest of Paul in this matter."

Intercession for Onesimus

8 **Therefore, although I have full authority in
Christ to command you to do what is
fitting, 9/ I prefer to beseech you for
love's sake. Since this is what I am, Paul,
an elderly man and moreover now a
prisoner of Christ Jesus, 10/ I beseech
you for my child, whom I have begotten
in prison, Onesimus, 11/ who was formerly useless to you, but now is very
useful to you and to me. 12/ Him I am
sending back to you, him, that is, my
very heart. 13/ I would have liked to keep
him with me so that he might serve me
in your place during my imprisonment
for the gospel; 14/ but I would not do
anything without your consent so that
your good deed might not stem from
compulsion, but from your own free
will. 15/ For, perhaps, the reason he has
been separated from you for a while is
that you might have him back forever,
16/ no longer as a slave, but as one
who is much more than a slave, as a
beloved brother, especially to me, but
how much more to you, both in the flesh
and in the Lord. 17/ Now then, if you
consider me your partner, receive him as
you would receive me. 18/If he has
wronged you or owes you anything,
charge that to my account—19/ I, Paul,
am writing this in my own hand, I will
make compensation for it—not to
mention to you that you owe me your
very life besides. 20/ Yes, brother, may I
have joy in you in the Lord. Refresh my
heart in Christ.**

If a slave ran away, he could be pursued by taking out a warrant against him.[1] If the slave were apprehended, he had to be taken back to his master, who could punish him at his discretion. In such a situation the intercession for the slave from a man who was an acquaintance or a friend of the master was of the greatest importance. In a similar case, Pliny the Younger writes to a certain Sabinianus[2] and intercedes with him for a freedman (*libertus*) who had run away from him and come to Pliny. The *libertus* is full of remorse and now must dread facing his master, who is bitterly angry with him. Pliny concedes that Sabinianus has every right to be angry. Nevertheless, he proposes to him that clemency is the more laudable, the greater the reason for anger, and asks him

1 A warrant of this kind is preserved in *P.Par* 10 (Wilcken *Ptol*. 121) which dates from the middle of the second century B.C.: in Alexandria a public notice was posted that a slave by the name of Hermon had run away from a certain Aristogenes. Then a description (and telltale marks) of the slave is given: he is a Syrian from Bambyke, 18 years old, of medium height. Next, the peculiarities of his physical appearance are listed. It is further noted that he has three *mnaieia* (gold coins), ten pearls, an iron ring, and is wearing a cloak and an undergarment. A reward is offered to anyone who apprehends him and brings him back, or who indicates that he has sought asylum at a temple. Whoever can give any leads as to the whereabouts of the slave should do so to the governor's office. A slave by the name of Bion, who belongs to Callicrates, ran away with Hermon. Bion, too, is briefly described, and a reward is offered for his capture. (The text may be found in Dibelius–Greeven, 111f. The text with a translation and commentary is available in Moule, 34–37).

2 Pliny the Younger, *Epist*. 9.21: "To Sabinianus. Your freedman, whom you lately mentioned as having displeased you, has been with me; he threw himself at my feet and clung there with as much submission as he could have done at yours. He earnestly

to forgive. He might also consider how young the *libertus* is and that he has shed many tears over his fault. The request to receive the guilty but repentant *libertus* and to treat him with clemency is repeated once more for emphasis. In a subsequent letter Pliny thanks Sabinianus[3] for heeding his request. Sabinianus had not been angry with the *libertus*, but had shown himself to be a forgiving man.[4]

Paul also intercedes for a runaway slave. He, however, does not say that the master should exercise the Stoic virtue of clemency and show himself to be mild-mannered. Rather, Paul speaks to him in terms of Christian love and faith. The Apostle weighs his words carefully and fashions the structure of the principal part of the

---

requested me with many tears, and even with the eloquence of silent sorrow, to intercede for him; in short, he convinced me by his whole behaviour, that he sincerely repents of his fault. And I am persuaded he is thoroughly reformed, because he seems entirely sensible of his delinquency. I know you are angry with him, and I know too, it is not without reason; but clemency can never exert itself with more applause, than when there is the justest cause for resentment. You once had an affection for this man, and, I hope, will have again: in the meanwhile, let me only prevail with you to pardon him. If he should incur your displeasure hereafter, you will have so much the stronger plea in excuse for your anger, as you shew yourself more exorable to him now. Allow something to his youth, to his tears, and to your own natural mildness of temper: do not make him uneasy any longer, and I will add too, do not make yourself so; for a man of your benevolence of heart cannot be angry without feeling great uneasiness. I am afraid, were I to join my entreaties with his, I should seem rather to compel, than request you to forgive him. Yet I will not scruple to do it; and so much the more fully and freely as I have very sharply and severely reproved him, positively threatening never to interpose again in his behalf. But though it was proper to say this to him, in order to make him more fearful of offending, I do not say it to you. I may, perhaps, again have occasion to entreat you upon his account, and again obtain your forgiveness; supposing, I mean, his error should be such as may become me to intercede for, and you to pardon. Farewell." (C. Plinius Sabiniano suo S. Libertus tuus, cui suscensere te dixeras, venit ad me advolutusque pedibus meis tamquam tuis haesit. Flevit multum, multum rogavit, multum etiam tacuit, in summa fecit mihi fidem paenitentiae. Vere credo emendatum, quia deliquisse se sentit. Irasceris, scio, et irasceris merito, id quoque scio; sed tunc praecipua mansuetudinis laus, cum irae causa iustissima est. Amasti hominem et, spero, amabis: interim sufficit, ut exorari te sinas. Licebit rursus irasci, si meruerit, quod exoratus excusatius facies. Remitte aliquid adulescentiae ipsius, remitte lacrimis, remitte indulgentiae tuae. Ne torseris illum, ne torseris etiam te; torqueris enim, cum tam lenis irasceris. Vereor, ne videar non rogare, sed cogere, si precibus eius meas iunxero: iungam tamen tanto plenius et effusius, quanto ipsum acrius severiusque corripui destricte minatus nunquam me postea rogaturum. Hoc illi, quem terreri oportebat, tibi non idem; nam fortasse iterum rogabo, impetrabo iterum: sit modo tale, ut rogare me, ut praestare te deceat. Vale.) [Also cf. Dibelius–Greeven, 111].

3 Pliny the Younger, *Epist.* 9.24: "To Sabinianus. I greatly approve of your having, under conduct of my letter, received again into your family and favour, a freedman, whom you once admitted into a share of your affection. It will afford you, I doubt not, great satisfaction. It certainly, at least, has me, both as it is a proof that you are capable of being governed in your anger, and as it is an instance of your paying so much regard to me, as either to obey my authority or to yield to my entreaty. You will accept therefore, at once, both of my applause and my thanks. At the same time, I must advise you for the future to be placable towards erring servants, though there should be none to interpose in their behalf. Farewell." (C. Plinius Sabiniano suo S. Bene fecisti, quod libertum aliquando tibi carum reducentibus epistulis meis in domum, in animum recepisti. Iuvabit hoc te: me certe iuvat, primum quod te tam tractabilem video, ut in ira regi possis, deinde quod tantum mihi tribuis, ut vel auctoritati meae pareas vel precibus indulgeas. Igitur et laudo et gratias ago; simul in posterum moneo, ut te erroribus tuorum, etsi non fuerit, qui deprecetur, placabilem praestes. Vale.) [Also cf. Dibelius–Greeven, 111].

4 The letter (fourth century A.D.) of a Christian priest in Hermupolis to a Christian officer in the Fayûm is preserved, in which he intercedes for a soldier who had deserted: "I would have thee know, lord, con[cerning] Paul the soldier, concerning his flight. Pardon him this once!" (γινόσκιν σε θέλω, κύριε, π[ερὶ] Παύλω τοῦ στρατιότη περὶ τῆς φυγῆς, συνχωρῆσε αὐτοῦ τοῦτω τὸ ἅβαξ) [trans. Deissmann]. This letter is *P.London* 2.417.5–8; cf. Deissmann, *LAE*, 216–21.

letter in such a way that the addressee is gradually led to the actual request.[5] First of all, he gives a brief description of his situation (vss 8–12). Before he mentions the name of the runaway slave, he speaks of him as his child whom he has begotten in prison (v 10) which stresses how dear and beloved he is to him. Then Paul looks back (vss 13–16) to the time when Onesimus came to him to seek refuge. Since Onesimus has accepted the Christian faith, Paul sends him back to Philemon "no longer as a slave, but as one who is much more than a slave, as a beloved brother" (**οὐκέτι ὡς δοῦλον ἀλλὰ ὑπὲρ δοῦλον, ἀδελφὸν ἀγαπητόν** v 16). Only after these careful preliminaries does Paul voice his request (vss 17–20) to receive him "as you would me" (**ὡς ἐμέ** v 17). The Apostle is certain that Philemon will comply with his request and he finally exhorts and beseeches Philemon once more "refresh my heart in Christ" (**ἀνάπαυσόν μου τὰ σπλάγχνα ἐν Χριστῷ** v 20).

■ **8** The particle "therefore" (**διό**)[6] forms a loose connection between this verse and the preceding thanksgiving.[7] The Apostle could make use of his authority and command what is fitting. The Greek word **παρρησία** designates Paul's frankness and openness toward men.[8] This candor is grounded in the openness (**παρρησία**) of Paul toward God (cf. 2 Cor 3:12; Phil 1:20). Since he can turn to God in undisguised openness, he can also associate with men in total freedom and fearlessness. At times **παρρησία** can mean that the relationship to other men is characterized by openness in the sense of affection. Here, however, **παρρησία** means much the same as "authority" (**ἐξουσία**).[9] Paul possesses full authority to issue commands. Had he issued a "command" (**ἐπιταγή**) on the basis of his apostolic authority, there would be nothing else to do than to obey this obligatory order unconditionally.[10] Therefore, the Apostle could simply command that "what is fitting" (**τὸ ἀνῆκον**)[11] be observed also in the affair about which he writes to Philemon. The reference to what is fitting does not mean here the generally valid moral commandment, but the duty that is imposed on the Christian. What this duty implies is made concrete by what follows. In his relationship to his slave Onesimus, Philemon will have to do that which is fitting for a Christian.

■ **9** The Apostle, however, does not want to enforce compliance with his word. Rather, he wants Philemon to perform this deed of love on the basis of his own free decision. Therefore, Paul says that he prefers to request[12] this from Philemon "for love's sake" (**διὰ τὴν ἀγάπην**). There is no reference to the Apostle's love or to that of Philemon,[13] but to "love" (**ἀγάπη**) as such, to the love which governs the Christians' dealings and association with one another.[14] To his request Paul joins a reference to the situation in which he is himself. The Greek adjective **τοιοῦτος**[15] (of such a kind) which precedes is first

5 Lohmeyer takes the artful, systematic development of the principal part of the letter as proof that this section is composed of poetic lines: "These sentences and lines are thought out in Aramaic, but spoken in Greek." (p. 183) Cf. also P.–L. Couchoud, "Le style rhythmé dans l'épître de Saint Paul à Philémon," *RHR* 96 (1927): 129–46, who takes the entire letter as a composition of eight strophes with eight lines each. There is no doubt that Paul writes in well–thought–out phrases, but there is no reason for considering this entire section to be a poetic composition.

6 Cf. Bauer, *s.v.*; Blass–Debrunner, par. 451,5.

7 Cf. Jack T. Sanders, "The Transition from Opening Epistolary Thanksgivings to Body in the Letters of the Pauline Corpus," *JBL* 81 (1962); 348–62, esp. p. 355.

8 Cf. Bauer, *s.v.*; Heinrich Schlier, *TDNT* 5, p. 883.

9 Cf. Schlier, *ibid.*, 883.

10 Cf. 1 Cor 7:6, 25; 2 Cor 8:8; Rom 16:26. Cf. further Gerhard Delling, *TWNT* 8, p. 37. The verb "to command" (**ἐπιτάσσειν**) does not occur again in Paul. In the Synoptics it frequently describes the authoritative command of Jesus addressed to the demons. Cf. Mk 1:27 par.; 9:25 par.; Lk 8:25; cf. further Mk 6:27, 39; Lk 14:22; Acts 23:2. Also cf. Ign. *Rom* 4:3: "I do not order you as did Peter and Paul; they were Apostles, I am a convict; they were free, I am even until now a slave" (**οὐχ ὡς Πέτρος καὶ Παῦλος διατάσσομαι ὑμῖν· ἐκεῖνοι ἀπόστολοι, ἐγὼ κατάκριτος· ἐκεῖνοι ἐλεύθεροι, ἐγὼ δὲ μέχρι νῦν δοῦλος**).

11 On this concept cf. p. 158, n. 23 above on Col 3:18 and Heinrich Schlier, *TDNT* 1, 360.

12 "That **παρακαλεῖν** has the note of 'entreaty' even when it means 'to admonish' may be seen from Phlm. 8f., where it is expressly distinguished from 'to command' (**ἐπιτάσσειν**) and is an outflowing of love" (Otto Schmitz, *TDNT* 5, 795 n. 166). Cf. further p. 80 above on Col 2:2; Bjerkelund, *Parakalô*, 188: "Paul uses **παρακαλῶ** (I entreat, request) when the question of authority must not present a problem and the Apostle can deal with the members of the community as his brothers in the consciousness that they want to acknowledge him as an apostle. Therefore, this entreaty indicates that Paul has

explained by the name "Paul." Attached to this is the designation *πρεσβύτης*. This Greek noun could be taken to mean "ambassador" and then would be an expression of the authority granted to Paul. In order to justify this translation it is not necessary to resort to the conjecture *πρεσβευτής*,[16] for *πρεσβύτης* is also used occasionally for envoys and ambassadors.[17] If one takes the term as referring to the Apostle's office, then Paul would be underlining the fact that he speaks as an ambassador of Christ[18] (cf. 2 Cor 5:20).[19] The Apostle, however, had just given express assurance that he would waive the "authority" (*παρρησία*) he had to give commands. Therefore, in saying that he is a *πρεσβύτης*, Paul is alluding to his age.[20] Paul is not employing his apostolic authority here; he is speaking to Philemon as an elderly man.[21] Moreover, as "a prisoner of Christ Jesus" (*δέσμιος Χριστοῦ 'Ιησοῦ* cf. v 1) he shares in the weakness and humiliation of Christ, for whose sake he is now[22] suffering. If Paul calls attention to his age and his imprisonment, he can expect that Philemon will pay due respect to his words.

■ **10** Once more Paul uses the verb "I beseech" (*παρακαλῶ* cf. v 9) and now also brings up the object of his request. His intercession is for[23] his child whom he has begotten in prison.[24] Only after the Apostle has affirmed the close ties that join him to Onesimus, does he mention Onesimus' name.[25] Onesimus had been the slave of a Christian master, but was not yet a member of the Christian community. After his escape, when he had come to Paul and had stayed with him, he had become a Christian. Paul states this fact before mentioning Onesimus' name, a name that surely would have conjured up bad memories in Philemon's mind.[26] Now, however, he can no longer bear ill–will toward Onesimus if the Apostle speaks of him as his "child" (*τέκνον*). Paul occasionally describes himself as the father of the entire community because he has begotten them in Christ Jesus (cf. 1 Cor 4:15; Gal 4:19) and says that Timothy is his "beloved and

---

a certain confidence in the community addressed."

13 This is the view of Dibelius–Greeven, *ad loc.*: "trusting in the love of Philemon mentioned in 7."

14 Cf. Wickert, "Philemonbrief," 236 n. 16: "The common love urges that the request be made."

15 The Greek phrase *τοιοῦτος ὤν* means "Since that is what I am." On the Greek particle *ὡς*, cf. Bauer, *s.v.*: "*ὡς* introduces the characteristic quality of a pers., thing, or action, etc., referred to in the context." Bauer, on *τοιοῦτος*, says that it is followed by *ὡς* in the meaning of "in my character as." Cf. e.g., 1 Cor 3:10: "like a skilled master builder" (*ὡς σοφὸς ἀρχιτέκτων*).

16 Lightfoot, Haupt, *ad loc.*

17 Cf. 2 Macc 11:34; LXX 2 Chr 32:31 (B); 1 Macc 14:22; 15:17 (א). Cf. also Günther Bornkamm, *TDNT* 6, 683 n. 2.

18 Cf. also Eph 6:20: "for which (*scil.* the Gospel) I am an ambassador in chains" (*ὑπὲρ οὗ πρεσβεύω ἐν ἁλύσει*); Ign.*Sm.* 11:2: "an ambassador of God" (*θεοπρεσβευτής*) [Trans.].

19 Cf. Lightfoot, Haupt, Lohmeyer, Moule, *ad loc.*; further Wickert, "Philemonbrief," 235; Kümmel, *Introduction*, 246.

20 Ps.–Hippocrates in *περὶ ἑβδομάδων* (quoted by Philo, *De opif. mundi* 105) uses *πρεσβύτης* to describe the sixth of the seven ages through which men pass. This sixth age occurs between the age of "mature man" (*ἀνήρ*) and "old man" (*γέρων*), that is, 49 to 56 years of age. According to Hippocrates, *Aphorismi* 3.30f, *πρεσβύτης* denotes the final stage in the span of a man's lifetime. Cf. Franz Boll, "Die Lebensalter," *Neue Jahrbücher für das Klassische Altertum* 31 (1913): 89–145, especially pp. 114–18. One cannot infer the exact age of Paul from this passage. Cf. Dibelius–Greeven, *ad loc.*

21 Vincent, Dibelius–Greeven, Friedrich, *ad loc.*, explain this passage in much the same way. Cf. further Bornkamm, *TDNT* 6, 683.

22 Instead of *νυνί* (now) manuscripts A pc have the less emphatic *νῦν* (now).

23 In this context, the Greek preposition *περί* does not mean "about, with reference to," but "for, on behalf of." Cf. 1 Cor 16:12; 2 Cor 12:8; 2 Thess 2:1 and consult Greeven, "Prüfung der Thesen von J. Knox zum Philemonbrief," col. 374. Paul does not want to make a request about Onesimus (this is the view of Knox, *Philemon*, 23f, n. 8); he is interceding on his behalf. Cf. Bjerkelund, *Parakalô*, 120f, 210 n. 4.

24 After *ὅν* (whom) manuscripts A 69 al sy^h add the Greek personal pronoun *ἐγώ* (I). Manuscripts C ℜ pl sy expand *ἐν τοῖς δεσμοῖς* (in bonds) by adding *μου* (my). "The shorter reading carries more weight!" (Lectio brevior potior!)

25 The name "Onesimus" (*'Ονήσιμος*) is frequently found as the name of a slave. Cf. Lightfoot, 308f; Bauer, *s.v.*

26 Cf. Theodoret, *ad loc.*: "then after these words of praise he gives the name" (*εἶτα μετὰ τὰ ἐγκώμια τὸ ὄνομα τέθεικεν*) [Trans.].

faithful child in the Lord" (τέκνον ἀγαπητὸν καὶ πιστὸν ἐν κυρίῳ 1 Cor 4:17). The image of father and child is sometimes employed in Rabbinic Judaism to describe the relationship that obtains between a teacher and the student whom he has instructed in the Torah.[27] In the mystery religions the mystagogue is considered the father of the initiate who remains bound to him.[28] Paul uses a similar mode of expression.[29] For the Apostle calls Onesimus his "child" (τέκνον) not only because he, like a father, is interceding for the slave (v 19),[30] but also because he has begotten him, that is, he has converted him to faith in Christ. Paul's child, therefore, is the brother of Philemon (v 16), who also was led to faith in Christ by Paul (v 19).[31]

■ **11** Earlier Onesimus might have been a useless slave to his master.[32] Now he has become quite a different person[33] who is really useful to the Apostle and also to Philemon.[34] The words ἄχρηστον/εὔχρηστον[35] (useless/useful), which describe this change of circumstances, allude to the word **Χριστός** (Christ), for **Χριστός** (Christ) in Hellenistic Greek would be pronounced exactly like **χρηστός** (useful).[36] This transformation has

27 Cf. *b. Sanh.* 99b: "He who teaches Torah to his neighbour's son is regarded by Scripture as though he had fashioned him" [trans. Epstein]. Cf. Billerbeck 3, p. 340f, where additional Rabbinic examples will be found. Cf. also Friedrich Büchsel, *TDNT* 1, 665f.

28 Cf. Apuleius, *Metamorph.* 11.25: "When I had ended my oration to the great goddess (*scil.* Isis), I went to embrace the great priest Mithras, now my spiritual father" (Ad istum modum deprecato summo numine [*scil.* Isis] complexus Mithram sacerdotem et meum iam parentem). Cf. further the evidence collected by Dibelius–Greeven, *ad loc.*: *IG* 14.1084.5f; *CIL* 3.882; 6.2278. The initiate is taken to be a child who has received initiation into the mysteries at the hands of the father. Cf. Reitzenstein, *Mysterienreligionen*, 40f.

29 Cf. Dibelius–Greeven, *ad loc.*

30 This is the opinion of Deissmann, *LAE*, 335f.

31 Although Ὀνήσιμον, τόν ποτέ σοι κτλ (Onesimus, who was formerly useless to you, etc.) is in apposition to περὶ τοῦ ἐμοῦ τέκνου (for my child) and should be in the genitive case, it is in the accusative. The accusative case here is explicable as attraction to the relative sentence ὃν ἐγέννησα κτλ (whom I have begotten, etc.). Cf. Moule, *ad loc.*

32 Phrygian slaves were generally considered useless. The evidence may be found in Lightfoot, 310 n. 2.

33 The καί (and) that occurs before σοί (to you) is omitted by manuscripts A C ℜ D pm it sy^{h}, but is adequately attested to by manuscripts ℵ* G 33 al vg sy^{p}. [Trans. note: This καί is omitted in the translation of this verse for stylistic reasons.]

34 Ὀνήσιμον (Onesimus) is modified by an appositional phrase which begins with the definite article: τόν ποτέ σοι ἄχρηστον κτλ (who was formerly useless to you, etc.). On this point of grammar cf. Radermacher, *Grammatik*, 116: "An attribute or an apposition that follows the word modified is more closely joined to it by the definite article even though the article itself is not necessarily demanded by the rules of grammar."

35 Cf. Plato, *Republic* 411A: "is made useful instead of useless . . ." (χρήσιμον ἐξ ἀχρήστου . . . ἐποίησεν). A similar play on words is also found in Rabbinic tradition: "It can be compared to a man who was about to purchase a slave and who said to the owner: 'This slave whom thou offerest me for sale—does he belong to the class of the mischievous (קאקוריסין which in Greek is κακὴ αἵρεσις), or to the well-behaved (קלוריסין which in Greek is καλὴ αἵρεσις)?' Said he to him: 'He belongs to the mischievous, and as such do I sell him to thee!'" (*Midr. Exod* 43 [99c] in the Freedman trans.). Cf. Billerbeck 3, p. 668. Many instances of the contrast ἄχρηστος/εὔχρηστος (useless/useful) are found in the Shepherd of Hermas: *Vis.* 3.6.1: ". . . they are not useful for the building." (οὐκ εἰσὶν εὔχρηστοι εἰς οἰκοδομήν); *Vis.* 3.6.2: "they are useless" (ἄχρηστοί εἰσιν); *Vis.* 3.6.7: "when you were rich, you were useless, but now you are useful . . . Be useful to God" (ὅτε ἐπλούτεις, ἄχρηστος ἦς, νῦν δὲ εὔχρηστος εἶ . . . εὔχρηστοι γίνεσθε τῷ θεῷ); *Mand.* 5.1.6: "long suffering . . . is useful to the Lord . . . ill temper . . . is useless" (ἡ μακροθυμία . . . εὔχρηστός ἐστι τῷ κυρίῳ . . . ἡ δὲ ὀξυχολία . . . ἄχρηστός ἐστιν). [*Vis.* 3.6.2 and *Mand.* 5.1.6 are rendered by Trans.].

36 Cf. Justin, *Apol.* 1.4.1: "from the name we are accused of, we are most excellent people" (ἐκ τοῦ κατηγορουμένου ἡμῶν ὀνόματος χρηστότατοι ὑπάρχομεν); 1.4.5: "For we are accused of being Christians, and to hate what is excellent [Chrestian] is unjust" (Χριστιανοὶ γὰρ εἶναι κατηγορούμεθα· τὸ δὲ χρηστὸν μισεῖσθαι οὐ δίκαιον trans. from ANF 1, 163–64). Cf. also Athenagoras, *Supplicatio pro Christianis* 2; Tertullian, *Apol.* 3.5: "But Christian, so far as the meaning of the word is concerned, is derived from anointing. Yes, and even when it is wrongly pronounced by you 'Chrestianus' [for you do not even know accurately the name you hate], it comes from sweetness and benignity" ("Christianus" vero, quantum interpretatio est, de unctione [*scil.* χρῖσις] deducitur. Sed et cum perperam "Chrestianus" pronuntiatur a vobis—nam nec no-

been accomplished by Onesimus' conversion to Christ as the Lord. The past has now been cancelled out. Only the present, which is determined by the fact that Onesimus belongs to Christ, is valid.[37] Also Philemon can corroborate this transformation, for Onesimus was once "useless"[38] to him, but now he will be "useful." It is true that Paul can only cite himself as witness to this transformation. Nevertheless, he puts: useful "to you" (σοί) before "to me" (ἐμοί). For Philemon will have to satisfy himself that Onesimus has become a different person.

■ **12** The Apostle is sending[39] Onesimus back to his master.[40] In doing this, he is fulfilling the requirements of the law.[41] Paul, though, is sending Onesimus to Philemon with the express assurance that this slave[42] means as much to him as his own heart.[43] When Onesimus returns to his master, it is as if the Apostle himself had come to him.[44] How then could he withhold from the slave what he owes the aging and suffering Paul?[45]

■ **13** In a few words Paul now tells what had transpired before he wrote his letter and sent Onesimus back. Paul would have liked[46] to keep[47] him with him. For Onesimus has rendered faithful service to him and could even

minis certa est notitia penes vos , de suavitate vel benignitate [*scil.* χρηστότης] compositum est [trans. from ANF 3, 20]).

37 On the contrast "formerly—now" in primitive Christian preaching and teaching, cf. p. 62 above on Col 1:21f.

38 Epictetus *Diss.* 1.19.19 mentions a cobbler, the slave of Epaphroditus, "whom he sold because he was useless" (ὃν διὰ τὸ ἄχρηστον εἶναι ἐπώλησεν).

39 The Greek verb ἀνέπεμψα is an epistolary aorist and is rendered "I am sending back." Cf. p. 171, n. 7 above on Col 4:8. ἀνέπεμψα does not mean that Paul is sending him up to a higher authority as one would send somebody up to the duly constituted law court where his case could be decided. Thus Knox, *Philemon*, ch. 1, holds that Paul wanted to retain Onesimus, but sends him to Archippus via Philemon. As his master, Archippus will pronounce judgment on the matter. The verb ἀναπέμπειν, however, clearly has the meaning here of "to send back." Cf. Lk 23:7, 11, 15; Acts 25:21.

40 The manuscript tradition has no uniform reading for this verse. After σοι (to you) manuscripts D* it vg^{cl} sy^{p} add σὺ δέ (you). Instead of σοι (to you) manuscripts P 𝔎 G pl vg^{codd} read σὺ δέ (you). At the end of the verse manuscripts C 𝔎 D (69 al) pl lat sy have προσλαβοῦ (welcome). "This reading clearly has its source in the desire to find the object of the request expressly mentioned earlier than it is actually given, i.e. in vs. 17" (Dibelius–Greeven, *ad loc.*).

41 For the corresponding Jewish legal prescriptions cf. Billerbeck 3, pp. 668–70. On this question cf. p. 187 above.

42 The construction ὃν—αὐτόν (whom) could be taken as a Semitism. Cf. Mk 7:25: γυνὴ . . . ἧς εἶχεν τὸ θυγάτριον αὐτῆς (a woman . . . whose little daughter of hers had) [Trans.]. For in a Hebrew sentence a personal pronoun or suffix always follows the relative אֲשֶׁר (that, which, who). It is probable, however, that αὐτόν (him) is placed here to pick up again the relative pronoun before the sentence continues: when I send him, I am thereby sending my very heart. Cf. Moule, *ad loc.*

43 The meaning of τὰ σπλάγχνα as "child" is out of the question in this context. On Philo, *Jos.* 25, which is occasionally (but without justification) adduced to corroborate such meaning, cf. Helmut Köster, *TWNT* 7, 553. Earlier in the text, Onesimus was already called the "child, whom I have begotten in prison" (τέκνον ὃν ἐγέννησα ἐν τοῖς δεσμοῖς v 10).

44 Cf. Köster, *TWNT* 7, 555.

45 On this intercession which Paul makes for Onesimus, cf. the letter of recommendation *P.Osl.* 55 (second–third century A.D.): "Diogenes to Pythagoras his brother, greetings. Know that Theon the Admirable, who is delivering my writings to you, stayed at my house. He regards me as his brother. Therefore, you will be well advised, brother, to receive him as you would me" (Διογένης Πυθαγόρᾳ τῷ ἀνδελφῷ χαίρειν. Ἴσθι Θέωνα τὸν παράδοξον τὸν ἀναδιδόντα σοι ταῦτά μου τὰ γράμματα οἰκεῖόν μου ὄντα καὶ σχέσιν ἀδελφικὴν ἔχοντα πρός με. Καλῶς οὖν ποιήσεις, ἀδελφέ, τοῦτον ὑποδειξάμενος ὡς ἂν ἐμέ) [Trans.]. Cf. Bjerkelund, *Parakalô*, 121f.

46 The verb "I would have liked" (ἐβουλόμην) expresses an attainable wish. Paul, however, foregoes its realization: I "would have liked, but I do not, or did not, do it" (Blass–Debrunner, par. 359, 2).

47 It is true that "to retain, to keep" (κατέχειν) also occurs as a technical term in the context of the sacral rights and duties of asylum where κατοχή means that the deity has sequestered the one entering. Nevertheless, "there is no doubt that Πρὸς ἐμαυτὸν κατέχειν in the context of Paul's letter can only mean 'to retain with me' " (Lienhard Delekat, *Katoche, Hierodulie und Adoptionsfreilassung*. Münchener Beiträge zur Papyrusforschung und Rechtsgeschichte 47 [München: 1964], 7f).

continue to give it in place of Philemon,[48] who doubtless would also gladly aid the Apostle. Paul, as an apostle, could have the right to claim[49] this service and is in great need of it, especially in the imprisonment which he must suffer for the sake of the Gospel.[50] Nevertheless, he does not want, under any circumstances, to encroach upon the decision which only Philemon, as the slave's rightful master, can make.

■ **14** The Apostle will do nothing without his consent.[51] For Philemon should not feel that he is forced to do this good deed, but should be free to decide for himself that he wants to do it. In speaking here of "your good deed" (**τὸ ἀγαθόν σου**), Paul again selects a quite general expression which does not restrict the letter's recipient to the fulfillment of a precise instruction. Rather he is encouraged to let love do its work, for love is resourceful enough to find the right way in accomplishing the good.[52] This, however, cannot happen if Philemon is compelled to act against his own will. Love can only express itself concretely on the basis of a decision that is freely arrived at.[53] Therefore, even the slightest suspicion that Paul might be intruding into a decision that can only be Philemon's must be avoided.[54]

■ **15** In reviewing Onesimus' flight, Paul chooses his words very carefully and wonders whether perhaps[55] the reason why Onesimus was separated from Philemon for a while[56] was that he should now receive him back forever. The passive verb "he was separated from" (**ἐχωρίσθη**) plainly intimates that God's hidden purpose may have been behind this incident which has caused Phile-

48 The Greek phrase ὑπὲρ σοῦ means "to be your representative." In ancient papyrus letters ὑπὲρ αὐτοῦ occurs frequently; a scribe, writing for an illiterate person, employs this phrase to indicate that he is representing him. Cf. Deissmann, *LAE*, 335 n. 4.

49 Cf. Acts 13:5: "And they had John to assist them" (εἶχον δὲ καὶ Ἰωάννην ὑπηρέτην). In Phil 2:25 Paul calls Epaphroditus, who is a member of the Philippian community and is staying with him, "your messenger and minister to my need" (ὑμῶν δὲ ἀπόστολον καὶ λειτουργὸν τῆς χρείας μου). He had even placed his life in jeopardy "to complete your service to me" (ἵνα ἀναπληρώσῃ τὸ ὑμῶν ὑστέρημα τῆς πρός με λειτουργίας Phil 2:30.).

50 Cf. above on v 1 and Ign. *Tr.* 12:2: "My bonds exhort you, which I carry about for the sake of Jesus Christ" (παρακαλεῖ ὑμᾶς τὰ δεσμά μου, ἃ ἕνεκα Ἰησοῦ Χριστοῦ περιφέρω).

51 Cf. Rudolf Bultmann, *TDNT* 1, 717; Bauer, *s.v.* On this meaning of the word γνώμη, which is frequently attested in the papyri (cf. Preisigke *Wört.* 1, col. 301), cf., e.g., *P.Oxy.* 10.1280.4–6: "I acknowledge that I have of my own free consent made a contract with you" (ὁμολογῶ ἑκουσίᾳ καὶ αὐθαιρέτῳ γνώμῃ συντεθῖσθαί με πρὸς σέ) [Trans.].

52 Cf. v 6: "in the knowledge of all the good that is in us for the glory of Christ" (ἐν ἐπιγνώσει παντὸς ἀγαθοῦ τοῦ ἐν ἡμῖν εἰς Χριστόν). The phrase "the good [deed] which is yours" (τὸ ἀγαθόν σου) can be explained grammatically: the definite article turns the adjective into a substantive. Cf. Blass–Debrunner, par. 263 and Moulton–Turner, 13; also see v 9 "that which is fitting" (τὸ ἀνῆκον).

53 On the contrast "not from compulsion—but from one's own free will" (μὴ ὡς κατὰ ἀνάγκην—ἀλλὰ κατὰ ἑκούσιον) cf. Thucydides 8.27.3: "of free will or through absolute necessity" (καθ' ἑκουσίαν [*scil.* γνώμην], ἢ πάνυ γε ἀνάγκῃ); cf. further 1 Pt 5:2: "not by constraint but willingly" (μὴ ἀναγκαστῶς ἀλλὰ ἑκουσίως). The adjective "willing, voluntary" (ἑκούσιος) occurs only here in the Pauline corpus. On "from one's own free will" (κατὰ ἑκούσιον) cf. LXX Num 15:3: "free–will [offering]" (καθ' ἑκούσιον); Heb 10:26: "deliberately" (ἑκουσίως); *P.Oxy.* 12.1426.14: "of free will" (ἑκουσίᾳ γνώμῃ); *P.Lips.* 1.26.5f: "We acknowledge that we have divided among [ou]rselves of our [own] free will and [ch]oice; we will not [go] back on our decision" (ὁμολογοῦμεν [ἑκο]υσίᾳ καὶ α[ὐ]θαιρέτῳ καὶ ἀμε-[τα]νοήτῳ γνώμῃ διῃ[ρ]ῆσθαι πρὸς [ἑ]αυτούς [trans.]). On *P.Oxy.* 10.1280.4f cf. n. 51 above.

54 For this reason the Greek particle ὡς (as if) is placed before κατὰ ἀνάγκην (from compulsion) here. Cf. Pliny the Younger *Epist.* 9.21: "I am afraid . . . I should seem rather to compel, than request you" (Vereor, ne videar non rogare sed cogere). Cf. p.196, n. 2 above.

55 The Greek adverb τάχα has the meaning of "perhaps." Cf. Xenophon, *Anab.* 5.2.17; Rom 5:7, and Bauer, *s.v.*

56 On the Greek phrase πρὸς ὥραν, which means "for a while, for a moment," cf. Gal 2:5: "to them we did not yield in submission even for a moment" (οἷς οὐδὲ πρὸς ὥραν εἴξαμεν τῇ ὑποταγῇ). Cf. further 2 Cor 7:8 and Bauer, *s.v.*

57 The Greek verb ἀπέχειν is the technical term for receiving a sum in full and giving a receipt for it. Cf. Phil. 4:18: "I have received full payment, and more" (ἀπέχω δὲ πάντα καὶ περισσεύω). Further examples may be found in Deissman, *LAE*, 110–12; Bauer, *s.v.*

58 Consequently, the word "forever" (αἰώνιον) is contrasted with "for a while" (πρὸς ὥραν). The עֶבֶד

mon so much annoyance. For now he will receive him back[57] so that he will no longer be separated from him. The separation had lasted for only a short time; the new relationship will endure forever.[58]

■ **16** Philemon and Onesimus are now related to one another as brothers in Christ. Therefore, Onesimus will be far more than a slave to his master.[59] The Apostle calls him "a beloved brother" (ἀδελφὸν ἀγαπητόν). This brotherhood will now characterize his relationship to his Christian master.[60] In saying this, Paul is not speaking in a Stoic sense about the equality of all men, who come from the same seed and breathe the same air.[61] Rather he is describing the new relationship of community that is grounded in union with Christ. Although Onesimus "in the flesh" (ἐν σαρκί) is, as a slave, the property of his master, this earthly relationship is now surpassed by the union "in the Lord" (ἐν κυρίῳ).[62] There is no doubt that earthly freedom is a great good. Nevertheless, in the last analysis it is of no significance to the Christian whether he is slave or free. The only thing that matters is this: to have accepted God's call and to follow him (1 Cor 7:21–24). The master of a slave also must be obedient to this call, for he, too, is subject to the command of the Kyrios. In this way, the relationship of master and slave has undergone a fundamental change. Although it might seem natural that Philemon grant Onesimus his freedom,[63] the Apostle can leave it to Philemon how he wants to decide. Under all circumstances Philemon is bound to the commandment of love which makes its renovating power effective in any case, since the slave who returns home is now a brother.

■ **17** Only at this point[64] does Paul make his request that Philemon receive Onesimus as he would welcome the Apostle. Paul bases his request on the fact that a close tie exists between him and Philemon and that he has the Apostle as his "partner" (κοινωνός). The Greek word κοινωνοί means partners who share common interests or who as comrades are engaged in the same endeavors.[65] When Paul calls himself a "partner," he is referring neither to business transactions nor simply to the ties of friendship. Their "fellowship" (κοινωνία) is grounded in their belonging to one Lord. This deeply binding relationship draws them together into common activities,

---

עולם (Deut 15:17) is the slave for life. Nevertheless, the meaning is certainly not that Onesimus should be a "slave for life" (οἰκέτης εἰς τὸν αἰῶνα) [cf. Hermann Sasse, *TDNT* 1, 209]. Rather, "forever" describes the new relationship of the master to his slave, a relationship that is grounded in Christ and not to be severed again. Now Onesimus is no longer the " 'property' (*res*) of his master" "which he was according to Roman law" (Merk, *Handeln*, 227).

59 On the phrase "no longer as a slave, but as one who is much more than a slave" (οὐκέτι ὡς δοῦλον ἀλλὰ ὑπὲρ δοῦλον), cf. von Soden, *ad loc.*: the particle " 'as' (ὡς) expresses the subjective evaluation of the relationship without calling its objective form into question . . . therefore the line of thought found in 1 Cor 7:20–24 is not exceeded."

60 The Greek adverb μάλιστα, which is superlative in form, is used here as an elative in the meaning of "especially." Therefore, the comparison can be heightened by "how much more" (πόσῳ μᾶλλον) which follows.

61 Cf. Seneca, *Epist.* 47.10: "Kindly remember that he whom you call your slave sprang from the same stock, is smiled upon by the same skies, and on equal terms with yourself breathes, lives and dies. It is just as possible for you to see in him a free-born man as for him to see in you a slave" (Vis tu cogitare istum, quem servum tuum vocas, ex eisdem seminibus ortum eodem frui caelo, aeque spirare, aeque vivere, aeque mori. Tam tu illum videre ingenuum potes quam ille te servum).

62 The expression ἐν σαρκὶ καὶ ἐν κυρίῳ, which according to Dibelius–Greeven, *ad loc.* means "as a man and as a Christian," occurs only here in Paul. Cf. Conzelmann, *Outline*, 174.

63 The view that all men have equal rights was advocated in the mystery religions. Consequently, a slave who had undergone the same initiation rites as his master, was no longer considered a slave, but stood alongside his former master as a free man. Cf. Philipp Seidensticker, *Lebendiges Opfer*. NTAbh 20, 1–3 (Münster in. W.: 1954), 15 n. 33.

64 The Greek connective οὖν (now then, therefore) is the second word in this verse. Cf. Bl-Debr par 451, 1: "After Parenthetical remarks οὖν indicates a return to the main theme."

65 Cf. Lightfoot, *ad loc.*: "Those are κοινωνοί, who have common interests, common feelings, common work." Cf. e.g., *PSI* 4.306.3: "to have received [. . .] as an equal partner" (προσειληφέναι τ[. . .]οην κοινωνὸν ἐξ ἴσου); *P.Amh.* 2.92.18f: "I will have neither a p[a]rtner nor a servant" (οὐχ ἕξω δὲ κ[ο]ινωνὸν οὐδὲ μίσθιον); 2.100.4: "he took Cornelius as his partner" (προσελάβετο τὸν Κορνήλιον κοι-

in faith and love.[66] On the basis of this bond, Paul makes his request in which he not only intercedes for Onesimus,[67] but even identifies himself with him.[68] All the love that Philemon will give to Onesimus will be considered as love that he had given to the Apostle himself.

■ **18** Of course, damages must be repaired or compensated for. If Onesimus has wronged his master or owes him anything, the Apostle will stand good for him. When Paul says this, he does not necessarily imply that the slave, in running away, had pilfered something from his master. For he had already caused injury to Philemon's property solely by running away, even if he did not steal anything. Philemon is asked to put the cost of the damages that resulted from Onesimus' flight, on the Apostle's bill.[69] Earlier, in employing the term "partner," Paul had used a word with juridical meaning. Now he once again makes use of a word that describes legal obligations. He requests that Philemon let the outstanding damages be charged to his account.[70] Philemon will realize that the Apostle has no earthly riches at his disposal and will consequently understand what he means when he declares that he is prepared to stand good for the damages.

■ **19** Writing in his own hand[71] Paul gives the declaration that he will make compensation for the damages.[72] In effect, he is giving a promissory note which is inserted in a parenthesis (v 19a) within the context. This promissory note obligates him to make the compensation which may be required.[73] Verse 19b picks up the thought expressed in v 18: if the discussion is going to center around debts, then Paul can make a contra-account[74] and re-

---

νωνόν) [papyri rendered by the Trans.]. Further examples may be found in Bauer, *s.v.*

66 Cf. Theodore of Mopsuestia, *ad loc.*: "on account of a common faith" (ob communem fidem); cf. further Friedrich Hauck, *TDNT* 3, 807.

67 On this point cf. the letter of Pliny the Younger to Sabinianus cited above p. 196, n. 2.

68 Cf. Friedrich, *ad loc.* On the phrase "him as me" (*αὐτὸν ὡς ἐμέ*), cf. *P.Osl.* 55 (see p. 201, n. 45 above): "Therefore, you will be well advised, brother, to receive him as you would me" (*Καλῶς οὖν ποιήσεις, ἀδελφέ, τοῦτον ὑποδεξάμενος ὡς ἂν ἐμέ*), and consult Bjerkelund, *Parakalô*, p. 52.

69 The oldest manuscripts read the irregular form *ἐλλόγα* (as if the verb were *ἐλλογᾶν*) instead of *ἐλλόγει* (from *ἐλλογεῖν*, "charge to one's account"), which is found in manuscripts 𝔎 pl; cf. Rom 5:13.

70 On the Greek verb *ἐλλογάω* or *ἐλλογέω* in the meaning of "to charge to one's account," cf. *P.Strassb.* 1.32.9f: "He should write out a bill for it (*scil.* for a plough), noting how much is owed him and that he has delivered it, so that in this way he can settle accounts with him" (*δότω λόγον, τί αὐτῷ ὀφείλ[ε]ται καὶ ποῦ παρέσχεν, ἵνα οὕτως αὐτῷ ἐνλογηθῇ*) [author's trans.]; *BGU* 1.140.28–33: "This bounty of mine it will be your duty to make well known both to my soldiers and to the veterans, not to enable me to take credit in their eyes, but in order that they may use this privilege, should they be ignorant of it" (*ταύτην μου τὴν δωρεὰν καὶ τοῖς στρατιώταις ἐμοῦ καὶ τοῖς οὐετρανοῖς εὔγνωστόν σε ποιῆσαι δεήσει, οὐχ ἕνεκα τοῦ δοκεῖν με αὐτοῖς ἐνλογεῖν, ἀλλὰ ἵνα τούτῳ χρῶνται, ἐὰν ἀγνοῶσι*) [Loeb]; *P.Grenf.* 2.67.16–18: "Therefo[re], the pledge is supplementary and will not [be] charg[e]d to y[ou]r account" (*ἐντεῦθε[ν] δὲ ἔσχες ὑπὲρ ἀραβῶνος [τοῦ] μὴ ἐλλογουμέν[ο]υ σ[ο]ι (δραχμάς)*) [Trans.]. Cf. further Bauer, *s.v.*; Herbert Preisker, *TDNT* 2, 517; Gerhard Friedrich, "*Ἁμαρτία οὐκ ἐλλογεῖται* Röm. 5, 13," *ThLZ* 77 (1952): 523–28.

71 The verb form *ἔγραψα* (I am writing) is an epistolary aorist. The parenthesis, v 19a, was surely written in his own hand. It can no longer be ascertained whether the rest of the letter was dictated (this is the view of Dibelius–Greeven, *ad loc.*) or whether it, too, was written by Paul himself.

72 The verb *ἀποτίνειν* means "to make compensation" and is also a juridical term. Cf. *P.Oxy.* 2.275. 24–28 where the following conditions are found in a one–year contract of apprenticeship: "and if there are any days on which the boy (the apprentice) fails to attend, Tryphon (the boy's father) shall produce him for an equivalent number of days after the period is over, or shall make a compensation of one drachma of silver for each day" (*ὅσας δ' ἐὰν ἐν τούτῳ ἀτακτήσῃ ἡμέρας ἐπὶ τὰς ἴσας αὐτὸν παρέξεται [με]τὰ τὸν χρόνον ἢ ἀ[πο]τεισάτω ἑκάσ[τ]ης ἡμέρας ἀργυρίου [δρ]αχμὴν μίαν*) [Trans.].

73 This clarification of the Apostle is to be construed legally as a private intercession. Cf. Otto Eger, *Rechtsgeschichtliches zum Neuen Testament.* Rektoratsprogramm der Universität Basel für das Jahr 1918 (Basel: 1919), 44.

74 On the phrase "not to mention, to say nothing" (*ἵνα μὴ λέγω*). Cf. 2 Cor 9:4: "to say nothing" (*ἵνα μὴ λέγωμεν*). Cf. Blass–Debrunner, par. 495, 1: "The orator pretends to pass over something which he in fact mentions."

75 Verse 19b is to be translated: "not to mention to you that you owe me your very life besides." Haupt, *ad loc.* and Jang, *Philemonbrief*, on the other hand, punctuate the sentence this way: *ἵνα μὴ λέγω· σοί* (*scil.* *ἐλλόγα*) [to say nothing. Charge it to your own

mind Philemon that it is in fact he who is indebted to the Apostle.[75] For it was through Paul [76] that he was won over to the Christian faith.[77] With this phrase the language of debt and compensation no longer remains within the domain of juridical obligations, but is used in a figurative sense to describe the relationship of Philemon to the Apostle.[78] Philemon will understand that within this relationship one can no longer balance debt against debt. Onesimus has experienced the same mercy of God by which Philemon first became a Christian. Therefore, he should receive him as a brother in Christ and squelch any stirring of anger, no matter how justifiable it may be.

■ **20** To strengthen[79] his request Paul adds one last sentence in which he once more addresses Philemon as brother and expresses the wish that he wants to have great joy in him in the Lord.[80] In giving voice to this desire, Paul employs an expression that is almost a fixed formula.[81] Consequently, a word–play on the name of Onesimus cannot be read out of ὀναίμην (may I have joy, profit, benefit in).[82] Nor can it be inferred that the Apostle expected that Philemon would grant his slave his freedom so that he could remain with Paul and serve him. Philemon is reminded of the "love" (ἀγάπη) in which he exists. By acting on the basis of this love, he will do what is right and will be able to make the Apostle happy. The question of the existing social order, in which there are masters and slaves, is not broached.[83] There is clear reference, however, to the fact that in Christ the relationship of human beings to one another has been radically renewed so that slave and master are one in Christ (Gal 3:28; 1 Cor 7:21–24; 12:13). Thus at the end of the two short sentences that comprise v 20 Paul places the phrases "in the Lord" (ἐν κυρίῳ) and "in Christ" (ἐν Χριστῷ).[84] The Kyrios demands that all, who are one in Christ, deal with each other in "love" (ἀγάπη).[85] With this in mind, Paul once again requests that Philemon refresh his heart in Christ. He had concluded the thanksgiving by saying that through Philemon's deeds of love "the hearts of the saints have been refreshed" (τὰ σπλάγχνα τῶν ἁγίων ἀναπέπαυται v 7). Now at the end of the principal section of the letter he uses this phrase once more, and voices the expectation that Philemon will also refresh the heart of the Apostle. In doing so, Paul indicates to Philemon that he is certain Philemon will heed his request and receive Onesimus as if the Apostle himself had come to him.

---

account]. Cf. also Blass–Debrunner, par. 495, 1. Nevertheless, "this way of taking the sentence removes the unassailable seriousness of the declaration of liability" (Lohmeyer, *ad loc.*).

76 Thus, a mutual set of obligations is established (cf. Rom 15:27). On the verb "you owe besides" (προσοφείλεις), cf. *P.Par.* 26.44–46: "And what debts are owed us besides, along with the periods for which they have been owing and the persons who owe them, he will force them to pay us" (καὶ τίνα πρὸς τίνας χρόνους προσωφείληται καὶ ὑπὸ τίνων, ἐπαναγκάσῃ αὐτοὺς ἀποδοῦναι ἡμῖν) [Trans.]; *P.Hibeh* 63.14f: "what you owe to me besides" (ὃ προσοφείλεις μοι) [Trans.].

77 Cf. p. 192, n. 9 above on v 5.

78 Manuscript D* adds "in the Lord" (ἐν κυρίῳ) at the end of v 19.

79 The particle "yes" (ναί) lends emphasis to the statement. Cf. Phil 4:3: "Yes, I ask you also" (ναὶ ἐρωτῶ καὶ σέ). Further examples may be found in Bauer, *s.v.*

80 The verb "may I have joy in" (ὀναίμην) is one of the rare optatives that occur in the NT. Cf. Radermacher, *Grammatik*, 165; Blass–Debrunner, par. 65, 2; 384. Moulton, *Prolegomena*, p. 195, writes: "is the only proper optative in the NT which is not 3rd person."

81 Cf. Bauer, *s.v.* (i.e., ὀνίνημι). The optative "may I have joy in" (ὀναίμην) occurs six times in Ignatius: *Eph.* 2:2; *Mag.* 2; 12:1; *Rom.* 5:2; *Pol.* 1:1; 6:2.

82 Cf. Blass–Debrunner, par. 488, 1b: "Paul is not playing upon the name of the slave Onesimus, although he uses ὀναίμην only here (Phlm 20); at most the recipient could make the obvious word–play himself from Ὀνήσιμον . . . ἄχρηστον 10f."

83 For this reason, criticisms have been leveled against Paul that are as subjective as they are unjust. On this criticism cf. p. 162, n. 73 above. On the question of slavery and primitive Christianity cf. Karl Heinrich Rengstorf, *TDNT* 2, 261–80, especially 270–73; Heinz Dietrich Wendland, "Sklaverei und Christentum," *RGG*³ 6, col. 101–04; H. Gülzow, *Kirche und Sklaverei in den ersten zwei Jahrhunderten*, Unpub. Diss. (Kiel: 1966 [with extensive bibliography]).

84 Manuscripts 𝔎 al vg also place "in the Lord" (ἐν κυρίῳ) at the end of the verse.

85 Cf. Preiss, *Life in Christ*, 32–42.

Conclusion and Greetings

21 **Confident of your obedience, I am writing to you; I know that you will do more than I say. 22/ At the same time, prepare a guest room for me, for I hope that, thanks to your prayers, I will be restored to you. 23/ Epaphras, my fellow prisoner in Christ, Jesus, 24/ Mark, Aristarchus, Demas, and Luke, my fellow workers, greet you. 25/ May the grace of the Lord Jesus Christ be with your spirit.**

With a few sentences Paul brings his letter to a conclusion. After he has stated his confidence that Philemon will certainly do what is right (v 21), he announces that he is planning to visit him (v 22). A short list of greetings (v 23f) and the wish for grace (v 25) end the letter.

■ **21** Paul has made a request of Philemon and has deliberately foregone giving a command on the basis of the authority of his office. The words of the Apostle, however, are not without binding force; they bind the recipient of the letter to the commandment of love. Therefore, Paul can be absolutely confident that his request will be fulfilled. It is this assured confidence that Paul expresses once again at the end of the letter. He has been writing this letter, confident of Philemon's obedience. Since this confidence is grounded in their common faith,[1] "obedience" (ὑπακοή) is the only appropriate response that the addressee can give to the word of the Apostle.[2] Therefore, it is not left to his discretion whether he is willing to act out of love or not.[3] Rather, he is obligated to obey the apostolic word.[4] Paul, however, is convinced that he will do more than what[5] he is told. Of course, here too the Apostle refrains from indicating what this "more" consists in.[6] Thus, not a single word is devoted to the question whether the slave should be given his freedom.[7] How Philemon will concretely express "love" (ἀγάπη) to his returning brother, is his responsibility.

■ **22** Paul at the same time[8] adds that Philemon should prepare quarters for him so that he can visit him soon. By announcing his visit, the Apostle lends a certain emphasis to his intercession for Onesimus. For he will come

1 Cf. Bultmann, *Theology*, p. 323 (vol. 1, sec. 35): "The trust which he places in a congregation (Gal. 5:10; II Cor. 1:15: 2:3; cf. 8:22) or a friend (Phlm. 21) is probably also to be understood as flowing out of his 'faith,' especially since he characterizes it as a confidence 'in the Lord' (Gal. 5:10 . . .)."

2 On ὑπακοή as obedience to the Apostle's word, cf. 2 Cor 7:15; 10:5f; further Phil 2:12. Consult Bultmann, *Theology*, 314f (vol. 1, sec. 35). On the obedience of faith cf. Rom 1:5; 5:19; 6:16; 16:19, 26; cf. Conzelmann, *Outline*, 172.

3 Dibelius–Greeven, *ad loc.* translate ὑπακοή by "readiness, willingness," instead of "obedience." Wickert, "Philemonbrief," 233, correctly argues against this translation.

4 On the concepts employed in Phlm 20f compare 2 Cor 7:13–15: "His [*scil.* Titus'] mind has been set at rest by you all . . . and his heart goes out all the more to you, as he remembers the obedience of you all, and the fear and trembling with which you received him" (ἀναπέπαυται τὸ πνεῦμα αὐτοῦ (*scil.* Τίτου) ἀπὸ πάντων ὑμῶν . . . καὶ τὰ σπλάγχνα αὐτοῦ περισσοτέρως εἰς ὑμᾶς ἐστιν ἀναμιμνῃσκομένου τὴν πάντων ὑμῶν ὑπακοήν, ὡς μετὰ φόβου καὶ τρόμου ἐδέξασθε αὐτόν). Also cf. above on v 7.

5 Instead of the Greek neuter plural relative ἅ (what) manuscripts ℜ D pm latt sy^p read the neuter singular relative ὅ (what).

6 Harrison, "Onesimus," 276–80, taking up ideas from Knox's *Philemon*, holds that Paul had expected Philemon to free Onesimus and to send him back to him. Philemon then did as Paul expected him to do. The text, however, says nothing about this expectation!

7 Dibelius–Greeven, *ad loc.*, remark: "The legal side of the matter is not in view at all." Cf. Heinrich Greeven, *Das Hauptproblem der Sozialethik in der neueren Stoa und im Urchristentum*. NF 3, 4 (Gütersloh: 1935), 52–55.

8 On the use of the adverb "at the same time" (ἅμα) for "denoting the coincidence of two actions in time" (Bauer, *s.v.*), cf. Blass–Debrunner, par. 425, 2.

9 On "I will be restored" (χαρισθήσομαι) cf. Test. Joseph 1:6: "I was in prison, and the Savior restored me; in bonds, and He released me" (ἐν φυλακῇ ἤμην, καὶ ὁ σωτὴρ ἐχαρίτωσέ με, ἐν δεσμοῖς, καὶ ἔλυσέ με) [Trans.].

and see for himself how things have gone. Paul is quite confident that he will soon be freed from prison. When and how this will occur, depends solely on God's decision. God's decision will restore him to the community.[9] Therefore, the intercession of the community, which entreats God for the imprisoned Apostle,[10] takes on great significance. For the cry of the community presses on God and can bring it about that the prison shackles be loosed and the Apostle regain his freedom. That is the object of his hope, not because he wants this for himself, but for the sake of the communities with which he wants to stay.[11]

■ **23** The Apostle tries to strengthen his bond with Philemon by the greetings[12] which he has to extend. The series of names, which reoccur without exception in Col,[13] begins with the name of Epaphras who is called "my fellow prisoner[14] in Christ" (*συναιχμάλωτός μου ἐν Χριστῷ*). Whereas in Col he was described as the founder of the community in Colossae (Col 1:7f; 4:12f), here it is said of him that he shares the Apostle's imprisonment.[15] It is highly probable to assume that, after Epaphras, is to be read the name of the same Jesus who is also mentioned in Col 4:11.[16]

■ **24** Mark,[17] Aristarchus,[18] Demas,[19] and Luke[20] are introduced as fellow workers of Paul (cf. Col 4:14). In contradistinction to the more detailed list of greetings in Col, no further information is given about the persons mentioned. The only fact mentioned is that they are at the Apostle's side as fellow workers. By greeting Philemon the "fellow worker" (*συνεργός*) [v 1], the "fellow workers" (*συνεργοί*) of Paul emphasize the mutual interest that binds them together as helpers in the same work.

■ **25** The wish for grace, which the Apostle extended to Philemon and his "house community" at the beginning of the letter, is once more given at the end.[21] Here it is

10 On the intercession of the community for the Apostle, cf. 1 Thess 5:25; 2 Cor 1:11; Rom 15:30; Phil 1:19; 2 Thess 3:1.

11 Cf. the use of the plural form of "you" in this verse: ὑμῶν—ὑμῖν!

12 Because of the fact that more than one name follows after the verb in the Greek, the Byzantine text has the plural form ἀσπάζονται (greet) instead of ἀσπάζεται (greets).

13 On the comparison of the list of greetings in Phlm and Col, cf. pp. 175–77 above.

14 On the concept "fellow prisoner" (συναιχμάλωτος), cf. above on Col 4:10.

15 On the other hand, Col 4:10 names Aristarchus as the "fellow prisoner" (συναιχμάλωτος) of Paul. The word "fellow prisoner" can also be taken in a figurative sense: one who, like Paul, is a prisoner of Christ (cf. p. 172, n. 20 above). Since, however, Paul repeatedly refers in Phlm to his "chains" (δεσμοί vss 1, 9f, 13), it is more probable to understand "fellow prisoner" in its non–figurative meaning, as a description of the companion who is staying with the imprisoned Apostle.

16 If one reads "in Christ Jesus" instead of ". . . in Christ, Jesus," this would be the only place in Phlm where Paul would be using the phrase "in Christ Jesus" (ἐν Χριστῷ Ἰησοῦ). He employs either "in Christ" (ἐν Χριστῷ) [vss 8, 20] or "in the Lord" (ἐν κυρίῳ) [vss 16, 20]. Cf. Ernst Amling, "Eine Konjektur im Philemonbrief," *ZNW* 10 (1909): 261f. It is likely that the last letter of the name Ἰησοῦς (Jesus) was omitted due to an oversight. Cf. Zahn, *Introduction*, p. 451 and see above on Col 4:11. In any case, the name Jesus was surely not yet considered a "sacred name" (nomen sacrum) at the time when Phlm was written and avoided for that reason. Cf. Erich Dinkler, *Signum Crucis: Aufsätze zum Neuen Testament und zur Christlichen Archäologie* (Tübingen, 1967), 30 n. 15.

17 Cf. above on Col 4:10.

18 Cf. above on Col 4:10.

19 Cf. above on Col 4:14.

20 Cf. above on Col 4:14.

21 Manuscripts A C 𝔎 D pl lat sy^p add ἡμῶν (our) to κυρίου (of the Lord). Manuscripts ℵ C 𝔎 pl lat sy place a concluding "Amen" (ἀμήν) at the end. Subscriptions, which were added later, give additional information. Some of this information was inferred from the letter (e.g., relative to the recipient of the letter and his slave Onesimus). Some was taken from tradition, e.g., the fact mentioned in manuscripts L P al that Phlm "was written from Rome" (ἐγράφη ἀπὸ Ῥώμης). According to minuscules 42 (390) Onesimus would have died as a martyr in Rome at a later date.

also extended to the entire community, to all those who along with Philemon heard the message and request of the Apostle. Instead of "with you" (μεθ' ὑμῶν) the fuller expression "with your spirit" (μετὰ τοῦ πνεύματος ὑμῶν) is used here as in Gal 6:18 and Phil 4:23.[22] The community's life stems from God's manifestation of grace. And the community will continue to exist only if the "grace of the Lord Jesus Christ" (χάρις τοῦ κυρίου Ἰησοῦ Χριστοῦ) remains with it.

22 "Spirit" (πνεῦμα) is thereby used in an anthropological sense. Therefore, no difference in meaning exists between the phrase used here and the shorter phrase "with you" (μεθ' ὑμῶν). For "in concluding salutations (Gl. 6:18; Phil. 4:23; Phlm. 25) 'your spirit' (πνεῦμα ὑμῶν) means exactly the same as 'you' (ὑμεῖς) [1 Th. 5:28]" (Eduard Schweizer, *TDNT* 6, 435). Cf. also Bultmann, *Theology*, 206 (vol. 1, sec. 18); Conzelmann, *Outline*, 180.

Bibliography
Indices

1. Commentaries
a/ Colossians[1]

The Ancient Church:

Ambrosiaster (Ps. Ambrose)
CSEL 81, 3, ed. Heinrich Josef Vogels, pp. 165–207 (Phlm: pp. 335–42).

John Chrysostom
MPG 62, col. 299–392 (Phlm: col. 701–20).

Theodore of Mopsuestia
Theodori episcopi Mopsuesteni in epistolas B. Pauli commentarii. The Latin Version with the Greek Fragments. With an Introduction, Notes and Indices, by H. B. Swete. Vol. 1 (Cambridge: University Press, 1880), pp. 253–312 (Phlm: Vol. 2, Cambridge, 1882, pp. 258–85).

Severian of Gabala
Pauluskommentare aus der griechischen Kirche, aus Katenenhandschriften gesammelt und herausgegeben von Karl Staab, NTAbh 15 (Münster i.W.: 1933), 314–28 (Phlm: p. 345).

Theodoret
MPG 82, col. 591–628 (Phlm: col. 871–78).

Oecumenius
MPG 119, col. 9–56 (Phlm: col. 261–73) and in Staab, *Pauluskommentare,* 453–55 (Phlm: p. 462).

John the Deacon (Ps. Jerome)
Texts and Studies, ed. J. Armitage Robinson, vol. 9, 2, ed. by Alexander Souter (Cambridge: University Press, 1926), 451–73 (Phlm: pp. 536–39). Also, *MPL* 30, col. 891–902 (Phlm: col. 945–46) and *Clavis Patrum Latinorum,* ed. E. Dekkers (Steenbrugge: [2]1961), no. 952 (p. 209).

The Middle Ages:

Cassiodorus (Ps. Primasius)
MPL 68, col. 651–60, and 70, col. 1351–2 (Phlm: 68, col. 683–86, and 70, 1355–58).

John of Damascus
MPG 95, col. 883–904 (Phlm: col. 1029–34).

Sedulius Scotus
MPL 103, col. 223–30 (Phlm: col. 249–52).

Photius of Constantinople
Staab, *Pauluskommentare,* 631–33 (Phlm: p. 637).

Haimo of Auxerre
MPL 117, col. 753–66 (Phlm: col. 813–20).

Hrabanus Maurus
MPL 112, col. 507–40 (Phlm: col. 693–712).

Florus the Deacon
MPL 119, col. 389–94 (Phlm: col. 411–12).

Atto of Vercelli
MPL 134, col. 607–44 (Phlm: col. 719–26).

Lanfranc
MPL 150, col. 319–32 (Phlm: col. 371–76).

Bruno the Carthusian
MPL 153, col. 373–98 (Phlm: col. 483–88).

Theophylact
MPG 124, col. 1205–78.

Hervaeus
MPL 181, col. 1313–56 (Phlm: col. 1505–20).

Peter Lombard
MPL 192, col. 393–98.

Euthymius Zigabenus
Commentarius in XIV epistolas Sancti Pauli et VII catholicas, ed. Nicephorus Calogeras, vol. 2 (Athens: 1887), 113–56 (Phlm: pp. 333–40).

Thomas Aquinas
Opera Omnia, vol. 13 (Parma: 1862), 530–55 (Phlm: pp. 661–65).

Dionysius the Carthusian
In omnes Beati Pauli epistolas commentaria, (Cologne: 1533), sheets 99–104 (Phlm: sheet 122); also, *Opera Omnia,* vol. 13 (Montreuil: 1901), 351–72 (Phlm: pp. 459–65.)

The 16th to 18th Centuries:

Erasmus, Desiderius
Opera Omnia, vol. 4 (Leiden: 1705, reprinted Hildesheim: 1962), 881–98 (Phlm: pp. 977–80).

Zwingli, Huldrich
Huldrici Zwinglii Opera, completa editio prima, ed. Melchior Schuler and Jo. Schulthess, vol. 6, 2 (Zürich: 1838), 220–28.

1 For the commentaries which appeared before 1800, page numbers are listed where relevant and, in addition, there are numbers in parentheses in case there was commentary on the Letter to Philemon. For the commentaries since 1800, these numbers are no longer necessary since it is clear from the title whether Philemon receives commentary. Parentheses are used only when the commentary on Philemon appears in another volume of the same work.

An asterisk (*) adjacent to an entry indicates that that work has appeared since 1968.

Calvin, John
Johannis Calvini in omnes Novi Testamenti epistolas commentarii, ed. A. Tholuck, vol. 2 (Halle: ²1834), 122–65 (Phlm: pp. 366–72); or *CR* 80, col. 77–132 (Phlm: col. 441–50).

Melanchthon, Philip
CR 15, col. 1223–82.

Bugenhagen, Johann
Annotationes Jo. Bugenhagii Pomerani in epistolas Pauli ad Galatas, Ephesios, Philippenses, Colossenses, Thessalonicenses I, II, Timotheum I, II, Titum, Philemonem, Hebraeos (Strassbourg: ²1534), 53–67 (Phlm: pp. 135–38).

Sasbout, Adam
In Omnes Fere, D. Pauli, et quorundam aliorum Apostolorum, epistolas explicatio (Louvain: 1556), pp. 304–32.

Musculus, Wolfgang
In Divi Pauli epistolas ad Philippenses, Colossenses, Thessalonicenses ambas, et primam ad Timotheum (Basel: 1565), 122–216.

Major Georg
Enarratio in duas epistolas Pauli, ad Philippenses et Colossenses (Wittenberg: 1561), 92–184.

Beza, Theodore
Jesu Christi domini nostri Novum Testamentum eiusdem Th. Bezae annotationes (Geneva: ⁴1598), 286–301 (Phlm: pp. 356–58).

Bullinger, Heinrich
Commentarii in omnes Pauli Apostoli epistolas, atque etiam in epistolam ad Hebraeos (Zürich: 1603), 363–81 (Phlm: pp. 487–90).

Hunnius, Aegidius
Opera, vol. 4 (Frankfurt: 1606), 641–92 (Phlm: pp. 858–66).

Balduin, Friedrich
Didactica apostolica, hoc est, S. Apostoli Pauli epistola ad Colossenses (Wittenberg: 1624).

Novarini, Luigi
Paulus expensus, notis, monitisque sacris (Lyons: 1645), 312–23 (Phlm: pp. 385–87).

Grotius, Hugo
Annotationes in Novum Testamentum, vol. 2 (Paris: 1646), 623–48 (Phlm: pp. 779–86).

Davenant, John
Expositio epistolae D. Pauli ad Colossenses (Geneva: 1655).

Crell, Johann
Opera Omnia Exegetica, vol. 1 (Amsterdam: 1656), 539–43 (Phlm: vol. 2, pp. 55–59).

Estius, Guilelmus
In omnes Beati Pauli et aliorum Apostolorum epistolas commentaria, vol. 1 (Paris: 1661), 680–712 (Phlm: pp. 880–86); or, *In Omnes Pauli Epistolas, item in Catholicas Commentarii*, ed. Francisus Sausen, vol. 4 (Paris and Louvain: 1843), 358–438 (Phlm: vol. 5 [Paris and London]), pp. 405–20).

Gomarus, Franciscus
Opera Theologica Omnia (Amsterdam: 1664), 547–76 (Phlm: pp. 594–99).

Alting, Jakob
Opera Omnia Theologica, vol. 4 (Amsterdam: 1686), 389–400.

Suicer, Johannes Hendricus
In epistolam S. Pauli ad Colossenses commentarius critico-exegeticus, theologiae Christianae compendium (Zürich: 1699).

Fell, John, ed.
A Paraphrase and Annotations upon all St. Paul's Epistles (London: ³1702), 259–82 (Phlm: pp. 361–63).

Alexander, Natalus
Commentarius litteralis et moralis in omnes epistolas Sancti Pauli Apostoli et in VII epistolas catholicas, vol. 1 (Rouen: 1710), 426–48 (Phlm: vol. 2, pp. 63–66).

Calov, Abraham
Biblia Novi Testamenti Illustrata, vol. 2 (Dresden and Leipzig: 1719), 796–850 (Phlm: pp. 1083–94).

Calmet, Augustin
Commentaire littéral sur tous les livres de l'ancien et du nouveau Testament, vol. 8 (Paris: 1726), 483–506 (Phlm: pp. 621–26).

Wetstenius, Johannes Jacobus
Novum Testamentum Graecum, vol. 2 (Amsterdam: 1752), 281–96 (Phlm: pp. 379–82).

Bengel, Johann Albrecht
Gnomon Novi Testamenti (³1773, reprinted Berlin: 1860), 508–17 (Phlm: pp. 556–7).

The 19th Century:

(Koppe–) Heinrichs, Johann Heinrich
Novum Testamentum Graece perpetua annotatione illustratum editionis Koppianae, vol. 2, partic. 2 continuit J. H. Heinrichs (Göttingen: 1803).

Flatt, Johann Friedrich von
Vorlesungen über die Briefe Pauli an die Philipper, Kolosser, Thessalonicher und an Philemon, ed. C. F. Kling (Tübingen: 1829).

Bähr, Karl Christian Wilhelm Felix
Commentar uber den Brief Pauli an die Kolosser (Basel: 1833).

Böhmer, Wilhelm
Theologische Auslegung des Sendschreibens an die Kolosser (Breslau: 1835).

Steiger, Wilhelm
Der Brief Pauli an die Kolosser (Erlangen: 1835).

Baumgarten–Crucius, L.F.O.
Commentar über den Brief Pauli an die Epheser und Kolosser, ed. E. J. Kimmel and J. C. Schauer, in Exegetische Schriften zum Neuen Testament, vol. 3, 1 (Jena: 1847).

de Wette, W. M. L.
Kurze Erklärung der Briefe an die Colosser, an Philemon, an die Epheser und Philipper, in Kurzgefasstes exegetisches Handbuch zum Neuen Testament 2, 4 (Leipzig: 1843).

Huther, Johann Eduard
Commentar über den Brief Pauli an die Colosser (Hamburg: 1841).

Cramer, J. A.
Catenae in Novum Testamentum, vol. 6 (Oxford: 1842), (Phlm: vol. 7 [Oxford: 1843]).

Ewald, Heinrich
Die Sendschreiben des Apostels Paulus (Göttingen: 1857).

Dalmer, Karl Eduard Friedrich
Auslegung des Briefes St. Pauli an die Colosser (Gotha: 1858).

Schenkel, Daniel
Die Briefe an die Epheser, Philipper, Kolosser, in Theologisch–homiletisches Bibelwerk, NT 9; ed. J. P. Lange (Bielefeld: 1862).

Bleek, Friedrich
Dr. Friedrich Bleek's Vorlesungen über die Briefe an die Kolosser, den Philemon und an die Epheser, ed. F. Nitsch (Berlin: 1865).

Braune, Karl
Die Briefe St. Pauli an die Epheser, Kolosser, Philipper, in Theologisch–homiletisches Bibelwerk, NT 9; ed. J. P. Lange (Bielefeld and Leipzig: 1867).

Hofmann, Johann Christian Konrad von
Die Briefe Pauli an die Kolosser und an Philemon, in Die heilige Schrift neuen Testaments 4, 2 (Nördlingen: 1870).

Meyer, Hein. Aug. Wilh.
Kritisch exegetisches Handbuch über die Briefe Pauli an die Philipper, Kolosser und an Philemon. KEK 9 (Göttingen: [4]1874).

Lightfoot, J. B.
St. Paul's Epistles to the Colossians and to Philemon (London and New York: Macmillan, [3]1879; [11]1892).

Klöpper, Albert
Der Brief an die Colosser, Kritisch untersucht und in seinem Verhältnisse zum paulinischen Lehrbegriff exegetisch und biblisch–theologisch erörtert (Berlin: 1882).

Franke, A. H.
Kritisch exegetisches Handbuch über die Briefe Pauli an die Philipper, Kolosser und Philemon. KEK9 (Göttingen: [5]1886).

Schnedermann, G.
Die Gefangenschaftsbriefe des Apostels Paulus, in Kurzgefasster Kommentar zu den heiligen Schriften Alten und Neuen Testaments sowie zu den Apokryphen B, 4 (Nördlingen: 1888).

Oltramare, Hugues
Commentaire sur les épîtres de S. Paul aux Colossiens, aux Éphésiens et à Philémon, vol. 1 (Paris: 1891): (Phlm: vol. 2, [Paris: 1892]).

Soden, H. von
Die Briefe an die Kolosser, Epheser, Philemon; die Pastoralbriefe, in Hand–Commentar zum Neuen Testament 3, 1 (Freiburg i.B. and Leipzig: [2]1893).

Abbott, T. K.
The Epistles to the Ephesians and to the Colossians. ICC (Edinburgh: T. & T. Clark, 1897; [8]1953).

The 20th Century:

Haupt, Erich
Die Gefangenschaftsbriefe. KEK 8–9 (Göttingen: [8]1902).

Peake, A. S.
The Epistle of Paul to the Colossians, in The Expositor's Greek Testament, vol. 3 (New York: Dodd, Mead & Co., 1903).

Williams, A. Lukyn
The Epistles of Paul the Apostle to the Colossians and to Philemon, in The Cambridge Greek Testament for Schools and Colleges (Cambridge: University Press, 1907).

Kühl, Ernst
Erläuterung der paulinischen Briefe unter Beibehaltung der Briefformen, vol. 2 (Die jüngeren paulinischen Briefe) (Gr. Lichterfelde–Berlin: 1909).

Schlatter, A.
Die Briefe des Paulus, in Erläuterungen zum Neuen Testament, vol. 2 (Stuttgart: 1909; [4]1928).

Ewald, Paul
Die Briefe des Paulus an die Epheser, Kolosser und Philemon in Kommentar zum Neuen Testament 10 (Leipzig: [2]1910).

Knabenbauer, Joseph
Commentarius in S. Pauli epistolas, Epistolae ad Ephesios, ad Philippenses et ad Colossenses in Cursus Scripturae Sacrae, NT 2, 4 (Paris: 1912).

Westcott, Frederick Brooke
A Letter to Asia: Being a Paraphrase and Brief Exposition of the Epistle of Paul the Apostle to the Believers at Colossae (London: Macmillan, 1914).

Lueken, Wilhelm
Die Briefe an Philemon, an die Kolosser und an die Epheser in Die Schriften des Neuen Testaments 2 (Göttingen: [3]1917).

Toussaint, C.
L'épître de saint Paul aux Colossiens (Paris: 1921).

van Leeuwen, J. A. C.
Paulus zendbrieven aan Efeze, Colosse, Filemon en Thessalonika in Kommentar op het Niewe Testament 10 (Amsterdam: 1926).

Moule, Handley C. G.
Colossian Stubies, Lessons in Faith and Holiness from St. Paul's Epıstles to the Colossians and Philemon (London: Pickering & Inglis, [2]1926).

Billerbeck, Paul
Die Briefe des Neuen Testaments und die Offenbarung Johannis erläutert aus Talmud und Midrasch, in Kommentar zum Neuen Testament aus Talmud und Midrasch 3 (Munich: 1926; [3]1961).

Hastings, E.
The Epistle to the Philippians and the Epistle to the Colossians (Edinburgh: 1930).

Scott, E. F.
The Epistles of Paul to the Colossians, to Philemon and to the Ephesians in The Moffatt New Testament Commentary (London: Hodder & Stoughton, 1930; [9]1958).

Meinertz, Max: Max Meinertz and Fritz Tillmann
Die Gefangenschaftsbriefe des heiligen Paulus in Die Heilige Schrift des Neuen Testaments 7 (Bonn: [4]1931).

Radford, Lewis B.
The Epistle to the Colossians and the Epistle to Philemon in The Westminster Commentary (London: Methuen, 1931; [2]1946).

le Seur, Paul
Der Brief an die Epheser, Kolosser und an Philemon übersetzt und ausgelegt in Bibelhilfe für die Gemeinde: Neues Testament 10 (Leipzig: 1936).

Bieder, Werner
Der Kolosserbrief, in Prophezei (Zürich: 1943).

Huby, Joseph
Saint Paul, Les Épîtres de la Captivité in Verbum Salutis 8 (Paris: [2]1947).

Gray, Crete
Epistles of Paul to the Colossians and Philemon (London: Lutterworth, 1948).

Benoit, P.
Les Épîtres de Saint Paul aux Philippiens, aux Colossiens, à Philémon, aux Éphésiens in La Sainte Bible, (Paris: 1949).

Masson, Charles
L'épître de Saint Paul aux Colossiens, in Commentaire du Nouveau Testament 10 (Neuchâtel and Paris: 1950).

Synge, F. C.
Philippians and Colossians, Introduction and Commentary. Torch Bible Commentaries (London: SCM Press, 1951; [2]1958).

Dibelius, Martin and Greeven, Heinrich
An die Kolosser, Epheser, an Philemon. HNT 12 (Tübingen: [3]1953).

Lohmeyer, Ernst
Die Briefe an die Philipper, an die Kolosser und an Philemon. KEK 9 (Göttingen: [8]1930; [9]1953, reprinted as [13]1964). Ninth Edition, 1953: Nach dem Handexemplar des Verfassers durchgesehene Ausgabe, for the Thirteenth Edition, 1964: Ergänzungsheft von W. Schmauch.

Beare, Francis W.
The Epistle to the Colossians. IB 11 (New York and Nashville: Abingdon Press, 1955).

Vine, W. E.
Epistles to the Philippians and Colossians (London: Oliphants, 1956).

Bruce, F. F.: E. K. Simpson and F. F. Bruce
Commentary on the Epistles to the Ephesians and Colossians, in The New London Commentary on the New Testament (London and Edinburgh: Marshall, Morgan & Scott, 1957).

Moule, C. F. D.
The Epistles of Paul the Apostle to the Colossians and to Philemon in The Cambridge Greek Testament Commentary (Cambridge: University Press, 1957).

Staab, Karl
Die Gefangenschaftsbriefe in Regensburger Neues Testament 7 (Regensburg: [3]1959).

Carson, Herbert M.
The Epistles of Paul to the Colossians and Philemon, An Introduction and Commentary in The Tyndale New Testament Commentaries (London: Tyndale, 1960; [2]1963).

Ridderbos, H.: F. W. Grosheide and H. Ridderbos
Efeziërs—Kolossenzen in Commentaar op het Niewe Testament (Kampen: 1960).

Johnson, S. Lewis, Jr.
"Studies in the Epistle to the Colossians," *Bibliotheca Sacra* 118 (1961): 239–50, 334–46; 119 (1962): 12–19, 139–49, 227–37, 302–11; 120 (1963): 13–23, 109–16, 205–213; 121 (1964): 22–33, 107–16, 311–20.

Conzelmann, Hans: Hermann W. Beyer, Paul Althaus, Hans Conzelmann, Gerhard Friedrich, Albrecht Oepke
Die kleineren Briefe des Apostels Paulus. NTD 8 (Göttingen: [10]1965).

Mussner, Franz
Der Brief an die Kolosser. Geistliche Schriftlesung 12, 1 (Düsseldorf: 1965).

Thompson, G. H. P.
The Letters of Paul to the Ephesians, to the Colossians and to Philemon in The Cambridge Bible Commentary on the New English Bible (Cambridge: University Press, 1967).

Johnston, George
Ephesians, Philippians, Colossians and Philemon in The Century Bible, New Edition (London: Nelson, 1967).

* Hugedé, Norbert
Commentaire de l'Épître aux Colossiens (Geneva: Labor et Fides, 1968).

b/ Philemon

The following commentaries must be listed in addition to the authors who also commented on Philemon and were thus listed in a) for Colossians.[1]

The 19th Century:

Hagenbach, C.R.
Pauli epistolae ad Philemonem interpretatio (Basel: 1829).

Rothe, M.
Pauli ad Philemonem epistolae interpretatio historico-exegetica (Bremen: 1844).

1 For the history of exegesis, cf. also the survey given in *RGG*[3] 5, col. 332.

van Oosterzee, J. J.
Die Pastoralbriefe und der Brief an Philemon, Theologisch–homiletisches Bibelwerk, NT 11 (Bielefeld: 1861).

Vincent, Marvin R.
The Epistles to the Philippians and to Philemon. ICC (Edinburgh: T. & T. Clark, 1897; [5]1955).

The 20th Century:

Schumann, Alexis
Paulus an Philemon, Betrachtungen zur Einführung in ein tieferes Verständnis des kleinsten Paulusbriefes und in die soziale Gedankenwelt des Neuen Testamentes (Leipzig: 1908).

Knabenbauer, Joseph
Commentarius in S. Pauli epistolas, Epistolae ad Thessalonicenses, ad Timotheum, ad Titum et ad Philemonem. Cursus Scripturae Sacrae, NT 2, 5 (Paris: 1913).

Eisentraut, Engelhard
Des heiligen Apostels Paulus Brief an Philemon, Eingehender Kommentar und zugleich Einführung in die Paulusbriefe (Würzburg: 1928).

Bieder, Werner
Der Philemonbrief, in Prophezei (Zürich: 1944).

Knox, John
The Epistle to Philemon, IB 11 (New York and Nashville: Abingdon Press, 1955).

Müller, Jac. J.
The Epistles of Paul to the Philippians and to Philemon in NIC and The New London Commentary (Grand Rapids, Mich.: Wm. B. Eerdmans, 1955).

Leaney, A. R. C.
The Epistles to Timothy, Titus and Philemon, Torch Bible Commentaries (London: SCM Press, 1960).

Friedrich, Gerhard: Hermann W. Beyer, Paul Althaus, Hans Conzelmann, Gerhard Friedrich, Albrecht Oepke
Die kleineren Briefe des Apostels Paulus. NTD 8 (Göttingen: [10]1965).

Stöger, Alois
Der Brief an Philemon, in Geistliche Schriftlesung 12, 2 (Düsseldorf: 1965).

2. Studies
a/ Colossians

Aalen, S.
"Begrepet plaeroma i Kolosser– og Efeserbrevet," *Tidsskrift for Teologi og Kirke* 23 (1952): 49–67.

* Allmen, Daniel von
"Réconciliation du monde et christologie Cosmique, de II Cor. 5:14–21 à Col. 1:15–23," RHPR 48 (1968): 32–45.

Anderson, Charles P.
"Who Wrote 'The Epistle from Laodicea'?," *JBL* 85 (1966): 436–440.

Anwander, Anton
"Zu Kol 2, 9," *BZ* 9 (1965): 278–280.

Argyle, A. W.
"πρωτότοκος πάσης κτίσεως (Colossians i.15)," *ExpT* 66 (1954–55): 61f.

Idem
"Colossians i.15," *ExpT* 66 (1954–55): 318f.

Baggott, Louis John
A New Approach to Colossians (London: Mowbray, 1961).

Bammel, Ernst
"Versuch zu Col 1:15–20," *ZNW* 52 (1961): 88–95.

* Barbour, R. S.
"Salvation and Cosmology: The Setting of the Epistle to the Colossians," *Scottish Journal of Theology* 20 (1967): 257–271.

Barclay, William
The All Sufficient Christ: Studies in Paul's Letter to the Colossians (Philadelphia: Westminster, 1963).

Benoit, Pierre
"Corps, tête et plérôme dans les épîtres de la captivité," *RB* 63 (1956): 5–44. Reprinted in *Exégèse et théologie* 2 (Paris: 1961), 107–53.

Idem
"Rapports littéraires entre les épîtres aux Colossiens et aux Éphésiens" in *Neutestamentliche Aufsätze: Festschrift für Prof. Josef Schmid zum 70 Geburtstag*, edited by Joseph Blinzler *et al.*, (Regensburg: 1963), 11–22. Reprinted in *Exégèse et théologie* 3 (Paris: 1968), 318–34.

Idem
"Paul, 1. Colossiens (Épître aux)," *Dictionnaire de la Bible: Supplément* 7 (Paris: 1966), col. 157–70.

Best, Ernest
One Body in Christ: A Study in the Relationship of the Church to Christ in the Epistles of the Apostle Paul (London: S.P.C.K., 1955).

Idem
A Historical Study of the Exegesis of Col 2, 14. Unpub. Diss., Gregorian University (Rome: 1956).

Bieder, Werner
Die kolossische Irrlehre und die Kirche von heute. Theologische Studien 33 (Zürich: 1952).

Blanchette, Oliva A.
"Does the *Cheirographon* of Col 2, 14 Represent Christ himself?," *CBQ* 23 (1961): 306–12.

Bornkamm, Günther
"Die Häresie des Kolosserbriefes," *ThLZ* 73 (1948): 11–20. Reprinted in *Aufsätze* 1, pp. 139–56.

Idem
"Die Hoffnung im Kolosserbrief—Zugleich ein Beitrag zur Frage der Echtheit des Briefe" in *Studien zum Neuen Testament und zur Patristik, Festschrift für Erich Klostermann.* TU 77 (Berlin, 1961:), 56–64.

Brinkmann, B. R.
The Prototokos Title and the Beginnings of its Exegesis. Unpub. Diss., Gregorian University (Rome: 1954).

Buckley, T. W.
The Phrase 'Firstborn of Every Creature' (Colossians I, 15) in the Light of its Hellenistic and Jewish Background. Unpub. Diss., Angelicum University (Rome: 1962).

Burney, C. F.
"Christ as the APXH of Creation. (Prov. viii 22, Col. i 15–18, Rev. iii 14," *JTS* 27 (1926): 160–77.

Camelot, P.-Th.
"Ressuscités avec le Christ," *La Vie Spirituelle* 84 (1951): 353–63.

Carrez, Maurice
"Souffrance et gloire dans les épîtres pauliniennes (Contribution à l'exégèse de Col. 1, 24–27)," *RHPR* 31 (1951): 343–53.

Casel, Odo
"Zur Kultsprache des heiligen Paulus," *Archiv für Liturgiewissenschaft* 1 (1950). 1–64.

Cerfaux, Lucien
"L'influence des 'Mystères' sur les épîtres de S. Paul aux Colossiens et aux Éphésiens." in *Sacra Pagina* II, Bibliotheca Ephemeridum Theologicorum Lovaniensum 13 (Paris and Gembloux: 1959), 373–79.

Cerny, Edward A.
Firstborn of Every Creature (Col. I:15), Diss., St. Mary's University (Baltimore: 1938)

Coutts, John
"The Relationship of Ephesians and Colossians," *NTS* 4 (1957–58): 201–07.

Craddock, Fred B.
" 'All Things in Him': A critical note on Col. I. 15–20," *NTS* 12 (1965–66): 78–80.

Dacquino, Petrus
"Epistola ad Colossenses in luce finis ab Apostolo intenti," *VD* 38 (1960): 16–27.

Deichgräber, Reinhard
Gotteshymnus und Christushymnus in der frühen Christenheit: Untersuchungen zu Form, Sprache und Stil der frühchristlichen Hymnen. Studien zur Umwelt des Neuen Testaments 5 (Göttingen: 1967).

Dibelius, Martin
Die Geisterwelt im Glauben des Paulus (Göttingen: 1909).

Idem
Die Isisweihe bei Apulejus und verwandte Initiations-

Riten. SAH (Heidelberg: 1917). Reprinted in *Aufsätze* 2, pp. 30–79.

Dupont, Jacques
Gnosis: La connaissance religieuse dans les épîtres de Saint Paul. UCL II, 40 (Louvain and Paris: [2]1960).

Eckart, Karl-Gottfried
"Exegetische Beobachtungen zu Kol 1, 9–20," *Theologia Viatorum* 7 (1959–60): 87–106.

Idem
"Urchristliche Tauf- und Ordinationsliturgie (Col 1:9–20, Act 26:18)," *Theologia Viatorum* 8 (1961–62): 23–37.

Eitrem, S.
"ΕΜΒΑΤΕΥΩ: Note sur Col. 2, 18," *ST* 2 (1948): 90–94.

Ellingworth, P.
"Colossians i. 15–20 and its Context," *ExpT* 73 (1961–62): 252f.

Feuillet, A.
"La Création de l'Univers 'dans le Christ' d'après l'Épître aux Colossiens (I. 16a)," *NTS* 12 (1965–66): 1–9.

Idem
Le Christ sagesse de Dieu d'après les épîtres Pauliniennes. Études Bibliques (Paris: 1966).

Foerster, Werner
"Die Irrlehrer des Kolosserbriefes" in *Studia Biblica et Semitica, Festschrift für Theodore Christian Vriezen* (Wageningen: 1966), 71–80.

Francis, Fred O.
"Humility and Angelic Worship in Col 2:18," *ST* 16 (1962): 109–34.

* *Idem*
"Visionary Discipline and Scriptural Tradition at Colossae," *Lexington Theological Quarterly* 2 (1967): 71–81.

Fridrichsen, Anton
"ΘΕΛΩΝ Col 2:18," *ZNW* 21 (1922): 135–37.

Idem
"Charité et perfection. Observation sur Col. 3, 14," *Symbolae Osloenses* 19 (1939): 41–45.

Gabathuler, Hans Jakob
Jesus Christus, Haupt der Kirche—Haupt der Welt: Der Christushymnus Colosser 1, 15–20 *in der theologischen Forschung der letzten* 130 *Jahre*. AThANT 45, (Zürich: 1965).

Gewiess, J.
Christus und das Heil nach dem Kolosserbrief. Partially published. Diss. (Breslau: 1932).

Idem
"Die Begriffe πληροῦν und πλήρωμα im Kolosser- und Epheserbrief" in *Vom Wort des Lebens, Festschrift für Max Meinertz*, ed. Nikolaus Adler. NTAbh Suppl. 1 (Münster i.W.: 1951), 128–41.

Idem
"Die apologetische Methode des Apostels Paulus im Kampf gegen die Irrlehre in Kolossä," *Bibel und Leben* 3 (1962): 258–70.

Glasson, T. Francis
"Colossians 1:18, 15 and Sirach 24," *JBL* 86 (1967): 214–16.

Grässer, Erich
"Kol 3, 1–4 als Beispiel einer Interpretation secundum homines recipientes," *ZThK* 64 (1967): 139–68.

Grosheide, F. W.
"Kol. 3:1–4; 1 Petr. 1:3–5; 1 Joh. 3:1–2," *Gereformeerd Theologisch Tijdschrift* 54 (1954): 139–47.

Hall, Bernard G.
"Colossians ii.23," *ExpT* 36 (1924–25): 285.

Hanson, Stig
The Unity of the Church in the New Testament: Colossians and Ephesians. ASNU 14 (Uppsala: 1946).

Hedley, P. L.
"Ad Colossenses 2:20–3:4," *ZNW* 27 (1928): 211–16.

Heikel, Ivar
"Kol 2, 16–18," *Theologische Studien und Kritiken* 107 (1936): 464f.

Henle, Franz Anton
Kolossä und der Brief des hl. Apostels Paulus an die Kolosser: Ein Beitrag zur Einleitung in den Kolosserbrief (München: 1887).

Hermann, Theodor
"Barbar und Skythe: Ein Erklärungsversuch zu Kol 3, 11," *Theologische Blätter* 9 (1930): 106f.

Hockel, Alfred
Christus der Erstgeborene: Zur Geschichte der Exegese von Kol 1, 15 (Düsseldorf: 1965).

Holtzmann, Heinrich Julius
Kritik der Epheser- und Kolosserbriefe: auf Grund einer Analyse ihres Verwandtschaftsverhältnisses (Leipzig: 1872).

Hough, Lynn Harold
"The Message of the Epistles: Colossians," *ExpT* 45 (1933–34): 103–08.

Joüon, P.
"Note sur Colossiens III, 5–11," *RechSR* 26 (1936): 185–89.

Käsemann, Ernst
"Eine urchristliche Taufliturgie" in *Festschrift für Rudolf Bultmann*, ed. E. Wolf (Stuttgart: 1949), 133–48. Reprinted in *Aufsätze* 1, 34–51. ET, "A Primitive Christian Baptismal Liturgy" in *Essays in New Testament Themes* tr. W. S. Montague, SBT 41 (Naperville: Alec R. Allenson, 1964).

Idem
"Kolosserbrief," *RGG*[3] 3 (1959), col. 1727f.

Kehl, Nikolaus
Der Christushymnus im Kolosserbrief: Eine motivgeschichtliche Untersuchung zu Kol 1, 12–20. Stuttgarter Biblische Monographien 1 (Stuttgart: 1967).

* *Idem*
"Erniedrigung und Erhöhung im Qumran und Colossä," *Zeitschrift für Katholische Theologie* 91 (1969): 364–94.

Kittel, Gerhard
"Kol 1, 24," *ZSTh* 18 (1941): 186–91.

Knox, John
"Philemon and the Authenticity of Colossians," *Journal of Religion* 18 (1938): 144–60.

Kremer, Jakob
Was an den Leiden Christi noch mangelt: Eine interpretationsgeschichtliche und exegetische Untersuchung zu Kol. 1, 24b. BBB 12 (Bonn: 1956).

* Lähnemann, Johannes
Der Kolosserbrief, Komposition, Situation und Argumentation. SNT (Gütersloh: 1971).

* Langkammer, Hugolinus
"Die Einwohnung der 'absoluten Seinsfülle' in Christus. Bemerkungen zu Kol 1, 19," *BZ* 12 (1968): 258–263.

Larsson, Edvin
Christus als Vorbild: Eine Untersuchung zu den paulinischen Tauf- und Eikontexten. ASNU 23 (Uppsala: 1962).

Leaney, Robert
"Colossians II.21–23 (The use of πρός)," *ExpT* 64 (1952–53): 92.

LeGrelle, G.
"La plénitude de la parole dans la pauvreté de la chair d'après Col. I, 24," *Nouvelle Revue Théologique* 81 (1959): 232–50.

Lewis, Edwin
"Paul and the Perverters of Christianity: Revelation Through the Epistle to the Colossians," *Interpretation* 2 (1948): 143–57.

Lohse, Eduard
"Christologie und Ethik im Kolosserbrief," in *Apophoreta, Festschrift für Ernst Haenchen*. BZNW 30 (Berlin: 1964), 156–168.

Idem
"Christusherrschaft und Kirche im Kolosserbrief," *NTS* 11 (1964–65): 203–16.

Idem
"Imago Dei bei Paulus" in *Libertas Christiana, Festschrift für Friedrich Johann Delekat*, ed. Walter Matthias. Beiträge zur Evangelischen Theologie 26. (München: 1957). 122–35.

* *Idem*
"Pauline Theology in the Letter to the Colossians," *NTS* 15 (1968–69): 211–220.

Lyonnet, S.
"L'étude du milieu littéraire et l'exégèse du Nouveau Testament: #4 Les adversaires de Paul à Colosses," *Biblica* 37 (1956): 27–38.

Idem
"L'hymne christologique de l'Épître aux Colossiens et la fête juive du Nouvel An (S. Paul, *Col.*, 1, 20 et Philon, *De spec. leg.*, 192)," *RechSR* 48 (1960): 93–100.

Idem
"L'Épître aux Colossiens (Col 2, 18) et les mystères d'Apollon Clarien," *Biblica* 43 (1962): 417–35.

Idem
"St. Paul et le gnosticisme: la lettre aux Colossiens" in *Le Origini dello Gnosticismo*, ed. U. Bianchi. Supplements to *Numen* 12 (Leiden: 1967), 538–51.

Masson, Charles
"L'hymne christologique de l'épître aux Colossiens I, 15–20," *Revue de Théologie et de Philosophie* NS 36 (1948): 138–42.

Maurer, Christian
"Die Begründung der Herrschaft Christi über die Mächte nach Kolosser 1, 15–20," *Wort und Dienst* NF 4 (1955): 79–93.

Mayerhoff, Ernst Theodor
Der Brief an die Colosser, mit vornehmlicher Berück sichtigung der drei Pastoralbriefe kritisch geprüft, ed. J. L. Mayerhoff (Berlin: 1838).

Megas, Georg
"Das χειρόγραφον Adams. Ein Beitrag zu Col 2:13–15," *ZNW* 27 (1928): 305–20.

Merk, Otto
Handeln aus Glauben: Die Motivierungen der paulinischen Ethik. Marburger Theologische Studien 5 (Marburg: 1968).

Meuzelaar, J. J.
Der Leib des Messias: Eine exegetische Studie über den Gedanken vom Leib Christi in den Paulusbriefen. van Gorcum's Theologische Bibliotheek 35 (Assen: 1961).

Michl, Johann
"Die 'Versöhnung' (Kol 1, 20)," *ThQ* 128 (1948): 442–62.

Moir, W. R. G.
"Colossians i.24," *ExpT* 42 (1930–31): 479f.

Münderlein, Gerhard
"Die Erwählung durch das Pleroma: Bemerkungen zu Kol i.19," *NTS* 8 (1961–62): 264–76.

Mussner, Franz
Christus, das All und die Kirche: Studien zur Theologie des Epheserbriefes. Trierer Theologische Studien 5 (Trier: 1955).

Ochel, Werner
Die Annahme einer Bearbeitung des Kolosser–Briefes im Epheser–Brief in einer Analyse des Epheser–Briefes untersucht. Unpub. Diss. (Marburg: 1934).

Oke, C. Clare
"A Hebraistic Construction in Colossians i.19–22," *ExpT* 63 (1951–52): 155f.

Percy, Ernst
Der Leib Christi (σῶμα Χριστοῦ) in den paulinischen Homologumena und Antilegomena. Lunds Universitets Årsskrift, NF Abt. 1, Bd. 38, 1 (Lund and Leipzig: 1942).

Idem
Die Probleme der Kolosser- und Epheserbriefe. Acta reg. Societatis Humaniorum Litterarum Lundensis 39 (Lund: 1946).

Idem
"Zu den Problemen des Kolosser- und Epheserbriefes," *ZNW* 43 (1950–51): 178–94.

Perels, Otto
"Kirche und Welt nach dem Epheser- und Kolosserbrief," *ThLZ* 76 (1951): 391–400.

Piper, Otto A.
"The Saviour's Eternal Work: An Exegesis of Col. 1:9–29," *Interpretation* 3 (1949): 286–98.

du Plessis, I. J.
Christus as hoof van kerk en kosmos: 'N eksegeties–teologiese studie van Christus se hoofskap veral in Efesiërs en Kolossense (Groningen: 1962).

Reicke, Bo
"Zum sprachlichen Verständnis von Kol. 2, 23," *ST* 6 (1952): 39–53.

Reuss, Joseph
"Die Kirche als 'Leib Christi' und die Herkunft dieser Vorstellung bei dem Apostel Paulus," *BZ*, NF 2 (1958): 103–27.

Robertson, Archibald Thomas
Paul and the Intellectuals: The Epistle to the Colossians. The Stone Lectures for 1926 (Garden City, New York: Doubleday, Doran & Co., 1928).

Robinson, James M.
"A Formal Analysis of Colossians 1:15–20," *JBL* 76 (1957): 270–87.

Rongy, H.
"Les erreurs combattues dans l'épître aux Colossiens II, 16–19," *Revue ecclésiastique de Liège* 30 (1938–39): 245–49.

Idem
"La divinité de Jesus. Col. I, 15–17," *Revue ecclésiastique de Liège* 31 (1939–40): 37–41.

Idem
"Le Christ et l'Église. Col. I, 18–20," *Ibid.*, 94–99.

Idem
"Le Mystère de l'Église. Col. I, 24–28," *Ibid.*, 166–72.

Idem
"La réfutation des erreurs de Colosses. Col. II, 8–15," *Ibid.*, 216–26.

Idem
"La vie supérieure dans le Christ. Col. II, 20–21 et III, 1–4," *Ibid.*, 284–90.

Idem
"L'authenticité de l'épître aux Colossiens," *Ibid.*, 338–49.

Rudberg, Gunnar
"Parallela. 2. Syndesmos," *Coniectanea Neotestamentica* 3 (1939): 19–21.

* Salas, Antonio
" 'Primogenitus omnis creaturae' (Col. 1, 15). Estudio Histórico-Redaccional," *Estudios Bíblicos* 28 (1969): 33–59.

Sanders, Ed Parish
"Literary Dependence in Colossians," *JBL* 85 (1966): 28–45.

Schenke, Hans–Martin
"Der Widerstreit gnostischer und kirchlicher Christologie im Spiegel des Kolosserbriefes," *ZThK* 61 (1964): 391–403.

Schierse, F. J.
" 'Suchet, was droben ist!'," *Geist und Leben* 31 (1958): 86–90.

Schleiermacher, Friedrich
"Ueber Koloss. 1, 15–20," *Theologische Studien und Kritiken* 5 (1832): 497–537.

Schmid, Josef
Zeit und Ort der paulinischen Gefangenschaftsbriefe: Mit einem Anhang über die Datierung der Pastoralbriefe. (Freiburg i.B.: 1931).

Idem
"Kol 1, 24," *BZ* 21 (1933): 330–44.

Schmid, M.
Die Leidensaussage in Kol 1, 24. Unpub. Diss. (Wien: 1956).

Schweizer, Eduard
"Zur Frage der Echtheit des Kolosser– und des Epheserbriefes," *ZNW* 47 (1956): 287. Reprinted in *Neotestamentica*, 429.

Idem
"Die Kirche als Leib Christi in den paulinischen Antilegomena," *ThLZ* 86 (1961): 241–56. Reprinted in *Neotestamentica*, 293–316.

Idem
"Die Kirche als Leib Christi in den paulinischen Homologumena," *ThLZ* 86 (1961): 161–74. Reprinted in *Neotestamentica*, 272–92.

Idem
"The Church as the Missionary Body of Christ," *NTS* 8 (1961–62): 1–11. Reprinted in *Neotestamentica*, 317–29.

von Soden, H.
"Der Kolosserbrief," *JPTh* 11 (1885): 320–68; 497–542; 672–702.

* Steinmetz, Franz-Josef
Protologische Heilszuversicht. Die Strukturen des soteriologischen und Christologischen Denkens im Kolosser- und Epheserbrief. Frankfurter Theologische Studien 2 (Frankfurt: Knecht, 1969).

* Testa, Emmanuele
"Gesù pacificatore universale. Inno liturgico della Chiesa Madre (Col. 1, 15–20+Ef. 2, 14–16)," Studii Biblici Franciscani Liber Annuus 19 (1969): 5–64.

Tromp, Sebastianus
" 'Caput influit sensum et motum.' Col. 2, 19 et Eph. 4, 16 in luce traditionis," *Gregorianum* 39 (1958): 353–66.

Unger, E.
Christus und der Kosmos: Exegetisch–religionsgeschichtliche Studie zu Kol 1, 15ff. Unpub. Diss. (Wien: 1953).

a Vallisoleto, Xaverius M.
" 'Delens . . . chirographum' (Col. 2, 14)," *VD* 12 (1932): 181–85.

Idem
" 'Et spolians principatus et potestates . . .' (Col. 2, 15)," *VD* 13 (1933): 187–92.

Vögtle, Anton
Die Tugend– und Lasterkataloge im Neuen Testament: Exegetisch, religions– und formgeschichtlich untersucht. NTAbh 16, 4.5 (Münster i.W.: 1936).

Wagenführer, Max Adolf
Die Bedeutung Christi für Welt und Kirche: Studien zum Kolosser- und Epheserbrief (Leipzig: 1941).

Wambacq, B. N.
" 'per eum reconciliare . . . quae in caelis sunt' (Col 1, 20)," *RB* 55 (1948): 35–42.

Idem
" 'Adimpleo ea quae desunt passionum Christi in carne mea . . .' (Col 1, 24)," *VD* 27 (1949): 17–22.

Weidinger, Karl
Die Haustafeln: Ein Stück urchristlicher Paränese. UNT 14 (Leipzig: 1928).

Wibbing, Siegfried
Die Tugend- und Lasterkataloge im Neuen Testament und ihre Traditionsgeschichte unter besonderer Berücksichtigung der Qumran-Texte. BZNW 25 (Berlin: 1959).

Wikenhauser, Alfred
Die Kirche als der mystische Leib Christi nach dem Apostel Paulus (Freiburg i.B.: ²1940).

Yamauchi, Edwin
"Sectarian Parallels: Qumran and Colossae," *Bibliotheca Sacra* 121 (1964): 141–52.

* Yates, Roy
"A Note on Colossians 1:24," *Evangelical Quarterly* 42 (1970): 88–92.

Zedda, S.
"Il carattere Gnostico e Giudaico dell' errore colossese nella luce dei manoscritti del Mar Morto," *Rivista Biblica* 5 (1957): 31–56.

b/ Philemon

Amling, Ernst
"Eine Konjektur im Philemonbrief," *ZNW* 10 (1909): 261f.

Couchoud, P.-L.
"Le style rhythmé dans l'épître de Saint Paul à Philémon," *RHR* 96 (1927): 129–46.

Goodenough, Erwin R.
"Paul and Onesimus," *HTR* 22 (1929): 181–83.

Greeven, Heinrich
"Prüfung der Thesen von J. Knox zum Philemonbrief," *ThLZ* 79 (1954): 373–78.

Harrison, P. N.
"Onesimus and Philemon," *ATR* 32 (1950): 268–94.

Holtzmann, Heinrich Julius
"Der Brief an den Philemon, kritisch untersucht," *Zeitschrift für wissenschaftliche Theologie* 16 (1873): 428–41.

Jang, L. Kh.
Der Philemonbrief im Zusammenhang mit dem theologischen Denken des Apostels Paulus. Unpub. Diss. (Bonn: 1964).

Knox, John
Philemon Among the Letters of Paul: A New View of its Place and Importance (New York and Nashville: Abingdon Press, ²1959).

Meinertz, Max
Der Philemonbrief und die Persönlichkeit des Apostels Paulus (Düsseldorf: 1921).

Müller-Bardorff, J.
"Philemonbrief," *RGG*³ 5 (1961), col. 331f.

Pommier, J.
"Autour du billet à Philémon," *RHPR* 8 (1928): 180f.

Preiss, Théo
"Vie en Christ et éthique sociale dans l'Épître à Philémon," in *Aux sources de la tradition chrétienne, Festschrift M. Goguel* (Neuchâtel and Paris: 1950), 171–179; reprinted in *La Vie en Christ.* Bibliothèque théologique (Neuchâtel and Paris: 1951), 65–73; ET: *Life in Christ*, tr. Harold Knight. SBT 13 (London: SCM Press, 1954), 32–42.

Roberti, M.
La lettera di S. Paolo a Filemone e la condizione giuridica dello schiavo fuggitivo. Pubblicazioni della Università cattolica del Sacro Cuore, Ser. II, 40 (Milan: 1933).

Verdam, P. J.
"St Paul et un serf fugitif (Étude sur l'épître à Philémon et le droit)" in *Symbolae ad Jus et Historiam Antiquitatis Pertinentes Julio Christiano van Oven Dedicatae* (*Symbolae van Oven*), ed. M. David *et al.* (Leiden: 1946), 211–30.

Wickert, Ulrich
"Der Philemonbrief—Privatbrief oder apostolisches Schreiben?," *ZNW* 52 (1961): 230–38.

Indices*

1. Passages

a/ Old Testament and Apocrypha

b/ Old Testament Pseudepigrapha and Other Jewish Literature

* Numbers in parentheses following page citations for this volume refer to footnotess.

d/ Early Christian Literature and the Ancient Church

e/ Greek and Latin Authors

2. Greek Words

3. Subjects

4. Modern Authors

Designer's Notes

In the design of the visual aspects of *Hermeneia,* consideration has been given to relating the form to the content by symbolic means.

The letters of the logotype *Hermeneia* are a fusion of forms alluding simultaneously to Hebrew (dotted vowel markings) and Greek (geometric round shapes) letter forms. In their modern treatment they remind us of the electronic age as well, the vantage point from which this investigation of the past begins.

The Lion of Judah used as a visual identification for the series is based on the Seal of Shema. The version for *Hermeneia* is again a fusion of Hebrew calligraphic forms, especially the legs of the lion, and Greek elements characterized by the geometric. In the sequence of arcs, which can be understood as scroll-like images, the first is the lion's mouth. It is reasserted and accelerated in the whorl and returns in the aggressively arched tail: tradition is passed from one age to the next, rediscovered and re-formed.

"Who is worthy to open the scroll and break its
seals . . ."
Then one of the elders said to me
"weep not; lo, the Lion of the tribe of David,
the Root of David, has conquered,
so that he can open the scroll and
its seven seals."
Rev. 5:2, 5

To celebrate the signal achievement in biblical scholarship which *Hermeneia* represents, the entire series will by its color constitute a signal on the theologian's bookshelf: the Old Testament will be bound in yellow and the New Testament in red, traceable to a commonly used color coding for synagogue and church in medieval painting; in pure color terms, varying degrees of intensity of the warm segment of the color spectrum. The colors interpenetrate when the binding color for the Old Testament is used to imprint volumes from the New and vice versa.

Wherever possible, a photograph of the oldest extant manuscript, or a historically significant document pertaining to the biblical sources, will be displayed on the end papers of each volume to give a feel for the tangible reality and beauty of the source material.

The title page motifs are expressive derivations from the *Hermeneia* logotype, repeated seven times to form a matrix and debossed on the cover of each volume. These sifted out elements will be seen to be in their exact positions within the parent matrix. These motifs and their expressional character are noted on the following page.

Horizontal markings at gradated levels on the spine will assist in grouping the volumes according to these conventional categories.

The type has been set with unjustified right margins so as to preserve the internal consistency of word spacing. This is a major factor in both legibility and aesthetic quality; the resultant uneven line endings are only slight impairments to legibility by comparison. In this respect the type resembles the hand written manuscript where the quality of the calligraphic writing is dependent on establishing and holding to integral spacing patterns.

All of the type faces in common use today have been designed between 1500 A.D. and the present. For the biblical text a face was chosen which does not arbitrarily date the text, but rather one which is uncompromisingly modern and unembellished so that its feel is of the universal. The type style is Univers 65 by Adrian Frutiger.

The expository texts and footnotes are set in Baskerville, chosen for its compatibility with the many brief Greek and Hebrew insertions. The double column format and the shorter line length facilitate speed reading and the wide margins to the left of footnotes provide for the scholar's own notations.

Kenneth Hiebert

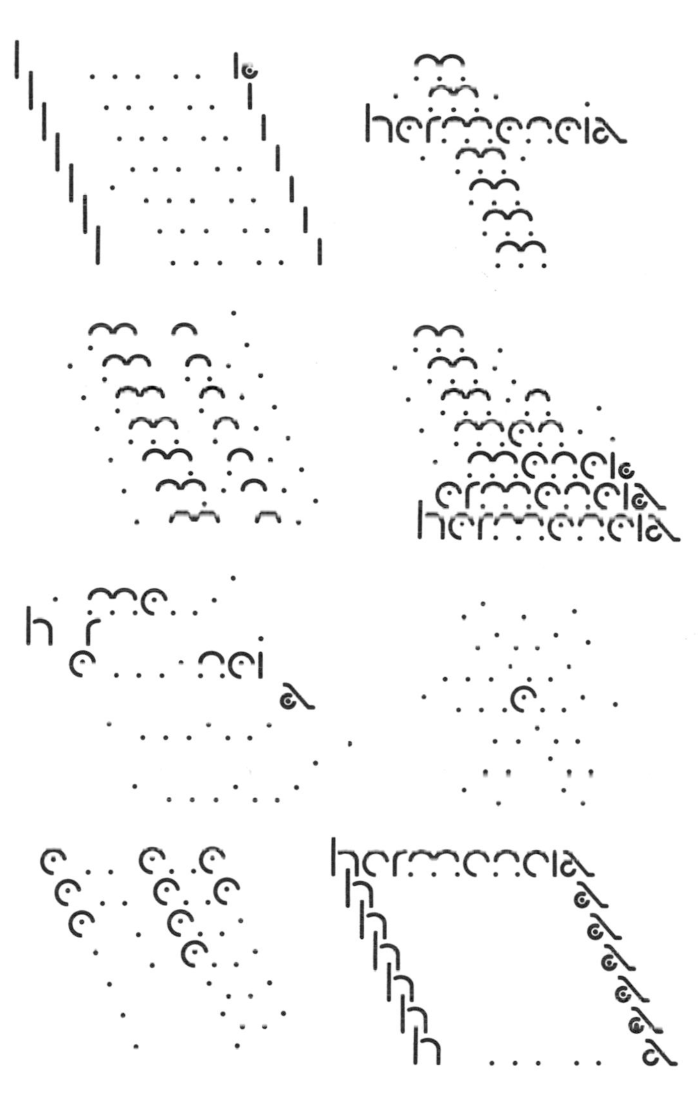

Category of biblical writing, key symbolic characteristic, and volumes so identified

1
Law
(boundaries described)
Genesis
Exodus
Leviticus
Numbers
Deuteronomy

2
History
(trek through time and space)
Joshua
Judges
Ruth
1 Samuel
2 Samuel
1 Kings
2 Kings
1 Chronicles
2 Chronicles
Ezra
Nehemiah
Esther

3
Poetry
(lyric emotional expression)
Job
Psalms
Proverbs
Ecclesiastes
Song of Songs

4
Prophets
(inspired seers)
Isaiah
Jeremiah
Lamentations
Ezekiel
Daniel
Hosea
Joel
Amos
Obadiah
Jonah
Micah
Nahum
Habakkuk
Zephaniah
Haggai
Zechariah
Malachi

5
New Testament Narrative
(focus on One)
Matthew
Mark
Luke
John
Acts

6
Epistles
(directed instruction)
Romans
1 Corinthians
2 Corinthians
Galatians
Ephesians
Philippians
Colossians
1 Thessalonians
2 Thessalonians
1 Timothy
2 Timothy
Titus
Philemon
Hebrews
James
1 Peter
2 Peter
1 John
2 John
3 John
Jude

7
Apocalypse
(vision of the future)
Revelation

8
Extracanonical Writings
(peripheral records)

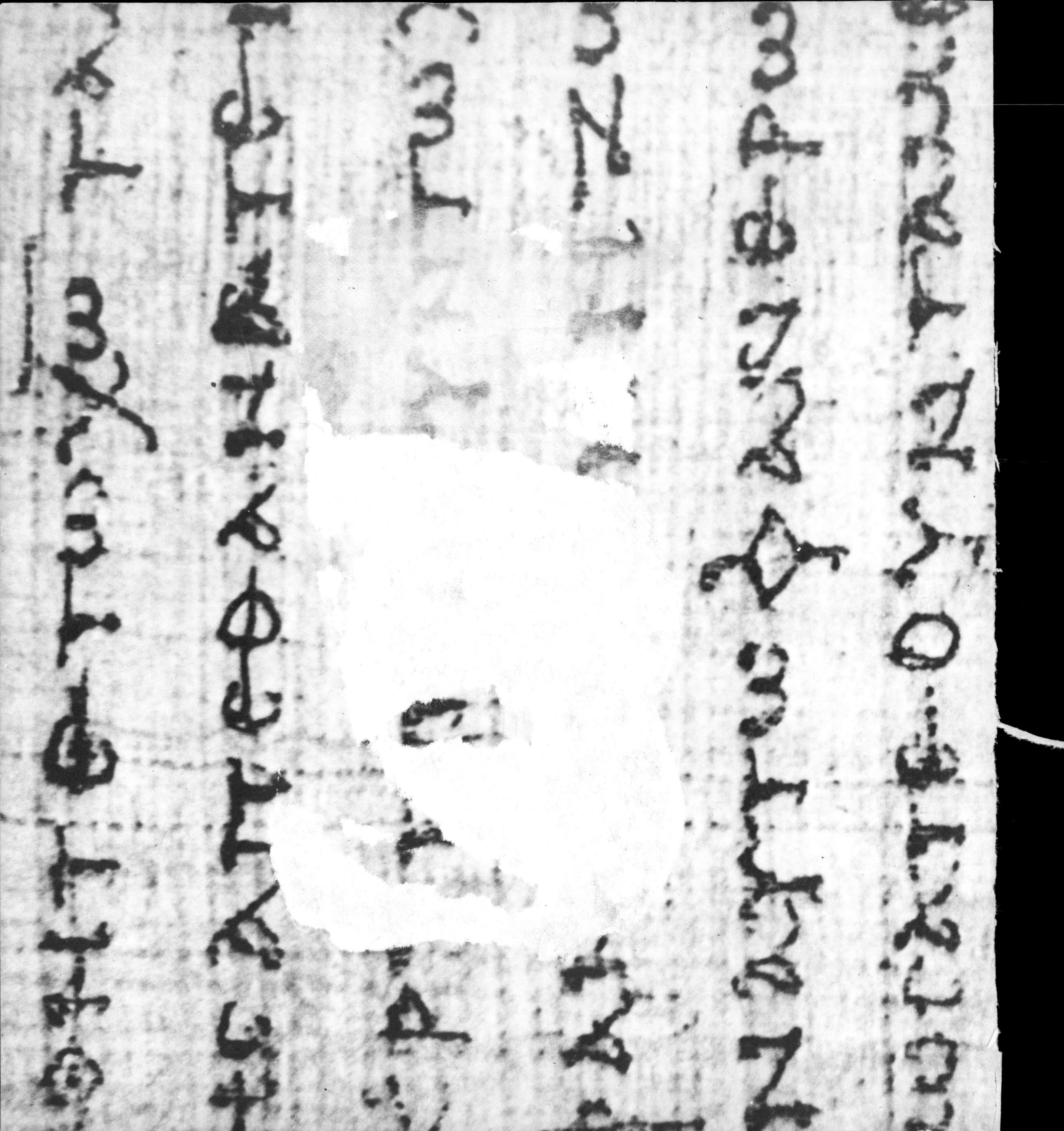